Equal Stages ze

C000200954

What Now? series editors

Nick Awde is founder of the Other National Theatre at Morecambe's Alhambra Theatre, where he created the Morecambe Goth Passion Play, and co-director of the UK Centre of the International Theatre Institute (Unesco). He is also international editor (non-staff) for *The Stage* newspaper, was head critic of *The Stage's* Edinburgh reviewing & awards team for many years, co-founder of the UK's first professional theatre review site *Theatre Guide London*, and he also worked for many years for *The Voice* Newspaper Group. He has written, illustrated or edited more than 50 books including: *Women in Islam, Chechen Phrasebook, Hausa Dictionary, Mellotron: The Machine and the Musicians That Revolutionised Rock, Singer-Songwriters Volume 1,* and the forthcoming *Avant-Hard in the UK, Finnish Rock,* and *Electric Guitarists & Bassists: Electrification of the Nation.* As a playwright/composer, dramatic works include *Pete and Dud Come Again* (with Chris Bartlett), *Andrew Lloyd Webber: The Musical* (book, lyrics & music), *Noddy Holder's Christmas Carol Unplugged,* and *The Europeans (Parts 1-3: Bruges, Antwerp, Tervuren).* As Nick Awde & Desert Hearts, music includes the albums *Blues for Blighty (Vols 1-3), Swimming in a Fish Bowl, Mellotronic Belgium Blues,* avant-garde opera *Belgium-737,* and the EPs *Selling England by the Pound, Close to the Edge b/w Meryl Streep/Rocket Man,* and the single 'European Man (I Do What I Can)'.

Isabel Appio is an established journalist and publisher with a focus on social inclusion in education, the workplace and arts & culture — primarily for under-represented and unheard young people, women and those with diverse abilities. Isabel worked as a leading journalist and publisher during the 1980s & 90s campaigning heydays of the Black British press. Isabel is the founder of Thrive 4.0 (Where Talent Meets Opportunity) which promotes inclusion and self-empowerment of marginalised groups in the new economy. She has worked on promoting diversity and inclusion with an extensive range of organisations including top corporates, self enterprises, local & central government departments, universities & colleges and leading charities & public bodies.

Also from Desert♥Hearts/Bennett & Bloom:

Solo: The Evolution of One-Person Theatre *(out in 2020)*
Nick Awde

Accidental Angel: Charity at Full Throttle *(out in 2020)*
Kate Copstick (of UK/Kenya charity Mama Biashara)

Critics: The Not So Dying Art of Theatre Criticism in the UK *(out in 2020)*
Nick Awde

Electric Guitarists and Bassists, Volume 1 *(out in 2020)*
Nick Awde

Singer-Songwriters, Volume 2: (including Peggy Seeger, Annie Haslam,
Judy Dyble & Judie Tzuke) *(out in 2020)*
Nick Awde

Singer-Songwriters, Volume 1: David Cousins, Arlo Guthrie, Iain Matthews,
Ralph McTell, Al Stewart, Richard Thompson
Nick Awde

Mellotron: The Machine and Musicians That Revolutionised Rock
Nick Awde

The Fifties Child: A Social History Through the Songs of Barclay James Harvest
Alex Torres

The Vibrators: 21 Years of Punk Mania
Ian M. Carnochan (aka "Knox")

The Thin Book of Poems
Lach (Fortified Publishing/Desert Hearts)

The Wholly Viable: An Autoblography
Phil Kay

Freeing the Edinburgh Fringe: The Quest to Make Performers Better Off
by Charging the Public Nothing
Peter Buckley Hill

A Floristry of Palpitations
George Stanworth

The Big Bardaid Book
edited by Donna Daniels-Moss

Quaking in Me Stackheels: A Beginner's Guide to Surviving Your First Public Performance
Paul Eccentric

The Commuter's Tale
Oliver Gozzard

The Little Big Woman Book
Llewella Gideon (illustrated by Nick Awde)

The Tattooing Arts of Tribal Women
Lars Krutak

Tattooed Mountain Women and Spoon Boxes of Daghestan: Magic Medicine Symbols in Silk,
Stone, Wood and Flesh
Robert Chenciner, Gabib Ismailov & Magomedkhan Magomedkhanov

The Elfin Pedlar: A Cycle of Ballads On Traditional Themes
Freye Gray (illustrated by Ian M. Carnochan)

Andrew Lloyd Webber: The Musical
book, lyrics & music by Nick Awde

What Now? Beyond Diversity and Inclusion Series

Series editors: Nick Awde & Isabel Appio

Equal Stages

Volume 1

Standing Up for Identity and
Integrity in the Performing Arts,

NICK AWDE

DESERT ♥ HEARTS

in association with
the Other National Theatre
& the International Theatre Institute

We need Champions not Gatekeepers!

This is the first volume in the **What Now? Beyond Diversity and Inclusion** series, kicked off by Nick Awde & Isabel Appio in response to the frustration of watching diversity and inclusion in the United Kingdom turn into a version of *Groundhog Day*.

For years now, the search for equality in our society has been descending into a self-fulfilling cycle of consultations leading to initiatives leading to consultations leading to . . .

At the same time diversity and inclusion have become big business, where talking about discrimination, gaps, disparity, ceilings fuels a highly influential and heavily funded sector that generates an impressive chunk of jobs, training, legislation, workplace culture, controls, hierarchies, elites.

Diversity and inclusion aren't a bad thing, of course, and we're living in a country that is a world leader at least in terms of their practice. But it's still visibly lacking, and a huge amount of achievements are being constantly undone. There's a cycle that needs to be broken and a lot of missing voices that need to be heard in the national decision-making processes that shape how we accept and live diversity in the United Kingdom.

Hopefully this series will add to the conversation and get the right people in the room.

First published
in 2020 by
DESERT♥HEARTS

www.deserthearts.com
www.bennettandbloom.com

info@deserthearts.com

© Nick Awde & the Interviewees 2020

Typeset & designed by Desert♥Hearts

Printed & bound by Printforce, United Kingdom

British Library Cataloguing in Publication Data
A catalogue record for this book is available from the British Library

ISBN 978-1908755-38-4

*

Contents

For everyone who teaches
the performing arts
in schools everywhere

the other national theatre

Exciting, inclusive, diverse, representative theatre for all performers and audiences...

Theatre for the deprived, cut-off, left-behind and excluded, for those needing dignity...

Theatre for the bored, couldn't-be-bothered, to make people welcome, to know it's their space, their voices, their faces up there — along with everyone else's...

The Other National Theatre is taking shape at the Alhambra Theatre in the West End of Morecambe, in the North West of England — and we'd like to take shape in minds all over the nation.

Because culture in our country is a postcode lottery, an accident of geography, we created the Other National Theatre at the Other End of England. In the West End of Morecambe, Lancashire, to be precise. We have no budget but big plans.

Internationally, as the hub of Alternative National Theatres, we are twinning the Other National Theatre with performing arts individuals and organisations in every country of the European Union. It will act as a channel to all those other nations. Nationally, we want the Other National Theatre to help the conversation about representation in theatre and to share this within the regions and nations of the United Kingdom, and also internationally — helped by the UK Centre of ITI.

Here in Morecambe, we would like to mirror and match show-for-show the London National Theatre's programme of shows. If they do Macbeth, we'll our own version. If they do a new play by an established playwright, we'll stage a homage or topical response without breaking copyright. A David Hare play about the NHS in London may inspire a local writers' groups up North to talk to healthworkers and come up with a staged response to the play's themes.

Our artists and activists, our disabled and marginalised, our schools and colleges, foodbanks and local businesses, all will have their responses too.

Giving non-professional actors of all ages and backgrounds a voice is central to the Other National Theatre, aided by DIY West End Theatre which draws on semi-professional and professional Northern-based actors, directors and writers.

Onboard we also have the input and collaboration of Swedish director Henrik Grimbäck.

othernationaltheatre.org.uk
info@deserthearts.com

 **International Theatre Institute ITI**
World Organization for the Performing Arts

Based in Shanghai & Paris, the International Theatre Institute is the world's largest performing arts organisation with centres in almost 100 countries. It is a part of the Unesco umbrella of culture organisations and is non-funding but works as a platform to network and share work globally.

Partner international organisations include the European Federation of Professional Circus Schools (FEDEC), the International Music Council (IMC) and the World Mime Organisation (WMO).

ITI UK is the UK Centre of the International Theatre Institute and is based at the Alhambra Theatre, Morecambe, in the North West of England.

ITI UK works to create within the UK that promote international spirit of the performing arts, and to create collaborations with ITI centres overseas. To make this happen, we are working on a UK-specific approach to international work that best allows UK performing arts interface with the rest of the ITI countries and vice-versa.

There was no ITI UK Centre for a number of years until we formed in 2017, and we're busily reconnecting the UK with the ITI world network.

ITI's vision includes projects such as creating a World Performing Arts Capital and a World Theatre Festival, and it also focuses on diversity, education, young people and empowering new audiences. Equal access, equal opportunities are the rule. ITI also organises World Theatre Day (March 27) & International Dance Day (April 29).

Facebook: UKCentreITI
itiuk@mail.com
iti-worldwide.org

Limitless Strategies

It's very European to have a manifesto, so here's one launched in 2019 as a plan of action from the Other National Theatre & Alternative National Theatres for today's local, national & international theatremakers to create theatre's future as small intelligent highly mobile units.

- othernationaltheatre.org.uk

ONE: Celebrate the difference within diversity, seek out the Other. Respond to each community's spectrum. Be inclusive yet share those stories without diluting them.

TWO: Balance the reality of money. Pay the creators, subsidise the audience, enrich the community by spending there. Embrace 'fringe' values, create 'EasyJet' circuits.

THREE: Local is national is international. Quality is in the mind and requires no more than an audience. To create meaningful hubs and circuits, everywhere is connected if you want it to be.

FOUR: Listen to your audience, learn their language. The language of dialect, class, education, generation, region and Otherness. Speak to your audience before, during and after.

FIVE: Children are the present, not 'the future'. NOW is the moment, always show them what is possible. Remember they will come if their parents also know what is possible.

SIX: Publish, disseminate, spread the word. Creativity demands a living legacy, to be discovered beyond the locale. Consider your audience's potential, let no one be missed out.

SEVEN: Leave a trail in plain view. Leave traces and tools to inspire the community, its talent, its visitors. A path to be picked up by those who follow you.

EIGHT: Community is the nation's true stage. A community is not there to be rescued but to be met on equal terms. The community has the same right to *Lion King* as it has to *Hamlet*.

NINE: Rediscover the idea of 'folk'. Think beyond living museums for past traditions. Find the lost voices, the emerging voices, the Other voices, the smaller nation's voices that speak within every nation.

TEN: Accept the cultural monoliths, the cosmopolitan hubs, the funding elites. Show them how it's done but don't let them take credit. And remember always that 'culture' assumes a meaning which is different wherever you find it, wherever you take it.

* * *

A touch of further reading

Four pieces written in the years leading up to 2020 that offer further food for thought on national identity and integrity in the UK today:

An Oxford Story *(2017)*
An observation by writer, producer & theatremaker Lauren Mooney (@lozopus) on applying to Oxford University:
medium.com/@lozopus/an-oxford-story-6262a1e7912

The Trouble with Outreach *(2018)*
Playwright & youth worker Nathan Lucky Wood (@lucky_wood) asks why work being made with 'hard-to-reach' groups is so closely focused around their most difficult experiences:
exeuntmagazine.com/features/trouble-outreach-work

The Cost of Doing Business: A Year at the Holbeck *(2019)*
Artistic director Alan Lane (@slunglowalan) assesses Slung Low's first year of running the Holbeck Working Men's Club and presenting theatre that represents a held-back area of Leeds:
alanlaneblog.wordpress.com/2020/01/06/blogpost-the-cost-of-doing-business-a-year-at-the-holbeck

We Need to Pay Very Close Attention to What Is Happening in Britain Now *(2020)*
Journalist & broadcaster Una Mullally (@UnaMullally) writes in *The Irish Times* on honesty and identity, subtitled 'A nation that does not confront its national identity will not be able to move forward':
irishtimes.com/opinion/we-need-to-pay-very-close-attention-to-what-is-happening-in-britain-now-1.4264046

*

0
Introduction

'No representation without a voice, no voice without visibility!'

Nick Awde is a writer, producer, musician & director of The Other National Theatre at the Alhambra, Morecambe. Based in London & Morecambe, he was raised in Nigeria, Sudan, Kenya, Lancashire & London. • othernationaltheatre.org.uk

A question of language

Across the forty interviews in this book, you'll hear the voices of forty-two people from the performing arts who talk about how their work and lives reflect diversity and inclusion. These aren't missing voices and many are loud, but each speaks directly for the other voices that haven't been invited to our nation's conversation on equality.

However, this may not be the book you think it is — if, that is, you're expecting a feelgood diversity manual or Arts Council-friendly handbook. Yes this is all about diversity and inclusion, but it's the reality of people who do it rather than people who prefer to talk about the theory. In fact, it's a platform of voices from around the British Isles — England, Scotland, Wales, Northern Ireland and Ireland — who show you how they're actively using the performing arts as a path to make society a more humane place for all.

I should begin by saying that the focus of the live performing arts in this book is mainly theatre with touches of stand-up comedy, music and the United Kingdom's own-brand avant-garde. Areas like dance, physical, children's, community, education, cabaret, musicals, circus, and the design, technical and backstage sectors and so on are not covered here, nor are a lot of minorities or groups such as UK-based migrant practitioners. We plan for their voices to be heard in future *Equal Stages*.

I should also make the disclaimer that as interviewer, my personal and professional opinions present in each interview should not be taken as the opinions of the interviewees, nor should the opinions of the other interviewees be taken as reflecting those of the others in this book.

Wonderfully, each interviewee chose their own narrative — it might be their work, their practice, their life experience, upbringing or views on the wider social/political context — and, when put together between two covers, they collectively offer an indepth snapshot of how people across our islands are standing up for diversity at present.

They share the conviction that if you want to make a difference then you need to be visible — which makes the performing arts a good place to be. Logically linked to this is the idea of access, which is why we have tried to make this a book that anyone can read. You don't need to know anything about the performing arts or diversity sectors to access the knowledge pool here. All the chapters are refreshingly jargon-free, plus at the back you'll find a glossary of commonly used terms relating to culture and society which may not appear obvious to readers from outside the sectors or who are from outside the UK. Your patience is sought for the bits of bracketed information dotted about in the text, but not everyone knows, for instance, that the Soho Theatre is in Central London rather than Glasgow, and not everyone knows it even exists. We especially wish details of places and locations to be readily available to help map out the geographical spread of where people work, where they're based, where they're from, highlighting the various levels of access and mobility in each of the country's regions and nations.

Progress in a snapshot

So, back to that snapshot idea. Viewed from one direction, this book forms an image of how our particular corner of the globe has succeeded and also failed to meet the momentous one-step-forward, two-steps-back changes in contemporary society, culture, economy and politics that shape the arts of today. The interviewees show how they're riding this perpetually uneven wave of progress, how they're shaping the performing arts into a launchpad for wider conversations on issues like prejudice and class that affect all of society — and which are actively used to exclude many parts of society.

However, for all the good work that's done in the UK, the conversation more than ever needs to be a honest one, conducted with integrity. The diversity and inclusion (i.e. equality) sector is still driven in many ways by ideals based on the notions of victimhood, of the perceived nobility of the Other, of arms-length charity. All too often assimilation is the real end, put into motion by an admittedly caring hand extended by the majority to the minority as an invitation to take their place in the comforting world of the mainstream as citizens who are protected, but ultimately second-class.

There's no small irony in the fact that the UK has one of the best overall records on diversity and inclusion on a world ranking. And that's the problem, because in no way does this mean that things are even halfway there — while so much has been *undone*. In fact the worsening attitudes towards minorities and excluded groups in the UK of 2020 *[pre-Coronavirus crisis]* come from well-meaning national policies that have lurched from the old 'multi-culturalism' (which resulted in the de facto exclusion by isolation of groups) to today's 'diversity' (resulting in their inclusion by assimilation). Particularly in the mid 1990s, a lot of battles were considered to be won for minorities, and people fell into thinking that they were integrating on their own terms, that there was no fight any more, that they didn't need their champions. But here we are in the 2020s still struggling with the idea of simple equality based on respect, understanding and *seeing* how life is on the O/other side.

This age of anxiety

In fact parity is a problem across the whole globe. This is after all an age of anxiety — when everyone knows it shouldn't be so. It seems the more we learn the more we unlearn, putting up walls in the vacuum left by the knowledge we've just discarded — and there's frustration to say the least in seeing hard-won social structures demolished and having to be rebuilt again and again.

In the UK we're living with the legacy of the arts being undermined from the late 1970s onwards by government policies that have deliberately targeted culture and society, the effect accelerated by a succession of crises, most prominently 9/11 in 2001, the global crisis in 2008, the pre-Brexit Referendum uncertainty from 2013, the post-Brexit Referendum uncertainty from 2016. Each has sparked a new wave of devastating austerity, each wave forcing the arts ever further down the priority list in a chain reaction between economics and culture, economics and diversity. If you financially starve culture, then it starts to disappear from view, and with it all sorts of groups disappear too.

At the moment, like so many other sectors throughout the country, people working in the performing arts have watched powerless over the past few years as the bedrock of our profession slips away in real time and our industry's platforms shrink. We're losing basic rights such as our ability to earn from what we're good at, what we're trained to do, what there is a demand for, doing what the rest of the world emulates and is inspired by.

The wider national backdrop has seen income diminish, rents for where we live and work rise, dividing our industry and damaging, even corrupting, our attitude to creating. Our social mobility has declined, our regional inequality has increased, viable entrepreneurship has faded, wealth inequality has skyrocketed, and postcode still determines higher poverty, worse health, class disadvantage and fewer opportunities in life. Inequality in Britain is "now entrenched from birth to work", to quote the government's own social mobility commission report from 2019.

There's irony in the fact that these existential threats have created the current situation for the majority of those working in the performing arts where they have become invisible in a highly visible sector. Those decades of chipping away at the status of what we do have created so many cracks in the system that when we're not working, we're so hidden in them that effectively we don't exist.

Still, there's a part of me that entertains the idea of the performing arts — and theatre in particular — as being like a weed. It'll come back to grow in those cracks no matter what happens. Sure it won't pay the bills and not everyone wants it to be there, but it'll always come back whatever they do to try to get rid of it.

Connecting up the issues

So how do we sort this?

A feature of theatre is the way it creates ways to confront and solve problems in society by getting people to talk, by connecting communities, platforming voices, raising issues, getting people in the room. Especially now that our local press network has been killed off — until recently local newspapers and local radio stations formed a integral pillar of our nation's democracy and transparency — the flow of bottom-to-top voices more than ever needs conduits such as the performing arts (along with social media of course). That's not to say that theatre has to be overtly political, but it does need to responsibly create spaces where people and opinions can be seen and heard.

Another feature of theatre is its ability to adapt. On a practical level, a good example is the multi-roling that distinguishes all the practitioners in this book, who add any number of 'slashes' to their job descriptions: artistic directors, directors, actors/performers, writers/devisers, producers, ASMs, marketers, front of house, critics and so on. That hands-on approach opens up opportunities for others, attracts audiences, spreading the message while entertaining, engaging and educating at the same time.

So instead of offering a tickbox list of earnest questions, most of the conversations in *Equal Stages* start with a simple question like "How did you get into all this?" or "How are you changing things?" From that, each conversation takes its own direction, shaped by career arc, specialty or background, or just thoughts on where the interviewees are at at the moment. They talk simply about what motivates them, the vision they embody and why it drives them. Although not always suggesting sustainable career models, since many have had to carve unique paths for themselves, they do show how the performing arts can work for people who want to make a difference in society.

As I've said, some of the interviewees are from minority, marginalised or excluded groups, some represent and work with those groups, but they are hardly marginalised voices. What they have to say is centred firmly and clearly on identity according to race, gender, ethnicity, disability, age, class, region and so on, coming from a generational range that spans seven decades, from people who are in their twenties to those in their eighties — and so the integrity of what they do and why they do it becomes self-evident.

A note on funding

There's some criticism of the UK's funding system in this book, mostly from me, but I hope it won't prove a distraction. More than half of the interviewees are able to do the work they do because of direct major funding, and everyone without exception has benefited from indirect funding, such as the supported venues across the country that put on their work.

Criticism of the funders is basically directed at how that funding is assigned and used across the country. Funding is given in the name of fairness and sustainability, yet often the results fail to achieve those outcomes or to support the industry with the equity it merits. More often than not, the reason is that those who need to be at the decision-making table aren't at that table, especially if they're the sort that ask awkward questions.

Since the economy is a constant sociopolitical weapon that sees funding wilfully cut off to the social side of society — health, education, social services, culture — the present state of arts funding in the UK represents a history of missed opportunities and destructive policies and legislation. Consequently there is confusion about who the funders actually speak for. Who do they want *us* to speak for? And how do we justify creating art when it is based on the deepening codependency of funders and creatives who push the illusion of a level playing-field?

From activism to fringe excellence

In the right hands, theatre can be a potent focus for activism even if hamstrung by funding or silenced by charitable status, and it's 'soft' activism that generally works the best and doesn't set limits on audiences. It goes without saying that everyone in this book is a soft activist, even if they don't self-describe as such, simply from the evidence of what they do.

The long interview format gives them the opportunity to go beyond the narrow bandwidth of strategy writing or promoting a specific show or project.

It gives them space to talk about what inspires or drives them. If you put together the different angles taken in these interviews, they create a wider yet detailed picture of how diversity and inclusion can work successfully within the performing arts to inspire other sectors. There's also a strong sense running through all the conversations in this book that integrity is key to sustained success, i.e. having and stating your values, being seen to believe in what you're doing and who you're doing it for, who you're standing up for.

So here's an overview of these conversations . . .

Advocacy is a particularly strong platform to drive creativity, and poet, theatremaker and disability activist Jackie Hagan explains why we fail to see people affected by poverty, class or disability and how her work helps to keep them in the sight of society. Improvised theatre provides an interesting framework for that visibility, and performer and director Stephen Davidson shows how improv helps open people up to each other's differences while also making a convincing ally for transgender awareness.

Growing up on council estates continues to throw up barriers in the UK particularly when race is combined with class. Actor, writer and musician Cleo Sylvestre describes how her upbringing on a North London estate provided her with the sense of identity and drive that propelled her to the National Theatre stage, yet was at odds with the low expectations of theatre from the community she grew up in. In South London, arriving as a child from Nigeria to live on a Bermondsey estate, writer and director Gbolahan Obisesan reveals how he learned to negotiate the complexities of inner-city prejudices and an overloaded school system, and in the process found his career path thanks to drama at school and the National Youth Theatre.

Director Chris Sonnex comes from a council estate in Pimlico, a visibly economically segregated area in Central/South London that has given him the tools to parse the class-based tradition of gatekeeping in theatre and allowed him to develop the groundbreaking open-access phenomenon that was London's Bunker Theatre. Northern Irish writer and theatremaker Kat Woods details the barriers that face people who have grown up as part of the benefits class, particularly in areas that are far from our cultural hubs, and why they represent the key themes of her plays.

A parallel perspective of class comes from Dan Allum, who is from the excluded community of the UK's Travellers and Romanies, and he looks at how he was able to enter mainstream society through acting school, which then gave him the building blocks to create and tour with the Romany Theatre Company, which he founded.

Finding new audiences and sustaining existing ones is a major challenge today, and there's a growing sector in the UK that is introducing international work at grassroots level as a way of holding up that mirror from a different direction to our national practice. Lora Krasteva, cultural producer and artistic director of Global Voices Theatre, shows how to create unexpected access for audiences and practitioners by bringing plays from across the world to the UK through a small-is-best model that celebrates cooperation. As co-director with Isla Aguilar of BE Festival, Miguel Oyarzun documents how they started an annual season of international experimental theatre in Birmingham from scratch — and he explains how food also plays an important part in breaking down barriers.

As co-directors of Voila! Europe Festival, Sharlit Deyzac & Amy Clare Tasker curate cutting-edge European work in London that wouldn't normally be seen here, while also showing how the DIY economy of UK fringe is no obstacle to mainstream excellence. In Dublin, Brian Merriman describes how the political backdrop to the decriminalisation of homosexuality in Ireland inspired and continues to inform the International Dublin Gay Theatre Festival, while also sharing the ups and downs of Irish funding.

From the North to new audiences

Within the UK, the divide between the South East and the North of England is a reality that represents deep-rooted economic, cultural and class exclusion. A late addition and the only Coronavirus Crisis interview/amendment to this book and introduction comes in the shape of Liverpool playwright and actor Luke Barnes, who five weeks into the lockdown set up Stories of the North, a virtual open town hall to kickstart an artistic response to defining the North's identity and how to positively tackle the issue of parity with London and the South East.

An academically-tinged viewpoint of North-South parity comes from Will Nelson, fringe director and lecturer at Manchester's Arden School of Theatre, who highlights the impact of brain drain and rising costs on the performing arts in the North, and how culture there reflects the wider national divide in politics, notably Brexit and the legacy of Thatcherism. Over in Yorkshire, Halifax-based director and actor Barrie Rutter describes how he put a different voice into the national — and international — conversation when he founded Northern Broadsides as 'Northern voices, doing classical work in non-velvet spaces', while also showing how core funding and touring can make good partners.

Based in Belfast, writer Rosemary Jenkinson offers an overview of the background that has led to the marginalisation of Northern Ireland by the rest of the UK, and the way politics and satire have provided a distinctive voice that allows her and a wave of fellow contemporary playwrights to tackle the complex society they live in. Viewing the UK from Dundee, director, producer and writer John-David Henshaw discusses how making theatre in Scotland has led to him to running Sweet as a major venue at both the Edinburgh Festival Fringe and in Brighton on the South Coast of England, at the same time balancing this with producing his own company's shows.

The performing arts are forever expanding their vocabulary, and creative ageing is a prominently growing area of innovation. In London Gavin Barlow, director of the Albany Deptford, and David Slater, director of Entelechy Arts, analyse the stages that built up to creating their Age Against the Machine festival, drawing on their wider efforts to make work with older people that reflects 'what is in the street'. A central part of that work is *The Home*, created by writer, theatremaker and performer Christopher Green, who describes how the inspiration for the 48-hour immersive show came out of questioning and restating the relationship between audience and performers, the resulting universality taking the show on a journey from Deptford to Tokyo.

The challenge of new audiences is definitely focal to the work of Guleraana Mir — London-based writer, theatremaker and part of The Thelmas theatre company — who writes from a South Asian perspective in order to create narratives that are open to all, while also working to strengthen theatre in the community and education. As head of new works at the Liverpool Everyman & Playhouse theatres, Francesca Peschier brings a venue's viewpoint of nurturing different levels of work that reflect the community's talent and aspirations, while also establishing a flexible home to stage, develop and train.

As executive director of Cardiff's Sherman Theatre/Theatr y Sherman, Julia Barry explains how the Sherman 5 scheme is attracting new audiences and how, in line with taking responsibility as a civic resource, the venue invests in Welsh and Wales-based artists. In the South West of England, Kate Wood — who is co-artistic director with Bill Gee of Inside Out Dorset festival — shows how the landscape itself becomes an inclusive space through performance and installations thanks to national and international artists and collaborations with organisations outside the arts sector.

Closed shops, bums on seats

Access is a constant challenge for those working in the performing arts, and writer and broadcaster John Byrne, in his capacity as *The Stage* newspaper's careers advisor and columnist, addresses the reason why lack of representation is an issue that refuses to go away in the industry, in particular due to an uneven level playing-field and closed-shop attitudes. Comedian, writer & musician Paul Ricketts takes a closer look at the closed-shop barriers on the stand-up comedy circuit both onstage and off due to race and class, in the process sharing his insights into how we claim, shape and reject identity.

Similarly addressing how identity is formed and assigned, comedian Tim Renkow discusses how disability can break down barriers onstage and onscreen without having to dominate the conversation for performer and audience alike. In Edinburgh, writer and performer Jo Clifford explains how identity set the stage for creating *The Gospel According to Jesus, Queen of Heaven*, a solo play that explores transgender rights and which has also become a rallying cry for LGBT rights in Brazil.

Information and awareness are crucial first steps for access, a process documented by critic and editor Sophia A Jackson's decade-long work in opening up theatre through Afridiziak Theatre News, the UK's only website dedicated to African-Caribbean theatre, and she talks about how educating theatres has opened them up to black critics. The next step in that journey, i.e. physically opening those doors and putting bums on seats, is taken up by Tobi Kyeremateng, who discusses the circumstances that inspired Black Ticket Project and why she has designed it to operate as a grassroots programme to make theatres more welcoming to audiences.

Making the stage itself a more welcoming space is director, writer and producer Yvonne Brewster, who shares highlights of her long career both in the UK and Jamaica, breaking down barriers for black actors and creatives, most notably as co-founder of Talawa Theatre Company. As former artistic director of Yellow Earth, director, writer and actor David K S Tse has not only created opportunities for British East Asians in theatre, but also integrated activism into the creative process. As David once told me, invisibility — of himself and his community — was exactly the reason he got into the performing arts.

As a talent agent addressing representation literally, Lola Williams offers her thoughts on the measurable step-by-step approaches agents can make to create a permanent place for diversity onstage and screen, and she explains how her New Wonder Management Talent Agency is helping producers to accept actors on the basis of their skill sets.

In London, Clean Break joint artistic director Anna Herrmann shows how a women's theatre company can provide a safe space where women in the criminal justice system can learn and make award-winning work, while also responding to potential for change by working in the prisons themselves. Based in Oldham, musician, actor and composer Faz Shah applies a Northern and Muslim perspective to question the idea of a fixed identity within cultural spaces, and as a result he identifies a major need for neutral safe spaces that are open to everyone to learn and explore the arts.

A peripatetic fringe venue is one answer to that lack of safe spaces. Comedian Bob Slayer founded Heroes and the mobile venue BlundaBus on the basis of pay-what-you-want, promoting an equitable system that supports performers especially in the context of the costly ecosphere of the Edinburgh Festival Fringe. Heroes co-artistic director Lucy Hopkins — a clown and director — sees venues as being able to develop in a holistic direction, offering a wider experience of creativity around performances and workshops while resisting the traditional models of festival growth and expansion. In Leeds,

Slung Low artistic director Alan Lane is redefining theatre in the community by creating a symbiotic relationship between his producing theatre company and The Holbeck working man's club to meet theatre's social remit out of a bricks and mortar base.

A crucial way of establishing a theatre's presence is through its archive, says Sanjit Chudha, marketing and communications manager for Croydon's Talawa Theatre Company, and he sees access to the past work of black theatremakers as an essential resource to inform and support conversations such as decolonising culture. Just as crucial is access to a future career in theatre via our schools, says theatre in education writer and critic Susan Elkin, who points to the value of schools that decide to commit to drama in the absence of government support and who therefore help break down the assumptions that there are no decent careers in the industry.

As a nation, the UK has a truly lamentable history of safeguarding its own indigenous languages, which have acquired a degree of legal recognition only recently. Director Paula Garfield documents almost two decades of putting British Sign Language on our stages with Deafinitely Theatre while creating new ways to stage bilingual productions that include English and other forms of signed language. Betsan Llwyd, artistic director of Welsh-language theatre company Bara Caws ('Bread & Cheese'), explains how Welsh identity and culture are linked to language as the number of Welsh speakers and users grows with official encouragement, and how theatre has a key role to play in giving a voice to the expanding arts scene of Wales.

(And here I shall declare that my personal contribution to diversity during the production of this volume has been to finally sit down and learn BSL and Welsh.)

Poverty and leadership

Overwhelmingly these are positive voices about the prospects for meaningful work and their continued ability to improve society. However, the fact remains that the arts in general and theatre in particular have been running on empty for an increasing number of practitioners. For a country that is the fifth largest economy in the world it simply doesn't add up, and it certainly doesn't help diversity. Without revenue (which in theatre often comes from a show whose development has been funded) there is no work, without work there is no visibility, and without visibility there is no protection. It needs to be repeated again and again that yes it would be wonderful if every show was a hit and made tons of money, but isn't that missing the point of why we should value the performing arts?

The reality is that when financial support is taken away, it is the minority, regional and working class creatives who are the first to go. Rising rates, rents, cost of living, tuition, vanishing career paths, eroded circuits, fewer tours and shorter runs, diminishing public awareness and new audiences, demolition of drama at schools, reduced access to even mainstream theatre almost anywhere that's not a large city — all this takes its toll on diversity.

Most work can't get made without support, and that support needs society's acceptance of seeing theatre as both a civic and social right, and therefore an obligation as a part of our wellbeing. You need from society expectation of representation, pride in the arts, trust in funding. Crucially culture is not just what's on that stage, it's the fact that there's actually a stage to put something on. And as for content, people have as much right to see *The Lion King* at their local community hall as they have to see some European director's *Hamlet* at the Barbican. But the reality is that the best, most meaningful, impactful theatre today is being made in the imaginations of our theatremakers, established and emerging alike. There simply aren't the resources to go round — even staging a show for free seems to cost money these days.

Culture is therefore a potent weapon for our politicians, and in the Austerity Kingdom of Great Britain & Northern Ireland, it has panned out as a battleground between the left and right, in whose cultural circles the decision-makers tend to be from the same social background and/or education system, regardless of ideology, and who move increasingly in the same social circles the higher you go. Culture war therefore becomes an exclusive arena where a common privilege is jealously guarded by both sides and our common cause is lost.

All of this has negatively affected people's capacity to think ahead. The power to influence theatre policies has transferred from those who control and weaponise the purse strings, i.e. the rightwing moral Establishment (always on behalf of the people who don't go to any of this stuff), to those who control the nation's moral censorship, i.e. the leftwing reactionary Establishment who have weaponised diversity and identity (again on behalf of the people they represent who are more likely to go to this stuff). Both claim to speak for the people, and neither side is prepared to share their duopoly unless by (temporary) invitation. Meanwhile, the left's kneejerk outrage has dangerously handed the right the excuse to co-opt diversity and identity as protection and justification for their closed groups and for hate and attacks on other groups.

As a result, underlying many of the conversations in this book is a lament for the lack of theatre leadership at the highest levels in the UK, i.e. the people who should actually represent the vast diversity of this industry. The commercial West End theatre, big festivals, opera, ballet and music are well organised, well represented, securely financed, but the rest of theatre and the other performing arts are the poor relation without much of a negotiable place at the table, where the unspoken rule in any case is that culture is a privilege, that 'successful' theatre is a club with rules of entry and a two-tiered subscription that requires annual renewal by the masses — and lifetime membership for the few.

Actually, instead of 'leaders' let's call the people perceived as such 'decision-makers' (or, even better, 'gatekeepers'). The challenge in our society is that fewer and fewer of our decision-makers/gatekeepers in politics, government, academia, the arts, health, social security, finance, every sector really, have been economically poor or lived a life that is culturally or educationally impoverished. In the arts it's a deep-rooted problem reflected mathematically in the composition of the boards of our funders and theatres, where the entrenchment of social iniquity and the lack of diversity of audiences is already pre-ordained thanks to the cloning of our decision-makers. Everyone agrees publicly that we're supposed to see ourselves up on the stage, yet it's more than problematic if we don't see ourselves in the people who decide who and what goes on that stage. Especially when it's people who all look like each other, sound like each other, yet talk about 'making a difference' and 'taking risks'.

When, for example, was the last time you heard of the 'theatre lobby' tackling the government in defence of our interests? Our industry (and arts funding) grandees chatting to their mates in the Cabinet over canapes at the posh launch of yet another privately sub-contracted national diversity initiative can't be the action plan any more.

I bring this up because it is the background to why we started the *What Now? Beyond Diversity and Inclusion* series, why you're reading *Equal Stages*, why we want to seek out people who are making that difference and taking those risks. People who can tell that story of passion, commitment, vision and hard work, people who are defining a living evolving policy for positivity and change, who represent the amazing community of the performing arts, who won't stop defining and redefining diversity and inclusion through their actions.

The voices here are proof that if you invest in the people's art, then you invest in the people. This is also why this book will be of relevance and interest far beyond the worlds of the performing arts and diversity/inclusion. Parts of it might even be a manual for change in a small way. It's certainly a unique window into a very British Isles response to using the performing arts to dispel inequality caused by poverty, austerity and blocks to opportunity. Although historical inequality has morphed into a feature of our modern times, it cannot still our country's voices wherever they are.

In the end, this book is all about visibility, about being heard. You need to see and hear Other/other people to know how they think and live — to learn how to connect and to understand that we are truly one nation — and I hope this snapshot inspires you to look further.

March 3, 2020

*

The Coronavirus postscript

For extremely obvious reasons, this book as a snapshot of the issues facing UK society seen through the eye of the performing arts has turned out to be an image seared on the back of our eyeballs, a #LastNormalPhoto of how things were before all the doors closed not only in the United Kingdom but in the rest of the world as the Coronavirus Crisis changed everything. The significance becomes all the more acute when you realise that almost all the interviews took place between the beginning of October 2019 and the end of February 2020.

The impact on the performing arts has been especially devastating. First to close, last to open, ours was already a fragile industry, belying the huge revenues it generates. Amidst all the uncertainty, what is certain is that the challenges to the performing arts addressed in this book remain the same: visibility, representation, equity, funding, the ability to make a living.

A result of the crisis is that it has allowed the different parts of the sector to finally join as (a sort of) one voice to publicly define not only the relevance of the arts industry but also the idea of culture itself. But when we go back to the New Normal will it be just the same Old Normal? Will the 'lessons learned' from the Great Pause change the lowly position that culture and the arts hold for any reordered structure of our society? Will society really want to establish a National Arts Services, just as the creation of the National Health Service was a response to the shattered world that emerged after the Second World War? It's more likely things will slide back to the old model as if nothing had happened. But that, of course, was a model of haves and have nots, and through the crisis it has been those who have the least who have lost the most.

All the talk from that one voice that "we need to change" just reminds us that this has been the rallying call in the UK for the past decade at least. And it makes us wonder who is actually making that call at decision-maker level?

So as our collective focus shifts, this book now becomes an exercise in a different kind of visibility, that of theatre leaders. Music and dance have always fought their corner, but in theatre it has been a case of increasingly disparate groups loudly announcing they are speaking on behalf of everyone while fighting for their own corners even when facing clear-cut threats that affect everyone, like austerity and Brexit. The crisis has amplified this disparity, the new development being merely that theatre decision-makers are now having to speak up in union because, while not quite facing ruin like the majority of the industry, they are confronting the consequences of the crisis on the *relevance* of their organisations.

Everyone is busily stating the obvious about the fragility of our industry but utterly failing to explain why this is the case for what even the government proudly states is a billion-pound sector nationally and internationally. It's never too late to stand up, never too late to speak up, but nothing will get done until someone actually states our case at the topmost levels with conviction.

Ask around anywhere in the performing arts and you'll hear familiar stories of reduced or no income, the economics that impose every level of personal and professional isolation, the struggle to crack remote production and digital/online access for work — but this was the state of the industry before the crisis arrived. Many of us were already in economic lockdown and we're not looking for a reset, we're looking for an honest change. So before we move on to whatever New Normal means, we really do need to get a public understanding of how we got to where we were before we can even think of how to get to where we need to be.

It's one crisis, therefore, but we aren't speaking with one voice. Not even our decision-makers, whose Twitter manifestos, press opinions, Zoom summits merely parrot the other industries: "Things need to change." "Let's not revert to what we were." "Let's think longterm." "We need to look to the young people." "The environment is fragile for artists and freelancers." "Who gets to imagine the future?"

More honest calls from their quarter on our behalf would be: "Pay us all a living wage." "Don't censor us with poverty." "Drop the rent/rates." "Theatre for all should mean theatre for all." "We'll share our money." "Here's a building, use it." Oh, and "Would you like to be in the room with us?"

Since diversity is linked to economics, it follows that with no economy, there is no diversity or inclusion, no parity. We as an industry need safeguards embedded in any proposed new economic model. But in the past eight weeks I've sat in on so many conferences and read so many manifestos and opinions only to realise that the 'official' lines are all controlled by people still on salaries, who are doing this because they're still in paid time, not even furloughed. And that makes me question their right to talk about artistic freedom, their right to demand that people get paid, and, again, their right to urge that things can't be the same. After all, it's not their jobs that are on the line.

So the problem facing our would-be leaders remains: that they have no answer to what the Old Normal means or the New Normal, nor, crucially, any explanation for what the changes they're pushing honestly mean for the rest of us. They have no context to explain what working in the performing arts actually means, simply because before the crisis they opted *not* to create a context for the performing arts as an industry, as a pillar of society. Hence they have no meaningful solutions, no voice that speaks for all, and so they're not actually at that government table (if they are there) representing us all.

There's another call: "We're all in this together." Well no, that's not true either, just as Coronavirus isn't actually a 'great leveller' but instead worst affects the key workers, the poor, the minorities and the marginalised. So no, we're not all in it together. What we all are is perfectly aware of how the crisis has exposed, with greater clarity than ever, the disparities and inequalities that existed before.

The interviewees in this book are exactly the sort of people who should be invited to the decision-making tables — and I hope that some of them have been or will be. We can trust their experience to reflect us and speak for us, and what is certain is that they will raise their voices for what is coming post-crisis. Much in the news already, for example, has been Alan Lane, who turned over his team and building at The Holbeck working men's club to help the community during the crisis. As the venue announced: "The Holbeck is closed. But we are still busy. We are the ward lead for social care referrals from the Leeds City Council Coronavirus helpline. We deliver food, call the lonely, sort prescriptions. Whatever is needed. Our commitment to our community is determined. If you need our help then get in touch."

There are many many more out there who have done the same, of course. Meanwhile, the Arts Council responded with speed in committing to redistributing funds. However, they were simply sharing out existing money — when the pot's gone it's gone and they'll have to join the government's lengthening money queue, probably somewhere near the back.

Even before the theatres closed, publications like *The Stage [thestage.co.uk]*, edited by Alistair Smith, and *Exeunt [exeuntmagazine.com]*, edited by Alice Saville, had embarked on documenting the collapse of the industry and the responses to counter, adapt and reconstruct. In the process they've offered a platform to voices from every level of representation.

And then today, as we go to press and I hasten to complete this Postscript, three intriguing things have just happened in a row . . .

This morning playwright & performer Jo Clifford posted an open letter to a theatre in Edinburgh highlighting the roles seen and unseen that our industry plays in society. This evening, playwright James Graham has just run through a convincing justification of theatre as a state industry on BBC's *Question Time*.

And in between, a number of our prominent theatre organisations finally came together under a single banner with 'An Open Letter to Theatre and Performance Makers'. The agenda includes calling on the government to extend the Self-Employment Income Support Scheme in line with furloughing for all self-employed workers, and for the specific case of theatre workers, until theatres are able to safely reopen, and to get criteria removed from the scheme which blocks many legitimate claims. They've also offered to 'facilitate the establishment of a national task force of self-employed theatre and performance makers'. It's more than a bit late compared to other sectors, and it doesn't look as if this group is present at the government's table, but of course more and more groups will start to speak up to state our case, including those who stand up for diversity in theatre and the performing arts.

Thinking it through a bit further, though . . . this is an open letter from organisations whose grouping is defined by very specific links between them (as will be the case for other groups following with their own open letters), so again I wonder who was invited to those Zoom meetings? Who was in the room? Who was really there speaking for the missing voices? And again back to that question, who really speaks for all of us?

*

So today, Thursday May 21, 2020, as midnight approaches and we go to press, it looks as if a certain tide is turning. The problem is finally named, 'leaders' are stepping up, if not quite standing up, speaking up at least to each other, and possibly communicating who we are to the government and the country. With a bit of luck, the conversations, actions and results that develop after this book's publication will cancel out the pessimism of this Coronavirus Postscript.

But they won't change the details of the snapshot here. Diversity and inclusion are unlikely to benefit from the readjustments to come and they will end up worse off. There are and will be so many missing voices in the cases that are being made for the survival of the performing arts in the United Kingdom.

Like so many others everywhere, people in the performing arts have already long suffered the dishonesty of our government's refusal to dignify and define their employment status along with all the other official exclusionary policies to massage employment figures through zero hour contracts, gig economy, self-employed net vs gross income, the trap of Universal Credit. The lockdown has ironically highlighted the scandal of our excluded professional status, but post-crisis, despite all that we know now, many will remain excluded, trapped in the same old cracks, slipping through the same old net.

Coronavirus has amplified the existing age of anxiety, and it has also amplified this age of political distraction, a total war against the people which pre-crisis threw billions and billions of pounds into targeting and altering our perception of what is 'Normal', an outcome based on undermining our ability to accept others (and so removing the resistance of our solidarity) by eroding our understanding of our own identities. (So don't get distracted!)

As a journalist I reckon I've refused to deliver to my editors no more than four or five interviews in a 30 years or so career. I knew I'd lose the money but it had to be done, because in each case the interviewees turned out to be utterly dishonest, devoid of integrity. Not materially, mind, nor as bad people, but in their perceptions of their job, role and vision, which made me question their attitude not just to culture but to other human beings. The last interview like this was just a year or so ago with the head of a big budget arts organisation, who simply had no fucking idea about the work problems that were already looming for artists. Seriously. No. Fucking. Idea. Just the confident ignorance and bullshit that comes from a life and career of privilege. And dangerous when placed in a position of responsibility. I wrote the interview up, then knew I had to dump it. And guess who's one of the government picks currently speaking on our Coronavirus behalf?

That's how things work, of course. It goes with their job and I'm not complaining. I'm certainly not outraged. But why should that mean there's little or no room for O/other voices up there where it really counts?

Where are our *champions*? When I hear people in positions of responsibility speaking on panels on our behalf (and appropriating what everyone else has been saying for years) I do wonder if they could find the honesty to answer questions like, "If you didn't have your full-time job with your full-time salary and a big office in the building you run, would you still be saying this? Would you still be doing this? Would you really still be here? Would you still be standing up for others if you couldn't pay your own rent or feed your kids?"

And that's how I would end this Postscript . . .

. . . To be honest though, I do a disservice to the legacy and present/future efforts of the remarkable people who speak in this book — and of all those of you out there who share their vision.

So here's that open letter by Jo Clifford who says it all in a far more lyrical way that's far more appropriate to a book about the performing arts. It's a Facebook post that addresses the threatened status of Edinburgh's Lyceum Theatre, shared on the day her new play was to have opened there. And when she says "We are all in this together", you know Jo means it.

May 21

Dear Lyceum,
I wrote this to you on Tuesday night when our play was due to open, and didn't. And I didn't know what to do with myself, so I thought I'd write to you and see if that helped me understand.
 Understand why you matter.
 The play is called Life Is a Dream and I sometimes wonder whether, to quote the play, you'll turn out to be one of life's good things that have passed away and that, as we look back at you, will feel just like a dream.
 The trouble with you, dear Lyceum, is that you're labour intensive in an economy that's capital intensive. You value people in a world where the so-called successful enterprises succeed by eliminating people as much as they can, and so cause great suffering.
 But you promote well-being, dear Lyceum, and you give pleasure, and that

just doesn't show up on balance sheets.

And you do financial good to the city you belong to, in fact you bring in millions, but that doesn't show up in your yearly returns either, and so people still somehow think you're a drain on the public purse.

But that's why you matter. You remind us that wealth is not just about getting rich at someone else's expense; that true wealth is collective.

And you point to a time when we will value more than just money. When we give more value to human happiness.

The man who wrote Life Is a Dream, Calderón, my hero and my inspiration, also wrote a play called The Great Theatre of the World, which is also about you.

About the way you remind us that we all depend upon each other, and we have to work together.

Because a play is the creation of everybody — writer, actors, designer, stage crew, director. Everybody. And that includes the audience.

In your space, even if only briefly, we can feel we all belong together.

And so you remind us of a deeper truth: the fact that's how it is on our planet earth.

We are all in this together.

And only if we understand and feel for each other, and work and co-operate with each other, that we'll ever get out of the mess we're in and make the world a better place.

The fact is, dear Lyceum, you're like a gym. Only in your space we don't lift weights, or run on treadmills to become fitter and stronger. Instead you're a place where we strengthen our capacity to feel for each other and to empathise.

And so you contradict the cruelty of our selfish world and you help us to resist it.

And that is also why you matter.

I wish our play was opening tonight. I wish I didn't fear for you.

There's a line in our play that's always helped when I'm struggling with a sense of despair or futility.

Someone says:

"The good you do is never lost. Not even in dreams . . ."

Let's remember that, dear Lyceum.

The good you do has not been lost. It counts for something.

Let's keep our hope alive. Let's believe that one day a way will be found to re-open you and that our beautiful play, alongside many others, will be seen and give pleasure and joy to the world.

With the deepest love,

Jo xxxx

*

Lockdown, May 21, 2020

*   *

Dan Allum • Gavin Barlow • Luke Barnes
Julia Barry • Yvonne Brewster • John Byrne
Sanjit Chudha • Jo Clifford • Stephen Davidson
Sharlit Deyzac • Susan Elkin • Paula Garfield
Christopher Green • Jackie Hagan
John-David Henshaw • Anna Herrmann
Lucy Hopkins • Sophia A Jackson
Rosemary Jenkinson • Lora Krasteva
Tobi Kyeremateng • Alan Lane • Betsan Llwyd
Brian Merriman • Guleraana Mir • Will Nelson
Gbolahan Obisesan • Miguel Oyarzun
Francesca Peschier • Tim Renkow • Paul Ricketts
Barrie Rutter • Faz Shah • Bob Slayer
David Slater • Chris Sonnex • Cleo Sylvestre
Amy Clare Tasker • David K S Tse
Lola Williams • Kate Wood • Kat Woods

1

Dan Allum

'It takes more than talent and determination. You also need craft'

Dan Allum is a writer, director, composer & artistic director/founder of Romany Theatre Company. Based in Cambridge, he was born in Chelmsford, Essex, & raised in the East Anglian region.
• danallum.co.uk, @RomanyTheatre

How did you get into theatre?

I was brought up in caravan and travelled around till I was in my mid 20s. I would describe myself as a writer, composer and producer, though I also direct. I was always into music, listening to the radio was my passion. I didn't meet any Travellers who did the romantic stuff singing around the campfire. That didn't happen in my experience. But in my early teens, I thought, well, I think I can sing so I'll learn to play the guitar. I brought a guitar and taught myself to play well enough to create a few songs. I couldn't read or write in those days so I'd make the songs up in my head and memorise the words and the tune. I wrote my first proper song when I was 16 or 17. I had it recorded at a studio and it was played on our local BBC radio station, which was great. But of course because my family was travelling around all over the place, I wasn't able to join a band, so I couldn't get anything off the ground.

I drifted out of music and did the Traveller thing, got married and had a couple of kids who I loved dearly. But something wasn't sitting right with me in my work life. Something inside was driving me in a different direction. It was hard. Then I was in Cambridge one day and walked past a school advertising a drama event. It was the Lamda trials. You did a little drama piece, learned the basics. I'd never thought about drama before, so I went in, auditioned and was accepted. Every Friday evening you would rehearse a monologue and at the end of three months, perform your piece in front of an examiner. You might even win a medal.

I learned the scripts, played a couple of characters and won two medals. I said, you know what, I quite like drama . . . So I auditioned for drama school in London and got in. Nobody was more surprised than me. I did a three-year degree course — I studied at the Arts Educational Schools [in Chiswick, West London] from 1990-3. Came out with a degree when I was in my late 20s. I didn't really want to be an actor, but I loved the theatre so I decided to write a play just to see if I could do it. I wrote my first play in 1997 and it won four awards at the local play festival. I thought, wow, I'm a writer! I hadn't realised I had that talent. Since then I've won a number of awards for my writing. In 2003 I founded the Romany Theatre Company, and I've been creating and touring original work and composing music ever since, alongside writing for radio and developing TV drama.

For the stage I've also created new work at the National Theatre, Royal Court Theatre and Royal Opera House. For the screen I've developed original TV drama series with the BBC, ITV and Left Bank Pictures (makers of *The Crown*). I've also been an established writer for BBC Radio 3 & 4 and 4extra for the last 12 years. Recently I decided to write a Gypsy folk opera, and it's being performed both in the UK and in Budapest in 2020. My show *Carmen: The Gypsy* is being performed in Madrid too, so it will be fantastic to have two of my plays performed internationally in 2020. I've also lectured at the Anglia Ruskin University, Cambridge, taught drama in various schools and I give inspirational talks.

Last year [2018] we took *Carmen: The Gypsy* on a UK tour, after developing it at the National Theatre. We've done some really great work. Just recently my music has been coming more and more to the fore. I'm about to take my own show on a live tour, probably next year, just me and a small band, so that will be a very different turn.

But basically for your first question, how did I get into it? Initially it was through music and writing a little here and there. But mainly I guess it was drama school. Of course my culture was shocked when I went there because very few Travellers had been to university before.

People expect to experience culture shock when confronted with the foreign or exotic, but no one expects someone from within their own society to feel it towards that very same society. And not just a shock for you, but the people around you at drama school necessarily wouldn't have the vocabulary to deal with your reaction. So it could have had a ricochet effect?

I think it was a shock for both sides really. I mean, it was a shock for me to find myself in a school situation for almost the first time ever. I could barely read or write. It was very difficult at first, but I loved the atmosphere of the place — they allowed me to express myself. And I was finally *performing*! But for some Travellers, it must have been a real shock, though they never spoke about it much, you know? They must have seen it as a complete step outside the culture. But I stepped back in when I left drama school.

But there was no actual continuity for you. You had to go back.

I kind of had to do that for me. I went out, learned a few things and then came back.

With the reading and writing, was that something that you were already working on or did the college help you out?

By the time I went to drama school, I could basically write, but I couldn't spell. I could hardly take notes. In fact, I'd never taken notes on anything in my life before, so I didn't know what they were. When I was growing up, I'd spent a few weeks here and there in schools. When you're a Traveller, your parents would tend to send you to school sometimes because they had to or risk prosecution. But everyone knew it would be a terrible situation because of the racism. We didn't stay long in any school anyway, only a few weeks.

But I wanted to learn to read. I felt like I was missing out on something. Nobody in my family could read, including my parents. So I taught myself by using comic books. I began with small words like 'if', 'and' and 'can' before tackling the bigger words. Soon I was reading the whole comic. Then I moved on to newspapers. I read my first book when I was about 17.

Can you remember it?

It was a self-help book called *Positive Imaging* by Norman Vincent-Peale: you imagine what you want to achieve in your life then go for it. It worked! Another book that had a profound influence on me was *Your Natural Gifts* by Margaret E Broadley. It was interesting because I'd kind of felt separate up until that point. I wondered how come very few of my friends wanted anything different. I did, and when I read these books I realised that there were lots of people out there who felt similar to me, they wanted something other than what they were supposed to want. It was a real eye-opener.

However that was taking you into the outer world, which was hostile towards you, and away from your community. So that must've been quite a brave step to take. If 'brave' is the right word, perhaps 'determined' is better?

It was a determined step to make. There was racism all around in those days. You didn't stop on sites back then because there were no sites, so you'd stop on the side of the road, in fields or a farmyard. We did lots of the farm labouring or scrap metal dealing to make a living. But there was always racism. It was everywhere you went. It was them and us. Going into drama school was taking me one step further, going out on my own, stepping out of my culture and into this whole other society that had been completely hostile toward me.

But I felt that I had to do it to learn what I wanted to learn. Strangely, when I got to drama school, it had an atmosphere all its own because it was an art culture. There were people there from all ethnicities and cultural backgrounds and it no longer mattered that I was a Gypsy. For the first time in my life, I was in a culture outside my own, but it was one where people weren't racist towards me. And of course in a drama school, what I had to offer was worth something, because if you're different in a drama setting you're interesting. I found that people were interested in me *because* I was a Gypsy, I was cool, which was totally different to anything that I'd ever known. So I thought maybe I have got something to contribute, not only to my own community but to the outside world. That was another big eye-opener for me.

In theatre, it's likely that you weren't seen as interesting because you were exotic but because you brought your difference to the table, which everyone probably did as well.

What they wanted was to see how someone from my background tackled a Shakespearean role and things like that. It was like, "How would you play Henry IV?" "How do you play a Chekhov character?" And "What about this guy with all his self-taught rawness? How will someone like him play Hamlet?" They'd never seen anything like me, I was completely new to them. And I'd hardly heard of Shakespeare before so it was really new to *me*! There was that fascination on both sides. But if you weren't very good in a role they didn't waste any time telling you so.

What were you bad at? What were you good at?

I was good at the darker roles. The characters of De Flores in Middleton & Rowley's Jacobean tragedy *The Changeling* and Krogstad in Ibsen's *A Doll's House* spring to mind. I wasn't that hot at Noel Coward or Oscar Wilde type characters. I could do a bit of comedy though. I wasn't bad in Feydeau's *A Flea in Her Ear* and an obscure but very funny American piece called *And Miss Reardon Drinks a Little*.

Was it enough in itself to have got the degree or did people have tons of suggestions for what you could do with it afterwards? And did you feel you needed to go back and give time to the community before working out what you wanted to do?

I guess all students adapt after they finish one way or another, and the college basically gave you tools to go out and make a living for yourself in the arts.

What were the job opportunities on offer? Did you find the working theatre world quite open to you or did the racism begin again? Or you just didn't go into those areas?

I didn't go into acting because I didn't really enjoy it. It was kind of instant, I knew that I didn't want to be an actor. But I loved the theatre, so it was well, what can I do now that I've had this training? I know I'm not going to be an actor, but I wonder what else I can do around theatre? I left London and got into local theatre. I lived near Bury St Edmunds for a while and I did some directing at the Theatre Royal there, and worked at Eye Theatre a short distance away. It was okay, but again it wasn't enough. I wondered what would happen if I tried to write a play. In 1997 I gave it a go. I booked myself into a local drama festival and purposely gave myself a very tight deadline. I wrote a comedy called *Bus Stop* in a couple of weeks, a short two-hander in one act. And it won four of the awards presented by the festival, including best new play. I took the show to the Edinburgh Festival Fringe the following year and it did well.

That was the first time I knew I could write, and that it was the road to go down. I had a local hit with a follow-up play called *Dead Innocence* and then I made a short film called *Killing Millie*. I sent a screenplay titled *The Boy's Grave* to a film initiative for new writers in Scotland called Opening Shots and I won a place on their programme. I worked on the script with a producer for a while but it didn't really lead anywhere. I didn't know enough about the business at the time. I got one or two theatre commissions, but I didn't like being told how or what to write. You'd hand in the first draft of your script, and they'd say, "That's great, but we want it like this or like that." I decided to set up own company and do it my way. Romany Theatre was born.

When you started up, were you based in Bury St Edmunds or elsewhere?

I was based near Bury St Edmunds at the time but later moved to Cambridge.

For family and community reasons?

That's right.

So East Anglia gives you a regional base, and I know you've worked a lot with the New Wolsey Theatre in Ipswich, which is a brilliant producing theatre that's made a diversity a byword for its work. When you started the Romany Theatre Company, did that mean everybody had to be a Romany to be in it?

They didn't have to be, but we tried to include as many as we could. There were very few who could do it or even wanted to. My plan was to work with people who were disciplined and focused, in order to create shows to a high professional standard. We used a mix of Romany and non-Romany artists. We still do.

Not a common practice in our theatres.

You don't see many Traveller performers in theatre productions.

Did you go out seeking the Traveller performers or did they find you?

We auditioned. We'd advertise: "We want Romany performers." We put the word out in the Romany community too.

Do any of them come to you who've been to acting school like you?

One or two, but in the early days there weren't many. There's one girl who's worked with us for about 12 years on and off, and she had been to drama school and done stuff. But most hadn't.

Does access to schools play a factor in that?

Certainly if Traveller kids had been to school they'd be more interested. They love drama and music, especially music. So if they'd been allowed to stay in school I'm sure there would have been many more involved. But they tend to leave at secondary and go to work because that's their culture.

You were contemplating setting up a theatre company during a significant period in the UK when a lot of other people who'd never set up theatre companies just said, let's do it. There was something in the air and, like you, I think they felt they had to do it. Was there any advice, any mentoring that came to you, or suggestions to "go and talk to so and so, they'll give you some money"?

When I first started, there wasn't any money so I just did my own thing. Spent a lot of my own money. Then somebody did say, "You do know you can get money to do this? Why don't you try applying to funding organisations?" So I got some money from the Arts Council and the Big Lottery Fund which meant we were finally able to put on something and get paid for it.

Around 2007 I was commissioned by Forest Forge Theatre to write a play about Gypsies in the New Forest. I called it *A Clearing* and it toured nationally. It was a great experience and one of my favourite pieces of work. Then Romany Theatre began a three-year project called *Atching Tan (Stopping Place)* and one of the elements was a 36-part radio drama series set in the Traveller community. That's when I first started working with the BBC, a collaboration that's carried on to this day. But in *Atching Tan* most of the performers I brought in were Travellers, who didn't have any drama experience. It gave people a chance to try something new, and good things came out of it. And they loved doing it.

That must have brought a lot of pressure on you to set up an actual venue, so that the rest of country could well-meaningly tick that one off their list. Did you ever think about that or did you just take each year as it came?

There was a time when I could have looked for a theatre to run. But I didn't want to go down that road. I preferred moving around, it allowed more freedom to do things differently. If I'd only got bricks and mortar, I'd have been stuck in one place and I didn't want that.

In a way though you have stuck in one place, by concentrating on sharing Travellers' stories.

I knew I had to put work on about Travellers. You'd never see anything done authentically. All the stuff that I'd seen had been put on by non-Travellers, it never came across with any kind of authenticity. People from my culture would just laugh at them, it was so ridiculous. So I thought, why don't we show them what it's really like, put something on that's truthful and then get some Travellers to come in and perform it.

I wanted to show the Traveller community with authenticity, but also to give other Travellers the chance to perform, a chance to show what they could do and maybe make a success of it, or at least give them the opportunity to try.

They had very few chances because they found it difficult to get into acting or performing or writing, with so little schooling. It could be intimidating. But with a theatre company run by Travellers, they were far more likely to come in. They recognised the truth of the work. They'd say, "We've never seen or heard anything like this. It's so real, as opposed to everything else out there, which is just false." Showing that authenticity gives other Travellers the chance to perform and connect with their identity. Most Traveller families were not taking the arts seriously, weren't seeing it as a viable work opportunity or career move. I wanted to show them that it might be, if you're very good and you're determined to do something different with your life.

But because suddenly you've piled all that responsibility on your shoulders to tell your community's stories, was it difficult to consistently come up with stuff?

I didn't find it difficult to come up with stories!

Because you actually chose to make your writing into something that was specific in a way that only you could do?

I suppose there was an element of that.

But just because you know it, it doesn't always mean that you can write it.

That's absolutely true. It takes more than talent and determination. You also need craft.

I'm not sure I could write about my background. I mean, to make it interesting.

I didn't know if I was going to make it interesting. I just felt that it was the area to go. I realised I could make a good job of it after I'd written those first two plays. Then I wanted to write about the community I knew, the people I knew. But I would choose the stories carefully. I know a good story when I hear one, or when I work something out in my head it almost always comes off. It was good to have that kind of freedom for a period of time because when I started working with the BBC I had to be very specific.

Working for Radio 4, I would come up with my own ideas and script editors would help me develop them. Producers at the BBC had strong ideas of their own and lots of experience of course. They were and are good to work with. Then I began working in television where you have to be even more structured, with lots more people involved. It has its good and bad points. As long as people know what they're doing, it's okay, but not everyone does.

Does it eventually kill your voice or . . . ?

There is a danger of doing the same thing over and over again. You have to be careful not to get pigeonholed. It's important to keep changing, trying new things.

What would you put in a crib sheet for non-Traveller audiences?

Well, the language for instance. We put quite a bit of Romani language in. Travellers would never really share their own language, so you would never see that on TV. The people who wrote about Travellers just thought, "We'll include Travellers in here" but you'd never hear them speaking Romani, when in reality they speak it a lot. So I put that in my stories. Also there's good and bad in every community and I wanted to show that. I often wondered how the community would take to me showing the bad as well, because of course when other people wrote about Travellers in dramas or whatever, Travellers were always the bad guys in many ways. But because I also show the good in a way Travellers can recognise, they're able to take the bad onboard and be absolutely fine with that. I try to be fair.

I also pick powerful stories to tell that create very dramatic pieces, for instance the last Travellers to be hanged in England for the then crime of simply being Gypsies, which became the play *Killimengro [2006]*. I think that's what's kept people hooked. *Our Big Land [2014]* was about Travellers losing their right to roam, which has been done before, but the way I was doing it was very different. I was trying to show that Travellers are perhaps different to a lot of other diverse groups because many of them don't particularly want to fit in. They're proud of their culture and don't see why they should be like everyone else. You know, "We're just going to be who we are, rather than become like you." Most Travellers I know want to stay true to their culture and do their own thing. Which is tricky, because there is a whole society out there which doesn't want you to do that.

Can we use the word 'assimilation'?

'Assimilation'? Yeah we can. And that's the sort of thing that shows how Travellers are. They've never wanted to be assimilated. They think, "If that's the price of a peaceful life, we won't pay it."

But then all the money that's thrown through the arts and public programmes at a group in UK society like the Traveller community, a lot of it's being done for the wrong reasons, isn't it?

Trying to assimilate them isn't going to work. Various societies have tried for over two thousand years.

Ultimately, any state has to have the people within its borders assimilate regardless of how they personally feel about it. It's the nature of a state. Get everyone into the same tickbox. That sort of thing can actually create obstacles for your sort of documentation onstage. Have you been able to attract a stable of writers?

It depends from project to project. I brought in other writers for a production called *Yellow Dress* recently. That was seven or eight different writers, most of them Travellers.

How about touring work?

If you want to do a UK tour, then it's got to appeal to a lot of people. I had that recently with *Carmen: The Gypsy*, for instance, where I took a show that I originally did on radio and re-adapted it for the stage. Everybody knows *Carmen* the opera, so that was a good start, but I decided to do it my own way. I updated it, set it in the Traveller community and made it a contemporary story. Put the Carmen character on a present-day Travellers' site and see how we go. It did really well, got good reviews, drew audiences in, and we were able to get a number of co-producers on board. I like taking shows around the country. We've done it with several productions.

With *Carmen: The Gypsy* I realised that if you're working with different partners, they have to see something that's going to draw audiences in and you have to respond to that. But your job is then to keep your integrity about doing it your own way. As I mentioned my next production is a folk opera, which is inspired by Shakespeare's *King Lear*. I'm writing the libretto and composing the music. I've never written an opera before so I'm very excited about it. Again it will be a contemporary story set on a Traveller site. We've already had a lot of interest both in the UK and internationally. It will probably be a Romany Theatre production but if another company wanted to produce it I'd be open to discuss it.

If it worked out with another producer, would it have the integrity of a Traveller production in terms of casting and stuff like that?

Other companies or producing venues would have their own ideas of course. If my main roles were to write the libretto and compose the music, I'd still have a substantial say in the production. When I work like that, I have to really trust the organisation, that they're going to do it in the right way. You find out as you go along that some are okay, some are not, and then if we're not on the same page so to speak, it can be difficult. The integrity of the production is crucial.

A drawback when you're working with Travellers or the culture is that it starts to feel like you're speaking on behalf of your community, and there's a lot of pressure to get it right. And no matter what you do, some are going to agree while others are not. You have to trust your instincts about what you reveal in order to make good drama. Most writers come up with an idea, write about it, and get the show put on. If it works it works, if it doesn't it doesn't. But if you've got a cultural thing going on, you're getting judged on that as well as everything else. But as a writer that's a decision you make. You either go with it or you don't.

Do you feel that you've left the door open in a way that it can't be closed, or you've just done what had to be done?

I would hope that I've done some good along the way. I hope that I've changed some things and maybe opened a few doors and given people a chance to see what might be possible. But who knows what the impact is really. You just have to follow your instincts and go with what you feel. You hope you're doing something good and that something positive is going to come of it. I mean, some people you collaborate with or who see your work might say, "It was an incredible experience," or "It's helped as a stepping stone in what I always wanted to do." But whether the impact is lasting, I don't know. I hope so.

Does that integrity lie in you the writer or in the subject of your work — or is it same thing?

To me it's the same thing. It's a bit of a cliché to say 'be true to yourself', but if it doesn't feel true, then it doesn't work. And if it doesn't work, it's usually because there's no centre to it, no core. All my work is about integrity, it's very important. The guiding light when I write about my culture is: what will Travellers think of it? Will they believe it? Will they recognise it? But of course at the same time I want to appeal to a wider audience.

But you've got a very specific bar to keep yourself above.

It has to be truthful. It won't work otherwise.

Especially when your real judges are the Travellers in that front row of seats.

As far as my cultural work is concerned, it's those people. If they say this didn't work or you got this or that wrong . . . well, it's never really happened. Most of the Travellers that have experienced my shows are pretty blown away because they *know* it's been written by a Traveller.

Then from an outsider's point of view, do you think it gives you an edge to your writing? Although I don't think 'edge' is the right word to use for your work.

I hope non-Travellers get it. I'm sure my work has a uniqueness to it because of my background, and I guess one of the ways that could be described is 'edgy'. I like to think my work makes people feel in a certain way that they haven't felt before.

You just made me think: given your body of work, have you seen any connections made from the Roma communities across Europe to your work?

I worked with a group of Roma from Slovakia, and there's a little theatre in Budapest, the Piccolo Theatre, which is Roma too. We took some Roma actors from there, brought them across here to do a show, very fine actors. We did a cross-European project and that worked really well. It was a mighty risk, that's for sure because when they arrived they could hardly speak any English.

Was there a cultural resonance?

Roma in Europe speak fluent Romani. Over here it's very broken, very much part Romani, part English. But over there it's full. And they do play music around the fire and sing, you know, and the food is very traditional. They've kept a lot more of the culture over there, it's amazing.

Then tell me about the music. That presumably must have a different edge to it as well?

I have created an original soundtrack for most of my shows. I didn't go out looking to do that at the beginning, but the reaction of audiences to my music has always been extremely positive, from both Travellers or non Travellers. Recently I thought, instead of getting actors and musicians to perform my music on the stage in a drama setting, why don't I take some of that music, get a band together and perform it myself? So I'm going to be doing that next year *[2020]*. I call my music 'Gypsy Folk', but it's been described as a fusion of folk and musical theatre. I'm looking forward to performing live because it's a very different challenge for me.

Do you think it's something that's far more accessible.

I do, yes — and I'm already getting a lot of interest. People are booking the show. It's a bit terrifying because I haven't played music live onstage before. Never sang with a band. I've just come from a meeting with someone who is helping me get the band together. I've also been asked to write my autobiography, so I'm wondering if I should narrate a little about my life on stage, you know, between the songs. I'll be interested to see how it all pans out. It should be fun.

Will the Traveller community come to your gigs in the same way they go to your theatre, or do they usually end up at the O2 or SSE Hydro?

Some go to those venues. But my music is definitely more theatrical. A lot of the songs are about people in dramatic situations and Gypsies seen through the prism of history. That inspires my music and also seems to reach people from the wider community.

I'd like to bring a new audience to theatre through music. Travellers very rarely go to theatre in large numbers because it can feel a little intimidating. Getting Travellers to the theatre has been one of my driving forces, so enticing them there via music is just another step on that road.

Yours is traditionally a very scattered community, so you've got the challenge of finding enough in one area to fill a hall.

Even if just a few come along at first and enjoy it, they'll tell their friends. I never had any hope of going to the theatre when I was a kid, so it'd be wonderful to bring crowds in, not just Travellers, or people who had a similar upbringing to mine, but anyone who enjoys music and theatre. I guess that's why I always wanted to tell the truth with my writing. So when an audience comes in, they know it's all there in those stories on stage, and that they can be excited and inspired. That it can be accessible to everyone.

*

2
Gavin Barlow & David Slater

'For the most exciting things, we should take a leap of faith'

Gavin Barlow is chief executive/artistic director of the Albany Deptford arts centre in Lewisham, South East London. Based in South East London, he was born & raised in Manchester.
• thealbany.org.uk, @gavinjbarlow

David Slater is director of Entelechy Arts, based at the Albany Deptford. He is based in South East London, where he was also born and raised.
• entelechyarts.org, @entelechyarts

• ageagainstthemachine.org.uk

Is there anything else similar that inspired you to do Age Against the Machine: Festival of Creative Ageing?

David: It's organisations like Luminate [*'Scotland's creative ageing organisation' which runs events nationwide across the year*], Gwanwyn [*'Celebrating creativity in older age', a month-long festival held in May all over Wales*], Arts and Age [*'Celebrating and strengthening the voice of older people through the arts', 19 projects across Northern Ireland*]. Interestingly they're all regional. There are similar events in England but probably none of them nationwide. In London, for a couple of years I also directed the Capital Age Festival, which took place from

2007 in the last years of *[London mayor]* Ken Livingstone's tenure in City Hall.

Livingstone had a small team dedicated to older citizens in the capital and they did a large festival over several weekends. I was festival director for three of those: two were at City Hall itself and we also worked a lot with Coin Street Festival *[just a bit further from City Hall along the South Bank of the River Thames in London]*. But that was basically bringing together in one place things that were already happening across the city that had a theatre edge. And then we did something together, didn't we?

Gavin: We were co-producing a show called *Home Sweet Home*. Well actually David was doing it in Bradford, Stockton and here in London. It was a show with Freedom Studios that involved older participants from those three areas. We decided to curate a bit of a festival around it — it was done on a few pennies. So that was the real spark that made us realise it was possible to do Age Against the Machine.

However, it's also fair to say that the idea of the festival was more organic, because there's a project called *Meet Me at the Albany* which Entelechy Arts and the Albany have been doing in partnership for the past six years. It's an older people's project based here. *[It grew out of a simple question 'What if isolated and lonely older people had the opportunity to go to an arts centre instead of a day centre?' — one day a week all year, formerly lonely older people meet in the Albany to work alongside artists.]* It's important that this space in the cafe now takes over the building. But it's really important that for us it was one of those things that brings together a group of people in a space here. It's part of the life of a building and of a community.

In fact *Meet Me at the Albany* came into reality because of a challenge from the local authority. Lewisham Council were having to close day centres and, unusually for a local authority, they challenged their local cultural organisations to come up with ideas that would help to somehow mitigate that loss.

David: It was a very real and powerful acknowledgement that we have what they'd like, which is imagination. "We've got these problems. What do you reckon? How can we solve them *together*?"

So it was almost a corporate problem-solving session.

David: Actually it was something rawer, it was really a complete recognition of the fact that this is what artists do all the time. They're putting themselves in the position of working with people who use imagination. Because of this, it was much more of a sticky relationship. They wanted to be involved. They wanted to *play* with us. As a result they wanted to keep us out of areas like commissioning structures. Instead they wanted to ask questions like, "What's a different way of doing things, how do we create a different relationship between a local authority and its cultural organisations?"

Gavin: Looking back, it feels more radical than it did at the time, in the sense that we were in a position where the local authorities were having to make awful cuts, but instead of just slicing things down and leaving it at that, they weren't afraid to ask us, "Well this is the reality. So is there a different way of doing this? Can we *imagine* something better?"

David: So we started the conversation a different way. We invited the senior team from the local authority here and we all sat around the table in our office. We had coffee and croissants. It was almost like they left part of their professional role hanging on the door outside and as a result they seemed to create a space with us that offered a different view, and that created a different kind of conversation.

> *You've said 'slicing it down', and we should perhaps point out that the majority of local authorities across the country are in ever deepening crisis because of government cuts in their funding, and they're forced into axing services. Regardless of political persuasion, they've all been hit the same way — even the Tory councils across the country aren't all like Westminster [in Central London] who voluntarily opted to cut their entire cultural budget, the assumption being that market forces would naturally take over or local businesses would sponsor what was needed. And of course with their location and catchment area, Westminster could afford to do that. But clearly this is Lewisham who didn't want to take that option. Someone somewhere thought let's try and not leave the borough holding the consequences of that zero option.*

Gavin: And it really does so often come down to individuals who spot the problem and are able to make things happen.

> *And was that the case you think?*

Gavin: I think it was, yeah.

David: We certainly saw key initiatives come from the council's community directorate, which interestingly held social care and arts/culture. So that was enormously helpful.

> *And why shouldn't a responsible borough find it in their remit to seek an answer*

elsewhere to the consequences of its unwilling actions? It wasn't just a cultural response that you were asked to generate, I'd say you needed to encompass a whole lot more because you had to address an essential social duty. So is that what art's really all about?

David: But they *are* the same thing!

Gavin: Of course they are. And it's always been that way at the Albany.

David: Entelechy started 30 years ago with an area health authority who was dismantling all these old asylums outside of town. In a really enlightened move, they were literally trying to find another community for the people they'd thrown out, some of them had been 60 years of their life in an institution. But the problem was where on earth is this community?

So the authority asked artists to join their multidisciplinary team to go and see. Of course 'community' is a really illusive commodity. You have to make it and remake it. It's a constantly evolving entity. We formed a company, which meant working in a participatory way with all those questions about who's not in the room — and why. It segues into all those jargonistic things too, like 'barriers to participation'. So we started with that and our life as a company has since seen us constantly doing work with older people.

Towards the beginning, we often found themselves in rooms full of white British women in their 70s. Now the make-up of the streets outside where we were meeting — this was in Walworth *[Southwark, South London]* — didn't match the groups we were working with. It was and is an incredibly diverse area.

So we set the groups an ultimatum: "We don't look like the street. Make us look like the street, and we'll carry on." Since they were involved in things like faith groups, they were able to bring in people who were representative of the area. We then asked them re-site where we were working and lots of things like that. The fact is that 'who is not here, whose voice is not heard' is a political act in itself. So it sounds a bit zealous, but it happened in an organic way and we gave the relationship with the authority a whole load of time to evolve.

In terms of talking about who's not in the room and your experience in tackling it, what do you think you two brought to your collective table to create initiatives for older people?

Gavin: The Albany has always been more than the sum of its parts. There are 26 resident organisations currently here including Entelechy and Heart & Soul, who work with learning disabled people. So it always feels like there's so much more on offer here. Entelechy have worked with older people amongst other groups for 25, 30 years. So they have that real expertise of going into communities, working in different ways and being at the forefront of co-creation, as we call it these days.

David: We're making it up as we go along, that's what.

Gavin: Well, exactly. The Albany itself has gone through all sorts of different versions of itself, but one of the key things that we have, apart from a building with lots of other people using it, is its wide-ranging arts programme.

When I first came to the Albany 16 years ago, it didn't have an arts programme. It had this amazing history but it was it was in serious trouble, in huge debt. There was literally nothing going on in the theatre and it was pretty deserted.

I remember us holding a few public meetings in my first couple of weeks, and in one of the first ones, a few people were standing up and shouting, screaming in my face. They were really angry about the place. I wasn't used to this exactly, but it made me realise that the Albany has been an important place in lots of people's lives locally for years and years. And so people have had all sorts of connections with the Albany growing up and it had been an important place in the community, and they were angry that it had been allowed to disintegrate in the way that it had and I as a new director, I was a representative of this. And so it didn't have much at that time apart from the building, but you realise one asset it did have is those connections and the fact that people cared about the place; and that they weren't your average arts attendee. They were people in the local area. We built it back up from that position and that strength.

David: To be honest, when we very first started this area of work, we had no idea what we were going to do, what would happen. And that's its strength and why it has continued to be successful. So suddenly on a Tuesday we had 15 people who'd been given a basic description of what we wanted to do. They were isolated and had been introduced to us by their families or GPs. And Age Against the Machine went from there to take over the whole building for three weeks.

One of the key things that the Albany brought to it was to rethink what it had done up to that point for all the little important things that improve accessibility. For example, the seats in the cafe weren't of any use for a lot of people — and not just older people — because they needed to have arms on the sides and to be a different size. The space was cold and needed heaters.

There weren't enough toilets that you could get to. By transforming those public spaces, all of the front-facing staff in the centre could be supported to engage and welcome people to the festival by making it an 'ordinary' place for them to spend the day.

Those changes happened because they needed to be a priority. And they were made to be a priority. Through those changes we were able to focus on the audience/participants. There's a flexibility in our partnership based on listening, which is what co-production is all about.

Gavin: It's interesting how you can start by focusing on a particular group of people — isolated, older people in this case — and then move out in different levels from there. There's what the staff learns, what the building learns, how we adapt everything, how we make the place more welcoming, more comfortable. And it really is simple things like the right heating and the right chairs that are the essential elements. Not only are you making that place into somewhere that is accessible and welcoming to that group, you're also improving it overall for all sorts of people.

David: By way of example, there's a pretty interesting group of people in this cafe at the moment. *[Mind the Gap's full-day event for learning-disabled artists and companies was in full swing.]*

> *We're looking at the proof happening around us right now in this cafe. But, despite what you say about making it up as you go along, of course this sort of thing also comes from your experience in bringing people together, your understanding of the building and the community — in a weird sort of way programming comes almost as an afterthought. If you can get people together in one place and they're comfortable with it, that's already a festival thing.*

David: Of course. What has also been invaluable from our point of view is the fact that I spent some time in Brazil with their Points of Culture programme in 2010. I was working alongside Brazilian artists who spoke about what we did in a completely different way with a different expectation. It was that sort of perspective that gives you the courage to step out of where you feel you ought to be. You notice the cultural structures within which you operate, and you do a little sidestep. In my case it was a tiny repositioning but it felt huge in terms of just being able to take a different look at the reason for art, that point of culture, like an acupuncture point that radiates energy then infects all the other energies not only within the culture space but also outside it. That perspective also gives the local authority the courage to maintain their investment — they get it, they're excited by the co-production, the co-conspiratorial understanding of the parts necessary to make it all come together.

So how did you mix all of that into creating an organic structure that makes Age Against the Machine?

David: I love the way that botanists rope off that square area of land and look up all the plants that are growing within those bounds. That's what we did. We took this moment in time and asked what have we got? So together we'd commissioned *[theatremaker & performer]* Christopher Green to create a show 18 months before the Age Against the Machine festival. He started an R&D phase for what was to become *The Home*, a 48-hour immersive piece of theatre that wrestles with the balance between care and control and how life can flourish if you are living in a care home. How can a piece of theatre tweak the nature of the conversation, for example if we're always talking about the next abuse case in care homes? How can we push this on? And so all that around us was pretty central to developing things.

Gavin: It was absolutely central to *The Home*, it's an example of what you were saying how the programme's enough to shape itself. Or to look it another way, it is bringing people together and different kinds of people with artists in a different environment. *The Home* is a good example of changing artists' perspectives and practice, and a lot of really interesting work has subsequently directly come out of *The Home*. We originally brought Christopher in for the 21st Century Tea Dances regular events that Entelechy puts on. He came in as a host and then also became an artist with Meet Me at the Albany.

Out of the conversations and interactions around those projects he came up with the idea for *The Home* — about residential care, drawing on our years of shared work with older people. It premiered as part of Age Against the Machine: Festival of Creative Ageing in Lewisham in September 2019 before touring to ARC Stockton Arts Centre, and then Tokyo's Saitama Arts Theatre in Japan in 2021.

Christopher created a care home where the audience are invited to spend two nights and become the 'cared for'. The staff are played by professional performers and community participants who are all older artists. The piece is based on stories told by residents and staff living and working in care homes. It's challenging on so many levels, and yet it very much came out of Meet Me at the Albany, i.e. a local project and lived experience. And then it evolved. It is absolutely a local project but we were keen that it be seen as making a contribution to an important national debate around care for older people. So from very early on, we determined that the conversations we had round it as well as the articles and interviews about it should be as important as the show itself. It would all be part of the same thing. So you had this very local thing — it also stayed local when we did it in Stockton with ARC — that also got a certain level of national impact and coverage.

Another interesting element comes from when David and I went a couple of years ago to Japan to work with the Saitama who produce work in a similar way *[its former artistic director, the late Yukio Ninagawa, founded Saitama Gold Theatre, a company catering solely to people aged 55 and over]*. That was *BED*, and as a result our co-production of *The Home* came about. We'd connected with the Saitama through the Future Arts Centres *[network co-founded by the Albany]* and I mentioned it then. We want to make those international connections and it feels that *The Home* is a model for that where the experience is being translated to a very different culture and different system. It's a good example of how something from a very local project has a wider impact and can translate internationally.

That's at the heart of the festival and what we do in general in the sense that there's a lot of ways to function as a regional arts centre and to get your audiences which aren't just regional — and it's like a badge of honour that you can reach wider audiences. But it just shows that working hyper-locally or in a very local context doesn't mean that it's not artistically ambitious or that it can't have a wider impact.

David: It's also a swapping of address books. We wouldn't have known Chris if he hadn't worked with our 21st Century Tea Dances, if Gavin hadn't said he thought Chris was an artist that we would find interesting. Entelechy had also been developing a relationship with Saitama Gold Company through *BED*, a show that we've been doing here for street performance, so I went over and worked with some of their company over there. The performers in the company are in their 70s and 80s, Kiyoshi is the oldest member of the company at 90. *[BED was performed on the streets of Saitama as part of World Gold Theatre 2018.]* It's this constant meshing of relationships which then allows all these chance collisions.

There's a sustainability for both of your organisations in just going for it rather than get caught up in the politics of juggling partners, funding and hierarchies. Clearly it's not gung-ho because of course you have the confidence of long experience of those politics and the relationships needed to make things work. It's interesting how adaptability to your audiences springs from that, taking the hyper-local to Japan — what's on your doorstep is probably on someone else's, which gives everyone a chance to find something in common.

David: There's something about the authenticity of relationships that gives our work its sustainability. It's also trust. So within *The Home* with a cast of 60, there are 12 professional performers plus six performers in their 70s and 80s who are older people. Some of them came in here as isolated and vulnerable older people. And so you say, "Do you fancy giving up five weeks of your life?" Only it's not 'giving up' five weeks. In fact it's, "Do you fancy being totally involved in this production? Do you fancy performing on a street in your night clothes in Dundee?" It's about a different relationship, which is . . .

A leap of faith?

David: Yes, a leap of faith. Which takes you to an intermingling of different energies and experiences. A whole network is created.

Gavin: Picking up on the word 'trust', it's interesting to think that over the 16 years I've been here *[speaking at the end of 2019]* — and David has been here with Entelechy for longer than that obviously — if I go back those years, my job was to come in and turn the place around, blah-dee-blah. My expectation was that I would move on — people in this position usually do — but I'm still here. Trust takes time to build and it's all about building relationships. What I've found is that for the most exciting things to come out, it can take quite a few years because we need a point where we should take a leap of faith, but it takes time to get there. Even just on the level of the local authority, you have to build those relationships for a while for them to finally be able to go, "Okay, I can take this leap of faith and I can trust these people to make it work." So it's nice to be able to say, "We're not burnt out." In fact, do you know, I feel more excited by working here than I did at any point over those 16 years. And for me that's the surprise.

David: That's a relationship which is, as you say, hyper-local, and again that's the point of culture. If you forensically pay attention to the hyper-local then you can find yourself working with a company in Japan because it has that universal resonance and things are able to happen organically despite the difference in cultures. People will to come wherever you are, and for a fortnight in Japan the building was full of artists — 120 people plus groups of artists from Taiwan. Somehow people end up on your doorstep and they learn from an experience of a group of people who are in their 70s and 80s here who are teaching all of these people who want to work in a different way that people recognise and value.

Sometimes you feel that it's all nonsense that you're writing in funding applications about the older generation being key and that we need to hear their voices. But Meet Me at the Albany was actually quoted as a project in a Department of Culture Media & Sport White Paper a couple of years ago and we found ourselves wondering how on earth did that happen? And then we realised, oh yeah, it was the moment when one of the older participants, Joan, headed around that corner and said three sentences to someone from the DCMS. One short moment that so focused all the other voices shaping the discourse.

Gavin: Working as a group on evolving things like *BED*, Age Against the Machine and *The Home* — creators, performers, audience, building, community — is the opposite of what we're used to in the arts, where the visionary artistic director comes in, they're there, they make a splash. Of course that becomes very time limited, you know, ten years maximum and then you have to move on. But this sort of process upends that by creating something lasting, by allowing the space where other voices come through as an organic process. But it's not so obvious. For example, when we started talking to Future Arts Centres about the work we do, there was a fear amongst some of the other venues that we're fulfilling a social agenda at the Albany that could be seen as a challenge that compromises our artistic mission. I guess that surprised me because our process seems the complete opposite of that.

What comes out as artistic work goes in lots of different directions, but it actually comes out of those networks of relationships, which means that a centre like the Albany is an anchor in a community or in an area. It's a place where we can then connect with different sectors or different people. It's a building in an area which has a lot of deprivation but that situation is also changing massively fast, which probably makes the Albany one of the few places where you will find an opportunity for everybody to come together. I don't think there are many other buildings in the UK that everybody uses in the same way, where there's that chance of 'traditional' interactions.

I'm finding it hard to think of anywhere in London at least that covers as much as the Albany. Pleasingly, it does what it says on the packet. Which gets me wondering about the timing of Age Against the Machine — do you think there's a particular reason why it's happened now, why it's taken so long for London to catch up with the rest of the country?

Gavin: The honest truth is that we could see that we had the materials for something like Age Against the Machine, as we had tried some of that in the past. But what made us see the opportunity was in the new Borough of Culture competition, so we pitched the idea as part of Lewisham's bid. Now Lewisham didn't become Borough of Culture, but the Mayor of London selected our festival idea for a specific award — and that was what enabled us to do it. So there was also a bit of money to do it.

Interestingly, they said that of all the 25 or so boroughs who put in complete programmes of culture for their whole communities, not one of the bids apart from Lewisham's mentioned working with older people. So the Mayor's Office felt it important to do a festival connected with this, because although working with older people has recently come onto the arts agenda, it was a good opportunity to showcase what we were doing and what was happening in Lewisham, and also to bring other work that was international or from around the country to London.

David: Another way of looking at it is this was an opportunity to flaunt it, because something as powerful as *The Home* would have happened anyway. We had already done all these other projects, like the crazy huge 21st Century Tea Dance that filled the whole building with people, the street performance of *BED* that we did in Japan. What really gave us *and* the local authority the opportunity to work together was looking at their small grants programme. What this meant is there were something like 67 applications for money from the council that uncovered the small tiny things — the hyper-local — that were attempting to flourish or were already flourishing in neighbourhoods across the borough. So it enabled the uncovering of all of that, and with that knowledge we were able to match our artists with different ideas and create more levels of more partnerships.

Gavin: So there were 23 commissions that came out of that small grant process, which were the backbone of the festival. If you look at the festival brochure, it would be a challenge to work out which are community-led commissions and which ones we programmed in elsewhere. They were all part of the same richness of the programme.

It was certainly an interesting process because of working with the council's small grants programme, where they said, "We'll put £30,000 out there." Local community groups applied to do their community events as part of the festival. And so we thought that was an opportunity to take that and do it slightly differently, because we wanted to challenge those groups to imagine something much more than they would normally put in to an application form. And we also wanted the groups who would never apply for those things to apply. I think we achieved both of those things.

We took it through a very deliberate process involving stages. So the first stage was that we just asked people to send in ideas, like any ideas they had. We got over a hundred that came in through artists, individuals, community groups. And then there came the stages of working with those people, giving them feedback, helping them to put the application in, challenging them, pairing them with artists or challenging them to push their ideas a bit further. So it was quite an indepth process of working with people, out of which came those 67 applications, out of which came those 23 commissions. It's an example of investing in a process, if you like, which brought huge richness, which actually became the mainstay of the festival.

That's the same process which on a much larger scale has made European Capital of Cultures like Matera and Leeuwarden such a success and given sustainability for their future cultural make-up. It was all about the hyper-local. It really does come down to people on all sides just going for it, doesn't it?

David: Of course. We want to mix it all up, challenge assumptions. There's a danger that in less guarded moments art is used as a sugar-coated pill to soften people's time living in under-resourced institutional settings in the last years of their lives But you have to constantly challenge, provoke, to avoid the constant danger of wanting to settle, allowing things to settle, wanting things to be 'safe'. Just the fact that we've used the word 'older people' should be challenged. We should reclaim the word 'old'.

Gavin: I'm always struggling with the problem of language. But the people we work with are struggling with that too.

It's impressive by any standards the way you've tracked and kept up with the changes in the community around you.

Gavin: Going back 15 years or so, when we were starting to build a programme back for the venue, our way of working came out of the fact that we had inherited an arts centre that was funded not to produce any expectations in some ways. It was certainly the case at that time because we would bring in touring work, but we could see that none of it resonated with the local audiences. So from that came the aim of working with the resident organisations, working with local people to create expectations, and out of that came a programme where 70 per cent of what's on the stage at the Albany has somehow been created in the building or through collaborations — and it came entirely out of that decision to create expectations. We knew we were going to have to make the work simply because there wasn't the work out there that would resonate with our local audiences. One of the things we're proud of is that, even if you look at the demographics of the ticket buyers, they actually are fairly representative of the demographics of Lewisham. I think that's unusual for most arts venues in the country.

David: It has a lot to do with arts culture as a leisure activity, and arts culture as a need. Because we're in a world with other people, there is this human need to make sense of the things that are happening to you. Whether it's growing older, your body doing weird things, maybe you are living in extreme poverty, you can actually find something creative in all of those. It becomes a case of people growing into possibilities . . . I don't need to finish the sentence because already it sounds too much like a funding application quote. But that's truly what happens.

I love the phrase 'what will become of me?' — it can either be total despair or total hope, and it's what comes to so many of the older people that we work with. They can ask that and work it out together in the company of other people and artists . . . but they're artists too! We've learned that there are so many people in their 80s here whose parents told them as teenagers, "Over my dead body will you go to theatre school", but then in their 60s and over they go to craft school, and then life happens. They pick it up again. Become creative again.

Gavin: I remember very consciously when we started that we were happy to start projects as a kind of trial with two elements to it: (a) we'll try it, and (b) if it works we'll keep doing it. So at the very beginning we made a commitment that if we started something like Meet Me at the Albany, we weren't going to stop it one way or another, and that we would do it every single week. But that's quite a weird commitment to make.

David: How did we do that? . . . But we did do it!

[both laugh]

Gavin: We did make that commitment. It felt like if we start this, unless it fails, if it does work, we can't stop it, because it builds a huge expectation and becomes important. There are so many arts projects — and you know this is always the temptation — that set a project up, advertise it through their normal channels, attract a particular group of people, and then they try and diversify it.

In our case, however, at the very beginning we said, "We don't want people who know they want to come to an arts project to be the people who decide what it is and develop it." What we decided therefore was to put the work in — talking to people, talking to GPs, working with health workers, just finding people through lots of different routes, then inviting them in so that they became the core of the project. And when it became successful, we then brought in lots of other different people. But the core of the project wasn't the normal kind of formal arts project that people expect, where that project is created before inviting people in.

David: It had to be done the other way round. With long-term health conditions, for example, the resulting isolation isn't discriminatory, it affects everyone. And that was why partly why people were going back again to that idea of need for culture.

It very much reminds me of the ongoing conversation I've been having about reviving the Alhambra Theatre in Morecambe and how we need to find ways to help the community to rediscover the idea that theatre could happen there, even without funding. And someone said, "Why don't you do shows that people can bring their dogs to?" I would never have thought of that: people who are isolated, many of them with long-term health conditions, for whom their dogs are central to their lives but who won't visit buildings that are there for them because those buildings won't let dogs in. With a bit of focus, a space like the Alhambra can easily become dog-friendly for a night, it's not such a strange step to make. Thinking out of the box for little things like that can make a massive difference and also help people understand that isolation affects us all.

David: Once people walk through the door that space is theirs. Recently we put on Bryony Lavery's *Frozen* by *[visual physical theatre company]* Fingersmiths, a signed performance with deaf performers. It was about domestic abuse and it was hard-hitting and difficult to watch. It had been programmed for a Tuesday when 70 and 80 year olds were here and we were worried about the effect it would have on the audience. We tried to describe a little bit beforehand, but in the end we just thought it was best for them to go and see the performance.

Afterwards, people were coming up and saying, "We got it. Why would we not want to see this? This is something happens in our society. This is something we're close to." So that was the process of getting through those stages where people say, "Oh, I didn't know I was allowed. I didn't know I was allowed to go into the culture space." But people discover that actually yeah, that's okay, this is your space.

Gavin: It's your space, and anything's possible.

*

3

Luke Barnes

'The minute people say "I like it here", bars pop up, theatre happens'

Luke Barnes is a writer. He's based in Liverpool, where he was born & raised.
• *lukeedwardbarnes.com*
@lukeybarnsey

Five weeks into the Coronavirus lockdown you found the virtual space to talk about the North as it existed pre-crisis via your open town hall Stories of the North: "We're going to be talking 'Northern identity', if there is such a thing. If there is or if there isn't, how do we talk about it, how do we frame it, how does it affect the nature of how we talk about it in stories and in life? What can 'Northern stories' look like moving forward, how can we be useful as 'Northern artists'?" What made you do it?

It's a number of things. I'm a writer, I write for theatre mostly, and when I go to meetings, I get asked a lot about this concept of 'Northernism'. As much as I try, I don't know what it is — and if I had an idea of what it is, I would have monetised it in my career. But I don't actually know what it means. What I thought it meant was this idea of stories set in the North and the way we tell those stories being what we have in common. But these stories, especially in television and film but also, weirdly, theatre recently, are found in post-industrial poverty, deprivation, drugs, sexual abuse. It seems like the mums are prostitutes, the dads are depressed taxi drivers, that's the sum total. But the real North that we actually see lies in the intersectionality of things like class and culture.

I'm working on projects at the minute about that and I'm now getting clearer on it and I understand that the word 'North' is useful in some ways and unuseful in others. There are similarities and commonalities among our Northern cities, each has their own cultural uniqueness and industry — a term I use loosely. So when we talk about the North, we have to think in terms of those individual cities in the context of Northernness, Englishness, Britishness, Europeanness and global.

So here I'm going to sum up that problem as being the long-established economic, social and cultural divide between North and South, an imbalance tipped in the South's favour, made most visible (at the time when the Coronavirus crisis broke) through the disproportionately negative impact on the North of Tory-imposed austerity, Brexit and the 2019 general election. With our politicians and captains of industry failing as expected with dead-end billion pound initiatives like Northern Powerhouse and the HS2 rail link, there's not much promise offered by the 'New Normal'. I also need to point out that while the North has a string of mighty theatres punctuated by gems like Opera North, Northern Stage, Home, Manchester International Festival, Hull Truck, Middle Child, Red Ladder and so many other groundbreaking organisations, companies and festivals (and the BBC's MediaCityUK of course), the way things stood pre-crisis none of them had ever been able to join up to create the cultural wholeness that's taken for granted in the South East of the UK.

Well, for the open town hall, there were two mains reasons I wanted to do it. The first was obviously from me personally not really knowing what 'Northern' meant or how useful it was. The second came from my interest in what a theatre company of the North without walls would look like, how it would function culturally and practically, what work it would make. If I do the open town hall again, I'll talk about that idea of a 'National Theatre of the North' in more depth because there's something in that shared commonality that could allow us to make a body of work that can travel amongst the regions, our towns, cities and villages. It's a useful conversation for the North to have that isn't the same as the one they can have down South or in Scotland, Wales and Northern Ireland. I was also keen to keep it artistic and not to descend into a decimation of the responsibilities of theatres, TV companies, drama schools and film companies

I moved back to Liverpool last year after being in London for ten years, and one of the big things that's got me interested is looking at how the North can have creative and artistic retention, and how we can empower people to stay and make work here — and not have to go to London. You see so many artists who are awesome, and they go down there and just get swallowed up and then give up. When actually they can have more impact and even make more money and have a better lifestyle if they actually stayed in one of the cities across the North. So right now how can we empower people to do that? In fact a big part of me coming back to Liverpool comes from wanting to stay in one place and make work at the highest level without the need to go to London and impose brain drain on the city.

So those are the basic reasons, but the practical objective of the open town hall was to try and identify ways to talk about all this in a way that's useful and accurate and empowering. There's the idea of talking about what the whole country would look like within the context of a Theatre of the North, and also finding a way to talk about how to empower people to not have to go to London.

How about the timing? Is this something that you would have brought people together for in any case, or did you just realise that as a result of the Coronavirus crisis, you've got a captive audience — you know, let's get people talking while they've still time to think?

A hundred per cent the latter! As I've got older, I've realised that I don't know the answers. When I was younger I was relying on white middle class male arrogance, just being like, "Fuck it, I've probably got it right, I'm awesome!" Now that I'm back, I've realised that everyone here's sitting around doing nothing, so why not get together and share resources? Like, if we don't start talking about shit like this, we're never going to be empowered to speak about it on a national level. But if we do, then maybe, maybe we can start to change our relationship with each other and start doing things that change the microcosm of the way we work in the North and talk about the North. The Coronavirus crisis lockdown is just a useful time, since we're just sitting around doing nothing, to have those conversations. And why not, you know?

How do you build on those conversations, to get people to transform them into action?

I can't speak for others, but for me it has to be how we talk about it in the work itself. And it's not just in the scriptwriting or production, it's how we approach the initial genesis of a project. So the impetus of work for someone in my position needs to be in reimagining the way we talk about Liverpool in popular media, or Liverpool in context with the North, or Liverpool in context with Europe. Because what usually always happens — not so much in theatre, because theatre's different, but in TV and film — is that you go in and you'll say, "I want to write about *[picturesque villagey part of Liverpool]* Little

Crosby", and they'll be "Brilliant. I get that Liverpool's got pebble streets, bla bla bla, but can you have all the lads in tracksuits?" And you're like, well lads in tracksuits are a small part of society, it doesn't do anything for the way that the world sees Liverpool as the city that we see.

Reimagining the narrative of the city is important when we think about things like audience retention and brain drain, because if you keep telling a place that it's shit and people think it is and they're feeling sad about themselves, they'll start to believe it — "Well it is shit!" — and then they'll fuck off saying they're never coming back. Whereas if we as artists can say, for example, "Look, let's celebrate human resilience against post-industrial poverty, right?", then suddenly we're talking about how *great* people are. Or we can take the point of view of a middle class part of the city that we don't normally see, and suddenly it's about people living in an environment that is safe and warm. Then eventually that's what we all start to see the city as.

There's also the international context, especially for a city like Liverpool. It's definitely not true for Manchester, but Liverpool is its own worst enemy because it can be incredibly introspective and parochial when it comes to the way it talks about itself and the work it makes. The international context is really important because Liverpool is a European city but it sees itself as Scouse and not English, it doesn't look out that much, it looks inwards. Liverpool would definitely benefit from the presence of international theatre to help change its cultural perspective.

So it's about identifying our objectives and using them to shape how we portray these places in generating projects. But it's not necessarily talking about the North, it's talking about our specific place in the context of England, Britain, Europe and the world. You have to think about Liverpool looking outwards and being inspired by Europe as a European city. It's also talking about form, in other words *how* we tell our stories in this specific place with specific issues, in the context of the world itself. At the same time we should stop playing to the contextual stereotypes.

So we need to think about how to tell these stories, questioning ourselves so we're dealing with the shit that is sitting in this place, finding our place in the world in a way that's informed by cultures that aren't necessarily what you would call traditional Scouse culture. And that fits the picture of a place that is outward looking, positive, celebratory, fully acknowledging what's going on here. Not looking inwards, but making things theatrically or cinematically progressive, it's obvious. But we're still at a point when we haven't quite got to that place where we can remove those well-trodden tropes or conversations. So that's what I'm trying to work towards, I guess.

In this first open town hall the conversation probably wasn't more structured in that direction, but I was glad I did it because what people said confirmed all these concerns. And it was worth doing from an artist's perspective of course.

Do you think there's any way of putting down the roots of that conversation in a practical way to create a permanent response, like a Theatre of the North without walls? Because the danger is that when the doors are opened and everyone goes back to 'normal' post-crisis, all the talk that's in every Zoom conference, Twitter thread or political handwringing about righting wrongs and changing everything, most of it won't happen and it'll just be the same old shit as the New Normal snaps back to the Old Normal — or, worse, they'll pretend they've sorted it. Plus all this further highlights the fact that we're losing out because there's an absence of viable leadership.

That is definitely my biggest concern, especially with the conversations around European theatre at the moment. People are asking for the sort of revolutions here that have been happening there, but who's going to be the person to do something? And *can* do something? Our responsibility as artists is to ask what can I physically control? I'm not producer, so what can I do to empower others? What I am going to do is to pitch projects that do everything I'm talking about in theatre but that are also specifically working with the community, sitting down with real people, involving real people, tangibly working out what the impact of this particular project and this particular place can be. It has to be thinking on those terms because I'm not one of those people who says I'm going to topple power and burn it all down.

I try instead to gently nudge conversations in a way that will make things more useful to their communities. My priority is always going to be the people we're serving — it's not to do with coup d'etats, we've got to do what's in our direct power. It's about the nature of the projects that bring people out, rather than imposing or starting companies. I also want to get people talking about the Theatre of the North idea, asking how it would be useful in terms of generating their own work or bringing a project to producers to do the work your company would do if you had a company.

You're talking about it as a writer, but this also obviously affects directors, venues, performers and audience too. I think London during the decade you were there lost its creative lead in terms of putting on visible work with relevance, but its centrifugal forces still won't let the rest of the country redress the balance. Where do you think the barriers stand now from the vantagepoint of where you are, i.e. regionally, mentally, socially, economically within the UK?

Well here I feel that I'm now in a better place to pitch projects to big theatres in London than, say, two years ago when I lived there. I hate to be blunt about it, but in London I was effectively another middle class twentysomething straight white male in a sea of straight white males who think they're clever in a world where no one wanted to hear from that. Whereas now I'm back, I'm living and conversing and having a dialogue with a community that's a *real* community.

It's interesting that I don't have any friends here who work in the arts particularly. My friends who are working in the arts, I talk with online, on WhatsApp, on the phone or whatever, but I feel my viewpoint is stronger here, I feel more connected with the real world, and therefore I feel more confident to talk about some of the things that I wouldn't have when I was living in London. The problems are geographical, the exposure to the best culture, for example, is hard even though we've got cultural centres like Manchester, Liverpool, Leeds, Newcastle — I go to Sheffield quite a lot to see stuff, for example. But it's expensive to get around to those cities. I go into London too. But I don't see as much theatre as I did, which is probably why I work more in TV and film at the moment, because I see more of that.

Of course it's not fair to criticise our institutions for not trying to make this change moment because most of them are not in a position to do anything because of the crisis. But the real barrier to starting out lies in our education and ability to challenge the narrow influences we're getting from theatre, film, television in the UK, opening up our exposure to a wider variety of ideas and cultures. That's easily solvable, it's just about knowing where to look.

In terms of making stuff, though, the barrier's always money, it's always money. But you're more likely to get Arts Council money for a project in any of these places in the North than you are in London, where it's saturated and all about getting longer runs and press coverage. An especially big problem that came out of the open town hall is access to press coverage — the well-trodden model for theatremakers is that you have to take work to a festival or to London in order to get a few critics in. That's the only way you can get a bit of attention and use it to instil confidence in producers to collaborate with you. In fact that's sadly going to be the case wherever you live in the country.

So yeah, money, exposure, culture . . . There's ways around all that stuff, it's just knowing how to do it. Another big thing that came up is the question of space, like where do you make work? We need more theatres, more non-conventional spaces. Other questions were how can we get theatre the same support that goes to cultural events? How we can attract new audiences? How we can have these conversations in the most popular way?

A lot of this is linked to finding ways to tell stories that don't really exist within the parameters of what the public hears in the overpriced semi-irrelevant static storytelling that we often have. There was the opinion at Stories of the North that we're going to see a rise in storytelling happen outside of theatre spaces for a lot of reasons. One being that theatre outside of a traditional space can be like a cultural event, which means that it's more accessible to audiences. I hope it doesn't work out that way, but my biggest fear is that the theatres will take even less risk post-crisis, while the more radical younger people will make work outside the buildings. I think that's what's going to happen. I think. *[laughs]* Don't know!

At the very least you've got people talking in one place at grassroots level. There were tons of people and it was amazing to watch all those thoughts just go whizzing down the Zoom comment bubbles. They weren't angry voices patched in from the Twitterverse but practitioners crystallising a powerful vision for coming together.

I probably know about four or five people who were there and I have no idea who the rest were! What a lot of people were definitely talking about was the need for a wider cultural relationship between the North and South. They were pointing at the national media culture where the people who work in that industry push their cultural preconceptions on us of what Northernness is. So it's a wider thing than angry Twitter feeds. If I have that conversation with my friends here about Northernness they'd say the same thing, where you'd get a lot of like, "I get looked down in London", "People think because I've got a shaved head and got this accent that I bla bla bla." You've got a lot of that stuff constantly going on. Look at football, for example, every time we have anyone come up to Anfield *[Liverpool Football Club's stadium]*, you always get the "Sign on! Sign on!" chants.

So it's talking about a cultural relationship here that's much wider than theatre and it's our responsibility to reimagine our place in a narrative that is not what we have at the moment. It's much wider than just the theatre because, as I say, it's everyone's responsibility, where the more we reimagine our homes and communities and the places we love, the more people can have self-confidence.

The example I always use is when I was working with Hull and in 2017 I did *All We Ever Wanted Was Everything* with Middle Child when the city was UK City of Culture — and a mad thing happened. You went there and everyone was like, "Hull's shit, but it's home. Like it's shit, but it's our shit." And then the City of Culture happened and they were like, "I like it here!" Big shift. It sounds fucking stupid, but it changed the entire mentality of the city. The minute people start going, "I like it here", bars pop up, cafes open, artists start making work. Theatre is happening.

That cultural confidence is a massive thing, improving the quality of life in places. A big part of our responsibility is empowering cultural confidence in our own towns. The more we carry on reimagining these places and the more it happens, the more confidence we can have in ourselves and our communities. And then the more money ends up being there and bla bla bla. It's a really important move to get us developing our hometown by talking about it in a way that's not pessimistic.

A lot of acknowledging Value Added Northern and flipping that narrative needs money, especially in the case of theatre as you say. But how does money get diverted to where it can do the most, to bring equity? Because if you had a mini UK City of Culture in every single town every couple of months in the North, the arts would stay for ever and also you'd create a permanent and growing audience as well — and pride of course.

Money is definitely the biggest thing. I read a stat recently which says the Arts Council give more money to Islington *[North London]* than they do to all the former coalfield towns in Britain. Obviously Islington has Sadler's Wells and the Almeida Theatre there, but that's still fucking mental, you know? So that's what you're competing with, I suppose. And it's not just Islington, there's fucking loads of areas like that in London like the South Bank.

I was particularly struck by someone at Stories of the North saying that everywhere in the country is the North apart from the London and the South East. Mind you, there's Northern places in the top rich lists like Alderley Edge, Hale and Harrogate, but they don't need funding in the same way.

But that sort of funding is something that I don't know enough about. I've a rough idea of how smaller theatre companies operate financially than national portfolio organisations, for example, but the Almeida or Sadler's Wells, fuck knows. Rich old ladies with big dresses, I reckon.

Based on the ideas and feedback from Stories of the North, what do you think people want to see as the next step for when the country opens up again and we're in a position to act? Theatre's going to be a challenge to kickstart at any level since it was first to close and will be last to open.

What we can do right now even before the theatres open is to change the way that we talk about our hometowns. That's the first stage. Change the negative fragmented way we talk about our town, shift it to talking about things like resilience and pride. Talking about it changes your thinking about it. So the minute you start doing that, people will find confidence in themselves and then grow to the second stage, which is making work in those places and finding a profile that defines it. So those are the two things: talk about it, then make work that does what you talk about. And it's not about waiting for permission from anyone else do that.

How important is theatre as a tool for that in terms of where you see it going?

At the moment? Not important enough, if I'm entirely honest, and that's not a Liverpool thing, that's a national thing. The reason being that people think of theatre as something that is for them or is fun or is a good thing to do. I think people still have this idea of theatre being like the altar to the genius where you go and see the best actor do the best part of the best play. Maybe that's well and good for some of the theatre sector but it can't be the sum total. We've got to find ways to make work that is socially, politically, philosophically and humanly resonant in a way that is accessible and sounds like something people would do, being innovative and progressive at the same time.

And those were the types of questions I wanted to ask everyone on the open town hall: how can we make the work we make into something that is important, that people can access and come to but is still pushing the medium? That's where we start working out what we'll do next. Of course people have been trying to do this for generations. John McGrath was doing it with 7:84 *[Glasgow-based agitprop theatre company]*, Joan Littlewood, John Godber to an extent, Alan Ayckbourn. These people have kept knocking on those doors for ages while keeping themselves open to influences from the rest of the world. And for us it's being inspired not just by them but also by the Milo Raus and Ostermeiers and all the artists like them.

But theatre's had no one in the driving seat for years and years. You could see it in the lack of any sustained joined-up response to Brexit, to the regional divides, to social inequality, where maybe theatre actually and genuinely has been a reflection of society by not dealing with the issues either. And now we're facing a literally existential situation because of the threatened collapse of the theatre ecosystem as a result of the Coronavirus crisis. Why do you think theatre's lost its way?

I don't think it's lost its way. I just think that theatre and mainstream culture now are operating within very narrow parameters because everything's so dispersed at the moment. Theatre as a medium especially isn't helped by practical limitations, like it taking so long to get things done and therefore losing what it's all about. We're also dealing with the more internal questions of why our theatre is less socially responsive than it has been. I do know there's loads of good things about, and I also know everyone wants it to be good, all these artists, directors, writers, actors who are pointing fingers at how they all want it to be awesome. No one's holding on to their pearl necklaces saying, "I wish the art would fuck off." All we ever want is to be good. So we should just keep asking loads of questions until we get there. And one day it will just click.

I like what a friend of mine said the other day. She said the responsibility is in becoming that annoying person who asks the questions. Sometimes sacrificing your privilege means you're able to annoy someone else in order to get bigger shit done. I think that's what we've got to do, just keep asking the questions until we get people in charge of their own work and eventually the cultural landscape will change to embrace that. Or people refuse to change and go in another direction. But what we have to do is ask the questions and hope for a response, right?

*

4
Julia Barry

'What we discovered was never underestimate new audiences'

Julia Barry is executive director of the Sherman Theatre/Theatr y Sherman. She is based in Cardiff, where she was born and raised.
• *shermantheatre.co.uk*

A good question to start with is 'what is the Sherman?'

What is the Sherman . . . ? The Sherman physically is one building which was built in the mid-1970s as part of Cardiff University. It occupies a space on the very edge of the city centre of Cardiff but still situated within the heart of university — we're next door to the student union. The theatre has been many many things in its time.

My history with it personally is that I grew up in Cardiff and it was my local theatre. I went there from a very young age. At that time it was a theatre that was very much known for making work with and for young people under the artistic directorship of Phil Clark, so it had a thriving youth theatre. It's morphed through the years. In 2007, it merged with Script Cymru, which was the then new writing company for Wales. Today it's very much set up with the ambition of becoming one of the leading producing houses in the UK, while putting our audiences and our communities at the heart of everything we do.

The new writing that has come from the Sherman is largely based in and around the communities which we serve, but not always. We want to give voice to those communities and very much see ourselves as a civic resource for Cardiff — so we are more than just a theatre. We are a space for people to belong, for people to find out what theatre is, for people to hone their craft, whether that's the four year olds that come to Sherman Sherbets on a Saturday morning, our youth theatre, our Sherman Players, which is our amateur company, or artists at whatever stage of their career. It's a home for them. We ensure that all of our practice is, as far as possible, informed by the communities that we serve. That's a big statement.

That's very much reflected in the Sherman 5, which gives you an extra focus to all that, doesn't it?

It does. The initial funding for the Sherman 5 was a gift from the Paul Hamlyn Foundation. It was celebrating its 25th anniversary and wanted to go right back to the root of it, which was the Paul Hamlyn clubs that used to happen at the Royal Opera House *[in London]*, where *[publisher & philanthropist]* Paul Hamlyn would buy out an entire house and give those tickets to people who wouldn't ordinarily have access to the opera house. The remit of the gift that we received, along with four other organisations across the UK, was to engage with our communities who are facing barriers to engagement and bring them into our buildings to see the work on our stages. It wasn't about parachuting into communities, doing community work with them and then leaving.

We completed five years of that funding and we're now in a second tranche of Paul Hamlyn Foundation Funding for a further four years to deepen that engagement. So it's not just about bringing people in to experience the work on our stages, we're now trying to widen access to careers in the arts, opportunities for volunteering, for developing new skills. We run behind-the-scenes sessions so that people can come in and see what our carpenter does, what the lighting designers do. And we're very much talking about storytelling and the importance of it along with the breadth of voices, how do we encourage people from every community across our city of Cardiff to pick up a pen and give writing a go.

So looking at those communities, how Welsh do people feel in Cardiff?

How Welsh do people feel? Cardiff is a really interesting city because it's incredibly diverse. As somebody who grew up in Cardiff, I feel very Welsh. I've always been proud that I'm Welsh. I learned Welsh to A-level standard and then left Wales for ten years *[laughs]* and since coming home, I'm trying to use my Welsh more and more and immerse myself back in the language. There is, of course, the ongoing conversation about language and culture and how they are intrinsically linked, and then what that means for non-Welsh speakers.

Which isn't an obvious conversation for non-Welsh people to get their heads around.

It's an important distinction to make, and it's a conversation that we're all having about Welsh culture, Welsh identity and the role of the Welsh language within that. As a theatre, we work hard to ensure that the Welsh language is represented, and at the same time we've worked hard to make sure that the Welsh language is as accessible as possible. So the Sherman two years ago made a decision that any Welsh language productions we produce will always be surtitled in the English language so that non-Welsh speakers have access to it — and we've seen a huge increase in people accessing that work. That chimes with the Welsh government goal to achieve a million Welsh speakers by 2050 *[Cymraeg 2050]*, and I think the only way we will get there is by people being exposed to the language, but in different settings. Not having to go to Welsh lessons, but being able to go to the theatre, to enjoy a piece of Welsh language work that they can follow because it's surtitled and immersing themselves in the language.

So while Cardiff is a multicultural city, there is a real sense of Welshness there, although perhaps not quite as strong as in the North of Wales — unless there's a rugby international!

What contribution is the Sherman making to the identity of Welsh theatre? It's always a shock to realise that Welsh theatre is not an ancient tradition as in the rest of the British Isles.

We talk about making work for Cardiff first and foremost because we're not a national organisation — our audience primarily is Cardiff then Wales, and then beyond. We invest in Welsh and Wales-based artists. Building on the past five years and going forward now to the next chapter, we're very much looking at creating the best of contemporary Welsh work about life in contemporary Wales. In early 2019, we produced *Woof*, a Welsh language play by Elgan Rhys that was fundamentally about a gay relationship but actually was about so much more, with universal themes. It was one of the most contemporary Welsh language plays that I think we've seen, and a large proportion of the audience were non-Welsh speaking, who were able to take advantage of the surtitles, but many reported that after a while they stopped using them and were able to immerse themselves in the piece, language aside.

We want to tell those stories equally, so we're also exploring how we can make bilingual work, because that's the lived experience of the Welsh language in Cardiff, where people use language very fluidly. If they're bilingual, they'll speak English to one person and Welsh to somebody else, there'll be flitting in and out of English and Welsh mid-sentence. That's the linguistic reality, the lived experience for how to bring that onto our stages.

The Welsh experience of the capital city also makes us work with our diverse communities — a good example is a community production we did called *Love, Cardiff: City Road Stories*. City Road is one of the main thoroughfares through the city. Historically it was full of car showrooms and fabric shops, but over the last 15 or 20 years it's become full of eateries. You can get 62 different world cuisines down that street.

We worked with people who live, work and just inhabit City Road on a day to day basis to create a community production with about 16 or 17 people on our stage that went from somebody who had only arrived in Cardiff from Poland about six months earlier, the woman who runs the sex shop on City Road, the man who oversees the community garden, a young man we discovered in the gym but who was an aspiring actor, a couple who were Cardiff born and bred and had met in Tito's, a nightclub that used to exist on City Road — and they told their stories to their peers in two sold-out houses. The beauty of it was that ethos spilled out from the theatre that day and into the foyer and suddenly everybody was sharing their stories and their experiences. You could feel the electricity of that multicultural, inclusive cohesive society, and it remains one of the most special evenings at the Sherman ever. For me that's what sums up Cardiff and the Welshness of it.

So you were genuinely reflecting the drama of life in the community around the Sherman, and you didn't have to force them onto that stage.

Oh goodness me, no! And so many of the people who came in to see it were people who had never set foot in any theatre, not just the Sherman. They came because their friends were in it, and they made it the most genuine shared experience I think I've ever experienced.

Audiences then . . . As a producer I've also put on shows where we've got in people who've never set foot in a theatre before, and the next question logically facing you is how do you get them back in? Or do you want to get them back in? I don't mean that cynically, but getting audiences like that back in is a huge commitment that requires huge resources.

We know that, and so we know we've been hugely fortunate to have the Sherman 5 funding. It's enabled us to put in structures, employ people specifically to go out and do this work, and also to financially support people's first, second, third visits to the theatre. Through that project we have engaged in the past five and a half years over 4,000 members of the scheme, which in the first five years resulted in nearly 15,000 attendances. Of course some of them were one-off — people came once, and didn't come back — but many became repeat attenders and also independent bookers.

Their first few visits were very much supported. People booked their tickets on their behalf, arranged transport, but as audience members became more confident in attending, they've become independent. We can see its impact and the diversity of our audiences on a day-to-day basis, and it has created a marked shift in the audience base of the Sherman theatre that I don't think we will go back from now. I think we will keep growing and diversifying.

We've talked a lot to those communities about why they didn't go to theatre before. Whilst they told us a lot about the cost of tickets and transport, fundamentally for many people the response was, "People like me don't go to the theatre." So it's been about breaking down those perceptions, answering questions like "Do I have to dress up to go to the theatre?" and bringing people in for familiarisation visits. The first time they come, it's not necessarily to see a show but simply to be shown the theatre — this is where the box office is, that's where the toilets are, that's the bar, and this is what the auditorium looks like. It takes the risk away a little bit. And reducing the ticket prices also reduced the sense of risk in terms of their first visits.

What we also discovered was never underestimate new audiences. Because they were hungry for work. In the early days of the project, one of the first pieces of work we brought in for them was a piece of Shakespeare, *Romeo and Juliet*. Not long after that we invited them to *Iphigenia in Splott [by Gary Owen]*, which on paper was a piece of new writing, a one-person show based on the classics, nobody famous in it. In terms of your traditional marketing, it was a hard sell to a new audience. But by that point we'd started building up that hunger within the Sherman 5 audiences that they were ready to try the next thing. And the fact that the play was set in Splott, which was a part of Cardiff that many of them knew well, and there was Gary's ability to create work that resonates with people by getting to the heart of the place and the people in it.

Not only did those audiences come and see that show, but they actively became involved in post-show discussions, talking about the themes of the show, talking about identifying with the play's character, whether they could see a bit of themselves in it, whether they knew that person, whether they see that person walking down Splott Road on a daily basis. I think what one of the important things is we've shown is that not only is theatre for people like them, it's about people like them and made by people like them. It's a universal thing. So we're going back to that idea of generating new voices from those different communities.

But you do have a core.

We do have a core. Interestingly one of the biggest benefits of the Sherman 5 funding is the fact we were able to create a team specifically dedicated to developing those audiences, with the result that the Sherman 5 audience isn't any different from our wider audience, in fact they are microcosm of that — their needs and requirements are actually the same. So the organisation has developed huge areas of its activity in response to Sherman 5, but knowing that it's benefiting the wider audience, like informing pricing policies, making sure that we have a breadth of prices.

And you know it works?

Yes, absolutely. If somebody just wants to go to a main house show and pay our top price ticket of £26, they can, but equally there's a £15 ticket in there, and if you're under 25, you halve both of those so it'll be between £7.50 and £13. It's the same on our bar, making sure there's a breadth of choice. The welcome has been really important too. When we first started out, we had specific Sherman 5 nights. Since a lot of the members were potentially first-time attenders, we had a number of Sherman 5 highly visible reps and volunteers to help people navigate the space, on the door to say hello and welcome.

In time that practice has evolved across all performances, and also the ethos of our front-of-house practice, so now we always have people on the door saying hello, making it a friendly and more accessible welcoming space for everyone. It does keep the audiences coming back. And going back to what you've said about programming, we do have a pattern so that people know what to expect at different times of the year. In the autumn we always do an adaptation of a classic text with a well-known title, but it would usually be a new adaptation or a contemporary adaptation of it. At Christmas our Main House show is always an actor-musician led familiar title, whilst in the Studio we create an intimate show specifically for ages three to six, which is performed in both Welsh and English.

The spring is the time for our new writing slots with one or two new pieces. And then alongside that we've brought in initiatives like 'Get It While It's Hot', which is a take on the 'A Play, a Pie & a Pint' scheme: £12.50 a ticket, half-past six show, you turn up, you get your pie, your pint and your play. Less conventional ways of enjoying theatre like that make it a bit more relaxed with certain audiences.

Equally, going back to that idea of civic resource, the space can offer itself for a variety of non-theatre uses. So we've got quiz nights and Welsh learners in the foyer who come in every Wednesday morning. We host a Repair Cafe once a month, which is where people bring along items that aren't working for volunteers to fix their Hoovers, irons or whatever it is. There's a sustainability thing going on there that is also very much bringing the community together in a community space.

So many other theatres around the country are doing the same, but it has to be said that not everyone hits the level of theatre you're producing.

We had this serendipitous moment where Rachel O'Riordan arrived as artistic director and the Sherman 5 project launched at the same time, they just dovetailed by chance. We'd received the funding for Sherman 5 and done a six month pilot, Rachel arrived, we launched the full scheme for Sherman 5 with her first production, *Romeo and Juliet*.

Suddenly we were bringing back people who had not attended the Sherman for a long time, at the same time as we were bringing in new audiences who'd never been, and they all coexist. There's no distinction now, they've just all morphed into one glorious audience base. Yes it does change and it will always change, but we have a breadth of programmes that adapts to that.

We hosted one of the guys from the TV programme *Who Dares Wins*, which brought in a whole new audience who'd never set foot in the Sherman — lots of big men in black hoodies who are all into the SAS. Suddenly you really are reaching out across all sorts of communities. And this doesn't all come down from the management team. The Repair Cafe came from our front of house manager saying, "This happens over in that part of Cardiff, but they're looking for a place for over here. And wouldn't it be good for us, because on a Saturday morning we could open up the theatre." And that's the beauty of it, our staff team who are completely invested, looking for opportunities to bring the building to life and engage with more people. And you never know, somebody who brings in their broken iron on Saturday morning who's never been to us before may pick up the brochure and come back. And if they never come back other than for the repair cafe, then that's okay too. They know where we are and they know the theatre exists.

At the end of last year *[2019]* we became the first theatre in Wales to be awarded 'Theatre of Sanctuary' status, which feels like the icing on the cake really and is testament to the team's work. It epitomises how we see the building, that it is a genuinely a space for everybody. And it shines a light on the work that we're doing with our refugee and asylum-seeking communities, really vibrant communities in Cardiff. It's challenging and can have a huge impact.

There's a passion and an enthusiasm within everybody who works at the Sherman to make sure that every audience interaction is as good as it can be. And that does sound like everybody says that, and they probably do, but I just think the Sherman team do it incredibly well.

However, you can see Rachel's arrival not necessarily leading to success because of circumstances.

Well yes. She also arrived as Cardiff Council removed a hundred per cent of our funding, so we went from a staff of 32 to 21 within two months of her starting due to necessity because Cardiff Council had just cut all their arts funding other than the two venues that they owned. And so actually Rachel started totally on the back foot,

There's the wider story as well. The fact that what happened to the Sherman was happening to theatres all over the country — and their collective survival and reinvention is a story that definitely needs to be told. But it seemed there was something a little more revolutionary happening at the Sherman.

Rachel certainly brought the revolution and then she got the people in the theatre to go along with her. Because she brought that vision.

Could you bottle it?

No, because it sounds really rudimentary, although it's clearly deeper than that, to say that she put audience at the heart — we need to make work that will appeal to audiences. It's not rocket science. It's really interesting now to how the Arts Council of Wales strategy has shifted. Their new corporate plan 2018-2023 is called 'For the Benefit of All', and it's now all about accessibility and quality of work and audiences, whereas before it was all about making work but nobody was thinking about the audience.

So there was the aspiration for the Sherman to be a leading producing house in the UK with the understanding that audiences had to be at the heart of what we were doing. There was an acknowledgement that audiences need a pattern of programming that honestly reflects them. Feels all really basic, but important!

But it wasn't being done before,

It wasn't. We had had a significant building redevelopment and the doors had been shut for two years, between 2010 and 2012, so we'd already been experiencing challenges reconnecting with audiences. When Rachel arrived, we started giving them familiar titles, a pattern of programming, and then pieces of new writing, alongside the brilliant work we knew could do with our Sherman 5 project.

The team bought into the vision pretty swiftly, so everybody was working towards the same goals. We knew it would be a tough time because there'd been that significant structural change. We had lost people, young people left, jobs had been lost. So it was challenging for the first six months, but once we went through that bit, there was no looking back.

You've described the Sherman as a 'civic resource', reflected in your commitment to the communities of Cardiff. As we're seeing across the country at the moment, theatres like yours have had to very much become extensions of the councils — and not just culturally — as they're having to step into the municipal responsibilities as the councils lose their government grants and in turn make cuts to services, with the arts first in the firing line.

We are fulfilling a lot of that through the work that we do with schools, through the work of our youth theatre, through being a theatre of sanctuary, through our volunteer scheme, and through our Sherman 5 scheme. We are fulfilling huge civic engagement responsibilities that historically would have sat with the council. But I also know how difficult it must be when you are a council. If you're looking at your social services provision, of course you have to prioritise it. That said, I don't think people should underestimate the value that a theatre like the Sherman can have in terms of positively affecting some of those issues.

We have bursaries that we've put in place for our youth theatre, which means that we have young people from disadvantaged backgrounds and young people who are looked after coming to youth theatre. The impact that youth theatre can have on an individual is extraordinary. Just watching our youth theatre and the way that they come together as a tribe and the support they offer one another within that safe space. The work that we do in schools in terms of addressing poverty of aspiration, introducing children from very disadvantaged backgrounds into theatre, sending writers out to work with them and them writing their own scripts and coming into the theatre to have them performed by professional actors — all of these things. It's the kind of big society thing isn't it?

This all must have an impact and I just sometimes think if only councils thought in more cross-disciplinary ways, for want of a better word, rather than in the silos of we must support social services, we must support health. But actually what's the return on our investment? If we put some money into a local theatre, what's the return on our investment in terms of what they deliver for our communities and what that might then prevent in the future? That's very optimistic, big picture and wishful thinking perhaps, but . . .

They may do it, I suppose, but it's usually an investment that goes to music, which always seems to be several steps ahead of everyone.

Cardiff Council responded to the music argument when a city centre street full of live music venues under threat of closure began a campaign. There were a number of protests, and the council have come full circle and not only is Womanby Street saved but it's thriving. They're also making Cardiff a City of Music. They've totally invested in it.

But music's a far easier sell. And opera and ballet too, even if all of us don't necessarily go to either.

But if we're talking specifically about theatre at the Sherman, I think we offer high quality entry-level theatre for a first experience, particularly with young children. So the work that we make at Christmas for ages three to six, is made specifically for that age group.

It's the parents and grandparents who are willing to put themselves outside of their comfort zone for their kids. Parents who haven't been to the theatre before will bring their three and four year olds. And when they've been in once, it sounds a cliché but you can take them on that journey.

We've been talking a lot recently about theatre being 'analogue'. I know it's not quite the right term, but we live in a world where everybody's glued to the screen all the time. And isn't the theatre the kind of most beautiful thing, where you go in and you sit amongst people and you have that shared experience, it's in front of you and it's live and it's tangible.

You can't snap it and save it, and file it away, you have to remember it.

Exactly. I don't know why theatre is the harder sell. But I do know that you have to experience it in the moment, to share that experience with someone else. And you can't do it without audiences!

*

5
Yvonne Brewster

'If you don't own your own house, they can throw you out'

Yvonne Brewster is a director, teacher, writer, producer & co-founder of Talawa Theatre Company. Based in North London, she was born & raised in Kingston, Jamaica.

It was radio that got you into the performing arts, wasn't it?

It was! The BBC used to broadcast a programme called *Topical Tapes* — they were to reel-to-reel tapes that they sent to Jamaica 'to entertain the natives'. It was always plays which they aired on the radio (there was no television in Jamaica at that time, remember) and then they just chucked them away. Now for some reason — I don't know how I managed this, or who it was, or what — but I got hold of some of these tapes. My father was always ahead of the game, so he had one of these big console TV units when they first came out, waiting for television to arrive. So it had this pathetic little screen in the middle with a record-player and a reel-to-reel player on top. So I somehow got all these tapes and I'd hide away and listen to the plays. And that's when I decided that's what I want to do, I wanted to be on those tapes.

So it when I did my Higher School Certificate, the equivalent of A-levels, I was asked, "So what do you want to do, Yvonne?" "Well I want to be on the *Topical Tapes*." "Oh Jesus, what we going to do with her?! You've got to become a nurse," said my mother. I said, "No, I do not. The thought of blood is too much for me." "Well, you could be a lawyer, you chat a lot." "Oh no, they're all liars, lawyers. I want to be on *Topical Tapes*." And because I was the child that you didn't bother to try and put off from what she wanted to do, they said, "Okay, however are you going to do that?" I said, "Well I have to go to England and study."

I used to go to drama classes on Saturday morning held at the British Council in Kingston, and I told Mr Murray there what I wanted to do. He was wonderful, he didn't laugh or anything, instead he said, "You mean you want to go to *drama school?*" And I thought, "No, no, no, no, no, I don't want to go to that . . . *What* is drama school, anyway?" He just said, "Yes, that's what you want to do. I will get you a place and then I will vouch for you, and you will do the interview here." He thought of Rose Bruford *[College of Theatre & Performance, in Sidcup, Kent]*, which was only seven years old at the time, and he told me, "Well that's the best one because they're trying to make a name, and they say they like overseas students. They don't have any, but let's see if we can get you in there." And he did.

So I was sent up with a chaperone in 1956 to New York to board the *RMS Queen Mary* on her last voyage before they fitted the liner with stabilisers. I was locked in this state room with this dreadful woman, I used to escape every evening. Now my father was a Mason and he had big friends in the UK, so when we arrived on the boat train, we were met at Waterloo with this man with a cap on, and we were shepherded into this Rolls-Royce, taken to Upper Brook Street *[in Central London]* and deposited at the hotel on the corner there. We were shown around London for a couple of days and then I was driven down to Rose Bruford in Sidcup. The chauffeur had a lot of trouble getting to Sidcup, there was no satnav and the maps were useless. But we did get there, he deposited me on the driveway, put the bags in the hall, and said farewell, sped off down the drive, anxious to get back to West One *[Central London]*. And so I was left.

I was called upstairs by what turned out to be Miss Bruford and her partner Lady Henniker-Heaton, and they said, "Are you the girl whose father has paid for her in its entirety?" And I asked, "What does that mean?" They said, "Well he's paid for the three years." I said, "Oh my God, that means he *really* doesn't want me back home!" Miss Bruford didn't think it was funny, and neither did I at the time, I just thought, "Oh they've abandoned me."

You see I come from a privileged family in Jamaica, let's face it — or well, I did, they're all gone now. And Miss Bruford said, *[posh accent]* "Well, we will take the money, but you know—" actually everybody quotes this, "—you know you'll *never* work." And some people say to me, "Oh what a fantastic thing to happen to you, because it *made* you." And I say, "Well it's all right in theory, but I tell you that could destroy a person as well as make a person."

Luckily it made me. I looked at this little round thing, she was a woman of some girth, dressed all in green, with that frizzy, frizzy permed hair, sort of semi grey, and she had a . . . not a kind face really. Even people who went to the school still don't know much about Miss Bruford. Of course she was gay. But she wasn't out then because she couldn't be. Her girlfriend Lady Henniker-Heaton funded the college, which started in 1950 with the help of poet laureate John Masefield, Laurence Olivier, and Peggy Ashcroft, who were governors *[Rose Bruford pioneered the first acting degree in 1976]*. They were two women against Masefield and all that lot who were trying to tell them how to do it. And they fought, so I have to admire them.

If only people knew that Rose Bruford was such a powerful woman. She had to be insensitive, of course, because she had to survive. She was a determined woman and I came to understand what she was trying to do, which was hellishly difficult at the time. She was trying to run a successful drama school when it was just men doing that. I realise that I should have admired her, and I do now, I didn't then. All I thought was, "Who is this woman who is telling me I'll never work. All I want to do is be on *Topical Tapes*!" They looked at me and I looked at them — and I went, "Well . . . we'll see."

In fact I was the first person in my year to get an Equity card and to work *[until 1988 no actor or dancer was allowed to perform without a card, with only limited numbers released every year]*, I pretended that I was studying but went off to the Mercury Theatre in Colchester *[in Essex]*. *[Mercury co-founder]* Robert Digby was doing an Aladdin pantomime, and I got the part. Provisional Equity card: four weeks work, plus four weeks rehearsal. How I did it, travelling all the way to Colchester while managing to do my course at the same time, nobody knew. But because this was over Christmas, I was eventually on holiday from the college, but rehearsals were difficult!

I got my Equity card, and it was in the back of my mind the whole time: You'll. Never. Work. And I thought, "Oh yeah? I'm going to *work*." And I did. I told this story 50 years later when they made me a fellow of Rose Bruford. I saw all these fancy people and all those young faces sitting down there in the college, and they'd just done this talking about me as if I wasn't there. They gave this long long spiel about me, and I thought, "What's Rose Bruford . . . ? They said I'd never work, what are they going on about?" I got so fed up with them rattling off things that I'd done that I had to respond to this citation, so I got up and I looked at the chaps and chapesses who were going to graduate, and I said, "Well that's very nice, I don't recognise myself at all of course. However, I only have a short time to speak here, but I only have very little to say. When I first came here in 1956, they told me I'd never work. Look here I am now . . . receiving this thing. So, here's the lesson: don't believe a word they say."

Well you could hear the people behind me on the platform, they were *furious*. I had told them I didn't want to be a Fellow, but my husband said to me, "You must. Because you keep turning down these honours, but you need to inspire other people." So I accepted the honour but still had to rebel. Don't believe a word they say, believe in yourself, believe that you're bigger and better and greater than they say you are. Or believe that you are exactly who you are. Whatever it is, whether it's right or it's wrong, or it's semi right, you've got to listen to *yourself*.

It's just happened like that the whole of my life, and I've had such terrible enemies, oh my God. I've had to fight, especially some of the people in the Caribbean artistic community . . . I mean the letters they used to write. When I got all that money to set up Talawa Theatre Company at the Cochrane Theatre *[in Holborn, Central London, Talawa was founded by Yvonne, Mona Hammond, Carmen Munroe and Inigo Espejel in 1986]*, I got it for the simple reason that we decided that we weren't going to take a tenth of the funding that was needed, I wanted the lot. So I did a video with Peter Palumbo, then chairman of the Arts Council, in it. I stole his cuff links *[laughs]* and did a scene of him writing me a cheque for the whole amount. He fell about when he saw it and I got the funding.

That was a bit rough on the rest, I suppose. But I thought if you've got, say, a million pounds and you divide it in ten, what are you going to do with a hundred thousand and a theatre company? Absolutely nothing, you're going to get some taxis aren't you or some pizzas? I wanted the lot because I wanted to do something that would give people work, and give me work as well. So that was the money for the Cochrane, but . . . why should *she* get everything? So they wrote these letters to the Arts Council, especially one person who I thought was my friend.

I had some supporters in the Arts Council and one phoned me up one day and said, "Look, I think you had better come and read this letter." And I said, "No", he said, "Yes." So down I went and I saw the letter written by this person, absolutely slagging me off. . . I mean, it was an *awful* letter. God that stays with you, because it was a Jamaican person, and you think, "I've never troubled this man — never employed him, mind you, but I've never troubled this man." And he didn't get anything out of attacking me, except for the Arts Council going, "Oh watch out for that guy." So it's not been that nice really, but every now and again something good does happens and you think, "Cha! That was all right."

At Talawa our policy was to offer roles to black actors that they weren't being offered. And there were moments that make you go on, like staging *Antony and Cleopatra* with Jeffrey Kissoon, and having *[director]* Peter Brook come up to me and say, "Where did you find him? I want to put him in *The Mahabharata*." Kissoon is just this brilliant actor, and what he had brought to Antony was, oh, such a sadness! He was in *The Mahabharata* for years as a result of that.

Moments like the other day, when the Royal Academy of Music said that they wanted to make me an Honorary Associate of the Academy. "No you've made a terrible mistake. I don't mind, and I won't tell anybody, but you can't give me this because I am tone deaf." This is the Royal Academy of Music, after all. They fell about, they called me in and said, "Look, we also do speech & drama and we do mime, and the board of governors have decided it may be late but we're going to pay some respect to you." I was presented with the ARAM. I thought, "Christ, after all these years". True I did sit for a couple of LRAMs in 1959 [*Licentiate of the Royal Academy of Music professional diploma*] because they were going to fail me at Rose Bruford for not speaking in an English accent. I *knew* I was going to fail, but I had to go back to Jamaica with a piece of paper, right? Because my father had said, "You want to be on *Topical Tapes*, show me!" And it was costing him a fortune.

So I got a couple of diplomas for Mime and Speech & Drama from the Royal Academy of Music, which at the time, let's face it, were worth much more than a Rose Bruford training college diploma, which is all they gave in those days. I used to dig off from Sidcup, cheat on the railways, go and have classes at the Academy by Baker Street, and come back to Sidcup. At Rose Bruford they always used to say, "She suffers from the cold, she's always ill." *[laughs]* You see, I used to have these fake chilblains and colds, just to be able to study at two places at the same time. I don't think that's for everyone, of course, but you just do what you have to do.

Well, you clearly have determination and vision . . . and an insatiable curiosity which took you out of Jamaica. You didn't say "I want to travel" but "I need to do this, so I have to go . . ."

Exactly. I'm going to go wherever. And London because it's English and all my family studied in England.

What did your parents do?

My father was quite a lot of things, he was a chartered surveyor, a civil engineer, and he came to London to study surveying. My mother used to say, "I'm a clerk", but she was an accountant actually. They made it a good family to be in.

When you started to work on the stage after you got your Equity card, did you see that there was a system that needed to be changed, or were you were just happy to be working?

I created my own opportunities for work. Nobody really ever offered me anything. I knew I had to make my own work because my reviews are almost always bad. Critics like Michael Billington weren't so bad to me, but that other one with the pink shirt, he absolutely hated me. Most of them thought that I didn't know my place, so their reviews were *always* shocking. When I did *The Importance of Being Earnest*, it got some good reviews for once, probably because it was done up in Newcastle in the Opera House.

A wonderful man, Andrew McKinnon *[director of Newcastle Opera House]*, gave me the opportunity to do the play in this enormous multi-tiered theatre *[Talawa's first co-production in 1989 with the Tyne Theatre and first to tour outside of London]*, and he said, "Well, we'll probably only open one level of the seating. But anyway, you should do this with your ideas." My designer Ellen Cairns, is just the most talented creature in the world, and we were in York railway station when she looked up at the iron and glass roof and she said, "That's the greenhouse." It filled the stage.

I was lucky to have some really wonderful designers, especially Ellen and Sue Mayes. When we did *The Road*, Sue put 13 crashed cars on the stage. Health & safety wouldn't allow you do to that now. That was the stage, and they had to be clambering over the cars. And that's where the women really excel. I've never found a male designer who excels. The women are much more practical *but* they can zoom off on an angle!

In Newcastle only was it a most amazing set that Ellen created, I also had the best actors around possible, there was nobody less than first class in that thing. They didn't half wipe the stage, and they were all British, because I know that in the time when Oscar Wilde was writing, there were black people in this country that lived in houses like that. I know that. My own family did, so don't tell me it's not possible. *[Yvonne said at the time, "My aim is not to attempt a West Indian version of the play but to stage this Oscar Wilde classic with Black actors"— reasoning that the theme of identity and working out one's origins made it relevant to all sectors of society in Britain, Black Britons in particular. No attempt was made to change the script to accommodate a version of 'blackness' or subvert the play's values.]*

Then Oscar Wilde's grandson and biographer Mervin Holland came up and said, "I need to say this to you—" and he wrote it in my copy, which I still keep: "You have given back 20 years of this play's life because you understood that my grandfather despised Lady Bracknell. She is a *vulgarian*." I said, "Well, of course she is." He said, "But most people don't realise that."

In every interview, Mervin has said that people take it as a general English play, but it's actually a play that deals desperately with English snobbery, where Lady Bracknell has come up by her bootstraps, and she's a vulgarian. If you realise that, then the whole play is different. Well, it was meat and drink to me, because Jamaica's *full* of that type of person, all of these expatriates who come from outside of London, pretending that they come from SW1 *[London postcode containing Buckingham Palace]*. The accent's all messed up, they're pretending because they have a bit of money, but underneath it you see the rumble of the regions. But why didn't they just speak the way they do, because Yorkshire's just as good as SW1 for Christ's sake.

I saw in the play that that was it, and that Lady Bracknell had 'arrived', and that's why she couldn't make those allowances for other people — to *lo-ose* one parent, and yes, carelessness — real toffee-nosed people as I have come to know over the years. Lady Bracknell is a vulgarian, but, as Melvin says, people do the play with Lady Bracknell as part of the aristocracy and she so clearly is not.

So it's those kind of things that I remember.

You gave Talawa an amazing reputation for scripts.

Well, number one, I never change a word. I can't write it and I have never been known to change a word in a play, except with permission of course. I've been lucky with writers who have helped me. I had a fight with Wole Soyinka over *The Road*. Oh, I went on for months because it was overwritten. He *overwrites*, right? But I would not cut it or change a word without his permission and he would not give me the permission. In the end he did. It was still overwritten, but he sat next to me on the first night, and every time a cut came up, he went, "ssss . . ." as if he was being cut himself. *[laughs]* He was gracious though, at the end he turned and said, "You're right. It's clearer." And not a word did I say, because I do admire him. He's such a wonderful and a political animal of the first order.

It was the same thing with Derek Walcott, who spoke like he wrote, you know, in poetry almost. He also helped me greatly by telling me not to listen to people criticising me and saying such terrible things about me. So it's lucky to have those kinds of people around you, those kinds of events happening to you, encouraging you, to remind you what Miss Bruford said, and to say up yours, no!

What made you decide that you could go from acting to directing and then producing? That's a very empowering decision to have made in those days.

When I was at college — I started a three-year course there in 1956 — I never got any parts. I was good at radio because I realised that's what I had come to study, because it was radio that made *Topical Tapes*, right? But at Rose Bruford I never got any parts on the stage. I remember being given the part of a troll in *Peer Gynt*, with no words, and in *Spring 1600* I was dressed up as some slave girl who wasn't really in the play at all. So it goes on. *[laughs]* They were taking the money, so they had to put me on the stage, right? I eventually realised that nobody wanted to do the directing, because all these other girls were debs really, let's face it, and wanted to be in front with their blonde hair all flowing and doing something like *The Boyfriend*.

So they were asking who was going to direct the next show? We had to have a student director so I put my hand up and thought, well, yes, that gets me off the stage. Now Tom Baker *[the fourth Doctor Who]* was in my year, I absolutely adore him, as well as people like Brian Bedford, he's been in *[BBC Radio 4 soap] The Archers* forever, and Nerys Kerfoot-Hughes, as she was called at the time — she became Nerys Hughes, who was in *[BBC sitcom] The Liver Birds* and *[BBC Wales/One TV series] The District Nurse*.

Tom wasn't much on the straightforward acting, he was too real, an angry young man. He said, "Why don't we just do *St Joan [by George Bernard Shaw]*, because you are a Joan of Arc?" Well, I'm not a real Joan of Arc, nobody's going to put me on the stake or burn me, but we did it, just a little scene from it, and Tom played the lead, and I directed. He was fabulous, and we got some others, and that was my first director's book. It's at the V&A now.

Unusually both you and Talawa have had a long relationship with the Theatre & Performance Department of the Victoria & Albert Museum.

I love them because they've always been kind to me. They've always *not* ignored me. When the Department was the Theatre Museum *[in Covent Garden, Central London]*, they came and recorded Talawa's 1994 *King Lear*. There were four *Lears* on in England at the time, and they had to decide which one they would record and they chose ours. They brought four cameras, so you can now see it from four angles. It was a modern version because Norman Beaton was supposed to do it. Nobody was offering black actors Shakespeare so we jumped right in. Norman was 60 and the right age, but we lost him *[he fell ill just before rehearsals and died the same year]*. We had two weeks to rethink the play, and I just turned to my favourite actor Ben Thomas, young, 40s, who was already in the cast. I said, "Well, if Donald Wolfit did at 40, you can do it."

It was completely off the wall, but that was one of the best attended shows because people understood that Shakespeare had this beat, ba-duh-duh, duh-duh-duh-duh-duh, like a heartbeat going through all the play, and I could see that the cast got it and the audience got it too. And that's where David Harewood who hadn't done any Shakespeare was so fantastic as Edmund. And Cathy Tyson as Regan, Lolita Chakrabarti as Goneril, Diane Parish as Cordelia and Mona Hammond as the Fool, oh my God! Norman came with me to see the production before he died. We slipped in at the back and I held his hand. He was weeping — and at the interval, he said, "I can't see the end. This is my play. I wanted to do Lear before I died."

Heartbreaking. But what that also shows is that you really took to directing.

Yes, because they *really* didn't want me on the stage. And I didn't want to be on the stage, because I don't regard myself as an actor. I did two years in a BBC daytime soap, when I was really broke. Two years. Christ, that was absolutely awful, and I was *so* bad. I was in the first cast of Doctors, and I had the job for a year, and then they repeated it for another year. It's the most successful thing that that particular producer ever did, it's a bit like his *EastEnders*. You didn't have to act, you just had to remember because we did sometimes 27 pages in a day, so it was "Yvonne this is the red one" and you say, "No, no, no". And then "This is the blue one", you say, "Yes, yes, yes". Then there's "This is the 'maybe' one." The lines were all written all up your arm, or over the other actor's shoulder. I mean, you can't study 27 pages with these odd stupid lines. So no, I didn't want to be an actor.

But I learned this as soon as I did *Saint Joan*, so I never really wanted to be on the stage, it set me up completely. Then I went back to Jamaica and I thought no, I'm going to do something else, so in 1965 I founded the Barn Theatre in Kingston with Trevor Rhone *[Jamaican writer and filmmaker who went to Rose Bruford in the 1960s]*. I persuaded my father to give me his garage, and it was the most successful little theatre Jamaica's ever had, because it was talking about post-independence, where the people are, where the arts can serve them.

And new writing always in there somewhere.

Always new writing, even from writers like *[white British playwright]* James Saunders, because I had met him through Sam Walters *[white English director who founded Jamaica's first full-time theatre company and drama school, and London's Orange Tree Theatre, London first purpose-built theatre in the round]*, and James was writing quite interesting stuff at the time. So I did James Saunders, I did Pinter. *[laughs]* Can you imagine? I did his *The Collection*, because it had a bearing on the situation in Jamaica in a strange way. It wasn't very successful, but it did have something to say there. From the Caribbean there were Derek Walcott's plays and the Guyanese writers.

As far as the people there were concerned, we were a set of young idiots who were doing plays, but my thing about what happened with The Barn was always that it's in a garage. It's situated at the back of the house. It seats 144 people when they're packed like sardines. It's low roof. It's high chairs. The fronts of the chairs were cut off. It was really something else. You have to be very brave to go in there, okay? I wrote a book in 2017 on the theatre, because I thought it needed to be recorded, this lovely little theatre in my father's garage. I called it *Vaulting Ambition* because I thought that's exactly what it was *[the subtitle is 'Jamaica's Barn Theatre 1965-2005'].*

In fact Jamaica is where I get my love for Shakespeare, from my grandfather, the Jew from Poland who trained as a lawyer and ended up in Jamaica as an undertaker, and who always used to teach me Shakespeare. He would shave, and he would go, "Out, damned spot! out, I say!" And you would have to answer, *"Macbeth."* *"No.* 'Scottish play', you can't say *Macbeth."* That kind of thing. What a life!

At The Barn, it started with the *[white]* expatriates. We had no chairs at first, and they would come and, *[posh accent]* "Oh, my Lord, how charming!" and I wanted to kill them. We soon got some chairs because my mother bought them. And then I noticed the chauffeurs — God, this is time capsule anyway! The expats turned up with their chauffeurs, who would come out of the cars while they were waiting and look in through the back window. *Yes!* That's where I come in. Because it's not talent or anything, I don't have much of that, it's looking at what is necessary, what works, and I watched these guys. Now, we didn't do the full week, it was Wednesday to Saturday and a matinee on Sunday when we had to black out the windows, because normally the windows were right open in the evenings.

I noticed this chauffeur driving a very famous set of people on the Thursday and he was watching from outside, and then the Sunday I saw him come in, not driving a big fancy car but with his wife or his ladyfriend, and they sat *in* the theatre. I thought, "Wait a minute, we're doing stuff that is dealing with this situation in Jamaica, in the Third World or the general colonial stuff, and here it is appealing to the very people that we are writing about." Oh, my God, that was a revelation. I don't think I really realised it until then, and I thought, "That's it, we're breaking through." So we went around and handed out free tickets to all these people who were driving these posh types to the theatre on Thursday and Fridays — they wouldn't go on Saturdays, of course, hoi poloi right? — and tell them, *[heavy Jamaican accent]* "Here you are. Come on and see the thing from the inside. Yeah man, here's a ticket. I give you one free ticket, and then you can buy the other one, half price."

And then it *changed*. It changed the whole sociological make-up of the audience. That was amazing. Really, it changed the *colour* of the audience. It changed the *reaction* of the audience. The danger of course was of going down to meet these people instead of meeting them on an equal playing-field, and not patronising them. It's very difficult not to do that. It's cheap and easy to put on plays that use dialect and stuff and you end up patronising your audience.

What happened then? You knew that when you set up The Barn you were setting up something extraordinary that would make a difference. But then you decided to return to the UK. Why did you decide that?

Because I got bored in Jamaica. *[laughs]* That's the truth. Once you've done it, why do you keep digging the same grave? Once those guys started turning up, I was very quiet with it, I don't go, "Well this is what I thought all along!" I just do it behind the scenes. I saw them turning up, "Man dress up?", and then they go, "Yes, we going to the theatre." I said, "Done!" Because that's what we wanted and it's got nowhere else to go.

But it won't go back into the bottle.

No, it can't go back in. But now it's out of the bottle, it has forgotten why it was in the bottle before. So now theatre there has become pure vulgarity, and that's why I sold The Barn. I was there in 2005 and I went to a show at the theatre which was banal, superficial, *extremely* insensitive — and it lacked any real originality. You could see they had been doing the same jokes, the same moves, the same characters and the same strange faces going up and down, everyone thinking it's funny caricature. I said to my sister who was running the theatre at the time, because I wasn't in Jamaica, and she was allowing all these people in to do their shows. I said, "But Valerie, this isn't what it should be about. I'm subsidising this place from England because I think it's important."

Within a month I went in and took down the lights. I gave them to a school that has a putative theatre and they needed some lights. I took down the sound and gave that to another institution, I think it was another school. The mural that was painted in the theatre, I took down and put it in my mother's house. She was most upset because it's an enormous thing, 24 foot wide, and eventually some man came and took it and put it up somewhere. It's supposed to be going to the nation at some stage because it's a *[Karl]* Parboosingh mural which is a big deal. And then I just stripped the place, the dressing room, everything. And that was the end of The Barn.

Now it's knocked down, it's a car park. I sold it to the richest man in Jamaica. "Haaa . . . That's what you must do. Don't sell it to no lickle funny man, he's going to knock it down because he has car agency." So who do you sell to? You sell to Butch Stewart who owns *[international hotel chain]* Sandals, right? And that's where he parks the inbound cars. And I say to him, "Well, when you build your building there you should call it the Barn, the Barnette or the Barn Hole or something. You should recognise what was there for 40 years." And I think he will. Or maybe not!

I suppose it's that thing about following your dream, following your mind. I never had any dreams myself, but I have followed what *I* think is right. It can make you rather opinionated, but I do listen to people.

When you set up to Talawa in London in 1986, did that happen because it was the times that demanded a response from you? Or was it you thinking, "I need new stimulation, I need a different platform"?

I need to go a step back first to answer that. I was working for Carib Theatre Company in 1982 *[founded in London in 1980 by Yvonne and actor & director Anton Phillips]*. I was a member of the board — it was Anton Phillips and his wife and me — and we did children's theatre, we did a very successful Barry Reckord musical *Streetwise* down in Bristol and it toured around. It was not even an Arts Council tour and I had to drive the van. The night they'd finished in Bristol, I had to drop all the cast home back in London and the set was in the back of this big hell of a white van.

I got back home in North London and I couldn't find anywhere to park this goddamned thing. I was so tired, and I thought sod it and left it in the middle of the road with the key in it. Next morning about 8 o'clock, the doorbell rang, it was a Sunday, we'd finished on the Saturday night. It was Ken Chubb from the Tricycle *[he co-founded the theatre with Shirley Barrie]* and he said, "I've parked the van and here are the keys. You left it in the middle of the road, you know, you could get done for that." I said, "Look Ken, I couldn't park it. I was so tired." He said, "Enough of this. You running around the country, you go on like you're a teenager. You're not. You need to find out how the system *works*. There's a job going at the Arts Council, and I'm going to get the application papers, I'm going to help you fill it in."

I knew Ken because I helped with the beginning of the Tricycle, digging out the stones and all of that business. Now I won't even go into the place. I won't even darken the doors of that wretched place because they changed it. They call it The Kiln. How insensitive, this is a place that actually burned down.

The job was Arts Council officer. I got an interview and I went. And there was director of arts & drama John Faulkner and arts administrator Jean Bullwinkle. I still speak to her. She's nearly 100 now, this amazing woman who kept the Arts Council going. I went into this interview with John and Jean and some other people, and they asked, "Why do you want to be an officer?" And I said, "I don't. I've never been in an office in my life. So why would I want to be an *officer*?" They liked that, and asked, "How do you think you could improve our work?" I said, "Well, you ask me a question like that? In the Arts Council, they give money to their friends. You don't look at the new work. You just put it into projects, and then if you like it you give it. That's ridiculous. If it's funding, well I come from a place where there's no funding for anything. You should be funding the people without it."

They offered me the job and I still didn't want to take it, but my husband said, "Well it's money. You're not making any money now, you're running around all over the place. You're parking things in the middle of the road. It's impossible because nobody is taking you seriously. You have to know Ken is right. You have to know how the system works."

So I got myself some tights, because I'm not really a great dresser, and some office clothes and I went to work. And I never regretted that. Jean called me in the first day and said, "You have no idea what you're doing, do you?" I said, "No, like I told you." She said, "You're going to have to come to work now." I said, " I tell you what I'm going to do, I'm coming in now. I will stay for exactly two years and then I will leave." They didn't believe me but I did. That's what it is to put down a thing and stick with it. I left two years to the day. But I learned such a lot and I thought, "Right, now I know how the system works. How can you be working somewhere like theatre and you don't know how the system works? And then you moan and groan." And that's why people became jealous and some hated me.

I didn't care because I had learned how it worked. They could have done that themselves. And I understood that to be totally and utterly and *brutally* honest about what your objectives are is the main thing. That's what I learned from the Arts Council. So many people come in and try to fool you up: "Oh, I'm going to do a mime extravaganza, and it's going to be based in the Yangtze River, so I need a grant to go to China." Yep. But they were wise in there — I don't know what they are like now — and they needed to see the money on the stage.

So when Talawa later got a grant for *Oh Babylon! [in 1988]* — it was a *big* grant for this Derek Walcott musical extravaganza — we went in to the Arts Council afterwards and we went to officer after officer to cost it out and do the reconciliation for every cent. We had no taxi expenses. Nobody was allowed to take a taxi. If I took a taxi, I paid for it myself. No jaunts. None of that, because it's the people's money. They need to see the money on the stage. There were 23 people on that flipping stage and some of them were high high profile and a lot of them are still in work, doing good work. I was always learning from challenges like that.

What would you say to the younger generations today who want to make a

career in a world where there are still barriers? Would you tell it like it is? What
would you tell someone wanting to start off in the world of theatre?

It's complicated. In one way you could even say it's more difficult now than it
once was for black theatre, because the people who can play the game have all
the chips. But really — and I'm sorry if it's boring but this is what I always say
— you have to call your own shots. If you are not in charge of what goes on,
if you are not given the important jobs like the scripts, the publicity, then you
are always a migrant. Because you have no power, and you will have to do what
other people want you to do.

So it will never happen where there will be a black company that is led by
somebody who is not intransigent, and it will not be led by someone who
thinks they are the answer to the world's problems because they are the only
one without a problem. That's what I was trying to do. But I think the
generation today, you've got better educated people, there's quite a
groundswell of people in drama school who have role models now that they
can look up to. I think somebody now has to put ego to one side and fight to
find a space, even if it is a shed, to create a new black theatre — but maybe
that's just my life's idea of how to operate.

So you have to be quite selfless but you have to have an opinion, and you
have to have an ultimate aim. And the ultimate aim is to be able to say, "We.
Will. Do. This. We. Will. Do. This. . . ."

They've tried it so often, like at The Factory down in Harrow Road *[North
West London]*, but there is nobody with any funding because everybody's lost
the funding now. When we did research maybe 20 years ago, there were 36
black and Asian companies. Tara and Tamasha are still riders, and Talawa
because its foundation was pretty strong. All the rest have been demolished.
The Tricycle isn't the answer because it is an all-comers thing, but that's fine
because it's multicultural and they did do a really good cross-section of work
giving people opportunities.

Also you do get fed up with the leading. It's a lot of hard work. And the
hope is that the next person maybe will have not necessarily a better view but
a broader view, because you must encompass *ownership*. If you don't own your
house, they can throw you out. That's what the African-American people have
learned and what they have shown us. They still have some idiots over there
who vote for Trump — you have to have some in the burrow — but they
understand it. We are not sophisticated or have enough longevity in this
country. Well, I know that Septimus was here in the fourth century BC but
I'm not talking about that. I'm talking about how in numbers we have only
been here since the 1940s really.

My uncle flew planes during the Second World War and afterwards he came back home to Jamaica. He said he was going back to England but my father and his father said to him, "You're going back nowhere. Because they don't want you now. You fly Battle of Britain, you finish. Stay here, and make you money." He was able to stay because of that support, but the rest came back here and now you see the Windrush where there is no reckoning, there is no appreciation, there is nothing, that's it.

So I think that one has to have faith and hope and just the tiniest bit of charity for people to realise that there are enough role models, and for people like Idris Elba and David Harewood to be able to formulate a caucus which cannot be ignored because, let's face it, they have television and film presence. If they can be persuaded that this is what is necessary, then we might come back to where we lost the plot because of the people who undermined the Cochrane, who undermined the New St James Theatre. Now it's a Lloyd Webber place but it was all our effort that turned that into a theatre, and in the end we saw it given to the Establishment instead.

One must not get bitter, but it needs that generation who are in their 40s. There are others, but they're not political, and they don't know how to activate that way. And none of them are big like Idris, David and so on. So one has to have patience. Rome was not built in a day, nor was a black theatre.

*

6

John Byrne

'If you are already up the ladder, pull somebody up with you'

John Byrne is a writer, broadcaster & careers advisor/columnist for The Stage newspaper. Based in Hertfordshire, he was born & raised in Dun Laoghaire (Dublin), Ireland.

• *performingcareers.com, @dearjohnbyrne*

Photo: Kirsten Reddington

Maybe let's start at the beginning?

Well I've been working over here in Britain for something like 27 years now . . . I still consider myself Irish and I have an Irish passport, but I'm certainly well past that point where my career in Britain has been longer than the one I had at home. I've made my living in the arts for most of that 27 years, but, like anybody who makes a living in the arts, that's been in a very broad range of areas. The 'glamorous' stuff like performing and broadcasting might get more attention but it was built on the back of my original career as a visual artist, where a good example of a typical job would be designing and drawing posters about forklift truck safety (this basically involved drawing 37 intricate images of forklift truck manoeuvres with very very minor adjustments to each image — this was well before the days when computers could do it at the click of a button).

In fact, starting out as cartoonist, there's been a whole side to my career that involved working for a vast range of trade magazines across almost every industry you could think of from *Plastics & Packaging* to *Bakery World* to *Concrete International* to *Hotel and Caterer*. I eventually started getting drawings into the *Irish Post* which is the Irish paper in UK and then into papers like *The Stage* and *The Guardian* and *Private Eye*, which is sort of the 'National

Theatre' of British cartooning now that *Punch* is gone, but it was usually the trade jobs rather than the high profile ones that paid the rent. I then developed a 'stand-up cartoons' act, in the course of which I began writing for and managing other comedians (mainly because they were better at getting the laughs than I was!). That expanded into managing singers in fields ranging from soul to opera as well as providing a career advice service for performers. So, from starting off by using my own artistic skills to make a living, for the last 15-20 years I've also tried to use the lessons that I've learnt to help other people make a living from their own skills.

If anybody asked me if I had a background in the arts in my own family, for a long time my answer would have been "no". My Dad was a lighthouse technician (a bit like a lighthouse keeper except he moved around a bit more, fixing them) and my Mum was a legal secretary until they got married, whereupon, because this was the 1960s, she left her job to raise me, my sister and brother while Dad went out to work.

I did have a distant uncle who could draw quite well and I suppose he was the family member I associated with the arts. He encouraged me with drawing and later with comedy writing, although he himself worked as an accountant — as a kid, I never quite understood why art was his hobby, not his job. Obviously, I now know that was probably because he wanted to eat and pay the rent more regularly than working in the arts might allow! My Mum and Dad are both in their 90s now so I go back to Ireland quite a lot to visit. And, as you do, particularly as you get older yourself, you find more time to reminisce with your parents — you're actually interested in what they have to say, which you never were when you were a grumpy teenager.

In one of those conversations with my Mum I was reminded that she actually could draw quite well but just *didn't* — because there was no way that a 'housewife' in 1960s Ireland could envisage make a living as an artist. And even though my picture of Dad was a 'blue-collar' worker going out to his job as a lighthouse technician, I was reminded that before I was born, he was always involved in amateur dramatics. He had a great tenor singing voice, and a gift for comedy and was in Gilbert & Sullivan and shows like that. I used to see the photos of him in costume as a kid, but never associated that with 'work'.

To my shame, it took nearly 40 years to dawn on me that actually both Mum and Dad could possibly have had careers in the arts, or at least had the opportunity to have careers in the arts if they'd been born into a different class, or if they had seen more people like themselves involved in the arts. And that's an interesting realisation for me, because a lot of the work that I've done has been aimed at helping people identify strategies to get through doors that they might not normally get through. Or, better yet, to build doors for themselves — because the system and the structure of the arts still blocks far too many people from whatever doors already exist.

Maybe there is some kind of subconscious motivation for that, because in my own family background there are people who had artistic talents but never got the chance to pursue them, simply because it just wasn't an option. Of course, people will say, "No, it's always an option, they could have made that choice" — just like I used to think about my uncle. But looking at the social structures, economy and the very closed nature of the arts in Ireland at the time, I don't think realistically that was the case.

I feel that it was only because of moving to Britain several decades ago, that led to opportunities I probably wouldn't have had in Ireland, at least back then when the arts were much more closed and clique-ridden. I'm grateful for the work I've had over here, although also very aware that it has its own rigid class structures and its own closed artistic environment. I was lucky enough to get off the boat in the era of Bono, *Riverdance* and boy bands, when the Irish were generally making waves in the performing world (as opposed to the literary world which was historically our 'field') and I kind of sneaked in with the backwash. But that makes me privileged too, because I happened to be Irish at a time when we had slightly moved up the pecking order and were the 'acceptable' immigrants compared to more recent arrivals.

In latter years I've also been working with actors and creatives in the United States, which has slightly different structures, but one thing that doesn't seem to be different whatever territory you work in is that, to make a career in the arts anywhere, it's easier for people who come from certain backgrounds, who have a certain financial standing, who have the right connections. People probably talk about that barrier now more openly than they used to, but talking about it and doing something about it are different things. Certainly, what we call 'diversity' or 'inclusion' shouldn't be just about a few small spaces becoming available at somebody else's table that the favoured one or two can access when given permission. If we are truly going to be diverse and inclusive then it should be everybody with an equal opportunity, full stop.

A lot of the flaws in terms of diversity initiatives and diversity panels is that, as far as I can see, they still seem to work on the assumption that the playing field is already level, but that for some reason certain people have not managed to avail of the opportunities that are available, so if we can 'just give them a helping hand' that will solve the problem. But the narrative of 'us on the inside being kinder to people on the outside', helping a few extra people squeeze through and then giving ourselves a big pat on the back for doing the bare minimum is from the outset designed to cover up the fact that the whole system is flawed and exclusive, rather than addressing it, let alone changing it.

I'd say that everyone knows that, but it hasn't meant that the inner core chooses to change no matter what progress is made on the periphery. After all the strides made in raising awareness, providing equal opps and changing legislation, underneath a lot still hasn't changed and actually has got worse in some sectors — like, for example, the statistics about actors where there's a direct correlation between success and privileged background.

To be a freelancer in the arts — let's take acting as an example — one of the prerequisites to having a chance of making your career is that you have to be able to afford to be unemployed for vast tracts of time. So that in itself is a barrier to anybody who doesn't come from a privileged financial background. If you don't have family money to comfortably draw on, you need to get something like a grant or a scholarship to study in the first place. But that's finite, and even if you get one, once that runs out, you'll end up having to get a day job which is either not going to let you go to auditions, or which will often be very poorly paid in exchange for whatever flexibility it offers.

Another issue — and anybody who works in the charity world will know this — is that it's really difficult to get anybody to give someone a grant for a second time. Organisations may give out grants and scholarships, but when it's next year and the next round of the giving cycle comes round, it becomes increasingly difficult for whoever's got that funding to get another grant or a scholarship because you've already got one.

There's also that 'pull yourself up by your bootstraps' myth where, having got your grant or your scholarship or your launchpad, you should then become sustainable. But that isn't always possible because one grant or scholarship is rarely enough to get you over the huge vast wall between organisations and individuals who can draw on privilege and those who can't.

Which again raises that word 'sustainability'. It's been a touchstone for quite a few years and yet you look around the country where so many great and good arts initiatives founder the moment the funding dips or disappears and out come the begging bowls and the blame game. The programmes, projects, initiatives all add up to the same sense as a doomed Soviet Five Year Plan, especially with the Arts Council's stream of increasingly unconvincing consultations. You can't see the sustainability when someone gets famous and rightly thanks the National Youth Theatre for getting them on track, but fails to mention the inherited socioeconomic base that gave them the confidence to go for it and sustain it afterwards.

Right. Whenever we talk about diversity, inclusion, sustainability, we talk in terms of initiatives and programmes and other philantrophic gestures. So it's almost like some people (usually white, middle to upper class and even more usually male) get to make movies and write plays and publish books because it is assumed they have a right to, while everybody who doesn't fall into that privileged category can only get in via initiatives and schemes and similar things. It's almost like there's all these walls — like the opening of the old TV series *Get Smart* where there's about 57 metal doors that you've got to get through before you get to actually do anything. It's very wearing to have to jump through all those hoops all the time. This is sadly true in almost every area where there are diversity or inclusion initiatives in place, based on gender, race, class, based on whatever. Inevitably the fact that some people get through the hoops and are accepted and other people who also applied aren't, creates divisions — no matter how positive and supportive of each other we all try and be. Even the process itself is divisive.

It's hard how to see how basics like talent, skillsets and merit fit into all this. People are proud to say that they've got to where they are because of their hard work and because of those around them, something that's not appreciated or even acknowledged by a lot of people in the industry or even the funding bodies. However counterbalancing that is that you can get there despite the system, outside of the 'this is how things are done' path, but that can undermine you because you haven't the experience of working your way up the system. There's a massive disconnect between the two sides, which the industry doesn't address because it will show it up. Lessons aren't learned, models not adopted and the lessons of individuals overcoming prejudice to get things done where institutions have failed is lost. We're impoverished as opposed to poor, conned by the privileged into aspiring to be 'entrepreneurial'. Whether we act on it or not, we all recognise the situation but now, in the 21st century, is this really what they mean by 'sustainability'?

We have ended up with two education systems which are alive and well even in the 21st century. There's the education system for the masses which is based on hard work. The implication being that you're educated to work hard for your elders and betters. Then there's the education that the 'betters' get, which is about utilising and maximising the resources that the rest of us supply to lift themselves even further to the top. And arts education is no different in that regard if you look at the culture, management and intake across many of the top courses.

Depending on where you're looking at the system from, your view of how high you can reach is going to be different. The sketch from *That Was The Week That Was [1960s BBC satirical series, which featured the 'Class sketch' or 'I know my place', performed by John Cleese, Ronnie Barker & Ronnie Corbett]* was a very visual way of illustrating that and it still holds true, and not just in terms of class politics. If you happen to fall into the category of 'the masses' then the 'reward' for your hard work is that you will at some point be able to stand among those who are privileged, and be with them and eat at their table. Not the same thing as actually *being* one of them, of course, which is probably why some of the people who have 'made it' this way seem to work so hard to keep others from their community out — possibly wary of guilt by association.

In my area of business advice or coaching, or whatever you want to call it, there is a lot of what is rightly called 'inspiration porn'. I'll use a recent meme I saw about Beyoncé as an example. This isn't intended as a criticism of her personally — I admire what she has done a lot — it just happens that she was the celebrity named in the Instagram post by some life coach or other I saw recently. It went something along the lines of "Beyoncé has as many hours in the day as you have, so stop complaining that you are short of time. You're just short of commitment." I'm sure there are other versions out there with other celebrity names in them, but the basic implication of this kind of post is that you can achieve anything if you just work hard enough — and that if you are not successful it is because you are somehow not committed enough. Well, yes, Beyoncé has worked hard to get to where she is and she deserves her success — but by definition she is already successful so she now has a team working for her, which means she can get a lot more done in 24 hours than somebody starting out on their own. Tweets and memes tend to take Beyoncé to where she is now, edit out the years of struggle and hard work she has put in to get to that place, and then put pressure on an artist starting out because they are not getting there in 'five easy steps' or whatever spurious empowerment program the motivational coach behind the meme is pushing. It is 'pull yourself up' philosophy monetised.

I know we don't want to make this conversation a completely negative one, but it has to be a realistic one and it's never going to be realistic if it doesn't acknowledge that the mythical 'level playing-field' just isn't out there. Even when you are gifted a little time in the limelight by the powers that be, if you are not a member of the 'old boys' club' you often won't get the longterm support to make something sustainable out of it.

Certainly in the UK's performing arts that seems to be a huge challenge. Here there's the current illusion of funding through the Arts Council — currently standing up for 'relevance in the arts' as opposed to its former 'excellence in the arts'. We've seen that over the past 10, possibly 15 years where the Arts Council of course hasn't gone bust or bankrupt, but what it's done is to come up with all these devices, branding and pretexts to avoid having to stay in one place and be skewered into committing the money it clearly hasn't got to share out (and which isn't its fault). So it's been: we're not going to do London, we're going to prioritise regions, we're rural touring, we're not, we'll give less to London, we'll give less to the regions, it's not excellence, it's relevance . . . What it is, is divide and rule, so no one compares notes because they're all either panicked because there's less where there wasn't much in the first place, or over-enthused because there's a little tantalising them where there was nothing before. There's the smoke and mirrors of customer service where 'we'll get back to you with an answer within five weeks' is simply deflecting lack of money with promise of efficiency, cementing the illusion that you actually had a chance. It's a situation not found in Europe — well for the moment at least — where the municipality and the regions traditionally hold a lot of the purse strings. But recent UK history has been all about Westminster throttling local authority at source on everything. A positive response obviously has been the growth of fringe. Much as it's battered financially and conceptually problematic, fringe in theory is an excellent answer to accessibility for the arts. Tellingly it's not a tradition in Europe, where the countries there tend not to have their own term to describe it. There's not the infrastructure, or even a perceived need for it. Led by Edinburgh, as it's become more corporate — which it has to be in the absence of the calming effect of funding — fringe is now being sold on the idea of 'level playing-field', which has now infiltrated the rest of the industry and contaminated the funding area. It's become a mantra: so long as they mention 'level playing-field', it doesn't matter if it isn't. As a 'self-tickbox', it's the ultimate open sesame, but all it seems to do is highlight the problems of access and the lengthening queues for it.

One of the most disempowering things in any profession, or indeed any aspiration, is to feel like you are 'waiting for permission', and it seems a lot of access in the performing arts is based on that: from an actor who's waiting for permission to have an audition to a playwright or director who's waiting for the green light to put on a show. In essence whether you are making a funding application or sending your casting profile out for a potential role, it's a request for permission. It's almost like the whole of our industry is predicated on asking for permission.

The only way that somebody's going to step outside that is to start making their own work and doing their own performing without waiting for permission. But to avoid being one of those 'inspiration pornographers' I was talking about earlier, I need to tell you that this is going to be a hell of a lot harder if you are not one of the 'anointed ones', not just because it will be harder financially but also because the system is set up to resist that.

I remember producing a big testimonial gig for a comedian quite a few years ago, somebody who was highly regarded in the industry although not necessarily a big name to the wider public. Since I run an agency myself, I did things 'by the book' approaching the celebrity guests via the proper channels — going through their agents and record labels even when either myself or the comic knew the acts personally and could have just sent them an email or picked up the phone (it was just before texting became a thing, which tells you how long ago it was). A lot of stars did come along and it turned into a great evening. But for quite a while afterwards I was having conversations with some of the other celebrities I had asked along the lines of "Why didn't you invite me to that gig, I would have loved to have been part of that." "Mate, I *did* invite you, but your agent/PR person/record label told me you wouldn't be interested because it wasn't on TV and there wasn't much money involved." Technology has moved on, but I am not sure the attitude has.

That perennial threat of ownership of your talent by others . . .

Our system is the opposite of level playing-field because it's totally slanted towards ownership, and it's slanted toward those who can at their will bestow or withdraw permission.

It's been a slow slide into a sort of land grab, a rights grab, image grab. Taylor Swift copyrighting her lyrics — except it's obviously not her but her 'people' — McDonald's copyrighting 'I'm lovin' it' and then Disney trying to copyright 'Day of the Dead' (Mexico) or 'Hakuna matata' (East Africa). All of which throws up a new form of appropriation which impacts on the integrity of talented people: are they a person or an entity? With 'Day of the Dead', it was a Mexican-American cartoonist Lalo Alcaraz, who stood up for the world's population and said "no" — it wasn't a politician, ministry, pillar of society, rights campaigner or NGO. The point is that it confirms what you say, that even if they can't copyright it, they will still try, because they assume that entitlement of ownership, pre-ownership even. And it's dictating how our future generations make their first move, more often as not hobbled when the long-term goal has already been defined, commodified and given a price.

It's art as commodity. And in any industry where there's a commodity involved, whether it's coffee, rice, whatever, you get the people who own the industry making the lion's share of the money. They're not the ones who grow the coffee or plant the rice. So many industries are structured so that the people who own the industry make the money, and the people who actually do the work may make some money but it is usually a lot less than the people who own the industry. Our industry isn't any different.

So it comes with the system: we need inequality because otherwise, so we're told, the system wouldn't work if we want something equal out of it.

You're absolutely right because, to a certain degree, as an audience we're paying for an experience that somebody else can give us that we can't give ourselves. And we're paying to hear and see talent that we genuinely 'love'. But if we're not careful we can end up prioritising our own enjoyment (or cultural upliftment if you want to be posh about it) above standing up for a more equitable system. A bit like somebody who is concerned about sweatshops but still 'must have' that beautiful T-shirt in the high street store or (and this is one of my own constant dilemmas) wants to support companies who treat workers well but has just spotted that deluxe edition DVD of a really hard-to-find old movie that is exclusively on Amazon.

The big lie is that if we don't support the existing system, we won't be able to enjoy those things we love . . . I think we will, but if we are serious we may have to forego them for a bit while they find their own ways to reach us. At the moment those new ways often involve streaming platforms and social media platforms which are themselves either owned by the same big media companies the artists are trying to break free from, or are becoming problematic in how they throw their own weight and influence around, so we are not quite there yet and it becomes a very tangled web.

While all that is going on, you find few people these days who openly oppose diversity and inclusion (if you don't count media pundits for whom being contrarian is their primary income stream) which can lead those of us who do want to see change living in a cosy bubble and assuming everyone in the arts feels the same. However, there are always occasional breaches of the code of silence when private emails or social media posts sneak out and reveal what is going on behind the scenes and they can be more reflective of industry attitudes than we might like to admit: the agents who tell white actors that the reason they are not getting work is that "everybody is looking for ethnic actors these days", or cis actors that "you'll get nowhere if you are not gay or transgender". That's just like the perception that "the country is being flooded with refugees" — it's a strongly held perception in many quarters, but absolutely not backed up by facts and statistics. But so long as that perception exists, there's always going to be resistance to inclusion, diversity, whatever you want to call it, not only from the top down but from actors who are themselves being exploited by the system but misdirected into blaming other people who are even more discriminated against instead of directing their anger at those who keep an iron grip on access.

On the other hand, generally in the performing arts there are more opportunities for specifically live performance for the very reason that there seems to be less ownership. Yes it can be carved up, and that's why we have the West End, but there's a whole load of other stuff out there that you can't necessarily sustain or make pots of money from, but which does let you get your voice and face out there. And it seems to me that if you do a one-hour play, by its very nature you can't package it into 280 characters in a few seconds, so already people have to come and accept it on its own terms as soon as they take their seat. There's also something about live performance, theatre most of all, in that you can video every single night if you like but there won't be much of a market for it. Plus you know that, no matter how robotic or teched-up you are, every night will be different if only because every audience is different. And so there is an unpredictability there that defies control, commodity, and at least becomes a level playing-field within that hour. But there's still something not quite connecting in all this.

Certainly that kind of fringe show, scratch or performance piece is as close as it's possible to get to something that isn't owned by anybody but the creator. To a certain degree, the screen equivalent of that is not indie movies or shorts anymore, it's the TikToks and other direct-to-audience platforms — but again, we have the problem that the platforms themselves look 'indie' and cool but are often owned by the same establishment that controls the rest of the industry.

It seems like there's no point in talking about diversity if you don't have empowerment. That's the real hardware to get equality going.

Absolutely. It reminds me of when I was working in Dublin years before I came over with a group of Travelling people which was unusual at the time because it was actually run by Travellers as opposed to do-gooders like me. We're going back to the 1980s when things like recycling were still a new thing but Travellers have always done a lot of recycling culturally. Back then, it was things like tin cans, cars, scrap paper and it wasn't necessarily called 'recycling' but that was what it was. This group received funding to put together a recycling resource warehouse in Dublin, which again was quite a new concept there at the time, where schools could come and buy art materials which were recycled things that had been collected by the Travellers.

It was a very successful project, but the constant struggle was that every time a particular funding ran out and there was an application made for new funding, the response would often be, "We want to fund something new. So we can't fund the thing you did last year even though it's really successful — if you want funding, you need to come up with something new, even if you are not ready, and even if the thing you are currently doing is 'new' to each new group of Travellers or each new group of settled schoolkids who engage with it."

Like the Arts Council in the UK, nothing changes. After the regions initiative failed, they went after the new audiences, which was then followed by the report that they're not getting in the new audiences.

What happens is that there's a drive to attract new audiences, but the people who are funded to attract new audiences are often the same people. So the new audiences often find they're not actually involved in the production or the creation, they're just an audience.

Doing interviews for *The Stage*, there's the familiar fact that when you interview an actor in Britain, it's often likely that when you ask them what their first motivation to get involved in the arts was, the answer comes back, "I was taken to see a panto when I was seven" or something like that.

What that means is that a young person went to see something and the idea was birthed that "I could be part of that, I'd love to do that." And that is a great thing. But with some exceptions, the panto business can be very limited to a certain audience and demographic. Stepping away from panto, the same thing applies to any form of creative arts. For the art form to develop and grow, there has to be a way in which the pieces coming out of it inspire people in the audience to feel "Well I could do that! Is there a way I could be involved in something like that?"

Often with this reach for new audiences it's like the audience is a resource to keep the productions going, but if there aren't enough elements of diversity, the new audience doesn't see itself reflected in the piece so it never births that idea of "I can do that! I've got permission to do that!" — and then even if the productions do keep going, the content tends to stagnate because the pool of influences never widens.

I had a very brief period as a children's presenter on Nickelodeon TV. There was a foot and mouth outbreak in the country, so they couldn't rely on that kids' show staple, bringing live zoo animals into the studio. Me and my live cartoon act were the stand in act for the Orangutans and the Pythons.

At the time I lived on an estate in Bermondsey, South London. I did my little stint for about six months in the afternoons on a Thursday for the channel. That was back in the day when Nickelodeon was quite new to Britain. At the time my kids were around eight, nine or ten, so I thought for one brief period in my life I'll be a cool dad. I spent lots of time waiting to get recognised by eight, nine or ten year olds at school gates . . . but that never happened. What did happen was that one day I was walking through this council estate in Bermondsey while I was still doing the show and two big 15 or 16 year old youths shouted "Oi mate!" I thought, "Okay what's going to happen here?" But then one of them said, "You're the bloke from Nickelodeon!" And his mate said, "No, he can't be, cos he lives *here*!"

The really telling thing for me was not so much that 15 to 16 year olds still watch kids' shows but that, as far as that particular lad was concerned, somebody who lived on his estate couldn't possibly be on television.

How did the 'Dear John' Stage column come into being? And since its longevity proves its continuing relevance, is it the same issues each year or are they changing?

I first started working for *The Stage* around 1997-98. The internet wasn't a common thing back then and I still remember faxing stuff into the newspaper which felt like 'magic' to me — I started off doing the cartoons for the letters page. What *The Stage* always has done — and it has been doing it for over 140 years now — is to pick up on what's happening in the industry and change with the industry. So the 1990s was the time when you were starting to see programmes that were the precursors of *The X Factor* and *America's Got Talent* and those kind of shows today. Shows like *Pop Idol* — I think there was even a *Soap Idol*! — these kinds of programmes were the genesis of the current type of TV talent shows which do two things, one positive and the other negative.

The positive thing they did and still do was to get more people interested in the process of making a career in show business, particularly younger people. And that is a very positive thing in terms of breaking the cliques. But the negative side was the unrealistic picture they presented: that if you walk in off the street with a sob story, this will guarantee you success. Obviously that isn't how any kind of entertainment industry works or should work, and *The Stage*'s editor at the time, Brian Attwood, realised that there was a constituency of younger performers as well as older aspiring performers who were interested in gaining usable information about how to break into the industry, but weren't being given a true picture by what was available to them at the time.

Brian had the idea of running an advice column which is how the 'Dear John' column idea launched itself. Initially it was monthly and then moved to weekly where it became more of what I describe as a 'chatshow on paper'. Basically someone would send in a query, I would give a response, then I would ask two other people who were familiar with the subject to give a response, then at the end I would do a Jerry Springer-type sum-up.

We ran it for a good ten years like that, and then it moved to the current 'Careers Clinic' format where people send in more detailed queries. By that time I was so well known as 'Dear John' it didn't really make sense to change my Twitter handle or email, which really confuses my American followers because they think I'm like the old 'Dear Abby' column and assume I give advice to the lovelorn!

It's a long time since I've had an actual handwritten letter to the column, but I do get a lot of email queries which can get quite long, detailed and personal. What I tend to do is either send the person a personal response based on what they've actually told me and then, for *The Stage* version, I redact the details that will identify the person, and keep in the advice that is more generally applicable. But the issues are real, and they keep coming in so I can confirm that making it in the business is no easier now than ever, just different.

The reason that format still works today is, I think, largely due to the fact that I can't think of any issue an individual somebody has presented to me over the years which doesn't have relevance to a lot of other people in the business- but for an industry which is perceived as quite outgoing, it is interesting how rarely people seem to speak to each other about what is actually challenging for them. Hopefully reading about somebody else going through the same thing helps, and even more so if we can offer a solution they may not have considered.

As for the second part of your question about whether the same issues come up, there are number of basic things that are always going to be the case. We'll always have an industry where there will be lots more people who want to work than jobs available for them. Obviously that's in the context of jobs which are being offered as opposed to making their own work, so you're always going to have more people looking for work than there is work.

The basic marketing tools in the industry are always going to be headshots, CVS showreels and things like that, even if the form they are available in changes. Maybe they will be virtual reality someday. Technology's changed a little bit already so whereas 15 years ago I might have been getting printed headshots and paper CVs sent in to comment on, now it's online casting profiles. But people will still want to know if they've got the right headshots, websites and marketing tools — or, if they change them, will it make a difference to the work coming in.

Another thing that has changed on the surface but also kind of stayed the same is that it's always been an industry based on 'who you know'. What's made things different now is that the online world has made it easier to connect with people that you don't directly know, with social media being most obvious avenue. If Cameron Mackintosh (the person, not the organisation) had a Twitter account, you could in theory tweet Cameron Mackintosh to contact him in a way that you couldn't have done back in the old days when you would have had to go through layers of gatekeepers.

Obviously it's not as simple as that. For a start, lots of successful people in the industry have social media managers, so you're not necessarily tweeting the individual, you're tweeting their social media department (although there certainly are very big names who do their own social themselves). But there's certainly the general *illusion* of more access. But the actual access that people have and work with is as it pretty much as it has always been.

If I think back on it, there are the two key problems that people raise or query more than any other. The first is, "I want to get more work as an actor, performer, writer, director. How can I do that because if I'm not in the right circles it's very difficult?" And then the second is one that has noticeably increased over the past few years — not increased in terms of it being a problem but in terms of people talking about it — the mental strain and frustration of trying to make a career in an industry which by its nature is quite unfair.

That's certainly got more pronounced. It's positive that more people are talking about it, but the forums that we use to talk about it, specifically social media, are the ones that often add to the problem. Because on social media *everybody* looks like they're successful and making connections, because we all present the best picture of ourselves on those platforms.

That's a conversation that everyone knows will run and run, and it clearly shows how the column has evolved with the changing industry. But then, 'evolved' is not the right word because you've been doing the same thing since the beginning but simply adapted the delivery and language of your answers.

That's a good way of putting it. Greater access via emails, Twitter, Instagram and so on, instead of old-fashioned letters, offers a wider space for people to express issues or problems because sitting down to write an actual letter can be difficult for people. It takes time, whereas dashing off a quick DM or Instagram message just makes it slightly quicker to express what you want to say.

To come back to that idea about everything changing yet many of the underlying issues remaining the same, it still must be a bit of a weird one where the industry's whizzing by you but it always ends up in the same place, and yet there is enduring change, just as we're seeing with the colleges and theatres coming up with steps forward like codes of practice and safeguarding, followed by the fringe and festivals, often jumping as an industry ahead of the legislation in areas like gender parity, wage practices, audition feedback.

What I do pick up is a level of frustration caused by the growing realisation that in this industry that 'raising an issue' and 'discussing an issue' are not the same as 'addressing the issue' — in fact sometimes, endless discussion is what we do to avoid actually addressing it. We're doing this interview in 2020 just after we've had probably one of the whitest Baftas and whitest Oscars that we've had for a couple of years, so all this raising of awareness isn't quite the same thing as changing the structures that are creating the inequalities in the first place.

So if you feel that you are excluded for any reason, the messages going out for people who are emerging, thinking of going to study or about to graduate, the message basically is that you can't rely on the system, you've got to go off and do it for yourself . . . or en masse.

That's true and you've made a good distinction there, because the truth is that you can't rely on the system. The American writer Audre Lorde said that "the master's tools will never dismantle the master's house". I've seen that quoted a lot and it's so true. Gatekeepers are never going to make themselves redundant, that's just not the way it works. So the truth of the matter is that I would encourage everybody, rather than basing their whole approach on trying to make their own way in this big structure, to try to create their own avenues, their own work and their own opportunities, but to go one step further and look at how they can genuinely use their work to create opportunities for others. And that can't be "when I am successful I will send the ladder back down". If you are already a few rungs up the ladder, you are in a position to pull somebody up with you.

In any case, making your own way sounds great in concept because it sounds very empowering, but the truth of the matter is that it can be very lonely. The key thing is that people have to make their individual way but they should do it in cohort with others. Not everybody agrees with me, but my perception is that the upcoming generation of artists — be they performing artists, creative artists, backstage people, writers — all seem to me to be a bit more generous and open to being collaborative rather than competitive than my generation was, and this is one area where social media has actually helped. Much as there are horrible trolls on social media, people can connect on social media and support each other's projects. A lot of people are starting to realise that if you support somebody's project it might not directly benefit you in the moment (well at least, materially) but it can create an atmosphere where when you have something going other people will also support you.

As with many things, it's much further developed in the United States than it is here, and often by the very communities who are most excluded from the existing system. I think of someone like the American filmmaker Ava DuVernay who constantly uses her own hard-won advances to generate openings for other people, creating collaborative community-based processes that really do move things on in a real way.

In addition to her own creative work she has set up a distribution company ARRAY which champions movies by women and filmmakers of colour, and the Amanda Cinema at ARRAY's LA campus which hosts events and festivals spotlighting work by those same filmmakers and many of their predecessors who never received the attention they deserved — very powerful because control of distribution and performance spaces is a big plank of the old paternal system.

There is similar work going on in Britain. Tobi Kyeremateng's Black Ticket Project is a recent example, aimed at allowing young black theatregoers to access theatre by removing the barriers which prevent them doing so, whether they are economic ones or the more insidious ones of simply not feeling welcome in white spaces. The more that happens the more those theatregoers may feel empowered to become theatremakers and the ones who are already making art may feel a bit more encouraged that the spaces where they can display their work are as much theirs as anyone else's.

But it takes a lot of courage and thinking outside the box to work in that way because the message that we're constantly giving in the industry is the old-fashioned one that you've got to establish yourself first before you create opportunities for other people. That's still very much a hierarchical method even if it's intended to be positive and empowering. I think it would work far more effectively if people say, "While I'm building my own avenues, I will take the opportunities to support as many people as I can, because at some point that will reciprocally come back to me. But I'm not doing it because it will come back to me — I'm doing it because it's the *right* thing to do."

It comes back to the idea that not everyone is meant to be an entrepreneur or multitasker and yet there's the pressure to make people feel guilty that they're not. You know: I work in theatre, I do everything, everyone knows that I work far more hours than I'm paid, that I multitask and multiskill and don't complain about it. The idea of having to be all things is another illusion that's been directly sold us since at least 1979 in the UK and people have been made to feel guilty for not being able to do it — or wanting to. You're absolutely right, people are beginning to embrace that collaborative spirit, however I suspect that a lot of people are still held down by the pressure to be all things to all people. How would you tell them that we don't have to be all that, that in fact it's okay to not be?

That message is quite radical. The reality is that some people are very entrepreneurial, and some people are very good at one particular thing, like acting or writing. So the real entrepreneurial spirit is everybody connecting with the other people to make effective work and to create effective communities but in a way that is not top down.

There's obviously a high degree of trust required for that. There will always be people who exploit other people and obviously we have the whole 'no pay low pay' problem where somebody says, "I want to make a show, I can't afford to pay anybody, but everybody should come and work for me for free anyhow because I'm an artist and I have the right to express myself." But that's not the way it works. The right to express yourself comes with the responsibility not to exploit everyone else. We have to value ourselves so that we're not working for free all the time, but equally be open to collaborations with people we feel we're on the same wavelength with, so that if we do work for something other than money, there is real value to both parties in the collaboration rather than the 'exposure' or 'better to be doing something than nothing' carrot that often drags performers and artists into exploitative relationships . . . "It's never going to be perfect, it's always going to be trial and error, but it is worth the journey to see where we can get to."

That's the sort of realistic way of working that needs to be reassessed and understood with each new generation or development. It can't just sit there, it always has to be picked up and reappraised. Is there anything through the columns that has given you any particular insights into what we can resolve and what remains problematic?

There are three kind of problems that people have always expressed to me in different forms. One is how do I move my career forward? The second is my career is stuck and how can I get it unstuck? The third one is more complex: it's the feeling that in order to move my career forward or unstick my career, I've got to put myself in a position where I may be exploited either economically, emotionally or even sexually. Whatever the specific problem being expressed is the reason the person often gives for being in the dilemma is ". . . my fear in this very insecure impermanent industry is if I do stand up to this, then I will never work in this industry again".

The encouragement that I give people who are in those kinds of dilemmas now is that our industry may not be anywhere near as diverse as it needs to be in terms of ethnicity or gender or class, but it has unquestionably diversified in terms of the different platforms, different channels and different avenues for making art which are now out there.

Even though there are still the major gatekeepers and big players who control lots of it, they can't possibly control all of it any more. What that means is that you don't have to take just one traditional path, and if any path is closed to you, you can find another or, if necessary, start building your own. The industry today is big enough that you can find your own path and even more importantly find your own 'tribe' — the likeminded tribe who will support each other along it.

At the end of the day, yes it'll be great if we could genuinely change the Baftas and the Oscars and all those institutions, and those of us who currently benefit from the exclusion should be the ones fighting hardest to change it, rather than leaving it up to the people being pushed out. But we can also look at creating other systems which are more egalitarian and community orientated.

We don't live in a perfect world, it's never going to be perfect, but it doesn't have to be as imperfect as it is right now, if we're prepared to be truthful that it ended up this way by design not by accident, and make sure we're just as deliberate in building a better model next time round.

*

7
Sanjit Chudha

'Nobody has to walk in and explain themselves'

Sanjit Chudha is marketing & communications manager for Talawa Theatre Company. Based in South East London, he was born in Mombasa & raised in Nairobi, Kenya.
• *talawa.com*

We're catching Talawa at possibly the biggest 'before and after' point in its 33-year history, as it moves into a permanent home at Croydon's newly renovated Fairfield Halls. That's quite a new chapter to be opening up for black theatre in the UK.

It is. We're now in our first theatre building since 1995 when we left the Cochrane Theatre in Central London — where we not only have a base but can produce and present. Having said that, Talawa was always set up to work with or without a building in order to bring black British stories to the stage.

The black British story is quite a distinct from equality, representation or diversity. People see a black person onstage, often a lone figure or the second spear carrier from the left or something awful like that, and that's a box ticked for a particular production. Well, that's not the way that we do it — we're about the story and the script being written by a black British writer, the director being a black British director, the producer likewise and as many of the team as possible, such as those who are offstage working on lighting, set design, make-up and wardrobe.

So in my case I might not be identified as black as such since I am of Indian origin, but I certainly fall into the 'BAME' category. I certainly have life experiences that mirror the ones that are being talked about onstage. So in that sense I have a sympathy for these stories and a passion to see them expressed and projected and brought to the fore.

We also look beyond to see what other factors we can bring to a production, particularly with our touring productions and particularly if they have a cultural reference that's incredibly strong, and we'll see if that can be echoed physically in the foyers and other parts of the buildings that we're getting into. So it's things like food, drinks, then decor. It doesn't always work, because some venues can be resistant, but luckily we've found that most are extremely happy to help make that change. They see the value in welcoming black British stories and audiences into their buildings.

That's something that just should *be*, rather than something to be celebrated as 'extraordinary'. The challenge is to make normal something that is seen as extraordinary or exceptional. It's the an obvious thing that people don't always get, but you know there's nothing unusual about being black in Britain today.

Most black people in this country were born here, and their parents were born in this country. If there is a story of immigration and family, it's quite often two or three generations back. Migration isn't assumed to be a direct lived experience, although in my case it actually is a direct lived experience. So that's why Talawa's focus on those black British stories matters as it counters attempts to erase that long-lived presence by defiantly saying 'we're here' in all our diversity.

We've been around since 1986 which means that we also have this wonderful thing called our archive. If you think about an archive, you might think of dusty boxes full of stuff, images and notes, old posters. You'll find all that of course, but you'll also be presented with ways to use the archive to help you understand that a lot of what we're talking about now has happened before. It may be in a different way but it has happened before. This is important because it can be lonely in theatre when you're endlessly replaying the role of the 'emerging' writer or artist, which is what black British artists and creators constantly experience. They find themselves on the loop of going from development scheme to development scheme. Those schemes are well meant but ultimately prove to be patronising, because it's only in a very few cases that those artists and creators are able to smash through the glass ceiling and actually lay claim to an artistic directorship or executive directorship on their own terms. We're starting to see that change, but this is 2020!

In fact, in the 33 years of Talawa's existence, you can probably count on the fingers of one hand the number of black or Asian artistic directors in charge of buildings until the extraordinary wave of appointments suddenly made in the last couple of years. The fact that it is changing is encouraging because once that sort of change happens, the lens starts to change and so does the filter through which stories are picked up and brought to fruition on the stage. This is precisely where the archive is important, in telling us that these struggles have always been here, that there is nothing new under the sun, but don't be scared because the fact that it's been done before means that we can do it again in today's circumstances and contexts. There is something to learn there — and there may also be something to react against.

Perhaps some of the work that was done in the past was great but of its time and therefore not appropriate for today. Perhaps that lesson from the past is a pointer to how we could adapt it now and do it better. But until you have that history and you know that you've got it and it's presented and it's there, you can't really learn from it and you're constantly doomed to go "oh everything's new and it's the first time it's ever happened" — and we end up, as happened at Glastonbury, with somebody striding onstage and going, "I am the first black British artist ever to appear on this main stage." Well actually it turned out that he wasn't, and it took someone else to point that out — the artist who actually had appeared there first [Skin with Skunk Anansie]. It was embarrassing but understandable because that's what happens when archives aren't there and histories aren't taught.

Archives take away the burden of having to constantly explain yourself — you have the support of somebody who has done it before. Archives explain that it's not you who's wrong or explaining it badly, it's actually the person you're speaking to who's failing to understand, failing to read that history, and failing to accept that you are the latest incarnation of that.

It's a concept that links into the growing conversation about decolonising culture, theatre, archives, museums and all of these things. It's a conversation that centres around, say, the repatriation of objects or the release of those objects in some way from the shackles that have been placed upon them — and we know that many objects are in museums because they were stolen. But one of the things that can't be stolen is our reaction to those objects, and Talawa's been working with lot of those institutions to animate some of the stories around those objects, to bring new fresh perspectives to bear on them, to articulate many of the discussions and emotions and thoughts and feelings that people have around how those objects have ended up in those spaces.

So we've done projects with the Victoria & Albert, the British Museum and the British Library, all of them are institutions which are beginning to explore those fields. And like Tamasha Theatre [based at East London's Rich Mix], we have also worked with the School of Oriental & Africa Studies [aka SOAS, part of London University] on deconstructing colonialism and that's something we're developing as a separate strand of theatre work. This is an area where we're constantly discovering interesting ways of having actors, writers, theatremakers interact and perform the work or perform the archive or respond to that archive. We make those objects relevant and make the stories of today resonate deeper and further.

This sort of work is important because theatre by Talawa is often associated with the big glossy stage productions starring big names like Don Warrington. But not all our productions are like that, in the same way as you'll find with any other theatre company of similar size and aspirations. So we also put on a whole range of smaller-scale productions that don't always get the oxygen of national press and publicity but hold the same value for audiences and the people involved in creating and staging them.

Apart from the shows, there's also the educational side, with strands like TYPT *[Talawa Young People's Theatre]* which involves devised theatre through working with participants aged around 18 to 25, many of whom have never been to drama school or for whom drama school was an impossibility. It's been relaunched this year as an eight-month long programme. On the one hand, you've got up to 30 participants who've never been to drama school, who don't have that expectation of what a rehearsal room should be like. On the other hand, you've got five to ten industry professionals at the peak of their game interacting with this group. It's as much a challenge for them as it is for the participants. That's a room full of magical possibility, right there.

The energy that drives this sort of intense learning experience comes from creating a safe space for those interactions to happen, and so lay down the seedbed for the stories that people need to see onstage that they're not seeing. Recently we've been reconfiguring TYPT, looking at widening participation — and obviously the whole change of moving to Croydon is a big driver in evolving the whole participation model.

Croydon has now embedded us within a community that has expectations of us, and we know that not everyone with those expectations fits neatly into the 18 to 25 age bracket. A pivotal point in our own story was the last time we had a sizeable theatre space that we could call our own was the Cochrane in 1995, and now we have this new 200-seat theatre space, which enables us to perform in the round, traverse or traditional set-up. The space means that once again we can offer access, open the doors to the community and platform their needs or hold interactions that identify needs and then help to tell those stories.

There's nine of us here, five are part-time, so having a small team means that logistically it's an issue because not everyone can specialise in participation or community engagement or the literary side of the business — about half of the team do that and, within that, they focus on specific areas. So linked to the move we've had a recruitment drive to expand the team and its skill-sets. That increases our bandwidth to build on interactions with the community, and in tandem we've created a series of engagement events, all of them free and aimed at the different groups we interact with.

We're working with black comedy improvisers, for example, because we know that many of the actors we work with want to flex that skill, improv is one of the performance muscles that can help keep you in shape. And for a lot of people who've never been to drama school, improv is also a great way to understand more about what's involved in the act of acting, the business of acting. There are master classes, again free, on producing participation and community engagement, marketing or fundraising, which is what I do. We've created rich listening opportunities too with Talawa Cafe, an online meeting space for black artists and creators to share tips, ideas, experiences, even the ups and downs of working in the field. We've designed all of these areas to overlap in one way, shape or form. Something interesting will come of that and at the same time give us more insights into what the community actually wants. We know that theatre and cultural production is at a tipping point so this kind of deep listening goes a long way towards helping us respond to what people really want.

Talawa's story has always been the way that we see all of those elements as working together, whereas in a lot of organisations at our level they're seen as quite separate. The fundraising message can turn out to be radically different to what's happening on the stage, which in turn is vastly different to what's happening in the participation and community engagement areas — and yet actually they should all be linked.

Now I don't know whether that story has evolved because it's been so long ago that we had a building and the obvious amount of changes of personnel since then. That's an important consideration. Our current longest standing member in the team is our artistic director Michael Buffong, who's been here since 2011. So comparatively not that long. I've been here six years now. I'm pleased to say that Talawa is even more fleet of foot, able to absorb change and respond meaningfully. But there are some organisations where people have been in place for 20 or 30 years. Talawa is definitely not one of them

The good side of long tenure is continuity, but if you've got a job for 20 years, then no one else is getting a job, especially if it's an organisation that doesn't have the capacity to grow for whatever reason. Talawa's continuity lies in handing the baton on pretty much every single minute of every single day while managing growth. Because we didn't have a permanent building and we were not able to expand our staff, we've had to think of other ways of passing on jobs and opportunities that come from other people and not generated by us. We've always been very generous about that and we always will be, because that's what we're here for, and that certainly benefits the whole sector. MAKE Online is an example of that as an online community to give black British theatre artists ownership and agency of their careers through a dedicated virtual space for artists at all stages of their careers.

A building also means we're able to host a lot more R&D work by our family of artists who have grown significantly in the past five years. With the new space, we're able to accelerate the outputs from those artists, which we hope will help make a bigger step-change in the industry.

That way it doesn't stop, it carries on, and exponentially. You're absolutely right about that baton being passed on — constant change and growth. When Michael joined, thanks to the efforts of Pat Cumper, the previous artistic director, the company got back its Arts Council funding, which it had lost ten years previously. We then regained our NPO [national portfolio organisation] status in 2012. In between 2000 and 2011 Talawa's story was one of wobbly survival, so if you think about it, it really is only over the last eight years that we have had the kind of stability to allow us to effectively develop and foster artists and grow new work.

So in fact you were on the way in any case. The new base is essentially a means to an end, it's not a building for the sake of having a building. The mission remains the mission regardless, to develop and produce black stories. Is that something that other people are doing?

Yes they are. But many of them are doing it as part of what they do along with lots of other stuff which doesn't involve black artists or developing black talent in the way that Talawa does, simply because that is the be-all-and-end-all of what we do. So I think there's something very different about the culture here at Talawa, nobody has to walk in and explain themselves — because we just get it.

An artist's ability to have those conversations with us and to make work with us is accelerated in a way that it isn't often found in other spaces where the first week is spent explaining what it is that you want to do, the perspective you're coming up from, fighting the challenges and myopia. Black artists and theatremakers are just not read in quite the same way in other spaces. I think there's something about the way that we enable meaningful conversations to be had within the first five minutes of them walking through the door that is unique.

It then means we can start working with artists in a very different way. A good example is our Studio Firsts strand — it's an opportunity for makers to create a new piece of work with our support, rather than playwrights or directors looking to explore an existing text. Artists apply to work with us to R&D in our space, with dramaturgy support and a small financial award from Talawa. Space is important because the possibilities are magnified when you have access to it, especially when hosted within a professional environment.

Another factor is that we can now start to do this in a way that we couldn't have done in recent years where we had to hire studio space. We all know that NPO funding has remained static. Now we've moved into a situation where a lot of the work that we're doing now can take place in our space. Prior to this, because we were having to hire studios, the financial costs of artist development were massive. We just sucked that one up and said, "Yes, of course we need to do that", but it did mean that there was very little financial capacity to meet demand. In fact we had to limit Talawa Firsts to three Studio Firsts artists, and three writers whose work was chosen from the 200-plus scripts that were sent to us through our script reading service. So money, or its lack, plays its part too. Having a space, rather than having to hire it, can be part of making the change we want to see, enabling more artists and writers to come through.

It's an important question of access.

It was the proverbial eye of the needle and we were trying to get a camel through it. It hasn't been limiting access as such, but having to find ways of selecting and enabling the work that we thought most needed to be seen in the here and now — but also had some kind of a future life. Those are hard decisions to make. Now with the new building and the spaces we can offer, we're suddenly in a position where we can accommodate, absorb and enable a lot more work that's also deserving of a platform. I hope this will have a knock-on effect throughout the industry. If it sounds a little unfocused at this stage, it's because we haven't done it before on this scale — instead of three, there's no reason why we can't help six, nine, or more new artists to develop and showcase their work in each Studio Firsts round.

Croydon is an interesting place to be because though it's within the London conurbation, it's not London. So you have all the benefits of the metropolis while actually being able to look out to the rest of the country.

I agree that outsider perspective is important. Croydon is definitely intriguing, you only have to walk in the streets and see the faces in this borough to immediately clock that there's something very special about this place. Socio-economically, it is massively diverse: in the south of the borough you have stockbroker mansions with a starting price of £2 million, set in an acre or two of land, while in the north part you have terraced and high-rise multiple occupancy buildings, and a degree of poverty that I think most people wouldn't expect of London at all. There's also the make-up of the population. The BAME population of London is around 40 per cent, while in Croydon, it's more like 55 per cent. Then add to the mix the fact that Lunar

House, the Home Office's immigration processing centre, is just 300 yards away from here.

When you say 'Croydon' there's many who hear 'Home Office'.

Exactly. And that makes it synonymous with the horrific Windrush and migration stories of today. But you know, there's something symbolic about the area . . . location is significant for a theatre company and there's something powerful about Talawa having a presence in a place like this where we've got this location and proximity to London on the one hand, and on the other hand there's this incredible and richly diverse community.

It's not just the local aspects though. We also have a remit to tour nationally. A lot of theatre organisations, particularly in London, are making some wonderful noises at the moment, and all power to them. But London is often as far as their work is going to go. Being in Croydon means that we get access to a community that is having conversations about things that people in the Central London watering holes aren't talking about. It puts us in tune with the rest of the country who don't think like Central London or are excluded from those metropolitan conversations. Interestingly, in the time when we were based more centrally in London, when we did call-outs for scripts or studio work, over a four-year period we saw a 'doughnut' effect where London applications were from outside of the centre. In fact, with the exception of some boroughs in the east of the city, the majority of applications came from Croydon, and that number grew and grew. We were destined to be in Croydon!

That along with a lot of other things started coming together and we had a series of meetings where Michael was talking about where he felt the organisation was ready to go next. We all agreed that bricks and mortar would be a great thing. But what we didn't want to change was the essence of the organisation, i.e. working with artists and working with communities to help create change. And therefore we didn't want the kinds of bricks and mortar that made us a building before it made us a theatre company, if that makes sense. Because the two are quite distinct in the DNA of Talawa's thinking. The beauty of what we now have here is exactly that. We don't have the pressure of having to be the Fairfield Halls. That's what the Fairfield Halls does and does very well. We do what we do within that, so we're liberated from the pressure of having to be something we're not.

How does the relationship work? Since it's the Fairfield's building, was there a remit you were asked to contribute to, or are you working it out as you go along with what you bring to the mix?

It's probably a bit of both. There's absolutely a commitment to make this work on the part of BH Live, the organisation that manages and programmes Fairfield Halls. The invitation came to us from Croydon Council who are the freeholders of the building and who are the people behind the drive to have it refurbished and reinstated to the community. So for us it's that interaction between Croydon Council and BH Live, both of whom have been incredibly welcoming. BH Live now have the building and are operating it on a daily basis. We're learning from our interactions with them. Of course, at the time of speaking, we haven't been here that long. A matter of weeks, and so at this stage we haven't had a weight of events and happenings going on. However, a few weeks after this conversation, that'll be the real test. but I don't envisage there being problems.

Are there any particular skills that you're now acquiring personally that you hadn't needed before?

I've worked in a lot of different environments and I came to Talawa from the corporate sector. You know, suited and booted with my own office, that kind of situation, and earning far more than I am now, that's for sure. The one thing I want to get across is that you don't work in theatre for the money, certainly not the supported sector. But of course I came to theatre because I've always loved theatre and working with people. In the corporate world, there is a certain kind of passion, but it's fairly shallow passion and doesn't sustain the soul in quite the same way as theatre does. It's a very different order of work where you're dealing with human emotions, human crises, human impulses and thought processes in a very immediate way, in a way that you're not, when you're talking about the packaging for Big Corp's latest product.

There's not much humanity there, whereas when you're talking about marketing a play, you're talking to the writer, to the actors, to the director, you're talking to a whole raft of people who have been involved in making that story live and breathe. And since Talawa isn't an organisation of 50 or 500 people, we're all far closer to the world of the play or piece of theatre and its creation— in fact we have to be for it to work. We know what's going on because it's happening pretty much in front of us, in the room next door or on the stage round the corner. Connecting with what is being done every step of the process means that marketing doesn't come as an afterthought — at the end of the process — as it usually does in bricks and mortar organisations.

So the way marketing functions for us is to listen to what's going on around us and act upon it, and so it gets fed back into the organisation. It's not just theatres that do this sort of thing of course, there are all sorts of organisations, including corporates that I've worked for, that do this. We're not only listening to what our artists and the wider communities around us are saying, we're also listening to what's happening across social media and other spheres, and absorbing all of it, which in turn becomes part of the other conversations that we're also listening to, at which point you can sit there and almost take an overview.

I referred to the filtering process and, in a funny sort of way, that's what we all do. We're filtering in vast amounts of information very quickly and there's no algorithm to take the place of that human connection. Even within the small team that we have here, the combination of ages and backgrounds we have also adds something to the magic that can make the brand what it is. That filtering process clearly helps in terms of the stories that are picked up and the artists that we've worked with.

I also encourage everyone out there to actually spreadsheet the hell out of everything because it does benefit you in the long run. Actually, maybe it goes back to what you mentioned earlier about this journey that Talawa has made and the way that it hasn't run before it could walk. We're planners at heart.

You are your own show in a way.

In a way which comes down to the brand having a responsibility, yes, plus there's something about the alchemy that we can't ever afford to lose!

*

8

Jo Clifford

'You refuse to be silenced, you do your best ... and things happen'

Jo Clifford is a writer, performer & transgender activist. Based in Edinburgh, she was born in Derby, Derbyshire, and raised in North Staffordshire.
* *teatrodomundo.com*
queenjesusproductions.com

On behalf of those who don't know your work, why theatre?

Why theatre? Well . . . Oh, why theatre? I've often said — and actually believe — that to create theatre is an act of resistance and that it's an act of resistance on many levels. An important thing is that when you create theatre, you're not creating an artifact, you're not creating an object. So it's not like creating a film on a reel or in a computer. It's not that. It's not a thing. It is a series of moments. It's a series of experiences. And in a world that is about buying and selling artifacts, things, objects, that in itself is a value.

The other fascinating thing about theatre is that it's something that happens cooperatively in a world that is supposed to be about competition. Theatre is collaborative, it happens collectively. It's a collective effort between the artists who are making it happen on the stage and the director, designer and everybody, but also the audience. In that sense it's a useful antidote to the very destructive individualism of the age.

And the other really important thing about theatre is that fact that because audience and performance are in the same room together, it is a particularly potent training ground for empathy. Every theatre artist has to be empathetic in order to begin to function as an artist, while the audience members are taken outside themselves and put into a different world, put into the shoes of different people. Empathy is incredibly important in a world and a culture that promotes competition and individualism that's founded on the lack of compassion.

In all these different ways, theatre is an act of resistance — a very important act of resistance, it seems to me. Obviously it's got its drawbacks. It's never quite managed to cope with the mechanics of mass reproduction and all that, but nonetheless at its heart there is something very important because it resists. It resists the world we live in and it helps us to dream of a different world, a different way of doing things, a different way of being in the world that is incredibly important and incredibly necessary.

Theatre is resistance and it's compassion — which are conflictive from any viewpoint, aren't they?

Absolutely. When I talk about it being resistance, then it *is* resistance. It's what good theatre does and it's something that runs counter to what a lot of theatre is today. That's one reason why a play like *The Gospel According to Jesus, Queen of Heaven [which reimagines the Gospels through Jesus as a trans woman]* causes such a lot of trouble in a country like Brazil, but it has caused a lot of trouble here in Britain as well because it runs counter to the prevailing values. And that really matters, it seems to me.

I'm increasingly using the play as a moral/cultural litmus test. Whenever the values of a particular country or culture come up in conversation, I'll put the question, could you put Jesus, Queen of Heaven on there? And if you can't, then I'm sorry, you've got to work on it.

In Brazil at this moment you can't put it on any more. It's very difficult to put it on in the UK in fact.

Obviously you struggled to put it on ten years ago when things were certainly very different, but even today you can't just put it on anywhere in this country, can you?

Well, no. It's very difficult to imagine a venue in London, for example, taking it on. Not because they're transphobic. Because if you said they were transphobic, they'd all go mad and say, "Oh, of course we're not. But . . . it just doesn't fit." I get told this over and over again, "Oh Jo, I love your work and it's fantastic but I can't see how to programme it, there doesn't seem to be a place for it. You know . . ." And I go, "Well fuck you" — under my breath of course. And that's precisely because the work has different values and is actually doing its job as a piece of theatre.

And why aren't they letting it do its job?

Because we think a lot about who we could take it to in, say, London. A lot of respectable venues were interested for a bit, but when it came down to it, they just wanted to put us on for a couple of nights in tiny spaces, they obviously had no faith in the show. And that certainly tells me something about the current theatre scene, that London is very resistant to work that does not conform to current values.

Draper Hall, Stefania Bochicchio's pioneering theatre in a community hall in Elephant & Castle, bucked that scene and sought you out to give you that London debut, for the simple fact that they and their audience got it and didn't see any risk. Unlike in Brazil of course.

Well what happens in Brazil is that you put the show on and a lorryload of armed police turn up, they invade the theatre, they try to stop the audience getting into the theatre, and when that fails they literally take the seats from under the audience's bums, make them stand up outside in the pouring rain, they cut the lights, they cut the sound. And you find a bomb is thrown into the theatre. The director finds that all the tyres on her car have been slashed. The actress has the most horrendous, horrible, nightmarish death threats. And insults thrown through online day after day after day after day after day. You get people with guns, literally people with guns, wandering around outside the theatre entrance saying, "I'm going to fucking kill that queer shit who thinks she's Jesus."

You get all this extraordinary violence, these terrifying attempts to silence the play, which at the moment has succeeded. But what you get in Britain is a kind of indifference. It is exactly that response of "Oh yes, Jo, I love your work, but I can't see how to programme it, I can't see where to place it." Which says very firmly, "There is no place for your work in contemporary British theatre." Obviously my job is to resist that as much as possible, and so we keep trying to programme it wherever we can. But it's never happening in the main venues, it's never happening in the centres. It's always happening in the periphery, which in many ways is a very good place to be, but also very frustrating place to be in other ways.

What was it at the time that made you think, "You know what, I'm ready to go with this, ready or not"?

Hmm . . . What was it? It was chance really. It wasn't a plan. What happened was early in the 2000s, I wrote and performed a play called *God's New Frock*, which was all about the God of the Old Testament. I'd done quite a bit of research and I'd come to understand that before we worshipped the Father God in the Sky, we worshipped the Mother Goddess on the Earth. And when patriarchy and the patriarchal religions took over, one of the first things they did was to very brutally and very thoroughly suppress all worship and memory of the Mother Goddess.

One of the ways of understanding the Old Testament is through that story. It's a story of the suppression of a female mother Goddess by the male father god Yahweh. I found that a really interesting story to tell — and I also saw a parallel between what happened to me when I was an adolescent and had to suppress myself. So I told the stories in parallel and performed it myself. It needed a trans performer — there were no trans performers at that time, and I felt it would be good for me. And it was. The shows did pretty well.

Then kinds of crazy things happened. I got commissioned to do a new version of *Faust*, I got commissioned to do *La Celestina [by Fernando de Rojas]* at the Edinburgh International Festival. And very tragically, my wife developed brain cancer and I had to nurse her through that. And then I fell ill myself.

In all this, I'd completely forgotten about *God's New Frock*, but somehow via Playwrights' Studio Scotland it had found its way to Italy to a theatre company in Florence called Teatro della Limonaia who had chosen it for a season of Scottish plays. They flew me over to see it. It sold out, then did a nationwide tour of Italy. I thought crikey, I must be on to something here, having forgotten all about it, and I said to them, "I tell you what, I'll write you a sequel based on the New Testament." I didn't have much faith in their capacity to give me a proper contract, so I said, "Look, if you find me a flat for free for three weeks in Florence, I'll stay there and I'll write the play for you." And they actually did. And I wrote *The Gospel According to Jesus, Queen of Heaven*.

This was in 2008. I gave it to them and they didn't reply, so I assumed they didn't like it. So I thought, okay, well this is a play, so let me put it on. I found a director Rachael Rayment, an old student of mine, then we found a producer whose name I have forgotten but who quite soon after joining us decided she wanted to be a stand-up comedian instead. But bless her though because before she did that, she went to Glasgay! *[LGBT arts festival that ran in Glasgow from 1993 to 2014]*, got £2000 out of them, and they scheduled it for 2009. Then we found an amazing composer and musician, Adam Clifford (no relation) and we put it on.

But, you know, that was all fortuitous. There was no plan involved. What also happened that year was the little bit of surgery that I had — and things changed for me. Suddenly I became much stronger in my own identity. People stopped yelling abuse at me in the street. And things were really looking up.

Meanwhile there was also something stirring in Glasgow at the time. There was an exhibition at the Gallery of Modern Art of trans and queer arts where one of the exhibits was a big old-fashioned family Bible. The idea of this came from a minister of the Metropolitan Community Church, Jane Clark, who said, "We queer people who've been excluded from the Bible, feel free to write in the margin, write yourself *back* into the book." There were some very beautiful things written there, but there were some very angry things. *The Daily Mail* picked it up and there was a huge scandal which really got the Christian traditionalists going. So when my play turned up a couple of months later at the Tron Theatre *[in Central Glasgow]*, they were all ready to pounce on it.

And they did. It was remarkable. It was a synergy in fact, the street outside the Tron was full of furious demonstrators. Catholics had brought along a statue of the Virgin Mary who they prayed to because apparently I was insulting her, and the Baptists and the Evangelicals brought along stern placards that said I was going to hell — "God says My Son is not a pervert", stuff like that. And so there was massive hatred on the street outside where I was performing my play.

It's very unusual in the UK that people get so cross about a play that they will protest against it. But they did. The BBC filmed a brief news report and it went on their website by the end of the week. Then the archbishop of Glasgow denounced the play, saying it was hard to imagine a greater affront to the Christian faith than my play. Well, if you googled the play at that point, you'd have already got about 600,000 hits. People all round the world had opinions about the play. Mostly they thought it was ridiculous. It was appalling, it was stupid. It was vile. It was disgusting.

But there was some support. There was certainly support from people who saw the play because they loved it, they were moved by it. But I was hideously traumatised because I wasn't expecting that level of hatred. I was terrified. I thought I was going to get beaten up. It's a very strange feeling when hundreds and hundreds and thousands of people hate you. You feel very exposed. You feel rubbed raw. But at the same time, I thought I must be on to something here. For people to get this cross about this idea it must really be working at some level.

Both the director and the producer in Glasgow were also traumatised. They were having an appalling time, death threats, people smashing windows of their office. All kinds of things had been going on for them. They said they didn't want to have anything to do with the play any more, and so I was on my own. It took a long time from there for me to slowly build it up. Again I was lucky because I met this amazing director, Susan Worsfold, a voice teacher who taught me how to use my voice on the stage. After about five years, I'd sold my house, bought a flat, so I had a bit of surplus which I could invest in putting the show on the *[Edinburgh Festival]* Fringe.

I have to say various venues had turned it down, and I hadn't been able to find a producer, they just weren't interested. But eventually we found Annabel Cooper, and the three of us put it on late at night at the fringe in 2014 in St Mark's Unitarian Church, very close to the Traverse Theatre. Natalia Mallo from Brazil came to see it and said, "I want to translate this play and put it on in Brazil." It was then partly on the strength of that that we were able to get Made in Scotland funding and take it to *[Edfringe venue]* Summerhall the following year. On the basis of that we got the invitation to perform the play in Brazil *[in English]*. And then Natalia's Brazilian version, *O Evangelho Segundo Jesus, Rainha do Céu*, started with trans actress Renata Carvalho performing it.

So *all* these things happened, one thing after another, and we've been doing *Jesus, Queen of Heaven* continually ever since in all sorts of places: hotel rooms, pubs, community centres, church halls, churches. And finally, in Christmas of 2018, in a theatre, in the main space, Traverse One, for the Traverse Theatre's Christmas show.

Last year *[2019]*, it was the tenth anniversary. We got a whole week, a wonderful week of work together in Glasgow at the Tron. We managed to get the Brazilian production across, which was fantastic — Renata had never been in this country before. We sold out on various occasions, we had a programme of workshops. We commissioned a play about that Bible exhibit that I mentioned earlier from a young queer writer with a queer cast, most of whom had never had the chance to perform as queers on the stage before. So it was an amazing event. Now we're regrouping and thinking about what to do next. Weirdly enough, in the last fortnight there have been invitations to present the show in Barcelona, interest in the Italian and Scandinavian rights. So suddenly, abroad is calling again. In fact very unexpectedly we got invited to present the show in a theatre festival in Sao Paulo, and the funding appeared from somewhere, and we managed to get there and perform and get back just before the Coronavirus *[first week of March — the government imposed the national lockdown on the evening of Monday March 23]*.

So yeah, that's all part of the story. If you want to know more, by the way, you should buy the book — we've brought out a special tenth anniversary edition.

But world domination seems a bit of a weird thing when you say that you still can't play every theatre, every town in your home country.

There's probably two strands to the work now. One is to continue to do it in community venues, which now includes universities as another source of interest. And then there are church venues, such as a very interesting retreat centre in the North of England that wants to put on the play as part of a big ecumenical conference in 2021.

What we've also discovered is that this is a show that really works in big theatres. It also works well within the context of the Brazilian show. So we now have to do a bit of thinking as to what's the best way of making all this work in the future.

What's perhaps unusual about us is that we definitely think along a very long timescale. One of the things that drives me mad about British theatre is that you rehearse a show for, say, four weeks if you're lucky, it then runs maybe for three weeks. It's never really ready when it opens for when the press come to see it, then just as it *is* ready, just as it's in the shape that it needs to be, *that's* when it closes and it's never seen again. It's wasteful, it's ridiculous, and it drives me crazy. That's one of the things we can change, because we have control over *Jesus*, no other management does. We can bring it back whenever we want to and however we want to. Hopefully that means we will get theatre venues eventually. It might take a long time, but I'm in this for the long game.

At the same time my other career continues. I'm creating a work, *The Not So Ugly Duckling*, with a storyteller actress Maria McDonell based on Hans Christian Anderson This comes from some years ago when. I went to a conference and this amazing *[Italian]* trans woman called Vladimir Luxuria was speaking. She said the thing about us trans people is that we have been around for centuries and centuries, but, given the extraordinary hostility and prejudice that there has been in Europe, we haven't been able to express ourselves openly. But there has always been an underground stream of trans expression. She said, why do you think Hans Christian Andersen was one of us? You can see it in his letters to the men he loved, and also in his stories. If you think about 'The Little Mermaid' or 'The Ugly Duckling' that's a really interesting theme for us to be exploring. So that's one thing I'm working on. The main thing is not to be silenced. And opportunities come up when you least expect them. So the work goes on, the struggle continues.

You recently did The Taming of the Shrew, which was a co-commission from the Sherman Theatre in Cardiff and the Tron in Glasgow.

Oh God. Yeah. That was *fabulous*. I loved that show. In that one. Katherina was a boy, Petruchio was a girl, I also hacked the text considerably. I completely changed it — you have to because it's a terrible text in many ways. But in order to turn that play into a queer play, wow, that really opens up all sorts of doors within it. and I'm very proud of that show. It's very funny, very provocative audiences loved it. But again, it's disappeared, which frustrates me.

You clearly did something quite different there. There've been all manner of gender swaps in Shakespeare — enough to make it a genre of its own — but it's always seemed to be quite pantomimey, even when it's meant to be serious.

As a play, *Taming of the Shrew* is really interesting. *Really* interesting because some of what goes on in that play is seriously horrific. The level of bullying and abuse is unbelievable and there's that really sad speech which Katherina gives at the end where she consents to her abuse. She internalises her oppression. Wow, that is *something*, and to try to rewrite it, to make it clear what's going on, was a fascinating thing to do — and a very powerful thing to do.

> *It seems to me that you came up with something that was an utterly contemporary response to the traditions of the play. But it's also a queer approach to a straight situation. It's a reminder that (a) that sort of subversion needs to be experienced live in a theatre, and (b) it needs a theatre with vision to get to a writer with vision on that stage with cast, creatives — and audience. Were there any placards and furious people outside this time?*

No. But it was interesting to compare the difference between the two theatres. At the Sherman I had the men sitting in a different place from the women in the audience so you have a sense of a bit of edginess in the battle of the sexes. The Tron wouldn't allow that, it would have freaked them out too much. I kept the prologue in where the woman who was going to play Petruchio was a female usher and she was subjected to sexist abuse from a drunken man in the audience — he eventually played Katherina. It was fascinating because at the Tron people did get very cross because they thought it was real. And so there were slow hand claps *[laughs]* and quite a bit of crossness. But nobody protested, I don't think. A shame really!

> *Maybe you wouldn't even have stumbled across the idea of doing the play if you'd been in London. It is a bit pointless to go back and think about that, but it seems that being based in Scotland does give you an edge.*

Well yes. It gives you a massive freedom.

> *And yet being in Scottish theatre has also involved massive resistance against you.*

Yes. But if I had done the sensible thing and moved down to London, I'd never have been able to get a single thing onstage. Seriously. I was very lucky in that I was able to be around at Edinburgh during a particularly lively and amazing phase in the Traverse's history. Jenny Killick was the director. It was astonishing the way she was open and took risks. She was certainly courageous and took risks with *me* in a way that no other theatre now would. That was an amazing bit of luck. But then, you know, that's how theatre is, isn't it? It's full of serendipity and unusual things happening when you least expect them. And

I don't think it's a coincidence the fact that I've never really managed to get a break through in London. I just think that my voice, which is in the end is a transgender voice, a trans woman's voice, London just can't deal with it.

Do you think there's also an element of it being perceived as a Scottish play. It doesn't have to have the themes of someone like David Greig, but its provenance is Scotland and therefore people south of the border, without bothering to look at it closely, will instinctively say, "Well, we've got enough of that of our own on this side of the border, so no offence but no thanks."

[chuckles] Of course what makes it all more complicated is that my other source of inspiration is Spain. So that makes me even more suspect — I'm not naturalistic. *Why* people imagine that the form of theatre that was progressive in the 19th century, naturalism, is still relevant now, I just cannot believe. It's astonishing how backward and reactionary theatre's reasoning is in this country. But there you go, I can't change that.

But in support of that, there is a long Scottish history of linking up with Catholic European cultures.

Exactly, *and* the music hall tradition is still very much alive. Even though I'm a bit alienated from it, Scottish theatre is in many ways far more interesting than England's. And always has been.

To come back to those ten years when you stumbled into the play, it took on a life of its own at the same time as there has been a wave through society, through the world over the same period. You've steered it through that time where there's been a mapping out of the debate, the acknowledgement and the laying down of acceptance, still not there, and the platform of transgender people within this country. And also awareness of what's happening in the rest of the world. Oh, and also connecting it with the way we are towards the Other in general. That awareness of transgender acceptance is being held up mirror to society. The parallel trajectory of the past decade of that process and of The Gospel According to Jesus, Queen of Heaven couldn't have been planned better even if you were able.

I think that's absolutely right. It's astonishing to have seen the rate of change. For instance, when I first performed that play, I believe I was the only out trans-gender theatre performer — certainly in Scotland but I suspect in the country. And just think about how much *that* has changed in the last few years. That's incredible. Incredible. There are massive changes and you're right, somehow I managed to stumble, I managed to be in the right place at the right time.

And that's all you can ask for really as a theatre artist. You're very much at the mercy of what is happening, you can't control it — unless you're a completely cynical artist. But if you're a proper artist you can't control it. You don't know what you're doing. You stumble along, you refuse to be silenced. Do your best and things happen. And certainly things have happened with that play with my work, which I am very proud of.

In bringing that act of resistance to the stage with that compassion, an appeal to love one another with a steely glint, what effect do you think it's had on other people in their actual lives?

I remember getting a letter very early on in the process, from a minister in Oxford and she said, "I know a trans woman who is dying of Aids, and I went to visit her in the hospital. I started to read your play out to her but she was a bit puzzled at first. Then she understood what was going on, and she was profoundly moved. She was clearly very inspired and strengthened by it." And that's remarkable to think about. And people in Brazil say the play has absolutely changed the course of Brazilian theatre. And I know because I've met so many trans women who have said, "Your play has transformed my life." Because it gives people a sense of hope and a sense of pride in themselves.

So in that way I know that theatre does change people, it's a massive affirmation of the beliefs I've had for many, many years. Just looking at the young queer artist who wrote the play about the book and the Bible. They came see me last week and they wanted a bit of mentoring, wanting to know what to do with the script next. It was very clear this was the first time that they have had any kind of support, that they'd be listened to as a queer playwright as opposed to a playwright that has had to pretend to be straight in order to get their work put on. And I thought, wow. Again, profoundly moved by that.

How do you see going onstage as a performer empowering you? The constant in your career has been as a writer moving on to be a playwright. But to then become a performer is quite a step. As a writer and playwright, I know I'd be unlikely to do it, no matter how close to my material I felt. But you had surges of confidence in yourself, for example after having had surgery, so going onstage must have been a lot more than simply getting your own words out there and connecting the message to the audience. It's been a true journey as well?

Yes it has been much more than that. I really discovered my vocation for the theatre when I was 14 years old. I was acting in school plays — and playing the girls' parts at an all-boys' boarding school. An extraordinary thing happened to me when I realised that the minute I was in the rehearsal room I just felt happy to be on the stage. I felt happy to be performing. I wasn't shy anymore. I felt confident. I felt I had a place in the world, and that was an incredibly liberating feeling.

Looking back on it, it is very clear that at that moment I found my vocation as a theatre artist, as a performer — not as a writer. But what I also discovered at the same time was that I would be so much happier wearing girl's clothes and living as a girl. And way back in 1964 that was about the most forbidden disgusting, disgraceful, vile, repulsive, unacceptable thing that I could be thinking, and I was profoundly, profoundly traumatised by it. I was frightened, I thought if anybody gets to know this — because the school I lived in was based on bullying and conformity — my life will be hell on earth. I also thought I would literally die of shame, so I thought the only thing I can do, is I will, I *must* repress this female identity that I seem to have and I must try with all my strength to live as a normal boy. I tried to go for male parts in the theatre, for example, but I couldn't, I just couldn't. I couldn't act those parts at all.

So I absolutely found my vocation at 14, and then within a year or so I lost it, and was blocked as a performer for another 40 years. But what has happened is that in the long, long process of overcoming that particular trauma, that shame, I slowly came to understand how I tried to escape from theatre all together and how I had tried to forget. I didn't know I was a playwright until I was 30 and didn't discover my voice as a playwright until I was 35 with *Losing Venice*, written in 1985. And then I wrote, and I wrote really fast because that was the only way to make a living, and slowly I understood that when I was writing I was performing everything in my imagination, I was becoming the actor or the actress on the stage, and *that* was how I knew if a character was good or not.

I realised, oh God, I've never lost that performer's instinct. And then, completely crazy idea, but I wanted to perform. I felt it was going to be an important part of discovering my identity, overcoming my shame and finding the courage and the strength to live as myself. And actually that was true. It was really when I was living as a woman and happily in my skin that I found the confidence to be able to perform. That was when I discovered the whole joy of performing that I'd last had all those years ago, when I was 14 and 15. That finally happened probably was when I was about 65, so that's 50 years. Then last year I had a bit of a crisis when I realised that I was no longer just a playwright any more. Performing is as important for me as writing. So there's an amazing, really miraculous process of discovery that's going on.

And that's where I am. That's kind of a weird place to be in your late 60s. But then life is weird don't you think?

*

9
Stephen Davidson

'It's tempting to want other people to walk in *your* shoes as an activist'

Stephen Davidson is an improviser, writer, performer, transgender activist & director. Based in North London, he was born in Kamloops & raised in Vancouver, British Columbia, Canada.
• impromiscuous.com

Improv is intriguing because it attracts so many different types of people and skills to the stage and empowers them. Could you do all of this without funding? And how central to your work is that idea of representation of the people you put on to that stage?

I guess I'd like to start by saying I *don't* get funding! I never have, nor have any of the UK groups that I work with. Improv is a very difficult thing to get funding for generally because I think people don't quite *trust* it. I think they don't quite trust the quality of it no matter how good the people involved are because it's much more difficult to quantify.

So I personally do a lot of diversity and outreach things just for free on my own time. One of the reasons I'm able to do that is because I've decided that the profits from my books *Improvising Gender* and *Play Like an Ally* will just go towards that. I therefore set up the Free London Improv Project and whenever there's enough money from book sales to put on a free class, I do it.

I also use that revenue to pay myself and colleagues to teach things that we already do for free, because although a lot of us initially want to scrap in and do our bit and teach for free and spread improv all around so that it can be accessible to everybody, past a certain point we're all professionals and have bills to pay and can only do our job for free for so many hours for so many years to make something happen — even if we're really passionate about it.

So the lack of funding for improv is a chronic issue, because you're right, it's such a perfect art form for diversity. If we could demonstrate that more and have it understood more by more mainstream funding bodies it would be really really helpful.

One of the reasons improv is so good for diversity is that any actor can play any part. You're not cast to look like a certain thing. For example, I could go into a scene and be a woman or a cat or a can of beans or literally anything that I want. That freedom is liberating, particularly for actors who might get typecast, whether because they're a minority — or in fact because they're a majority. If you're a young attractive female actress you're also getting typecast in a really unhelpful way, and maybe you want to spend the show being a surly old army captain, which is also a really lovely thing that improv offers.

And it also means that we can give people more freedom to experiment. So, for example, I'm transgender and I really love it when other actors play trans characters in an improv set. In any other scripted theatre it's obviously not a good thing to cast a cisgender actor as a trans character, for the same reason you wouldn't cast a white person as a black character, because it's taking that part away from somebody who otherwise could-slash-should have had it. But for improv there's no quid pro quo or reverse obligation, because I could play any part, a person of colour could play any part, none of us are limited, which means everybody gets to have that chance.

The opportunities for an actor to play a character that's so far removed from their personal experience is or can be, if you're an empathetic human, a really useful tool for understanding. One of the diversity classes I teach is called 'Improvising Gender' and it's about performing as characters of all different genders and understanding the make-up of skills and experiences your character might have. So it's not just the physical characteristics but also the emotional skills your character might have: do they know how to create communities or flirt or be confident in the face of their own ignorance? All of those skills are also extremely useful just for an actor-improviser to round out what they can do.

When people go to classes like that they need to develop a bit as an improviser, while also spending that time thinking about the way how we learn and experience gender can be an interesting human growth experience. Just to have that moment of stepping back and thinking, "What actually *is* a man or a woman or a non-binary person? How do I know that? What does that mean about this person's life experience?" And having taken the time to step back and evaluate that, we're in a much better place to not just to try a character who's trans or non-binary but also to maybe understand what that experience might be like for our friends or colleagues or people who are walking past on the streets. It's a really good experiential diversity effort because we *write* about diversity a lot and we *preach* about it and how important it is, but I think a lot of the time we learn and understand better by actually *doing* things.

So to the extent that you can try being a different person, taking the time to put yourself in those shoes is really valuable. That's a thing that improv offers that other art forms don't always, and I really wish that yeah, we could spread that a little bit wider. The trouble with improv as an art form is that it can be hit or miss. Even a really good performer can have a bad night and if you have that sort of pressure of 'a reviewer is in' or something like that, it can go off. But that uncertainty also means that an average performer can have a really fucking amazing night!

There's also a reasonably low bar to entry. You can do a couple of classes and get on stage, which means there's a widely varied quality level. I do think sometimes people go to see one show in a pub and think, "Oh no . . . ! Improv is *not* for me. That was *awful*." But it's a huge and varied community and art form. There are different styles of improv, there are all different schools of improv.

So that all makes for quite a complex community. But it's that common approach to performance that opens it up to everyone as a community tool. Improv is very feminine in that respect, it's not just geared towards that one moment put on the stage.

I'm curious why you would classify that as 'feminine'.

Well, it's not that 'testosterone' approach to drama. Improv is not about slaying the audience by always striving to build up to that final killer scene.

[laughs] Oh all right!

Perhaps 'holistic' would work better, because improv does so much more than what happens on the stage — it's an art form that isn't just about 60 minutes in front of an audience. You can do it here, you can do it in your front room, in that pub back room, community centre, old people's home, school, in the hallway . . . Even discussing it is part of the process, it's totally holistic.

You're right about most of that, yeah!

But that's important because it helps people understand that improv is more than an art form in itself.

Absolutely. The end product of learning to improvise is not an improv show. It's *yourself* as an improviser and the *community* that you build around that. Improv is often described as being a bit of a cult, because you come into it and you feel warm and welcome and accepted, and we work hard to make sure that it's true, because people perform better in that headspace. So it's very much a conscious tool set that we use and give to make that happen. It's things like having open body language or being in service to what the group needs rather than what you need, these are all good for improv and have the fortunate byproduct of being good community builders.

We do have a lot of people who come to improv classes initially because they want to be more confident or improve their social skills or straight-up stage fright. But a lot of it has to do with social interaction, which is where I think a lot of people feel anxiety. Improv is very very good for all that because although there are ostensibly some rules to it, they all have exceptions. That means it's something that you need to take time to learn how to do through repetition, and through learning to navigate a new and challenging world each time you play. It's a very social thing in that aspect; there are no absolutes, the outcome depends on the people you are doing it with, the place, the time, your mood. The social side is learned through gentle guidance and structuring rather than by handing people a user's manual.

I wrote my master's thesis on how people learn to improvise and a lot of it was through the lens of queer theory, which has to do with how we learn behaviours, such as gender by looking at people around us. So, for example, nobody will have given you a manual on how to be a man, but you learn it by watching your male family members, TV, reading books, looking at people outside. There's a constant feedback loop there where everyone is creating and reinforcing the idea of what masculinity is.

Improv is very much the same thing, where improvisers learn to be open and empathetic and accepting and confident and good community builders, just because that's the real skill set of improv. We can talk about things like story structure or different strategies for starting a scene or creating a character, but for me improv is that community sense and that attitude towards the world in general which we've learned through repetition and reinforcement in improv classes and shows.

Is queer theory still relevant to that or was only when you made those first steps in analysing improv?

It's absolutely still relevant. It informs my pedagogy a lot, because that idea of reinforcement and repetition of behaviour means that we need to be structuring classes and socialising in break times and going to the pub after in a similar way — group bonding etc to create the group of humans that we need for the show that we want, and for the wider community that we want.

So in every exercise that I teach, I will explicitly say things about attitude, how we're treating each other, how we're showing our own interest. Little things like eye contact, smiling and nodding sound very basic, but when they're constantly reinforced in our feedback loop, we feel accepted and listened to, welcomed in a different sort of way than we would otherwise.

I'm often tweaking little things about that community structure in a class. So for example, if we're doing a word association thing and you say your word and I then take a moment to go "aaaah . . . oooh . . . urrrgh . . . errr . . . um . . . *this*, I guess: potato!" Firstly, it's problematic because I'm not being spontaneous and allowing myself to say the first thing that pops into my head, but also you could very conceivably think that I didn't like your word and beat yourself up about it. Really in improv, I should be spontaneous and cheerful and just say whatever first comes into my head: "potato!" If I accept your offer immediately, there's a feedback loop there where you feel like your offer was good and maybe the next offer you make will also be good and you should be a little bit more confident about that. We can feed each other's confidence by being accepting and spontaneous.

> *It's making people know that as a concept they are willingly in the same room and not trapped in there. You're there because you want to keep the energy ball going around a ring of people you've chosen to be with for that moment and who will help you, not just the director in the trad hierarchy. Why shouldn't you want to do it?*

And that's a good illustration of why improv is so good as a diversity tool, because the more of those diversity boxes you tick, whether you're female or queer or a person of colour or disabled, the more people will treat you in your day-to-day life like you're less-than or Other. So you're more frequently obliged to prove that you're a competent adult rather than people just assuming that you are.

For example, as a man I'm definitely left in charge of all kinds of things without any question in a way that did not happen before (when I was female). There used to be much more need to prove that I was going to do a good job before people could just leave me to do it. Conversationally, as well, the way people listen to you changes and the way people give you physical space changes. When people walk into our office they often assume that I'm in charge. And I *am* in charge but I'm not wearing a name tag, *[laughs]* I'm just a middle class white guy.

So in the same way that we learn masculinity or the skill set of improv, if you're a person out in the world constantly being obliged to prove your competency, you learn to be more hesitant and back-footed sometimes and/or you learn to go in all guns blazing. Both of which are unhelpful for improv and both of which are needless emotional labour, if I'm honest. So if you're a quote-unquote diverse person who is treated that way and then you come to an improv class, if it's a well run improv class you get to enjoy the novelty of being listened to and respected and having your ideas built on without question, and that can be very powerful.

It also means that we need to structure classes to make sure that we're setting people up for success and actively nurturing those skills, because that same quote-unquote diverse person who needs to prove themselves has more to lose emotionally by going onstage and feeling a bit stupid. Whereas if you're a straight white cisgendered middle class man, everyone treats you like you're competent and everything more or less goes your way or seems feasible. Then if you go onstage and somebody tells you that you're crap or you've failed, it's less emotionally devastating and more of a challenge to overcome. We experience that differently because we experience the world differently.

I like that because you're not dumping people. If you have a formal director with the sort of hierarchy that it involves and a formal stage, everything becomes predetermined, other members of the cast should always be in the same place without variation, and you also have an audience with the same expectations. But without any of that, it looks as if you are just throwing people in, whereas in fact there is a safety net as you've said, i.e. trust in other people and in yourself, and that's what drives improv and if everything goes right on the night, that's the cream on top of the icing. So when did you first sense the attraction of improv and realise that it was going to be permanent?

In my previous life I was an improvising musician. I did my master's degree in contemporary solo bass clarinet performance which is very *niche* — in fact I might be the only person in the world with that degree! My thesis was about how people learn to freely improvise music, so music with no rules. Which is how I branched into this queer theory angle. I'd done a lot of queer theory and critical studies in sexuality and so on as an undergrad, and the lens of that was helpful to try and figure out why some people are better at free improv than others if there are ostensibly no rules and how we can teach that more effectively.

That was specifically improvisation in music to begin with?

My degree was music, but the thesis included improvised theatre and dance.

But at the time you were looking already at improv as part of a much wider thing?

Yes, because the resources of pedagogy don't exist for that. Even today, if you look for resources about how to learn to improvise music, you get jazz improv with chords and structure which is . . . different. So as part of that thesis, which I wrote in 2008 at McGill *[university in Montreal, Canada]*, I read a lot of dance and theatre pedagogy because to me both of those were closer to what I was looking at in music. And through reading that I thought, "This would be really good for me, I should do this." So I took up improv at Impro Montreal in 2008.

How did you end up in the UK?

I came to the UK because there's a bigger arts scene, it's more varied. When you get to a certain level in Canada most people leave the country and/or things become very specialised. For example, Vancouver has a very big TV industry, so if you're a set designer that's a great place to go to for that specific career, but it's not great for a lot of other artists. Whereas in London there's more cross-pollination and opportunity to see and be involved in really good art in many different disciplines. And to travel, particularly in Europe, to experience different cultures. I teach abroad once a month at least and I get to go and work particularly on diversity with communities all around Europe, some of which are already very diverse and some of which are very much monocultures struggling to adapt. That's a really interesting opportunity.

So the next question I suppose would be, where do you go from here? It's turned out to be quite a hostile culture out there despite all of the positive strides made. Where do you think people should take things from here? Doing the same thing, trying to expand it, trying to knock heads together or . . . ?

Wow. I mean, the world broadly is going a bit to shit. But for me improv is gently but steadily growing and expanding in a way that I find really heartening. For me as a quote-unquote activist I think one of the most valuable things I can do is to just be visible and positive. So for example Ellen DeGeneres came out a decade ago and there was a whole big to-do, but she was relentlessly nice and lovely and now everybody likes her and there's a much wider acceptance in America for LGBTQ people. I think that that style of activism is one of the most effective, because a lot of intolerance is based on fear.

For me as a trans person, I work hard to be as visible as I can, because to look at me most people don't guess that. So I make the effort of speaking about it and writing it frequently because people have a mental image of what trans looks like and it isn't me. In a lot of cases when people think of trans people they imagine bad stereotypes from movies, some scary unknown who is going to follow them into the bathroom, someone who doesn't fit in . . . I don't need to rage at anyone to be an effective activist, I just need them to see me as I am.

Largely for the same reason that I think positive visibility is important in improv. None of us are rich or famous — yet — in the UK. When people imagine improv they also imagine bad stereotypes from movies and TV: painfully awkward shows, bad puns, games designed to mess people up. People need to know it's not just silly games in a pub. It can be of course, and that's beautiful, but it's much more. And the more people that know that, the more encouraged I am. As lots of things in the world are going poorly, it can be heartening and appealing to all kinds of people who wouldn't necessarily have said, "Yes I want to be a comedian" or "Yes I'd like to be an actor." It's an inclusive community and it's an optimistic community. It's also a set of valuable skills. And it's art! And I think people need art particularly in difficult times.

What can other people learn from this . . . you're a transgender activist but you're also an improv activist it would seem.

Yes absolutely.

It's seems obvious but not everyone talks that way or acts on it. How does that combination of soft activisms become a model that other people can learn from?

For me the overriding thing as an activist is just to be visible and relentlessly lovely as a baseline.

So, back to the idea of funding . . .

Having never gotten any, it's still a bit of a bafflement to me how it works. If they want to fund improv and/or diversity broadly, they should just hire people who know about it because there's a lot of frustration with the lack of information about what it is and isn't as an art form and who we are. Unlike other art forms, when we apply for funding a big part of the application is justifying the existence of our art, whereas somebody applying for scripted theatre can spend their whole application talking about their specific project, secure in the knowledge that whomever is reading the application understands how putting on a play works.

But what's the block on that? If we're sitting in a pub taking to other people who don't know about this, as 'ordinary citizens' they'd agree they're also baffled by that. As you say, hire someone who knows about it, because not only is it logical but it's also the best practice that people are striving for officially. But it's not as simple as it looks, clearly.

The more we can make things personal to ourselves the more we can understand them. For example, what I was saying about trying characters of different genders. The more you put yourself into something, the more interesting and visceral it becomes. Part of the reason why the transgender movement in the last decade has had success is because there have been a lot of realisations about things like toxic masculinity, which make the concept of gender as a construct or a fluid thing much more relevant to everybody. Because we take that moment, even if we're not trans or anywhere close to it, to think, "I could have learned to express my feelings better. That's the thing that this societal construct has done to me personally." And then you understand a little bit more.

With improv, there are lots of things in that neighbourhood that people could and should understand in the same visceral way. Things about being spontaneous and emotionally open, being all right with failing as an emotional skill, being empathetic towards other people, knowing how your body language and way of communicating affects other people. These are skills that all of us should have, especially anyone remotely connected to theatre.

And improv is a very effective way of learning them. So for me, if I want to explain what improv is and why it's important to somebody who's not a performer or who is not maybe going to come and take a class, I would start talking about what do you need to learn as a human to be happy and create connections with people. And to tie it in with diversity, one of the things you learn is to not make assumptions.

It's another really nice thing about improv where, if we walk into a scene, I wouldn't assume that you look like that. You could be absolutely anything, we could be absolutely anywhere, have magical powers, we could be telekinetic — that way of looking at the world in a slightly more flexible way. For a start, it's obviously good for diversity that I'm not looking at you and only seeing what you physically look like — it can also be really powerful as a tool for flexible thinking and the way you view the world.

I think part of why the funding thing is so difficult is because improv ticks so many boxes, oddly. It's a performance art, and it's a community practice, and it's personal development, and it's outreach. The fact that it's such a useful skill set is oddly against us.

So you applied queer theory to music improvisation and came up with improv and transgender activism. Added to which, you threw in the dance and theatre side to music, although I can imagine the dance being a bit more useful perhaps . . .

They're both really useful, but different. One thing that I really liked about the dance pedagogy is the mixture of abstract and concrete, because it's difficult to write down a physical movement. Learning the vocabulary to do that isn't always the best way forward. You learn different ways of communicating, things like Viewpoints *[the Six Viewpoints, created in 1978 by theatremaker Mary Overlie in New York, a theatre/dance composition technique along the acronym SSTEMS: Space, Shape, Time, Emotion, Movement, and Story]*, the repetition of shape and the architecture. We use that in theatre as well, because it's a valuable and easily transferable vocabulary to learn as a skill rather than as a script, if that makes sense. If you're paying attention to things like that then you'd notice them in any situation — rather than if you learned *Hamlet*, where you'd probably learn some transferable skills, but mostly you just learn *Hamlet*.

So I think in terms of mental flexibility and artistic practice and flexibility, that kind of thing is very useful and also informs my practice. It's a good illustration of the process and the skill set being more what the product actually is, being more than the show. So people who have been improvising for a long time will have that intuitive understanding of staging and tempo and rhythm in a piece, something that I think often other actors need to be coached much more explicitly on. Improv performers also bring a loveliness and a connection in a scene where scripted actors often need to be heavily coached to learn how to do it, possibly in a slightly more clunky way.

There was a really interesting article that I read about dance when I was doing my thesis. It was about the feeling of freedom when you're out clubbing, how people go to a club and they feel like they can lose themselves in the music and just be there doing that for a couple of hours of their life. But actually the *first* time you go clubbing it's often not that way, it's terrifying. You have to learn how to do it, to find the freedom. That's a really useful parallel for learning improv because your average person on the street, if you told them, "Come do this thing, we're going to put you on a stage and you're just going to make a show up", they would be terrified. But when we take them through classes and, later on, jams and shows, we use that repetition of skill set and positive reinforcement. Things like making an offer and having it be supported, or consciously listening actively and building on what you hear, or being surprised in a scene when information is different than you assumed and choosing to be positively surprised rather than angry that you were wrong about what you thought was going on.

Those skills can make us much freer and happier onstage definitely but also in our lives and I think that's a really valuable thing that I took from that pedagogy. So that also moves forward and again — sorry to bang on about it — but in terms of diversity, if we're thinking about diverse people who are not always treated that way in their day-to-day life, the more we can impart that sense of freedom and confidence and awareness, the more we can affect the positive social change. Because it's not just "look there are lots of people of colour on our stage" — it's "look we are creating a community where lots of people of colour are happy and confident and outgoing and will be positive representations of our community and their community and bring more people in".

Because improv makes everybody involved. If you stay in it and it suits you, it makes you more confident, more outgoing, often happier, relaxed, spontaneous and for me those are qualities that make a good activist, a visible activist. I look at other trans activists and I often see people who are very brittle and angry and I absolutely understand why. But for me that's not an effective way forward in terms of acceptance and visibility and communicating your needs and your personhood to other people.

So for example if somebody uses offensive language with me, I am much more equipped to gently set it right and/or make a joke about it that will make the ethos clear. I think sometimes activists who have been activists for a long time and/or who are really feeling the effects of their Otherness, have a harder time taking something like that in their stride. And we become combative very easily — within our own communities as well. I can think of countless instances of infighting amongst queer activists certainly.

It happens less in improv but as schools split off into different schools of thought there are, well, not major conflicts but *different* approaches. In terms of queer activism, for example there's a trans Pride in London this year and within about a month of the committee being formed they'd split into two committees doing events on the same day because they couldn't agree about some minor detail. Which is very typical and *so* unhelpful in the grander scheme of things in terms of us as a community. The queer community broadly is very good at the concept of a chosen family, a chosen community and creating those connections, but as it's gotten bigger and more diverse we split off from each other sometimes. We create rifts that are really unnecessary and we get things like simultaneous trans Pride events or there's a bisexual Pride movement now going on that are saying cis white gay men are not even queer any more because it's so accepted, which is fucking galling for so many reasons and also really unnecessary to their core point of bisexual pride and visibility. Why do they have to attack anyone? No reason!

I see a lot of this parallelled in the improv community as it grows and diversifies. The skill set of improv is one that encourages co-operation, but as our numbers grow past the point where we could conceivably all know each other we create smaller sub-communities. If we're not careful, they could become closed and combative.

So the best activism is often the one that deflects anger and so works for all sides. I mean, channelling anger obviously opens a lot of doors but with the growing confidence of a marginalised community you get as a result, anger doesn't always have a place.

For broader community acceptance no I don't think it works. There are lots of reasons to be angry as a trans activist, and I think being angry in the general direction of the government and people who can do things about that is a very good strategy and very relevant and needed. But in terms of broader societal acceptance, you catch more flies with honey, dealing with angrier people or people who have very different views from you. It's a bit like dealing with a heckler or somebody who shouts a really unhelpful suggestion at an improv show. In stand-up comedy, if somebody shouts something unhelpful, you usually put it back to them with a putdown and that's like part of the banter of it, but in improv we try really hard to make sure our audiences feel taken care of to the best of our abilities. So if somebody shouts out "dildo!" as a suggestion *[as the theme of a performance]*, I wouldn't push back with an insult. I might at the most say, "Do you really want to see a whole show about *that*? Have you thought it through?" Usually the answer is no.

But at least you have the audience on your side — and the show — even if that suggestion gets a laugh.

Yeah. So there's that. In a way angry activism or put down culture can be counterproductive to that sort of encounter too though. If I'm used to interacting with people who constantly police each other I might get used to calling prejudice out and having them immediately retract the offending statement. If I find myself in a conversation with somebody who is actually a racist, though, that card doesn't work in the same way. Because I would say, "Oh fuck, that sounds a bit racist", and they would go, "Yes." It means that my tools are not suited to that situation.

You can't always have something for everything.

No. So we need to create and practise different tools for dealing with that person — and for me empathy and thinking about the experiences of people who are different from myself means that I could have a conversation with that person. I might not convince them to stop being a racist in a 20-minute conversation, but I can engage with them and hopefully gently chip away at that a little bit.

For example, I'm rehearsing a show that's an improvised Tennessee Williams, and because it's set in the 1930s and 40s in the Deep South in America, a lot of the themes that we see coming up again and again in Williams' work are to do with gender and race. For us to authentically improvise that, we end up with characters and situations that are actually quite sexist. We've had scenes and relationships onstage that have been quite violent, we've had straight-up rape scenes. That is often not what improv is, but here we have an example of a very specific genre and an ensemble that has been together for a couple of years and is trusted and bonding and everyone's okay with this being the show. As a diversity precursor, all of these people are having a nice time, I promise! *[laughs]* I checked, repeatedly.

But it's interesting to put yourself in the characters like that again and again. To try to see the world through their lens. Because it's very tempting to want other people to walk in *your* shoes as an activist. And particularly as a left-wing, very liberal activist, it's very very easy to be judgemental of those who don't share your opinion. So although I'm never going to be sympathetic to a sexist viewpoint, spending a lot of time as a male character who feels pressure to provide and has not been taught how to express their feelings or has been taught to express their feelings in one particular way their whole life can be a really interesting experience. And it means that if I'm then talking to somebody in real life who's a bit sexist, I can empathise potentially with those things where they don't have the tools to express themselves or they feel under pressure to be a breadwinner in a world where that is difficult to do or if they don't quite have the skill set to interact with all of the people around them in a meaningful way. For me elements like this that humanise somebody are a much better place to start an interaction than "hey stop being such a sexist!" If you gently get people on your side and suggest things, I've often found that progress can be made, even if it's slow.

It is palpable. I travel a lot to teach about diversity in different countries, especially Europe, where things like gender equality and LGBTQ rights are in very different places than they are here in the UK. Me having the tools to talk about that has proven much more helpful than being combative when someone initiates a scene that's very sexist or they're constantly playing female characters who only want a boyfriend — which in any one scene if that's your character's motivation is fine, but if it has been the last ten scenes then we maybe have a lack of insight. *[laughs]*

So I can have that discussion with that person about the improv skills behind that and the gender construct behind that and what else it might mean to play a female character or to interact with a female character or maybe to play an LGBTQ character not as a joke. I can have a long and productive discussion with that person to help make them a slightly better improviser and also, I hope, a slightly less sexist human being because they take in a little bit of time to think about it. Does that make sense?

Sure. But because we're working our way towards a world where at least in theory there's normality in society, more and more people feel they need the right words, attitudes and to do the right thing, yet without real actual experience, it all adds to the pressure. Is it okay to tell them that's okay? Or is this still not the time?

It's important as humans that we maintain a sense of curiosity about the world and the people in it. So whether or not you're out there to actively try and be in activism and push things on people, we can worry about people who stop reading and meeting new people at any point in their life. We need to be actively encouraged. It can be hard to look at activism as a task or a bar that you have to hit. So things like not feeling you're enough of an activist can be a big hurdle. But if we look away from that, if we stop thinking about whether we're good enough, in fact we stop thinking about what you should or shouldn't be doing, we can push for intellectual and emotional curiosity about the world. We keep learning and we keep meeting new people and that is how we build those bridges and gradually expand that knowledge because you'll never know all the things you need to know.

There's terminology about gender, for example, that I don't know — because I'm *so* old at the age of 35, and there's a whole generation of people with a whole other way of doing it and expressing it. I did once make a note and tried to learn those things, but I have friends in context in that generation and that world so I don't need to be an expert on it to interact with them in a meaningful way. I learn what I need to learn when I need to learn it because of who is directly in front of me because that's how you make that human connection. I certainly couldn't write you a whole list of all of those terms and their definitions, and if even somebody in my position can't, then probably nobody else needs to feel bad about that. *[laughs]* Like, we're all humans, go about your business!

Everybody doesn't need to read a glossary or wander around holding a sign at a march. Both of which actions I respect and are very useful, but that's not everybody. But like I said, everybody is a human and connected to other humans. So there's something really valuable to be gained from the practice of meeting a new human and understanding their point of view and their experience. You'll never fully understand it, but taking that time to just have a conversation to me feels like something that's much more doable than being a quote-unquote activist. And if you take the time in that conversation to share a little bit of yourself as well, you're effectively being an activist for whatever group you represent or are seen to represent.

For me the skills of improv can deeply inform that approach of being able to meet a person who is very different from you and to find one thing you have in common. That's where you make the connection. So if somebody is fervently religious, I as an atheist am probably not going to get onto that boat but maybe I also have strong feelings about standing up for your beliefs, putting your money where your mouth is. And maybe that's where I connect to that person. Because I take that extra little mental step of thinking, "Well, who are you and what are you really saying?" And then I find a way to connect.

It's not activism in the traditional sense to have that sort of conversation but it's just a different type of activism, because it's very easy to be in a little bit of a bubble despite how connected the world is now. And it's easy to forget that skill of human interaction. I think a lot of people who are very far right-wing or otherwise have gone off the deep end in terms of their own beliefs or activism, what they've lost is that ability to connect to different humans.

So if I take the time to connect to them, it's a step towards something — and if they want to come to an improv class and learn that skill properly, they're very welcome! Improvisers tend to be quite left-wing, but I definitely know people in the improv community who are very religious or conservative or . . . I know some improvisers who voted for Brexit. Not many but they exist. And some of them are lovely humans and they're all welcome in the community, because that's how we do as improvisers.

*

10
Sharlit Deyzac &
Amy Clare Tasker

'We bring people together to share ideas ... and make it not scary'

Sharlit Deyzac is a writer, actor & co-director/founder of Voila! Europe Festival. Based in Porto, Portugal, she was born in Marignane, Côte d'Azur, France, and raised in the Middle East.
• *@Sunshinesharlit*

Amy Clare Tasker is a theatremaker, producer & co-director of Voila! Europe Festival. Based in North London, she was born in Stockport, Greater Manchester, & raised in California, USA.
• *amyclaretasker.com, @AmyClareTasker*
• *voilafestival.co.uk*

Voila! seems very much to have come of age this year [2019] and it's good to take this snapshot of you in action. Do you feel that it has always been a work in progress or was the plan to go from stage to stage?

Sharlit: An interesting question . . . With the bilingual English-French festival, as Voila! originally was, the Brexit Referendum in 2016 was such a slap in the face for everyone. There were so many people affected that it felt that being a French-English festival was just not enough so it had to go European.

That was the last year when we were in just one venue when everything sold out, so it made sense to grow. But in a way, by going European we also took a few steps back, because there was a lot more to learn. Now we are definitely gaining momentum and it feels now like that 'coming of age' — we haven't actually coined it that way but I think it's a good way to describe where we are right now.

Amy: The festival has developed on the producing side as well. Sharlit for five or six years has done it on her own essentially, with the support of the Cockpit Theatre. And then I came on last year *[2018]* as the deputy director. So this is now my second year with the festival. I certainly know a lot more about what we're doing now. Last year it was a big learning curve: to jump in and go, "Cool, I will help you programme this and we'll produce it together!"

We've learned a lot from doing a complete cycle and also from the Piece of the Continent Festival we did in April this year in partnership with the Actors Centre *[in London]*. So when it came to programming this year's festival and making a new venue partnership with Rich Mix, I feel personally that I've levelled up as a producer, which has allowed the festival to be better supported and grow.

This year we've been a bit more specific in the programming, and we've got two venues instead of three. Because the festival is spread outside just one location, creating a sense of hub is really important. We want each space to be where the audience can feel in their element, to sit around, see two shows on the night and then in the middle have a drink and chat in the bar with other people who've seen the shows.

Sharlit: It's creating that festival atmosphere, because there's no denying that, as opposed to the Edinburgh Festival Fringe or Camden Fringe and all that kind of stuff, we're a winter festival really, which means we don't have any outside 'courtyard' spaces where people can hang out. And so it's finding that buzz within both venues while also making sure that these venues are complementary to each other.

Amy: That's the development of the festival isn't it? Maybe something else to say is that late 2018 was the first time that venues have actively approached us to say, "Will you bring your European programme to my venue?" The Actors Centre and Rich Mix both came to us, saying, "This is really interesting, clearly an important thing to be doing right now."

Obviously this is not to diminish the Cockpit Theatre's support because it all started there. Dave Wybrow *[artistic director of the Cockpit]* has been so, so supportive of us. Not just co-producing the festival, but also mentoring me and Sharlit and encouraging the festival to be the best that it can be. But it's also nice to be on the receiving end of that interest and people recognising that Voila! is something important to be doing right now.

Sharlit: This is also because Voila! has become a community for the artists and the audiences that have been following us for a while now. It's something that Amy and I also want to develop since we don't want it to just be a once a year festival for two weeks, but a constant presence whether it be online or through events or talks and conferences throughout the year.

We would be able to offer a safe place for Europeans and Brits who want to keep London a European city with European theatre present on its stages. To have a year-round space for this purpose is important. Apart from BE Festival up in Birmingham — who've been doing it for a while as well — it's weird that there really aren't that many platforms looking at this as a niche, looking at the self-contained theme of Europeanness.

It's sad that, for all of the 'enlightened' Brits' talk of being international and taking the lead in global arts, that it took something as divisive as Brexit and our inability to tackle it for us to miraculously see so many people claim European credentials overnight. With Voila! you convincingly nailed your colours to the masthead a long time before that, as part of that wave of awareness that started around 2008 onwards, post global crisis, when people everywhere started to look for ways to reconcile the idea of national identity with being a citizen of the world. In the years that have followed, the established festival response hasn't been particularly impressive — the Edinburgh International Festival seems to get more provincial every year, while new initiatives like Manchester International Festival and London's Greenwich+Docklands International Festival are great but struggling to find a focus. The Edinburgh fringe is a de facto international festival but it's not a model that can sustain a year-on focus the way Voila! or BE Festival have the potential to develop. Are you picking up on the Euro model or does the UK being the UK, London being London in fact mean that you just have to go with what you've got? You must now have so much feedback and ideas being thrown at you, so how's it working in terms of balancing and bringing that European element into an area where, as you said, there isn't much on the landscape?

Sharlit: It's funny because the original Voila! started on its own really. Dave had booked some shows at the Cockpit which happened to have all these French themes, and he was kind of like, "Oh hang on, I think there's something going on here. Maybe we should make a festival out of all this?" And suddenly it just snowballed.

There are a lot of French people in London and there was no one doing a festival for them. Of course it's not just for French people it's for French lovers too — there's loads of Brits that love France, there's loads of Europeans that love French stuff. And so it was born out of the desire in people to see it all in one place, to have it under one roof. It would probably have made itself, even without us. It would have all happened at some point.

We've seen some European seasons here and there creep up. The Yard did Brexit Stage Left *[2019]*, which was more of a Brexit festival with readings, but you're right, there are a lot of ideas and it's interesting that you're talking about the European model because one of the things we like about Voila! is the whole idea of fringe — and fringe is actually a very British concept.

So one of the cool things about Voila! is that when Brexit wasn't around we weren't too worried about that but our idea was how can we help companies that are in Europe? Companies who are working in subsidised theatre and therefore take a long time before they can put a project up on stage. How can we get the most pressing issues and the most urgent plays to be staged as soon as possible, like we do on the fringe?

We were looking for the companies who were falling through the cracks in Europe and needed a platform to say what they wanted to say that wasn't being said in their own countries. In that sense the UK is extremely bold and has a lot of young emerging companies making work no matter what, with or without funding, the theatres going, "All right I'll take the risk with you, fifty-fifty. Let's do the thing!" Now that is virtually unheard of in a lot of European countries but it's a super strength of the UK. Yes it's precarious, yes it probably exists for not so noble reasons — where artists are having to pay venues in order to put a show on — but at least the opportunity is there.

So what we try to do is make that experience worthwhile to them. Amy and I are a bit more than programmers, we give a lot more to the companies: tips on how to market themselves, programming them in a way that will help so they're on double bills and they can work collaboratively, to get audiences to come and watch two shows at the festival and help those companies outreach to more new audiences. It makes it worth their while to understand the rationale for why they're doing a fifty-fifty split on the show with the venue.

So this is playing to the strengths of what fringe theatre can be, the empathy that Amy and I have for emerging companies and the passion that we have for European collaborations and watching Europeans collaborate, sharing their different skills and methods of acting and ideas and cultures and stories. That's what I think makes Voila! unique because we think a lot about the acts, the artists.

We are an artists' festival probably to the detriment of the theatres in a sense. They're like, "You really should be thinking about audiences and so on . . ." and of course, we do. But for us it's like, "As long as there's still support for the artists, then there will still be work made that needs to be made." Because the audiences will come. It's interesting to take a step back in terms of audience, because the festival had sold out in the last year when it was just the French one and we then hopefully retained most of that audience when it became the European fest. But also there's a new audience to go and find.

In fact a few people were not so happy with the changes in the identity of the festival. We actually got complaints last year from someone who received our newsletter who said, "Where are all the French shows? What is this new thing you're doing, which is such a weird mix of strange shows?" And we replied and said, "Well, those shows are the reason why we chose to make it a European festival, and if you like we can take you off the newsletter." In fact there were nine French shows out of 36, so I don't think it was like we were taking anything away from this person. But she wrote back and said, "I don't want you taking me off your newsletter, I just want to see your French shows and I would like you to not do this festival but instead bring back the French festival!"

I suppose if you're going to go European, you also need to negotiate the tricky cultural rivalries that already exist between the different nations.

Sharlit: For everyone person who feels that way about the festival, hopefully we've got 20 more from different cultural backgrounds within London who are excited by the European expansion of Voila!

It's Europe in microcosm on your doorstep! Proof that you're tapping into more than a fleeting zeitgeist. Talk to us then about the relationship between that international element and your programming. If you're an international artist what do you get when you come to the festival? And if you're a national artist what do you get from the international people coming over? Which are quite different things.

Sharlit: Around 70 per cent of the companies at the festival are UK-based: they're Europeans who are mainly based in London who have come out here to the UK to try and make it as actors, creatives, theatremakers, and who have banded together. Sometimes they are from the same country, but a lot of them are multinational European companies. And they all complain that they feel there is no place for them onstage, that it's very hard for them as individuals to be cast in companies for having an accent or things like that, and as collectives they encounter the same barriers or resistance.

What I've found when speaking to the theatres themselves is that there's a worry, there's just a misunderstanding of putting on a show that is foreign. A foreign accent is already a bit of a hurdle let alone a foreign language, and that's something very tricky for a programmer to put on. They'll only put on a show with that sort of element for a day or two, they're never going to put it on for weeks on end or anything like that.

The Cockpit has put on a lot of shows in translation in the sense that they're surtitled. They do a lot of Russian work for example, but it all comes with challenges such as the surtitles. And also a lot of the theatres are still like "Oh I feel like I don't know any Europeans, can you put me in touch with them?"

So we have both of those things: the companies saying, "Nobody knows about us, they don't want to hear about us" and the theatres saying, "Oh we don't know anybody . . ." That was the case with the Actors Centre where they were, "We love what you're doing but we just don't know where they are. Can you help us reach out to them?" So it's basically giving a platform with a safe umbrella festival that makes everybody comfortable: the company feels like "Oh my gosh, this is where we belong!" and the theatre feels like "Oh this is great they've got an umbrella! We don't know everything about European culture but these guys know what they're doing, they're going to bring it and that's cool."

But you know there's other experience to bring. For example, a theatre might suddenly get a rush of hundreds of audience members who don't speak English with a British accent and it can be a challenge for the staff, because you don't always understand what they're saying, they're not pronouncing very well the name of the show that they want to see, everyone needs to be prepared a little bit more.

That's the sort of thing we take into account each year, looking at how we can streamline and make it easier, from everything like picking up tickets to writing the newsletter in a way that it can be read by loads of different people. There's all sorts of unexpected things that need to be Europeanised in a way.

Amy: Making our information accessible to speakers of languages other than English who need to read it in English is especially important. It's something that we do in tailoring the information that we send to the companies. I'm a native English speaker and only speak English, but I'm learning German because now I'm so embarrassed to be a monolingual person working on a multilingual festival! Sharlit however speaks French and English, and Portuguese now as well, so she is really good at reading the emails that I send to companies and going, "Okay, well that's a really cute thing to say and everybody who's a native English speaker will get your joke, but don't write it that way because you're just going to confuse the hell out of everyone else!"

Sharlit: Or there'll be subtleties obvious to someone in Britain that might need to be said clearer for someone who isn't. So that's a just a part of how to manage the different cultures and make things accessible to everyone — and enjoyable too. The main thing is that they want to come back again next year — not only the artists but also the venues.

With artists coming over from abroad, we try and house them with artists who are based in London who are also appearing at the festival. To help create those kind of links, we obviously also organise an opening party that gets everybody together, and we take into account the fact that the international companies can't all always come to that — maybe they're playing at the end of the festival. So we encourage all the companies to go and see each other's shows for free, we really push them to go and do that and support each other. We also do an advance meet and greet event as a way for them to find out who else is in the programme with similar skills or ways of working.

It's awesome to see them go on supporting each other online and being like "I'm doing this theme and there's this company coming out from Lithuania but they're doing it in this way. Come and catch the double bill!" You get this camaraderie which is really lovely, something we try and cultivate a lot. Even the audiences have always been telling us that there's a really warm friendly atmosphere at Voila!, and I think that's precisely because of this acceptance of cultural differences, that we're all in the same boat kind of thing. It's something we want to make sure that we can continue doing in the future.

As for the more conceptual question, where we're talking about tapping into culture, Europe, zeitgeist, you probably need another ten years before you can sit down and look back to work out what you've been doing instinctively at the moment, what you're responding to, the timing of it all, whether it's the politics or economics or a combination that mould the festival, or whether you're responding actively along with other people to a vision in society. But we're lucky to be talking about theatre, which is regaining some of its voice precisely through festivals like yours and BE Festival. Certainly in the couple of years leading up to the Brexit referendum in 2016, the performing arts had a predictable and rubbish response — and it wasn't much better after the result. But 2018-2019 have seen responses from unexpected directions, sustainable, better serving and perfectly formed, like Voila! — which is logical since you've hardly come from nowhere. At the moment it really seems to be fringe and dance that haven't disappointed. Do you feel that theatre honestly does have something to say, a role to play at the moment, to step into the breach as an instrument of reflecting how society thinks and making connections in ways that other parts of society/culture can't?

Amy: Theatre is not so direct and immediate that it's going to change what Parliament does in the next year or so — and that's why I go on marches — but theatre can change what happens in the next ten years. That's because of the way it can affect the people who come and sit in a room all together, how it can show people that it's not scary to come and engage with our European neighbours.

Also there's a lot of talk amongst theatremakers about "Oh, it's not worth it to preach to the choir and everyone who comes to see your political show already agrees with you." Hopefully, we're doing some audience development work — although that's not always possible — but even if the bulk of our audience are people who already care about Europe and who are already open-hearted and outward-looking, it's important for us to get together regardless. Otherwise, making your individual voice heard can feel very lonely and very discouraging.

So from a personal point of view, it has been helpful for me just psychologically to be working on the festival during this time *[of Brexit chaos]*. I feel like I'm doing something to help in the way that I am able to do it. I'm not an MP, and though I write to my MP, she doesn't agree with me. So I do this.

Theatre works because it is a deeply human thing that we do — we gather around the fire, we tell stories that change the way we feel and change the way we interact with the people around us. We go out into the night after we see something and we go, "Okay, I feel ready to reach out", and that changes things.

Hopefully you're right when you say we need ten years from now to go and study this — and I'll leave that to someone else because I'll still be busy doing the thing itself! I couldn't tell you if we're responding or trailblazing or whatever, but we are definitely part of a zeitgeist. This isn't happening in a vacuum and we are all of us absolutely affected in the long term on a massive cultural level.

So we do what we can, where we are, to bring people together to share ideas and make it not scary, to encourage people to learn languages, to be curious and open and find out about who's around them in this amazing multicultural city. And to spread that in the sense of expansive open arms. Just because we have borders between our countries, we don't need to have borders in our minds and in our relationships.

I do think that theatre is unique in its ability to spread like that. Yes, film can spread much wider but there's something about the liveness of theatre. We in fact have quite a lot of interactive shows in the programme this year, and theatre in that way is literally rehearsal for life: "What would you do in that situation? Okay, do it! And see in a safe way what happens when you do it."

I'm particularly excited about *European Freaks* in the programme by Stereo Akt, a company that we are bringing from Hungary with the support of the Hungarian Cultural Centre in London. They're doing an interactive show fronted by dysfunctional humanoid robots. It's about how we can resuscitate Europe and asks what is democracy, what does it mean to be a responsible citizen? This kind of work clearly has a direct effect, but even something that is on the surface that may seem "oh it's just a play" . . . well, you know there's no such thing as "just a play". The stories stay with us and they change how we behave.

Any other examples from the current programme that you can single out as having a particular resonance?

Sharlit: We were just discussing two of the shows where the companies have taken the start of their work in the community. They've gone out, made interviews with the community and then made the shows out of that.

Mags is about the relationship between mother and daughter. It's from Wales, by Cardiff-based Cwmni Pluen *[literally 'Feather/Plume Company' in Welsh]*, and is a devised piece that's been developed over two years through work with three community groups across Wales. The show asks how far family bonds can be pushed, and how it feels to belong, through following the story of Mags and her return to her hometown after chasing a hedonistic escape from life events. It's multi-genre with music and bilingual in Welsh and English.

The other one is *Forbidden Stories* from Cyprus by Ludens Ensemble where the artists went out and interviewed people in Cyprus from the Turkish side and the Greek side. Faced with all these stories where everybody thinks that they hate each other across the border, what they actually discovered were amazing stories of collaboration, of people helping each other, of creating a community and getting on with life. They missed out the war and the political situation, instead on a daily basis it was "I need you and you need me and we're the same and we can all help each other out."

So these are the sort of stories of hope and people coming together that theatre brings to you, showing you that these big countries with their borders hardly represent the smaller communities inside them, the smaller places where it's just humans interacting with each other and wanting to support each other and having loads of similar stories to share. It's also an interesting theme that links these shows, since they're completely different in form — the Cyprus one is very digital with a load of tech and projections onstage, and then the piece from Wales is bilingual Welsh-English with a live band onstage.

Amy: So they both use research in similar ways yet are very different pieces of art. And then of course environmental climate change means that we get a lot of projects about that from people in very different disciplines. For example aerial artist Hazel Lam, she's from Belgium and Hong Kong, has a piece, *Lighthouse*, where she's doing acrobatics with long tubes and looking at our relationship to plastic — it's a show without words.

At the same time we have *Medea One Standing* by the Washing Machine

Collective. This is a London-based company of five artists who all have different cultural backgrounds, from Italy to Japan, and represent different techniques as well — so one's a musician, one's a visual designer, some are actors and writers. The piece they've created is in response to an actual climate theory, the Medea Hypothesis, which has the idea that maybe Mother Earth is not an all-nurturing mother figure but actually more like Medea who will kill her children. So that's taking the myth of Medea from the Greek classics and twisting it together with the modern crisis of the environmental change, with a mix of performance techniques. They've already made a couple of shows before that are something between performance art, gallery installation and theatre.

Sharlit: That's a lot of what we do, the kind of things we look for are multidisciplinary multilingual and multicultural, so our classic Voila company is a group of mixed Europeans from different backgrounds each having different skills and sharing those skills and coming up with something really motivated.

This year we have a play called *Back to Berlin*, by CB4 Theatre which is essentially marking the Fall of the Berlin Wall which will be celebrated in November of this year — it's been 30 years since the Wall fell and it's the story of the dad of one of the performers. He came from Germany and was at uni in the UK and couldn't believe that the Wall was finally coming down so he made his way over there to just watch it falling down. He recorded the whole story of what it was like for those communities to finally see this border get busted. It's a story that is relevant to us all today because we're building walls everywhere, whether it be Trump or soon to be maybe somewhere in Ireland.

All excellent left-field steps forward into the issues facing us today! We're also talking about how you are very accessible in the way you're set up: you're not doing stuff that you enjoy for the sake of it or that you feel you have to do or that you feel needs to be out there just for its own sake. Also it seems that in your programming there is a major forethought about accessibility to a UK audience to begin with but also anyone else in town because London is a completely international town in any case.

Amy: Absolutely. And you know, we take an absolutely ridiculous amount of time to programme — we have an extensive number of attributions and codes that we use, because we look at everything like where's the company at, who's in it, is it diverse, is it pledging to gender diversity, is it using a lot of different skills? And then aspects like do they need us, can we help them in their project, can we make their voice heard more? How can we help them get new audiences that they don't know? And, of course, how can Voila! through these companies get new audiences who might not up until now venture to go and see European work?

Sharlit: We're now receiving 200 applications, which I'm sure is nothing compared to some, but for us it's just me and Amy doing everything, so we take a great care in looking at every one of those applications. Matching up shows is part of Voila! — we love double bills, where two shows are somehow complementary and yet at the same time very different. One's from Croatia, one's from Hungary and you get an explosion of cultures in one evening. That creates an amazing buzz because people have so much to talk about after seeing a couple of shows programmed like that.

Amy: Ticket price reflects access in that works in progress are £8, and everything else in the programme is £10. So that offers you a cross-section of international work you wouldn't otherwise see. On the main stages you're looking at £30-£40-£50-more, and, like you said, it's 'EU-RO-PE-AN WORK!'

Sharlit: Obviously we're not knocking what the main stages are doing.

> *Well I can always knock them for you. Quality and relevant considerations aside, their shows usually pander to elite audiences no matter what ticket scheme they have going — we all know we're not welcome. And that's a white middle-class middle-aged male speaking here. 'European' on our main stages just means 'fringe with a budget'.*

Sharlit: Sometimes you do just have to go, "Bloody hell, they wasted all their money on *this*?" You're right and I think a lot of people — at least from my generation, in their 30s and probably below — are just a bit, "Oh well, it's a bit pompous and I don't know if I'll feel comfortable going to some huge famous venue with the way I'm dressed or the way I think." They just see it as inaccessible to them in so many different ways, and it's not only financial. It's good that you were making the point, Nick, by saying that we do try and make the programme have a little bit for everyone on all those levels.

Amy: We do consider UK audiences as an additional collaborator on these shows, in particular the shows that are in development. We absolutely want people to use multiple languages, but most of the shows will use mainly English with other languages sprinkled in a way that's accessible to English speakers.

And as UK audiences we're so used to narrative as the driver of performance, we do encourage companies of course to use projections, movement and music, it doesn't even have to be done with words, but a narrative is really important.

Sharlit: We do know that of our audiences. We're careful in programming work that might be considered a bit too European, a bit too out there. But that doesn't mean we're not willing to challenge our audiences. But because we feel we know our audience now, we take great care in the work we choose to present.

> *Looking at the bigger picture, which you've touched on all the way through, if we view the UK through London theatre, it's strange how the capital hasn't reached out and really grasped the international thing. London really does contain the whole world and on every corner you'll hear a different accent or language — and all the world Englishes too. But there's a tendency to see that as an opaque wall or, bizarrely (the more liberal you get!), not to notice it at all. That linguistic and therefore cultural lack of representation onstage seems silly, and there's definitely a cultural block there that needs to be addressed.*

Sharlit: You're right, but when you go to the theatre you just never hear them. I know the Brits themselves complain that there's not enough Scottish or Welsh or Northern Irish or even Northern or whatever, let alone the Europeans. You very rarely hear European accents onstage or on TV, and when you do hear them they're usually thick and false. And often not even one by a real European but by a Brit.

So professionally speaking, we're saying there are enough European practitioners working crosscultural, crossdiscipline etc here in London just to run a festival every day for a whole year that would be entirely represented by non-Brits. I know there is a measurable problem for them on the London stages for various reasons, but Edinburgh will always look good if you add up all the foreign practitioners who are UK-based you'll measurably have the biggest festival in the world with that international element — most of them probably London-based ironically.

> *So how integral is that home-grown/home-based international creativity to your programming? Or it is less relevant as the festival's reputation grows and those connections with other countries solidify?*

Amy: Given the reality of the competitiveness required by any fringe festival in London, we need the local companies and we thrive on them. They're easier for us to support in a way they have accommodation in London, and they're familiar with the logistics of what it means to be part of a festival in the UK. They're also in a position to take advantage of new opportunities when members of the industry come and see their shows, or other programmers to help them get on tours, so we definitely feel like we can be more of help to them.

Sharlit: Which is why we programme more of them. To be honest, they have a much bigger following and we can't really afford to bring in only international companies from outside of the UK, because Amy and I would have to do all the selling and that's not our speciality. Our speciality is finding the gems and giving them the support that they need to do it themselves, to sell themselves and to be in a place where they can do that. We find it hard the fact that we can only afford to take a handful of companies from abroad. However we do partner with cultural institutes, and they help us to a degree, but there is also something satisfying in finding and helping Europeans who are based in London because we know the struggles that they have of being in London and making it in London. Both Amy and I are performers as well and we feel that struggle with them. But you're absolutely right, they're out there and they are making stuff and there are theatres programming them, but it is really nice to be able to have an umbrella festival kind of home for them all. And like you say, there's the idea of making Voila! a more year-round community rather than just a festival that happens two weeks a year, so it helps if we have a lot of London-based artists in our network

Amy: It's great to have that mix as well. As we've said, the London artists sometimes host the artists who come from aboard and that becomes even more interesting because these London-based companies are often people of different cultural backgrounds and nationalities drawn together in London to make something that is completely mixed and new and hybrid. And then on the other side, it's really nice to have an all-Hungarian company from Hungary who come over and work with the Hungarian Cultural Centre to get to know our London audience and the London-based artists get to meet Hungarian theatremakers who are representative of the cutting edge of contemporary Hungarian performance. So it's not really one or the other, but both together is a really powerful mix.

Sharlit: There's another thing which is complicated to talk about. We have to kind of fight our case with the cultural institutions of other countries because they want us to bring what they want to bring. Obviously they want to represent their country with the best, but we're like, "No, we want the guys in the shadows that you haven't represented in your country and who we know are amazing." People like the Hungarian Cultural Centre are very relaxed about this, happy to support their very contemporary and cutting edge artists, but they still have to carefully consider who we want to bring over. The French Institute have been supporting us for years, but even then we have to make our case every year to bring over the underdog because we're not interested in the company that's been touring the same show for five years in France and whose story for us is dead.

You often find yourself thinking that you've already saw a similar show in London made by someone else ten years ago. London in that sense is high high high quality, and the Europeans who come here need to be ready to show something that is really original — because in the 'official' subsidised world, no matter how great it is on many levels it can be also extremely limiting.

Amy: What you said about the zeitgeist, Nick, is relevant here because artists in many ways seek to see the future. A lot of the time we're tuned into what is going on in the culture and ask what we need to talk about next. Someone for example wrote an article about how nobody was doing any Brexit shows at Edinburgh Fringe this year because we've moved on already. Artists are way ahead — particularly fringe theatre. If you see something today at the fringe you'll see something derivative of it at a subsidised theatre ten years from now.

And really we'd expect it to be the other way round if the 'subsidised theatre' had ever done its job in the first place.

Amy: That's very true. As Sharlit's said, the fringe is where we go to make emerging work that has an emergency to it, work that has to be done right now because *now* is when it's relevant and there exists the passion to drive it. And there's also the factor that the more artists encounter these kinds of bureaucratic systems like funding where they have to get through to the powers that be, then get their approval, the longer it takes, the more delayed and out of date the projects get.

Sharlit: We don't have to be fortunetellers to know that if you start now with something that way, if it's a two-year process to get it onstage, that's how long it'll take.

And there's also the puzzle of defining your audiences.

Amy: There's certainly something to finding audiences for these shows. It's not really that people will come and see a show that speaks only to them. Sometimes a French person will come to see a show because it's a French show. But lots of other times someone will see a show because they're interested in the theme of family, burn-out, robotics or any of all the sorts of things you'd expect to find at a festival.

You don't come to a Voila! show because it's a European festival or you're a European — that's a really broad umbrella — but because you identify with the theme of the show and you say, "Okay, I'm interested in this theme about Greek myth and climate change, so let's see what happens." And what happens is you get a bunch of different people in the theatre united by this idea that we're all from different cultural backgrounds who are there for a common purpose. The audience doesn't come because it's a European festival but because we programme a European festival for lots of other reasons. And we also hope that people will come because the shows are well made, obviously.

Sharlit: Widening the festival physically is important too. The Cockpit and now Rich Mix have been essential in this, and we'll see what other venues might be interested in taking part in the festival, because there's definitely scope for it to grow and be a London-wide festival — and to go on for longer.

We're exploring all sorts of different potential models. We took the number of shows down from last year *[2018]*, because we had 36 shows and we almost felt like it was too much. Sometimes audiences and press don't really know where to go when there's too much. This year *[2019]* we have 23, ten or so less than last year and it feels much more manageable for Amy and I.

If we wanted more we would have to get more funding. The funny thing is that everybody is going why don't you guys get European funding and our reply is well because that's not how Creative Europe works, you need to have three different countries involved. And we do this in London with people from all over the world but that's not a country! You know we went to IETM this year in Hull *[IETM — the 'international network for contemporary performing arts' — is a Euro-funded performing arts network that advocates the value of arts and culture, holding two plenary conferences annually and smaller meetings all over the world]* and it was really interesting because there were a lot of words about Europe and oh my God what are we going to do and all kind of this stuff, and what I didn't know is that of *all* the Creative Europe bids, the UK is present in 50 per cent of them or something like that — they're either lead or secondary country. And that's because everyone wants to make work with people in the UK because there is something incredible about the way that theatre is made in this country.

All the Europeans who are based in London and who are making work are very conscious of how the UK has helped them in their method and the amazing training that you get here and the strong ethics of working with British-trained actors is second to none. I worked for an international theatre company with a French cast last year, and I wanted to shake every one of them. They were just so undisciplined, rude, entitled and a bit self-involved really. There's definitely something the UK can teach Europeans in terms of company ethics and making the most of what the whole team has to give.

All over Europe people have been panicking for a while, I think, because their theatre systems have been losing funding for all sorts of reasons but with the same effect. Starting with the European Union downwards, things there are sliding inextricably towards the UK's uneven Arts Council funding model, which is scary territory but the only alternative really if you want to get anything done — although the other countries are probably having to work out how the starving bit fits in. What European governments are counting on is that no one twigs why there is no money in the UK for the arts yet it's one of the world's richest countries — where the arts are such a significant industry. The message that practitioners based here, regardless of nationality, have always tried to put forward is that fringe is the way forward. And if they don't hear that message, theatremakers in a lot of those other countries where state and municipal funding is on the point of collapse are going to have to make that transition. It's a message that's boldly at the fore of Voila!

Sharlit: Absolutely. If you think about it, it's significant the way the British fringe model is now starting to spread across Europe. There are the Nordic fringes that began with Stockholm, the Prague Fringe and even in Paris they had a fringe which was actually just shows in English.

They're absolutely inspired — but Paris is a truly massive challenge since fringe is more than a bit counterintuitive to the way culture is actually done there.

Sharlit: Sure, but they have already got a year or two out of it and they're back for 2020, so that's good!

They've just done the first Istanbul Fringe and that looks as if it's going to develop extremely well. Their audiences know that theatre there really has to think in international terms.

Sharlit: I think Prague Fringe is a good way to go. It seems like they've always got the concept. But you're right, it is something that countries like France are going to have to get their heads round, it's true that it doesn't necessarily sit with a socialist model.

Amy: Sometimes artists based in Europe who are used to that subsidised model will respond to our call-out and say, "I can't believe it!"

Sharlit: "How dare you!"

Amy: "How can you ask us to share, to split the box office and not offer me a fee?!" But you know, it's a totally fair response, and so we have this discussion with them where we try and explain how the system works and why it is the way it is. Why if you want to come to London, you're just going to have to do it like that or good luck to you. Because yeah, it is tough for it to be any other way really — unless of course they're big enough to go to the Barbican.

I'm working on an annual zero-budget European programme for the Other National Theatre, and part of the conversation is to convince companies in Europe that it's 'EasyJet theatre' — can you get to Morecambe by budget airline, ferry or train, sleep on our sofas, eat with the local community? Welcome to the UK!

Sharlit: Exactly. It's so important that we make clear how we do it here in the UK. We ended up this year putting a huge section on our website which spells out who we are, what we do, why we do it, and what to expect. And we make sure that we say to them, "You know, you have to go and read this, because when you sign the contract we need you to understand what things are like here in the UK." That sort of advance warning is great because in the end the people who apply totally get it and are really on board to do that and they're the best. That way we don't need to deal with those who can't handle all that, and you know maybe in the future when we get funding, we'll be able to reach out to those other people.

People who create shows like *European Freaks* are fully subsidised and are really willing to come over — they have that freedom. But most of the time the companies from abroad will say to us, "You know what? The best experience for me was learning what it means to be my own producer and reaching out to new audiences and doing the work in working on my image and understanding that I can't just sit back on what I've always done." In countries like France, it's the job of the theatres to fill the space, to find the audiences — and so the artists who come over here really appreciate the chance to learn how to get those skills for themselves.

Amy: There's probably another week-long conversation that we could have about the way that artists should consider their audience much earlier at the very beginning of the project. Questions like who am I making the show for, why would they come, what experience would I want them to have? That makes for better theatre. I've seen a lot of theatre in the UK as well as around Europe where I just go, "Wow, that wasn't for me and you don't give a damn if I liked it — or if I understood it."

Sharlit: These artists are not considering equally the experience of the audience, and if you as the artist have to sell the tickets then you've got to know why anyone would want to come and what they're going to get out if it. Not only does that make better art, it makes more accessible art. In fact I think 'better' is a bit meaningless. What is important is that it makes an audience experience, if they go away thinking that it was worth going to.

Amy: Art is actually having an effect on them, rather than sitting there after three hours going, "Okay cool, if that is what your theatre is about, then I understand that you're naked and you're a very very cool physical performer and I'm covered in glitter now. And that's it . . . That's all I've got from your three-hour show. I don't know what you want me to feel."

   And we can end on that sound bite.

Amy: Oh no! I do think that there's room for every kind of thing in the world of theatre and that the companies shouldn't have to only consider what's going to sell. Because obviously the other end of the spectrum is the West End, where you're having people create pieces of art based on how many tickets they think they can sell and what artistic choice will make it the most marketable show.

   We wouldn't advocate for that, either . . . These people who get to make work however the hell they want and they do it by taking as long as they want with all the resources they could possibly wish for. Of course by creating these expensive ideas, they also contribute to the world of theatremaking in that you can go oh wow! You'd never have thought you could have scores of projectors in the ceiling while the floor of the theatre is its own live performance responding to the motion of the performers. You know you won't see it on the fringe because you know you can't do it.

   The show with the projectors was actually a main stage show that I saw at a Polish festival. I have to say it was extraordinary — they were also naked, though I didn't get covered in glitter at that one. That's another thing with European theatre, performers getting naked. Because it's such a rarity for me, you know growing up in the States you hardly ever see naked people onstage and then you come to Europe and there's butts everywhere.

Sharlit: And since I'm French, I'm like, yeah, and . . . ? But I concede we might need to put a warning on the website!

                                   *

11

Susan Elkin

'You've go to get people who know in front of people who don't'

Susan Elkin, is a theatre in education writer, critic & former secondary teacher of English. Born in Oxford, she is based in South East London, where she was raised.
• *susanelkin.co.uk, @SusanElkinJourn*

You got the idea that you could write very early, didn't you? It's interesting, the idea of access to writing. You can't go to drama school when you're little. It's not quite the same thing is it?

Not at all for a budding writer. In my case, I entered a television writing competition when I was eleven a few times and I kept winning. My Dad made jokes that perhaps nobody else had gone in for it, but he was very encouraging. Writing's hard work, as you know, so I didn't really bother after, but as I got older I'd find myself reading the newspapers and thinking, "I could have written that!"

I became a teacher, secondary school English literature, so I ended up working with words all the time anyway. Every week I used to read the *TES [Times Educational Supplement newspaper]* and I thought that maybe I could write a column article for them. In 1990 I'd just trained a load of prefects and almost nobody trains prefects, so what about a piece about management training for teachers on prefects? So I wrote it and sent it to the *TES* and to my astonishment they published it *and* they paid me! Forty. Eight. Pounds. At the time it seemed like an absolute fortune.

I kept on teaching while sending things on spec to national newspapers. I know you're not supposed to do that and I would never advise any young journalist to do it, but it worked for me. And I had pieces very quickly published in the *Telegraph*, *Times*, *Guardian*, *Sunday Times*, and it all built from there. I finally stopped teaching in 2004 after having gone part time and doing the two jobs in parallel for eleven years.

The theatre thing, then . . . ?

Well the theatre thing was because I was looking for outlets. The writing got into education which got into writing about education but I was well aware that I could write about almost anything. And of course, I'd been an English teacher — teaching plays from a literary point of view, not drama. Taking kids to the theatre, and also going to the theatre a lot myself. And that got me thinking about writing about theatre too.

So I wrote to *[then editor of The Stage newspaper]* Brian Attwood and said, "I've got an idea. Can I write about taking school parties to the theatre?" He rang me up, which was unheard of — and I don't think Brian ever rang me up again for the next 20 years. *[laughs]* He said, "Good idea, do that!" And that was how it all began. Of course once I'd done one, I did another and then another, and then Brian asked me to be education editor. Would I like a column? And that's what I did until the columns were stopped in 2016. I still do features and other articles for the paper.

There's reviewing too and stuff?

I used to do a lot of reviewing for *The Stage* but that's gone now. So I'm doing it for other publications.

Starting around 1990, you've helped develop a whole area in the UK of writing about the performing arts from an education point of view. Crucially, it's not from an academic perspective—

—and some people don't like it. Like the time I was visiting a particular drama school in the North a few years ago. When I arrived I was warned by the head that a man on their staff had written a letter to *The Stage* a couple of weeks earlier — I knew about this because *[present editor of The Stage]* Alistair Smith had warned me about it. The lecturer had basically said who on earth did I think I was to have all these opinions and to express them in *The Stage*? As far as he could work out, all I was a secondary school English teacher. But that obviously is a view some people held.

Why would they have that view? Especially coming from the performing arts where so many people traditionally have had a history of entering it from so many left-field directions?

I suppose he thought I didn't know enough about the subject. I hadn't been an actor, I hadn't been a director. I hadn't actually worked at the coal face in the theatrical industry.

Is someone like this qualified to say that? It's not a question of an opinion being offered but a professional judgement.

I suppose he had done the things he'd done in theatre and there he is teaching at a top drama school, so he regarded himself as more qualified than me. I wrote something he didn't like, which was why he was allowed to say this. But if you are writing a regular column in a paper you have to be prepared to say things that some people are not going to like. Of course you do. Just read any columnist.

Still, that's refusing to accept The Stage's trust in you and your own experience. But there is that attitude around the industry that you have to have worked at that particular coal face to be taken seriously, which I suppose is just one of the things that goes with being a performing arts industry writer.

And also the fact that readers know that they have to trust you, and go with you even if they don't necessarily agree with you. But they shouldn't knock you down with what you're standing up for. Like anyone else in the industry, it's in the nature of a writer that you can't be an expert in everything, but no one expects an actor to have experience of being a Tudor to play a Tudor, do they? Sometimes it could be argued it actually helps if you haven't done it. Because you have to go out and find out and so you're coming at it fresh. *[laughs]* I used to write a lot of stuff in woodwork magazines. I barely knew a nail from a screw but I could talk to woodworkers to find out their interesting back histories, what had brought them to that. So I did a lot of personality pieces which went down well — and I also eventually learnt a lot about woodwork!

Not to do woodwork a disservice, but the performing arts can take you in any direction — was it The Stage that was drawing you in or did you find that the more you got into it the more you found your own definition of where you stood?

The latter. *The Stage* was obviously a springboard for it but I wasn't regular in the paper in the beginning. I was a 'frequent contributor'. The columns which I started in 2005 were a bit of a departure really, and I did blogs too when there wasn't a great mystique about them. I'd said to Brian, "I've got far more to say than I can get into this column, which doesn't even run every week because advertising often gets the space in any case. So can I have a blog?" "A blog? Oh yes, you can have a blog although we won't be able to pay you extra for it." So that's really how that started, incredibly casually. After a bit they found some money and paid me for the blogs too.

How do you get your head around the industry, keeping up with the changes? It's hard enough getting London covered, let alone the rest of the country.

The more you do it, the more you learn, the more you understand. I always used to feature Lamda, RADA and Mountview a lot because they're close at hand in London. But then I told Brian that it would be a good idea if I actually went and visited the rest of the country, and would *The Stage* pay for it? And they did.

I didn't do it in a very expensive way. When I went to somewhere like Glasgow, I had to stay overnight obviously. Many of the other places I managed to do in a day. But I did actually go and see *all* the drama schools in the country which gave me useful contacts in every single one of them. It's the only way really to be aware of what's going on. As soon you get your toe in the door and show your face, their PR and marketing people are especially pleased to see you and they'll send you every press release and tell what's going on although what they send is often a bit glossy. But it really helps you pick up on trends and work out what is actually going on.

It's interesting because you were picking up on something as a lot of our generation of writers were doing, Brian especially, which was that the old way of doing show business was winding down as an industry—

—or even the *industries* in theatre!

Exactly. A hugely complex organism was evolving into something else in front of our eyes. In response The Stage started to drop a lot of specialist sections over a period of time — unwillingly we have to add — but also coming up with more contemporary replacements. Eventually it stopped reviewing the student showcases, for example.

Which I think is very regrettable. Interestingly, I didn't actually like reviewing showcases very much but when I wasn't doing them I missed them. *[laughs]*

Now that you say it, I think I miss them too!

Well I contacted the drama schools and said, "Look, would you like me to do what I was doing for *The Stage* and I'll put the reviews on my own website. I'll publish them." And do you know, most of them said no. I was surprised. Most of the schools now have come round to the view that they don't want their showcases reviewed. They don't want students exposed to criticism. Now most of them won't even allow people to review their graduate shows, something we used to do a lot too.

Why do you think that's changing? Is it th element of safeguarding that's a growing feature of further education and people starting out in work?

No, I think it's entirely commercial. They want to give students an even-handed value for money. The reason I've been given from one school is, "We try to treat all our students equally so we don't want one student singled out over another."

Blimey, but it was precisely the marathon of mentioning every performer and giving them equal weight that made writing student showcases important as an entry into the industry.

And when does the real work start then? The following year they are certainly going to be singled out if A is better than B. That's the reality of what happens. But that particular acting school — and many more like it — won't take responsibility for that fact of life while they're still students, because it's deemed in some way to be inequitable. And that's a very odd way of looking at it.

I'm not shocked by that because we've witnessed and documented a whole industry reinventing itself and yet there are serious disconnects everywhere. Like all those leaflets the government was handing out a couple of years ago to all the secondary schools proudly announcing that a career in the arts is good because it's an economy that generates billions — yet at the same time they were cutting exactly the same curriculum and resources throughout the nation's school system. The new GCSE curriculum certainly isn't getting many takers.

Young students, 17-18 years old, are telling me they get no careers advice at all about the arts at their particular schools. At things like TheatreCraft or the National Theatre Creative Careers you'll meet hundreds of young people who are as keen as mustard and who have actually been brought to the events by their schools, but they're lucky because there are thousands out there who are just not getting the information.

And it's not that they're getting blocked — they're literally not getting it?

Careers advisers know nothing about the performing arts, never did, and teachers are still telling students they're just going to be unemployed if they're going down that route. Or telling them to go to university, which is usually hopeless advice if they want to act. It might work for some aspects of the industry, but if you want to act, university is probably not the best place to go. And the colleges which are parts of universities, who wisely or unwisely were merged a few years ago? Well they're beginning to have problems.

We're increasingly hearing about drama courses closed down. The word they use is 'suspended' while they 'review' it. I'm sure what that means is people at some senate meeting saying, "Oh come now, why do these drama students need 30 hours a week? It's costing a ridiculous amount of money. We're an arts university. We can train our fine artists on six, ten hours a week, so why do drama students have to have all this extra? No no no, we're going to *review* this!"

That's the thin edge of the wedge for conservatoire training. When you look at the number of performing arts colleges which have merged with universities, so many are having serious problems now and don't have a good relationship with their parent university, while drama courses at the universities themselves are being questioned.

Back to secondary schools — amidst the nationwide chaos over the recent changes in the GCSE curriculum, we were at the school open day where they were trying to help parents navigate the imposed mess of trying to choose subjects for our kids. And my kid's drama teacher — a seriously amazing, motivating person — just came out with it and told us all, "I actually recommend that you don't do it." Utterly heartbreaking. He said, "I can't teach this and the students are not going to enjoy it or get much out of it. There's far less practical work, which removes the point of drama, and I don't think they're going to get good results." And that was at exactly the same time as those government leaflets were being handed out. And they couldn't timetable drama GCSE either!

So if you have a dramatically inclined kid, send them to youth theatre? But you'd have to pay for it.

We haven't gone that far. I'm sure the parents in that position would have already done it. The teacher said that he could offer twilights with the kids, which they were used to doing in any case because they've done things like working with professional dance groups and the Shakespeare Schools Festival. But obviously once you start doing GCSEs, the kids are doing twilights for other subjects because they're trying to cram everything in. Anyway, so my kid chose not to, which was heartbreaking for him. He chose music instead, which was on the timetable, plus the school had just spent a shed load on keyboards and new Macs and so they had to use them, didn't they?

It's a funny thing how patchy this all is. Some school heads are totally committed to drama and somehow find a way of doing it. I've visited schools where the arts really are alive and well. I was at primary school in the Isle of Dogs *[East London]* not that long ago where the whole place was fizzing with all aspects of the arts. The reason was simple: the head there is committed to organising the curriculum so that the arts get delivered and making it clear that a lot of other benefits get delivered through the arts — it's doable.

Since they don't get any extra money, it really does come down to the choice of an individual there to make a difference. And despite those choices, we're watching the decimation of theatre in the school system happen in real time.

And things slip so quickly now. There's no slow decline to head off or take tactical action. And a lot of it is allowed to happen because people in the UK are numb nowadays. There's the idea that culture is a disposable thing and maybe you should go to university instead. That's what we're funding at the moment. But people aren't even bothering to go to university any more and I can understand that. The buzzword now is apprenticeship — there are some wonderful apprenticeships in the performing arts — and that certainly is not something that the school students or school leavers are told about.

But apprenticeships are still quite limited in number, which raises questions of access. My impression is that the lucky ones with talent from every background will seek the courses out and get in, but then . . .

It tends to be the deprived ones, but yes I'm wondering whether, once everyone else notices that they're on to a good thing, that the people who are far from deprived start getting in. I don't want to be cynical but it seems to me that if you don't promote it and make it available to everyone, it won't be taken by everyone. It wouldn't be difficult for the government to make the money available, and it wouldn't be expensive in government terms.

Apprenticeships are good for technical theatre. At the Royal Opera House's production park down at Thurrock *[in Essex]* they have up to 40 apprentices because the place is so big and they have so many different departments. At the National Theatre apprentices come and work in specialties like scenic construction for a couple of years. In fact they have some extraordinary departments, they've actually got a concrete management department — and an apprentice working there. Big companies like these mean that whatever your interests are, there is something for you — health & safety, production accountancy, all those sorts of things you can do.

How do we manage to tell people that there is a career but it needs to be seen within the context and scale of an entire industry of supply and demand with multi-levelled sectors that can offer sustained employment?

How you get the word out is a challenge. I suppose you have to train careers advisors — and that's a career in itself isn't it? Then you have to get them to understand the importance of bringing people who really do matter to the schools. If you were a careers advisor working in, say, Kilburn in North West London, and you wanted to tell your kids about apprenticeships in theatre, if you rang the National Theatre *[in Central London]*, I'm sure they would send you a speaker.

Well they have a remit to do that sort of thing, plus a budget, plus Kilburn is a lot cheaper and quicker to get to from where the Nat is based on the South Bank rather than to a school up in East Kilbride in Scotland.

Obviously the big companies have a lot more apprenticeships — the National, the Royal Shakespeare Company, English National Opera — but equally places like the Marlowe Theatre in Canterbury *[in Kent]*. They run an apprenticeship scheme for two or three at any one time for areas like technical theatre, front of house and marketing. The Queen's Theatre in Hornchurch *[Havering, East London]*, Theatre Royal York *[Yorkshire]* . . . I'm just scratching the surface.

   Somehow you've got to get people who know in front of people who don't. That's why my book *So You Want to Work in Theatre?* is not about acting. Its aim is to try and get to parents, teachers and careers advisors. No 14 year old is going to read it, but we just hope for the sort of people who would read, then take it to their 14 year old and say, "Look, you can do this!" We — *[publisher]* Nick Hern Books and I — knew we needed to get to the adults because you somehow have to break down this ridiculous prejudice about there being no decent careers in theatre, because there are. There are very good careers in backstage theatre, for example, and plenty of money.

Where does this prejudice come from?

I suppose it's part of this whole 'luvvie' thing, isn't it? A word I never use but

I'm using it now in inverted commas. It's this perception that theatre is people prancing about and is not serious. And people saying, "That's not what I want for my child!" It's that sort of blind prejudice really.

Which still persists.

Of course it does and it's usually strongest in people who rarely go to theatre — and if they did, it would be to see something very traditional. There's still a lot of that around today.

It's funny how the more theatre becomes accessible to everyone, the more that sort of attitude refuses to go away.

Of course that prejudice about apprenticeships is absolutely widespread too. If I may be anecdotal for a moment, my granddaughter's 22-year-old boyfriend had four good A-levels and a place to do business management at the University of East Anglia. At the very last minute he was offered an apprenticeship with a local firm to work in building management with day release to go to college. So he'll get a degree just the same and earn £11,000 a year meanwhile. Well it was a no-brainer. At the end of four years he knew that he'd be way ahead of his mates anyway, because he would have four years' experience and no debt. What's not to like?

That's for a completely different industry but the same thing applies to theatre — although acting is one area it doesn't really apply to. The performing arts are like an iceberg. People only see the tip, the performer on stage. They don't see the infrastructure that gets the actor there, and I'm not sure you can learn acting through apprenticeship like the other areas of theatre.

Conversely, Paul Roseby down at the National Youth Theatre will tell you that of course you can. He says, "You don't need to train to be an actor. Give me young people and I'll teach them how to be actors but I won't teach them how to act because they already know it." A bit controversial but an interesting way of looking at it. He argues they don't need three years at acting school because he didn't go himself but he became quite a good leading actor.

Just go and see the young people in the National Youth Theatre Rep Company. I've just seen them in *Midsummer Night's Dream* and *As You Like It*. Already in the first two plays in this year's season they've achieved an extraordinary high standard. At end of each season these young actors nearly all get agents and go on to work. You see them on television and all sorts of places afterwards. Crucially they didn't go to drama school.

Paul works for every single one of them. He takes them on around March and gives conventional training classes. Then they work on a repertory of plays for the autumn which runs in the West End and major fringe venues in the area. So it's effectively a Central London season for these young people. And that's how apprenticeship should work for actors really — what he's doing is replicating the old repertory system, which a lot of veteran actors will tell you is the best way to learn. And the actors pay nothing. The NYT gives each of them a bursary.

> *There's certainly the problem that everyone's squeezed by the lack of student money and, increasingly, the training institutions. There isn't much of a bursary system any more, let alone the free tuition that was around when the modern course system as we know it was developed. Plus there's the weight of society on students saying there isn't a sustained career awaiting them after they graduate.*

But what are drama schools teaching them? They should be trying to encourage them to think about this buzz thing of 'creating your own work', so rather than sitting at home waiting for the phone to ring you get on your feet and you form a company with your friends, devise something and take it to Edinburgh. And every drama school will tell you that they're the only one doing this but actually they're all doing it — some more effectively than others.

Look at *The Play That Goes Wrong* or *Six*, classic cases of doing exactly that. The first was a group of Lamda students and the two that wrote *Six* were Cambridge students. You might be successful, but even if you're not, you are out and about, meeting people, making the right contacts. If you can get your play up, that's what all the drama schools are encouraging you to do. They're training you to be entrepreneurial rather than sitting at home waiting for the phone to ring or working at a job that won't let you go to auditions.

Drama schools are *reactive* rather than proactive. So they're always a bit behind. And I'm not sure that's anybody's fault. I'm sure it wouldn't be any different no matter who was running a drama school. How else can you predict what's necessary?

> *Areas like music and art can always bounce back or at least drift along but drama education is more complex and requires a bit more steel to get you through the initial hoops I think.*

Music does too. There's the discussion about how useful it is to read music notation. Of course it is, it should be taught in every primary school. But instead we go on telling children that the last thing that matters when you're making music is notation. You've got people like *[comedian, composer & lyricist]* Tim Minchin saying he doesn't read music and it doesn't matter. But it does matter.

Minchin creates good music, and I'm not knocking what he does, but it would probably be even better if he could read notation. I mean you wouldn't expect somebody to write *War and Peace* if they couldn't read or write, would you? It's nonsense and actually reading music is not all that difficult. If you have a class of alert seven/eight year olds you can make it into ever such fun, and you could get them all reading and writing music very quickly. The reason we don't do it is, of course, because the teachers can't do it. So there's nobody to teach it.

But this is the 21st century, the world's fifth largest economy, a country that the rest of the world looks to as a cultural beacon . . .

And still looks to us for things like music conservatoires and for providing international musicians. But other countries like South Korea and China are catching up fast — because they fund it.

In terms of theatre do you think they'll start to upstage UK theatre?

Probably not, because there's the challenge of language, although this is diminishing. With music, if you're playing Beethoven or Mozart it doesn't matter if you can't speak a word of English or German. You could turn up at the Festival Hall and play the Beethoven Violin Concerto and communicate at the rehearsal with the orchestra and conductor through the music and a bit of arm waving. That's never going to be the case with acting is it, because most acting is going to be language-based. I know there's mime and non-verbal companies and of course other languages are growing, but English is very much the international language and not just in the arts obviously.

Writers? Where are all the writers in all this? We've mentioned all the others so far, including the concrete specialists.

Playwrights have a totally different skill and there are a lot of schemes around now to encourage them.

Such as the university courses, which are now becoming an important seedbed for playwrights?

If you really want to write a play, or possibly direct, university could be a far better place for you than drama school, initially. It's as if somebody came to me, as my English Lit students often did, and said they wanted to be a novelist. I would say go away and read as many books as you possibly can. It's the same with plays. I'm not saying that you have to go to university, that it's the only place to become a playwright, but if somebody at the age of 16 said to me, "I want to be a playwright, what should I do?", I think that's probably what I'd say. You need to study and read as wide a variety of plays as you possibly can. And a university course about drama as opposed to doing drama is probably a good starting point.

Don't go to Lamda to do it then.

No. Go to somewhere like University of Birmingham and study dramatic text because that is probably a better way in.

So the writers are slightly hived off in the formative years.

Not necessarily, because an awful lot of actors write plays. I interviewed David Haig recently. He's a very good example of somebody who writes as well as acts, and he's successful at both. I asked him, "If push came to shove and you had to concentrate on one or the other, which would it be?" He replied, "Oh, I'd write." Which I thought was interesting.

Which brings us to the other sort of writer, the critic. It's the sort of invisible-visible thing, where no one wants to pay for it but everyone needs it. So what is the role of a critic?

Basically to tell the public about plays that I have seen — plays that most readers won't see because once a show at a theatre is gone it's usually gone. Live screenings are changing that a bit, but that's the reality of live performance. So the critic describes the show for people who haven't seen it and who might, on the basis of your review, decide (a) "I might see it", (b) "I might not to see it", or (c) "well it's not practical at the moment so I won't go but I do know a bit about the show because I've read this".

Is there another aspect to it?

It's certainly not about trying to be unpleasant to people. When I'm asked to talk to groups of potential young critics, I always tell them that if you go and see a show and you really don't like it, it might simply be because it's not your cup of tea. Sometimes that happens to me too. So you have to approach the show by understanding that it can be good in its way, that you wouldn't have necessarily chosen to see it, but you can't slate it out of hand for being a bad show.

If there's something terribly wrong with it, you still have remember that a lot of people will have worked hard on that show. A critic always has to consider that before writing what you want to write. It doesn't mean you can't say negative things, but think carefully about being personal. This is somebody's work. A lot of critics will probably say I'm being soft. But I think that's an important part of our work.

You do need to learn on the job if you want to be a critic, which means your first few reviews are going to be awful and you do need mentoring, someone to literally look over your shoulder and say that's fine but lop off the first para, rewrite that bit in the middle, check the names and then it'll be good to go.

It's a bit like an apprenticeship to become a stage electrician in some ways, you need that monitoring until you can do it yourself. You can't just learn it by yourself and indeed you run then risk of danger. You need to be walked around with it. And in any apprenticeship you usually start by watching the boss. You simply stand there and pass the tools and watch what they're doing. Until eventually you can do it yourself.

It's learning by doing, isn't it? So I don't think I could help a young critic apart from giving very general advice. I'd say, well you write something, write what you think, and I'll tell you how to write it better. It's a very difficult thing to teach from scratch. No two critics are the same. I don't mean that they won't have the same opinion, but they won't express it in the same way.

Well there's no Stanislavsky method for critics, and I'll confess I have no idea what they teach on the courses.

As I've said: it's somebody's work, keep it brief, don't try and be clever. Coming from the English teacher part of my profession, it's definitely the more you read — and I mean fiction mostly — the more you know. Because every fiction book has to be about something, so you're going to learn stuff without meaning to. And you just soak up vocabulary effortlessly. It's a shame for any young people who don't do that, and that must be the same for critics, playwrights and anybody else of any age. Because if you want to learn to be a critic, what you should do is learn criticism in the same way that somebody who wants to be a novelist has to read novels. In short: read reviews.

And for any readers out there who plan on pitching a review or article for a site, magazine or newspaper, remember to read at least a couple of editions of the publication before you pitch! But back to the state of the industry . . . If people are still being denied access because of the postcode lottery, things are hardly getting any better are they?

Not really. There is a pendulum effect where we have sunk to a very low ebb at the moment. It will probably one way or another swing back and improve, because as you've said, the arts industry isn't going to go away. It's a huge part of people's lives and even these very poor kids have access to it via their phones and so on. *Everybody* is affected by the arts, even if they're not in a position to go out and do it, it's still there. And anything can change.

The thought, for example, of local authorities shelling out for audition fees may seem like a pipe dream, but in fact they used to. Paul Roseby of the National Youth Theatre, is from North Norfolk, and when he was first starting out, he got a place to go away and study on a three-week course with the National Youth Theatre. North Norfolk District Council were so excited — "Our local boy got this wonderful place!" They paid all his fees for six years. Six summers he went away. And now that Roseby is the head of the NYT, he makes sure that he takes outreach back to North Norfolk — they were there for him and he wants the boys and girls there to have the same opportunity.

Maybe outreach is the way forward, because all these theatres are under pressure to get funding, and some of what they can get is specifically to go out into schools. Granddaughter No. 3, who is eight and lives in Brighton, went to Glyndebourne *[countryside opera house in East Sussex]* to see a schools production of *L'elisir d'amore [by Gaetano Donizetti]* with her mum at half term. A thousand kids went, including a coachload of kids from her school. The best thing was that the Glyndebourne education department had gone to her school and taught the kids the songs. So she was going along full of music. Her mum had bought the CD and played them with her as well, and so she was familiar with all the songs and able to tell them apart and sing some of them, and also able to tell me the story of the opera she was seeing. Now that can't have cost that much, really?

That's just one example and of course the National Theatre, Royal Shakespeare Company and Royal Opera House are doing outreach as well, going out into schools. And Brighton is close to London obviously. But what's happening in somewhere like Coalville, in Leicestershire? I went there to visit a primary school stuck right out in the middle of nowhere, where not a single child at the school played an instrument or knew anything about any instruments. But there was an outreach project run by three very dynamic young people who were singing to the children and teaching them songs. In fact they were creating an opera about Coalville, the closure of the mines and the building of a new forest there in the centre of England. Of course it was a good thing because they were teaching children who weren't getting any arts tuition. But what was also important was that the school was enlightened enough to have them in.

Another time, I went with the RSC to a primary school in Stoke-on-Trent, like Coalville, another place that hasn't been renowned for its arts provision. This particular school had become an RSC partnership school, so that's an obvious commitment to outreach. There I saw how the company had spent a whole term with the whole school on a project around *The Tempest*, because the RSC were also doing their reduced version of the play at the school.

The headmaster asked if I would like to be shown around the school. I said yes please. So he sent me off with a group of children, and they showed me all the lovely things they'd done. They'd built Miranda's cave in one corner. Elsewhere they'd written the sort of poems that Miranda would have written to Ferdinand. They'd also done a geography project on storms and lots of other cross-curricular things. Once again it was a project that mattered because the head in that school was committed. The RSC was welcome and none of that stopped him from delivering the national curriculum.

Interestingly I've been to a number of schools with the RSC because they actually do a lot of outreach beyond Stratford and London. For example, each spring a reduced version of a Shakespeare play goes round to schools in the wider region. And when I went to see *The Tempest* at the Stoke-on-Trent primary, they had invited other schools to see it during the day, and then did it again in the evening so the parents could come.

That regional divide however isn't helping people in London to realise what people in the rest of the country are missing out on. Up in Morecambe, in the North West of England, I co-started Morecambe Fringe as way of getting a held-back community back into theatre as an idea and also physically. We'd reopened the Alhambra Theatre there, a huge great big blank canvas of a building that had been rebuilt internally as a giant club-style black box after the interior was gutted in a fire in the early 1970s. I tried to use the fringe as a way of setting up a kids programme throughout the year, and for the follow-up Fringemas and Story Festival that followed in the Christmas and Easter periods, I co-wrote with Chris Bartlett a panto Red Riding Hood — sadly there was no panto in Morecambe — and we used Morecambe issues and topography, and also the way that people speak locally. Over these three initiatives we managed to get kids in who saw live theatre for the first time ever — it was hard to get their parents motivated — so we all got very excited about that and got funding on the back of that. And then we couldn't get any more funding. Too late, I realised that everyone else still wanted to push how deprived the area was and how we were bringing the salvation of culture to the deprived kids, but I knew it was really, "Hang on the kids have seen theatre now, you can't go back from that. So when a kid has seen theatre for the first time, what do you do next?" And the funders certainly weren't interested in taking those kids on to the next step. Maybe if I'd shown an appropriate level of saviour complex they might have carried on for a bit more. Which made me realise the word sustainability is a complete con in terms of funding. They don't mean it. This isn't the 19th century, we're living in the 21st century, and it's appalling that we need to convince the powers that be that theatre, as part of culture, is integral to the wellbeing of communities and their struggling schools and that there needs to be hard cash to back it up, since there's no slot for a commercial model to work.

I suppose you need to send in drama teachers of course. But where are they?

Well there isn't a drama teacher at my 11 year old's primary school, which happens to be in London's Theatreland. Outreach is a bare handful of workshop mornings and a single theatre show across the whole year — and even that seems to be limited to KS2. They have a very high number of kids on free school meals, so that's a telling correlation.

We need to be thinking more laterally. All the big franchise companies are desperately trying to get more franchisees, but though they do really good work it still costs you £85-£100 a month per child to go on a theatre course. Which most of the parents at a school like yours haven't got. But there's the idea of support from the local authorities, who could do a deal with the schools to bring that cost right down so that it was affordable or *free* even. To subsidise stage schools, franchised or independent, to run after-school clubs in their local schools, that would be a way of opening up. We need more thinking along those lines for a way of getting access to drama.

A more hands-on approach would be your production of *Red Riding Hood*. Take the actors to visit the schools in the area while the production is on, so the children actually meet actors. They'll realise that this is the person who played Red Riding Hood but actually she has a name of her own. She's a real person and she's going to tell me about her life as an actor and maybe sing some songs with me. There's a lot to be said for that. Children see the actors on television and they don't understand that actors are real people. They have things like pets and mortgages like anybody else.

But it doesn't seem there are any magic solutions for the foreseeable future. Who knows where the arts will be over the next few years? Probably as marginalised as those children, whatever happens.

*

12
Paula Garfield

'With bilingual theatre everyone has to work doubly hard'

Paula Garfield is an actor, director & artistic director of Deafinitely Theatre. She is based in North West London, where she was born & raised.
• *deafinitelytheatre.co.uk, @DeafinitelyT, @paula_garfield*

English really is a foreign language for you?

I would say yes. My first language was actually English but I found it very difficult to access. It was a huge struggle and, to be honest, it really made me struggle with my identity as well. It was much later on in my teenage years that I was able to look up British Sign Language and to start to use it. I still use the English language for reading and writing but my preferred language is BSL — but I can't say I'm a first language user because I grew up, as people would say, an oralist.

At the moment there's a lot of children who tend to use BSL as a second language because they were raised like me. For example, I would read in English, I would write in English with limited access to fully understanding that language, then in my later years I moved on to sign in BSL. However, my children *[Paula's daughters are deaf]* have had a very different experience because they've learned BSL initially as a first language at home, and then when they come to learn to read and write, they do that through English, and their understanding of English is strengthened by having a solid and accessible first language to learn through.

I would say for my own generation, growing up with oralism and learning BSL later on in life meant that the parity of your English was relatively low because you weren't taught English very well back then. Education provision was quite poor for deaf children, whereas now for my own children they get taught English at a much higher level as well as their BSL. So they're at much more of an academic level than I was at their age, absolutely. I mean for example, when I left school at the age of 17, my reading age was equivalent to that of an eight year old! And that was not a unique experience, you'll find it quite common with deaf people of my generation at that time. So I would say BSL is definitely my preferred language.

So these are good times for a bilingual company like Deafinitely Theatre to produce work because of the growing BSL audience — including of course the increased awareness within society and the hearing people who also use BSL or learn it.

To be honest, you'd be surprised. I would say there are only a few deaf schools in the UK that encourage sign language while teaching. So there's now around 90 per cent of deaf children who come from families who are hearing and don't have any BSL to start with. They struggle to learn sign language, because in their family home all they have is spoken English. In my own case, my parents thought it would be better to send me off to a school where I could learn how to speak rather than learn how to sign.

It's ironic because theatre welcomes the use of sign language, and theatregoers think it's amazing to see. But it's so different in education, because there are still so many schools that try to stop children from using sign language.

But now BSL is much more prevalent, you'll see it much more. But it's sad historically for the education system, and there's still a problem with the perspective of a lot of schools that if you teach a child BSL or a child learns in BSL, they will become less able in English where actually it's the other way around. If they get to learn in BSL, which is for a lot of deaf children an easier language to access, it means that they will be able to take on much more and that they'll actually learn a lot more as well. So I would say the world of theatre is such a good place for Deafinitely Theatre to be because we are opening children's eyes and showing them, "Okay, in your school you might not be allowed to sign, but actually here it's allowed onstage. You can *perform* in BSL!" For some deaf children it may be the first exposure to BSL they've had.

What gave you your first notion that a deaf person could go into theatre, that you could overcome those linguistic barriers?

I grew up in the 1970s and 80s, when knowledge of sign language back then was very very limited. It was new to a lot of people, research was only just starting to take place in the 1970s into what sign language actually was, where it came from, where it originated from and so on. When I was growing up, people were quite oppressive about sign language. They thought it made you stupid and meant that you weren't going be 'intellectual'. That's what the view was back then in education, that if you're able to speak well then you're incredibly intellectual — and you know that isn't true at all. It can be quite the opposite to be honest.

So when I was growing up, I didn't see deafness in the theatre at all. My twin sister Fifi *[who is also deaf]* was much more confident, however, and she was involved in the London Deaf Drama Group, an amateur group that still exists today. I was just gobsmacked, it really blew me away because I didn't think that sort of thing was possible. That was that moment that made me realise, "Wow, I want to be on the stage, I want to be there." At that time my sister and everyone in the LDDG was using Sign Supported English *[signing that follows the structure of spoken/written English]* rather than British Sign Language because that was what school had taught — it was, "Okay, here are a few signs now and then to support your learning of the English language."

In 1988 I went to what is now the University of Reading and I started a course called 'Theatre of the Deaf'. It was a year-long course and as a part of it we were all taught British Sign Language. I remember the teacher saying, "Oh, British Sign Language is this, that and the other, it's got its own grammatical structure, it's got its own syntax." I was really shocked to learn this, as all my life I'd been told that sign language makes you look stupid, it's not a *real* language like English is, and I just couldn't believe that BSL was an entirely different language with its own grammar structure, etc. It took me a long time to accept that I had been denied a proper language of my own until that point. Learning BSL changed me as a person, and changed my life.

I then became a freelance actor after college for the next ten years, which at the start was so exciting. I was truly fortunate to work on some brilliant productions with some fantastic directors. After my one-year course I then learned so much more in the following years by working with hearing actors in various productions. I would ask my deaf friends to come and watch me performing, but a lot of them couldn't understand or follow what was going on, and I started to realise that the majority of these shows were not actually aimed at a deaf audience. I also felt a significant lack of deaf representation within the industry. That was when I thought, right, do you know what, there are no deaf directors at all in the UK, I need a deaf theatre company which is a good representation of deaf theatremakers but also so that we can present something to deaf theatregoers as well and create a deaf audience who have access to something in their own language.

It must have been quite a step to even think of setting up a deaf theatre company.

It was incredibly difficult. I was around 35 at the time and my most recent acting work was in a theatre company where I felt very uncomfortable. There was bullying that went on and, due to me being the only deaf actor, I felt incredibly isolated. So that was the final straw, I just didn't want to be involved with theatre anymore. It wasn't what it was supposed to be, and my deaf identity, my representation of who I was, just wasn't there.

I then bumped into Jo Hemmant, who was an arts officer for Arts Council England. She remembered me from previous jobs we had done years before when we were working for a theatre company — I was acting and she was office administrator. She told me that I was the only deaf actress she'd seen and that she had wanted to learn sign language because she realised that no one else was able to communicate with me, but we had lost contact. In fact she had learned sign language a couple of years before we met up again and started to work at the Arts Council where she would encourage deaf artists to access and apply for funding.

So we just met randomly and Jo asked me what was I doing at the moment. I said, "Well, I'm thinking about changing my career because I just can't cope with the theatre industry anymore the way it is." And she then said, "Why don't you apply for some funding to set up your own company?" Of course, I laughed the idea off because I just thought that it was impossible. How would I set up a company? My English isn't very good, my knowledge is probably quite limited, I don't know how to get funding, I don't know how to do a bid for funding at all. But she gave me a business card and said, "Look, give me a call, come into the office, we'll have a chat."

I thought about the idea for a while, and finally decided it might be worth a look. I took my friend along, Kate Furby — we became the co-founders with Steven Webb, of Deafinitely Theatre. Kate, who is hearing and works as a BSL interpreter, knew that maybe I could do with an ally to really get this off the ground. We talked my concept and ideas through, she understood what I wanted, what I was really visualising, and then she put together the funding application with me.

Our first performance was in 2002, but the last deaf professional theatre company in Britain before Deafinitely was the British Theatre of the Deaf which ran from 1960-1977. They were a deaf professional theatre company that used mime, so they weren't actually using sign language. After that there have been many deaf amateur dramatic productions and some deaf actors in the mainstream, but there had been nothing else professional and deaf-led for 30 odd years.

For that first performance by Deafinitely Theatre, the amount of deaf people we had through the doors was just amazing, we were sold out. They were desperate to see something in their own language, and that's when I realised we'd done the right thing — and we'd only put on the three performances. The Arts Council then recognised the popularity and continued to fund us for another three years, and then we became an NPO [national portfolio organisation]. We've been established now for 17 years, and we're still going. It's important to note that during this period, in 2003, the government officially recognised British Sign Language as a language of the UK in its own right.

How has the concept of making deaf theatre changed over the past two decades? Have you stuck to one style or adapted and changed your methods as you've gone along?

That's a very good question. When we started out, our first few productions were all devised work. Then we changed our process over to using scripts. In 2019 we toured a production of *Horrible Histories: Dreadful Deaf,* and although we had a skeleton script that was co-written with Birmingham Stage Company, we used a lot of devising again to create the show so it was a mixture of the two methods after many years of just using scripted work.

I have definitely seen a shift in the last ten years regarding challenges and attitudes. There are more and more deaf actors being cast in the mainstream which is brilliant. However I still see a lack of deaf people being frontrunners — where are the deaf creatives, directors, visionaries, people that make things happen?

Over the years Deafinitely Theatre's reputation has grown and more theatre companies seem keen to co-produce shows with deaf and disabled creatives and artists.. We have recently worked with some smaller companies, who have taken the risk and been willing to co-produce with us. It is as though the bigger, more high-profile companies wait to see how successful our productions are and see what the reviews are, before considering whether they would want to do something similar. My ultimate dream would be for Deafinitely Theatre to be a flagship name to co-produce a show with a company such as the National Theatre.

This is the problem that won't go away, isn't it? It's that two steps forward, one step back thing, and it can be discouraging, you see companies and practitioners throughout the industry just giving up. How do you help deaf

people deal with those situations and attitudes, especially people such as
emerging artists?

When we started off there were very few deaf actors, or hearing actors with
fluent sign language skills, but now there are a lot more of both. Now that
there's a positive influence from companies like Deafinitely, I can speak for
my own community and confidently say that deaf people now feel that they
are able to do this, that they can act, and they are beginning to have a
presence in some of the bigger theatre companies. Nadia Nadarajah has for
the last few years been working at the Globe Theatre, Charlotte Arrowsmith
has been working with the Royal Shakespeare Company *[the first deaf actor to
perform as understudy for a hearing principal actor]*, Sophie Stone was part of the
fierce and talented cast of *Emilia*, on the West End in 2019, and several more
deaf actors, but I can't possibly name them all here! Opportunities for deaf
actors have certainly grown compared to ten years ago, which is helped all
the more by inclusive theatre companies such as Ramps on the Moon, Graeae
and so on.

A lot of these actors started with Deafinitely Theatre, and there's a lot more
now who have started in the industry after having their first professional
acting job with us. They have had the opportunity for exposure and to have
their talent noticed from the shows that we put on, and then been able to go
out and apply to these other bigger theatre companies. I am hopeful that the
wider theatre industry will acknowledge Deafinitely Theatre, the important
platform that it has, and the stepping stones it provides for deaf talent. We
also have Deafinitely Youth Theatre, which is aimed our younger deaf
aspiring actors, by which actors such as William Grint and Rose Ayling-Ellis
have come through the ranks and have had stints on TV, as well as established
theatre companies such as the Royal Shakespeare Company.

For deaf actors the reality in terms of training is that a lot of the drama
schools in the UK are not fully accessible for them. We not only provide
them the opportunity to learn how to work with hearing professionals but
also how to get the best out of their own language. It's about building their
confidence to see that they can go out there into the mainstream theatre
industry to work with other companies. What's interesting is that I'm still in
touch with the actors that come through our doors and go on to work in the
mainstream, and although they enjoy moving up in their careers and
branching out, they often tell me that they miss working in an environment
that is totally accessible for them, with creatives and actors, deaf or hearing,
that can sign fluently. Often professional deaf actors will find themselves
being the only deaf person there, and so it is valuable to them to have a team
who can relate to them and talk to them about how to use their language in

the right way, who understands deaf culture, deaf identity, and how this relates to their work.

If we put the label of disability to one side, BSL represents a distinct linguistic group spread all over the UK. Does the impetus of hearing companies increasingly working with deaf actors necessarily create more deaf-aware work?

The problem is that the actors that I've worked with are involved with companies that don't specifically aim for performances for deaf audiences. I had to leave one production recently in the interval because the style of it was the same as it's been for the last 40 years. There was nothing new, they hadn't thought, "Oh, let's do a new take on it. Let's think about accessibility. Let's think about how it happens that a character is deaf? How they happen to know BSL?" The deaf character's sister knew a little bit of sign language to communicate with the deaf character, but in fact the actress playing the sister had never signed before so she'd had to learn on the job and maybe had just rehearsed the seven weeks. So it just meant the quality of sign language on the stage from this sister character was just awful. It didn't make any sense at all to a deaf person watching it.

It seems when productions like this are made and hearing companies want to include deaf actors it is with good intention, and it has some positive outcomes in that it raises awareness for the hearing audience of deaf talent and the richness of BSL on stage, it invites deaf performers into a 'hearing space' and frames them in a positive light, which is good. However, if a deaf audience had gone along to see a show like this, they wouldn't really have been able to access it. That's a good example of a sort of tokenism and that's where we struggle. And that's probably why theatres don't pull in a huge number of deaf audiences because they're still inaccessible performances that rely on the deaf audience reading captions or looking at an interpreter on the side of the stage to actually understand everything. So although they include deaf actors, they are in fact still aimed at a hearing audience.

But do you get called in, in a positive way, by people who will admit, "Look, we realise we don't really know what we're doing and we want to do it well, so can you come in and talk us through it all the way?"

Well, you'd be surprised that I *don't* get asked. I've had requests where it's been a director asking me to meet with them. We have a chat and then they'll text me like, "Ooh, do you think it's possible to do this bilingually?" "Yeah, absolutely, of course, because we do this all the time." And then they'll constantly ask me the same couple of questions, it's almost as if they just want reassurance that they're thinking that they're on the right line and then that's it. There'll be one or two conversations and they'll just go off and dominate the play. Again the result will be inaccessible, and again they don't really want that consultation.

But if you are going to commit to doing a bilingual production, it would make sense to have a consultant on side all the way who actually knows about how to do that successfully, who brings the sort of perspective, for example, that I've seen actors learning to sign in just the rehearsal period. If you're going to incorporate BSL into a performance, you need to have proficient BSL users. Obviously a deaf actor in a deaf role will be this, but if you need a hearing character to be able to sign, it needs to be someone who knows BSL to a good standard already. Just as you expect to have good hearing actors who have proficient use of English, you need exactly the same level of BSL proficiency if you truly want the deaf audience to be able to be able to understand and follow. If you were to have a French-speaking part and if the audience could tell that the actor is speaking French very badly, then it just would not be a quality performance and it's likely that the actor wouldn't have been cast in that role in the first place, in order to keep the quality high.

Unfortunately that's what you just don't see happening with BSL roles. Perhaps people don't treat BSL with the same respect because there is a lack of awareness out there that it is a proper language, that it takes years to learn and achieve fluency, and when thinking about performing to a deaf audience you need to have awareness not just of the language, but of deaf culture and community and identity in order to connect. My suggestion if you want to cast actors who will use BSL in your show is to book a deaf BSL consultant for the auditions so that they can give feedback if the actor's level of BSL is intelligible and good enough to follow from a deaf perspective.

There's a parallel linguistically with Welsh-language theatre. As Betsan Llwyd of Bara Caws Theatr points out, though there's a few young people giving bilingual shows a go on the stages in Wales, the more established practitioners find it difficult to find their audiences with the format, and so they stick with one or the other language. And yet there's something genuinely magical about a bilingual performance involving BSL that brings a whole other dimension to what you usually experience on stage.

I completely agree. I think it really does. With bilingual productions everyone has to work doubly hard because you are thinking about both audiences, about accessibility for both audiences — whether it's somebody who's never signed before, someone who's never seen sign language, you have to think about how they would all access the performance. So the production has to happen in a different way.

We create bilingual productions, but for us BSL is always the prime language. I could keep our shows as BSL only, aimed at an entirely deaf audience but the reason I want to make the productions bilingual is because of my past of being told sign language makes you look stupid, speaking is best, and generally having experienced the oppression of BSL. So I want to add English captions, spoken English or visual animations, etc, so that the hearing audience can access the show and feel the full impact of how powerful BSL is onstage, without feeling completely lost and not understanding what is going on.

When we did Sarah Kane's *4.48 Psychosis*, for the monologues I wanted the deaf actors to use not only BSL but also Visual Vernacular, which is a very visually detailed rhythmic poetic performative way of signing. Because of the combination it would be impossible to voice over because you just wouldn't get the language right. So what I did instead of a voice-over was to select key phrases from the monologue itself with good iconic signs that you can see clearly and which make it really visual. So for a devil, for example, you can bring in the pitchfork, the horns, the tail to make it visual. There were parts of the monologues that we captioned in the background as well as having the BSL actor really giving a visual performance. I also picked a few lines from the top, middle and end of the monologue to caption so that you've got some selected parts shown in the English language as well as the visual element of the British Sign Language. It's still a bilingual production but it's not bilingual per se in terms of voicing over every single word you sign.

A bilingual production should depend on the context of the production and as well as the content. And it always has to change. It's something you have to be flexible with it. There's no written rules.

There are a lot of theatremakers out there who are missing a trick because this is four-dimensional theatre, isn't it?

Absolutely. A previous production of ours was Mike Bartlett's play *Contractions*. The manager character was a deaf character who used BSL, and the employee was a hearing person who used speech but she could sign as well. She used Sign Supported English as part of her character, who was passive and innocent, whereas the manager was a very dominant assertive character. It shocked the audience because they'd never seen two languages working side by side like that all the way through. The deaf manager would use objects in the room as well to make it really visual and also to reiterate what was being said, the hearing character would respond but also incorporate what the deaf person had said, and so there was never any element of the audience misunderstanding what was going on. It was completely bilingual on more than one level and it really hit home for a lot of people. So it is possible.

> *The long-term commitment to diversity and disability by the BBC and, historically at least, Channel 4 created a platform on television that has helped create theatre audiences and inspire people to go into the performing arts. Even though the government has relentlessly cut what they set up, particularly in the past ten years, things like See Hear are still cutting-edge [BBC monthly magazine programme for the deaf launched in 1981, presented in BSL with English voice-over & subtitles], and in terms of legacy Switch remains one of the best series I've seen [See Hear drama series from 2001 about people in the deaf community, also launched at the time was The House on the Hill for young deaf children]. In fact a show like Switch must have been incredibly influential, given the quality of writing and acting.*

Oh yes, absolutely. It was so important to have a show like that. I'm reminiscing now! *[Paula was in Switch]* The representation of deaf people in the deaf community, it was lovely. And you're absolutely right, they've now cut down the funding so See Hear can't afford to keep putting on these series. There isn't that commitment at the BBC or elsewhere anymore unfortunately — and you're absolutely right, in the last ten years we've seen such a huge decrease in funding there. It's very fashionable at the moment to sign or to know some sign language, but they're not actually thinking about the long-term effect that the lack of cultural investment has on the deaf community. It's exactly the same that they're doing with disabled actors and disabled people in general.

> *But without that representation in mainstream theatre and with reduced representation on TV there must be (positive) pressure on Deafinitely to tour even if the funding isn't there. Which makes me think that the deaf experience of touring must be quite a strange one.*

I would say from my own personal experience that it's a lonely and isolating experience because you're away from home anyway. When you're touring with a company and you're the only deaf actor, you encounter a lot more difficulties. I remember one of my friends had been touring almost a year in a company where she was the only deaf actor. Even though she speaks very well for herself, she was very isolated. But there was one time that I toured in another company where we were two deaf actors and two hearing actors and it was a lovely experience. It was obviously a much smaller company, we were working together, we were teaching each other to sign and so on.

And of course with Deafinitely Theatre we're very comfortable, we're very free, we've employed hearing actors, but they can sign fluently, they have Level 6 BSL *[top certificate level of BSL language qualifications]*. They understand deaf awareness, culture, identity, so there's no issues there. For other companies it can be difficult. You have to teach them how to be with deaf people. At first they're quite excited — "Ooh, how do I sign my name? How do I swear? How do I sign rude bits?" And so on. But the interest then wanes. Obviously that commitment depends on the individual actors. Some are confident to clown around and try to encourage that level of connection.

Also for being on tour, you don't always get interpreters provided, so you're kind of on your own. At the same time you don't want an interpreter with you 24-7, it's like having a third wheel constantly there. And, of course, when touring or just working in one place with a hearing company it can be difficult to do all the basic things like the get-in, the get-out, dress rehearsals.

While deaf practitioners are trying educate the rest of the industry, how do you educate the audiences into knowing that there's quality there, for audiences who are not deaf?

In the first few years of Deafinitely Theatre when we were performing our devised work, we put on very short runs, a few days or a week long, and the audiences were predominantly deaf — it was very rare for us to have any hearing audience at that time. As we were always sold out, we wanted to start to raise our profile and try four-week runs in a well established venue, bring in the press for reviews etc, so we then had to think of how we could expand our audience to sell enough tickets to achieve this.

We decided to put on a well-known already scripted piece, and so we chose George Brant's *Grounded*, and that gave us a successful four week run. Then we did *Contractions* which gave us such a huge surge in hearing audience members because they wanted to see what the difference was between BSL, English, how were we going to incorporate the two? There was so much more interest, and we had exactly the same reaction with *4.48 Psychosis*, where a lot of the audience are familiar with the play and they wanted to see how the BSL adaptation would look like and how it actually worked. From our feedback and evaluation forms of our performances over the last few years, it seems we attract around 50 per cent deaf audience and 50 per cent hearing, which is pretty good.

In terms of educating hearing audiences that there is inherent quality in deaf productions, we achieved this spectacularly when in 2012 we performed

Shakespeare's *Love's Labour's Lost* entirely in BSL as part of the Globe to Globe Festival *[part of the World Shakespeare Festival, itself part of the 2012 Cultural Olympiad, featuring 37 productions of Shakespeare's plays in 37 different languages over six weeks]*. There was no spoken English voice-over, just the occasional plotline summary shown on the caption screens, but through use of BSL, Visual Vernacular, body language, gestures and visual art forms, we created a piece of 'Sign Theatre' that the hearing audience absolutely loved and enjoyed — and I'm sure it was an eye-opening and educational experience for many of them as to the quality and possibilities of using deaf talent.

Our passion and aim continues to be that of exposure, education, entertainment, and to encourage the embracing of deaf culture and language in the theatre industry. When the two worlds come together and work as one, it is a powerful, creative place to be.

*

13
Christopher Green

'The invitation is there to rebel or take over'

Christopher Green is a writer, experiential theatremaker & performer. Based in North London, he was born in Sheffield, Yorkshire, & raised in Derbyshire.
• *christophergreen.net*

I picked up on The Home because of its theme of older people in care homes. At 48 hours and a cast of thousands it looks like a massive project and a hugely long time in the making, so how did you first get into it?

It came out of working as an associate with Entelechy Arts *[based at the Albany Deptford in South East London]*. I'd hosted their 21st Century Tea Dances *[live arts knees-ups]* a couple of times a year for a long time and I've also been involved in Meet Me at the Albany *[weekly arts and crafts gatherings for older people]* from the start, not that I'm there that often. But I'm a sort of regular and in the process I've got to know some of the participants who are older people very well. I had also done a project of mine called *Ida Barr's Mash Up*, where as Ida Barr I worked with little kids and older people. We make two separate choirs and then bring them together for a giant choir, which I did for five years and went to lots of care homes and old people's clubs as part of it.

At the same time as doing that kind of work, my immersive shows were getting bigger and more ambitious every time. So *The Home* was just one of those very natural ideas, where everybody's terrified of growing older and being dependent and vulnerable. So it was like, "Oh I'll do an immersive show where you go and live in a fake care home and experience what it's like to be looked after." And so that was the start of the process.

I went to David Slater at Entelechy as the logical partner, he very quickly spoke to Gavin Barlow at the Albany, so then we became three producers *[David & Gavin are artistic directors of the two organisations]*. And you're absolutely right, the R&D process is the longest I've ever done — it's taken around three years, lots of care home visits, lots of talking to stakeholders in the industry, you know that whole kind of world, going to conferences presenting the idea. We then did a work in progress in 2018 at (B)old, the festival on age and creativity by Southbank, who were very supportive. Jude Kelly *[Southbank artistic director at the time]* was a big supporter of the project — I'd just done *Prurience* there — and I did a ten-minute version of *The Home*.

It's kind of weird to do a ten-minute version of a 48-hour show, but that was the moment when we were like, "Holy shit, it really works! It works in ten minutes, it's *really* going to work as a show." So it was exciting to know that I was on to something.

That's the gestation of it, starting in 2018, and now we've done it twice in the UK — first as part of Age Against the Machine, Entelechy an the Albany's festival of creative ageing in 2019, and at ARC Stockton Arts Centre *[Stockon-on-Tees, County Durham]*. We're doing it in Japan in April 2021, and we were going to ISPA *[International Society for the Performing Arts trade fair]* in Taipei this summer *[cancelled because of the Coronavirus crisis]* and ISPA New York in January the next year. I think it's going to be one of those projects that will have a life. It needs money to stage it obviously, but more than anything else I've done, it's creating the sort of ripples outwards that are much bigger than the work itself.

Before we get onto the international trajectory, give us a potted summary of how the 48 hours work.

It's a fictional care home, but it's very real. The audience is looked after by staff who are over 70 years old, and the idea is that this is a commercial company founded by someone who works in the City. They've got 20 care homes across the country, so they're a small provider but dynamic with a luxury product. They've got this innovative idea of a 'taster wing' so they've built a 30-bed unit next to one of their homes for you to go and experience it for yourself.

So if you come along, you're not pretending to be 80 and have dementia. There's no acting required from you. Instead you are being given the experience of what it might be like to be an older person in a care home. Crucially you're also being given that experience in a way that's a bit like time share, so you can sign up for the private insurance package. So it's two things I've always wanted to do: it's about vulnerability and it's about capitalism equally. In the care home you are encouraged to be vulnerable so there's the constant balance between care and control. And there's lots about health & safety and things like that.

You are part of a group of 30 people who stay overnight and have the taster experience, and then during the weekend there are four shows with up to 80 people coming from the outside — they are 'community visitors'. They come to participate in the Saturday afternoon talent show, the Saturday night bingo, non-denominational worship on Sunday morning and the open afternoon later that day. Each of those is 90 minutes and is livestreamed so they function like shows but also fit within the 48-hour immersive taster experience.

So that's the general shape and it's a lot about groups. I've been fascinated with groups for a long time — without it becoming therapy, because it's not! But I think we're all odd with groups. Even if we love them we have to establish a relationship with them, and I'm always alive to how groups work, group dynamics, the power of groups. And that's what my work's about really, the audience as a group.

Does your theatre work get picked up overseas much? That exploration of group dynamics is something people in places like Europe and East Asia are particularly interested in.

Historically I've travelled a lot when I was doing a lot more cabaret and my solo shows. I So I did lots of international touring in that way, went to Australia a lot and America quite a bit. And then the biggest shows have gone to places at times, for example with Duckie *[aka C'Est Duckie, created with Ursula Martinez, Miss High Leg Kick & Marissa Carnesky]* we went all over the place, New York, Sydney, Berlin, Tokyo and Kyoto. A pivotal point was when *Prurience*, which is the porn addiction show, went to New York and the Guggenheim Museum picked it up. They'd never done a piece of theatre before and for me it was the first time that I relished the idea of remaking a piece for a cultural context and spend.

So I went on a trip to New York purely just to be around and go to AA meetings and things like that — obviously there were some production meetings too. I was going like, "Yeah, the show *works*, but I'm going to rewrite it in this way and I'm going to change the *provocation*" — because the way groups work, as you say, is different. What's exciting now is the supersizing I'm doing for *The Home* in Japan, at the Saitama Arts Theatre *[which came together with Entelechy and Saitama connecting through the Future Arts Centres network]*. It's such a great provocation although remember that I'm not directing it, I'm there as advisor.

Because the show's designed to be in Japanese presumably.

Yes — whenever we do the show, if it's in English I will direct it, if it's not, then I will be advisor to the production. I'm not interested in directing through a translator. It's too weird and too odd and too culturally specific. *The Home* in particular is all about minute detail, which I love. It's all about, "No no this is wrong, those colours aren't right, there's *no way* that company would have those colours!" *[laughs]* But it is really important! It's the tiny little things that pull you out of the art of it.

In Japan, how does it work? Is it just one show or a run of several shows? And how does one do a run of a 48-hour show in any case?

Initially they're doing one show, which I'm fully aware is crazy in any case because it's such a big production. But again the ripples go outwards in a big way — you have all these different audiences coming in, and there's the online presence. The idea is after that, it'll be restaged but we're focusing on this first one.

I think we've already quite a lot of interest, from places and of course we're going to ISPA in Taiwan and New York, the trade fair where you go and sell it. We'll see how it's going to work internationally on a wider scale. ISPA is a straightforward presentation and then I'll do my ten-minute version which I really like. So yes it's nice to talk about that one.

It's nice to have this slow gestation, it's such a different rhythm from the other shows that I've made. I think it deserves it because of the scale, and what that also means is it gets rid of that half life of a show where you usually know that, yeah, by 2025 no one's going to want it any more because it'll be old hat. I don't think that's going to be the case with *The Home*, it's got an urgency about it but it also has a solidity to it.

But at the same time, that decision to produce the show overseas means you need to adapt it to a new context — and hand it over to a director in another company. It becomes a completely changed process.

Yes. It then becomes about me interrogating the structure that I'm making, with all the attention to detail rather than what theatremakers often focus on, which is the noise the show makes. In Japan it's been a very different process from the outset: endless meetings with interpreters, lots of people in the room, all very formal. I think they understood very quickly which were the non-negotiable bits of the show for me and the bits that absolutely need to be negotiated, need to be culturally relevant. It's been exciting to go, "It won't work if we don't do this, but all of this is just texture, culturally specific and therefore is literally your territory."

It make you think of the way they put on the big international operas for just a handful of nights across the year. Which must be the complete opposite of you doing the cabaret circuit — "I'll do three in a night, in three different venues if need be."

Three different *characters*! I've done all of that in that old music hall model. Absolutely done that.

On the other hand, if you need to work overseas on a big project this, it actually makes you a far more attractive proposition — that flexibility of 'have characters will tour'.

Or fly to Sydney for one gig, which I have done. In the old days, of course. Now, everyone would shoot you for doing that. But I have done that all those kinds of crazy things.

So now we're talking about the reverse of all that, something which takes three years just to do a handful of shows. Not to be negative, but how does it work to convince a theatre on the other side of the world to put The Home on, where there's not only a totally different culture but also different theatre practice?

That's absolutely not to be negative. Something like this is absolutely about the idea, it's about the way people talk about it at all stages of the project. *The Home* is absolutely the point where people go, "What? You want me go and live there for three days, and you will feed me and I won't be allowed out and I can't drink and . . . *what*? I'm not doing that!" That reaction is as much part of the work as any of the 30 participants who actually go and do it. And then there's the way people who experience it talk and write about it afterwards. There's the people who watch it streaming, which we make available at certain times.

So it's the whole thing as well as the moment of theatricality, all of it gently but persistently questioning, well what is theatre? Is *The Home* just those 90 minutes where you're sitting front of a performer, or is it the whole idea of it? You know, the things that people are drawn to and the things that they are horrified by. If somebody says, "There's no way I will go and see a show set in a care home" — even then, they'll file that away in the back of their brain and maybe in 10 or 20 years' time when they're told, "Oh, I'm afraid you've got a degenerative thing, you might need to get a carer in," and their response is, "This is what I don't like, I said I didn't want to go and do that thing." It's all part of making theatre broader and relevant through the simple fact that all that is going on and is part of the work.

So how did the Japanese part of the project get set up? Was it a gradual coming together?

It happened very practically through the connection with Entelechy and Saitama and Future Arts Centres. That came together quite quickly, because Saitama were involved in the UK production by coming over and observing. So Japan has been embedded in the project from the start, which totally makes sense. The involvement of Saitama Gold Theatre makes it even more interesting — it's a group of non-professional older performers *[founded in 2006 by Saitama]* just for people over 55 years old. I see there being three constituencies of performers for *The Home*: firstly, professional actors; secondly, a subset who are professional older actors, people over 75 but who have had a whole career in the industry or training in the way that we'd understand; and thirdly non-professional older performers — Saitama Gold will be that group in Japan.

For the London production that third group came through Entelechy, and then we sourced them through the Stockton ARC and I did a lot of work with them in each case. The Entelechy group obviously were the ones who I've known for a long time. A lot of the feedback after that show was people asking, "How did you work with them? How did you get them to do so much? How did you get them to be so confident and so immersed and their performance so subtle?" To which the boring answer is that I've known them for eight or nine years and so they trust me, and that gave me the confidence to know how to supercharge their presence in the show.

In Stockton, I worked with a group that I didn't know, but over four workshops I was in a position to say, "Trust me this will work, just be yourself in this moment, just react as you react, be small, don't perform." This is a really important part of the project and there's no reason why it shouldn't work. If there's a really confident 30 year old person who you, as an audience member, suspect is an actor, then a part of you can't help but sit back and wait to appreciate the performance. All of my theatre work reflects my fascination with the way that, whether it's staged, we all go, "Oh the show's starting now, great!" so if as professional actor dresses as a careworker does this whole thing starts this routine on you, you're like, great this is happening fantastic, deep inside you sit back and the lights have gone down and you're like, brilliant!, you're performing and I'm being the audience, therefore I am passive. But if an 85 year old goes, "Oh, um, I'll get a cup of tea for you", and you're like, "Are they . . . ? Is this part of the show? Or is this just an old person offering to get me a cup of tea? Should I let them?" Do you know what I mean, it's really messes up what is performance and what is theatre and all of that.

But in a very real and relevant way. You're breaking down barriers, not just to make people emerge looking at older people in a different way but sharing the realisation that it will all come to us — if you live that long of course — especially given the loss of the extended family in our society.

Intergenerational living, exactly. We don't have that any more, we don't have the advice those relationships have to offer, we don't have any of that. I'm not massively oversentimentalising *The Home* but there are some beautiful moments. I've witnessed conversations like an old lady taking a participant's hand and going, "It's not that bad you know!" *[laughs]* That's good because we need to be told that there's good and bad about being a child, there's good and bad about being 50, and there's good and bad about being 80. That's the human experience, and to hear that from someone who'll hold your hand and tell you, that's great isn't it?

Even if you're not directing, it's still a huge amount of work.

Yes it is absolutely. But in Japan it's very straightforward. For example, I've just done a couple of weeks over there to do recruitment and a bit of casting. Now I'm handing over to the director, and I'll do everything by Skype from now on until I go over for three weeks of rehearsal. So in terms of my involvement, it doesn't dominate everything, and that's the way it needs to be. I need to clearly let them direct it otherwise it will be a mishmash — it's my show, but it's being restaged with me as an advisor, it's not purely my vision any more

The Japanese director Naoki Sugawara is interesting because he heads a theatre company OiBokkeShi — which means 'Ageing, Dementia, Death'. And as an actor and writer, he's really a pioneer in working with older people in theatre.

What's your impression of the set-up of the theatre itself, in view of the fact that I presume you've not worked with a Japanese theatre before.

I've performed in Japan, bringing shows there, but I haven't made work there. Saitama are an enormous organisation, very formal and very organised, it's very like going to the National Theatre. At the moment they're coming to the end of their vision of doing every Shakespeare play. When I was there they were doing *Henry VIII*. I went into the massive rehearsal room and found thousands of people in there, all these TV actors and everything, and this very esteemed director asks, "Ah could we ask you some questions about . . . ?" And I was like "*Don't* ask me questions about *Henry VIII*! No one does *Henry VIII* so please do not look upon me as an expert. You can ask me about a couple of words but . . ." That was funny.

So they're super-organised, very funded, very structural, as the cliché of the Japanese company would be, and it's an absolute delight. There was a beautiful moment on the very first day when they had provided a translator, really smart. About 20 minutes in, she said, "Just so you know, I won't translate your jokes, just to save time. I mean, I think they're funny, but it's just going to slow everything down because they won't really understand, and then everyone will be embarrassed that they don't know how to react. So I'm just going to cut that out, but carry on. I just won't translate the jokes." And of course that's fascinating for me, because I'm like, "Well who am I if I'm not being flippant? Because that's who I am. I quite organised and serious, but then I subvert everything with lighthearted British self-effacing self-loathing. So I don't know who I am!" So that was a ontological wobble. But it was also a beautifully Japanese moment and rightly so. She did the right thing, that's her job as a cultural translator.

They're putting it in a community centre on the edge of Tokyo. That doesn't mean community centre in the way that we understand it. It's an enormous, incredibly funded building that looks like a bank headquarters. It's on an extraordinary scale with lots of rooms and restaurants — not like our idea of a room where there's some old fellow who's got the keys and opens it for two hours a week.

That's bound to create interesting ripples in Japan.

I think it comes down to leaving space, having the confidence to leave that space. It's all very well to say we're doing this immersive theatre show where the audience join in and there's the entertainment, but in my experience — and this is not a criticism — most shows like that are a different form of theatre. They don't leave space for the audience, so it is prescribed that you will go, you will do this, you will interact in this way, and then you will leave and be happy. A bit like going to a theme park, where you walk around, you'll buy a hotdog and go on the rollercoaster, then you'll leave going, "Oh yeah, that's what I expected."

But my whole trajectory — and it's lovely to realise that I've had one — is about having the confidence to leave space, so the invitation is there to rebel or take over, to say no or let's do it like this, or yeah we get what you're doing but we just don't want to, we just want to leave, whatever. But if you don't have the confidence to leave the space then they won't react and you are prescribing, even if you feel you're not.

Which brings us to *No Show [2020]*, which is all about openly allowing the audience the space. Actually it relates to what you've been saying about funding. I've always been clear — well, not always, but certainly for the last 15 years — that I want to offer work in different ways. As a result I've been a one-man band in many ways, arriving with suitcase and an entire show in it. My cabaret work, for example, is all unfunded and rightly so.

Because so much of my work is done within that capitalist structure — I have something to sell you, you buy it, great, straightforward — then I feel it's justified now to say that some works *cannot* exist without funding. In fact I have the confidence to say that since a show like *The Home* can't exist without funding, I'm going to ask for a lot of it because all of *this* that we're doing without funding.

So *No Show* is on a totally different scale. It's about the basic relationship between a solo performer and a group of people who have decided to be called the audience, and what happens when one person is here, a group of people are there, what happens in that relationship. The breakthrough linked to this, after The Yard [*theatre in East London*] asked me if I wanted to create a show, was the observation that culturally there are so many people absolving responsibility for their roles. Politicians want to be politicians but they don't want to have that breadth of leadership, the Royal Family don't want to be the Royal Family at the moment, where they're like, "It's all so difficult at the moment, innit? I'm going to go and live somewhere else."

There's lots of examples of that throughout our society, and I as a performer quite often don't want to be a performer, which is why my work has become what it is. I don't want to be that person facing a hundred or a thousand people or a load a of drunk people at a wedding. Sometimes I just don't want to do that. So what happens when I decide not to? Normally we can rely on a performer, especially a cabaret performer or someone who's come from entertainment, to always want to go, [*singsong*] "Look at *me*!! Look at *me*!!! I'll tell you a *joke*! I'll sing you a *song*! I'll do the *splits*! I'll do *anything* to make you *hap-pee* . . . !" What happens when that person goes, "You know what? I'm not just feeling it tonight. Is that all right?" And that is *deeply* problematic for what is theatre, what is performance, what is entertainment, and so that's the starting point for *No Show* — but it obviously fits in with all of my work, just on a different scale.

For your largescale work, does that mean that you have to come up with a minimalist approach?

Yes it's the same idea done in a very different way.

And No Show doesn't need funding?

It's got a *little* bit.

Sorry, an inadvertently sneaky question.

No no, it's a very good question, a very specific question, because I made it sound like it didn't have any funding. And, no you're right, it's got a tiny bit of Arts Council money but it's mainly a commission from The Yard so it's got a little bit of top-up.

So indirect funding really, which is one of the ways that Arts Council funding does benefit people — support work through places to show and share it.

Yes. It's mainly through the venue and the way they work.

But it's not a funded vehicle where Christopher Green has this amazing concept and the world is gagging for it and it simply must have money thrown at it so you can turn up to flash your arse with a conceptual twinkle and run away . . . or something along those lines.

[laughs] Which is an idea!

An idea like No Show is pleasingly minimalist conceptually, and probably quite a timely approach — which is hardly surprising since you generate zeitgeisty shows. You're also helped because of the structure of what you do — working solo, ensembles, collaborations, groups and institutions, and the performance art/installation undercurrent of your work got picked by the Guggenheim. You're in a good position to strip it all down.

I think a lot of where I am now is that an audience, whether they know it or not, the people I work with and the performers that I employ and the teams of people like *The Home*, I think they quickly realise that I know what I'm doing and I *could* do it. I could do a two-hour solo show. I've got the skills to do it, but I am not doing that. I'm employing other people to do it. I'm saying to an 85 year old who's never really performed before, *I* can show you a few tricks [chuckles] and *you* can do it.

But what happens is that people then ask me all the time, aren't you frustrated that you're not performing? I'm like, I am *so* happy not doing performing. [laughs] So there's something about that, as well. And there is that confidence to ask what is this show? Am I going to do it or not? Am I going to turn up? And if I do, do I do the show or not? And then leave the space? But the audience has got to know that I could leave if I wanted to. It's very different from being 22 and going *ac-tual-ly* I'm nervous, because I'm not sure I can pull it off. No, I can do it. So there's something in all of that, which only comes from a certain degree of confidence, and it makes me really happy to be doing it at this stage.

> *Without trying to push a theory, and you can just offer a one-word answer like 'no', but do you think that sort of reflects the growing malaise in theatre, the fact that most of the stuff up there is mostly, for want of a better word, vision-free. It may be technically good but the ever increasing barrier of cost means that the vision of today's theatre seems to be taking place in social media. There's definitely a Twitterverse of simply amazing theatremakers out there with amazing ideas for creativity and change, but very little of it is getting on to the stage, and most of the stuff that does get on to the stage doesn't join up and creates a disconnect with the audiences who aren't able to share or question the message, the politics or whatever.*

'Yes.' And I will interrupt you at this point because brilliantly I've been commissioned to write a book about the audience which I'm slowly working on. What it's going to be about — and this is the publisher's aim — is that virtually everybody who makes work on any scale will go, oh have you read that thin book by that guy? Because it's saying have you really thought about the audience, have you really thought about what you're asking them to be? And if the answer to that question is we're asking them to be the audience, then great go ahead, but *have* you asked that question, and if so what do you think the audience should *be?*

Anybody starting a cabaret act, somebody taking their first show to Edinburgh, somebody directing a show for the Royal Shakespeare Company, they should all be asking these questions, because I think, exactly as you're saying, we're not asking those questions and that's why we're getting the sterility. There's some great stuff on stage, there's some great ideas and it all looks lovely and all that kind of stuff, amazing performances, but we're just really ignoring the audience, we're not properly interrogating what that relationship is.

Going back to the international thing, when you go to a different place, we often believe theatre has been exported to other places in ways we understand, and then when you go to somewhere and discover that it hasn't, it's totally amazing. I was lucky enough to be taken to the sumo championships in Tokyo — you can't get a ticket — and it was a great guide to a community. We were two rows back and the experience was totally thrilling. What was also brilliant for me was that a week later they sent the link to the live TV footage which I didn't know they did. There's shots of things of me going *[clutching interviewer in mock shock/awe]* "aaaaargh! ohhhhhhh!" I was massively reacting, but so was everyone else, we're all like "aaaargh!" because that's what you do, because there's two massive people trying to throw each other off the stage and they might land on you.

And they did! There was this old lady in front who suddenly got this big 200 kilo oversized bloke on her. We're all like clutching each other, ooorgh! There's all of this shit going on and I'm like, wow that interaction with the audience is really great, and they're all chatting to me and saying can I touch your hair and it's like, yeah okay sure. It was exciting and was one of the best audiences I've been in. It was a *proper* audience. But that sort of experience was so different, it's never going to happen in most theatres here. Everyone would go, "Hm-yeah-that-was-very-good-are-you-getting-the-Tube-home?" It's just a shame that we've had that programmed into us.

> *So the final question then would be a sort of standard question. And since you're a non-standard sort of person I know that if I ask you a standard question I'll probably get a non-standard sort of answer.*

[laughs] That's my career in a nutshell!

> *So here comes the earnest Alan Yentob question: apart from No Show and The Home, if there was one show that sums everything in your work, including all the cabaret, what would it be?*

That's a really good question, and I'll be slightly bland and say I can think of a '*Desert Island Discs* Eight' off the top of my head. And of that, I'll pick one. It's from a while ago, during the Iraq War when I was in Australia at the Melbourne Comedy Festival and I was doing Tina C and it was a massive gala. I kind of knew it at the time, but I now realise that at the heart of what I was doing with Tina was like "look how attractive I am look how seductive I am" — which is what happened both physically, and with the songs and the demeanor.

Because this was during the Iraq War, I come out in this amazing khaki outfit with a huge dress and the stars & stripes singing a patriotic song and I'm like *[silky Tina C American drawl]* "You know I'm going to do this for our, uh, you know troops, and I know you didn't, as *Australasia* didn't wanna send your troops out there, and that's fine, we're not judging you, you're WRONG, but we're not judging you, okay? I'm still here to sell you product . . ." And so we're doing this whole thing and it's thrilling, and then this group of guys start shouting, "Fuck off you American bitch! Fuck you! Fuck you!" — and they just go mad in this massive gala that was being televised.

The show people are panicking but I'm like, *[as Tina C]* "Oh! Oka-ay . . . I don't understand what you're talking about, but okay . . . ." So I'm thrilled, but they have to stop the show, and I'm saying, "Don't stop the show, this is *great!*" And then they made the guys leave, and I was like, "*Why* are you making them leave?" And I realised in that moment that what I'd been wanting to do with Tina all the time was just to get someone to say "NO!! You're nice and everything and you look pretty and I would . . . but NO!!" And I was like oh my God that's *exactly* what I want, and so now so much of my work is about kind of saying yeah how much will I do until you say no, until you say I don't want this or can we do this in another way?

Obviously you don't want complete anarchy onstage the whole time, like you can't go to the National Theatre and you know the opening scene exactly, and when Lesley Manville makes her entrance, you can't then shout, "NO! Lesley NO!" But actually why not? At some degree, why don't we just then go, "Listen for me, I'm not really getting this . . ." And we don't do that.

I've always angled for bringing back tomatoes and soft fruit. It's what you've paid for.

Well we might mumble about it as we walk home, but there's something about that state of saying NO! So that would be the moment of my Eight that I would pick. It was thrilling and everyone was like, "Oh I'm so sorry Chris that must have been awful for you." I'm like, "Oh my God that was the best thing that's ever happened to me!" Brilliant, I'm part of an anti-war process.

What it also shows is that they had totally believed who Tina was, so it's also the biggest compliment that they had not seen any layers of theatricality, they *believed* who the character was. And that's the most thrilling thing too: they had said, "Yeah, we see who you are, we don't want you." And I was like, "Great, if we all did that, the world would be a much better place." So yeah, power to the people.

Oh, and can you come and see *No Show*? I mean I might not be there but you might be . . .

*

14

Jackie Hagan

'We don't have time to be lazy, we have to crack on with this'

Jackie Hagan is a writer, performer and queer & disability activist. Based in Manchester, she was born & raised in Skelmersdale (aka Skem), Lancashire.
• jackiehagan.org, @jackiehagan

How does your background give you the ability to see what's needed in terms of equal treatment in the UK?

I'm from a council estate in a spill-over town that is now studied on the GCSE syllabus as a failed town. It's like Alan Bennett says his inheritance was coming from Leeds, mine is coming from Skem. I've got a *lot* of art out of it, it's a very singular place, the streets are in alphabetical order.

My family still lives there, my brother works in a factory like my Dad did, and my Mum and her boyfriend have major mental health conditions. In fact they met on a psychiatric ward, it was a lithium romance. My Dad had one leg and spent a lot of time in a wheelchair after a stroke that left him paralysed on one side, he died when I was a teenager. My Mum spent time in psychiatric ward when I was a kid. I'm also bisexual. So there's a lot of reasons I've been sat on the edges of society looking in. I was diagnosed with bipolar early on, and when I suddenly had to have my leg off I realised it was make or break mentally, and so I decided to be vigilantly optimistic and see the bleak comedy and absurdity in everything while also remaining realistic and optimistic, see the potential, see how we can sort stuff out, how we can bolster folk and improve morale, help people who are angry find empathy.

I've gone from proper council estate to spending a lot of time in the arts industry and media industry. I've essentially a foot in both camps (no pun intended). I don't agree but I understand why working class people vote for Brexit, I see how they get to voting Tory, I understand why the so-called undeserving poor have big tellies and spend benefit money on drugs and fags and booze and I understand neglect. I'm touring my fourth show *This Is Not a Safe Space* at the moment, which is, in part, a explanation of the underserving poor, it's not a defence, it's just "here's this information, do with it what you will".

I don't just use my own mind as research, I interviewed 80 people living on disability benefits for that show, and I interweave the audio of those interviews with frustration comedy, absurd poetry, But I think I wouldn't get let into those people's houses, I wouldn't get to have the frank chats with folk, if it wasn't for my council estate gob and wheelchair bones. It's useful, I'm a conduit. I also explain other social phenomena — dragging up as middle class in order to get by in certain jobs, the effects of social mobility, the reasons disabled people are frustrated, and the ways in which we are all related.

I also did a philosophy degree and have been sectioned, and both lend themselves to dismantling society and everything we think. It helps with understanding life and condensing it down to its essence, which is great for everything from writing children's plays to talking at conferences or writing poetry — that on its surface it's entertaining and odd, but on second hearing has a lot of depth.

So how does what you perform reflect who you are?

There's a saying about the Irish that they won't tell the truth when there's prettier words to say. It's meant to be a slur but I like it, I've an Irish background — there's a lot of truth in lies, people get mixed up between truth and honesty, truth about humanity is what we aim for in art.

It's also well known that Scousers don't shut up, we're all comedians and storytellers no matter our jobs, it's the docks. The men would all sit on the sea wall waiting for a boat to come in, and one would jump to the front and tell a story and the next fella would try to outdo him and so on until the boat came.

My performance is an extension of my personality and worldview. I'm always aiming for truth and authenticity, what that means has changed over the years. My skillset and confidence has grown and so that means my intuition has improved as to what questions I need to ask in my art and the form an idea should take.

There's various sides to what I perform. There's the odd cabaret persona that dresses up her stump as various celebrities, it's normalising disability in an abnormal way, it's warm with a cheeky wink, it's not shocking, it's charming. That's very authentic. Moments of weirdness among broader humour like downing cheap lager from my false leg. All of that stuff is to remove the pity from viewing disabled people — we are normal, we get drunk, we can be dickheads, we're people. I'd say that reflects accurately who I am in the pub, except it's more meticulously planned out obviously.

My worldview is down-to-earth and is born of never trusting the mainstream narrative. It isn't angry and childish, it's interested and considered, I'm not trying to force feed audiences specific messages, it's more a case of "huh! have you seen this?" or presenting people and ideas we vilify in an informed, realistic way. Theatre is often a way of peering into other people's lives without being seen, it's being invisible and improving your worldview by understanding more people and situations. I do try to meet the audience halfway, but certainly not the whole way. I don't make art that is just for me, but it is always authentic.

The first hour-long show I toured back in 2013 was an odd situation. It was my first commission and very soon afterwards I was in hospital with a mystery disease, and came out three months later with one less leg, a new lover and loads more maturity. I wrote the script in hospital when we weren't sure if I was going to survive. I started touring it before I'd fully learnt to walk and found a place to live. It was crackers.

At first I did a strategic rural tour where actually lots of people knew folk who'd had a leg off in farming accidents. It was a poetic comedy for 13 yrs-plus called *Some People Have Too Many Legs*. There was a dream sequence with volunteer unicorns from the audience and bubble machines and disco lights at the point I'm having my leg off, with the theme tune to *[BBC TV sitcom] One Foot in the Grave* in the background all raved up. Not only was I making it palatable for the young audience but it isn't a million miles from how you feel on diamorphine. I was very aware of the audience at that time, I didn't want this show to be shock tactics or lazy, it was optimistic, it was weird and found the good in everything, which mirrors accurately the mindset I had to have at that time.

Sometimes there's a crossover between you and the audience. However the show I tour now, I say, "I used to want to make stories alright for you, but I don't anymore" — and that's true, the world has got harsher, and so I want to present people to the audience, ways people live, but I don't want to coat things in unicorn fluff. But then there's the children's work I do and obviously that is fluffy, but I've found a way to be hardcore while kid-friendly. I tour as part of a drag troupe now called Fantabulosa! who put on a hour-long drag extravaganza, I perform as Freya Bentos (like the pie). I have to do work that is important.

There's a thing about vulnerability. We love seeing characters be vulnerable. But when you're on stage and not on telly you need to ensure no one feels the urge to look after you right there and then . . . they can't sit back and relax if they feel like they need to hold you up. You have to show command of the room while remaining vulnerable. I love that. I love that in everyday conversation, it's something you have to master early on in life so that you can be close with people you are talking to. I was very close to my family, so I am always wanting to replicate that, it's a good lifetime urge to have and understand if you're going to make live art.

A brilliant poet, Gerry Potter [from Manchester], asked me once why I was always trying to find the meaning of life. I think he asked because I was really suffering with it at the time. I think I never trusted anything as a kid and so I invented an imaginary land and then got very into philosophy and got lost. Since then I've been trying to figure out what the world is all about, like a lot of people, and so the best way for that to be a joyous thing that involves lots of other people is to be an artist.

When they asked you to appear at the IETM plenary in Hull [IETM — the 'international network for contemporary performing arts' — is a Euro-funded performing arts network that advocates the value of arts and culture, holding two plenary conferences annually and smaller meetings all over the world], what particular qualities do you think they were looking for in your show?

I'm a bit like a mum on stage, but a weird funny one. I'm very likeable and it's instantly very welcoming. The show will go off in a different direction and it will alienate you at times and go strange and bring you back home but it's just cosy enough for people to stay with me. In that way, international audiences don't feel entirely alienated. I think that's why IETM invited me to perform at their conference. In the show they wanted, *This Is Not a Safe Space*, I talk directly to the audience for a lot of it, not in an old school drag queen way or an old school comedian way, in that I don't pick on anyone, everyone is safe so that we can talk about other people's lives who are very unsafe.

I've never been nervous of going on stage, it's like meditation for mad people for me, it's the one place I focus and stop trying to figure things out, I'm there to read the audience and deliver this stuff in the best way that night. It's when I get to breath out. I think that relaxed atmosphere is great for audiences. If English is your second or even not your language at all, if you are reading captions, or your culture is a million miles from mine, you definitely understand the relaxed vibe. I represented the UK in an international poetry slam in Rio de Janeiro, there were captions which we had to stick to — no ad libbing! So I won the crowd over by just saying "Ola!" in various ways. When I was younger I wanted to be liked by everyone, so I had lots of practice figuring out how to be relatable to a diverse crowd.

Plus, re: IETM, it's always a plus that I do a lot of wraparounds i.e. workshops and Q&As etc! Theatres like that. If you are an emerging artist I'd suggest shadowing a really good facilitator. Workshops can be really effective — but bad workshops can put people off art.

At home I've done well over two thousand workshops with people in prisons and psych wards and with refugee groups and a hundred more supposed 'hard to reach' groups, and so you get used to working with people in different ways. It means you can deal well with working with translators, unexpected problems, challenging behaviour, people being people. I used to run a not for profit organisation putting on workshops and publishing people with mental health and other problems, and you realise it's not always about the writing or about the play we're all creating, it's about people expressing themselves which is a huge and crucial area, especially with people who are ignored or looked down on.

You must encounter a forest of terminology every way you turn as it's all evolving in front of us, like the change in perspective from multicultural to intersectional. 'Marginalised' is one word that's being used a lot at the moment that relates to what you're about, isn't it?

In the theatre industry we are becoming more and more informed and equipped to handle the fear-born ways in which humans keep each other down or divided. In terms of what we would put on stage, we went through the phase where didn't tell stories about certain groups, then we identified who we were excluding (to some degree, some groups are seen as 'worthier' than others) and we told stories about them that were not informed by them, then we told stories based on stories we collected from them and we started to give marginalised people opportunities to tell their own stories however it would be in bit-form — for instance a non-refugee writing the skeleton of a show and slotting refugees into it, then we started to give opportunities to marginalised artists in a way such that they can create the art themselves, this is where we are now.

I believe we need to look more into the support that we offer marginalised artists. Often people enter the industry through schemes that are built to bring in marginalised artists, and people expect them to have pre-requisite knowledge of it, it increases imposter syndrome, makes asking for support difficult. This is true of non-marginalised artists too. However, if there is previous experience of oppression, then there is more increased chance of low self esteem. Simply coming from a different background to many people in the industry means that we have learnt a different way of surviving in the world that is difficult to unlearn when it has been integral to us, a different way of interacting and talking, we might have a different concept of what it means to be professional, and then when we act out of turn the criticism can hit harder due to lack of self-esteem, and so instead of simply correcting the supposed problem it causes more problems.

I've known a lot of other marginalised artists who have had mental health problems as a result of entering an industry that doesn't know how to deal with them. Obviously I've always had mental health problems so there's that, but I did take a serious overdose of morphine that I feel is in part due to the experience I was having with the industry at that time. From my heart-to-hearts with other artists, this isn't uncommon.

Obviously it's difficult, but we need to understand that people are suffering because of how our industry is and we truly believe we can change it. A lot of people are really tired, and that's because society at large needs an overhaul, but we can only do it in small, hugely important ways a bit at a time. Do you remember Mr Trebus? He was a pensioner on TV in the 1990s who had a home whose walls were coming apart because he had hoarded so much stuff. I feel like we're sorting out his home one binbag at a time and it's arduous and the building is falling down around us but we have to keep going because what else?

There's an urgency and we don't have time to be lazy, we have to crack on with this. Organisations can't rely on an A4 sheet of questions for feedback. Feedback is paramount but needs to be addressed in a sensitive and effective way. There is a big case of big dog/little dog, marginalised artists who are disenfranchised or feel small, find it difficult to address this directly to those who need to hear it. As marginalised artists we need to stop swilling in a pool of the unhelpful form of gratitude, and stop bowing down on our back legs like a chihuahua, and we need to tell the big dog organisations that the next time someone like us comes along, please treat them as people who just had different experiences, we don't need pity or kid gloves, just an open mind, someone who is happy to ask questions and be genuinely interested in our experiences and not in a tokenistic "wow aren't you exotic" way but in a ordinary human way.

It gets awkward, like we aren't meant to point out that someone is black or using a wheelchair, like the respectful thing to do is to pretend that everyone is a white, non-disabled, straight, middle class, person. It's the same politeness rule that means you don't say that someone has one leg or a wig or has just given you a drink in the wrong glass. It looks like it comes from a good place but it creates all sorts of problems. It actually comes from this place where it is shameful if you divert in any way from the default (white, cis, straight, etc) person. This default person shaves their legs, buys a new couch at Christmas in case the neighbours see their raggedy-ann threadbare couch that they actually love, this person goes on holiday to impressive places and has their photo taken jumping up in the air on a beach, they are wrinkle-free and smell like jojoba oil, they drive a fancy car, they bleach their sink a lot and eat eight a day, and are always hydrated.

They sound like a nightmare to me, but that's because they don't exist, no one can be that 'perfect', that's why people keep on trying, they keep buying the stuff and feeling ashamed when they can't. I'm obviously going to say next that it's created by capitalism, and then I think you think I'm going to jump on top of a police van waving some fire around. I'm not. Money is idolised because it is sometimes incredibly useful, it can buy you a lot of freedom, but we as humans are crazy and so we make something god-like and forget that other things are more important. Shame is a useful marketing tool.

Where we are heading in the theatre industry, I hope and I push for this, is that we start to help each other to recognise and shrug off all of this. We calm down and stop trying to be so polite in an unuseful way. We dismantle the bits us that were created by this 'default person' dream, and we think about what we are really interested in and what is really important — people, the environment, ensuring that we have a future and that we DO NOT LEAVE ANYONE BEHIND.

We need to really listen to artists who have been there. We will ask questions of new artists that are not due to politeness but because we are genuinely interested in other cultures and ways of living — I know people are, because they spend loads of money on going travelling — we absolutely don't tilt our heads to one side and use a singsong lilt and a high-pitched patronising tone when we speak to marginalised artists. We need to get rid of the 'awwwwwww factor' when it comes to people we think of as being lesser able than us. We need to realise that everyone is equal and that includes not just race, sexuality, gender, class, ethnicity, but also how long the person has been involved in the industry. We need a atmosphere that is warmly forthright and doesn't beat around the bush.

Once we know how to support people, we can do that. Once we know how other people handle situations, we can go further, we can start to adapt the way the industry does things, change networking and make it more effective and less awkward and frustrating by people by bringing in dinner ladies with dinner lady attitudes to deliver compassion — kick people up the bum when they are being highfalutin, introduce reticent people to who they need to talk to. Or bring the crip-time idea from the disability arts community into offices, i.e. the understanding that people have things they have to prioritise over that working day, that everyone wants to and will get the work done, but that you have to flexible and trust people to work as hard as they have to.

The stage I want us to head for is using our understanding of marginalised artists' lives to make the industry a more effective and comfortable place for everybody.

Diversity initiatives don't always help that, and they especially appear to be vague about including class — why do you think that is?

Say we join Weight Watchers and want someone to go with but we daren't ask any of our friends because it's like calling them fat. That makes sense to us because we think of fat as a bad thing. Something we should try to stop being, and if we try hard enough we will succeed to stop being fat. Any failure is nothing to do with the make-up of society, it's just another symptom of the default person stuff I was talking about, that and other systems of power.

Basically, calling someone 'working class' is a slur that obviously I don't believe in. I also think fat is extraordinarily overly vilified. I don't believe that 'everyone is beautiful', unless we mean that humans are so intricate and weird that they are beautiful — like Angela Chase in *My So-Called Life [USA TV teen drama series]* — I mean that physically, most of the time, being attractive is irrelevant, I preach body irrelevance not body positivity. That's another story for another day though.

Things associated with being working class is being unsophisticated, lazy, stupid, untravelled, unattractive, unprofessional, a school bully. People respond to the idea presented in LGBTQ politics that you are born gay, you are born trans, this helps people be more empathic, if someone can't 'help' what they are then we have to at least accept that they *are* this thing, right? But with being working class, people believe we just need to try harder to be middle class. We can change this, we weren't born like this.

Not only is the game rigged in that sense but let's entertain the idea that being working class is not a bad thing, and we, as working class people, often do not necessarily want to be middle class, in fact wanting to be middle class can often be fueled by internal classism. We can want to have enough money that we are not in poverty, we can want a job that isn't classed as a working class job, we can want to go on a fancy holiday, we can eat a bit of hummus, but these are things in isolation. To lose your accent and deny your background is something we do to be accepted by people who should just accept us as we are, it is something we do because we feel shame for who we were, it something we do because we have been told too many times that middle class is better than working class.

This is why initiatives shy away from it, either from abhorrent classism, but often from an embarrassment over terms, what term to use that doesn't insult? It's these areas — those where someone sees the group as lesser, where we get euphemism-crazy. I get it a lot over having one leg, I'm asked, "I'm so sorry to ask a personal question but when did you, ahem, lose your leg?" every time I'm in public. People call my stump (great, forthright, to-the-point, down to earth word) a residual limb, a 'small leg', or (bluergh) a leglet! I think in words that are to the point and that do not encompass the idea that the group is lesser or imply unuseful stereotypes. People like saying that the words we use don't matter and that there are more important things we can do to make life better. You can do both. One doesn't exclude the other.

People make this mistake often — "How can you be campaigning for period awareness in this country when there are still women experiencing FGM in other countries?" — because one doesn't exclude the other. There are plenty of people, if everyone campaigns for the thing that really pisses them off in whatever way is authentic to them — not everyone can or wants to march, campaigning doesn't have to be a slog, do something you love — then we're getting somewhere.

Theatre initiatives get stuck on 'socio-economically disadvantaged', which only mentions money. There's more to class than money. When society doesn't value you, it's hard to value yourself and society. We have to be clever and sensitive with our words, we need them to make society better for people it isn't working for, rather than just accurate. I favour 'working class', but it has its problems too. For instance, when I would do earlier versions of the show I'm touring at the moment, there would be a row of people afterwards who I thought wanted to compliment me — ha! But they needed to explain to me that they were middle class but their dad was a plumber or their family lost most of their money or they had cared for their disabled father etc.

What was happening was that I hadn't addressed the problem of how incredibly overly binary the terms middle and working class are, they in no way capture the nuance and complexity of human experience. It felt to people like I was dismissing the suffering they had experienced. I eventually worked in a whole comedy bit about how I know middle class people have problems too. There was also the problem that calling someone middle class can sound like you are dismissing how much they have tried in life — that they have been handed it on a plate rather than tried and worked really hard.

Binary terms don't work either. They don't work for gender, white and black doesn't capture ethnicity and race, when we group bisexuals into two groups — gay or straight — we deny people's sexuality. Binaries are how we think when we are young and naive, as we get older we know life is much more than that.

So working class is a dodgy term, but if we legitimise it then we can make a lot of people feel like they are important, that their suffering and trying is important, if we class it as a marginalised group, which it absolutely is, then we allow thousands of people to breath out and let some of our anger subside, it is not an apology, but it does acknowledge that being working class is hard.

*

15
John-David Henshaw

'You want to tell people how things can be, not how things *will* be'

John-David Henshaw is a director, writer & artistic director of Edinburgh/Brighton fringe venue Sweet Venues. Based in Dundee, he was born in Glasgow & raised in Stirling, all in Scotland.
● *sweetvenues.com*

Do you see yourself as a Scottish theatremaker?

Yes I do. I've been making theatre in Scotland since my first plays went up.

So that identity comes from the simple fact that you're creating in Scotland or is there a sense of fulfilling a need?

My concept of being a *Scottish* creative has probably grown alongside being a creative — it was creative first. The idea of nation is a bit of a complicated thing in and of itself, isn't it? And I'm not entirely sure at times how positive or negative that can be. But there's certainly a sense of space that's linked to where you come from, and that starts feeding what you do. At the end of the day when you are a creative, there's no way your geography doesn't affect you. It could be the geography that you've grown up in or the geography that you choose to go to. But the culture and society, the landscape and countryside that you're in, that's all going to affect how you think and the work you make.

So in which landscape did you start off creatively?

Dundee. Which is also where I live now.

Why didn't you make the move to somewhere like Glasgow or London?

I can think a lot of reasons not to go to London in particular and do what people do there. But the first answer is the simplest one, which is I was at university in Dundee, and it's here I first began properly engaging with theatre. Whilst my university didn't do drama as a degree, there was the sort of amateur slash semi-professional university theatre society, which I ended up becoming president of and running for four and a half years.

Interestingly, I'd been approached to join the society as a writer. But it's a theatre company, so you act, you do backstage, you do a bit of everything, you start learning. And there I learned a lot about where I wanted to be in theatre. From doing some acting, for example, I realised that there are people who are better at it than I am. Much as I did enjoy it, I didn't enjoy it anywhere near as much as I enjoyed directing and the creating, the tech side of things, designing light, building sets.

That's the environment of 'learn something then learn everything', which I found encouraging and nurturing because it was always challenging. I ended up in the tradition of writing/directing but also with my sleeves also rolled up, building a set, power tools in hand, designing it all. But remember this was still uni, and so there came the moment where you have to go, "Is this what I want to do with my life or is it just a very lovely hobby?" The end of the end of the beginning of my story was that I ended up quitting my PhD (in 2006/7] and going into theatreland forever.

I set up my own production company, and I was very lucky because I could do that with the folk that I'd worked with at uni — we're still together, we still make shows together all these years later. We had that unique moment where the right people are there at the right time. It was luck. And I think theatre does involve a lot of luck — and luck has different flavours.

I suppose the challenge with theatre is that it's meant to be the place for ideas and to bring your vision to other people — whether it's purely entertainment or something deeper. But you can't force it, can you?

No. That's where it falls apart is when you force it. Theatre can't be an engineered process.

But then that becomes a problem when you're faced with channelling issues through your work as a theatremaker. Especially when faced with all the constraints that come out of the fact that you can't control the money.

That's a huge factor, sadly. At the end of the day, you have to be able to at the very least *afford* to make the work. Whether you can afford to eat or not afterwards is your own choice — although it shouldn't be! But there is ultimately a fundamental cost in materials, renting a space, paying people that need to be paid even if you yourself are doing it for free.

What was it that you set up in Dundee that wasn't already there?

I went to Dundee thinking I would do my degree and then move on. And then I realised that it was a place that had a fundamental sense of community and society based on people caring about each other. Small 's' socialism, and all that, It has a very creative heart. And yes Dundee Rep is based there, as well as Scottish Dance Theatre, so there is theatre there, however I wouldn't say that it's got a thick vein of theatre. That sounds ironic because obviously you've got some amazing work that is generated from there, and fantastic community theatre, but it's not as if there's tons of little fringe venues, and it's in that scale where I've always tried to work.

And the right people were there. I guess that's it, it comes back to community. I was able to find my tribe, make that decision to — and it is a decision — to put down those life roots as well as creative roots in a place and find that people want you to succeed, which is an amazing attitude. Certainly Dundee faced an awful lot of economic and social difficulties, especially in the 1970s and 80s, and that has created a place that wants people to win. However big or small, they want people to do well and they want to turn around to you and go, "Well done. How can I help you do that? Let's do this together." It doesn't always work, but I think there's a spirit of trying and a spirit of support that is just unbreakable and it's a great city to be part of. Not to sound like I'm doing a tourist board advert, but it is.

However, the road to making theatre there is not always easy, which is why I make a lot of theatre in Brighton rather than in Dundee. The buildings want their money. We're back to money. The funding structures are complicated and the dialectics of the cultural direction of Dundee are very much in design, new sciences and new media. Theatre can struggle to fit into that. But Dundee gave me the opportunity to be *somewhere*, a place where the cost of living was maintainable enough that you could make work.

And I'll bang on about it again: there was a positive attitude to help you make that work. People are willing to give up time, energy, *advice* — never underestimate the power of someone who's just willing to sit there and listen over a cup of tea. And from there it gave us the opportunity to work locally — and you're in striking distance of Edinburgh, which makes the Edinburgh fringe very easy — *[chuckles]* in relative terms of course, again those financial barriers. We have accessibility in terms of 'you're allowed to be here', as long as you can afford it. That barrier we've solved thanks to the can-do attitude of the people around us. Things like, "We can all put our hands in our pockets for the rent for a space." We'd all flip the bits together and share the risk. I'd love to say share the profit, but profit doesn't always happen, does it? But if it does, you do.

So the Scottish scene for me was work in Dundee, creating work in Dundee, putting on productions in places like Dundee Botanic Gardens, doing the Edinburgh Festival Fringe. I was also creating work, teaching drama, and writing up in Inverness. So Scotland was very much the focus.

So here's a question I'm not actually sure what the answer is, but how do you respond to that in what you programme? Without that wider theatre ecosystem, is the idea to throw out a wider net, like making sure to include at least one panto and one Kafka per season?

From a programming perspective rather than from that of creating work, when I started out I had all these big grown-up ideas about looking for things which Make Money. But I quickly found out that the shows you think are going to be commercial successes often aren't. Sometimes that can be utterly absurd because you go, "Well, we did all the right things, everything's in place, and yet no one wants to see it." But how do you break that to the person who's created the work? It's not that their work was bad and you know they've done their homework because they've laid out the thing in front of you and it definitely looked like a business plan. But it's still creative work, so they didn't sit there and go, "I have created a thing to make money." No, they've sat there and said, "I've created a thing and I think it will work. I also think it will be good business." So I gave up on 'business' and my programming approach is always heart and gut. And that's come from where I am, it's come from the people around me.

Basically people need a chance to make the work. What it sometimes means is that I have worked with shows in the past that needed improvement, but the creatives making it were just great. They were passionate and maybe this wasn't the project that was going to be the winner. But the next one probably will be, and if they never got the chance to do it, they were never going to make the second piece of work. So someone has to turn around and say yes, because *you* are worth the risk. You are worth that investment of time and energy.

So you go with your gut. You know what is 'failure' and realise it is rarely actually failure so long as you learn from it. Rather than just looking at the money, I would much rather have a show that doesn't make its financials but know that we had a positive relationship, that we nailed the things creatively, that the people involved leave that fringe experience — since that's typically what I'm talking about — with a better knowledge of their work themselves. That has to be the fundamental baseline of what we're doing.

And all driven by that gut feeling of course.

Yes. Sometimes you just have to accept you're in a Philip Marlowe novel and you go with it.

You used to have an actual physical venue in Dundee and now don't, which I suppose sums up theatre being that cycle of you set something up and then it ends and then you set something up again . . .

Sometimes that's it. Hopefully we're about to start a new chapter of that life in a different space, but it's that case of you trying to find somewhere where you can make a different sort of deal when you don't have a bag of money. There's not always deep pockets, but you're trying to create something that will then become sustainable, so you're looking for people who are either able to offer a peppercorn rent or are able to meet us in the middle on a bar share or something like that. Basically you're trying to find that 'I'll scratch your back if you scratch mine' meeting point. When we had the previous permanent venue, we had found our deal like that, which sadly then didn't work out because, well . . . not everyone holds up their end of the bargain. You have to roll with that though, don't you?

So we were always on a bit of a time limit with the space, but in the time when we had it, if we could make it work and create a sustainable model, well then there'd be income that we could then use to pay the rent on the space. The fact that it didn't work out is a typical story of the arts today. The folk that I've worked with all these years, all the actors and people who work backstage, all came together and started scrubbing, painting out this old bar-like club space, converted the dance floor area into the stage area. I rewired it, we put up new walls up in bathrooms and replumbed it. We began doing teas and coffees out of the old bar, that sort of thing, working towards eventually being able to open the bar properly for when we were doing shows. It was very hands on and very Challenge Anneka-type thing *[BBC reality game show]*. But no Anneka Rice. If only she turned up to help!

So that's what we did, and it was an incredibly positive experience. We came together as an artistic community and the folk in Dundee were really interested in what we were setting up. The good thing was it proved the space was wanted, that there was room in the city for spaces catering for fringe theatre with a small 'f' — seatings of 50, shows that run an hour, that don't have a wine break. And that was a big deal for Dundee.

We opened our doors with the cry of "the space exists, everybody let's use it!" to having international productions, workshops, rehearsals, debuts of work that then have gone on to tour internationally, all within the space of six weeks. The international side comes from having worked hard in fringe and having connections and the confidence to go, "Look this exists, do you want to try it?" But that doesn't create things like rehearsal spaces and people running classes. Those come locally, which they did. So it really did prove that the space was feasible. And then sadly it went away, but that's what happens with landlords sometimes isn't it? *[laughs]* One can't dictate their needs.

But it was an exciting period that we want to achieve again. I've very much done that down in Brighton, but I obviously want to recreate it in Dundee since that's where I'm from. You always want to be able to represent yourself where you come from, don't you? That's important to us, at that primal level. It also speaks about the ethos that we've always tried to make art in, that is a collaborative thing. It's not existing in a vacuum. You're not on your own. If you're doing it on your own and nobody else is talking to you, then probably something's gone a little bit wrong. So that's how we built a space out of nothing, and then it went back to nothing. Ironically enough, it ended up being my accountant's office. So I would sit doing spreadsheets with my accountant in what used to be our stage space.

What do you do after setting something up and then having it snatched away like that? Can you take that experience and make it a positive one or is it something that just rankles and you need to reset your vision?

It makes you wary. But I think you have to as quickly as possible put that behind you. You want to work from a position of trust all the time, but sometimes you need to work from a position of paperwork. It does rankle, but you have to move on. Otherwise you're not going to make anything new. You'll just sit there and fester and I just don't see the point. Take the good anecdotes from it, find the positives. Of course, if you've got a particularly good horror story that you want to share with someone, well that's okay too — if your life lesson helps provide a life lesson for someone else. So we moved on — I do stuff in Brighton while still looking for that space in Dundee. I suppose what you learn is to try and keep making it better than it was the last time.

At the same time you took over running Sweet Venues at the Edinburgh Festival Fringe — at the last one you were up to 80 shows. For those who don't have experience of Edinburgh, we need to explain that for the month of shows in August, a venue puts in a good year's work to make it work. But you can do that because you're tied to the reality of a venue that is bricks and mortar. And you know that you're going to also get kicked out at the end of the month, part of the cycle which sets up an alternative universe to the experience of the Dundee venue.

Yes, and my fringe experience, which has fed heavily into having a bricks and mortar venue, probably made it easier to get over the rankle. In fact my arts mentality has always been a little impermanent. As you've said, our work is typically ephemeral and weirdly for me so are the buildings. All very liminal spaces. At Edinburgh, for example, the spaces exist all the time, but they're not always theatres. Which seems a bit mad.

The impermanence of the fringe, whatever that term ends up meaning year to year, sets you up to be fairly robust. You bounce back from the things that kick you down relatively quickly in comparison to if you're sitting there going, "Ah, but this was solid and it was forever." It's going back to doing a bit of everything in a way. I have designed and built and painted gorgeous sets, and then the show finishes and you put it all in the bin or recycle it into the next set, and people are like, "Oh, that must be heartbreaking." Well the first time is probably harder than the second time, and then by the fifth, it's just how it is — none of these things are forever and they've done everything they were supposed to do and they were wonderful and audiences were entertained and it's done its job. It's the same way that I don't expect every actor that's been in a show to spend every week afterwards reciting their lines randomly. Of course that would be weird. So why would I have a storage unit with every set I ever built sitting in the back of it? That'd be weird too. And there's a bit of that attitude that you've got to adapt to where you make your art, because not all spaces are permanent. And that's okay.

That explains why you could make the move to setting up Sweet Venues in Brighton as well as Edinburgh. But why Brighton? From the point of view of London, which is just up the road, it's traditionally been a hard sell.

It's not a hard sell.

Okay. So tell us about that. Your objectivity obviously won't be London-centric.

Why Brighton? I was invited. Yeah. People asked me to come down and be part of it. There's that community thing again, people inviting people to be part of something. Brighton Fringe is a vibrant fringe and that's where I started my relationship with Brighton. The people I was working with were interesting and positive. Brighton Fringe felt like an opportunity for artists to gain impact for their work. Things like reviews — access to actually sit and have a cup of tea with an editor from reviewing press is a huge deal that you don't get in Edinburgh at all. So it felt like less is more, it was smaller, the access was better. There were creative opportunities of progressing work, tutoring, finding your feet, getting on with it.

Yes there's problems, there's flaws. It's getting better, but there are probably still a few too many shows at Brighton Fringe that are work in progress and not polished-up objects. Not that any show's ever finished, but there's a few shows that use Brighton in a way where they're going, "Oh, it'll be okay, and then I'll use that as a step to the next show." I think they forget that the reviewers that are in Brighton are the same professional reviewers in Edinburgh and they aren't informing those reviewers by putting 'work in progress' on that work. They'll review you like you're ready product, that the show is all good to go. I think some people do themselves harm by accident because they don't take it seriously enough. But that's by the by, because people make mistakes of all different kinds. In fact expectation management at Sweet Venues is one of our biggest jobs as a venue. You want to tell people how things *can* be, not how things *will* be, and to try and make sure that you've given them as much opportunity and information to get out there and make the best happen.

But why am I also here in Brighton making and presenting work all year round? The opportunity was there and the right people were to make work with — again, positive attitudes to community forming an artistic community. The creativity down there is pretty high. It's like-minded people; we're all speaking the same language, just in different accents. I'd much rather be somewhere that is eager to make work than not, which sums up both Dundee and Brighton for me. It does mean that the geography is a bit crazy and it does stretch you sometimes and it means you have to make choices between projects and that's hard. But I think I'd rather probably be in a position where I'm having to make hard choices than not make any choices at all.

You don't hear people quite describe London in the same way.

I think the problem is probably that everybody is there. Not that everybody actually *is* there, but everybody tells you that *you* should be there.

That fear of missing out thing.

Yes, and it's also very expensive. I know we're back to money, but it's a fact. London is a very expensive place to try and exist *and* make work. That's a very complicated thing. People go there to follow their creative dream because "It's London! All of it will happen!" and instead they find themselves working not just nine to five, but nine to everything — just to pay for a flat to make sure they're in the right space to be able to make their work. And then they find it hard to make that work. They find themselves caught in this rat race, which may seem a cliched term to use, but it's true. Then three years pass, they've not made the work they should be doing, they're out of their practice, and they've become locked into that cycle. How do you get back out of that?

I do think London can be great for people. There are people like stage technicians and stage managers who have trained and worked with me and they've gone on to amazing careers in London. So I'm not saying London's terrible, that's not it. It's hard and it's its own thing and you've got to be able to go into that with your eyes wide open. I just don't think it's the be-all-and-end-all which some people would paint it as — "Oh you haven't made it unless you're in London" or "The only way you're going to make it is in London." I would much rather make work in those other places that aren't the place that I'm being told I need to be.

Well, certainly your audiences will be different.

Yes, and that's true of audiences everywhere. Those audiences in other places that are not London deserve to have work. They also deserve work that has a different voice from all those which are London-centric. This isn't me saying for a moment that everything is one note out of London, but it is coming from one cultural centre. Inevitably with any work there's something in the DNA, there will be an experience that has cut into that show somewhere along the line that's come from that place. That's not a bad thing, not at all. But isn't it interesting to put a show in your eyes that's got a different DNA, that's carrying that different flavour, that different colour, and is coming from a different life experience?

Young people need to able to access the arts, for example. You can't tell every 17 year old who's sitting there thinking, "I wonder what it's like to write a play/direct a play/be in a play?" that they need to be in London to do that. That those are the only types of play there is. You want things to happen grassroots that speak to everybody, and the only way you're going to get that wide voice is to support and create outwith the areas you're told to be in. I'm not saying anything I think is revolutionary or groundbreaking. There's plenty of us that are creating who know that we are happy and proud to be creating in the place we've been born or the place we've settled or because we travel round. We are happy to be creating out of the environment that we find ourselves in.

It's imperative that work is being generated everywhere. It's got to be holistic by including London, meaning that there is a true to and fro of ideas. So I'm happy to be part of that other voice, just as I'm happy to eat brilliant work that comes out of London up with a spoon like it's the best ice cream because I want to see shows wherever they've come from. I just don't want to necessarily create them everywhere.

In all of this, how do you know that your own voice is actually hitting the audiences as it should be? Or finding the space to make your own work? It must be particularly difficult in view of your calendar across the year and the length of the country. This is a bit more than your traditional actor-manager would be doing.

It's nearly impossible. I'm not going to pretend. It's been so busy that it has meant putting a hold on my creative projects, my personal journey on that road. I've made some time this year to start that again — but only because I made a deliberate decision to do that. I feel that's 'selfish', but that's probably my own nagging sense of guilt from spending the last few years facilitating other people's dreams and their opportunities. But in any case, you have to put that to one side because that's you trying to shake the habitual. And am I allowed to go and make some work? Of course I am, because nobody would wish me not to.

I suppose I've always kept my hand in and always made sure I had work coming out of my company every year in any case. But I've felt there's been a tendency towards work we've done before and not necessarily creating massive amounts of new material, so it's good to be making again. It does make the process slower because I still have other areas to look after which are a priority in terms of responsibility. There are people you work with a lot and you want to look after them, you want to be there to make all of that work properly for them, which is exactly why there can be the tendency to put your own project on the backburner. You need to make a space, create a gap in that schedule to go "right, breathe, make some work". Because it's important, you want to be connected to the wheres and whys that you started doing what you do — it's a little bit of a journey back to finding that journey forward, if that makes sense.

Sure. So any tips on making that sort of creative space within the admin, the managing and the travelling?

What I've found is to just try and be kind to yourself. That's actually the only advice I've got. You're not always going to get it right. You're going to make mistakes along the way because you always have, and you can magnify those mistakes in your head. I think it's very easy for us to burden our brains with everything we should have done or could have done a bit better. For me, the thing is, if you go, "oh right, that didn't work properly, I got my timings wrong, I don't want to do it again", well take the lesson from it, learn it, move on. But move on, move forwards, use it properly — as energy not as a barrier. That's not a reason to stop trying to make the work, it's a reason to go, okay, I need to think about how that worked for me. Change that behaviour. Find a new road.

So what you're saying is that you can productively multi-task — that creating, producing and managing are not incompatible.

No, they're not at all incompatible.

I suppose we know that, but we need to hear it from someone who lives it.

They are absolutely compatible. You may have some late nights, you may have some stress, you may find yourself in a place where you go, gosh, I've not spoken to that person for four months who I used to see regularly, because you know, you're losing your social time because you decided to make work again. Some of the sacrifices you're willing to make, some of them you aren't, but the only way you find that red line is by crossing it. It's all completely compatible as long as you are genuinely being present and taking those lessons.

By virtue of what you do, you'll have an indepth overview that's constantly updating of where small to medium work lies on a national scale at any given point, and you'll probably agree that in many respects that over the past decade UK theatre, like the nation, has lost a lot of its direction. Well that's speaking overall, because Scottish theatre is maintaining if not its quality then at least its identity. It's not necessarily the speech or issues, but the simple fact of Scotland being a different ecosystem system as you've outlined which has carried on regardless, whereas the rest of the country has fallen by the wayside to a degree. Of course every year we see great theatremakers emerge nationally, but so much of the work that's being made isn't connecting, certainly in England — where it's significant that Arts Council England's latest last gasp is to focus on funding theatre that has relevance. Is Scottish theatre relevant nowadays to people in Scotland as opposed to what you've witnessed elsewhere in the UK? Or is discussing relevance a pointless exercise because theatre is always a different animal for different communities?

That's a really tough question because I think there's also a language of scale that cuts across everything. The theatre that I specialise in is typically looking to create audience sizes of 50 on average at most. So my Scotland and Brighton experiences are probably relatively similar in the sense that the people who want to meet and challenge and consume that work are there to meet, challenge and consume. They want it, they're excited for it. So they are switched on. They're also being drawn in by a different level of price of ticket — obviously you are hitting a different audience to the one that a West End show is going to hit. There's absolutely a creative and audience difference that happens when you shift those ticket prices around, regardless of geography.

Now what the final statement is on that and the relevance of the work is, that's a really complicated thing. But certainly on the scale I work at, where you're seeing ticket prices averaging around 10 quid, there's a good chance that people you're pulling in are potentially not as financially fluid as others. What you're giving them is an opportunity to access work — and, importantly, you also have the opportunity to put on work that isn't risking all the money that you've got. That's in relative terms of course, but you're not laying on a multimillion pound show. There's a directness and a *life* in this sort of theatre that is different. It's not any less well-crafted, it's not any less professional, and it can say different things in a different way.

I struggle to say that theatre is a strictly regional thing. The Scottish scene is the Scottish scene. The Brighton scene is the Brighton scene, which makes it sound like Brighton is the equivalent of a country, which isn't the case. The Edinburgh scene is different to the Glasgow scene, as you rightly said, so does being in Scotland make them more relevant? Are they more connected than elsewhere? I think that's a nigh impossible statement without me spending time watching work happening in Hull, watching work happening in Liverpool, watching work here, there and everywhere, being able to get a real gauge, temperature of a community and how engaged with theatre they are.

There are so many factors that it's very difficult to see the effect of one simple idea of 'relevance'. I guess relevance is contextual. It's quite easy to talk about a Scottish scene, but that Scottish scene is built up out of different communities, different cities, different towns. The Highlands & Islands experience is very, very different to that of Central Region. There's a perception that lots of things go to Central that don't happen up in Highlands & Islands, in much the same way that people might say, "Oh, everything ends up in London and not in the North."

We could argue whether that's true or not — it's probably is on some levels, while on others the grass is always greener. That sort of stance means you risk missing the unique advantages that you get from where you are. Tribal, contextual, these are the key bits, aren't they? And we can only contextualise ourselves within ourselves.

There is definitely passion and a desire for a Scottish identity to be there in theatre, and the way that sort of process stretches out is in many ways tribal. But how that tribe reaches out is through friends, family, friends of friends — that's obviously where your first audiences begin. If there's a passion around a piece of new work it's because the people around it are somehow connected to it and then you hope that ripples out because the work's got quality. That's a different, positive form of tribalism.

*

16
Anna Herrmann
'You really do get a sense of theatre being transformative'

Anna Herrmann is joint artistic director of Clean Break, a women's theatre company working with women in the criminal justice system. She is based in North London, which is where she was born & raised.
* *cleanbreak.org.uk*

Clean Break would seem to be a very natural home for you.

My commitment to social justice began as a young person, not through my own lived experience of inequality (although neither of my parents were born in the UK so I did have a sense of outsider-ness when growing up) but through an awareness and profound desire to live in an equal and fair society and a recognition that this wasn't happening around me. From this emerging politicisation spurred a real commitment and drive to make change happen through theatre and the arts.

And that's been the through line of my career ever since I began. I working initially with homeless young people for a project called Leap Theatre Workshop, part of the Leaveners, a Quaker based arts charity, and then I worked for four years around race and identity in Greenwich — this was after Stephen Lawrence's murder which was one of three racist murders in Greenwich in the 1990s.

Greenwich Council was trying to shift culture and understanding in the borough and in a partnership with Charlton Athletic *[football club in South East London]* they created an arts and sports initiative to tackle racism in the borough. We approached it looking at identity. There were a lot of white working class young people in the borough that we needed to reach alongside young black people as part of building community cohesion.

So I began with a particular lens around young people and housing inequality and then around race and diversity, completing my postgraduate studies to inform the practice that I was doing. And then I moved here to Clean Break in 2002. And again, that came out of a strong sense of recognition around women's inequality, and the interlinked issues of multiple disadvantage, and a desire to be part of a women-only space. I hadn't had that experience before, but I felt committed to the principle of why it was important and what I could contribute to it.

What's significant from the performing arts side of things is that you came sideways into it, since that wasn't the focus of what you'd been doing before.

I actually did train in theatre, but my interest in it was always as a transformative tool, as something that could be powerful to create personal and societal change. I did a degree in Birmingham University in Drama and Theatre Studies and went straight to working with social and development issues and as an actor/workshop leader in theatre-in-education.

So it was a collaborative approach that you sought in your practice as soon as you could?

It was always about that — about creating spaces that could be transformative — but the passion for theatre was definitely there. There have been moments in my career when I've asked myself if I would be better placed working for an NGO, contributing on a more practical level. But I've always come back to a feeling that on a personal level I need theatre in my life. Collaborating in a creative process is one of the spaces where I feel most able and alive, finding meaning when people are creating and imagining together. So at periodic intervals I would think "the world's too terrible, I've got to do something more urgent", and then I'd reflect, no I can't leave theatre behind, it has to be part of my purpose as well.

So theatre makes a difference.

Absolutely. And you see it when you're in an organisation over a long period of time. There are Clean Break Members who no longer attend here, but who we remain in touch with, who I have had relationships with for 18 years because when I started they were students here on our former education programme. We've maintained a commitment to these connections, we've continued the relationships with Members, and been privileged to really see individuals' journeys. *[Clean Break's Members Programme is available to women aged 17 and above who have lived experience of the criminal justice system or are at risk of offending due to drug alcohol or mental health issues. It offers Members a foundation of learning and skills in theatre performance, creativity and wellbeing, and opportunities to engage in professional, public facing performance projects.]*

I also believe you can see the *potential* for change in a short space of time. We go into prisons, delivering over three days — and you already see people's creativity expand and where that lives for them in that moment, when they're feeling really proud and valued. I question how sustainable that is, but at Clean Break through the relationship with Members over many years you really do get a sense of theatre being transformative because you witness the change in their lives. You know, they become more skilled, complete degrees, they become empowered as women. It's not necessarily that they all have a career in the theatre industry, but they make their own progress and it's just as meaningful.

It's a measurable step to empowerment.

Yes. But it's not linear, and that's always what makes it so hard to measure. People's lives aren't linear — if people relapse, they can always return to Clean Break. We're there, alongside them and that's long term, and that does really feel transformative.

When you first came to Clean Break it was an organisation that had already been through several transitions. In good ways, meeting challenges. So almost two decades, even if it sounds artificial time period, must give you quite a perspective not only on how things have changed with the people you work with but also the way Clean Break has adapted and evolved and expanded. But not in a capitalistic sort of way, of course.

No, although finding diverse ways to generate income is on the top of all of our agendas! 2019 was particularly special for us as we turned 40 and spent the year celebrating our birthday. We created a heritage project to look back over our history, connect with the founders and delve into the story of the company from a multitude of perspectives. Interestingly, the narrative does fall quite neatly into decades. The first ten years of the company was about self-organisation: it was about women ex-prisoners making work, a self-organised company claiming space and being part of the political theatre movement, the women's movement and changing the shape of criminal justice and its perception of women.

And then the next decade after the founders moved on, saw us commissioning professional playwrights — the first was Bryony Lavery, in 1989. These were predominantly women without experience of the criminal justice system immersing themselves in the lives of women with experience and writing a play that we then produced.

And then the education programme burgeoned alongside the artistic work to make Clean Break a safe space where women could really upskill themselves, to receive support and gain the skills and confidence to move forward positively with their lives. When I joined in 2002, the company had renovated an old piano factory into a permanent home and been delivering education courses there for a number of years. There were a lot of strong partnerships with education providers (e.g. City & Islington College) and criminal justice charities too, including Women in Prison and CAST *[Creative & Supportive Trust]*. There was European money, and we got money from the Ministry of Justice and trusts and foundations to offer training for women on probation. I never thought at the time that our resources were that plentiful, our ambition always seemed greater than the resources we had. But when I look back on that period, up until 2009 when there was the financial crash and then austerity stepped in, it seems that we were very well funded because we could deliver this substantial programme.

The last decade has certainly not felt like that. We've seen resources cut, partner organisations fold that we're working with, support agencies for women shrinking, needs growing, foodbanks becoming much more prevalent, you know, all those things. The impact of austerity on women's lives and on poor women's lives has been horrendous. At the same time as we stopped receiving funding from Camden Council, there was no longer any European Social Funding *[ESF]* and other statutory funding also started shrinking. So we had to rethink what was unique about us, what was the thing that only we could do, because we didn't have the resources that we did a decade ago to deliver across these different areas.

Lack of resources was one of the drivers to our current restructuring and model, but certainly not the only one. It was also a recognition of the need to unknot a persistent theme that had niggled for decades, that of the lack of artistic involvement of our Members in our produced work. This became the right moment to foreground our Members — to ensure that the women at the heart of the company were being valued as theatre makers, not only students or learners but as women who are actively part of leading the work. So we reframed ourselves as a theatre company that places participation at the centre and always makes work with our Memberships' involvement.

That's quite radical, but on the other hand it does create a single direction that's not only true to your vision but also highlights the tools you have.

It does. Resources were limited, we had to change to survive, but we weren't just closing and cutting. We were making it into something that we felt was also stronger — placing our Members at the heart of the company and making sure that when we produce work, that if they are not the writer, then they're the cast, if they're not the cast then they're the creative team or all of the above. And that feels right. So that wasn't about just stripping back, it was about evolving.

Well into something that you actually always were.

And want to be again. It was aspirational and we feel like we're on a journey towards making ourselves truly a co-produced company — valuing both Members and artists equally for what they both bring to the story.

Having to find income is the existential problem today facing organisations like Clean Break which by their very nature need funding to do what they do because they step in to do what the government and authorities aren't doing. Is there a danger under those circumstances that in trying to retain funding or attract new funding that you're forced into altering the vision of your work or your wider practice to become tickbox-friendly? As we've seen from so many other organisations, that sort of decision starts to feed back on them and eventually they become those tickboxes. You lose your core identity — and if the funders suddenly remove those tickboxes, you're left with no identity at all. Has that been an issue?

You know what, it hasn't been, and that's because we have always had such a strong social mission as well as an artistic mission and had stable leadership *[with Lucy Perman at the helm for 21 years]*. But although we haven't had to go down that route, we have had to make sure that our decision making is not funding-led and remains mission aligned. The women that we work with have needs and there is a mission and strong values around how we are working with and for those needs. And that does help us stay focused, even though the hard thing now is how best to diversify our funding sources to respond to the changed economic landscape.

This has led us to expand how we work with corporates, including exploring what we can offer to the corporate sector. What aspect of our practice translates well to the business world and can we monetise it to generate unrestricted income? How do we retain our values whilst doing that? Where is the benefit? Where is the benefit for Members in that? It can't just be about income. If we're investing resources in it, it has to move our mission forward. It's a question of integrity too. That's at our core.

How does it work then theatrically? What should we be seeing across the year now with the changes in strategy?

We launched our new strategy in 2018, and interestingly leading up to 2019 when we were making these changes internally, we were also working with an artist, Stacey Gregg, who was on commission with us as a playwright to work in the traditional way that we used to work. Stacey came into prisons with us, led writing workshops on the education programme and undertook research to help develop the idea for her play. But she arrived at a decision that it didn't sit right with her to be writing this story when she was working with women who she felt could be the writers themselves.

The process she was going through was mirroring our own discussions as an organisation at the time. Because we were saying we've got to be braver about women telling their own stories, about them creating the work and us believing that our audiences will want to see this, based on our 40-year track history. There has also been a similar conversation going on in theatre which is very much about that — about representation, about whose voices are given space, about whose work we see, about whose stories are being told.

Stacey wanted to bring in another collaborator Deborah Pearson, who was more of a performance artist, to work with our Members and to co-create a piece. Their process of co-creation offered a tangible expression of our new plans, so we were proud to launch our 40th year with the play they had created. That was *Inside Bitch*, which was performed at the Royal Court Theatre *[Sloane Square, Central London]* with four of our Members onstage who had devised it with these two theatre artists.

And the two artists were happy?

I believe so — they were committed to a collaborative process and were able to achieve this with the work and we had a great response from audiences. It was also a brilliant spring board for us to 'announce' our new model, to be followed by *[BLANK]*, our autumn co-production for 2019 with Donmar Warehouse, *[originally a co-commission with the National Theatre]* which continued to push the boundaries of what a Clean Break play looks like and where you might see our work. So *[BLANK]* was on the Donmar Warehouse stage *[Covent Garden, Central London]* with a 14-strong cast. The playwright was Alice Birch and two of the cast out of the 12 adults were our Members. It wasn't a big number, it wasn't six, it wasn't 50 per cent, but it felt significant as part of our moving forward. What we're doing now is investing in our Members developing skills as playwrights, and at the same time we're commissioning women playwrights because we have a commitment to both introduce our Members to the industry and create opportunities for female theatre artists.

We're also looking at different ways of creating work, and bringing in theatre makers that we might not have worked with before, for example, we worked with Paula Varjack in a partnership project with Cardboard Citizens as part of our anniversary year. We are pushing the idea of form to find the right fit for autobiographical storytelling that enables Members to tell their stories in a way that doesn't require the same discipline as a traditional play, with the involvement of a playwright. It's a different approach where they can be freer and thrive in that form. So we're trialling different forms and hopefully what you will see on our stages is a much broader variety of work: a diversity of form and story. People used to know what a Clean Break play was like. And our canon of work is brilliant so it's not to judge what came before, but it did tend to be a two-hander/three-hander studio play told via a darkly traumatic naturalistic-rooted story. We can really play with that now, and *Inside Bitch* was a perfect example of how we can tell stories differently.

Is there a formula that you have for explaining how women in the criminal justice system are the core of your social mission?

Our plays are our main way of commenting, sharing and reflecting on women's lives. But we extend that for audiences with the post-show talks, events and workshops that we curate around the plays as well as via research/ learning and partnerships that we create with academics and universities. We are part of two big research projects happening currently to better understand our work within the context of the criminal justice system and the arts. In terms of the plays themselves, a good example of how we use our plays to advance our mission is *Not Pretty Like the Rainbow*, written by one of our Members, Daisy King. It specifically looks at short prison sentences and the impact of these sentences on women's lives. It was performed by our Members, who toured it to criminal justice conferences and to universities in February-March 2020.

The majority of women in the UK are in prison for nonviolent offences and they get sentences of less than six months which completely disrupts their lives. They lose their children, they lose their homes, they lose their employment — if they had it. And this is for nonviolent petty crimes. We're spending a huge amount of money as a society sending women to prison. We can use some of our plays, as with *Not Pretty Like the Rainbow* to comment on this, to highlight that this is what's happening. This isn't right. Let's do something about it. It's a call to action. Giving a writer a specific brief like that allows us to be more explicit about the system and how it impacts on women, asking people to think about alternatives — because our position as an organisation is about advocating alternatives to prison for women.

So if we're talking about what we believe as an organisation, it's that the majority of women should not be in prison. Their crimes are low-level, they're non-violent and they are caused largely out of poverty. Fifty per cent of women prisoners say that they committed a crime to support somebody else's drug use or because of poor relationships linked to coercion. Our position is that if you support women to attend independently run women's centres, offering gender specific support to manage their health, possible drug use, their relationships, to look after their children, then we will get better outcomes. We do try and embed this messaging in our communications in general, but occasionally it will be a very specific part of an artists' brief. Otherwise, it's just ephemeral, it's kind of *there, but it's not explicit.

That all explains exactly why you can be reactive because of the depth and continuity of what you've done as an organisation. In the UK we have so many things with an impact on national policy that owe their origins to one or two individuals who simply woke up one day and said we've got to do something. And so often it's for completely obvious issues that no one else is addressing. Clean Break's story is especially affirming because it came out of two women who were in the criminal justice system, so they really understood the wrongs that need to be righted. But on the other hand, it's 40 years on and a lot of things haven't changed. If you think about it, your visibility is as important as ever in order to remind everyone that there is so much that needs to be done.

It's true that in criminal justice in many ways things haven't changed — and things are worse and more entrenched; there's self-harm in prison, significant mental distress and there are tragic suicides. But when you look back at when the women who started Clean Break *[Jacqui Holborough & Jenny Hicks founded the company in 1979]*, they were initially in Durham prison, which is a maximum security prison, and they were in for minor offences, and completely misplaced in that environment. Their experience then was that the system did not recognise women's different needs. There was *nothing* gendered about the criminal justice system then.

Now it's 40 years later, and there are still examples of shocking treatment of women but everyone at least understands the importance of holistic, trauma-informed services. So that has shifted. But that's one of the most frustrating things as well; how long change takes to happen. 13 years ago

Baroness Corston [*Jean Corston was commissioned by the Home Office to conduct a report into vulnerable women in the UK criminal justice system, published in 2007*], recommended that we reduce incarceration, and establish a network of community-based women's centres, with a gendered approach. But we still have a Government that talks about building more prisons rather than investing in community resources. And that's because politics is always short term, isn't it? It's for the cycle of the next four years and no one is ever brave enough to commit to change that is longer term.

Race is another question which attracts a lot of talk but it's hard to see much commitment to meaningful investment in resources.

Race is such an important conversation in theatre (as elsewhere) as we're an industry which has for far too long been dominated by white (male) voices. And for Clean Break it's important as well because black people as a group are disproportionately over-represented in the criminal justice system. So racial discrimination is vital to consider and we're making a major shift to better represent culturally diverse voices and to produce work made by diverse artists. We have made a commitment that 50 per cent of our commissions will go to women of colour in order to ensure that the stories we tell don't ignore the lens of race and how it impacts on black women in the system.

We have always been aware of this, it's always been part of our story. But it is significant now that we're consciously and actively trying to shift the status quo in relation to colour, class and socioeconomic position. We've got a particular lens on women with a criminal record, but it's the intersectionality of it that is really significant.

How has the reaction to the reorganisation and recentring been from the Members who've come through Clean Break?

It has shifted. We undertook a carefully planned change process, where we engaged and consulted with our Members. We took quite a long time, with a lot of care because it was important that the change happened in partnership and through dialogue. There was quite a bit of hurt and loss from Members attending at the time — and again, we created space to listen and hold this. I think there's still a bit of disappointment remaining, which bubbles to the surface every now and then. But the company has always changed and evolved, this was not the first time. People still talk about how we used to run an Access to Higher Education course which we had to stop in 2011/2012 when tuition fees came in. We still have Members who say, "Why don't you run the Access course anymore?"

Consequently, for our membership and those who have a long-term connection with us, there is a sense of loss about the courses we no longer run. And equally we have to manage expectations because we did say, "We're changing, and there will be more opportunities for you." For those who have had these opportunities, there's a lot of goodwill and excitement but there are women who feel left out. Working out how to manage this is part of our new challenge. But we couldn't sustain the programme we had and grow and take risks as a theatre company. We had to narrow our focus to make the changes we believed were right.

The other obvious strength is the fact that you have your own purpose-built building. I've realised how it can become so many different things — one moment a safe space and secure, the next an open-doors venue for one and all.

The building provides us with a workspace. Absolutely. And it's also a home — it has been a very private space for much of our history. Audiences in general know about our work through the theatre they see in venues, but it's our Members and our referral and producing partners who know about what goes on here. It's been private for a reason to keep women safe, but now we want to make it more public, for people to come and experience us a little bit more. It's just finding the right way to do it.

So that is quite a major shift then, isn't it? Because you have the double responsibility of being a space for women and for women connected to the criminal justice system.

We do things with a lot of care. It's finding the right moments, looking at how we've done it historically. We've taken part in Open House *[annual London weekend which opens buildings to the public]* in the past, we've celebrated Fun Palaces and brought audiences in for one off performances. We are also part of the community of Camden, so we're in conversation a lot about what is the right way to be a civic space in the borough. We are planning a Members' festival, our first, where members will co-produce a festival of theatre. It's for our Members principally, but then we're going to open it out to wider audiences and for the local community to come in and see what our Members are doing, see their work. It's opening the doors but at selected moments for us to work out what it feels like and how it impacts, because it's important that we remain a safe space — and in a way we have an anonymity about being here. So any kind of trumpet blowing has to be really carefully and sensitively done.

One particular thing connecting all of Clean Break's work is language and definitions. If you're going to give people a voice, they need the language and the organisation needs a language as well. You're ahead of the terminology and helping to define it, so it follows you.

The terminology is shifting very slowly. When I came into the organisation 18 years ago, words like 'offenders' and 'ex-offenders' were very much the language used. Defining someone with that label ignores the fact that they are a human being, a person with that experience. Giving them that noun 'offender' is so dehumanising and so oppositional to their transformation. It has always been important to me that we talk about women with experience in the criminal justice system as 'women' foremost. So we, alongside our women's sector partners, have helped this to shift in public sector-speak.

Interestingly, when we co-produced *Inside Bitch*, we put out a glossary for press and the media of the terms that we prefer and the terms that we don't find acceptable or don't use. We were tired of having a conversation with the press and then seeing the newspaper caption with 'Cons do theatre' or 'inmates act out'. People aren't 'cons', we just don't describe people like that, that isn't what we said. But headlines are headlines and they'll use a provocative word if they can, no matter whether it's wrong. So we now lead with saying "this is the terminology that we use, it's the terminology we'd like you to use when you're reviewing our work and talking about what we do."

That has been interesting because it's also about being braver and more confident as a company and saying, "Okay, we don't just have to do it internally. We can also say to other people *you* adopt this language, because this is the right language to use."

So we are beginning a new chapter of the next forty years of the company's life, with renewed confidence, a strong profile and greater audiences and yet the same core values and commitments to women whose lives have been affected by the criminal justice system. This will never change.

*

17

Lucy Hopkins

'Getting your energy field in a room, that's what live performers do'

Lucy Hopkins, clown, director, workshop leader & co-director with Bob Slayer of fringe venue Heroes. Based in Worcestershire, she was born in Bolton, Lancashire, and raised in Leicestershire.
• **lucyhopkins.com, heroesoffringe.com, @lucyehopkins**

Photo: Matthew Highton

Where's the structure of your shows evolved from?

The work that I'm doing at the moment happens in a ceremonial frame, but the first show I made in 2013, which I still do and really enjoy, was completely different. *Le Foulard [Art Show]* is about an artist trying to make a Great Work and then the characters she creates destroy her show, transform it into a new thing and the artist fights that the whole way through, it's about the creative process. It became very scripted — it had to be, the interactions between the characters are fast and there's an ending to get to! I toured it a lot, in English and French versions, but ultimately I realised that I missed and longed for that space where things are happening in the moment, being created in the moment, being improvised — which is how I had developed the show, fixing the things that worked as I went along. And I realised working in the moment, with the moment is my absolute favourite.

And so I made a show called *Surprise Event.* I billed it as "an hour-long, interactive, human installation" and reasoned that anyone that came to a show on the back of such a description would be ready for anything basically. I did it a few times here and there and the fun of it was that it was honest — honestly loose and improvised, and always a surprise, for me as well as them — and at the same time it gave me a framework in which to develop new ideas.

I wanted to play about with certain elements, for example I would switch the lights off with a movement of my hands, using it to give structure to the hour, punctuate the moments, have a problem with, it was really fun. It created a frame to play in so I could try out all the little things that were tickling my mind. And having a frame, rather than a script, felt really helpful.

Then I encountered this amazing lecture by a Franco-Algerian eco-philosopher called Mohammed Taleb, where he conceived of the world in terms of Mythos and Logos, and I wanted to present that content — and *Powerful Women Are About* was the show that resulted from that.

The lecture was all about how all of the problems of our world could be traced back to the imbalance between 'mythos' and 'logos' — logos being logic and order and reason, mythos being wonder and enchantment and the arts, the subconscious, intuition, all of that side. And in that way, mythos is more commonly associated with the feminine, and logos with the masculine. But it's right brain and left brain essentially. And mythos has been systematically denigrated, shunned, denied, demonised by our logos world.

So the imbalances of our world — between the genders, between the sexes, the rationalisation and justification of colonialism, the burning of witches, the dismissal and attempted elimination of indigenous culture, the dismissal of anything that can't be explained by the logical mind — comes from the over-importance we have given to logos over time. That blew my mind. I thought it was brilliant and it totally spoke to the part of me that has always felt that this world isn't just the surface, the part we can see, but that there are loads of dimensions to it — how we *feel* things, how we *live* things — there's so much we don't understand about the universe.

So for *Powerful Women* I used this wonderful content from Mohammed Taleb — and a Theremin [*electronic musical instrument controlled without physical contact*]. There was lots of playing with the audience, getting the audience to sing at the Theremin, trying to get them involved. About halfway through the Edinburgh fringe run, I rearranged the room so the audience sat on four sides and I performed in the centre. That totally changed the piece, because then the audience could see each other, it was impossible not to interact in a way, even if that interaction was just watching the audience in front of you. I realised at the end of that run that this was my favourite thing of the whole show: getting the audience involved in that way. So I went on to make *Secrt Circl*, where I kept the ceremonial setting and said, right this is a ceremony, but the content was the interaction. Everyone sat in a circle, it's one of the reasons why we created our SpiegelYurt, a beautiful little 55-seater circular venue for 'intimate cabaret'. The central action of *Secrt Circl* was that I would gather objects from everyone in the audience, cast them on the ground and do a reading of the 'collective unconscious' of the group. I use divination methods in my own practice when

I'm stuck on something — Tarot cards or the I-Ching, or else just pay attention to stuff I see around — you can make meaning from anything, if you want. In doing a reading of objects I'd try to make meaning from the big old pile of shit in the middle of the room, *[laughs]* there'd be sometimes actions to do, things to resolve, there was this cantankerous witch who'd turn up and frighten people (that was me), it'd be a kind of guided improvisation. I could say and do what I wanted basically, talk about whatever came up, interact with the people. The trick was to do it in a way that made sense to people, so they'd stay with me. And so I had this play space where everything was possible simply by saying, "This is a ceremony, anything goes. I'm the priestess of this ceremony, so it's whatever I think needs to happen next."

So, like *Surprise Event*, it was a structured playground which allowed improvisation, connection with the audience, and where I could play around with my ideas. But it was also a circle with this idea of upholding mythos, the unexplained and unexplainable, magic, wonder, there were always lots of magic moments, as there always are in improvisation, but in that setting it became a conscious, collective act of manifesting and honouring those mythos vibes which have been suppressed and dismissed for so long. That was the thing that Mohammed Taleb was saying in his lecture, that the dismissal of mythos also leads to our devaluing the arts and our own creativity, our own need for spontaneity and wild cards and how healing it is to be able to live wildly and creatively. Not all the time, you know . . .

I'm still working in that ceremonial space. I made another show, *Ceremony of Golden Truth*, which is another circle show but the focus is less witchy and more sacred. It's about upholding the sacred in every moment, because our time here on earth is fleeting! At the same time it's completely preposterous. I don't think those elements are mutually exclusive. I'm working on a third circle show at the minute, working title *The Unknown*, which will be about bringing all of that ceremony and mysticism right back into reality, so it's really grounded. It's about dealing with the darkness, in a way. So I'm working out how to play with that and not get lost in it.

Bringing clown into a ceremonial space, being in the present moment, acknowledging reality whatever that might be, accepting it fully and playing with it all, laughing at it all, encouraging people's imaginations to spin out and not be confined by my own, hopefully, to go ever wider, deeper, higher, I really stand by that. It's important to have feelings of the sacred and wonder without being dictated to, without it being, "This is religion and here are the rules." It's like, "No, this is your being, your mind, your definition of soul, do with it what you will and feel your own power as creation in the moment, because that's what life actually is." Creating every moment in the moment, taking the moments that went before, leading up to the moments that will come after. The present moment is simply the result of every decision ever made by every being that ever lived. That's all it is. *[laughs]* So that's what I do. I'm a Modern Day High Priestess of Sacred Idiocy. Why not?

It's interesting the way you mix physicality with the intellectual — well actually that's the logos and the mythos isn't it? But you really do do that in your shows.

Great. I'm delighted that you see so.

But also what's important is the audience. You can't do this without an audience — and it can't be a congregation-style one. They're not there to be merely a foil for you, are they? They're more than that.

Absolutely. They're the point. I feel really strongly that anything an artist does is for people. That's our work. It can be for yourself too of course, but if you want to make a living out of it you're doing it for people. So I try to listen to them. To find out what they like or how to best play with them. Not to pander to them, but to invite them into territory they didn't know they'd enjoy.

A fashion designer friend of mine, Tom Cawson, once said to me, the trick is not giving the audience what it wants, but giving the audience what they don't yet know that they want. And that has always stayed with me, because it's always like going *beyond* preparing a surprise party, thinking of what could be amazing, things they won't be expecting, secrets, surprise twists. More and more I've come to see that when I stay open to that possibility in the moment, those surprises are always there. It's trying to stay connected to your own true mind in a way because that's always surprising if you follow that. It's also surprising to be in a space that feels like it's for our wellbeing, but that doesn't need to be serious or really pious, it can also be hilarious and preposterous. And still feel really good. I think we're being bombarded with so many crazy healthless messages so we have to identify the set of muscles that help us see things healthfully, for our own good. We have to actively work if we want to see life as "we're alive, we're living beings on this living planet and that's amazing".

And all of the structures of society, the imbalances, built up over hundreds of imbalanced years . . . so many people are being shafted . . . and we're trying to make space for more voices being heard and more visibility for the folk that get invisibilised. With *[mobile fringe venue]* Heroes that I host with Bob Slayer, we have an emphasis on platforming original voices, we're always trying to platform diverse work, and we're seeing now the new work we need to do to go further.

Bob has done lots to challenge the huge financial barriers that exist at the fringe, but we need to do more to address the cultural barriers, to find out why certain people might not even think it's for them. So now we're seeing, oh-kay . . . we're going to have to actively go out into other communities to find those artists who share the values of Heroes and say, "We programme independent artists, we support independence and an alternative, financially sustainable approach." It's not a stepping stone to the mainstream, although many Heroes acts have gone on to do all sorts of brilliance in mainstream ways — but it's about building a path that's financially sustainable for the artists, and then letting everybody know that it's for everyone.

We're working out how to reach out without tokenism and be more accessible to people so artists go, "Oh, that could be for me, that feels like me!" Particularly we have really few applications from people of colour. And the more research I've done into how we might work towards redressing that, again not to tick a box but to really connect with communities, and then the more research I've done into the imbalances of the world, ecology, gender, peoples, etc, it's clear that the next big invisible root problem to recognise is that of the deep-down white supremacy vibe of the whole planet, which comes from our telling the story of colonialism as one of adventurers and pioneers rather than thieves and bullies who were unwilling to listen and exchange. Harsh isn't it! And when things feel harsh, the natural thing is to step back from it, or run! And that leads to denial, or bargaining, which we see a lot of.

And I mean invisible to white people of course, not to everyone by any means. It's difficult for white people to perceive this imbalance because everything is set up to stop us seeing it, even the writing of history, and especially our own psyches because it's so hideously uncomfortable to face. Thinking, "Of course everybody's equal, I agree, definitely, I don't disagree that" — that's the absolute lowest bar. Beyond that, if we want to get equal and have everyone having a good time at the big old Party of Life we — white people — need to educate ourselves consciously about the white history that has been imposed and read, watch, listen to the experiences of people of colour, for example, and learn from it. It's all out there! It's a big old unpick, there's generations of normalised inequality in our very DNA, it feels like walking downstairs backwards, unpicking that experience and being prepared to look at it and being prepared to feel *shame* at it. Because that's the great transformer actually. It's not about beating ourselves up, but I do think acknowledging the shame is kind of important. A friend of mine who is studying a Master's in race and social justice at Goldsmiths, University of London, talks about being willing to sit in the discomfort rather than fleeing from it — and I've found that helpful. Ha! It's full on isn't it? But it *is* full on. And once you start to see it, you can see it everywhere and it's awful and complex and won't be undone by one diverse fringe programme. We need to be able to look at it and accept a telling of history that is completely different to the one we were brought up with, to carefully unpick the pieces of our identity that have been built on this erroneous telling. And rebuild an outlook with the real history in mind. Simple, right?!

But if we've not got the learning and education and the courage to face the awful ugliness of how the world has become and the benefits we white people are still receiving from it, then there's no point in talking about diversity, it will always be token. It can't be done on the surface, it's too big, we're going to have to go deeper to heal it. Heal our vision and heal our outlook and heal our perspective and grow from it. And that's an absolutely ginormous work that could take generations and generations. But healing takes time! All we have to do is the next healing action, then the next one after that, and so on.

So how does that influence you in going out there looking for the sort of the things that you know Heroes needs to programme?

Good question. Heroes has always been about variety, the programme has always been influenced heavily by recommendations from our existing performers. But we're recognising the importance of being truly inclusive, and that means spreading the net wider of where we source those recommendations. And of course it has to be stuff we love.

I've been going to two fantastic nights when I can: Wacky Racists, hosted by Sophie Duker, and FOC IT UP! *[FOC = Femmes of Colour]*, hosted by Kemah Bob. Wacky Racists platforms performers of colour and any perspectives that are underrepresented on the mainstream circuit. FOC IT UP! platforms women and female-identifying performers of colour and was set up as a response to there generally being one token slot offered to a woman of colour in a mainstream comedy gig: fuck your token slots, we'll have them all, thanks. It's great. All the nights I've been to have been great vibes, great acts and I really appreciate being in an environment where the tone isn't set by or for white people, it feels like I get some deprogramming from a white-centered experience. Siân Docksey runs a great night called Permitted Fruit, the nights are out there, and the community is vibrant! So I try to go to them when I can, and speak to folk, and harvest more recommendations, reach deeper, further . . . There's still loads more to be done but I'm in this for longterm change, not just trying to look good fast.

A lot of what you're talking about rises above New Ageism or whatever, it's just common sense. And while change doesn't come without hard work, you don't have to be a Calvinist to put in the hard work. But society in the past couple of decades has not rewarded people's hard work, and certainly things like putting diversity on next year's programme need everyone on all sides to make the effort.

Exactly, do the work! How are we going to rebalance society? Do the work of reading up about it. It's grim. But I feel like I *have* to read up about other experiences, otherwise how will I know? And that's the thing, it's always been an *option*, and more and more I don't think that should be an option because all those experiences of other people who we don't necessarily relate to, whose experience we'll never share, we give them less importance. I think teaching the history of colonialism in schools would be a good start, and how it basically exported capitalism and destroyed our connection to the planet. But for those of us who'd like the world to shift and didn't learn that in school, I think we need to put the work in, bottom line. And the work is deep and long. So it's just about chipping away, doing the weeding, and trying to make a garden that everyone can grow in on their own terms. Flipping heck. No quick fixes for that.

You also do workshops and residencies around the country and in Europe, and Heroes has now also become very much a focus across the year for you.

Heroes enables me to do Edinburgh again and again, because the Heroes model means I can afford to. When I brought *Le Foulard* to the fringe in 2013 (under the name *The Veil*), I played to sold-out rooms at the Pleasance *[one of the 'Big Four' paid-for Edinburgh fringe venues]*, got some great press, but I was lonely and exhausted and the whole experience cost me £3,000. I was told I'd had "a great fringe". I thought, fuck that, if that's great then this is a broken festival. I didn't even visit for the next two years. Then someone told me about Heroes and I thought, yes I know Bob, I'll go and check it out . . .

The Heroes model has enabled me to take risks and explore creatively — it becomes a delight if the show does well rather than a desperate necessity — and I can try things that are more interesting, less guaranteed, more exciting. I use Edinburgh as a forum, I gather all the elements throughout the year and set out a solid start point, then bring the show into being during the month of the festival. That happened sort of by accident with *Powerful Women* and I've done it more consciously from *Secrt Circl* onwards. *Powerful Women* wasn't 'ready' for the fringe, and I found what made it work about halfway through — putting the audience on all sides. Ultimately this led to a different show and a different experience of the fringe which I liked — and I've realised it's actually quite stressful trying to fit into a model where success means everything being fixed and finished. So now I prepare my shows differently. They're ready for the fringe. But they have space to really take advantage of the uniqueness of Edinburgh and grow and evolve throughout the month, and that way they're never finished and there's always maximum fun potential for me and the audience. I work like this on principle because the Heroes model allows me room to experiment, and because I want to contribute to a fringe that is a creative hotbed not just a marketplace.

My favourite thing about live performance, the whole wonderful magic of the arts, is the bubbling creativity of it. And that's what's wonderful about Edinburgh, those late-night events where you never know what you're going to get and people are like, "Shit it's really difficult and brilliant and creative and exciting." Those moments, they switch us all alive in a really special way that I think is imperative for life. As an artist I want those moments, that's how I want to work, and that's how I want to *live*.

The workshops I do on clowning *[The Art of Being an Idiot & Circle of Idiots]* and other stuff such as mentoring and directing bring in income and there's also the touring that we do with the BlundaBus *[the Heroes mobile bus venue]* and the SpiegelYurt, that all funds things as well, and there's other work like being in other people's creations like *Spencer Jones' The Mind of Herbert Clunkerdunk* for the BBC, of course that I do. We don't make loads of money. But I don't need loads of money. I need enough money to have a good and simple lifestyle and put a tiny bit away. You just don't need loads. Which is also the bottom line.

Here's a question then, do you need to be funded?

Oh very good. Funding . . . I've never gone down that path as yet. Because I'd rather make work and find a way to do business than write a proposal for funding, basically. Grant application writing isn't my skill set and I don't like doing it. I'm in front of the computer enough doing emails and admin and dates and diaries and planning. And I'm making my life work otherwise. No judgement against it, I just haven't chosen to engage that way. Also I think more and more, especially with our changing world, whether we transform it in uplift direction or catastrophe direction (and probably it'll be both simultaneously), funding isn't something to be relied upon.

I've seen theatre practitioners that I know have their funding pulled and they suffer, their idea of themselves, even their identity suffers. Something I found very interesting in a David Mamet book — and I see it happen often — is that well-funded theatre can give a false idea to practitioners and audiences alike. It's saying that there is a group of people who know better than the audience what art is.

So a show is funded and sometimes tickets are cheaper or free, especially to 'audiences in need', then the audiences come and they're like, "Oh yeah, thanks, grateful for the ticket, didn't really get it" — but they're not empowered to say, "Oi that was bullshit, I want my fiver back." It's what attracted me to Heroes *[which is a pioneer of the 'pay-what-you-want' model]* which is constantly exploring how to make models that are sustainable. So that the audience are empowered, so that audiences pay the performer directly. And the exchange of money — or something else — is right and good, so that audiences have the value of the work and performers have the value of the work as well — "Together we're going to make something, let's be honest about how we value it and let's make that work together."

In terms of funding, we consider it all the time. I'm not against it in principle. In a way it's wonderful, but it's almost like people haven't got the discipline to use it well enough. *[laughs long & hard]* Do you know what I mean? Sometimes it makes it too easy, too swiftly, so that people believe they're doing more than they're actually doing. It can give a false sense of the importance of your work, and for me at the end of the day the belief in my work has to come from the interaction with the audience and what the audience say when they walk out.

In Europe the concept of funding is completely different — it's embedded bottom up and fringe economics are an uneasy fit. Funding in Europe isn't a carrot, it's an integral part of civic society, a willing obligation. So something like the BlundaBus will be paid for by people's taxes and everyone will have access to it and directly see where their taxes have gone. There's a confidence about having that at the heart of the community as opposed to a perpetual anxiety which we have here about anything funded. The caveat is that they've already begun to slash culture over there quietly, or not so quietly. How does that square with your experience of Europe?

I've worked quite a lot in the French-speaking part of Switzerland, there's really interesting arts culture all over the place. Society is comfortable, wealthy, has good healthcare and so is happy and relaxed enough to go, "Yeah let's go and take a punt, let's learn from an experience, let's educate our minds and beings as well." And so people are empowered to have an opinion on it, and if they don't like it, it didn't break the bank, so to speak.

But my main experience is in France where I lived for ten years. While I was there they had a system where you could declare yourself as an 'intermittent de spectacle' *['casual entertainment worker']*, whether you were an artist, director, technician, composer, anyone in performing arts. It basically means that you declare all of the work you do which pays you in a way recognised by that system, and the following year the state tops you up to that amount of hours if you don't get the work — but you have to hit that amount of hours per year. It sounds like an amazing system and I have friends who it has really served. But I've also known artists who have become very jaded by their whole artistic career because in order to keep that benefit, you have to take on projects that make up your hours, which often take you away from your own creative practice, so you get trapped in the system. Artists aim to be in that system rather than developing their own practice and fighting to make the work that they love. As a result there's very little risk taking in the artistic environment in France.

And another knock-on effect is that, because artistic practice is funded by the state, the artists become insiders. For me the artist is the person on the outside reflecting back, the jester or the fool saying, "Hey society, this is what you are, this is what you could be." When you're funded by the state or a body connected with the state, it's going to cut your tongue a little bit, it's going to shut you up a little bit. Because anything that isn't seen as conforming to society, even on a subconscious level, is going to be "that's not quite right, even if it is good". That goes back to that "give them what they don't yet know they want" thing.

It's like in the early 1800s when Joseph Grimaldi expanded the part of being a clown. He built on the legacy developed from the Restoration when basically you were only allowed to speak *[i.e. perform 'serious' drama]* in the Theatre Royals dotted about the country — London had just two, in Holborn and Drury Lane — and the rest of them had to be 'silent' because their theatres weren't sanctioned by the king. And one of the things that developed as a result of that constraint was physical comedy. It was 'illegitimate theatre' and outside of the Establishment, so there has always been that outsider flavour to the street stuff, the physical stuff, circus, the bit where there's the ribald, the rowdy or the uncontrolled, the free, the libertarian, the wild, the *un*tidy. All of that world is where things can happen to make people remember that we're all connected to life and each other in a way that's so much wider and more exciting and profound than anything that society could tell us. Or will tell us. Because the point of society is that it all hangs together. Which is very good, because I'm no anarchist. On the other hand I totally am.

Taking a model like Heroes . . . why don't we have Heroes-style venues on every corner?

Because . . . because we are a society that is mostly about money-making. We've gone mad. We've gone mad for money. And that's been upheld as the thing: business is the thing, profit is the thing. Which goes back to capitalism which goes back to colonialism. It's not about humanity, it's not about good times, it's not about being well and whole, it's not about living independently in harmony with the environment and it's certainly not about diving into your cosmic depths — unless of course that'll increase your productivity as a worker — and the reality is that most of those choices and decisions come from people who aren't going to be affected by the absence of communities in small towns or the grounded, rounded wellness of the population as a whole.

There are people who have become sick for this money. We call the hoarders mad who don't throw anything away and cram their homes with everything they find, but we don't say that about people when they're hoarding all of that cash that they'll never realistically be able to use. But it's a sickness of the human condition and it takes a certain sort of outlook to say, "Actually, let's do something for the wellbeing of ourselves and others." It takes courage to be prepared to stand apart from society and offer that, especially because it takes hard work and it might fail. So you have to be a bit mad do it. But that's 'mad' in the way society calls people mad who don't really conform to society and its own madness.

But I don't know, Nick, why we don't have more Heroes. Business rates are probably something to do with it. Although, I say that, they do exist, The Bill Murray in London, The Stand in Edinburgh, small independent venues and projects of all kinds do exist. But it's hard work, so you have to want to live it, then it feels less like hard work and more like a great life! And you can't mass-produce it, it's love, it's independent spirit.

You know, there are times I think the whole system is created to wear people down. People are knackered, people have got lives to lead, they've got a sick mum or they've got kids or they've had a problem at school or need to go somewhere because a friend really needs them. Life just spins you through a series of big life events and if all society is going to do is say, "Above all else, you have to work, you have to drive the machine forward or you're worthless. And buy this shit, and pay that bill . . .", well I think we can do better, that's all. It's possible to run larger models in a fairer way. It's possible!

It's difficult to believe in your own thing and you do have to have a lot of support. I've always had very good support from my parents. I've always known that if things got really bad I would have a degree of financial support and emotional support. I've always known that and so I've not needed to use it too much. But I'm very aware of the value of it. And it's an absolute privilege. I think it's the backbone of me doing things my own way. It's not all a merry stroll in the park, don't get me wrong, but having parents that say, "Do what makes you happy", and knowing that I can take a risk on something that I love and if it fucks up then I'm not going to be on the street, that's enormous, that's a massive privileged position to be in, I feel it is. So if I can take these risks with my life and grow that way of thinking, the support I've had has been a big part of that. Of course it's possible to do all sorts of amazing things with much less familial support, with none, but it's one of those things we don't recognise enough I think. I don't think it can be understated.

That's effectively reclaiming the word 'community', which is another word that has been twisted and turned for funding purposes, for isolating groups, political processes, regional divisions and all the rest of it. What you're saying is that a venue such as Heroes has the possibility to be a community, one that gives you identity, purpose and a level of power even if that's not recognised by society. If you're a community, then your audience becomes a part of you. And you know what? Every year, of all the shows I end up seeing across the genres, venues and festivals, I really have to say that the majority of them show little or no consideration for their audiences no matter how much they say they do.

I agree. Last night we opened in Harrogate, we took the BlundaBus and the SpiegelYurt there in association with Harrogate Theatre, and we did the launch show in the little SpiegelYurt. We were a small audience of 30-odd people with me and Bob and Laurence Marshall and Phoebe Douthwaite, otherwise known as the Old Time Rags — Phoebe's a step dancer and Lawrence is a musician, they're mad talented. Together we made this very loose flowing show where all the audience were speaking as well. We talked about nonsense and we did some acts, some music and dancing, and afterwards the comment that came up a lot from people was how refreshing it was. How refreshing to be there and be actually present, be invited to be present. How it wasn't a show where you sit back and just receive something, it's like we were all *making* this happen in this little magical round space next to a bar in a bus. And I love that idea of creative work being refreshing to the people that experience it. But the fact they said it implies they hadn't felt it for a while!

I think the changes that could bring this different world that we long for are right there, right there behind every tiny little . . . tiny wink of the eye, flick of the hair they're right there behind every moment. We don't have to rewrite everything, we don't have to undertake massive works, we have to work on our individual exchanges with people, put ourselves in situations where we wouldn't normally be and learn from them. And look too at that idea of how to serve. A lot of these ideas, I realise that they're quite old school Christian concepts — like service and compassion and kindness, forgiveness — but those concepts existed way before Christianity claimed them, didn't they!

And charity . . .

Yes all of that good stuff. We need it don't we, it's so healthful, it's so good for us. Like if I think "how can I serve?" then I feel like I'm contributing and then I feel better. Like, "Oh great, then I can be here, I don't need to be having this feeling that I need to justify my existence or excuse it or something." *[laughs]* That's probably just an ego trap too though. Oh I don't know Nick. It's like all the little secrets to life, it isn't rocket science, but it isn't straightforward. But quality of life isn't more complicated than trying to live truly as you are, and loving that, and being grateful for it, it's ancient stuff — and the experience of art is an ancient human dynamic. Since the beginning of consciousness, humans have sought to express or gather together in song or rhythm or story. Those arts are ancient and important for us all.

When I started to become aware of the impossible contradictions of the world, which was about 15 years ago, I remember thinking I should be a nurse. "If you feel so strongly about helping, if you feel all these things, then be a nurse. Do something concretely helpful." But that would practically never work, I'm not good around injuries, and I don't like hospitals, I'd be a terrible, miserable nurse. So then I had to consider the worth of what I loved doing, and at some point it sort of dropped in, bam! — the arts are something that have always *been*, humanity has always made art in one form or another, so then why not try to create amazing and unique moments, which in turn meant I had to define that on my own terms and to accept that the pursuit of amazingness on my own terms might not lead me on a path of fame and glory, it might just mean working away on these intimate shows and happenings that exist in the moment for the rest of my life.

Maybe that's what life could look like, maybe that's what work could look like. And then I came to the idea that the artistic environment, like all environments, is about healthy ecology. Part of the problem that we have with our world ecology is that we don't value the small and tiny beings, we limit diversity to get mega single crops of beef, wheat, sheep, corn, coffee . . . A strong, healthy ecology is human beings and everything in nature living together in harmony, a bit less of that, a bit more of that, that next to that because they help each other, that sort of thing. If making art is my work and that work brings me joy and impacts all those around me in a way that is good — uplifting to the world or encouraging or refreshing, then that's my role, and that's just A-okay.

I don't need to be a 'mega crop'. And that's exactly why the ecology is in crisis, it's the madness that we're seeing in the environment, it underlies all of our systems. In the arts there's always a push, a desire for superstars. Well, it isn't just about superstars. It's about real connection happening now and unexpected moments of being inspired by surprising things and all of that sort of magic. It's also tiny and inclusive and beautiful and inspiring and honest and raw and true. If that's my path, very well then! And I'll try my best to live up to my values and not trash myself when I don't, which is a very easy thing to say.

You're not a nurse but working within the performing arts, and you're holding out not just for your own commitment to live performance but you're working, through Heroes, on actively improving that live experience. Based on where society finds itself at the moment, how does the idea make sense that live performance won't and can't go away, even if you can't make any money out of it?

I experience live performance as 'energetic', and in that sense it's a spiritual exchange, although 'spiritual' is the wrong word, 'of the soul' is perhaps better? I mean that with the live arts, practitioners learn, through training or experience, to affect their energy field, and therefore the energy of the space and perhaps of the people who are there. We use music, light, colour, set, the space, how we interact with the space, the form of the connection between performer and audience (fourth wall, direct address, etc), the quality of that connection and, most significantly, our physical, mental, emotional, energetic presences. Human presence is incredibly powerful. One of the most significant things I've learned from performing is how sensitive we are as humans. We read, feel and gather information from each other all the time, and the performance space amplifies that. People see *everything*. We're taught to screen it out, out of respect for one another and I think also to try to limit the amount of information we receive, so we don't become overwhelmed. Also because it's too complex to process.

But anyone who's ever tried to do something in front of a group of people will have felt how sensitive the people watching them are. You do one little thing that's a tiny bit inauthentic and everyone in the room feels it. It's a nightmare. But there's nothing like it . . . I like to think performing is like surfing, but you can also summon the waves and influence their flavour, and the creatures that lurk beneath! Some performers like a choppy sea, others like it calm. And there are so many different ways to approach it, from the most constructed, where there have been precise choices made about every element of the performance, to the loosest, where the moment unfolds and is created in real time. I love it, I *love* this work.

And it's all about sharing a moment together, winkling a little bit closer into ourselves, into our experience of life, into the things that make us all tick, the things between the heartbeats, the moment, sharing a moment of existence with each other and remembering who we are. I mean it can be if we want it to be, it can be whatever, but for me it's got to bring us to life, to our humanity, because if not then what's the point?

Which brings us back to the audience. We know that an audience can get the same out of a show as the performer. But the problem is that it sort of gets lost as everyone bangs on about bringing in new audiences without actually taking them into consideration, or pandering to the same audiences over and over again, or, worst of all, pandering to an audience that only exists in the imagination of the Arts Council. Is it just a case of it is what it is, or is it possible to truly work on building those audiences and to bring in not only people who normally don't go to live performance but also people who would never normally cross genres?

Yes! Why not. It's good if there are lots of ways to interact with the place we're trying to bring them to. At Heroes we run a bar with booze and soft drinks — it funds our model and gives people who might not usually come by a clear way in, since most people have experience of the transaction of a bar. You buy a drink and you've paid your way, simple as that, you feel a right to be there. And the whole space is set up so it's very easy to speak with people you don't know necessarily — big benches and tables outside, there's a piano downstairs on the BlundaBus with a sign that says 'Pianist Wanted'. But of course the Edinburgh fringe is just for a month and I think to build audience you really need to build a relationship with a place. Bob and I have just moved to Worcester and we're looking at setting up something more longterm here, lots of possible options at the moment so I can't say more than that! But to really reach out, I think it takes time, legwork and a real will to make it happen. It's about putting yourself into places where you might not usually go, putting yourself out there, literally, sharing something about your organisation and seeing who it attracts. And if that doesn't attract a wide enough range of folk, then it's about reviewing the process and having another go. And keep questioning yourself. It's a work we have to do on ourselves, or it won't stick. Which people do you want to exclude, who doesn't attract you, who do you think "oh no they'll be a pain!", and just question the shiv out of it all. Try and be better i'n't it!

So for me now it's something about not just the performances and the workshops, but what we offer around that. We're looking at setting up a space that could be a venue but there are workshops around it, people working with their hands on things like woodwork, arts, practical skills and people growing things in the garden. You know, something that gives a really wide experience of creativity and how the expression of it can be so so good for us, healing actually. We're in this massive moment of planetary transformation, and as well as being enormous, the shift is actually really tiny. We've already got everything we need to improve the lives of all the living systems on the planet. It looks like it starts with slow down, check your priorities, eat well, grow things, buy less, reach out, be kind, include folk — we all know it. It's a practice. Healing! It's healing. And the arts totally have their place there. Laughing together with a group of people at something that lifts our hearts up, that's healing. See? I still haven't managed to let go of that nurse thing.

But obviously it's also about good schools, healthcare, a society that agrees to take care of its vulnerable and uphold each other, so you know there's lots to do there too, isn't there? And in the time being, while we're not living in that society, it's about keeping your principles, your creativity, your being radiating out, or tending to its quiet light, whichever. I've talked about it for a while now in terms of 'keeping the torch lit'. Even when times feel really dark, keep your torch burning, give a light to other people whose torches are out, stick your torches together sometimes and blaze them up a bit, rebind the handle. Just keep the torch of your values burning bright and beautiful. And pass them on! We've been doing it for time. They're the big old ancient values. So however best possible, I try to keep my torch lit. *[laughs]* It's all I can see there is to do really. And the more people the better.

But then at the end of the day, everyone's torch is their own business isn't it?

*

18
Sophia A Jackson

'Always work from the basics, and be as *honest* as possible'

Sophia A Jackson is the editor of Afridiziak Theatre News, the UK's only website dedicated to African-Caribbean theatre. Based in South London, she was born & raised in West Bromwich, West Midlands. • afridiziak.com, @Afridiziak

Photo: Adrian Pope

There's been a string of constantly downwards turning-points for critics in the UK, but the last few years have seen rather a lot of them. I suspect we're discovering that it's in the nature of theatre criticism to go with the changing times. And that there's no such thing as a typical critic today. So was it an atypical route that got you into theatre?

I moved to London from West Bromwich when I was 16. I went to South Thames College, University and in my late 20s I did an MA in journalism studies at Westminster University. From there I did a few freelance gigs including working at the *Weekly Journal [sibling to The Voice]* and *New Nation* newspapers. When *New Nation* went bust, I had all these contacts within the theatre industry but I didn't know what to do with them. At the same I realised that there were a lot of African-Caribbean productions taking place, but there wasn't one place where you could find out where these shows were. So I decided to launch *Afridiziak Theatre News* as a one-stop shop for African-Caribbean theatre.

Was there anything that inspired you? Any similar site or publication?

I enjoyed being the listing editor at *New Nation* and I wanted to look for an outlet for working with that. But instead I thought, "Oh, I'll just set up my own publication." So that was really the inspiration I suppose, plus I saw that there was a gap in the market as well. Although there were lots of African-Caribbean productions, nobody was really talking about them. They seemed to be quite niche and even underground, and I wanted to raise awareness, basically.

Where were the challenges?

I found press offices officers were often reluctant to give us press nights, like for the big shows, and I'd struggle. It would be like, "Oh. Well. Press night's full. But you can come another night." Or I'd be sat in the lap of the gods with terrible seats and views. It was only with more experience that I came to realise that I'd been treated quite badly. Once we became more established, we would be invited to press nights without me having to say, "Hi, could we come along to your show *please*?" They become more receptive, but it took a good few years to get to that stage — and also to get decent seats on press nights!

Was that down to the fact that it's an African-Caribbean site or because it's not The Guardian?

I don't know, to be honest. I felt that it could have been both, because even now when I go to press nights, they're not overly diverse in terms of the critics that are there. It's all still very elitist, and that crosses over in terms of the publications that get invited to press night or publications that productions want to go to press night. And that's connected with the reviews that we've done every year, they're quality reviews but *Afridiziak Theatre News* is rarely quoted. When they quote five stars, it's from *The Times*, or from *The Guardian*.

It's not just a problem of access for the reviewers and reviews, it's the audience's access as well, isn't it?

That's a massive issue. But a barrier like that will be there so long as theatres aren't representing the audience, who should be represented by who's actually on the stage. And we're certainly not there at all.

Do you see Afridiziak as a pioneer in what you set out to do?

Yes, I do. We launched in September 2008 and that was an exciting time. There are a few publications that started off around the same period as

Afridiziak, however they didn't solely focus on African-Caribbean theatre but general black event listings. Most of them are gone now, unfortunately.

Even in those days most people were a critic-slash-something else. How have you kept the something else going?

I'm an events manager by day. When I started out, the theatre was a labour of love. Now, I am just as passionate, but I don't have as much time as I did when I first launched. I have a team of reviewers, interviewers, whereas before I was trying to do everything myself. But I still basically put the content together with my brother Basil Lumsden, who is the web developer. But even if I did have the time, it's impossible now to personally go to every single production for the very good reason that there are more productions that have black actors. There are more black directors, there's more black productions as a whole, which is great because it means that theatre is stepping up in terms of diversity. The stories that are being told are proof of how massively things have changed over the past decade. So we're very busy.

Would your remit let you expand to review white productions and filter them through African-Caribbean eyes?

Of course, and over the last few years we've worked hard to open that up a lot more. Obviously, there are lots of quality productions that aren't African-Caribbean productions. When press night opportunities like that come up, I'll always forward them to the team and if somebody wants to go and review, then they can, they're more than welcome to review. Those shows don't need as much support from us. We'll include them to broaden the remit of the site, but it's not an essential part of what we need to do.

Would it be important though to broaden the horizons of your readership into the general world of theatre?

The last few years have been important because we have seen, not exactly an explosion, but a very steady programme to get black performers on the stage. And then, by default we've seen the directors follow through, and now we've got the artistic directors coming through and the playwrights. Although they have always been around, playwrights are now being given more of a context. So the next step is, well . . . we've all been to shows in which we've seen either completely black or a very high percentage cast and sometimes very brave programming. But you still look around the audience and everyone's white.

If your role is to help change things and to chart how others are doing that, how do you do it in practice?

My role is making sure that our readers know that there is a wide range of plays out there and that they are for black people too, and making sure that those productions are accessible to them. Some theatres will regularly contact us to offer our readers discounted tickets. That's usually very successful — those are the newsletters that get the most opened because theatre is expensive. So even when you've got a well-paid job, it's still considered a treat to go to the theatre. It's not as cheap as a lot of other cultural or social activities. But you do get more offers now, there's definitely a lot more £10 offers, and that kind of premise measurably opens it up and does get more diverse bums on seats.

If we go back to growing up in West Bromwich, what was your experience of theatre there?

I developed my interest in theatre after coming to London. It wasn't something I did in Birmingham. I played the clarinet so I played in the woodwind orchestra.

So what was it that made you click into theatre when you went to London?

I think it was simply coming to London and finding more access to black people generally. And then more events and activities and culture. There was obviously a lot more going on in London than there was in West Bromwich/ Birmingham in any case, and because I was becoming a writer/journalist, I started off doing lots of reviews for other publications before I set up my own. Anyway, the interest sort of peaked through that entry to London.

How did you learn your craft as a critic? Was it through university or did it just happen as you did what you did?

It was really my master's in journalism studies which involved quite a lot of going out and reviewing various art forms. Not necessarily theatre, just generally going to arts exhibitions galleries, crafting our own voice and being confident in that voice. The concept of how to actually write a review or news story was also all through my master's. I don't think I would have set up my had I not done the degree, I wouldn't have had the confidence to do that. I did obviously read other reviews and still do. We used to have more free papers in London in the evening like *London Lite* and also the *Metro*, which we still have, so when I was commuting, I read a lot of reviews in the free papers, definitely. And then because of my course, I read *The Guardian* a lot.

When you started going to the theatre with your critic's hat on, did you bump into any other critics? Was there any sort of solidarity that you felt out there?

Oh, no, no. Even now I don't talk to any critics when I go. Sometimes I think it's probably imposter syndrome, because when I look around, there's hardly anyone that looks like me and also because theatre's so elitist, as I've pointed out, it affects the way a lot of other critics are. To be honest, if I do talk to someone, it's because I know them from the wider industry and it will most likely be another black writer. But generally I don't have chitchats with other critics.

Do any of them come up and talk to you?

No. What about you? Do you find that people don't talk to you either? I don't think that they're a very warm bunch of people.

No they don't talk to me. And when I started out, the ones working for the big press titles in the old days were the worst. I'm white but I started off as a reviewer in the national black press while I worked at The Voice newspaper as well as The Weekly Journal and Pride Magazine. You were there a bit too. But there was never enough black theatre to kick music or film off the front page of the culture section, unless it was heavy hitters like Talawa Theatre or Oliver Samuels. I don't think I got any Talawa gigs but for pleasure I did go the Samuels farces that came in every year from Jamaica to do London and the big cities. But aside from the black theatre companies that were starting up, at that time coverage of theatre otherwise was usually someone had told someone who'd told someone that there was a black actor or actress in a West End show, even if it was a tiny role. But at that time black people tended to go the West End for the clubs and the musicals, not theatre — and you can still understand why. So I'd be told, "Oh, Nick, you can go." "Why me?" "Well, one, you know about theatre. Two, you're white. And three, it's on your way home." Then, weirdly, the big theatres suddenly jumped from ignoring the black sector to desperately flooding it with tickets and offers as diversity drives started to kick in. It was like, "Oh my God, you're THE VOICE! You simply must come . . ." The rather loud silent coda being, ". . . so we can say that we have someone who's black in the house." To see me turn up, the PRs and producers were . . .

. . . disappointed? *[laughs]*

'Infuriated' is likely a better word. It was funny watching them trying not to show it. Whatever I wrote was usually transmuted by the editors into a more newsy sort of piece. The growth in black theatre got the younger or trainee journalists interested and some of them wanted to do reviews. So the editors would let them go too. What was heartbreaking is that most of those writers had so little theatre education or experience that they found it hard to write structured reviews. For example, a young journalist would come back from a Macbeth and her review would be simply a recounting of the plot. There are all sorts of divides in our society, but the gaps created by our uneven educational system really do need looking at.

In fact I still feel like that about opera. I find opera, and also ballet, extremely daunting. I'd much rather send a reviewer who would be more confident with it, and then I can go along and just enjoy the performance. That's because I don't have the right experience, I think. For me it presents an educational barrier, I wouldn't feel comfortable giving a good review of an opera.

I suspect the majority of critics would agree with you on that one. They just might not put it as bluntly. Or even admit it. But that elitism can present a positive challenge sometimes. Since my time at The Voice I've always asked why can't we send complete beginners to review opera? Forget about the West End stuff if our readership won't ever go to it. But there's a lot of people I know who'll put on a bit of opera when they're at home. There's probably more reason to have African-Caribbean critics for opera than for West End drama.

Interestingly, the English National Opera first approached me when they announced their new season for 2018. They were perfectly honest about what they wanted: "We're trying to reach different audiences. Would you come along to our launch?" For the reasons just explained, I was adamant that I would come along to the launch and promote the season on my social media, but I wasn't doing any sort of review. But that didn't stop them from offering complimentary tickets to see one of the shows in the season, so of course they're aware. I did suggest to them that they probably need to do some sort of training course about wording for opera reviews in order to train black writers to know exactly what they should be looking for, and they said they were up for it. There was no follow-through, but I think that would really helpful to be honest

It would make more sense with a mentoring process. How do you give feedback to your own team?

I tell them to always work from the basics: write about what you see, why you liked it and why you didn't, and be as *honest* as possible. A critic's role is to give that honest opinion about a production, and hopefully encourage people to see it and tell their friends to see it. To raise awareness of shows and to show people the diversity that exists in the productions out there. Without reviews, a lot of people wouldn't go to see a show. They might see an advert or poster for it, but having read a review they're more likely to go and see the show.

Which is how a lot of critics from all backgrounds have always gotten into the business. It's a perfectly acceptable provenance. In fact, for every critic I've spoken to, there's no common background. Very few of them are 'trained' writers. It's interesting to compare notes on how we all fit our other jobs into it, and also how we fit our family and kids into what is clearly an incredibly antisocial cycle of life/work.

Since having my daughter, I basically stopped going to regular theatre for a few years but I go more frequently now she's older. That doesn't mean I have stopped going to the theatre entirely, what it means is that I've started going to *children's* theatre. My daughter has loved theatre from a very early age because of my passion for it. I've adapted, so now I'm going to matinees instead of going at 7:30 on a weekday, but if it's a show that I'm really interested in, then I'll definitely try to go along. I think I'm okay with not going to the theatre as much as I used to. As long as somebody is there representing *Afridiziak* then I'm fine. I think the main thing is that we're there and on press night and it doesn't have to be me.

Are you at least reviewing the kids' shows?

I started off reviewing them but now it's easier to just buy tickets. It was a bit like how I feel about reviewing opera — I just want to go along for the pleasure of it. It's like, "Oh, that was nice. My daughter enjoyed it. She laughed. End of review."

A lot of us have been there. In fact now you're actually paying to go to the theatre, has that been a rude awakening?

[laughs] I didn't realise how expensive it is! We went to see *Rumpelstiltskin* at the Southbank Centre. It was like 30 quid for the adult tickets and £10 for children, and I was like, "Oh, is this *how* much?!" It was a bit of a shock to be honest.

Has that given you any perspective on the problem with audiences? The fact that you look around and it's not just a question of white faces, it's also people who have the educational, financial and social confidence to be there.

Apart from the Southbank show, we also went to Theatre Peckham *[South East London]* around the same time. The friends that we went with to the Southbank weren't black, and when I looked around, it was just my daughter and I who were black in that audience, which is obviously very depressing. But when I went to see *Robin Hood* at Theatre Peckham, the audience there was more diverse. But it's Peckham, so we'd expect a Peckham audience to look like the neighbourhood where they live. But yes, it has been a shock to the system, and I think children's theatre also needs a lot of work in terms of the audience because I do feel that the audience is very middle class white families enjoying those shows. It shouldn't really be like that.

So do you think that a lot of those people sitting there feel entitled?

Um . . . *[laughs]* Yeah . . . possibly.

I get very angry, to be honest, with that and it puts me off a lot of shows. I'm not sure I have the right to get angry though, which might be the point.

Well you have got a right, of course. It's not exclusive on who can be angry, it's about empathy, isn't it? And I guess you can see that there's actually some sort of social injustice there.

As Afridiziak's role as a critical force has grown within UK theatre, is there anything that you're particularly proud of from seeing that co-relationship develop?

I'm definitely proud of the fact that the website still exists and that we are quoted more on theatre posters, and in promo, on social media. I'm especially proud that we get invited to press night at the same time as everybody else rather than having to knock on people's doors to say, "Hey, we exist!" That's definitely something I'm proud of. We also get lots of nice emails from readers that say how much they appreciate the newsletter and the special offers. So I'm glad that we are there, providing the service that is appreciated.

How viable is a professional theatre reviews site?

Well I'm not at the stage where I could give up my day job, although some

people would disagree and say it's because I *haven't* given up my day job that
the website hasn't elevated itself to financial viability. Yes there are
advertisements on the site, but that's not enough give up my day job. So, yes,
it's precarious, but maybe it's precarious because I have not invested in it with
that financial focus. I'm happy for people to come to the site, ask if they can
advertise and I say yes, welcome aboard. Whereas I could be proactive and
count out the business opportunities, build up the brand. Instead it has moved
along nicely each year. *Afridiziak* has never embarked on a big marketing
campaign for itself, and perhaps if that sort of thing had happened or will
happen, the site would be financially successful.

>   *Do you have any thoughts on what the role of the critic is, particularly as it's
>   changing so rapidly? Can theatre survive without professional-level critics?*

I don't think so. Not for long, because theatre relies on the importance of
press night. There's so much difference between the nature of a production
before press night and a production after press night. Press night is a big deal
in theatre. Before press night, it's in preview and the tickets are often on
special offer, and it's not such a big deal what people think of the show. But as
soon as press night is over and the reviews are out then often that's when the
production starts selling so, no, I don't think they could do without press
night, not right now.

>   *Basically you're saying that the critic is an integral part of a production. Which
>   is a funny thing to try and tell people outside of the business, but from our point
>   of view it's logical. Which is a problem if you have to say something less than
>   positive about a production.*

That's always been a problem. There is a lot of pressure, I always gulp
whenever a review comes in and it's one star. I'm just like, "Oh dear, I cannot
cope with having to send the producers or the PR a one-star review." But it is
what it is.

>   *One of the running debates is whether you would drop running a one-star if you
>   felt that it really didn't help. If you witnessed people who had a story to tell or a
>   vision, and that needed to be commended and supported, and to give them a one-
>   star would send out the wrong signals. Well, it would be the right signals to the
>   company, but the wrong signals to the audience.*

In the past I've never dropped as review in my capacity as editor. If I've had to
drop anything, it's because the writer has insisted on it for some reason. I've

had to ask a critic to reword what they've written — perhaps it was slightly offensive or not well structured, particularly when somebody's seen a show that's really bad and they've slipped with the professionalism by just writing whatever they wanted. So you send it back and ask, "Please can you remove this?' and they've not agreed. I'd be reluctant to remove a review, but I've tried not to upset anyone either.

Is there anything you've written yourself that has caused a problem or helped a success. Did you write the review that made people come back to you a couple of years later and say, "That was our breakthrough review, thanks!"

Indeed there have been. One was *Julius Caesar*, an all-black production by the RSC with Paterson Joseph, and the company loved the review so much that they used it in a book that he's got out at the moment and quoted it. That was really nice. Mind you, I didn't write the review — that was Gillian Fisher.

Another reason I struggle with writing reviews myself is because I'm at the stage where I hate the actual process of sitting down to write them. So that's probably another reason why I don't go to the theatre very much. Thankfully, the team write fantastically so I'm much happier overseeing press nights and making sure that *Afridiziak* is there.

And where do you think the direction is now for Afridiziak?

I would like it to be better known. If you know about it, you know about it, and there are lots of people that know about it and come to the site time and time again to see the reviews, the interviews, the special offers, listings, etc. But we need to tap into the people that don't know about it. And like you've said, we could even start reviewing more mainstream productions that don't have a black cast or writers to broaden the awareness.

How does this reflect the nation's ability to make diversity a reality?

One challenge we're facing is the term BAME, because diversity and inclusion often comes across as a tickbox exercise. However, in terms of diversity, theatre is in a much better place than we were 11 years ago when I founded *Afridiziak*, in the sense that we have black playwrights not just in the fringe theatres but in the mainstream theatres and really owning those spaces when they haven't been encouraged to in the past — and they're not just talking about race issues.

So there has been progress . . .

There's definitely been progress.

Is that a result of tokenism or more realistic motives? I know the white people in this country like the idea of 'quotas' but that's basically an American concept which seems pointless in the UK.

It may have stemmed from a tickbox exercise, but black creatives consistently prove their worth.

Of course alongside the playwrights we've seen the performers — which is where the first main push came for visibility and representation — but also the directors and the artistic directors. And it seems that they also finally managed to make a convincing move on the lack of female representation at the same time. So clearly there was something happening. But has this come about from fulfilling their funding commitments or have institutions been really listening and thinking that it is time to make a change?

It's probably a combination. Certainly the institutions want themselves to be more reflective of this society that we live in. It's not sustainable to only cater to people that look like you, at the very least it's quite archaic to work like that.

There are the cyclical conversations about class, its representation both in audience and onstage, how within an audience — white obviously — there continues to be a rarefied pool that isn't reflective of the population and which just isn't shifting despite admittedly half-arsed efforts to shift it. There are also the age divisions in many areas where the bright young things go the fringe, the old ones go to the West End regional tour, and the rest of us of any age go panto in between if we have kids or a musical if we can afford the babysitter. Again, that's mostly the white people since theatre is a very specifically safe space for white people. I'm not sure even a move like Fringe of Colour ['spotlighting black & brown performers at Ed Fringe & running a free ticket scheme'] will make any difference to the cultural/class exclusion of the level playing-field of somewhere like the Edinburgh Festival Fringe.

But it will make a difference, because at least we're talking about it. And something like Fringe of Colour hasn't happened before. I imagine, as the years go by, it will also start to have an impact. But it does go back to your first question of what the issues in theatre are from a black person's perspective, and I would say it's simply those bums on seats. But not just *white* bums on seats.

That's an insightful way of looking at theatre, where it's not just about the craft and the art of the performance, although livestreaming is changing this — but I'm not sure it will change much in the long run.

It makes a difference if you've missed a sold-out production of *Small Island* at the National Theatre *[adaptation of Andrea Levy's novel by white writer Helen Edmundson]* and the only way you can watch it is livestreamed in the cinema. *[laughs]* That happened to me . . .

Me too . . . those ticket prices, eh? I should mention to our readers that a lot of recordings are available for free at the Victoria & Albert's Theatre & Performance Department, either by going there in person or via your institutions, depending on copyright. Access like this is about the business of getting people to witness what's on that stage — whether it's a free community play or a hard-nosed bottom-line West End musical, you still need to have a trusted system to get people in, regardless of who they are I suppose.

Where improvement is needed is for more black people to think that going to the theatre is for them. To know and assume that going to the theatre is for them. And let's remember that theatre is still very elitist across the board in any case. The prices are elitist. But you do have new organisations such as the Black Ticket Project which manage to get £10 tickets out there. They have a mailing list and they send the offers out, and if you're lucky enough then you can go and see a production that would normally cost you £50-£60 for a fifth of the price. I think that's the sort of thing which is being encouraged across the West End as well, where organisations like theatres and producers are becoming really positive about this.

Anecdotally or from what you're actually seeing, do you think there'll be a wider knock-on effect from a project like that? Can it create a new theatregoing community from scratch, hit that critical mass, whatever it might be that keeps that community going of its own accord and which then, most importantly, integrates? Or do you need more projects like Black Ticket Project to amplify it? Plus how do you launch out of the London/West End orbit without leaving it all behind?

It is London-centric. Obviously there's more scope for ticket offer schemes to branch out across the country. *Afridiziak* has always had theatre offers, and those are our newsletters that get the most opened because everyone's like "oh great you've got an offer on thank you". We also get quite a few emails from subscribers who say, "I always book your offers, thank you!" — so the way to get people in, at the moment at least, is to continue offering discounts for tickets. Bums on seats!

To return to the idea of the past decade of change, there came a before and after point for UK theatre criticism that was sort of marked by Lyn Gardner losing her position as theatre critic & commentator at The Guardian newspaper, which removed the hope of any critics in the UK making a living out of the job. It reflected a zeitgeist of the idea of criticism metamorphosing into a form of 'modern' criticism — the fall of the nationals, the rise of the websites and the blogs — and latterly the audience reviewer. It's been quite a turnaround and not always a happy one, which seems to have matched the lifespan to date of Afridiziak. Do you have a sense that you've ridden this wave — even if people haven't given you the space you've actually earned — to get to where you are now? Is there so much more to do?

When I first started, I was definitely hungry for more and more and more and more. But now there is more and more, it's not that I don't feel the hunger's not there, but it's now hunger for *where's* the next black production, because I can see there's a steady stream of black productions and a lot of them are getting on the stages where they should be — but not all of them. Theatres like Hackney Empire and Theatre Royal Stratford East *[both in East London]* have done so much. But it shouldn't be just them. It's great that in London, for example, main stages like the National Theatre, the Royal Court, the Young Vic are staging all black productions. And those things were not happening ten years ago. In 2009 there was the all black cast of *Cat on a Hot Tin Roof* at the Novello Theatre *[in London]* and I remember that *everyone* was talking about it. It was just like, "Oh my God, what a bold move an all black cast on the West End stage." And now we have black playwrights filling out West End stages.

Theatre has definitely evolved and *Afridiziak* has evolved with it. But though I'm happy to see all the developments in the theatre industry, I just think that what's missing is a more diverse audience. The productions are there, now it's about making sure more people are seeing theatre and not just the usual suspects.

*

19

Rosemary Jenkinson

'If we can just get our plays seen here, then we're doing well'

Rosemary Jenkinson is a playwright, poet and short fiction writer. Based in Belfast, Northern Ireland, where she was born, she was raised in Belfast & Dundrum, County Down.

- *@rosemaryj77*

You've done a fair bit of travelling, haven't you?

Yes I have. I went to university in 1986, Durham University, and then, just as I was leaving Durham, my parents moved from Northern Ireland to Berwick-upon-Tweed because my dad got a job there. I didn't go back to Northern Ireland until 2002. I moved around the UK quite a lot: I did a postgrad in Keele, I lived in Newcastle upon Tyne, in Gillingham *[Kent]*, Dundee, so I was all over the place for a long time. I also taught abroad, places like Prague, Athens, Warsaw. So I was away a long time.

You didn't end up in London.

No! I always thought London would be probably too big for me and I'd be depressed there in some shabby little bedsit. So no, I never wanted to go to London. It's funny that, I don't know why, because I was happy to go to other big European cities but London just never never appealed. *[laughs]* I know Londoners probably think it's the metropolis, the centre of the universe, and to me it's fun if I'm in London for a few days, but if it's any longer all I think of is *depression* when I'm there!

So you never found the type of work that lured you to London, in a performing arts way?

Well I wasn't into theatre until I came back to Northern Ireland after 2002. Otherwise I would have probably been lured down by the bright lights. Afterwards from Belfast I had a tiny connection with London through an initiative with the Royal Court and one with the Soho Theatre. But very very little connection. I'd actually have loved to have had a connection to London, but it seems a very closed world. The way theatre is, you have to be meeting people all the time to be thought of. If you're not in the London scene it's virtually impossible to break in. And I don't have a London agent now — I did have one at the very start but that went badly. They stopped answering my emails and that was the end of that really. I never bothered to get another London agent though it would probably have helped me a lot.

You bounced back to Northern Ireland though.

Yes and I think it was a lot to do with the fact I felt I had been wrenched from Northern Ireland. I wanted to go back after university but that didn't happen because my parents were no longer there, and I felt taken away by circumstance. It was also because in England I had been writing prose and short stories and trying novels, and I felt I couldn't find my voice. Then when I went back to Northern Ireland I felt much more connected to my voice, the local dialect just was *richer* to me, I just felt more rooted to it.

That idea of voice is important, isn't it? It's not just 'your' voice, it really is a lifeblood thing for many people, to be surrounded by people who speak the same way and an audience that speaks that way.

Possibly, though I also find that Americans absolutely go wild for anything Irish. Well, that's my experience — I've had a lot of plays on out there and they adore it. But I feel that being in Northern Ireland means I can have more richness in my language and more of an authenticity of place, so it just feels right. When I was in England I didn't feel that I belonged to any part of England, Scotland, Wales or anywhere. I felt totally disconnected and that came through in my writing.

Which is an interesting thing to run with, isn't it?

It is, it is! It's that whole thing of locality but with a universality. That's the best you can achieve as a writer, particularly in playwriting because it's all to do with dialogue. It's so much more important than prose to be in a society where you find people's language fascinating — and I do find Northern Irish language fascinating, all the dialects, so that really helps.

So after your international wandering, you went local to find your universal.

Exactly.

How's it been going then?

It's been getting better. It was very very slow in the beginning to establish myself when I came back — a lot of false starts if we're talking about theatre specifically. My very first play, *The Bonefire*, got bad reviews and that really knocked me back — that was 2006. But then I just kept going forward and getting into the local Belfast scene and overall it's gone well — some big plays on at the Lyric Theatre in Belfast and I was writer-in-residence there two years ago. So many playwrights get immediately lauded as the greatest, but it never really happened to me, it's been an incremental thing and me refusing to go away in spite of any bad reviews and knockbacks. *[laughs]* I think that's really the story.

That's a period in which a lot of our political and economic ills have taken root, and yet at the same time we've seen huge strides in social awareness and calls for change. Certainly in Northern Ireland, it's been a momentous couple of decades. In mapping that change, the trajectory of your plays sort of makes you symbolic of Northern Ireland's recent history.

[laughs] Oh I would love to be a symbol! No, with the Peace Process I was writing plays that took a wider perspective because I'd come back from living outside of Northern Ireland. I wasn't writing about the Troubles, and living in England really helped as it meant I could see the sectarianism afresh and with more focus. I was also looking at more modern and general themes which most writers in Northern Ireland weren't doing, like climate change and homelessness. I've also done a lot of political themes that are not just about Northern Ireland, so again I think that's helped. Brexit has been a wonderful thing for me because it's put us Northern Irish writers in the spotlight so I think that whole Irish border argument has been a positive for us.

A great thing for me personally was Waking the Feminists, that whole Dublin movement *[grassroots campaign formed in protest against the male-dominated lineup at the Abbey in Dublin for its 2016 centenary programme, supporting a new wave of female playwrights, directors and other creatives]* and I joined the movement in Belfast as well. That probably resulted in me getting my first play on a Lyric main stage and for sure as a woman I would never have had that chance before. So that gave me a boost even if it's questionable whether the Waking the Feminists scene has been a shortterm boost or a longterm one. Either way it's certainly better for a woman working in theatre than before.

> *In trying to explain Northern Ireland to people who have never been there, it's not a cliché to say there's something of an edge to everything there. Sure everyone speaks English there, but words like 'politics', 'religion', 'language', 'history' carry another level of meaning that they can never have in the rest of the UK. Well some of that is shared with a community like Glasgow ('religion') and obviously the Republic of Ireland ('history', 'language'), but certainly you'd draw a blank if you applied the word 'sectarian' to anywhere else. There's also the fact that Northern Ireland, though a devolved 'nation' within the UK, has become something else through being ignored by the rest of the UK and not engaged by the Republic to become a quasi 'small nation', i.e. a sovereign nation too small in population and resources to independently function in the way big nations do. So I'd say Northern Ireland has been forced to be both inward and outward-looking in a way that, again, the rest of the UK could never have a concept of. That must give you a very different worldview to draw on — no matter how woke or politically aware or climatically conscious someone in London is, they just won't find that edge in their arsenal.*

The level of political hatred in Northern Ireland is just so much deeper than in most of the UK. Though I do feel that some hatred has recently come into English politics in the Brexit argument between Remainers and Leavers. It was interesting that because of those two divided Brexit strands, England could finally understood how vitriolic our politics are.

The whole thing about Northern Ireland, as you say, is that we are a small nation and have to look out. I would look to the UK more — although I do look South *[Ireland]* as well, so both, but some people wouldn't look to the UK at all. That's another thing you have to remember, they'll only look to Ireland, they hate the UK. As a result there are so many tensions here in Northern Ireland, and I suppose when I write I'm picking at those tensions. Sometimes I want to inflame them and other times maybe I want to transcend them for different dramatic purposes.

I certainly remember when I came back in 2002, a lot of people in the theatre were saying, "Oh we don't want anything more about the Troubles, we've gone past that." But it's funny how the Troubles are back in vogue, it's to do with the centenaries coming up of Northern Ireland *[2021, the centenary of the creation of Northern Ireland]* and of course we had 1916 *[the Easter Rising in Ireland]*. The past is being stirred up really badly, and of the course the whole border issue of Brexit has brought up the past as well, so we're now returning to the past and analysing it. That's interesting for a writer although I've over the past years I've been writing about more general topics.

Across Europe there's been a major EU-driven wave over the years to put culture at the centre as a softly political way of unifying people in the different regions and nations. It seems to me that Northern Ireland would be in a wonderful position to be able to interface on its own terms with the other nations of the UK, the South and Europe. Even if it hasn't turned out that way, do you feel that there's a responsibility regardless for Northern Irish writers to look for things that need to be out there, because as things stand you can say things in a way that the politicians, commentators, newspapers and the communities themselves can't?

Yes I do. The more my work is produced, the more I am asked to be a political or cultural commentator and I think it was particularly Brexit that gave me the opportunity to talk more about politics, about those incendiary points and question them. I do feel we're all being pushed politically, but it's a good push, especially as the DUP *[Democratic Unionist Party, Protestant]* and Sinn Féin *[Catholic & Republican party]* have lost touch.

Maybe I'll just talk for myself and say, as a Protestant, that we don't really appreciate the backward-looking elements of the DUP opposed to abortion and gay marriage, so therefore we are talking about a different Protestant view that is not represented by a political party. That's exactly where writers can be useful because we can give a bigger broader perspective of what it means to be Protestant or someone who votes Unionist, and we don't see everything through very harsh binary political lines. Our job is to show the nuances of political opinion right now and how it's complicated. We all have links with the South and the UK and it's not a simple issue about wanting to be with one or the other.

So I do think our role as writers in Northern Ireland is to show that there's a middle way, it gives more dimension to us and we have to do this now when our politicians are being very very quiet because they weren't in government for three years *[the Northern Ireland Assembly suspended itself from January 2017 to January 2020 after policy disagreements between its power-sharing leadership]*. That has given us a bigger voice and helped us to become more politically confident. Because in Northern Ireland traditionally you're told, "Say nothing, don't put your colours on the line and try not to upset people." I think that's negative and it's frustrating to me to have to hide my views all the time. Here we're very much encouraged in the arts to suppress our politics, but recently we've been pushing much more against that.

Viewing that in black and white, it makes you sound like a purely political writer whereas clearly you're not. And yet you are by sheer virtue of context — who you are, where you are, your birthright. So really by the act of just being and doing in Northern Ireland, you're making a political statement.

That's true. And it's interesting how I've always loved satire. It's a huge thing in Northern Ireland and always has been, it's the way we deal with our politics. Satirical theatre has come out more recently in my work — I've written more satires since our politicians refused to go back to Stormont because it was something to rail against. So the politics has pushed me into being more political. But I also agree that anything created in Northern Ireland right now can be a political act because we're at the centre of Brexit tension because of the whole border thing — is it going to be a sea border, is it going to be a land border — and the Lyra McKee shooting *[journalist who was killed in 2019 during rioting in Derry~Londonderry]*. Everything is much more edgy. Like you said, there is always that edge somewhere and it has come back, forcing us into a political situation. I mean, *[Northern Irish playwright & poet]* Seamus Heaney was forced in the 1970s to politically comment and he did so. I also feel that I need to say stuff about what's happening, because who else is going to?

And yet it's viewed as a small corner of the country, wilfully ignored by Westminster, hobbled by Stormont and funding cuts, so logically people's ability to get work made is going to be adversely affected — as is the ability of audiences to see that work.

The cuts have been terrible, particularly since 2015-16, and we've had no culture minister for three years. It's a dreadful situation. One of the problems particularly for theatres at the moment is that there is no touring money so we can't take plays from here to the rest of the UK or Ireland. It has limited what we can do. So I feel frustrated that I'm trapped in my own corner — I mean, I can write articles that can maybe go to *The Irish Times [based in Dublin]* or whatever, but I can't get the actual theatre out.

And there are the practical things . . . I am only allowed so many actors, and my last play only had two characters, which is so frustrating. But people still go to the theatre and have a huge appetite for plays. So the audiences are still good but there's just no money to put work on. And because of the art cuts here, everything is much more commercial so there's very little that's ambitious politically, very little new writing, but an awful lot of revivals. If I want to do something political, I'll put it on anyway, on a shoestring in a black box, just because I think it needs to be on. I did a satire about Theresa May in 2019 and I wanted that out because it's current. Current topics are the most exciting thing to do, to do the whole Dario Fo thing.

You're speaking from a Belfast base of operations, which highlights the internal divide that's Belfast versus the rest of Northern Ireland.

Sure, but at the moment there is a little bit of money for touring. In fact I have a play on right now, *Dream, Sleep, Connect*, that is touring round Lisburn, Armagh, Newry, Cushendall even. The Arts Council *[of Northern Ireland]* will give money to tour around Northern Ireland and they actively support that. So that's a good thing, but to go outside of here, no, not happening.

So people are actively trying to make those connections everywhere as everything's conspiring to keep them stuck in one place. If you're struggling to stage even the smallest of black box productions, that's not good for the message is it?

No, the message doesn't get that far, and that is one of the problems. The only benefit I see to getting those shows out is that I can also talk to the papers so I can get my message out through the press. That's the way to go if you want to talk about social change, and it's always valuable to do even though your audiences are really small.

So theatre becomes part of a much larger vehicle, and needs to be in order to do its job. Are there any particular plays that you've done that you think have made an impact perhaps in ways that other plays haven't?

My first play *The Bonefire*, which didn't get good reviews, did make an impact. It was a satire on sectarianism and paramilitarism produced in Dublin by Rough Magic, which is a great theatre company, and it did at least shake things up. In a way it was ignored because it was uncomfortable, but I still think it was completely worth doing because it made an impact historically — not at that time in 2006 but looking back perspective-wise it can be seen as an important play because it just took the piss out of our politics and it was the right time to say how ridiculous the Troubles were.

Another play I'd say is *Here Comes the Night*, which was on the main stage of the Lyric. It was about the street where I am living right now in Belfast and how Catholics were forced out of it in the early 1970s when they were told to leave by the UDA *[Ulster Defence Army, an Ulster loyalist paramilitary group]*, though I set the play earlier back in 1966. I wanted to confront the history of your community in the history of your own street. It got great audience numbers so it felt like it made an impact.

The homelessness play *May the Road Rise Up* has also probably made an impact even though it's only a monologue play because it came at the right moment. It was about a woman and it coincided with the surge of interest in *Waking the Feminists*. It's unusual because most homeless plays are about men and I thought it changed people's perspective a bit. I also wrote *Lives in Translation* about a Somali asylum-seeker which was sympathetic to a cause but was more about the flaws in the system that assesses asylum-seekers. I think it was a big eye-opener for people about the asylum-seeking system. There was touring money to Dublin but it was very very brief and it also toured to a couple of venues down South, but it was good that the production made it out of Northern Ireland. Very rare, but because of its universal aspect it was able to tour. It helps that academics are interested in work on asylum seekers, so it had wider appeal, again because of the universal aspect.

If we talk about a national voice of the performing arts in somewhere like Scotland, theatre in particular, that strong definition certainly focuses funding wherever it comes from. But the National Theatre of Scotland confidently rests on all the city and regional theatres there and I suspect they're not really that bothered whether a Scottish show travels over the border. It's not essential to Scotland's capacity to create and sustain its ecosystem of creatives, performers, companies and festivals who are all on message. But still, whatever you do in your local black box in Scotland can easily go up the ladder to the main stage in Glasgow — and beyond, nationally or internationally. In Wales they're slowly building up a similar structure and establishing a Welsh identity for theatre, and obviously Ireland, being a country with ownership of its history, is confident enough not to have a national theatre if they don't want one, which they do and they don't, because they've got a string of amazing theatres and companies old and new with unassailable Irish identities. It's strange that Belfast at least, with its opera house and theatres historically, has struggled to keep its head up as a hub for Northern Irish theatre. At the moment it's the Lyric in Belfast that's flying the flag, but from an outsider's viewpoint it's hard to catch a definable voice.

But there is a distinctive Northern Irish voice. I suppose you would think of me, David Ireland, Owen McCafferty, Marie Jones, Abbie Spallen — there's a lot of us and we have a similar voice which is sardonic and dark, but also highly humorous. So there is a voice that comes out but that's not necessarily one that's fostered through theatres, it's just something natural within us. We have cynical voices because of our country's politics.

Theatre here is not well connected up as plays in the black boxes aren't being transferred to the main stage of the Lyric. Still, the Lyric would be our national theatre clearly because it is a seedbed of some talent, but also there are a lot of theatre companies who don't see the big picture. They are happy to operate only in their own little circle and have their own audience without venturing out. But from my perspective as a writer that's terrible, the writers aren't benefiting because of the lack of ambitiousness of local companies. It's not that there's any money for ambition either — we all realise that as playwrights if we can just get our plays seen here then we're doing well.

Are there discernable Catholic and Protestant voices at the moment, or even voices for Belfast and the rest of Northern Ireland?

Yes, and the rural voice would be quite different from Belfast. Obviously the Belfast voice is faster and much more acerbic, while the country voice is of course slower and more colourful with more metaphors. As for differences between the Catholic and Protestant voices I don't think there are any, even though Catholics might say Protestants are a bit more dour. *[laughs]* But I think that's not actually true.

We all went through similar feelings through the Troubles, and that comes through in our voices, the fact that we like the same black humour. I will say that there would be some competitiveness between Catholic and Protestant writers. I remember hearing about a Catholic writer who complained to the Lyric that there were too many Protestant writers being produced there, so yeah, there could be a bit of competitiveness about, because there are two different political perspectives. I suppose theatres are aware of this and know they can't put on too many plays depicting one side at the expense of the other. It's a tricky balance.

A barrier the Catholic bloc definitely has the right to complain about is the fight for the legal recognition of the Irish language, a key statement of identity which as we know is linked to why the Stormont shut-down. Do you think there's room for Irish language theatre in Northern Ireland?

Of course. I went recently a couple of months ago to a show, *The Story of the Shaw's Road Gaeltacht*, at the Cultúrlann McAdam Ó Fiaich *[Irish language cultural centre on the Falls Road, Belfast]* — produced by Aisling Ghéar, the Irish language theatre company *[based in Belfast]*. The play was in Irish and surtitled in English, about the origins of Irish language activism in Belfast. There's also been a huge explosion over the past few years in Irish language schools so they've got a great market for it. So of course it's important and absolutely I support that. I'm all for different perspectives, and most theatre practitioners want to reflect as many diverse voices as possible.

Theatre is very insular in each country and each city has their own scene, and I suppose that's what I feel too. It's just hard to get Northern Irish voices out to the rest of the UK. Maybe the sea is a complete mental block for some people. My opinion was that after Jez Butterworth's big Northern Irish play *The Ferryman* was a hit in London, you would have thought London theatres would be clamouring and reaching out to Northern Irish artists to find out more if only because of this whole Brexit thing, and keeping an eye out for us. But we just don't feel they're connecting with us and we're still very cast-off in a way.

What's been coming into Northern Ireland from the Republic and the rest of the UK in terms of theatre? Are you on anyone's touring budget or transfer list, or does it feel like there's a block?

There is a block here and it's a two-way block. Of course there are things happening, for instance at the Lyric the small studio is used for touring theatre, and you get lot of UK and Southern Irish shows. The big shows we should be seeing rarely come here and if they do again it would be at the Lyric — something like an Abbey Theatre *[Dublin]* co-production of a Conor McPherson play. The Grand Opera House is closed at the minute for refurbishment, but that's where you would get big English successful West End shows touring. So we do get a glimpse of London theatre, but it's not huge. We certainly don't get to see much of the cutting edge theatre that is on at the likes of the Soho, the Royal Court and the other London theatres.

You can't just jump on a train in either direction . . .

Exactly and now that *[UK airline]* Flybe's gone it's going to be even worse. *[laughs]* It means it's much more of an overnight stay for us and a bigger financial commitment to come over. It's practical things like that.

Which is a situation that speaks loads.

It does. I make sure I buy a lot of plays and keep an eye on what's coming up, what subjects are covered in London, because otherwise we won't be exposed to those ideas. Not that I would say I'm reactive or I kowtow to London as some superior hub of drama — in fact I know the zeitgeist as well as anyone in London, but we all have to feed into each other. It's important that it should be a two-way thing, and so the rest of the UK should be looking at what we're doing as well.

*

20

Lora Krasteva

'Here's a model. We know it works. And then it happens'

Lora Krasteva is a cultural producer & artistic director of Global Voices Theatre. Based in East London, she was born in Sofia, Bulgaria, and raised in Algeria, Bulgaria, Tunisia & Spain.
• *globalvoicestheatre.com, @GlobalVoicesTh*

I'm guessing it was theatre that landed you in the UK . . .

Not quite, but it has kept me here. I grew up in a family where the arts and theatre are well regarded but mostly regarded as hobbies, so it's not something that I pursued professionally until I came to London where I was finishing a master's in political science. I did a double degree between Paris and London, where I was at the London School of Economics studying European Studies, of all things. I was born in Bulgaria but my parents emigrated when I was a baby, so I lived in Algeria, Tunisia and Spain before going to study in France.

It became apparent that I didn't want to pursue the typical sort of European Studies careers path, you know, European Parliament, Commission or consultancy. But I had always done theatre on the side at uni, and my course had a Latin American programme and I had spent some time in Argentina. So when I bumped into this amazing project in London, the CASA Latin American Theatre Festival, I asked the director Daniel Goldman if I could get involved. I started working with CASA in 2011/12, and that was the start of me seriously considering the arts and theatre as a professional opportunity.

I spent five years working at CASA, starting as a volunteer and then ended up effectively producing the festival with Daniel. Throughout that time, I managed to balance my personal budget by doing freelance work and other side gigs that had nothing to do with the arts. So I was finding that flow of being able to manage several projects, and it came to a point where I felt I had reached my growth in CASA and needed to do my own thing, whatever that meant. The festival was in a good position, it was starting a new chapter — either I could leave it in safe hands or stay for the next 20 years.

So I left, and by a myriad of circumstances, I ended up working at the Arcola Theatre *[in Hackney, East London]* where I started a duty manager job to keep the finances afloat, but at the Arcola there's a big community, and things are very porous, so there were lots of opportunities. Meanwhile I also ended up working in individual giving and was in touch with Streetwise Opera where I started working on With One Voice, the international arts and homelessness movement in a similar capacity doing development. That's how I ended up exploring fundraising in depth, learning very fast to work with corporates and trusts and foundations, adding that string to my producing bow.

So Global Voices didn't come out of nowhere?

Nothing comes out of nowhere. Especially nowadays. It actually started with William Gregory, he's a UK-based translator from Spanish who brought to the Arcola the idea of doing play readings of queer plays from around the world. He knew that the queer work you usually see in the UK, specifically in London, was mostly British or from the United States. And so he pitched to the Arcola to do a series of international play readings from around the world, and open a call for it.

The result was Global Queer Plays *[2018]*, a weekend of plays from around the world in English. The format was a call-out and then plays were read in full as a double-bill, followed by discussion. At that point I was working at the Arcola helping produce the Creative Disruption Festival, which Global Queer Plays was part of. There was a lot of queer work happening in the programme because we were also celebrating the Queer Collective, and the first performance of the Women's Company also happened to be in the festival. Along with Bec Martin-Williams (then participation manager) at the Arcola, and Robin Skyer, who is now programmes producer of Global Voices, we were thinking wouldn't it be great to do a similar call and response and have a Global 'Something' event that focused on female work.

It was quite late in the day to be able to put something in the festival programme that followed the same format — we knew that the call-out for Global Queer Plays had taken such a long time — so we ended up putting on Global Female Voices at the end of the same festival, in April. It was a reading of excerpts of plays rather than complete works because we didn't have sufficient time to do a significant call-out. It was more about tapping into a network of international friends and asking, "Do you have that play that's sitting on your desk and you know it's brilliant but you just haven't got the time or the means to read it and can we read it, is that okay?" These are people who work in international theatre or in theatre in translation that need to be heard, have really great plays that just haven't got a reading, just haven't got that exposure. We got some really good suggestions, and that's how the very first Global Voices event happened.

We had five excerpts of 15 minutes, and because it was all tied into the festival, everyone just came on the day to rehearse, and the model was born. That was in April 2018. It was a free event, everyone volunteered, most of the people who read were part of the community theatre groups that are at the Arcola, we didn't charge entrance. And it was fabulous, people turned up people were engaged with the material the creatives absolutely loved it. So we were all buzzing at the end of the night. And inevitably we had a Q&A and people were asking, "Well what's next?"

We were looking at the audience and creatives and going, "We don't quite know. But let's figure it out together." So we put our heads together with Zhui Ning Chang, who is now connections producer of Global Voices, and we realised it would be great to run this event a bit more properly, with a formal call-out for new writing by female writers across the world, and see what comes back.

With the support of the participation department of the Arcola, a few months later we put that Global Female Voices again. It was a paid event with the format of five plays, a call-out, a selection process with the directors, and so Global Voices was launched.

Where's it going now?

The events we've done to date have been testing the model. Learning how the platform works in gathering people together. How we curate it with an accumulation of voices feeding into the process. A lot of that comes from what I've learned in the arts of homelessness and the idea of co-production, that idea of 'nothing about us without us'. So we're always bringing in people from the community or the geographical area to curate the event. We know now that we have the evidence that the model works as a one-off event, so with the backing of the Roundhouse *[in North London]* we're presenting a few more events like that.

Events like the Latin American one *[2019]* bring me back to CASA and networks in Latin America, which helps to link with the writers and the creatives here in the UK and people like more established organisations, and I hope that people like the International Theatre Institute who have the experience and knowledge can feed back into this. People are interested in exploring the excerpts we're doing as full readings which could lead on to potential productions or collaborations with the writers, perhaps inviting them over in an exchange with UK creators. There's also the hope that Global Voices can help producers and venues in the UK to lose the fear they may have of international theatre and to infiltrate UK stages with stories of Otherness, stories of elsewhere, because we're now in a time when we really need to be as open as we can be and bring those stories to life here in the UK.

We do the call-outs in English at the moment purely because of capacity and funding. I would love to be able to open the call-out to other languages and I'm just figuring out how best to go about it.

All of which makes you think, since we're talking in October 2019, that things have been happening remarkably swiftly.

It has been a blur, especially the last few months. But anyway that's where the first one came from.

It's interesting how even in such a short space of time, you've decided to do the events short and sweet and as they come, rather than slot them rigidly into another theatre or festival's seasons. Is that dictated by circumstances and resources or is it an intentional let's-see-what-happens approach — or a happy mixture of both? It makes sense to me, but it is unusual for these times, especially as you're not trying to soak up funding by shoehorning Global Voices into something like a week at the end of the year.

It's been a combination of things, and probably the major factor for me is that I've always had another job. Purely because of capacity, it's not possible for me to commit to doing a Global Voices once a month or a whole season of works. When I was working at the Arcola, I was working more than full-time each week in any case, especially when I started doing Global Voices as a 'let's give it a go'.

So that's one factor which is purely practical. Secondly, it's how the opportunities came about, and how it was easy to make those decisions from speaking to people who had seen what we do or who had heard about it. After the first Female Voices we did the second Female Voices saying can we look at this model that's emerging where the audience pays and to see if it works outside of a festival setting, as a stand-alone event.

So it really came about by testing and trialling it, and then chatting to people around it. When we did the first two Female Voices, we asked the audiences what other Global 'Something' Voices event would they like to see. At the first one, we read a Kenyan play and afterwards the cast were chatting with the audience and going, "Wouldn't it be great to do a Global *Black* Voices?" And I heard that and said, "Great, let's do it."

Of course that meant we still had to work on it. The geographical spread was ambitious, we needed to find the right curator, bla bla bla. And then there were the conversations with venues and other organisations who were interested in the work, like Malú Ansaldo at the Roundhouse: "I love what you do, I know your work, I trust you, these are the dates that I have in the programme, does that work for you?" "Yes/no." And I guess that's what gave the rhythm.

I'm assuming that money hasn't been a priority in order to have got this far?

Not at first. That idea originally came about because it was in the setting of a community festival so there was the understanding that it was okay to just put it in the programme and get everyone in the community to join in with curating and reading. There wasn't the pressure to 'professionalising' it.

The second time around obviously we did 'professionalise' it, but that's 'professionalise' with the sense of 'put a tag price on the skill'. Everyone from the outset is a 'professional' because they have taken on the project as a passion and brought in their talent. So we were now paying for a few things, like the photographer, because we now had a bit of box office — and the support of the theatre obviously.

After that, I was thinking wouldn't it be great if Global Voices 'Theatre' existed? Taking on that initial model, how else can we use those skills, those platforms, those writers? So money wasn't an issue in the beginning, but it is a thing now. One reason is that seeking funding and getting funding puts it on people's agendas. There is an art to packaging and selling this. We can be more or less successful doing it just by ourselves, but we gain from having other people getting behind us and saying yes this is important. The more they do that the more the stories of the voices of the people that we put onstage gain credibility in this country. They have a value set in themselves but having that backing from funders' adds.

You're framing it from a society point of view, to nail it in terms of British society.

Society, and also industry. You once asked me why does the industry need this? And I felt Bridget's reply summed it up: "They should want it, rather than need it." And showing that you have funding and backing does that. That there is a need or that there is a want for that work. That it's not just me.

[Talking to Nick/The Stage newspaper about Global Black Voices ('Meet the black

theatremakers amplifying global voices', September 6, 2019), poet & journalist Bridget Minamore, who curated the event, said: "I think the idea of what the theatre industry 'needs' is a bit more difficult than people like to admit. It's easy to repeat platitudes about how our industry needs diversity when it comes to race — or gender, or class, or disability — but the truth is the industry doesn't really need it. Instead, I think the industry should want diversity, and should want things like Global Black Voices to thrive. We should want black stories from across the diaspora, as well as want black British stories to be told on our stages. If there's one thing GBV can teach us all, it's that people want these stories. We might or might not 'need' them, but since theatre is this beautiful art form, why can't simply wanting something be enough? Why should we have to justify the importance of seeing a wide range of stories with words like 'need'?"] It's interesting the way Bridget leapt on that. And it's interesting that you've brought it up too. It backs up what you're saying about how this can't work at a professional level if it's not being done at community level — although 'community' isn't quite the right word.

Theatre brings people together, and it isn't a coincidence that I also work with homelessness, helping creativity and self-expression and forums where art is available can really save someone's life.

As I've mentioned, besides Global Voices, I also work for With One Voice. It's an international arts and homelessness movement, and we've been working in Japan for quite a few years supporting the arts and homelessness sector here. We were involved with the Cultural Olympiad in 2012 in London, and then participated at the 2016 Olympic Games in Rio de Janeiro showcasing homeless people's creativity. We give a platform to the changing perceptions about homelessness and we've been working on doing the same in Tokyo for the Olympics there.

I'm guessing that's an interesting adjunct to how Global Voices runs.

What I do on one side of my work, I practise on the other, definitely. It's all mixed up. I was talking about this to my colleague David Tovey, who also works at With One Voice, and I was like, "I've only just realised that all the co-production and co-creation, which is now very much starting to be in vogue but has always been the raison d'etre and the heart of With One Voice, is the heart of Global Voices and a lot of my other, past projects."

Global Voices came about because people *wanted* it. It wasn't the vision from me or the team that said, "We're going to put this out there and it's going to be a success!" It was because people said, "We want this, we've enjoyed this, this works, we want more of that." And along every step of the process, more and more people become involved.

In fact the choices and decisions and the legwork spread across so many layers mean that the end result, even if it's just people with a piece of paper reading bits of plays, is actually quite exciting. Because so many voices are making it and because the next item on the agenda, the next event, the next set of voices that we focus on is based on somehow being plugged into the community and what they want to hear.

Now that we're got ourselves established, even in such a short time, people are writing or messaging or chatting about, "Oh have you thought about this? We'd really love to get involved if you do it." It's a communal effort. "You want to do a Global Asian Voices? Fabulous, let's go. Here's a model, here's how we've tested it out, we know that it works." And then it happens.

It's very easy for you to just say that it happens, but the amount of advance effort required for a single night isn't that much different to what's needed for a full run. Especially when you're coordinating five directors and casts in one go. And especially in a metropolis like London with the logistics of trying to get everybody in the same room can be daunting, plus of course the ever present danger of people who made the commitment well in advance suddenly phoning in on the morning to say, "Really sorry, something else has come up" — i.e. something better paid.

People still do that and we're used to juggling stuff like that. But a project like this is a lot of years in the making. I've been in the UK nine years or so, and I know that with time, even if you don't realise it, you do make friends and networks, you do get to know people and you learn how it works, you learn from the people you work with. But it often needs a lot of grafting here in London.

Does that change, every week it's different?

You do have to be a grafter. Since I came to the UK I haven't stopped working, any type of job just to pay the bills. Everyone has been talking about Brexit obviously, but I remember coming here and having to do paperwork to be able to stay and counting points at a time when my country Bulgaria wasn't fully in the European Union yet *[Bulgaria became a member state of the EU in 2007 but UK work restrictions weren't lifted until 2014]*, not knowing if I could stay, if it was okay to stay, and if I stayed how would I be able to do things like go to the doctor? Today I feel like I'm living in a repeat where I'm back to where I started in the UK nine years ago. One of the things you learn from migrating is that you have to work twice as hard because you're not from here. And you have to work twice as hard on top of all that in my case because I'm a woman. So that kind of triples the amount of work.

Or quadrupled, because if we're taking about theatre, then it's something based on rarely ever getting paid for the effort put in as you would in other industries. But you do it regardless, unthinkingly and possibly selflessly — if only by result than intent. Maybe this reflects the social role that theatre can play in society. How does that influence the evolving direction for Global Voices? Could it be a whole two-week annual festival with editions elsewhere in the UK, Europe or beyond?

I don't think that we've gone for it yet. I do see a lot of possible futures — obviously there's that question of capacity and funding, and you can't do all the things at the same time, but I don't think that if we do one thing or the other we'll be losing out. And you know why? Because no one says that we should.

There is no formal structure as such, so your response is what your response is. It looks like something you can't quantify though you know it has an impact?

You can quantify the impact. But I don't think that you, me, people around us would know that impact yet. Obviously there's the immediate stuff, whatever that may be, but there are also things that I did five years ago that now I realise have prepared me for this moment. That's the process of growing up because you have the experience and objectivity. It's all linked. And it never stops.

In terms of the people you've brought in and given this exposure to, there's a slightly more quantifiable impact on them presumably and also the performers. At the moment you're visibly involving playwrights, translators, performers, directors and curators. The mere act of bringing everyone together will have an impact in itself. Something has been set in motion.

There are several things at play. For each of those roles that you've mentioned, there are a set of things that we are trying to achieve which the platform is useful for. So for writers there's the fact that they have a credit that the play's been read even if it's just an excerpt. In London in a lot of countries that still is a cachet and something that you can put forward and put on the biog of the play. The fact that we're hoping especially now and in the future to get full plays produced and published has an impact.

From working on one of the first Global Female Voices plays, the team really clicked and decided to do a full length at Vault *[Central London venue/festival]*. And from there they really clicked again and now as the same collective they're putting new plays together, You can trace that back to them meeting at Global Female Voices — and that's just one story. For directors it's always interesting to come across new surprising material that they didn't know. Sometimes they cast themselves, and sometimes we recommend actors so they get to play around with new talent that they wouldn't have met before. That way we expand everyone's network for the people who are local, right? And that's valuable in itself.

It's a similar situation for the actors. They get to play around with new material, meet new people, get seen by other people. Something interesting was Global Latin American Voices where people came because they need Latinx performers and they want to see people in action. And when you have fun you can really tell that person you would like to work with them in the future.

The translators as well get recognised in a space where we make a point of highlighting the fact that we do have translated texts in a way that doesn't often happen in London. The curators as creatives get to do something that maybe they don't get to do necessarily in their day-to-day work, and they also get to recommend their networks. So although there's not a lot of money if any in all this, we are creating employment for people even if it is just one day at the moment.

And then there's representation, seeing people like you onstage working with people like you onstage on a text that is about you that you recognise yourself in — because you're queer, because you're black, because you're female, because you're Arab, because you're Indigenous, and you go, oh yeah this is me. So I'm working with people like me about putting on stage stories about us and we're presenting it to people that understand it or want to understand it and are here to *hear* us.

It's super privilege being the person with the Global Voices team creating that space — it goes back to the question of do you get what you put in? And I do. It's seeing people creating a home for people in the space of a night, we're just reading some texts but we feel that we're a community together in that space and I think that's pretty awesome.

That sort of accessibility needs to be put into the context of where the UK currently finds itself. So many people talk about being international but rarely are. You're doing all this at an in-yer-face community level but bringing in international texts and international voices.

It is funny isn't it? You have to go all the way to Ghana to bring a story for black people in the UK to feel at home. I'm exaggerating, but I think that's the point, right? Accepting that sometimes far away is closer than your neighbour. We're privileged to be in a world where 'far away' is less inaccessible than only a few decades ago. Now you get a director and a writer in different continents who are communicating via WhatsApp and Skype about what excerpt to read, how to put it onstage, how they see the characters . . . It shows that the foreigner is not a stranger. There is culture, there is difference in that culture, but the gap is an imaginary gap.

But because you have that multicultural, multinational background and work, plus the perspective of a migrant, it's easy for you to point that out.

But I don't do that. That would be arrogant — and I would hope that I'm not arrogant in my communicating this! It's about practising it. I don't go wagging my finger at people judgementally going, "What you're doing is wrong and your country needs sorting out and this is all crazy or crap." No, I say there are issues and I have a perspective and I'm critical, but I work really hard to be aware and to be knowledgeable and to understand and to listen and to observe and adapt. Being an immigrant is like being super adaptable. You have to be water, like they say, take the form of where you put it.

So you are what you do.

Aren't we all? Sometimes I forget that I'm foreign and I don't think about it at all. I'm not hyper aware of myself all the time and then something will happen and I'll be like, "Oh yeah, I just forgot that I'm Bulgarian and so that was a really weird situation I just found myself in." Or maybe I just forgot that you're British and created another weird situation . . .

Yes, there are other people in theatre making noises in different ways. I can understand their frustration and anger, I can understand what their position is and that they have lived experiences that might justify that. But that's not how I see it for myself.

Could Global Voices go to Europe? It's a logical if not essential next step. They're ready for it there.

Well, first of all we are in Europe . . .

I'm exposing my geocultural identity here.

I'm not wagging my finger . . . But people have been asking me about doing this elsewhere. It is part of what the next step should be — and this is exactly how it starts, with someone suggesting something and it starts rolling from there. If the idea keeps coming back, then there's only one way to know, which is to try it out by doing it. And then we'll see. Either we'll fall flat on our faces and there'll be two people there and it'll be really sad, or we won't fall flat and we'll carry on tinkering with the model.

A good example is Daniela Cristo, who said, "I want to do this in Colombia. I love the name, I love the concept, I've seen the events and I want to do this in Colombia and present regional theatre in Bogotá where I have contacts because I want to do 'Voces Amazonas or Voces Pacíficas', whatever that might turn out to be. And then expand and do maybe all of Latin America." Exactly as it should be, and so we will have at some point a Colombian 'chapter'. *[Update! Voces Globales Colombia, GVT's sister company was created in May 2020]* I would also love a Caravan of Global European Voices, to test it out in different countries.

A physical caravan like a roadshow?

It's metaphorical caravan. Don't ask me why, but I like the idea of doing things in fives, so maybe the caravan could do five different cities from London to Sofia or Istanbul depending on where you see the 'edge' of Europe. You take and then test it out in different countries and do a single call-out for all of the countries and then get every city to have a good curator in. So from the same call-out you're putting out 15 different projects. It might be that in one country there's a Roma theme and in another it's migrants or queer, whatever is relevant to the local community that is curating.

It's almost *not* our job to impose those themes, but it's finding the likeminded individuals who resonate with what can be done and how it can be done.

But if your model goes down on paper it'll probably turn out as 'have idea, let's do it'. In fact if you formularised it you'd probably kill it.

I can sit and explain to someone how it happens but it's boring because it happens with a spreadsheet and a budget with things like when to fund it or email people. But essentially it happens by telling a story to someone.

And that's really how everything has happened. That's how revolution happens. that's how starting a business happens, what you're going to have for dinner. It starts with two people chatting about something and making a decision to bring everything together.

We've been lucky that people that have seen it or heard about it have said this is really nice, really interesting, here's some space, I'm going to come and do your photography for less money because I like what you do, I am going to spend a day in a rehearsal space because I love it and because I recognise that this is something that's worth it. Everyone is taking one for the team to make it happen. It does sound like, oh you just go and do it and it's successful. But it's still really tiny and fragile, and exists only because a lot of people have put a lot of effort into it.

And a lot of that Factor X — the day job. As you've already said, With One Voice in particular has helped give you the framework to focus your ability on the theatre side to bring people together and to take those leaps.

I am really lucky that I now have a proper job, one with a contract, but also it's working for an organisation that has the culture of seeing you as more than a member of staff. It sees you as a creative, as an artist, as an individual who has a lot going on and it's supportive of that. The director and the board and everyone around us see everything that we do outside With One Voice as a benefit to With One Voice. As a practical example, I work there with a lot of venues and we have a cultural spaces responses to homelessness programme, so already I'm a perpetual ambassador for two things I think are important: working with the arts and working within homelessness in an international setting. It helps us remember that there are issues everywhere and people can realise that their issues are found elsewhere. When we talk about homelessness in the UK, we point out that this is the fifth global economy but we're still talking about homelessness, and then when we talk in the UK about homelessness in Japan, people are like, "What, *Japan?*" So it's that care and awareness of knowing that we're all far closer together and more similar than we think — in our good things and our bad things.

There's also the idea of co-production. We're arriving at the point now where co-creation has led to co-production being formalised — it has a name and we're understanding it. We're starting to think about co-production more in terms of how we pass the knowledge on to other people and how it's all about equity. So how do you make sure that the people involved in the project are equitable? So it's about voices, where your voice counts and it's not me helping you out . . . What's the thing that people pick up on now that's really annoying? "Find your voice!" Well no, people have their voice. It's about amplifying it. They already have their voice and you may have to be the one who needs to listen harder.

*

21
Tobi Kyeremateng
'It's making people think about the ways they welcome audiences'

Tobi Kyeremateng is a cultural producer for live performance, festivals, film and community engagement & founder of the Black Ticket Project. She is based in South London, where she was born & raised.
• *tobikyere.com*

Was there anything specific that got you into theatre?

It's hard trying to recall a specific moment of 'falling' into theatre. I had sporadic moments of contact with it here and there — the Shakespeare play I saw at school, a Theatre in Education performance, going to see *Wicked* and that being my first time going to the West End, a pantomime with my family when my mum won tickets in a competition. But none of these necessarily feels like the moment of 'falling'.

At college I did a Performing Arts BTEC. It was a last-minute decision and I initially intended to stay at my sixth form college and do A-levels. I didn't even know what a BTEC was, but that was my commitment to wanting to be in this sector, to really wanting to understand what that meant and what that looked like. I still didn't know what exactly I wanted to do, but at the same time I started at Ovalhouse *[theatre in South London]* as a young associate after meeting *[director]* Toby Clarke who convinced me to interview for it. I had no idea what it was or where Ovalhouse was, but I trusted Toby and that was enough.

At Ovalhouse, I was working with 12 and 13 year olds at risk of being excluded from school. I think this was the moment I started to understand the different elements of theatre beyond the stage — things like boosting self-esteem and confidence, building relationships and making friends, finding joy and fun. I found that interesting and I wanted to know more about that in particular. After college, I started at Battersea Arts Centre *[in South London]* as an apprentice producer, and I would say this was my formal introduction to theatre — being thrust into the heart of it all and constantly surrounded by it. It was chaos and I was very lost, ha. After the first year of my apprenticeship, I think that's when I was like, "yeah, this is what I wanna do".

Did you feel there was any pressure on you to conform to other expectations of society?

Ha — where do I even begin? I'm the eldest daughter of two parents that grew up in a different continent, I'm the first in my family to be born and bred in Britain. Going into the arts wasn't really the expectation from my parents, and largely because, you know, what does a career in the arts even mean?

Historically, theatre hasn't presented itself as an art form for people who look like me or people who've grown up the way I grew up, and all that. Even now when I tell people I work in theatre, they're like, "Oh wow!" — because it's just not the expectation. There's also a context that comes with the word 'theatre' and what springs immediately to mind when people hear that word. More and more I'm pulling away from telling people I work in 'theatre' until we (the sector) can unwrap the multitude of things that means.

In the time I was growing up, a lot was changing in terms of the things that young people had access to, and some of that meant trying to figure out all the different options that were in place. There has been a shift in the idea of professional qualifications and careers that people might want to do.

The linear structure for 'success' has gone to shit. The trajectory that's been heralded for such a long time is: you're born, you go to school, you go to college, you go to university, you get a degree in something academic or academically adjacent, you go into a stable career. You do that and you live comfortably and that's it. That rhetoric was always a pipedream for specific racially and economically marginalised communities, but now more than ever, it's feels like a myth.

Does looking at the industry that way mean there are less barriers?

I don't think there's been a time where there's never not been a barrier, and I don't think there will be a time when there'll ever not be a barrier. What that barrier is will shift because things change — economics change, politics change, finances change. These barriers are built into the foundation of how this sector and our society operates.

I don't know if there's any real legacy plan in place for the things that are happening now to make sure that they're not just a 'spur of the moment' thing. The whole diversity conversation comes up as a recurring thing, which means that every now and again we'll get these bursts of more writers, more directors, more actors. But none of what's happening now has been sustainable or had a legacy, because if it did, it would mean that we wouldn't be having the same conversation over and over again.

Not being cynical, but so many of the changes — visionary or otherwise — are so dependent on funding that when the funding goes they just disappear.

Funding has gotten tighter. Not just for artists, companies and venues, but across the board in terms of education, youth services and so on. Cuts in other sectors also affects the arts and how we operate as a sector. There are areas that we've started to compensate because of added pressure from other directions. For example, when I was working with young people at Battersea Arts Centre, all of a sudden we were called on to compensate for the lack of youth services because all the youth clubs had been shut down by government cuts across social services. We were suddenly in a position where we were supporting young people effectively as youth workers — which we weren't necessarily trained to do.

One could argue that that should be the role of arts centres and theatres anyway — that there should be more civic spaces, and it shouldn't just be about young people coming in and doing theatre projects, but they should also want to come in and fix their CV or find a job. But at the same time, people aren't trained to do that work as well. And all of that just comes from the stress of lack of funding across all the areas of the arts. You are expected to deliver the same as you've always delivered, or more, for less resources and less funding and less capacity. It's really tough. I've also noticed in a lot of conversations recently how some artists feel that they have to defend the nature of their work to see it within those funding criteria. That's an interesting conversation.

Some of that criticism is very valid, and as an artist I guess you just want to make the work that you want to make. But the way that our society is now, we all have a responsibility to think about things in a wider sense than just art. Everything is political. The choice to exist outside of the politics is political.

Can implementing 'accessibility' and 'engagement' in your work be a bad thing? And if so, why is it a bad thing? Hard questions, but this is a precarious time. It's always been precarious, but I think we're starting to see the shift now. All these are important factors, and we all have some responsibility, especially when it comes to public funding. We all have a responsibility to society in some way.

I don't know what people were doing before the Arts Council and things like the Arts Council existed. I don't know how people were making work and whether people still had the same incentives to make that work. Arts Council might not exist in the next 10-20 years, and we'd be forced to evolve with that. I can't even imagine what that would look like, but it's something we have to think about.

The organisations you've worked in are a good who's who of organisations which, despite the precariousness of it all, have seriously tried to make things happen. Is it all of them being based in London that gives them the ability to do that? Or do you think it's the unique inherited culture and attitude of organisations like Battersea Arts Centre, Ovalhouse, Bush and Royal Court? I suppose though, they get the funding and the audiences by virtue of being in London in any case, and they also get the guaranteed profile and feedback. But if you took away the money, I'm not sure they would be able to still make it happen.

Being in the capital is a bonus to some extent, but there are lots of buildings in London that still aren't doing the work that we should be doing. Funders see organisations flourishing on very little money — they tend to be smaller organisations with barely any resources and are led by the artistic directors of the future, run by people who are all willingly breaking their backs to try and make some change. The funders will say, "Oh, they're doing great things. We should just leave them as they are instead of looking at investing more of an infrastructure in them." To be able to do that brilliant work *independently* you need infrastructure and you need resources. And if you don't have those, eventually the foundation will crumble.

You can have as much funding in the world, but if the people working as a part of your organisation ultimately don't share a similar ethos in terms of the change that they want to create and the legacy behind it, then that funding won't make any difference. Your productions become futile, or they have no legacy to them.

When I was at the Bush *[in West London]*, I saw this at every level of organisation, whether it was front of house or the artistic director, every single person had a shared value of what the organisation should achieve within the community. That's the way to create something that is sustainable.

You'd talked about things making a shift diversity-wise. Even compared to five years ago, there have been huge changes in theatre's commitment to this. How you view where that shift is going and whether it's going in the right direction?

How the industry is shifting? I don't know where it's going, to be honest! I really don't. I feel like we've ended up here by accident and that everyone's sort of like, "Oh, okay, we're here now, what do we do?" You know, I don't think we planned to be where we are now. We've got incredible shows like Inua Ellams' *Barber Shop Chronicles*, Arinzé Kene's *Misty* and Natasha Gordon's *Nine Night*, we've got people like Gbolahan Obisesan, Kwame Kwei-Armah, Lynette Linton in positions of power in theatres. But I don't think that it was a deliberate choice as a sector that got us all working towards it. It's just sort of happened, which means that no one knows what's going to happen next.

However, a really good example of a good shift was Madani Younis' time at the Bush through to Lynette coming in. From the capital project and taking the building to a more financially stable place, having shows like *Misty* come through that building and then have a legacy in the West End, that all created some history there. When Madani left the Bush, he left it in the best position possible, which made it possible for Lynette, who I think was 28 at the time, to come in and take over the space. Lynette wasn't coming to fix a crisis. She was coming in to be given the resources to actually be totally creative and think about what she wanted that space to operate as. Those kinds of shifts and changes can only happen once you've built that up the sort of succession plan that Madani had, ensuring that these places are set up to allow *people* to flourish in those positions.

I don't know how many buildings are thinking about their succession plans. We've clearly still got an issue with people staying in organisations for way too long. We're looking at 25-plus years for some of these people. I don't know how that lines up with the theatre that is happening in the wider sector, but everything gets get cut off at a certain point, like you might have a rotation of administrative staff and producers. But once you get to senior-level execs' level, everyone's in there for a very very long time.

So I don't think anyone really knows what's going on at the moment, what they're all just doing is bigging the changes up as they happen and saying it's a really positive thing — but no one actually knows what's going to happen next. No one knows how we got here! There's nothing that we're actively learning from. Obviously, I would like the changes to continue and I would like more diverse people — racially, class-wise, disability-wise — coming into positions of power around the country. And people being allowed to take all kinds of creative risks and to shape buildings to fit with the way our society is evolving and to meet the needs of our society. But whether that will happen, I'm not sure.

Okay. if you could wave a magic wand, what would be the first thing that you would do?

Oh gosh, what would be the first thing I would do? I think I would debate the necessity of the board. I would either change the way that boards operate or I'd just get rid of them altogether. The hierarchy of theatre at the moment doesn't really make sense to me, and I don't think it allows for something that's a bit more diplomatic and a bit more community in spirit. Ideally, I would completely change what they're there to do and who they're there to work with and serve.

So against that backdrop, how did Black Ticket Project come about?

It started in early 2018 — well, it artificially started at end of 2017 when *Barber Shop Chronicles* went to the National Theatre for the first time. I went to see it and there was still a very predominately white middle class National Theatre-type audience. For a show that's set in barbershops around the world, with 12 black men onstage talking about all these things, I found it really strange and but predictable at the same time. I certainly found it frustrating to wonder. "Why aren't my friends here? Why isn't my Dad here? Why aren't my brothers here? And the people that spend their every Saturday in a barber shop, why are they not here?" So I bought 30 tickets and handed them out to young black men to go see the show.

That was the first time all of them had ever gone to the theatre. So I guess a part of this is saying, "If a show like *Barber Shop Chronicles* is the first ever show that I saw in theatre and not Shakespeare, what does that reveal about my viewership of theatre as being something completely different?" So that's what I did. But was no expectation or anything of it. The aim was that they went to see the show and that was it.

Then in 2018, *Nine Night* came to the National and I got in touch with the theatre directly this time. I said, "This is what I did for *Barber Shop Chronicles*, I want to do this again for *Nine Night* — but I want it to be to be a bit more constructive. I actually think that you need to be involved in this because it's your job, essentially. It's not mine. I'm not getting paid to do your job for you." So we worked together on that and they subsidised a couple of tickets, I put out a fundraiser for the rest, and we fundraised far more money than we intended. That meant that over the course of the run 250 black people came to see that show, and it evolved from there.

But I feel like the project is very much a community project and a lot of what it's about have been suggested by other people. For example, we now have a Patreon account where people donate monthly because people told us that this what they wanted to do. There's that naming of the product — someone else named it. So it's very much been about what people think is necessary.

And then there's the idea that theatre is the main thing that it works on. But I'm not particularly precious about the art form or how many people see a show. So for some shows people have had a couple of tickets, five tickets, 10 tickets, and that's fine. For other shows, there's hundreds and that's fine as well. In fact I only have two things to tell organisations.

The first is that they need to have really good seats. They've got to be in the stalls, they can't be in the back or in the gods somewhere, because people need to feel like they're welcome in that space and have a sense of ownership over that space.

And secondly, they need to work out how to make this sustainable and embed it into their infrastructure. So if tomorrow I decide that I don't want to do the project anymore, they need to make sure that these relationship won't just fall through the cracks and disappear overnight. The organisations should work out how to continue those relationships with these young people and these community groups. It's things like how to like brief front of house to know how to communicate with people that have never been to your venue before.

All these things are really important. But this is making people think about other old ways in which their system welcomes audience members, because things like finance are simply one barrier. Another barrier is the way other audience members treat you, and there were a couple of times at the National where members of the audience were being quite disrespectful to our young people. That's a whole other problem that needs to be figured out. But yeah, that's the project in a nutshell.

This is voluntary work that you're doing, and you respond as the opportunity demands. The weird thing is that this exactly why it seems to be sustainable, which is not the expected result from something that's neither funded nor commercial.

Sort of. It's more about the content of the show. Growing up in South London, I spent a lot of time in barber shops with my dad and my brothers. It's a very male-dominated space, a space for black men to gather and to talk about anything and everything. It's a ritual and there are people who carry out this ritual every other Saturday. It's this little space that they see as a home for them. They should be able to go to a theatre and feel that it's that space for them as well. For that particular show, *Barber Shop Chronicles*, it was important that the young men we gave the tickets to that they saw their everyday on stage as well. So that was the reasoning for that show.

If it came up, would you send people to a dead white man play like a Shakespeare if the production had something worthy to offer?

People ask all the time if a show we offer tickets to has to be written by a black person or directed by a black person. I think the first show that people see through us has to be reflective of who they are. Most of the time, we start with the Shakespeares and then in my case, eight years later, you see *Misty* or *Barbershop* and you're like, Oh, okay, this is possible, and I want it to be the other way around for these groups.

> *There's that thing about funding being linked to outcomes and so on. But with Black Ticket Project it is what it is, you either see an effect or you don't, but either way it can't stop you from continuing. The funny thing is, it looks like a perfectly logical thing to do but not everyone's doing it. What's the insanity that led you to this?*

[laughs] To be honest, I don't know. Sometimes I'm like, "Why am I doing this? I could just stop. I could just stop right now . . . !" I don't know. I'm just eager to see some sort of tangible change, and it's frustrating especially for a lot of young people nowadays because it doesn't feel like we can see any tangible change. You see a lot of talking, you see conversations all the time, but we are yet to see any really *tangible* that's actually happened that lets you say, "Okay, this is the thing that's changed or this is a thing that has shifted."

Black Ticket Project comes mainly from a place of that frustration and wanting to bring a little bit of hope. There's the risk that you will switch off if you see nothing happening, but if you can practically see the changes, it's more than effective to stick with what works in that direction. To some extent, something about Black Ticket Project works, so I want to keep doing it like that. I have certain milestones that I want to achieve along the way and as long as I can see those things approaching in the distance, there's no reason to stop.

But things like having to create outcomes are frustrating and that's definitely why I've stayed away from public funding. A lot of people have been like, "Oh why don't you talk to the Arts Council? Why don't you go and see people with money?" But I find it detrimental the way that organisations engage with young people who they haven't engaged with before. They always see them as 'participants', which means that you're not an active member in the work. So if you're a young person trying to get into the arts or you want to see a bit of theatre, you probably have to do a week-long drama course first or you've got to participate in their building in some capacity. And some people just don't want to do that.

What Black Ticket Project is doing is to contribute to building the sustainability of the sector. We're building the future audience members that are hopefully going to start coming to your venues after your current audience members are all wiped out. It's about sustainability. But a lot of people don't see other people as active or future audience members who will carry on the sector, they just see them as 'participants'. That's frustrating and I don't want to have to make people do a workshop just so they can go see work. There's all the other required outcomes as well, like that huge saviour complex about you having to talk about how much this thing has changed the young person's life, why they decided to go and see art because it was art, bla bla bla bla bla.

That's not the aim of Black Ticket Project. The aim is that you get a ticket, you go see something. If you've gone to see a show, then you've achieved what we want to do. It's not about trying to 'change people's lives'. Don't use the experience to get people to say, "You know what, I didn't like that show" or "I don't feel that that show related to me" or "I would have done this differently or that differently." More often than not when you ask people, "How you feel about the show?" after they've seen a piece of work, they'll probably just say, "Oh yeah it was interesting" — which doesn't mean anything. It's not significant. Because they have no reason to say, "I didn't like it" — because you feel like you have to love the thing that you're going to see. And it always feels like that's phenomenal.

Black Ticket Project isn't a numbers game. I can tell you how many tickets are being distributed but I couldn't tell you how many people have gone to see work. Because the idea is that we work with the same people over a long period of time because it's about building a culture around going to see work. So it's not that you go and see this fun show, it's a phenomenon and you're never going to the theatre again — or need to. Instead, you might see five, six, seven, eight shows through us because it's about building a thing that makes you say, "Oh, actually do you know what? I might go to the theatre today — because I know I can do that, because it's just a part of what I do as a hobby." Those numbers things, those anecdotal things, they're just not relevant.

Do you think there's something in Black Ticket Project that can be built on as a vehicle for wider social change?

I think there would be if it was as democratic as that. To be honest, my idea of what theatre is, is perhaps different to what the sector would call theatre. People that I've grown up around have always used the word 'theatre' and it hasn't necessarily been in the context of a building or a stage. Sometimes it's been on the school playground, sometimes it's been on the bus, sometimes it's been in the car on the way to church. It's happening around us all the time. But the only time the sector usually recognises that is if it's on a stage in a venue. But theatre elsewhere can be really powerful.

Sometimes we fall short in terms of that recognition where if you did want to make a piece of work it becomes about who has the access to do that in the first place. Can anyone call a venue right now and say, "Hey, I want to put on a performance tomorrow, can I have the place?" Does everyone have that sort o relationship? And are all the shows that we see written by the people whose voices really need to be heard? We're obsessed with giving people voices. It's problematic to say we've given someone a voice when people have always had their voices, why they aren't being heard is the problem. I don't want to give anyone their own voice back to them. I want to enable people to speak for themselves.

There is something incredibly powerful when people just say, "Do you know what? This is where my mind is right now. This is what I'm thinking about. This is what I'm battling. I'm going to gather people in the space and make something happen." There is something beautiful and powerful about being able to do that through the lens of creativity. It doesn't necessarily have to be within that strict theatre context. The act of making a performance can create change within our society — even within our sector — more so than the art form itself.

*

22

Alan Lane

'We should *compete* in your imagination'

Alan Lane, artistic director of Slung Low & The Holbeck working men's club. Based in Leeds, Yorkshire, he was born in RAF Gatow West Berlin, West Germany, and raised in West Berlin & Lincolnshire.
• *slunglow.org, @slunglowalan*

Combining big projects with a working men's club might not make much sense to a lot of people, especially in Europe, but you've just done your first year of it. So I suppose the first question has to be how's it going?

It's going very well. And also it's very hard. And both of those things are true at the same time. We've been here a year and a bit now, and . . . well there's a great story about Greg Dyke when he took over *[BBC show]* Breakfast TV. It was his first proper programme but there was no editor for the show. So he was completely in charge without taking the blame and got them to run documentaries on things like shoe factories and Estonia and all sorts. It was just the most dull dreary nonsense that you could find. Viewing figures plummeted. And then the first day he puts Roland Rat on the show, obviously the viewing figures rocketed. He turns around and says to his bosses, "Look, I've doubled our audience!" He'd driven it so much into the ground that any increase in viewers looked amazing. So there's the same sense of that measure of success for us because when we moved into the club, we didn't have very much in the first place in the area around us — although there are four or five other organisations that are also really slogging away, and they are absolutely heroic.

But for us there was a sense of being a bit of a desert, until we told ourselves,

"In fact, you can do whatever you want!" So we just inundated the club with what we could do, from African weddings to first holy communions, queer cabaret, because we're the only place within quite a distance where you can put on an event, plus there's a community who want to help you do that. Slung Low always tried to remove all the barriers. If you sent an email to me now saying, "I want to put on a poetry reading evening and I want to do it *tomorrow night*" — if this space is free, it's happening. And that obviously leads to some *proper* disasters, but it also mostly leads to a lot of just stuff happening.

It also leads to an awful lot of just removing the amount of paperwork you have to do. We have about four questions we ask you before you do your event. Once you've answered those four questions, you can crack on. It's unlikely that we say you can't come back if it's wasn't very good, because you probably aren't going to come back in any case — you mostly know if you were not very good. We had one guy with a bad night, but he was just lazy, hadn't done the work, and as a result just wasn't very good. And he's never come back. Whereas we have had four or five band nights run by people who you would be more than happy with if they wanted to run them like a business — they thought they had to make a profit. But we're basically trying to take the commercial pressure off.

So we take on lots of events that don't make us money, where the community needs that space because they have nowhere else. It is an unbelievable privilege that we decide not to worry about whether it makes any money or not, but just say let's give it a go. We've got an event coming up this week in which an asylum seeker network will feed 250 people upstairs. It will probably cost the club just to host the event. But actually we don't care because we'll have 250 people who wouldn't have come here otherwise. So that's the bragging side of things: more people doing more things, they're in charge of more of that, and because they're in charge of more of the stuff, it means that we can also put the stuff we want on, because it's now in the mix rather than being the only thing on.

What this means is that when that happens, more people are coming to a wider range of stuff. So, for example, our audience are seeing a much better quality of theatre than they might have done before because we can leverage our contacts in the industry they're watching work that people might say is 'demanding'. And actually you can find the audience for it. We talk about everything, you know, we don't distinguish between high or low art or whatever the current phrases are that define that. So what we find is that people are really keen to see a wide, broad range of things, but they're much more keen to put their own events on and to drive them. And that combination has been really helpful to us as making a difference. — it increases both the range of events and the range of people who come to the club.

The downside is that it's fucking hard work. It's not the hoovering and the emptying and carrying things upstairs. It's the emotional, political work of being in a community that has just been badly led for five decades. And I don't mean by the [city] councillors, who are actually quite good, but by national strategy. The national strategy of Britain is that places like Holbeck can get to fuck basically. They are just seen as the cost of doing business. Holbeck has had its ups and downs. It was at the heart of the Industrial Revolution, then there was an attempt in the middle of the 20th century with Kays Catalogue and various light industries, then service industry, then retail. And then that just ran out.

What we've got is an unbelievable amount of mobility, people moving in and out. The council housing here is in bad state of repair. We've got drugs, we've got unemployment, we've got a very old *and* a very young population. We've got asylum seekers and unbelievable amounts of long-term sick and all of those things aren't because the people of Holbeck are any more or any less morally or physically strong than you are or I.

But the cost of having a late-stage capitalist post-industrial nation is that there are going to be places like Holbeck. And that's an accidental decision, it doesn't mean anybody takes any delight in it. It's just the consequences. What you end up with is groups of people who are incredibly angry, incredibly distrusting, incredibly tribal, incredibly aggressive and, at the same time, people who are incredibly desperate. Our bins are regularly dismantled, we've been done over now three or four times, our bus got smashed up just before Christmas. This is being done by people who are absolutely at the very end of society. It's hard to hold a space in all that, it involves a lot more shouting than being a theatre director really should.

There are times when you stand up in meetings to talk about this and people are saying genuinely horrible things and you realise you are responsible for that space. Do you become the person who lets them say it or the person who stops them? What is the voice you are silencing? I'm a big lad, I'm six foot three, I'm white, I'm straight, I'm middle class, I am everything that we know that is problematic. But I also know that to let that person carry on with that destructiveness would be a moral failure at the very least. It's always tricky trying to ensure you avoid the shark moments.

We have saved the club with our money. [*Slung Low paid The Holbeck's debts to the brewery off with VAT credit from Flood (Hull UK City of Culture 2017), ensured that staff working behind the bar etc were paid a living wage and returned the deeds to the membership. They manage the club and it is owned by its members.*] That is a fact, but the club is still full of people who say some really horrible bloody things, really horrible. And therefore at some point on some level if we're being grown-ups and thinking about this beyond, you know, the day-to-day life of running an arts centre, running a community centre, is we're a bit responsible for that, aren't we? We are, we just are, we're a bit responsible for keeping this space where those men sit there and say those things about women. And that means that it's just the realisation that neither choice (to stop them or to let them say hateful things) is morally free — is morally pure, rather. So, a very longwinded answer to your question, but that's how we doing, that's where we're at, which is exciting and also quite tiring.

So you asked yourself the question how did you get into this? A lot of people not from the North might think you insane to do it because this isn't easy to pigeonhole. Neither social crusade nor artistic-political journey, neither fish nor fowl?

Well we are a theatre company, Slung Low, that over the last ten years has made large-scale outdoor political pieces of theatre with very large groups of people, which we define as people's theatre. It's the combination of people who've spent their lives making theatre and people who fancy doing it for a little bit of time because they understand that it's an interesting hobby or something. You end up with both groups of people doing much better than they would be if they were just working without the other group of people. And we've done that all over most major Northern cities in one way or another. And if you look at the process of that, the play has to be really amazing because they normally cost a lot of money and they're normally part of some big event like Hull 17 *[Flood]* or the centenary of the Battle of the Somme *[Somme 100 Manchester]*.

It has to be great art and to have an impact on our cultural conversation. All that stuff, because that's the gig. But it also has to be worthwhile to 250 performers of all backgrounds who are coming to stand in the pouring rain for hours on end because they have to be part of that process. So you're having to deliver a really high-end product that can sit within a conversation of theatre around mainstage productions and all that stuff. And you're also having to deliver the concept of the community actor. For me it's an act of politics, and it's also an act of creating a gang, creating a self-supporting group of people who believe in a core mission for a period of time.

We do that under commission. Whoever wants us, we go and do that and we have a set of values that we do that by. But obviously our funders are like, "You need to have an office. You can't just go wandering around spending millions of pounds." So we applied exactly the same sort of thinking to the subject of where we're going to be based administratively. We were like, "Well there's no point having an office if it just sits there being empty, can we find a larger space? Can we share that space with other people? What happens if we just start saying yes to everyone? Can we change all the locks so they're just numbers rather than keys? So we don't even have to be there if you rang us to use it. We just say yes, you can let yourself in?"

And then obviously we have to be somewhere quite cheap if that's going to happen. We're also a Northern company, it goes without saying that we're based in the North of England and all the values and aesthetics that come with that. A lot of those are political but a lot are to do with size. Our last show *[Flood, which was a four-part epic]* was on a hundred square metres of water. Now, there is no stage in the land that big. We have lead actors coming in on speed boats. So from a purely artistic point of view, working just within traditional culture and industry parameters is tedious.

If I want performers to come on in a Land Rover even on the biggest stage of the National Theatre, and they're like, "Oh, like you can't do that." I'm like, "Well then why am I bothering?" If you tell me that I shouldn't do my work in Hull because I'll never become famous that way, I'm telling you you haven't got what we need to match our artistic ambition — so Hull is actually better.

So we ended up in Holbeck, in South Leeds, which is an inner city area, very deprived and right next to an area of lots of affluence. We took over five railway arches as a base. But after a little while, we starting to think well hang on, we're helping all these people rehearse and all these other things — we could start sharing that work. So we built up to becoming a local little theatre. Our audiences were diverse socially and economically, they weren't particularly diverse in any other way.

We noticed that there was a huge population living really close to us who weren't using us as often as we wanted, no matter what we did marketing-wise. So we asked them why, did a big survey, and they all said, "You're right bang in the middle of the industrial area, it's dark, it's scary. There are a lot of sex workers around. There are a number of women who have been murdered. We're not going to *walk* to your theatre. That's just mad." At the same time, we were rehearsing a show for someone else in the big room at the local working men's club — the Holbeck — and they'd left all their bank statements out. We were looking at them and we realised they were in a lot of trouble financially. We talked to them about that. They were a bunch of volunteers. They owed a lot of money. They'd been going for years and they were knackered. And so what we looked at was a scheme by which we paid off all their debts

We have a company wage here, we all get paid the same and we can't own anything. Owning stuff isn't very useful to us because if we owned it, what would we do with it? But we earn a lot of money from our big projects — when we work for the BBC or the government or whatever, we don't charge them the company wage that we pay ourselves, which is the average wage of the nation, around 540 quid a week, we charge them the going rate. So our producer Joanna Resnick sells the production for, say, 30 grand, we now have this money, pay ourselves and are left with what's basically profit. We gave it to the club and wrote off all their debts and then said, "Let us move in and manage you. We'll keep the bar exactly as it was." It's a classic 1970s working man's club in the main part but the rest of the building is a flat, some offices and a 300-seater cabaret space which were all derelict. "We will renovate and turn this place back into a community arts centre. And because of where we are, no club can sell beer to make a profit, there simply aren't enough people with money and there aren't enough people who drink. So we will guarantee you against loss." So here's the plan: they lose about 25 grand a year, so every year we reset their books to zero and then we give them £3,000 so they can carry on doing their community events. From their point of view, they're still the club, most of the club, although a lot of them are still thinking there's another, better deal out there. They just don't know which one it is. If they find it, I think they might become rich one day.

But most people look at it and go, "These guys just walked in, wrote off a hundred thousand pounds worth of debt, guaranteed it against loss and, more importantly, secured the membership its ownership of the club and our long-term future." That is an amazing deal. If you look at it from our point of view, we just moved into the middle of our community, the community we had been trying to get to come to this railway arch between 2010 and 2018. And it's without changing a single thing we're doing: no spending on marketing or programming or anything else. At the Holbeck, our audience just tripled literally overnight. Now we're obviously writing down their debt which was a load of money. But we *know* because of our values that we can't spend that money on ourselves. We can't give ourselves a bonus. You have to do some good with the cash, so we've done that. Then every year we write off against a loss of £25,000 pounds. The annual rent in the old place with the five railway arches was more than the money we paid to save the Holbeck.

So we save money. Now if you're the Arts Council, who we announced these things to really clearly and really transparently, everyone's going, "Oh my God, that's such a brilliant thing." But then there are more than a few people in the industry going, "Oh, that's an act of folly. Oh that's a bit too generous. Oh, that's a bit too . . ." They're the people who also say, "You can't behave like that because that's not how you behave." But what would they say if we sit down and go, "Well, what point of view would you like us to take if you were our funders? We just tripled our audience and reduced our overheads."

Now I personally am the worst businessman in the world. I mean literally. I've done nothing in my life but lose millions of pounds on culture. But I'm pretty sure that if a chief executive came to you and said, "I'll turn your business around, I'm going to triple your audience and I'll reduce your overheads in three weeks." They'd tell you you're a genius. For the sake of argument let's say that's actually correct, but it is also true that it's simply an act of generosity, and it is also true that this is an act of politics, and it's also true that it's all those things.

So that's how we ended up here, because we just kept chasing our values. We just kept chasing the idea that if you're a theatre company and you're making work, you should have a social reason to do it. Again, this idea that there are parts of the country which nobody has any interest in doing culture with, and it's not that they actively don't want people to come. If you're the nearest big theatre, you'll have positioned and priced yourself in such a way that, no matter what your values are, no matter how many *schemes* you have, no matter what you do, you do know that the kids of Holbeck are never fucking coming to you. You just know that.

Now you're not a *bad* person for knowing that. It's just your business model because somebody spent 12 million quid on a building in the city centre where the parking is eight pound fifty an hour, where the buses don't run after your show's closed, and because of your business model, because of all the things you have to do, trying to be a good person without being radical, you *have* to charge them £32 a ticket, you then compensate for that by putting on a few schemes, and on a Tuesday you can sort it if they're willing to queue for three hours that they can get in for just three quid. You do of all that because you're not a bad person, you're just a fucking dull one, you've got a set of problems and you're going to work through them, and then when you get to the end, then you're like, "Oh my God, yeah, this is the best we can do." It isn't the best you can do, it's just the best you can do without paying an incredible price for it. And I don't blame anyone for that. It's just frustratingly lazy fucking thinking. But anyway, that's why we're in Holbeck.

And working men's clubs . . . ?

There's a couple of immediate answers to what working men's clubs are. The last 50 years, they are basically subsidised drinking environments that sit at the heart of communities, traditionally working class Northern communities, but not always. So they're member-owned spaces where people go and drink. The club directly buys their beer from the brewery — as a result, in order to go in, you need to be a member. So your licence is slightly different and it's actually slightly easier to be a licensee. And then your beer is slightly less than the market rate and the idea is that the profit that's driven by you drinking there then goes back into the club and into activities. Most clubs now that still exist are really struggling and getting by on a basic model of "we're a pub and we're open maybe three sessions a week at a time that a certain type of person really wants to drink". So certainly lunchtime is massive in the world of working men's clubs.

Where they were in the middle of the 20th century is a really interesting model, whereby all the money would be spent. And we're talking about men who spent an awful lot of their wage in the club, and the profit generated there would be spent for community good, not necessarily social good. For example, as they did here, they could hire 20 buses to take everyone on holiday to Blackpool for a week. So you're a member of a club where you've raised so much money that you can go on holiday for free — well, not for free, but for being a member — that's quite an interesting model. Except now increasingly we're surrounded by an Asian and African community, neither of which really wants to drink, and then an awful lot of the rest of our community simply don't have the money to buy beer, no matter how cheap it is.

So what we're talking about is servicing what in any other community would be seen as white middle class men. But here they're not. They're white *retired* men. If you go all the way back to the very beginning of working men's clubs — and we argue very passionately with our blue plaque that we're the oldest working men's club, which might not actually be a fact, but we are the oldest one still working as a club — they were places where people came to be free of work, of market pressures.

The first thing that was built here at the Holbeck was a lecture hall. For the first 30 years, there wasn't a bar, there were classrooms and billiards rooms and lecture halls. They were places where people didn't have to play the roles of capitalism, they didn't have to be customers. The club was members-owned and people came to learn new things, lectures were given, people would learn new games, you had a sports team or football, their cricket team was really big here in the beginning. This would be your base as well, so you would come and your mind and body would be exercised. And then after about 30, 40 years, the money started to run out. So they put the bars in these clubs in order to generate profit.

It's 150 years later, but all we're really doing is exactly what this place is set up to do, you come here and we run a cultural community college, everything from bread baking to Irish dancing. You can learn Indian cooking, how to whittle wood, and there's a bar for sure, entertainment upstairs and you can use it for your own events too. Our cabaret room doubles as a classroom, there's a double-decker bus in the car park that does the same. All of the workshops are funded by the Paul Hamlyn Foundation and we charge on a pay what you decide, so no one's left out.

So when people go, "Oh God, how did you come up with it?" Well we didn't come up with anything, we just reset it back to what it originally was. The obvious social political model of the working men's club is really clear to me.

And it's also really clear why you had to grab it by the horns — it's not like it's a cheap subsidised converted warehouse somewhere like Hackney in East London. Not only have you got to seek it out but you have to really want to settle there. You have to want to speak the language. And also keep track of the changing communities that you find there — and find a way of respecting their worldviews. Now how do you balance all of that? You're fulfilling the remit by preserving the idea of a working men's club by evolving it, and at the same time functioning as a largescale theatremaker Slung Low. You've explained the mechanics of it, but you still need to explain how you actually make it work.

Because I honestly can't think of anything else that would be worth my effort. You know, there's four of them in the team at the minute, and I'm pretty sure they would all say it slightly differently. It's my job to talk about this stuff, but we talk about it within ourselves a lot. And I can't think of a better thing to do with my 40s. And, you know, as a person of some energy and, thanks now to our belief in training, the company's considerable CV of skills, we're not likely to get trapped in doing something that we don't want to do or that doesn't have a reason. I mean, I know a lot of people who work in theatre who are just miserable. They're endlessly miserable about the state of theatre. You'll never make an actor more unhappy than when you give them what they want.

But you'll come up against the feeling everywhere that you can't really change anything. Well, okay, but what you *can* do, and I suppose this is the central mission, is find a small bit of land and say, right, within this bubble we're going to exist like this. We're going to believe in these values. We're going to find those things that are important . . . It is my genuine belief that you can have a day-to-day social conscience that can be right at the heart of your artistic activity and still make it work. The whole premise of the theatre is when you come and see it, it shouldn't be, "Oh, I really love the political and social conscience of this company, which is why I like this work." We should blow your fucking socks off.

I know we don't like to use the word 'compete', but we should *compete* in your imagination for everything you've ever seen. We should stick up for giving you work as vivid, as powerful, as likely to drive you to action as any work of art you've ever seen. If we're not going to succeed in that, then the world is full of better artists than us, but that's our *ambition*. We should push for this on a day-to-day basis with our values and we should scrutinise those values. We get to choose them, but once we've chosen them, we should pay all the possible prices necessary to keep our promises. I think that that's worth a life, it's worth an effort, it's worth it, because if you work in theatre, it's going to be hard anyway.

I remember speaking to a very very important director — and he ran a massive theatre, I mean like a huge one — and he said, "If it was up to me, I'd be making ensemble devised pieces, putting physical theatre at the heart of it." At the time he was putting on *Twelfth Night* with some fucker from the telly you've never heard of, and I was like, "I don't believe it. If you're not going to do it, then *who* is if you can't?" That idea of climbing a career ladder and getting to the point where finally you get to do what you want, it's not true. You climb the career ladder till finally you get to the point where you don't have to come to work as often. It's just not a worthy ambition for your effort.

We work incredibly hard here, but that's something that anyone I ever met in theatre would say — I've literally never met anybody who isn't turning up and putting a shift in well beyond what most industries would think was normal. It's going to be hard no matter what you do, so it might as well be hard for a reason and we don't always get the balance right here. We do know that we deal with a lot of stuff ("hang on a minute, you're about 30 seconds away from burnout, let's see if we can find you a holiday . . .") But we also have some pretty solid stuff here: company wage, saying yes to everyone, sharing everything we have with everyone. They're all things that people like to see and like to say but actually living it means that well we get robbed quite a bit. And those two things are actually reasonably connected. Not because we're robbed by the people we share with but because if you're that open and transparent at some point you leave a hole in which someone comes through and so when we get robbed, of course it hurts when we get smashed up.

Of course it hurts. But there's also part of it that shows it's working. Making things and facilities available increases risk, and we calculate with that risk in mind. The bus is there, out, not in a locked compound which would be easier, which would be cheaper, which would be less work, but it's out. It is out in the community. Yes, once a year someone is going to take a sledgehammer and do it over and we'll repair it, because that's our job.

I've been based in the North pretty much all my working life, working this way, but I've experienced the other side a few times and I realise I don't like it and come back. That idea of making theatre because one day you hope it catches fire and then goes somewhere and starts to make you money, I've never understood that as a driving motivation. I do know lots of people who that is a driving motivation for, but I've never understood it because there are much easier and simpler ways of making money. There just are. And moral ones! And the idea of chasing newspaper reviews . . . Having met some critics, they're very lovely but I wouldn't trust them to evaluate anything out of five. Not because they're not important or useful but simply because how would you set your life to that?

It was like that in much of my early career where the company would make a show in the hope that someone would give us permission to make another show. Because Lyn Gardner had said this and you would go "YES!" and you would take this to someone who hadn't seen the show. But you're basically saying to them, "Lyn Gardner and some other people say this, so now can I have a go at your place?"

But there is the joy and wonder that you can get when it does work. When a group of people walk into a space and you tell them a story with all your tricks and all your craft and all your honesty and all the stuff that you can do, and you see them get it and you're like, got them, got them, got them in a way that you genuinely don't believe that a computer game ever could, got them in a way that . . . maybe pop music does as well. I'll allow that. And okay, the most amazing food you've ever had in your life too. But we're talking about so few things in life that truly have the ability to change someone. You walk in here three hours ago and you're leaving now and the DNA is saying that there is a process of thought that you will never have in the same way as a result of what we've just done for you.

Now my wife is a completely different beast and very successful in commercial theatre, so I don't say this with any disrespect to anybody working there. But just looking at it, I personally can't spend a life playing this game. At the same time, I don't want to give up on the idea that art and culture can genuinely shift someone's DNA and can bring them joy in a way that a lot of life doesn't. So if those few things are true, well what do you do? What we decided was you become Don Quixote, you find the nearest windmill, you call it a giant and go for it. And you build your own little land and you go within this land, "These are the rules, and we will pay the price of these values."

And that's why we're here. I could genuinely have been somewhere else. Now I'm here, I am Holbeck through and through and if you were here, I'd take you on the most boring four-hour walk around the area where I would tell you all the joyful things here. You'd be looking at me going, "Oh you're in love aren't you? That's what makes people boring, you're in love with it!" But before we moved here, it could have been anywhere, but it's not, it's here now. And as a result, this is the hill that I'll die on because, you know, you've got to pick one, eventually you have to just pick a hill and go, "We don't move from here."

Yeah, that's a bit ominous. It sounds a bit like us and Morecambe . . .

I think you've got your hill. You've got your hill!

Indeed. A sea-drenched mudflats kind of hill. And what you're doing completely resonates with what we're trying to do with our theatre, the Alhambra, in trying to make a space that reflects the heart of your community. What I've realised from Morecambe and from that general Northern perspective is that there's resistance from London and the South to doing it for the community without it being 'community'. We want it to be quality but we also want people to come and feel at home. We all see people getting the funding to just do the 'Legs Akimbo' thing, but to be perfectly honest, in this day and age it's wrong. A community

*theatre should strive to be everything the community specifically needs but it
should also look at offering what, say, London takes for granted. In a realistic way
of course, which is where that ambition in programming comes in.*

For us, I completely agree that it's the kind of central challenge. Because who
decides? How do we decide? How do you decide what's the most popular? Ant
and Dec are the most watched television programme on telly. So it has to be
that? We say no, of course not. That's so ridiculous. Mostly how we measure
the success of theatre is that it moves on to be able to play to more people. So
actually we're saying that popularity is an important thing. But it's a very
confused, very personal thing. The way we've squared that circle has been to
ensure that everybody gets what they want, but they don't get to say what
other people don't want.

There's also our belief that genuinely quality does out. So one night a club
deejay is going make us all want to dance. The next night *[writer & performer]*
Chris Thorpe is going to do *Status* which is difficult and not immediately
accessible. But if I set up an experimental studio in Holbeck and charge everyone
25 quid a ticket, I'll be closed in seconds. The best example is the cabaret. After
three months we'd put on a cabaret. So if you're the Arts Council now with its
with its consideration of 'connection', I put on what was basically a 1970s classic
cabaret which delighted the local residents. I got a drag queen to compere, a
magician, some comedians, a woman playing classical music on a cello. I put it
on and served them their supper in the middle and everybody was happy. I did
something so classically popular as to basically be Saturday night television at
eight o'clock on ITV. The house band was Jamie Fletcher and her band with
Davina de Campo, a runner-up to RuPaul's *Drag Race UK [TV series, season
1]*. They also wrote an *unbelievable* experimental musical, a kind of contemporary
art musical about queerness, which they played the songs from. And then we had
The School of Night, who were Ken Campbell's Hard Bardic improvisers
improvising in rigorous meter and delighted the fuck out of everyone, and so on.
I turned to Darren Henley, CEO of Arts Council England, who was there for
the cabaret, and I said, "You fund all of these people and you fund all of these
people because they are genuinely excellent. These are all avant-garde artists
and they're here with pasta and garlic bread and free Bombay mix and everybody
is loving it." I don't think labels are very useful because I don't think those
people are any of those things you want to label them as. They are artists who
are endlessly thinking and developing their craft and thinking about the form.
And they are artists who want people to enjoy what they're doing. Be provoked
by what they're doing for all sorts of reasons. But there's the tragedy of the
failing marketing system in theatre of "but we know performers who are like this
and we know audiences who are like this". And you're like, "Well no, you people

were like this 40 years ago. You just keep trying to sell to those same people. But it's 40 years on, so you're actually selling to the *children* of the people of your audience for 40 years ago and the world has changed." "Yeah. But if you live in Harrogate 1, you love *Twelfth Night*." "Forty years ago you did. The world has changed." And I think how we get around that is (a) we put it all on, and (b) we don't call it any of the things that you're meant to call it.

We just tell people what it's about, what's going to happen to them. And then we find the best quality of *anything*, we call in every possible favour. So if we're going to have a band, we've got a gig coming up, it's going to be Rash Dash. We're going to have people singing. It's going to be the finest people who we know as singers. There are cheaper and easier ways round, but the ability to leverage our experience and connections as artists is vital to this. If I was doing this 15 years ago with the same amount of money, I wouldn't be doing it as well.

Why?

Because I didn't know anyone. Because why would Chris Thorpe want to play here? Who's this Alan Lane? Well now they might think I'm a wanker, but they definitely go, "Well he can be trusted to put it on. He can be trusted." People come here and 100 per cent of the box office goes to the artists. There are people on tours, on fees for big theatres who end up with more money in their pocket at the end of a gig here than they do in the studios of the biggest theatres in the North because by the time all the costed items have been worked out, I've handed you an envelope and it's got 485 quid in it. You're like, "Jesus I've made more money here than . . ." Then I go, "Yeah, *and* we cooked you lunch *and* there was an audience." Because increasingly if you're on the studio circuit, there isn't an audience. So that's how we've squared the circle. Mostly by not really caring, mostly just by making sure it's good. So if we do a Christmas fair, we want to just be the best Christmas fair in the world. There's no art in a Christmas fair, and it is arguably culture but there's no art. Okay. What are we going to do? Well we want to sing carols. Wow. The most amazing band. Well yes, we could, but actually that won't make people sing will it? Well no, we should get the loveliest community choirs. Yes! That's actually the right thing for that particular moment. It's not the most excellent but it is the one that will encourage more people to sing and that's how we do it. You can see high art here too. We've got an opera coming, I hate high and low, it doesn't make any sense in any case, but the next week there's going to be a bunch of happy kids running around as clowns.

I don't think it's the answer to your question about community and theatre. I think it's just how we've tried to answer it.

I think that's an answer to the question, and I relate to that, and if I relate to that then the rest of the fucking country can too.

Are you listening, the rest of the fucking country? *Relate to that!*

It's a bit of a skewed image of culture though to see it as grassroots pitted against highbrow, the lowly community theatres against the big mighty houses.

I don't think they are any better than us, but I do know they get funded a lot more. And I think that's the thing as I get older I get more and more chippy. I get more and more angry about it, not less. It is possible to completely reimagine how we engage with culture. But the cost is high for everybody and it will involve us getting rid of some stuff, and it will involve getting rid of some people who had really beautiful careers mapped out because that's what they were promised from an early age. They're going to have to shift their worldview . . . and we've got to stop how they do the funding. There are organisations that simply don't work. It doesn't mean they don't do what they think they're meant to be doing. They simply don't work cause they're not doing any of the things that the rest of us want doing. And they don't serve audiences. They don't serve artists. I don't really know what they're for, but they *can* demonstrate that they are successfully doing the thing that they've always done for the last 40 years. Those people need to stop being given so much money, and that really is the only way. This idea we're not in competition is laughable. We are.

I'm working with a team of four and realistically we need a team of seven, so where am I going to get my three other people from? And yes, we'll do all the things that we can possibly do, but at some point the funders are going to have to take the other three people off someone else and give them to me. Or choose not to do that. And accept that that tells themselves a lot about what their values are. Someone said, "Oh we should have one of these in every town." "Yeah, great. Go for it. You've got to give them 185 grand, *[laughs]* each!" So you've got to work out where that's coming from.

It's hard to argue down South exactly why you need that funding if they haven't seen it with their own eyes. Of course you don't need to give money to those big places, just let them die naturally. And of course what's needed is a centre like the Holbeck in every town — even in London where, for a metropolis with so many excluded areas of its own, there are ridiculously few buildings like the Albany Deptford. In London I certainly can't take my kids to the theatre because I can't afford it. I live in a borough where there isn't anywhere like the Holbeck for me to take my kids to, and we live really centrally but we don't have a local theatre or arts centre. Well there's one up the road, but that's highbrow, not for anyone under

*50 or twentysomething. I can take the kids to the West End, I suppose, which is
wonderful, a world experience they're not going to get because I can't afford to take
them. Certainly not once a month. And prices being what they are, I'd much
rather take them to the cinema, and even then I struggle to do that unless I go
halfway across the city to find a cinema with cheaper tickets — but that doesn't stop
the popcorn being astronomical wherever you go. We bring in our own drinks and
snacks, but that can dampen the experience! So I can't take them anywhere locally
where the performing arts in a wider sense bring together the community in all its
different shapes and forms. If that's London, it's proof that the cuts are everywhere,
at least relatively speaking. But how do you articulate that need without falling
into the trap of, "Well, we need to give you the funding and then you need to be
up on your feet and then you need to be sustainable." Because 'sustainable' has been
morphed and corrupted and used as the goal to take away funding.*

I think you have to directly deny it. We're lucky because we're small enough
that nobody's really interested in watching us fail, and therefore we do operate
beyond the normal bounds. We don't have a board because . . . well in fact we
do have a lot of boards: a community advisory board, a club board, a
professional board. But they don't have any legal responsibility. If you are as
risk-taking as we are, you don't want to hand your responsibility to anyone
else. You want to keep it as close to you as possible. In fact we're not a charity
for lots of reasons, but that only works because we have complete commitment
to transparency and we're locked into this company wage. If we weren't,
there's no way that we would be as popularly supported as we are. People
know that when they give us money, they know exactly where it's going
because they can come in and see the accounting book.

Now all of this is the context for having to fight the logic of what arts
funding is for. That's really difficult because naturally you have to meet the
criteria in order to be given arts funding. So you're meeting your criteria for
your funding but at the same time you're also trying to smash the system
down. And that is a very difficult trick. We only get away with it, to be honest,
because our work is unusual.

We're not impossible to cut by any stretch of the imagination, but it would
be a strange decision because nobody really does what we do. It's not like
there are ten other companies like us. So we feel we can say: do not use Arts
Council funding to prime the pumps of commercial models. It's the stupidest
thing that we've all collectively allowed to happen for 20 years. I've sat on
boards of theatres who are having to demonstrate they don't need their
funding in the run-up to a funding round. And we're like, "You didn't know
that you just made the argument for your own cuts. Right?" You know, it
happened and the leadership at that level did it for a reason.

We're now seeing the pump priming argument grow as we see more and more theatres getting into bed with commercial producers to test product, then that's what it goes on and makes a lot of money. The next big question for the industry will be to say, where does that money go? So if I am the artistic director of the recently created 'Durham Playhouse', where does that money go, what does it do? What's it for, how does it serve that original organisation? Are we saying that when that show goes on and it's a commercial success, then the money goes back to the theatre that originally co-produced it and took the financial risk? So now what we're saying is we really want artistic directors and chief executives who are good at guessing where's the next popular hit will come from? Well, here at the Durham Playhouse we don't make popular hits, it's just the theatre paid for that show because we wanted that show, and then its producers brought it in and made money from it. What, so the theatre didn't make any money from it then? However hard we try, whichever way we look at it: it's a shitty system.

So the question is why are you making *Breakfast at Tiffany's*? Not accusing you, but *why* are you doing that? You're doing it for lots of reasons, but I'm *not* convinced why you're doing it. You're doing it because your audience might want it for definite, but you're not doing it because that's what the public funding is intended for. But that is what public funding currently *is* exactly for. And my argument is we need to change that.

If the market is failing our communities culturally — and it is — then that's because the market doesn't give a fuck about communities culturally, because that's not what the market does. The market doesn't care. The market is abstract. It just gets on with doing things that might make money. So everything that's left has to be picked up by subsidy. And the point of subsidies, surely, is to ask important things like where do you live? And so let's go and put the money there. But what we've made instead is a bunch of chief executives who are now *investors*. "Here is two million quid. We expect you to turn it into eight million." Well that's fucking ridiculous. "No, you're just going to need to have all of the following skills." But why? Surely we don't want big regional theatres getting involved in commercial. "Yes, but the National Theatre made all this money from *War Horse*." Yes, but surely it was not doing *War Horse* because it thought it might make all that money. It was doing *War Horse* for a load of other reasons, and if it wasn't then it needs to stop it immediately.

Fundamentally the idea of funding as pump-priming for additional funding is just nuts. Because it encourages you to re-model yourself into markets where that's possible. And that isn't even possible in most parts of the country, because they're not London. Poor buggers who are asked to try shouldn't be made to try. But then to be honest, change your resource, change the point of the funding. Then look back at where we put funding where it was pump-priming and understand that's not a very good use of what we've got. Not while so much of the country is not getting the culture that we hope and want it to have.

But I don't think you win the argument. You just keep throwing yourself at a wall and hope that eventually cracks will show. You just have to keep going because the system surrounding the status quo is huge and hard to crack. There are a few things in this industry that we are unwilling to talk about and this is the kind of core one where we really need to shift the conversation. It boils down to questions like why do we have the same leaders at the top of our organisations? It's because of that, that boards look at something and go, "What do we need to do? We have a substitute strategy obligation to do X, Y and Z. Get me someone that can do X, Y and Z." Well the X, Y and Zs are wrong, you've got the wrong template. And until we shift that, we're going to keep finding people who've been there a long long time running those organisations in a certain specific way. And lo and behold, they all look the same as well.

You've said that the ultimate justification for doing all this is "just feed the kids". That's exactly why I got into all this, so I know what you mean. You recently wrote in your blog: "Last summer there was a group of kids who had been identified by the council as at risk of returning to school after the summer holiday suffering from malnutrition. There was the money to feed them. And to provide a health activity and arts programme. But nowhere for it be hosted. Of course we said yes. For five weeks kids got fed. Kids that would not have got fed did. The kids got fed." Lay it out exactly why this is so important.

There's a real privilege and responsibility to running anything in this life. There's all these people, right up to the prime minister, who are supposed pumped up with their own pomposity because they're supposed to be in charge. But actually when pressed they're like, "God, no, I don't have any *real* authority." Well we do. We really do. We can be the difference. Our team here can be the difference between whether some kids eat or not. They will go back to school, malnourished. Some of them will be officially starved. The opportunity walks through the door and says can you do this thing? And we say yes.

There are other things we can do. We can be more open. We can be more ready. We can be more eager to see those moments. We can be willing. I mean, in this particular instance, it was a no brainer. But there are times when you'll be like, "Oh fucking hell, this is going to take up my whole weekend, isn't it?" Yeah. It is! But that thing's going to happen. That little moment is going to happen. Those people are going to get to have that experience with a family in at the weekend when they had a wake — at the last minute they needed a place. It wasn't my rota but the team basically got there. We can take the burden off them. That family got somewhere to grieve and they didn't have any money. And with the exception of this conversation we're having now, it will never have an impact. Like us getting a reward for it. But it did have an impact because that family got somewhere to grieve.

And as ridiculous as this sounds, it makes us really p*owerful* and we should carry that power as gently and as humbly and whatever, . . . generously and at times [laughs] self-sacrificingly as we can. That doesn't mean anyone is more important or better than anybody else. Except for a very small part of the population, pretty much everyone is as powerful but they just refuse to accept it. There is a system in place, not to sound like an old Marxist, to teach us to look to the idea of the customer as the most powerful role in society because it keeps us on the tramlines. I refuse to accept that's true. I'm a citizen and I've got a van and a bus and a club and a load of kit and me and mine can do so much with that simply by saying, if you want it, it's yours.

Obviously that sounds easy, but then we pay the price of having said that. And that makes us powerful. That makes us have influence on the world. But of course, [laughs] there is another way of being us, and that's where you're like, "Well, hang on a minute. I've got my strict rules of engagement, I'm going to hit my responsibilities but I do have my work-life balance." Okay, you have hit your responsibilities, but there is a wider responsibility and mostly it's the responsibility to *imagine* what you can do and then go and *do* it.

I remember literally stepping over a homeless person to get into a theatre, where the artistic director said to me, "Actually, we do want to talk to you about the homeless problem. Should we make a play about it?" And I was thinking, "Well, we might open a fucking hostel in your theatre." But you couldn't do that because the chair of the board would be like, "Well, hang on a minute. We've got a statuary obligation that says we're . . ." Are you out of your mind? All I can say to that is what are you doing with your life? What are you doing? Personally I'm terrified I'm going to get to the end and be like, "Fucking wasted that."

So yes, 'feeding the kids'. I didn't even feed them. We literally just held the room while someone else fed them. But holding the room for those 24 kids to get fed every day for five weeks, well that'll do me for a bit. And then let's find the next opportunity to do something like that. Well, how can we help you?

Because that's part of how theatre is: it comes and goes. It doesn't exist for long. And the idea that I get to the end, I'm like, "Oh, all that energy, all that heartache, all that cheese I didn't eat, I wasted it all . . ." — and that genuinely, genuinely motivates me. And that's why I hold onto "the kids got fed" in the middle of all of it. When you're tired and you want to go home and you want to see your own kids and all that other stuff, I'm like, "Have the kids got fed now?" So yeah, that's the answer to that one.

*

23
Betsan Llwyd

'Two languages are better than one ... the world opens its doors wider'

Betsan Llwyd is a director, actor & artistic director of Theatr Bara Caws. She lives in Cardiff and works in Caernarfon, Gwynedd. Born in Llanidloes in Powys, she was raised in Staylittle, Bagillt, Holywell & Mold, all in Wales. • theatrbaracaws.com

Theatre in Wales hasn't enjoyed quite the same start as in the rest of the country?

Professional Welsh-language theatre as an industry is comparatively young — especially compared to the rest of the UK. It's generally assumed that this is mainly down to the effects of the Revival *[of Christianity in Wales, which triggered similar revivals across the world]* at the beginning of the 1900s which frowned upon 'entertainment' as such, so we have achieved a lot in a fairly short period of time.

I was appointed artistic director of Bara Caws *['Bread and Cheese' in Welsh]* about seven years ago. It was an interesting time as there seemed to be more political awareness in general, similar to how it was at the beginning of the 1980s when I started in the business. I'm not sure whether or not that's actually followed through because things have got pretty crazy since.

[TV channel] S4C was established *[in 1982]* — this was fantastic for the Welsh language and culture, and it has been extraordinarily successful, although, to be honest I'm not quite sure where it stands at the moment — policies have changed, society has changed. I feel that S4C hasn't managed to exploit all the opportunities that came its way over the years, and now with so many digital channels and platforms it can be difficult for the channel. But at the very beginning it was such an exciting venture and had a huge impact.

How did theatre fit in with all of that explosion of culture? Was Welsh-language theatre — and English-language theatre in Wales — given a boost by the focus and pride generated by S4C?

It was great for the Welsh language industry as far as actors were concerned because there was so much more work around, *diverse* work, which meant that you could learn new skills. You could be working in the theatre, then go on to work in television, and radio too — it was a fantastic opportunity for all of us to play a part in that mix.

At that particular point, TV was absolutely integral to empowering the Welsh performing arts. When it came along, what did it offer you personally as an actor?

For me, I was just about leaving university and trying to find a foothold in the profession. I was one of a group of friends who made a conscious decision to work in theatre for the first few years of our professional lives, then when the offers of television work came along we were confident to go for it. It gave us different experiences and different opportunities, and opened out the acting world in a different direction. I was extraordinarily fortunate because I managed to keep on doing both, and I've had wonderful opportunities to work on a diverse range of television, film and theatre productions.

You stayed in Wales for university, but when you finished, you must have had a lot of people telling you to go to London, Manchester, Glasgow, Bristol . . .

At the time we didn't really consider it. There were five of us leaving uni at the same time — three from Aberystwyth and two from the Welsh College in Cardiff — and we established a Welsh-language theatre company creating new work primarily for young people. So Theatr Ystwyth came into being, and as well as new works we re-looked at some of the classics and gave them a twist to push the agenda — e.g. swapping genders of characters. But it was a conscious decision to stay in Wales.

I think this emphasis for people to train beyond Wales, though it has been happening for a good few years, became more prevalent about 10-15 years ago. This issue of where you train and where you're offered work can be tricky. The problem arises mainly with agents who will want to steer their clients to work in England, or in the English-speaking world in general. It can be difficult to argue the point that some people truly want to stay in Wales and work through the medium of Welsh.

The difficulty for young actors today, especially if they haven't been on a training course in an accredited college, is getting signed up with an agency — because the emphasis in the whole industry is that if you haven't got an agent you're not going to get seen. So, unless you're a director, like me, who goes to the theatre to see actors on stage, it becomes impossible. It doesn't seem so long ago, in my experience, that there seemed to be many more directors, producers, casting directors going to the theatre to see what talent was there.

You personally must have had some weird moments along the way too. Not just the ignorance about Wales and Welsh but also the stereotypes of the magical mystical valleys filled with choirs and druids and the odd noble coal mine.

I did, in a sense, at Theatr Clwyd *[in Mold, Flintshire]*, when we did this play in 1993 called *Full Moon [adapted from the Welsh-language novel Un Nos Ola Leuad/One Moonlit Night by Caradog Prichard]*. I'd been in the film version a couple of years before and was asked to take part in this English adaption for the stage, which transferred to the Young Vic. The director, the wonderful Helena Kaut-Howson, asked if I would do some media interviews but that I also had to be aware that people didn't know that you could have a successful career in a language they didn't even know existed. The media wanted to couch everything in this mythological mystical Wales full of ghosts and spirits — I was so exasperated! It's changed somewhat by now because you've got extraordinarily successful high-profile actors who are Welsh, and who are proud to proclaim the fact, and that's been really good for us.

Wales is also becoming more prominent due to the many TV series that have Welsh themes and characters — though often starring English actors whose accents are atrocious! But I will point out that people still tend to think that Wales is just 'The Valleys'. Years ago, at an audition, this guy asked, "Can you be a bit more like a welcoming Welsh woman from the valleys or the hills?" But I don't have an obvious accent, which obviously worked against me. (I was born and brought up in Mold *[in Flintshire, North Wales]* — on the border with Cheshire.) So I'm afraid I waved goodbye to my chances of securing the part there and then, and told him, in no uncertain terms, that not every woman from Wales is 'welcoming' and we don't all come from "the valleys or the hills". There's still that little bit of stereotyping going on, but hopefully that will eventually change.

And Bara Caws has long experience in helping make that change happen, hasn't it?

As a small touring theatre company, Bara Caws has been going for over 40 years *[founded in 1976]* and was the first company that ever took Welsh-language theatre into the heart of the communities. Last year *[2019]* we won the main award from the National Rural Touring Forum, and all of a sudden we came into prominence for English speakers in Wales and beyond, people who didn't know Bara Caws existed, even though we have this record of success, because we simply didn't come across their radar. This was wonderful for a small company like ours, because recognition like that is the kind of thing that raises awareness of Welsh language theatre, and now another faction knows that there are people producing and performing work for and in the community, and doing so on a small scale and on a tiny budget but still succeeding in drawing in the crowds.

How does producing work fit in at Bara Caws?

We do offer production support to new artists/companies whenever possible, e.g. we have produced numerous shows for a local company, Seren Ddu a Mwnci *['Black Star & Monkey' in Welsh]*, which was performed in locations throughout North Wales. After performing in the National Slate Museum, Llanberis and Penrhyn Castle, Bangor tourists showed an interest in seeing English versions of the shows, but that is not within our Arts Council Wales remit.

But are you allowed to tour outside of the Welsh-speaking areas?

We could, provided the productions are in Welsh, but with the cost of touring and the call on our services within Wales, it's not a feasible option at the moment. Welsh language theatre used to tour to England on many occasions, doing particularly well in Liverpool, for instance, because of the strong Welsh-language community there. We have been invited to London to perform but the cost is prohibitive. If we received a large cash injection we'd love to hit the Welsh-language societies that exist in towns and cities around Britain.

And around the world too.

And around the world, yes that would be fabulous. In the past the company has forged links with the Oerol Festival in the Netherlands and performed in festivals in Ireland, and it would be great if we once again spread our geographical wings — but as always it comes down to cost.

But the UK isn't the rest of the world, and it's incredible that we're just talking about getting from one part of the country to another part. London isn't that far away. It isn't not like you're Aberdeen or even Liverpool, you're closer and it's heartbreaking to see that companies like Bara Caws can't get the work to the capital.

Interestingly, we did this production recently, *Lleu Llaw Gyffes [a hero of Welsh mythology who appears in the tales of the Mabinogion]* by Aled Jones Williams, and photos were posted up on social media. This guy tweeted saying, "Fantastic photos. It breaks my heart that I can't see this production." So I replied, "Please come, there's an English precis!" — to which he replied, "It's not that, it's the geographical problem." And that was only London to Wales. Now if something piques my interest I'll travel, but I do appreciate that it can be expensive. This is why our provision goes down so well in Wales itself as we go right into the heart of communities.

Apart from the inescapable centrifugal force that London has on the rest of the country, on a more practical level, there's also the fact that if you go to London you can do more than just see a show — shopping, sights, professional catch-ups, even personal since everyone seems to have a friend or family member living there at one point or other. Whereas someone going to Caernarfon, for example, and who's not from Wales or who doesn't venture far out of the big urban areas, they'll struggle to work out what to do with their time there. In my case I don't drive, which is a barrier if there's not much public transport, plus I have a perfectly logical phobia of rural buses.

I appreciate that, but in an ideal world it could be possible to curate a 'package' for this neck of the woods because there are a couple of great art venues and cinemas in the area, and the landscape itself it second to none. The opportunities for walkers, climbers, sailors, etc are on the doorstep. And we do have a Michelin-starred restaurant in the vicinity! The odd Shakespeare production is staged in the castle — which appeals to tourists — and summer seasons used to be held in Bangor which attracted full houses — I don't know whether this is something which could be brought back.

Looking at the idea of Welsh language theatre beyond Wales, it's a bit surreal to think of the reception that a Welsh language theatre production gets if it plays London, where it's usually a small festival or the Welsh Centre or maybe a studio in a bigger theatre that decides to put it on. You wouldn't think of the National Theatre offering a stage even though they have the designation 'of Great Britain', but then none of the arts centres or mid-level theatres would be likely to either. And yet Welsh-language theatre is by and for people who have the same issues and general experiences as the people in London, be it Brexit, Coronavirus,

Aldi vs Morrisons, or who really should have won the last edition of The Voice, but it won't be accepted as 'British' simply because it's in another language — and in the UK, language of course is perceived as foreign and not Other. Your average non-Welsh-speaking theatregoing Londoner would most likely feel a minority in your audience and not really understand that this is a perfect experience to learn about coexisting. Some will understand of course, others might go out of a sense of solidarity, others out of the quest for exotica or out of pure curiosity. And also those who think because it's in a foreign language, it must be highbrow art. And how many will be likely to go back again? So selling a show in the capital of the country that Wales is a part of must be a surreal proposition. I suppose someone dedicated from London could pop over regularly to Wales to see theatre in context and so better understand it, but then that sort of reduces the freedom on your side to take it to the rest of the country to put it on and say, "This is British theatre, it belongs to us all, here's all the context you need, enjoy it!"

Well, the acceptance and understanding that Welsh is a living language, through which many people live their daily lives, is a UK-wide problem, and it's probably fair to say that it's primarily a problem for the English. It's a similar attitude to "why bother learning any other language, because everyone speaks English anyway?" that you hear when travelling abroad.

And you're right about the difficulty of attracting people to see plays in a language they don't understand. It has been mooted that a primarily Welsh-language drama festival could be held here, as used to happen 30-35 years ago. Indeed Arad Goch from Aberystwyth have been phenomenally successful with their Open Doors Festival which is a theatre festival for children/young people, and companies from all over the world perform there. It maddens me when I see work in the Welsh language which is much better produced and more engaging than some work in English — wherever in the UK that work is performed — not achieving wider recognition. Some critics from London do visit the larger venues in Wales on a regular basis, but very rarely do they see work in Welsh, and I could probably safely say that they would never come to a community venue.

I should point out that, accessibility-wise, we always provide an English precis of every show, and other theatre companies have developed their own modus operandi. For instance, Theatr Genedlaethol Cymru *[the Welsh language national theatre of Wales in Carmarthen, its English language counterpart is National Theatre Wales in Cardiff]* have produced an app called Sibrwd *['Whisper']* which you can download on your phone, which then provides an English spoken/written translation while you watch. We trialled it on one production, but it was an expensive option for us because of needing extra staff to operate it. We also asked our audiences what their preference would be for a Bara Caws production, and most came down in favour of the written precis — a much more viable option for us.

So it really does need a festival format rather than touring to grab that audience?

Well, a festival vibe is very attractive, where you can dip in and out of shows. We see this a lot at the National Eisteddfod *[held annually, the largest music & poetry festival in Europe]* and it is a fabulous window to the Welsh-speaking world. But it is a shame that the English-speaking audience aren't generally more open-minded. I've been in productions myself where audience members who didn't understand the language have been genuinely astounded at the production values of Welsh-language theatre. You have to open your eyes to see what's out there — and ears to hear it too! — but unless people want to see it, it is a difficult sell.

And it's a question of also anticipating what is it they think they want to see, what their own idea is of Welsh theatre.

I suppose that's true, but to be honest with you as a company we don't target English-speaking audiences when deciding upon our artistic programme, though some productions can be attractive to them thematically e.g. we performed a show called *Hwyliau'n Codi [literally 'The Raising of the Sails', also meaning 'An Uplifting of the Spirits']* some years ago based on the shipbuilding industry in North Wales, and that generated interest among English speakers who enjoyed the historical aspect of the piece.

But we are actively aware of what our own audiences would appreciate. Our next production is *Draenen Ddu [postponed because of the Coronavirus crisis]*, a Welsh-language adaption of *Blackthorn* by Charley Miles, translated by Angharad Tomos. The original play was a great success at the Edinburgh fringe a couple of years ago, and what interested Angharad when she saw it is that it's about a small community in North Yorkshire but could have been written about any small community in Wales. In fact, it has worldwide relevance. Hopefully Charley Miles will eventually get the chance to see this production and spread the word about the Welsh-language theatre sector.

We depend a lot on word of mouth to generate long-term interest, and we have started to see Welsh learners return to our productions. As for 'giving people what they want', one of the mainstays at Bara Caws for years has been *The Club Show*. It's an X-rated show, in the Welsh language, which is performed in pubs and clubs throughout the land. We're the only company that offers this kind of provision, and the exciting thing is that the audiences don't realise they're watching theatre as such. It's a phenomenally successful part of our programme.

So Bara Caws is just doing what any self-respecting theatre needs to do, responding to the needs of the community, speaking their language — and not just linguistically.

We feel very strongly about that. Since it was established in 1976 the company has continued to evolve, but the main responsibility has always been to keep on performing plays that are relevant to the communities of Wales *in* the very hearts of those communities. We have a network of local organisers which has been nurtured over the years and always ask them for advice and feedback.

One of our most important playwrights, Siôn Eirian, has written his third play now for us called *Fienna ['Vienna']*. It's the last of a political triptych that he's written for the company *[the others are Garw/literally 'Rough/Rugged' and Yfory/'Tomorrow']* and that's really looking at Europe and exploring boundaries and identities. We played *Yfory* in Pontardawe in South Wales and during the Q&A afterwards an audience member (who was not a fluent Welsh speaker) asked us to translate the piece into English to take it to the South Wales Valleys, as the contemporary political scene was so relevant she wanted as many people as possible to see it.

Next year we will be staging a play marking 30 years since the Greenham Common Peace Camp which was established by a group of women from South Wales. We will definitely try to extend our audience reach with this one. Given endless resources there are so many opportunities to which we'd like to respond, and we do try to push the boundaries in certain areas, but ultimately our responsibility is to our Welsh-language grassroots audiences.

Our remit is challenging — we have to produce at least three shows a year aimed at different target audiences. Our more 'challenging' work is performed mostly in more official theatrical venues, making the most of tech specs and so on — but we do prefer studio spaces than the main auditorium. Then we tour specifically targeted productions to community halls and try to give new practitioners the opportunity to get a foothold in the professional world. For instance, last year we commissioned three young writers who had formed their own community theatre company, Cwmni Tebot, to write a revue-type play on a subject close to their hearts, and *Costa Byw ['Cost of Living']* was born. It focused on the dearth of housing for local people in the Llyn Peninsula in North Wales (this was literally a two men and a plank production — two actors, a ladder and a pile of books!). Some people come to see every single one of our productions, others will just come to their local village hall, and others just to see the pub shows.

If you take the two chairs and a plank idea for a show and blitz the northern communities with one nighters, what sort of spaces would you be playing?

These are always targeted at community or village halls. Bara Caws is greatly loved by its communities, and we work hard on nurturing that feeling of ownership they have on the company, so it's crucial that we still visit the hearts of those communities and play in the smallest venues possible.

Can we talk a bit more about language? We should explain to the rest of the country that Welsh is a living indigenous language of the British Isles — one of the seven languages that have always existed here: Welsh, Irish Gaelic, Scottish Gaelic, Manx, Cornish (all related Celtic languages), English and British Sign Language. And rather than being this fanciful tongue of spirits and legends, Welsh is a living language and by far the healthiest of the Celtic languages. Anyone who speaks Welsh is bilingual in a strange way — the language is as different to English in terms of grammar and vocabulary as French or Hindi, and yet it's a language whose speakers share the same basic culture, economy and societal norms as the rest of the country. You order your groceries in Tesco, drink a pint, complain about your internet provider in exactly the same way as the rest of the country. That's a subtle distinction which is easy to understand in most other countries where bilingualism and/or the co-existence of national languages is perfectly normal — Belgium, Hungary, India, Iran, Nigeria, Morocco, the list goes on. So how do you get people, even in Wales, to accept that Welsh is neither foreign nor exotic, but was here before English, is an integral part of our nation, and which, along with BSL of course, we should be learning in all our schools?

[laughs] The million dollar question! But, for a lot of us the co-existence of Welsh and English is normal! It's very difficult to keep a cool head when you hear people asking what's the point? The obvious reason is that two languages are better than one, three better than two and so on — and the world opens its doors wider so that more diverse opportunities come your way — that's the message we need to get across.

It's wonderful that the language is growing phenomenally down in South Wales in the Cardiff, Swansea, Newport area *[where Welsh was lost]* and the number of Welsh schools opening there is very heartening. Some people have had a bad educational experience, obviously, and have battened down the hatches regards learning Welsh *[in Wales, it is compulsory for children from age five to 16 to learn Welsh, at least as a second language]*, but nowadays I draw people's attention to resources such as the Duolingo app (which I'm using to learn Spanish) — and it's surprising how many are already using it to learn Welsh. It's only five minutes a day, so very user and time-friendly.

Which I'm already doing — 'Dych ch'in hoffi cyri?' 'Draig dw i.' ['Do you want a curry?' 'I am a dragon.'] Again something very obvious to point out, but your first language is Welsh, it's your mother tongue. English is your second language.

Yes, I had no English until I was about five, but after that, to be honest with you, because I was brought up on the borders *[the parts of Wales bordering with England]*, while we spoke Welsh at home I spoke a lot of English in school even though the schools were Welsh medium. I never truly understood the threat to the language until I went to Aberystwyth Uni and had a bit of an eureka moment. S4C was to have been established when Margaret Thatcher did her U-turn. *[During the 1970s, Welsh-language activists had campaigned for a dedicated TV service, and both the Conservative and Labour parties included this in their manifestos for the 1979 general election. After the Conservatives won a majority, they decided against a Welsh fourth channel, leading to acts of civil disobedience, sit-ins at BBC and HTV studios, and attacks on television transmitters in Welsh-speaking areas.]* As a result Gwynfor Evans, the president of Plaid Cymru *['Party of Wales', advocating independence from the UK]*, threatened to go on hunger strike, and as a protest we were all asked not to pay our TV licence.

One evening we were asked to go to a meeting to discuss this, and the president of the students' union stated categorically that if we didn't pay he, and many others, would end up in jail! I was stunned. This was a bare-faced lie. I found myself, one of about 350 out of a thousand students who wanted a Welsh channel, voted down by people who had no interest in the language, or the culture, most of whom who would, most likely, leave Wales at the end of their courses. That was when I realised what it was all about.

My children were educated in Welsh medium schools and colleges, and now they live abroad and are mindful and respectful of their respective cultures, and as a result are multilingual. I live as much as possible of my life through the medium of Welsh, both personally and professionally.

As I touched on before, languages in most other countries live side by side with other languages, they can't get away from them unless they're divided by extreme geography. On an island with no porous land borders, a dominant language/culture like English in the British Isles can just squash the others out, especially if the smaller linguistic communities don't have a larger related group beyond the sea to offer support or a comparison to what's happening in other countries. It's both the tyranny and apathy caused by the accident of geography, but, given the chance, context and lessons of history, we English can still learn to embrace the languages and cultures that were here long long before we arrived.

We were discussing this years ago over a pint, and somebody asked why, as a general rule, the Scots seem to have a more patriotic sense of identity as a whole than the Welsh, though they've lost their language. The consensus was that the decisive factor was probably geography — it's a larger country and there's a significant mountain range between England and Scotland, whereas Wales is tiny and has always been 'squashed' to one side. Whether or not there is some truth in that I don't know.

But there seems to be more of an awareness of the language these days, thanks to the celebrity culture we live in, and programmes such as *Game of Thrones*, and the fact that Robert Downey Jr used a Welsh accent in *Dolittle*. But we can't ignore the fact that the awareness regarding the use of the language is a major problem here in Wales. For example, I can't tell you how many times people can be disrespectful, or even downright rude, about some of our indigenous names — while abroad people have no trouble at all with the pronunciation! And the sentiment of preferring English over Welsh 'to get on in the world', which was highly prevalent years ago, unfortunately still rears its ugly head from time to time.

It's shocking the way theatre in both languages in Wales historically never received the support given to theatre in most other parts of the country. Has there developed a common idea of Welsh theatre as a reactionary movement or is there a specific voice for each language . . . or is it pretty pointless to discuss, the most important thing being to just get on with it?

Regarding specific voices for each language — it's tricky. Of course, many plays performed are translations or adaptations of classics which are relevant in both languages, but obviously nuances can be explored and exploited when that piece is in your mother tongue. And I guess Welsh language theatre has the opportunity to be more political because we're working in a minority language, which is in itself political.

I sometimes feel that Welsh writing in English can seem a bit condescending, especially when put in the hands of non-Welsh-speaking people. There are people working hard at trying to find a truly bilingual solution, and some young practitioners, like Stephan Donelly through his own company Invertigo, are exploring different ways of making theatre and of exploring their own identity as Welsh people. But at the moment, you feel that once one avenue has been explored, that's that, and anyway I've been in this business a long time now and things seem to come round in circles — there's nothing new under the sun is there? But I look forward to being proved wrong!

*

24
Brian Merriman

'Have we got the courage to tell our stories — truthfully?'

Brian Merriman is a producer, director, actor, writer, singer & artistic director/ founder of the International Dublin Gay Theatre Festival. Based in Dublin, where he was born, he was raised in Wexford & Waterford. • gaytheatre.ie, @brianm179

I always seem to be facing a losing battle with people who want to categorise Irish theatre as 'foreign'.

It's funny you know, when we're trying to get rights to a play here in Ireland, we're considered to be UK. People say, "Oh no you can't do that play because it's on in Britain." And we're going, "So what? Unless there's a bus, a plane, or a boat daily, it's not going to matter." So, they do disadvantage Irish companies if it's on anywhere in Britain. It's really weird. I'm trying to get that through to rights holders. And then others will say, "Oh they're foreign, they're international." Whatever. We are still here as an independent nation for the past hundred years, you know.

The pitfalls of running an international festival, one for which you pushed out the boat in 2018 on celebrating your 15th anniversary along with the 25th anniversary of decriminalisation.

And they both were highly influential in getting something done. But the festival came about quite simply. After working in theatre doing musicals and things like that, a couple of hundred productions, I came back to Dublin in the 1990s thinking that it was over — after a certain time living out of suitcases you begin to hit a bit of a wall. I got a decade of work in Dublin's Olympia Theatre and then, I decided I would do a master's degree in equality studies, because I was working in that area for some time and we were ten years decriminalised then. [*Homosexuality was decriminalised in Ireland in 1993, and most forms of discrimination based on sexual orientation are now outlawed. Ireland also forbids incitement to hatred based on sexual orientation.*]

The spark for the International Dublin Gay Theatre Festival came around the 150th anniversary of the birth of the birth of Oscar Wilde. I went to a photography exhibition celebrating Pride and every image I saw there was gay people still wearing a mask, even though we were ten years decriminalised. And if you have your moment when something all comes together, that was mine, and I said, "We really have to assert our citizenship if we're going to have more change and progress. Everyone thinks the theatre is full of queens. They enjoy the theatre and yet they don't link that positive together as a gift from LGBT artists." So I said, "Roll our stories out into the mainstream, warts and all. Our livelihoods and our lifestyles will not be scrubbed up to make us more acceptable. Let us tell the full story of our diverse identity." And that's where the genesis of the whole thing came from. Wilde, equality, artistic visibility and Pride.

Presumably it was easier than if you had done it before 1993. On the other hand you still must have encountered opposition.

I did, and I found opposition in the strangest of places to the festival. I would have to say some of the 'opposition' or objection came from the gay community and the artistic community — LGBT people who had survived or felt that they had survived in the arts without their sexual orientation becoming what they would describe as an 'issue'. They felt that it was drawing attention to their 'issue' by seeking an artistic credit for the things we all do very well. Others said of course, "Oh I wish I'd thought of that."

I would have to say it was a very mixed bag. I found well-meaning straight people smiling at me saying about the programme, "Well done." And then saying, "But there's nothing in that for me." And they were not coming to the shows. But they were the whole point of the event: getting the straight people to come. That's changed, and now we do have about 50-50 . . . maybe even a little more straight to gay these days.

People are coming in (a) because they know people in the cast, and (b) because straight actors and straight companies are looking at the repertoire and saying, "There's some really cool parts there." It's now fashionable to play gay. And there's (c) because we are out in the mainstream venues — and from day one we have been.

But I remember at the beginning that those venues were not so convinced either. One day I walked into one of them and the manager said to me, "Oh dear, we've only sold two seats for tonight." I turned around to her and I said, "It's just as well I sold the remaining 68." Now this was the cutting-edge venue in Dublin, but it didn't even connect with their audiences at first. You have to work to change things.

Was there any model that you took?

No, I have to say. Because I can't find ourselves exactly anywhere else. Like having had to say to the Edinburgh Festival Fringe in the early days, "Where's your LGBT programme?" They were extremely positive and said, "Oh, right, let's put this in as a category." I often shared my lists with them. But there was the Gay Arts Festival in Columbus, Ohio, but *[USA President]* George Bush's backlash against the arts and LGBT visibility shrank funding sources and closed that down.

To start an international festival was . . . well, let me tell you the fun thing. I have a very good friend in London, Mark Pollard, he's an agent and a director. And when I got this idea to do the festival, I wrote to him and I said, "Mark, bring a play from London so I can call it 'international'." So, we got one international play the first year, two the second year and by the third year, 66 per cent of the programme was international. In fact, in the third year alone I had something like 80 applications from America, just on word of mouth. Because they could not speak there and they would not be listened to under a George Bush presidency (he now looks like a moderate compared to a certain person), they had no space to get funding anymore, he cut out the funding for the arts, for gay rights, etcetera, etcetera. We've had plays from Zimbabwe, Taiwan, Ukraine, we've had performers who are Iranian, Venezuelan, South African. That's very important to us and I don't knock it, but this amount of applications is hard work when we do them a voluntary level. It really is.

A constant in the festival is that it has always been run by volunteers, so it's an important part of what you do.

I don't even get my phone bill paid. And you see, this is where people confuse the terms. I am a *professional* director, and producer and writer. But I knew in order to do this, I was going to have to do what I often say: "*Donate* something!" I'm very lucky that I've gotten other people from other walks of life to donate too, but very few from active theatre. Still, I've been trying out a succession plan for some time and I do want to find a theatre person (who's really good) who will *donate* their time to bring their own stamp on the festival in the future to succeed me.

Having produced professionally, I do value equality and transparency. We publish our terms and conditions on our website where there's no secret deals, no negotiations, and anything we get, we pump it back in — for example, to be able to provide the venues for free. And when I see what other festivals need to charge in order to survive, we have a huge bonus here. At any American festival I've been in touch with, they charge you to read your submission. I not only read them for free, but I dramaturg them when I can, for free. This is about getting gay artists onto the main stage and getting their voices heard. I literally have gone through my stage crews and staff and said, "You have an interesting story, write me a short play." And a year later it's on a stage somewhere.

That idea of donating at a professional level then brings as many challenges as benefits then.

Of course. For example, our grant applications are still at the minimal level. I can understand them saying, "Well, if we just give them this, they're going to make it stretch so far. So why don't we just do that, so that we can invest in all the others that charge per word, for everything that's said and done."

And you know I would feel a little bit miffed about that, having proven to be so open about the things that we do. It's not just obviously that we have proper governance structures, but every single producer at the end of the run gets a printed read-out from our online booking service per day, per complimentaries, per everything, with an entire financial reconciliation on their last night. They don't wait for weeks for this. When the last show goes on at 9pm, my team gather and they have everything ready by 10:30pm for any producer, and they *offer* to settle with them then. And while they're still in the country, they can go, "No I know that we had ten more people there" — and we have a little bag of ticket stubs per performance and they can be physically counted immediately. We're in this not to create barriers but to give additional support to companies, because so often new companies in particular can fall on the basis of the fact that they don't often know what they're doing business-wise.

One example is the amount of new companies whose raison d'etre is to create a 'new space for new voices' in the theatre — laudable. Why are they all doing the same thing? Every young company has that same mission statement, but if they pooled their resources instead, they would do better quality work. They could put the ego of theatre aside for a moment, come together, make an annual programme of say three productions, give three writers and three directors one go each during the year. But instead they're all looking to raise money for writing, directing, venues, publicity, marketing. And that's killing younger people's opportunities to go on to the next step.

How is filtering that sort of support reflected in the festival programme?

When I saw the final programme in front of me for this year 2020, all I could imagine was, "This is so full of good theatre, probably nobody will want to come." You only have to think of the struggle *Angels in America* had before it took off in the next generation, or the trouble that Sondheim had in his early time. 2019 was a very theatrical programme, ranging from Wilde and Tennessee Williams right up to the modern day, and there's the fact that we're still reaching out to new foreign companies. But behind every play in the programme there's another dozen plays that, had I got more resources, I could have given them more help to get them from more obscure or hostile environments, safely to Ireland. And that's always the sadness for me behind any programme. We can do more but we need more resources and audience.

Gay life is more visible now, it's more commercially defined — and we have the landmarks of how we got here, to commemorate. Our 25th anniversary year of decriminalisation *[2018]* was also the 35th anniversary *[1982]* of the most important and visible gay murder in Ireland when Declan Flynn was murdered in Fairview Park *[in Dublin]* by six men. They were brought to court but got off and they got no prison sentence because gay people shouldn't be there in Irish society in the 1980s.

That prompted an angry reaction in Ireland, which brought forward what was later called the first Pride parade — the parade to protest about the court's actions. So that was a very important year for us to see whether we can reflect who we are, and put it on a mainstream stage? And not in a boring, lecturing, or purely an historical perspective — but what it means for us today in theatrical relevance.

In *Pride*, the movie *[2014]*, when I saw the credits, I realised if Mark Ashton, the young advocate hero, had lived, he'd be the exact same age as me. And it really hit me, the generation that we lost at that stage. And did they really work this hard for the gay life and culture we have today? I'm not convinced. That's the theme of my short play *The Off Switch* — so there's an opportunity to unpack that in some of our plays. It's a time to reflect, because I don't want people to be going around genuflecting to everyone over 50 and going, "Thank you, Sir/Madam." They need not only to know but never to take their eye off the duty of us all to prevent discrimination.

We did these things for a reason. We were fighting against oppression. But within oppression and discrimination there are wonderful stories, and I don't think people should be sad about survival. Survival is the greatest triumph when it's in the face of adversity, and I think some of our plays capture that. So I always hope people will engage with the festival and not just at the entertainment level, which is also important of course, particularly a gay theatre festival where they expect to see a bit of flesh — and there's a bit — but with the transformative side of our stories too.

But there are also fabulous stories. And I think the fact that men will do naked plays in a gay theatre festival is also very liberating, because in mainstream theatre it is primarily the female form that is exploited. And I have to say even for a gay theatre festival you will find actors can be very brave, and that includes the straight men playing gay to gay audiences. *Party Boy* was the first Irish play to achieve this and it took 16 years!

I remember a Canadian guy who had a naked shower scene in the show, which was in the mainstream back in Canada. But the first night he was here, he had the towel 'superglued' on to him. But as he gained confidence in understanding who our audience is, the 'superglue' was removed. He told me that the impact of the experience on his own understanding of masculinity was profound. So, it is interesting to see how we've brought, in a pretty inhibited country, not just gay themes but gay physicality to the stage as well.

How do you manage to pack so much theatre in there? The temptation for a festival with your budget to max out on the cabaret must be painful to resist.

Because we pay a price for that. That is my worry every time I see the final programme and say, "Oh my God, it's just so much theatre." We've always premiered new writing: 95 per cent of our programme every year is new writing. But then, how do you engage the people on the gay scene (heavily into drag shows) and indeed the parallel straight scene, because without them we're not going to survive or be relevant to the wider arts. Every year it's all ahead of us for the next two or three weeks thinking "have we done the right thing?" with the programme, and every year I hope we have.

There is no automatic recipe for success but we do see it in the results. Like with the transfers to the Edinburgh fringe. The play that won the best LGBT play *Five Guys Chillin' [by Peter Darney]* and the one that got the British Council's '10 Most to Watch' was *Gypsy Queen [by Rob Ward]*, they were with us first. Some shows are going on to the Brighton Fringe after Dublin as well and we encourage that by saying to a foreign artist, "If you want to try and stretch things — the airfare cost, etc — talk to Brighton, come back to me and I will oblige so that you can do both."

What's particularly interesting is the way the mainstream theatres in Ireland over the last few years — and they're not going to admit this now — are promoting more 'gay friendly or gay themed' theatre around the time of the festival. Shows like *Assassins* in the Gate, a Quentin Crisp play in Smock Alley, Noel Coward plays, Oscar Wilde plays in the Abbey, gay theatre programmes more frequently in April/May. I can't believe it's coincidence anymore because they're always popping up in April and May now. But I hope it doesn't take away from our opportunity, because we have so little, we wouldn't have the marketing budget of even one of those theatres. But the purpose of the festival is to mainstream our art form and if that's what happens, great. And it's great to see that it helps establish us as more of a recognised genre — and now it all spills over into Pride in June, who have decided to sponsor us this year, so we're delighted with that.

The festival at the moment seems male-heavy in terms of the writing and the topics. Is that deliberate or is it simply what comes up in the mix?

It's 'anti-deliberate'. And you can quote that. We have pioneered feminist writing since day one. I saw Waking the Feminists *[grassroots campaign formed in protest against the male-dominated lineup at the Abbey in Dublin for its 2016 centenary programme, supporting a new wave of female playwrights, directors and other creatives]* happen in Ireland some years ago — and more people now say they attended the launch at the Abbey Theatre than actually could have attended — and their support for young women writers has made such a difference. On our side we have prioritised women writing since 2004 but they get such little box office support. I was thrilled to see five out of five of the nominees in the writing category in our festival awards were all women one year. But actually we've had too few women coming forward with plays and each year is a worry.

People will complain if there's an absence in the programme, but we do actively help plays get on the stage for women's lesbian or feminist theatre. If I do struggle some years to programme, I am always working on the support that we need to offer. We've had to work on it — men will go to the women's plays in the gay theatre festival but women often will not do it in the same way, in relation to the men's work. In the early programmes, for a theme of coming out or something like that, I'd put a male story and a female story together in the one ticket. Now if I put the woman's half on first, some of the female audience will leave afterwards. They won't stay. The men tended to stay for both plays. But that just encouraged me more to go from the highways to the byways to place some presence in the programme for new female writing, and I got lucky in 2004 when Irish Oscar nominee Emma Donoghue, who wrote *Room*, offered me her catalogue of plays to get this going.

Across the board, we've got some great people engaging, but at times you really want to shake them and say, "It's not just once that you stick your head above the theatrical parapet, you must commit to doing it every year. And there is a space, a stage, a welcome and assistance with that in our festival."

Do you have the time/space to come up with grand strategies for the future?

Well I have a line on my forehead for every year since we started. But seriously, my hope is that we will get an injection of new blood. I've never been short of ideas, but I am short of people to help me see them through. What we'll always be about is trying for wider audiences for our stories and to make them more welcome. We have an open door policy, you don't have to know anyone. You don't have to feel threatened by anyone. Just submit your company's choice of play and we will take it from there!

We practise what we preach within our team. We've had wonderful interns from Britain like the two lads that founded the HandleBards — Callum Cheatle and Paul Moss later produced Shakespeare on bikes. They now do British tours and international tours. If somebody wants to be an intern, we'll feed you and give you a bed, work you into the ground and you will have a great time. We also work hard on creating a great atmosphere that's accessible: we put two plays on in every venue every night, we share audience by having venue tickets, where if you want to go to see one play, you get a discount if you see the other play in the same venue. We have a festival club every single night that's free, where everybody comes together in one venue to network, review and get audience reaction. It's hard to track someone down in Edinburgh, but you'll know where we are in Dublin.

The best thing about the festival is the way people continually from abroad make huge sacrifices to make us their primary destination every year. So, take New York's oldest LGBT theatre company, TOSOS (The Other Side of Silence) or Theatre Outre, a company from rural Leithbridge which is really cutting-edge in Canada. They fundraise and work on grants where the focus of their artistic year is to appear in Dublin. The opportunity to be a part of our festival is truly wide open. We are not a clique within a clique, we are the exact opposite, we're open and transparent and welcoming, we say, "Hello, walk in the door!" And our audience/tourists are helped and welcomed too. And all that makes it a great place for young people to learn theatrecraft from our LGBT theatre heroes who have developed this genre.

Any theatre festival worthy of the name needs funding or sponsorship to be sustainable. But doing it for free doesn't protect you when the plug gets pulled on you, does it? The awarding and withdrawing of funding is always a minefield, but you've hit particularly major problems there?

We got a letter in June 2018 confirming that we qualified for what's called Band C funding of the Festivals Grants under the Irish Arts Council Festivals scheme — good news. At 20-30k euros it's modest for what we're trying to do. They granted us 15k for our fortnight of new theatre. We got a letter at Pride weekend in 2109 to say 2020 was the second year in a row that we qualified for Band C, we got a higher mark. Despite qualifying for Band C again, they didn't fund us within the band, they gave us 50 per cent less than 2019. This was following our most successful festival in years and that absolutely savaged us. Instead they gave us a small grant and ringfenced it for new and additional Irish work. Nothing could be spent on our international participants from whom we all learn so much.

The maths meant that I had to find that 15k to even sustain what I had done and then come up with the new projects on top of it. The new 'condition' was a terrible message too at a time when populism stokes up the unwelcome and fear for the 'foreigner'.

It wasn't the end of the festival and it was a place many have found themselves and us too previously. But in a country as small as Ireland with little in the way of major sponsors, for a headliner like International Dublin Gay Theatre Festival that punches way above its weight, it's a questionable position to be in. The minister for culture at our 2019 launch particularly noted the fact that when Ireland fell off the economic cliff a decade before, and has been recovering since, dozens of huge festivals crashed, but we kept going.

Basically for 2020, they gave us a zero to sustain the standards that had qualified us for this Band C. Then they gave us a ringfenced 7,500 euros grant for only new Irish work and new Irish theatre and artists. I don't know what 'new' means for them. The previous year, they had challenged us to 'develop partnerships' as a result of the grant, and we had gotten six different international events and festivals offering work to Irish and other artists throughout the year, and that has just been dismissed completely.

Everyone here of course understands that funding from one year doesn't guarantee funding the next. But meeting the challenges of the criteria is a difficult enough task, and then, if we're given new criteria after the fact, it's impossible. So their challenge to us today is to find the money they gave us last year and also to do additional work. And it's very hard to put two and two together.

IDGTF has been poorly funded since it kicked off in 2004, which is reflective of the fact that options elsewhere for state funding are limited. Dublin City Council Arts Office has a very modest budget and they always helped us out around 4k per year — so I have to run a two-week long event with ten plays a night in the event they give me 4k. Their events side gave us 8,500 euros for 2020. So the challenge of sustainability starts all over again. Happily, Dublin's LGBTQ Pride Committee did offer us some support this year for the first time and that was very fortunate and welcome.

If you look at the escalating costs of putting on a festival, most visibly at Edinburgh, they're making people question the wisdom and nature of growth for growth's sake. The reality should be that you hit your natural level and then sustainability comes from your excellence, impact and influence, and it follows that funding has to be an evolving part of this. Certainly, sponsorship per se can't cover everything for a festival set in a small nation like Ireland, where LGBT theatre has a limited market, since it comes itself from a minority. But IDGTF really does punch above its weight in mentoring new Irish writing and raising Ireland's profile, by creating partnerships with international companies and showcasing them. What's not to fund?

That's for others to answer — it's clear they have other ideas. I remember setting a counter challenge to the companies we had supported in Dublin already, a few years ago: "Look, Dublin is hosting all of you. So is there any chance that you'd host Irish LGBT theatre abroad — because that's how you sustain employment for people who commit themselves to their genre." And when we achieved the most successful outcome ever of reciprocated invitations, the first thing the Arts Council *[of Ireland]* did was try to kill it with their 'Irish only' condition, which they also checked up on, before they issued payment this year.

I really wonder why people who invest so much time and effort in creating new theatre get kicked in the stomach so much, because theatre is crying out for people to seriously invest in it and believe in its future, to create new genres, new opportunities, new writing and new partnerships and not for profit — and this seems to have zero value.

Does that sometimes make you want to jack it in? After all you could so easily make a graceful withdrawal based on what you've achieved with the festival so far.

Yes but no, no. We always evolve — reinvent our survival strategies to best the bigots — because I have felt either prejudice or worse, snobbery at times. When you grow up experiencing all that discrimination throws at you — these things today are just irritants. I've dealt with worse in my life's journey! And that latest grant crisis made me shift my priority to survival from our next plan to see if we can get some bursaries together so that Irish companies can put on new stuff and we can give internationals a bit of extra assistance to come over. I need an angel or two to fly in!

At the moment, we're doing short and shorter plays (10-75 minutes max), and my ambition had been to do at least two full-length plays in 2020. The cuts prevented that from happening too. Theatre is something that must reflect modern society, must be relevant to it and engage in its issues and values. If you're put in a position of responsibility in an administration capacity, your duty is to enable, not to prevent or destroy. I don't always see that shared by all the individuals I encounter in some of the bodies that the arts depend upon, but I am very happy when I do see and experience it — and I have.

I feel that by promoting this minority genre and developing it, I've been cast into the role of a beggar. I am very conscious that the companies that stage their work in the festival are also investing in it — and I know there's no pot of gold at the end of it. And I'm very conscious that their investment is to be respected. And I do resent at times the fact that the artists, by virtue of their art, are also turned into the beggar. I don't believe that's a healthy place for art to be. And I have begged for 16 solid years and more.

Every year we've been able to get professionals to volunteer for this festival because it's important. But I have to say, as a professional, that it is wearing always to have to beg for something that I and other people know what to do and believe in, but is not acknowledged sufficiently. So, I believe that unfocused funding by the likes of the Arts Council is perpetuating the notion that artists must starve for their art. And I reject that one hundred per cent. At the same time as they cut us, they launched a laudable 'pay the artist' campaign — the irony wasn't lost on me!

That's like a multi-pronged attack on any idea of sustainability.

Well it's not for want of recognition. The Taoiseach *[prime minister]* Leo Varadkar, who is gay, bought two tickets in 2019 to see *Velvet* by Tom Ratcliffe. The festival itself was launched by our minister for culture Josepha Madigan, who praised IDGTF for its model as well as purpose. Official endorsement can't get any higher in Ireland. Even that won't open the minds of those with an agenda — and they are not all straight by any means. LGBT arts events can often experience inverted homophobia, where the gay administrator tries to prove their 'impartiality' by cutting the gay events to seemingly conform in their straight work environment. Yet, many straight administrators just see the artform!

The King's Head *[theatre in London]* came over and attended the entire festival and offered many a play a rental opportunity to perform in London. There are discussions to take Irish and international plays to other venues and festivals in the UK, Sweden, South Africa at present — it's getting bigger every year. But in one year, when we're given conditioned reduced grants to establish international partnerships after we've gotten this great results, and the next year we're told not to do that but to develop only local work. Let's face it, we specialise in new work, which is really hard to sell as well — but we've absolutely proven we can do it. So, what do you want us to do? In the absence of external consistency — we can only follow our mission.

As we're turning into our 17th year now, this is turning me into a grumpy old man . . . but I would really like a room which the festival could work from, a desk, a computer and even a part-time member of staff to show for our 8,000 performances of new LGBT theatre over 17 years. That would be fabulous. That and our own permanent performance space is the wish list. Then I could run a specialist small theatre year round!

It seems that politics and society can't be divorced from the performing arts in Ireland, particularly theatre. If you take one seriously, you have to take the other as well.

Can it be divorced anywhere? But it's more than that. Maybe I'm romantically looking back, but people could be defined either by their wealth or values, talents, potential previously, and now it's about their brand and their image — their strategies and frameworks. Even though defining people by their wealth wasn't a very proper thing to do, at least there was space for *values and talents*, and that showed in the work. Today, everybody presents themselves on social media like they're a rock star, and that's what has become and replaced the value — the merit. It's a malaise all over the world I'm afraid. But we still haven't lost the vantage point and insightful eye that live arts give you. What we're taking about is to get away from the fleeting clicks and the likes, to see something take place in front of you, which remains with you and you consider and talk about what you actually saw and experienced. It is not 'fake news'.

Values are being rapidly eroded in front of us all, yet you and the festival seem to have grown in values and affirmed them as other values have been stripped away from society. Values can't be bought — on the other hand, are you only as worthy as the funding you get if you're a minority?

I think you've hit the nail on the head. It's been interesting to see the Establishment confront the fact that now there are generations that are no longer going to accept that difference is bad, that difference is to be feared. The embracing by the Establishment of that difference — like with minimal dependency funding — has actually been a strategic way to seek to control it.

I used to work in a youth work organisation and I often put the challenge to them then: is a youth club a place where children can be liberated, or is it a tool of social control? And I think it would be very fair to say that part of the acceptance — and I hate the word — of the existence of LGBT culture is either a way to control it or to liberate it. They are conforming us and we must resist that because the real gift of a minority is that sometimes it gives the majority the opportunity 'to do the right thing' and that when accepted, it makes society better e.g. the marriage equality campaign in Ireland. It made us more inclusive and perhaps kinder.

So they say in their heads, "Well, that's a minority issue so they will get a minority funding." Of course an activist LGBT artist could write a mainstream major important work, but its chances of happening are structurally reduced, if they're treated in a minority or limited way. And so, I worry sometimes about where the incredible courage, the incredible comprehension of identity that went with coming out has gone. That term 'coming out' itself is misnamed because we weren't allowed to come out, instead we were allowed to embrace the negative preordained definition of what being gay was, in a heteronormative society and saying, "Well, that's who you say I am", rather than saying, "Listen, and I will tell you. This is who I am."

And that's the critical element of identity. We have no right to impose identity, but we can listen, we can ask people to tell us who they are. But the LGBT and other identities, that have had this marvellous courage to be visible and are now included in limited funding to the point of respectability, that we are no longer that threat to overall society, has led to an acceptance or an opportunity for exploration of limitless identities.

And in doing that, I am concerned about the imposition of language. As a people, we Irish had a language imposed on us *[English on Gaelic]* and I'm concerned at the fact that we're still now seeking to impose language on others. You see it in the mainstreaming and the giving of permission. When we 'came out' first, we didn't ask anyone's permission, but by virtue of the fact that we're now being funded in the broader sense of the word, we are actually now seeking permission, even though we have already done all the work.

And there's the danger that we LGBT can still pose. By telling our own stories in theatre, for others to learn the truth of who we are, we, who have been oppressed deliberately for so long, to suit the agendas of political ideology or religion, can now self-identify without limits or permission. That's too big an opportunity and responsibility to compromise — it has been hard won.

Within Ireland, as in Britain, the creative industries have been key in providing a semi-safe space over the ages not just for LGBT but also all Other identities. In Ireland did that initial breaking through of civil liberties come through the performing arts?

It made a contribution throughout our history, and of course setting up the festival in 2004 was a political act. I've said that publicly. I was countering the imposed norms by presenting the truth not just to the gay community but to my society. We positioned ourselves from day one in a small but mainstream setting. We opened the doors and said come in — this is who we are and this is what we have a right and duty to say. And that was critically important.

And it was a step up, standing on the shoulders of many. So rather than accept the constructed negative definitions in which we were 'blamed' for everything, the challenge was, have we got the courage to tell our stories — truthfully? Not the Disney version of our stories, not to scrub it up but our life stories. To simply demonstrate that we are as complex and as flawed as anybody else. And that's not as a result of our sexual orientation, that's as a consequence of the constructed inequality that was imposed on us. That too is our common bond with other minorities. The language of oppression and discrimination needs no translation — we all recognise it and understand its intent. Hence our international presentations work in Ireland.

Because of the timing and confluence of events in Ireland, were you in the right time, right place? I know you've said that you knew it was the right moment to start the festival, but it can't have been apparent at the time that things were going to happen as quickly as they did — or even in the desired direction.

Ha! Yet another tool used by the majority — even though they see the inevitable, and sometimes even acknowledge the truth in what the minority is saying — they decided to use and to hope campaign fatigue would wear us out. And in Ireland we were fantastic at campaign fatigue. It took so long to bring about any change and at that stage, as the first crumb fell off the table, I will never complain about the heroes who basically ate it and then collapsed with exhaustion. Really effective campaigns cultivate their invigorated successors who will continue the fight and I really so want that to be my legacy to the festival. I want someone to want it for the right reasons and bring it onto another plain without compromising our identity or conforming to the cancer of blandness that is killing the dependent grant aided arts sector — you can't create by committee. Let the administrative committee recognise creativity and do their job to enable and support it. I will probably fail in that ambition.

And what was really interesting about the creating of the festival was a couple of things that happened to me. We were the last country in Western Europe to decriminalise homosexuality in 1993. And that was the year I decided that I would try to stage the Irish premiere of *La Cage aux Folles*, the musical. The original production *[1983]* did very well in the United States, but it coincided with the Aids crisis in the UK and closed, and it had never been done in Ireland. Since I did musicals, I went, "I'm going to do this one, six weeks after decriminalisation, in mainstream theatre."

The young gay men were quite willing to become *[chorus line]* Les Cagelles and train and dance, that was fine — anonymity in numbers. The difficulty however was with my own generation and the generation older than mine. And so we found ourselves in rehearsal without the lead, Albin [the aging star of La Cage aux Folles club who performs as the drag queen Zaza]. Meanwhile a straight man was actually playing George [the owner and master of ceremonies of La Cage & Albin's husband of over 20 years] — seven gay actors had turned down the Albin role.

Now Albin is a dream of a role, right? But even though we were being decriminalised at the time, the gay actor's experience of life was that once you play gay, you *are* gay. It's like playing Jesus Christ on film: once people see you as Jesus, they can never see you as anything else. But then another director who was working with me turned around and said, "Myself and my wife have cast the part of Albin." And I said, "Oh great, who?" And they said, "You!" And I said, "No, no. Under no circumstances." And they said, "Why?" "Because I'd be crap."

And I remember him then saying to me, "You've a long weekend ahead of you, Brian. Because you've had the courage to put on this show and if you don't actually play the part no one else will, the show is not going to go ahead."

So I played the part. I found it very difficult because part of my own identity was not necessarily to identify with the feminine side of being gay — there's nothing wrong with it and they're the most courageous of all the pioneering campaigners as they had 'nowhere to hide' — so they didn't. But I went and I played it. In my admittedly controversial theatrical career, I have never seen so many audiences stand up the moment I arrived for my curtain call. I brought it to my hometown in the Waterford International Festival Light Opera, which had been running for 30-odd years at the time with Irish and British and American companies. I won the best performer award there. It then transferred into Dublin's Olympia Theatre and I got standing ovations every night . . .

. . . and I never got a part again. I never ever got a part again. Oh, doors were opened for me. I was on radio stations for two hour-long interviews. I was all over the press. But . . . I. Never. Got. A. Part. Again. Those seven gay actors who said no to the part were wise. I am glad I did it though — it changed me — in many ways, it was the exhausting end of my own coming out story — and I reconciled that in public when I portrayed that amazing role onstage in a more hostile and voyeuristic Ireland.

So, rapidly go forward ten years. We have gotten decriminalisation — and an equal age of consent at 17. So many people came out to me, particularly older people, during the run of that show. And not only do we now in Ireland have decriminalisation, we also have an employment equality act and an equal status act, so we have protection from discrimination in goods, facilities, services and the workplace. As a result, I did my master's degree in equality, so that I could understand the construct of inequality and the purpose of its imposition on minorities.

But back in 2003, I found myself at that Pride exhibition, holding my head in my hands because everyone in the photos was still wearing a mask. And everybody was. Physical masks, make-up, drag. Despite a decade of decriminalisation, everyone was still in masks. And that was the major prompt for me to say that, having gotten over the exhaustion of the first campaigns and the crumbs we were given in relation to decriminalisation and later protection at the workplace and services, etc, we had more to do. *We must tell people who we are.*

I'm proud that Dublin has been allowed to have its own identity as a modern city by virtue of the fact that our oppressors imploded. They imploded politically and religiously — and particularly religion imploded on the basis of the fact that it actually had no value, and no values, because what it said — it did not do. It concealed and protected the rape of children, and no matter what your moral barometer is, we all share the rejection of that one. And when the interests of the institution was put ahead of the well-being of the child, that was the final straw that broke the camel's back in Ireland.

Politically we had a single party that had run the country for 75 of the 90 years who would not have been liberally disposed to our well-being as such, and they were at that time, running the country into the ground economically. So they lost their mandate. So my political and religious oppressors were no longer as powerful. And within that space we were timely, we added our voice to that new Ireland, to say, "Right, we're no longer being controlled, we're no longer a dominion of the church, so we have to quickly tell people who we are and on that basis build the new inclusive Ireland." And that has happened. My play *Eirebrushed* outs the gay and lesbian heroes of the 1916 Irish Revolution and places their yearning for equality for an oppressed people at its core. We were never taught about them in history class in school!

Well, we should absorb that about a million different ways. That double foe of church and government is quite a thing. You couldn't take them out of the performing arts without bleeding, could you? Do you think Ireland had it easy — not that that's the right word — in being able to make that leap directly into the future, that idea of floodgates bursting so you were able to make several generational leaps in one go compared the other Western European countries?

If I was a 28 year old director of the festival I would tell you yes. But as a 59 year old director of the festival, who lived through the 1970s and the 80s, there was nothing easy about it. There really wasn't. It was a dreadful, dreadful, dark hypocritical place to live or to exist. You basically coped by *not hoping* if you were gay and stayed in Ireland. And if you could do that, you survived it. Some couldn't. I'm not saying my youth was miserable — I had the theatre and that cocooned me from most of the constructed hatred designed to sustain my exclusion from love, family and dignity.

A lot of my contemporaries would have emigrated, and some of them couldn't come home or even say that they had Aids and so they died in the care of strangers in Britain and America. Others married in the full knowledge that they weren't straight, which certainly didn't help fulfil their own lives. But you know, if any girlfriend ever asked me had I been with a man, I answered yes, even in the times of darkest criminalisation. Today, we have a legacy of their modern open-minded children and grandchildren. My God, we're very lucky people because they no longer consider being gay to be a fault and they voted in droves for marriage equality 62.38 per cent in 2015 to prove it.

So, it wasn't easy, is the answer of the 59 year old. But the 28 year old will tell you it was, because so much work had been done. Maybe that's the real success of what we did, today it's the norm for the younger generations — and that was our intent back then.

And in fact you've had a Taoiseach who is not only gay but not completely white. How has that come about?

At times I pinch myself! I was very involved with politics as a young person but I knew there was one thing stopping me from doing it. Firstly, I still hadn't figured my own sexual identity because I had no reference points or role models in a Catholic-ridden society. Secondly, it was the impact that being outed would have had on those I loved. You know, could you bring your parents and brothers and sisters out campaigning for you on the doorsteps while making all the sacrifices that being in a political life that that entails for a family? I had relations in politics. And then suddenly to be called a pariah. Or some absolute lowlife who didn't share any of your values might use that information to try to compromise you. If somebody tried to blackmail me, I know I would come out and say I am being blackmailed because of this and I will not be blackmailed because of this. That much I knew for certain, but I left the political party and took up journalism as an early career, and yet I remain a political being.

Now, fast forward on and I was casting a show once again at the Olympia Theatre, Dublin. It was *Rockin' Hood the Christmas Panto* (I had to earn a living!) and the two best kids who came to be in it was a boy called Peter Smith and a girl called Samantha Mumba (who later went on to pop/TV careers). They were first-generation Irish and black. And I cast them as Robin Hood and Maid Marion. And that caused consternation in the production group to the point in fact that one person — this is about 1996 or 97 — came up and said, "Oh Brian, they're black." I said, "That's right. The job description for Robin Hood is 'can he rob from the rich and give to the poor?' And with the right training I'm confident a black person could do that too."

But five sets of auditions later when weaker (whiter actors) came forward, I turned to the executive producer at the time and I said, "You know if this doesn't happen, you lose me too." And to be fair to him, he turned to me and said, "It needed to be teased out, but you are getting your way now because you are right on this one." And I got Ireland's first black Robin Hood and a black Maid Marion. Danny Donoghue from [Irish rock band] The Script also made his debut in that show.

In their review, The Irish Times referred to them as the 'black actors'. And that was the first and only time I've written to a newspaper about a review. I just wrote a very short sentence: "Dear Editor, Thank so and so for his views on the black actors. I wonder what he thought the white ones were like? Yours sincerely . . ." Obviously they didn't publish it.

So it hasn't been easily won, any of it. However it has been embraced by a generation of children and young people that do not have the religious guilt and the ideological baggage that was imposed on a newly liberated country back then. The Catholic Church didn't actually support the 1916 struggles and Easter Rising but, just like later in Poland in the 1980s when suddenly they all became 'trades unionists' backing Solidarity, they saw in Ireland the opportunity to replace the political oppressor by positioning themselves into a place of absolute power over an innocent and inexperienced people. Britain had executed the leaders of the 1916 Rising, and the bishops filled the power vacuum. So it's about a vulnerable fledgling state, and a new and torn people, that space allows for another dominant force to take over. And in our situation, it was the Catholic Church. They ensured their dogma was inserted in our constitutional laws and by their public control it meant they could deliver votes for conservative political parties. Checkmate the new state.

Our political parties, even if they had an instinct to be more liberal, could not — because, at a time when every single person was herded into a church on Sundays and every child was conscripted into a religion before they actually could reach the age of contractual consent, etc, you needed the approval of the church for everything. And the Catholic church pulled down a few governments in Ireland in the 20th century — politicians remembered that.

Not any more. Our answer now at the ballotbox in 2015 is we had 62 per cent voting in favour of equal marriage. What was critical there was not to call it 'same sex' marriage but to show that it was how we perceive the rights of every citizen and not just LGBT. And then we had the staggering vote of 66 per cent in favour of legislating for abortion. I think you can say there's actually a trajectory there. And I don't believe we're going back.

Every single person who came out in Ireland up to then was the person who won the marriage equality campaign. Because it's very hard to fear or hate the person you're looking in the eye. And, thankfully, we have enough gay people to make a critical mass to prove we are part of your families, we are part of your workforces, we are part of Ireland. And everybody knew a gay person when the time came to vote. And people did the decent thing. That's why Leo Varadkar is accepted by many. It was all our work. You know Leo Varadkar never came to the gay theatre festival while he was not out before 2015, but he did after he became Taoiseach in 2018. And he came with his partner. We appreciated that, it was a symbol or our embedded progress.

If we look at the festival as encapsulating all that built-up energy, what do you bring to it — not you as the activist but you as the curator, as the performing arts professional? Is it just holding the flame or are you generating tools that the rest of society can learn to use, even if it's just inspiring acceptance of things like equal-opportunities role-play theatre in a corporate environment?

I think you've put your finger on something there. When I set out to encourage others to put our stories in the mainstream it was not to mainstream the stories, it was to give the opportunity to the mainstream to witness and listen to what makes up our complete identity. What I try to counterbalance with my small festival is that so much writing in the performing arts is now by formula, agreement and by committee. Even in these writers' programmes, they dramaturg them to death, get new writers to write the same play, even persuade a writer that this isn't the play they intended to write in the first place. You never write another person's play. You can help with the structure and advise but it is their play and they get the right to tell their story, even if it's not great in the beginning — they learn from being free to say it their way.

If I advise as a dramaturg, I provide it from a different perspective. My first line is, "I am not going to write your play for you. I will tell you what I think, I will tell what I see in it, and I might say look that character is superfluous to your plot — a frequent flaw in a first play etc, but I won't tell you what to do. I will answer your questions honestly. I also may be wrong, but I'm offering the best advice I can! I've taken the time to read it and engage with it so here goes . . ."

There's a lot of youngsters who want to tell stories. That's great, it's the essential future of theatre. But, as I've said, why does every kid coming out of a drama school form their own company instead of collaborating with each other, with their meagre resources, to enable all of them to do new and innovative theatre? Why don't they get together, learn from each other and support equally three new plays in a year? That's better than putting on one or two but then dying and indeed becoming very disheartened in the art form because they perceive they've failed. They haven't failed, they have just taken the wrong structure. And what really and truly breaks my heart is this thing that's happening in drama schools, where they're being told that they've invented the wheel. There are loads of wheels. What also is it about what we do, that the young ones don't see a space for them in what is being done already? Is it because they value only the 'leading' role? But everyone needs time to develop and learn their craft. Real learning can take time — an actor's life is a lifetime. Just because you can write an essay on a play it doesn't mean you can produce, direct or play in it.

What we need is for people to sit on the vehicle and power them forward. And we need to collaborate and share the meagre resources we have in order to enable us all to get better. And instead, much of what's happening at the moment, in mainstream and particularly LGBT theatre, is they are putting a cake in front of us but they're slicing it so thin — you get a wafer at the end of it. Therefore many eat a little, but everyone remains hungry. If there is a cake still, are we generous enough to share it? We're not. We are set against each other in the grants process and the clever form-filler is often more successful than the clever creative.

And that's quite across the performing arts, because the greatest knockers of what I do would be other gay artists who see the festival as beneath them because we encourage new voices, or as 'competition' for the LGBT identity when there is so much to share rather than as a collaborative opportunity where we can progress together. So it's like artistic Thatcherism. In the 1970s we were all being educated for leisure — ha ha! — and you were a good person if you contributed to the value of society and the overall well-being of yourself and others. Thatcher came along and said climb on top of everybody and get to the top at all costs. And today's diversity in the arts is a bit like artistic Thatcherism. Because what happens is, our own will knock us first because they too are being starved — and then one or two of them who are acceptable will be fed, anointed as 'diversity-inclusion', as the only voice. What a huge creative loss, when our job is to create space not shrink it or hoard it.

Look at the top of the LGBT commercial arts structure — and I'm not saying that these identities are not critically important — but we still have the men in frocks, we still have the camp men, the victim, the shamed loner. Where's the plain ordinary decent person? Where's the person who's the gay builder? Where's the person who's the gay mother? Where's the person who's the gay victim of the domestic violence? Where are the Other stories that actually make good theatre? But to some, if you're not in a frock, you do not get into an awards ceremony *[in Ireland]*, and you do not get lauded, you are there because there is still that voyeuristic element to our identity I endured in 1993 in *La Cage* — and that basis for inclusion is *not* diversity.

You've described this great big loop of everyone patting themselves on the back, the funders, the recipients, the gongs, the praise for representing the 'community'. There's a grim logic to it all, isn't there?

Well, I hope I have also described the many positive and creative things too, because they are what matter. There are brilliant engaged enablers in the arts and in grant bodies and I salute them. Yes, creative minds often concentrate on the one negative rather than enjoying the many positives. We tend to look for and brood over the one bad critique too often. I do ask though what transformative thing has ever come out of a meeting or a reception over glasses of wine and cheeseboards, amongst people who have never been responsible for actually delivering the page to the stage? What of real creative value has ever happened there? How can agreeing a 'framework' liberate an artform or channel for new ideas to flourish and teach us? If we can all agree a 'framework' we are limiting ourselves to what has already been thought about or done — we are not opening ourselves to doing things differently — the lifeblood of any genre surviving into the future. 'Frameworks' may protect the present but they never invent the way to the next creative future.

Too much still comes from the image of the artist in the garret who was unfortunately made to starve by the people who are drinking the wine and eating the cheese. There is nothing noble for society in ensuring a starving artist is the norm. There is nothing sustainable in dependency. But ultimately those artistic images and messages are what have lasted and been accepted as a norm in the performing arts and in the wider arts structure. The fact is that, unless you are at the table, you are not considered — and you need permission to be at the table. What we need to question is who gives anyone the right to grant the permission to create and be heard? And why is that permission necessary to the future of the creative arts?

It's a direct contradiction of what liberating arts should be about. And those who are at the table or drinking the wine, are only embraced after their success has been made. And I challenge them: you are failing to see out of your offices, you are failing to hear those who may not be your friends, you are failing to *listen* to what you don't know and you are not discovering that despite this, there is a lot still going on!

*

25

Guleraana Mir

'There's many more ways of telling stories than we see on stages'

Guleraana Mir is a writer, theatremaker & one half of The Thelmas. She is based in Havering, East London, where she was born & raised.
• *thethelmas.co.uk, @g_ting*

Why did you pick theatre? Or did theatre pick you?

That's a really good question. My parents love the theatre. I guess that's probably the honest answer to that. It was the medium that I was introduced to earliest and given, I don't want to say an introduction to, but the most exposure or understanding of how to get into. We started by going to see musicals when I was really young, and then as my brother and I got slightly older, that then transitioned into seeing plays mostly on the West End, mostly with famous people in them — but still plays. And of course, every school has drama GCSEs, drama A-levels, opportunities to do drama (although I got a D in GCSE Drama and didn't study any theatre at A-level!)

At university I studied English and creative studies. I had always loved film but it seemed an impenetrable medium because there's no concept of how you get into film, especially as a writer as opposed to an auteur. Since I wasn't interested in holding a camera or looking at things from a filmic point of view, theatre just felt natural. I actually did want to be a journalist for a really long time, and while I was at uni I was doing a lot of reviewing or talking about art as opposed to considering being an artist myself, which only really came around when I started doing participatory work. And then I thought, well, actually I'm apparently quite good at this, so maybe I might want to try being an artist myself. Or there's an art in working with people and helping them to facilitate art. Does that answer the question?

That does answer the question, but it leads on to asking why you ended up doing applied and educational theatre?

This again comes from family. I come from a family of educators. Both my grandparents in Pakistan ran schools. My maternal grandmother ran a primary school, my maternal grandfather ran a secondary school. My mum is a Montessori teacher. We also spent a lot of time in Pakistan during the summers and their school holidays differ to England, so sometimes school would be in session when we were over there. We spent a whole winter in Pakistan because my granddad had a heart attack. And my mum was just like, I'm just going to take the kids and go and look after him.

I felt like whatever I ended up doing in life, there'd be an aspect of education to it. And for a really long time I argued or rebelled against that. It was only when I was doing my degree that there was one module where I just didn't know what to choose for it. And my tutor was like, "Why don't you do a community theatre module? That will get you in a school where you can lead some drama workshops." A good friend and colleague wanted to do the same thing because she in fact wanted to be a drama teacher. And then that just sort of set that ball rolling.

When I graduated I had this dilemma of do I want to be a journalist? Do I want to work in theatre? I did what you would call an apprenticeship at the Queen's Theatre Hornchurch *[Havering, East London]* where I ended up working on their theatre in education show. So that kind of cemented the idea of theatre and education. I then travelled and when I came back, I thought I wanted to be a nurse because I had this inherent need to do something with people that were vulnerable. Obviously that, coming from a family of educators, had implanted itself subconsciously. But I was still really reluctant to be a teacher.

I applied for a nursing degree, but they said that it had been a long time since I'd worked with anyone because I was just doing temp and office jobs. So I ended up volunteering at a special needs school, doing creative exercises with the one-to-one students that I was working with. I didn't really know what applied theatre was until I ended up studying it. However, I realised that though I wasn't ready to let go of creativity, I also wasn't ready to let go of education. But I didn't want to be a drama teacher and I didn't want to work in a school. Luckily, whilst I was faffing about in New York, I heard about an educational theatre programme at New York University. And I was like, this is the best way to put all my interests and my skills together.

That was a yearlong master's, and what really got me on track was the applied side of theatre. I ended up having a work placement at a really great youth theatre in New York, which got me looking at the diverse makeup there and the way that the city's education system is and how they use theatre far more in their curriculum than we do. It's really interesting in middle school and high school how much theatre is integrated into the curriculum and what opportunities there are. It drove home in me the sense that there are people that could benefit from art that are not having access to it. And it doesn't have to be professional. It can just be youth theatre or the opportunity to put on a play or write some stuff, just to really engage. Being creative facilitates so many other things in your brain.

I actually started by mistake on the teacher training route and it was only when I was a few weeks into the course that I realised the mistake I'd made, but I'd already signed up to the introduction to teaching and learning course, which was really neuroscience-based. It was deeply interesting with practical placements as well as lectures and seminars. So I decided I wasn't going to drop out of that course, I was going to finish it through, which cemented my interest in applied theatre because I saw that it needs to be inside the classroom — except I wasn't the person to do that. It also needs to be outside the classroom — and I wanted to be the person that did *that*. So I gained this really great grounding of how people learn, how people's brains work, how creativity and imagination facilitates learning. And then you just take it outside of the classroom. That's where I got most of my work and most of my fun in New York. And then hilariously I got back to London and ended up working in schools again.

So how did you apply creativity outside of the particular field that you trained in and were working in?

Outside of being in schools, and thinking about what I do now, I was just trying to find work with non-professional groups, working with adults or elders, and in youth companies. Anything that's not specifically in the schools tends to peak my interest. Like in 2017-18, I was working with Rightful Place Theatre Company *[all-female theatre by and for minority ethnic women aged 16+]* — they're made up of alumni and staff who have been through Mulberry School for Girls in Tower Hamlets *[in East London]*. That was an amazing experience of adult Bangladeshi women who knew that they wanted to do something in their spare time and wanted to be creative, but hadn't necessarily ever made a show before. It was leading them through a six-week workshop period and then writing a piece specifically for them and then watching them rehearse it and perform it *[Mano's, set in a female-run car mechanic's in East*

London, was at Rich Mix in Hackney]. That was really really exciting. And really cemented the idea that actually anyone can engage with theatre and that everyone will get something different from it.

> *But if everyone can engage with theatre, it doesn't actually mean that everyone is putting it into practice, or is able to, even simply as a member of the audience.*

We're not putting it into practice really, because if you look at theatre in London, for example, one barrier is that it's expensive. Another is that the stories that we see represented on stage don't necessarily call out to everyone. I'm privileged enough that I have parents who were interested to go and see shows regardless of what was out there. But you have loads of communities that don't know how to access art because it's not part of their day-to-day life or they'll walk past a theatre and be like, "Well, I don't really know. I've never been into a theatre and I literally don't know how to go." So, no, people aren't going to see the theatre because they don't have the money to, or they don't know how to, or there's not something that's appealing to them on stage.

My parents now sometimes will just buy season passes for the Queen's Theatre Hornchurch, because for the price of one West End ticket you can see three shows in the Queen's season, which is phenomenal. That makes it financially accessible, but you still go okay, there are loads of ethnicities that live in the area but the audience is still white, old and white. I don't want to talk disparagingly about them or mean this in a negative sense, but how do we change that? There is outreach and there is professional work, but where do we find the physical meeting of those two things? Queen's did a massive funded project with lots of local people, and that's great, but what's the next step after that? It's a longstanding project which goes on for a few nights, that's great. But what's next after that? How do you develop that participatory work?

> *Work that also reflects your audience. We have seen an extraordinary drive to put representation and diversity on the stage. But it tends to be that this is reflected in the audiences for the first night or preview when people are there for whoever is representative on that stage rather than the transfer of theatre. So you're selling seats to white older people of a certain class or people with aspirations to that class. Even panto has its limits for audiences. To be honest, what you see in a lot of the suburban and regional theatres will basically mirror the West End. And any perceived diversity in the West End comes from tourists rather than out-of-towners or people who a show sets out to talk to. Theatre is more than ever about 'who's in the room', and for all the initiatives, policies and funding, they've not managed to crack it.*

They haven't, and I don't know what the solution is. I feel there's this worrying trend of just putting on work that's underdeveloped but is there because it's representative onstage. That happens because the people making the decisions are 'panic buying'. So when they receive a script, they receive the prospect of a show that's different to what might have been on their stages before. There's very limited development for that writer even if they're told, "This is a great idea, this is a voice that we haven't heard before, a concept that we haven't seen before. Let's make it!" I don't want to say 'make it better' because then that then opens up conversations about eurocentric modes of storytelling and what is 'good' and why we have to have a three-act structure for a play to be good? Why can't it just be about feeling or an emotion or a sentiment, whatever? Which is a whole other conversation.

But if you are receiving something that's new and maybe different, where's the support for that writer or that production company to make the work 'good enough' that it will sell and not fall flat on its face? I do feel that part of it is due to the fact that the people who are buying the work just don't know, and they get excited by the mere fact that it's different. I went to the Writers' Guild Literary Managers' Forum last year and that made me realise there are probably no literary managers that aren't white in the country. We've got a couple of executives, a couple of artistic directors, but who are the people really looking at work, those programmers and literary managers who are the ones that essentially have a lot of the control, especially in terms of development?

Where do they get their empowerment from? We've seen the gradual growth of the literary managers as a distinct class and a lot of them come up through the academic side of things, after they get their MAs and PhDs. Similar to the other parts of theatre, get any large group together and factors like white, middle class, London, Oxbridge inevitably become more apparent the more salaried the group. They reflect the industry and the industry reflects them. If there's actually to be a drive to change everything, then the first thing to do is ask what's driving that drive? If we're not seeing every part of the performing arts industry change, we won't be seeing any true audience change. Such as representation at artistic director level reflecting what's happening backstage.

Backstage is a whole other conversation! To be honest, the thing that needs to change is nepotism. Because even if someone who is not a white man takes a position of power in a building, they will then resort to getting their friends in because they can trust the work that they make or that is the work that they want to put on.

Cloning being a subject that the established theatres really prefer to not talk about.

Basically what you end up with is people just calling on their friends to put work on. So it's the perpetuation of the process and the system but in a different gender or a different ethnicity or a different other minority form. It's frustrating to see people that you think are going to be champions of newness and then it's not new at all in any way, shape or form because it's just the people that they were associated with previously, who now come with them to their new building or their new position, and so it just keeps going around. What *then* happens is that the 'traditional theatre person' is frustrated at the incoming diverse theatre people, because they're essentially doing the same thing that they had previously been doing for ages, but they're now shut out. And of course you've got everyone else going, "We're still not getting a look in."

It's like waves but they're all closed off, whereas a real wave should be all mixed up. Anybody can physically see it — there's a new thing going on there, but you know it's got a beginning and there's going to be an end, by which time the next thing comes along. Maybe that's one of the reasons why theatres don't communicate through to their audiences because it's not a question of seeing their faces up there or their so-called voices, but they're just not seeing any coherence up there or sense of how did that person get there? If someone has their play staged at a well known institution because the director is a friend of theirs or that director has gone and picked up that play because it reflects them, we're happy for them, but basically the rest of us are sitting here and going, "Well, when will they come and see my work?" or "When will I stop getting the passive-aggressive 'well have you ever applied?' "

It's that passive-aggressive email that they send: "We've received your invitation, and if we are able to, we'll come on our own ticket." That sense of no indication whether they're actually interested or invested in coming to see your work. And if they do come, how will you know if they've come to see your work, how do you follow it up? So then what happens is this perpetual loop of sending people emails, inviting them to come and see things, nothing progressing forward. And then on the other hand, people get their debut plays on.

Well we can bring it round positively to something like your play Coconut. Now that was a breakthrough . . . presumably?

I love the play obviously. And I know it's flawed obviously because in the time that I finished writing it to the time that it was produced, I had transitioned into completely different writer. When it went up, I already knew that if I were to tell that story again I would tell it in a completely different way. However, there were two really important things to be noted.

The first is when we decided to make that show, we wanted it to be really, really accessible to the aunties that never leave their houses let alone go to the theatre, to anyone who thought that theatre wasn't for them, to anyone who didn't want to go and see a piece of like high concept theatre. Interestingly, it got likened to TV — and actually I've got loads of potential TV work out of it because the play is just really simple. We got excellent feedback from audiences and some really great reviews. We also received some really tepid reviews — I think it was that idea again of what people expect to be good theatre and *Coconut* didn't follow that outline for them or it wasn't tidy enough for them. And that was more important than seeing an almost sold-out show full of the most diverse audience I've ever come across at Ovalhouse. It was the biggest selling show there for two years.

And then when we took it on tour, every venue said that there was a percentage of people in the audience that they had never seen before. It sold out at Derby Theatre and I remember them saying at least 30 per cent of that audience had never engaged with the theatre before. So that to me is important. That to me is success. It's just slightly upsetting that it's not recognised. *[laughs]* But I also feel that way about Ovalhouse — it's one of the most exciting venues in London and nobody pays attention to what they do. All of the literary managers of the bigger theatres or anyone who's looking for new talent will make a list of places they will go to see new work, and Ovalhouse won't be on that list. And that's a shame because our industry would change radically if people paid attention to what goes on at places like Ovalhouse.

And that's a comparatively central London venue right on the doorstep of so many gatekeepers.

Exactly. Now what needs to change first is nepotism, regardless of which community we're talking about. And what then needs to change is this bandwagoning of the hot new thing. What you'll find is that something will do reasonably well and then for that writer or that production company suddenly they're everywhere. They're getting all the commissions, they're on all the schemes or they jump from scheme to scheme until they finally get a permanent position and you're like, well, what have you actually *done*? It sort of becomes, "Let's fill all of the spaces that we had for new people with this one thing, which is the new hot thing, and then we don't need to look anywhere for another three years because this momentum will sustain itself for three years."

You've set out very deliberately to work with people who want to understand what theatre is, you can't take theatre for granted. Every group you go to, you have to put yourself in their shoes.

Yes. And it comes from both Maddy *[Madelaine Moore]*, the other Thelma, and I. Maddy set up The Thelmas before me because she was sick and tired of seeing feminist theatre that was feminist in quotation marks that only looks to women's issues of infertility or periods or the things that we're supposed to care about as women. I joined The Thelmas when we realised that *Coconut* was going to go full steam ahead into a full production. Both of us come from participatory backgrounds, both of us came to theatre from a non-traditional route. And both of us are *makers*. We just want to get things done. If I sat around waiting for someone to give me a commission, I wouldn't have done anything. So that ethos is what I am applying to everything, that I'm going to do it until either I can't do it anymore or something happens to stop me from doing it. Things like a terrible review will just galvanise me even more, to say actually no, *this* is why you don't understand the work that I'm trying to make.

You were involved in the Decolonising History digital project by Tamasha and the School of Oriental & African Studies, University of London [both based in London]. I did my degree at SOAS and I do appreciate it as a perfect setting to address decolonisation via art, however I wasn't convinced by the approach or the content at first and thought it wasn't personal enough. But then I realised that it was the empowerment of the writers of the five audio plays that was central to it not only being successful as theatre but also creating a tangible bridge for others to walk over into other areas. What brief did they give you?

All of us got the same brief, which was we were allowed to take whatever classes at SOAS in BA History that we wanted to for one term. We were allowed to talk to anybody, students or staff, and we were to write a response to that. My piece, *The Bigger Picture*, came from being overwhelmed with the amount of history that I had consumed at the college in the space of two months — and struggling with the grief of having lost two grandmothers. In fact I had lost three grandparents within three years, and that was my connection to the motherland and learning history. And taking the Partition course *[the division of British India in 1947 into two independent dominion states, India and Pakistan, by the UK]* with Eleanor Newbigin *[senior lecturer in the history of Modern South Asia]* — she also came up with the project idea, her passion for history is personal, and that added to the loss I had in my life, made me understand how world history can be personal history.

So that's where the piece came from, centred on the young woman who's just lost her grandma, and is trying and failing to write her dissertation. She's wanting to feel a connection to her grandma, but is also overwhelmed with how you should talk about world history when there's just so much of it.

There's the need to find the bits that are missing, which are always women, because women are persistently written out of history.

So that was my very personal approach to Decolonising History. I know the rest of the writers approached it differently. Like Amy Ng, who wrote *A Form of Colonisation*, is a historian anyway, she's got PhD in history, while Bushra Laskar who wrote *The Questions You Ask*, about a mother having a stroke, was going through something very personal around the time that we were doing that project and her piece had a very personal connection to history.

Decolonising is such an intellectual idea, but also when you break it down, it's not. It's the idea that there is more than one history that you're taught in school, and what we need to do is to start injecting multiple perspectives into our curriculum. You could say the same for theatre, there are more than the stories that we are allowed to see on stages and there's many more ways of telling stories than we see on stages, and what we need to do is just allow other voices in, and maybe be influenced by them.

It's possibly a weird thing to say, but I think theatre is missing a major side to things where the idea of oral transmission, of passing on histories and experiences sidesteps the nepotism that can come with a script that fixes in writing the permission granted by class, background, expectations, privilege. That permission was pre-written long ago, whereas the oral thing is what you do in educational theatre, for example, which makes you go in and talk to people first and be defined by what they have to say. It's not finding those voices, it's not moulding them, but setting up lines of transmission by talking to people, asking them what they want and offering what you have. A big block to actually talking to people is theatre's expropriation of terminology. Like 'finding voices', which really means taking other people's voices, so the dismantling there needs to be accepting that their voices are always there and don't need permission from anybody.

I'll go with that! I applied what I'd learned through that decolonising history process into the way that we told the story of *Santi & Naz*. We called it 'a Partition play that isn't about Partition'. It's about two young women who are best friends in a Punjabi village leading up to Partition. Essentially it's a story of their friendship that is heavily influenced by the fact that Partition is coming and in the end they're ripped apart. But the number of people that came to see it and said, "Well, I didn't get enough information from the play." But it's not my job to teach you history. If you are interested in that period, in that passage of time, then go and read about it. What I want you to do is to learn how these two women felt, or what they experienced around Partition. It's not a 'history play', it's not me telling you what happened. It's me telling you what happened to those two women.

If you apply that to the wider idea of theatre, it becomes that notion of what voices are allowed to talk about what, and what is expected of them. I still feel my minority voices are only allowed to or expected to write about a subject like trauma or oppression. Anytime you try to bring something else into the mix, it's like, "But why don't you talk about that trauma?" Because I'm bored of talking about it, or I talk about it in my personal life but in my creative life couldn't I do something that's more fun or exciting or interesting?

Anyone from ten years ago listening to this conversation would be shocked that so little seems to have changed.

Well we're still having that conversation. I do feel like the 1990s did really well in setting up change, and then somehow we shut down. But now it's coming back.

Will your next steps be via your practical work or your creative work?

Well it's both. It's partly in the stories that I want to tell. A lot of minority writers want to write about the universal experience, but I've decided that's not what I'm interested in. I want to write about the Asian experience but really lean into it in weird and experimental ways. I'm working on a piece about Qandeel Baloch, the Pakistani social media star who was murdered by her brother. So I'm talking about honour killing and how that relates to society in England today and how actually honour violence is just toxic masculinity, it has nothing to do with religion. But I'll tell that from a South Asian perspective. I'm going to start making stories that are super relevant, but tell them from my perspective.

I also work with emerging writers and young people. I'm doing a project at the moment at Southwark Playhouse *[in South London]* called Future Voices. I'm working with a group of nine 13 to 16 year olds and for me it's about getting past their first impulses. They're of different heritages but all identify as black, and it's immediately like minority voices want to write about identity politics. I think that's fine because of course my first play was about identity politics, but then what we do is we feed the beast. We just churn out the plays about oppression, and then they want us to stop there. So if you stop giving it to them, then maybe they'll start paying more attention.

I've also been running the Vault Festival New Writers Programme where it's the same thing. I've got a really diverse group and it's trying to get past that first impulse of "I just want to write about my experiences." It's like, yes, write about your experiences, but how do we do that, making the most of our theatricality? How do we do that so it doesn't resemble a TV show? How do we do that in a way that a literary manager might read it and be like, "Oh, that's really exciting." The writer won't mind because the ideas are still there, like, for example, if you talk about slavery using a magic cucumber to transport you back in time. I'm trying to help the next generation of writers to think creatively about what stories they want to tell and how they want to tell them.

What's the real big block in theatre in general?

The biggest thing for me is still that persisting traditional power structure. And that connects of course with the idea of what stories get to be told and who gets to tell them, and very much telling people what they're allowed to write or make. And just not taking risks. I also feel that a big thing is not doing the audience development work. You should be able to go to see a show by a writer of a certain heritage that has won a prize, and see that the audience reflect that heritage. When we made *Coconut* and to some extent when we made *Santi & Naz*, I spent days doing audience development work, finding the women's associations, finding the people who these stories are for but may not get the chance to see them normally. Going to talk to them, having tea with them, taking posters around. Just doing the work to say, "Hey, this venue is for you. This story is for you, come and see it." Discount codes, all that jazz, whatever it takes to get people into a building. When you see shows that are intended for a specific audience and you don't see that reflected, that's really upsetting.

And once you've cracked it, sharing that work across theatres is pretty essential too.

Yes. For example, Derby Theatre and In Good Company *[East Midlands artist support programme]* are great, they supported *Coconut* and understood what we're doing. What I love about In Good Company specifically is the money. They back everything up with money. That tour for us was *not* a financial risk — they took that risk. I can't imagine that they recouped the money they gave us to do the tour but we were able to take the play to East Midlands and Lincolnshire venues, some really really white towns. The cast said there would just be one brown person in town and then they'd see that brown person in the audience later. There was such satisfaction of having got that person interested and actually having them come see the show. It's heartwarming not only for us as a creative team but also for the theatre that's done the work to get them in there. So taking risks and putting money where your mouth is, paying people to tour and get the work out there is really important.

But there's obviously the financial block posed by the cost of putting on theatre. If a main theatre doesn't take the risk to put your show on, the present model says you have to stage your show yourself and then go back to square one afterwards. And if you want to take your existing show somewhere else, it'll cost you a huge amount, so you might as well go and put on a new untested show. And then it becomes a self-perpetuating cycle. It also eats away at the idea of trust in the work you've already done as a company or as a writer. And if the economics mean that the show isn't properly seen, then where's the trust to say that it's worth seeing elsewhere or that your next show will be worth getting out there. But the financial blocks are just one of many in the way of accessibility.

Especially with regional venues, when you still rely on Arts Council funding so much. Again at that literary manager forum, they said that ticket sales aren't enough to do the work that they want to do. They need funding. Where is this money coming from? And if *they're* getting it from the Arts Council, it means that the individual artists aren't getting it from the Arts Council. So then what are we saying? It's a play-off between venues and small companies, but that doesn't seem fair, but how many pots can there reasonably be? Is there a better system of working out venue support for the smaller companies, for example? We can all see the problems, but I don't know how we fix it.

The problem is that there is no solution, or at least I can't see any solution. There's a part of me that says I just want to burn it all down. And interestingly I did Dismantle the Room last year *[an immersive escape-the-room experience that asks the questions about privilege: how can we dismantle existing power structures?]*, which was by Project 2036 and started at the Bush then went to the Royal Court. It's an interactive game about how you change the system. I ended up being in one of the (apparently only very few) groups that decided to quit, which was very much not my decision. But unanimously the group that I was with decided that we would just not do it anymore, that we would live quiet lives and try again later. I think that actually galvanised me more because I was like, "I know it's a game, but even if you guys are all willing to quit, I'm not. It's very easy for you to just say I'm not doing it. But it's not easy for me to quit changing the system because this is my job and this is what I do every single day."

I feel the only way to change it is to just burn it down. Otherwise keep working at it and helping other people that are on the rungs under you on the ladder. That's also an issue, people that get somewhere and then pull the ladder up behind them. So to combat it, at The Thelmas, we run a writer's group, I run workshops, Maddy runs workshops. We try and engage with the next generation as much as we can and just be like, this is how we're doing it, hopefully you might get something from us and that will help you do it too. And then if there's enough of us, we can just tear it all down.

*

26
Will Nelson

'Do you take a risk for your art, or play safe and pay the rent?'

Will Nelson is a fringe director & lecturer at the Arden School of Theatre. Based in Manchester & Bury, he was born in Preston & raised in Wigan.

I don't have a long list of questions. All I've really got for you is what's the problem with the North — or rather, what's the problem with the South?

[laughs long & hard] It's always been that there's a geographical distance that needs to be overcome. But that is also linked to class. And to privilege. There is a virtuous circle of funding in the arts in education where those that have the best opportunity are funded the best because they've produced the best work. And because they are funded the best, they produced the best work. Certainly it's been the case in all my working life. And it seems to be getting worse. But there are so many barriers to inclusion and achievement for young people across the North, and we are also losing our next generation of working class performers because of the demands on their time and money that they can't contemplate going into the performing as a career any more. Anecdotally, 30 or 40 years ago, you could subsist while you got your career off the ground. Now, you need to be independently wealthy to even have a hope in hell. Or fabulously lucky.

In terms of live performance or even recorded, a look at the backgrounds of our current top actors under the age of 40 will reveal that diversity seems to be if you've got the one who went to Cambridge and not Oxford — although of course you might get the occasional 'earthy' actor with slightly different roots. It's the same with our directors, essentially it's all the same dinner party. And the next generation now will be from the same dinner party.

The problem is that I don't know how to fix it. You're talking about an ideological issue, and there's nobody really at the moment who is able to counter that ideology. You see it manifest in the economics, where everything has a price, everything has a cost, everything must be able to pay its own way. If it can't prove it can pay its own way, it won't be funded. Hence my 'virtual circle' comments. But there is no art without struggle, of course.

> *Well no one's got an answer at the moment, but could there not be one that comes from within the performing arts in the shape of work that is done locally and picks up on the 'issues', the inequalities, and actually hits the audiences it's supposed to hit? On the other hand, there seems to be a dwindling number of places to do it in any case.*

Again, it's a combination of things. Is there an appetite for an activist theatre any more? I'm not sure there is. Socially, it feels like you can make the argument that things today are as bad as at any point from the 1980s onwards. And yet people seem to care a hell of a lot less. When I'm trying to analyse any of these concerns or problems, I don't know how much of this is me becoming some caricature of an old Northern curmudgeon. I'm not saying it was any better when I was 15 years younger, but what seems to be the prevailing attitude now is not one of solidarity or raising standards for all. It's just, to go crude for a moment, people who are quite happy to down a pint of piss so long as their neighbours are made to down three. It's not a case that people want everyone to be better off. We're living in a time where people just want to make sure that everyone else is as badly off as they are.

> *You're not exactly curmudgeonly—*

But I'm definitely Northern.

> *—but the point is that you've professionally fought to stay up North, you've resisted the pull to go to London. But it's really been stacked up against everyone who's also trying to stay-work-teach-create in the North where they belong, where there's people who understand them. And it seems that you're a very good/bad example of the effect of that divide, that lack of solidarity and of that totally misguided concept of what funding and fair distribution means.*

The Arts Council is a perfect example of that lack of solidarity between established and emerging companies, where you have established, well-regarded and well-funded institutions who bank on that funding just as another revenue stream rather than saying, "Well, actually we don't really *need* this." The majority of the cultural spend still goes inside the M25 *[London's ring road]* per head. It's comically higher than the rest of the country.

Ironically, however, if you were looking at this cultural solidarity at a grassroots level, I'd say it's more prevalent in London than it is outside the capital. In Manchester, where I'm working now, anything that we try to get off the ground is viewed with suspicion here. And that's not good, because we are now starting to see that the young people coming through to form the next generation are infected with the ideology that everything has to have a monetary value. So even in the cultural industries, training is now less about learning skills or providing a platform for expression but, "Well, I'm buying this qualification that will enable me to earn more money in a career or it'll buy me a ticket to the Lottery, where I might be one of the ones is who is lucky enough to get a career."

Teaching theatre is a wonderful job, but I teach at a regional drama school that finds itself more and more having to fight the pull of London. If we took our institution and just dropped it somewhere in the South East, we would immediately be more attractive just from the location — not for what we do. But what we actually do in terms of things like student surveys, studies and quality of teaching, we're up there with the likes of ArtsEd, Guildford and Guildhall and all the rest. But we're in the North West.

So there's not even a chance by virtue of postcode lottery, it really is just postcode.

Yes. It's totally a 'regional' thing. There's things that could be done. I've often had as a hobby-horse for years this idea of a 'National Theatre of England'. Now, I'm suspicious in the extreme of anything that involves waving the flag, but it is strange that we have a National Theatre of Scotland, a National Theatre of Wales, and the 'National' Theatre itself is located with all the rest of the London theatres. Diversifying culture away from the capital has to be at the heart of any strategy and as much as I would like it to be a specifically Northern thing, and base it in Manchester, Liverpool, or Leeds, the North culturally speaking could apply to anywhere that isn't the South East.

And, not to criticise it, the National in London doesn't actually represent anyone.

No, of course not. But such things moving away from the capital would start to create their own cultural ecosystems in the rest of the country. But, wahey, that's very pie in the sky thinking, isn't it? One of the arguments that has always been difficult to reconcile, particularly on the left, is the concept of regional and national identities within the United Kingdom. Scotland has its concept of civic nationalism and Wales has the benefit of its own culture and language. The idea of English nationalism has always been problematic, hijacked as it often is by the far right, but the question of an arts and cultural identity for England will help with this. I mean, what is English culture? Is it Shakespeare — of course but it always is — but in 2019, is it not Jim Cartwright, Sheelagh Delaney, the Beatles, Alan Bennett? I feel a National Theatre of England would help us to work that out.

If you did have a National Theatre of England, what would it do? Aside from considerations of the other three nations needing their own institutions after centuries of dominance — and systematic cultural obliteration — by England, we're actually uneasy (well, 48 per cent of the population probably) about vaunting England culturally or politically. Would you do theatre in one place or do it all over the constituent nation? And then there's the problem about major shows where the economics of access and touring become a barrier. To be honest, we're just not very good at confronting that monetary side of it, and we let it dictate what we create, which would ruin the whole point.

I would treat it like the Olympics. It would move. The organisation would take over an existing building, whether that'd be a theatre space or just 'a space' and it would be based there for two, three years. Its remit would then be to bring on new work to a presumption to use local talent. To try to build a legacy everywhere it goes, and then in three years' time go off and do it somewhere else.

So the National Theatre of England to my mind would not be a physical building but be more of a company that turns up somewhere, helps to regenerate, physically and culturally, and then moves on. Ridiculously, this is the model that professional wrestling in the United States has started to use. The WrestleMania event, every year in March/April has more often than not in the last few years been placed in areas requiring regeneration. It started in Orlando in the mid 2000s, where they go to a town, spend a lot of money there, bring committed people to it, do it up then move on, and next year it's somewhere else.

That's actually far more streamlined and manageable than the Olympics model, isn't it? You don't actually need an infrastructure, whereas with the Olympics you do need an infrastructure, which is cost-prohibitive and also encourages national and local corruption that eclipses the long-term viability of the exercise.

Yes, and I'm not saying it's always the case that if you build it, they will come. But if you build something then there will at least be something when you've left — and people will have the option to come. The difficulty is if you made it a physical permanent building in one place then you run the risk of it becoming just another white elephant.

So the idea of a separate National Theatre of the North, tempting as it is, would be a divisive step?

Yes, of course. It's divisive. As I've said, anything that says this is the National Theatre of a particular region or a particular constituent part of the United Kingdom is going to necessarily be divisive. Since, particularly in England, less so in the North, that whole notion of an English cultural identity has been very much coopted by the far right, if you consider that a lot of people who are likely to be implementing this or conceptualising this are going to be from the political left or centre, they will probably run away from the notion of an English theatre because people will jump to the conclusion that it will be and this summer we are going to be doing our season of Al Garnett pieces [*reactionary London white working class character in 1960s/70s BBC sitcom Till Death Us Do Part*] or a retrospective of *Love Thy Neighbour* [*1970s ITV sitcom about a white working class couple and a black couple as next-door neighbours in suburban London*].

But it shouldn't have to be that. In fact it should be a proving ground for the development of a specific English cultural identity because Scotland and Wales have managed to develop their own. But England, if anything, is too diverse for there to be a uniform identity. So I'm kind of arguing with myself now! But I do lean away from the idea of a specific National Theatre of the North because, again, of that idea that the North can refer to anywhere that isn't South East — and very specific parts of the South East. You could say that Suffolk or Cornwall are in the North, that parts of Kent even are in the North. We have a very large cultural and financial centre in London that dominates absolutely everything and that everything else is always going to be secondary.

The North does have its institutions like Opera North, which at least employs talent in the North, and then there's the likes of Northern Broadsides, which was set up to platform regional voices. Or are these not relevant?

Well in the case of Opera North, it's like saying Manchester United provide a platform for people just in Manchester to play football. But that's not what it does. Its location becomes a brand. Opera North are a very good brand no doubt. And everybody is always going to want the *best* people, and the best people coincidentally seem to always be the ones who are from the old institutions of the South East.

Northern Broadsides, I'd say, was of its time because I don't think you'd get something like that off the ground now. It comes back to what we were saying that there is a financial reality that has come for so many practitioners and performers since 1993, where the best will still gravitate towards London because the training institutions there will try and pick up them up. So in somewhere like the North you're drawing from a smaller pool of talent. But a big institution to can only work if it becomes and remains financially viable, so you have to spend a number of years trying to build it up. And it's clear that you can have all the artistic drive in the world but if you are trying to work full time on something that isn't even paying you enough to pay rent at the end of the month, then you're always going to fall away.

It's our perfect storm again. The difference in cultural spend inside and outside of London is hilariously different, and after 2010 when we especially needed more investment, investment was actually taken away. So I'm not saying they would have had it easy, but a company setting up in 1993 would have still had a network of growing cultural institutions who were willing to invest in local talent and local practitioners. The big chop that came in the funding for these places, mainly through Arts Council England, happened just shortly after 2010 — post the global crisis of 2008 — and after that, there was very little support for anything that wasn't going to turn a profit. Is my understanding, working off somewhere like the Duke's in Lancaster, for example, or the Octagon in Bolton, theatres all had to diversify their income and become more touring, less production.

We've lost a lot of solidarity across the country and it seems to me that theatre in particular, but also other aspects of the live performing arts like stand-up, hasn't managed to get to grips with much really bar the odd flash of brilliance like the Bunker Theatre in London. It's particularly galling at the moment because, like they used to say, it was good for the UK to have a rightwing government because everyone gets creative because there's something to react against. But we've lost that.

I think we absolutely have.

Why?

Gentrification. Let's use Thatcher as the most recent equivalent of what we have now, although, looking at the figures, I don't think actually her time was anything like as bad as it is now. The people railing against Thatcher were coming from the middle and working classes, because the idea of cultural work as a career was not ridiculous. She still had the Youth Training Scheme *[on the job training scheme for 16 to 17-year-old school leavers launched in 1983]* and there were still avenues to do that activism. There are stories of councils funding projects specifically to annoy the national government.

Firstly, those avenues have now been closed off. Secondly, the class effect, of which stand-up comedy is a good example. Traditionally stand-up was a working class pursuit, now it's a middle class and private school pursuit. It's like everything else and has become as gentrified as acting and music have. You need that cultural capital, that financial basis to be able to make a career out of the arts. You need to be able to afford to *not* earn money for a few years to get yourself established. And people no longer have that opportunity.

To me it's a materialistic argument, which is that people wherever they are need to be able to live first, and then create. If they can't create because they're too busy trying to live, then the only stories that are going to get told are the stories of those who don't have the same pressures on them. There's a wonderful interview with Chris Morris *[YouTube, Channel 4 News channel, 'Chris Morris on satire in the Trump era...']* where he says that comedians have become court jesters. They're no longer challenging the Establishment, they *are* the Establishment, enabling the Establishment to chuckle about its own contradictions and its own eccentricities but never enough to actually change anything.

Today even the stand-ups who like to be seen as the most subversive have become court jesters, like the Frankie Boyles of this world. They have now hidden under the safety of the umbrella of the state broadcaster to get on a panel show and say, "Oh hee hee, aren't we silly?" But never in such a way that will ever have people go, "Good grief that's appalling!" A perfect example, being *The Last Leg [Channel 4 comedy talk show with disabled presenters that started as an end of day discussion show for the 2012 London Summer Paralympics]*. When it came in, it was a *great* idea. It's now been around for what, eight years, but just does the same trick — it's subversive in the sense that it has let some marginalised people through the gate, and has seen its job done and left it at that. Featuring more minority Establishment figures is not changing that Establishment. So that is why you're not getting the cultural resurgence now.

Mind you, it all probably comes down to 'can you pay your rent or not?' But if you can pay your rent and create, you'd most likely be living somewhere where there's no audience. Well, obviously there will be an audience, but they won't have the money to go off and see anything, or necessarily have it on their list of priorities, or feel it's for them of course. That's an immense block on any resurgence.

True, and if there is going to be any kind of resurgence it's not going down in history as an epoch. You may find when this period is written about in 50 years' time, nobody will be talking about a 'Red Wedge' *[collective of musicians formed in 1985 to engage young people with Labour Party policies leading up to the 1987 general election, in the hope of ousting Margaret Thatcher's Tory government]* or nobody will be talking about a 'Channel 4' *[launched in 1982, committing itself to providing an alternative to the existing TV channels, its remit requiring the provision of programming to minority groups along with alternative arts]*. If they are talking at all, people will be talking about very small-scale crossover contemporary theatre performance art pieces of our times, no more.

I suppose there always have been those pieces. You know, like the way people reference some obscure 1970s avant-garde, agitprop or community group which was incredibly influential but virtually no one saw. There'd be one in Ulverston and Barnet and another one in Glasgow. There's nothing much that's new. What we have now is that you get the bones of innovation but there's no flesh there. In this day and age, we don't have things like Red Wedge or Extinction Rebellion for the arts, even though everything is starkly defined. For the last few years it's just like wading through treacle to get anything done in your general life, so to get something creative up and running is a huge barrier no matter how good or worthy it might be. It's hard to mobilise people. Is it because the majority of us are distracted by having to pay the rent because Mummy and Daddy aren't paying for us to pursue a creative life? Is that what it's all about?

Erm, yes! Unless you have stability you have no agency, because you are constantly beholden to a landlord or to a job that will click its fingers and demand that you come running. That's unless we can pay people to just create, but not pay them in the sense that we pay them based on output. The most ridiculous statement in a career full of ridiculous statements that *[former Tory prime minister]* David Cameron ever made was that the British Film Institute would from now on only be funding things that 'will be successful'. Well, how the hell do you know if something 'will be successful' until you've actually made it?

A colleague of mine says, "Sometimes you have to shovel a ton of shit to get a pound of gold", and that's absolutely true. I just see barriers everywhere you look. And it depresses the hell out of me that part of my job is to sell people the lie that barriers aren't as high as they look. I'm always realistic, I always will say the barriers are there, but I still have to downplay how big they are. And I hate having to do that.

We could just leave the next ten pages of blank and let the reader slowly flip them over and ponder the enormity of that. The irony is that we've got more theatre than ever, more people than ever empowered to do theatre, in the sense that they have the training, they know that they can do it, they know where the opportunities are, but again none of it seems to join up and it seems to be getting more and more fragmented. And I think it's especially difficult to explain this to people in the South East and in Europe, because they'll just be viewing this homogenous country where amazing theatre just happens. They'll see the West End, fringe and community theatre in every nook, all the rural and regional touring, our national and producing theatres, all the festivals — and of course the education and training. But physically step outside of the M25 and it rapidly becomes something that is fragmented, not because it's been shattered but very carefully chipped away. It's depressing, but it shouldn't have to be negative because it could change overnight for the better. It could be a company, it could be a show, it could be an event that suddenly makes that difference and everything changes. What's the one that's going to cause a revolution?

That's interesting isn't it, because I think the ones that are going to cause a revolution are probably already out there. But has there ever been that show? Realistically, in the 1950s, did *Look Back in Anger [quintessential angry young man play by John Osborne (from London), written in the North over 17 days in a deckchair on a pier in Morecambe where he was performing in a rep show, Seagulls over Sorrento]* have any effect outside of the pages of *The Manchester Guardian*?

No. But then I've never seen it, read it or needed to have an interest in it. Pinter's stuff either. So I suppose that makes me living proof.

[both laugh]

But to read those history books! It's the same with music, it's this deterministic dealing with history that one day, a 'great man' — because it is usually a man, let's be honest, and he's often white as well and middle-aged — came along and he did this great piece of work and then that changed it, and the next day everything was different. Boom! Practically, that's never really happened as far as I can tell. When the Sex Pistols, I dunno, I'm on dangerous territory now, but when they released 'God Save the Queen' *[1977]*, not everybody became a punk overnight. But to read the histories of that time, you'd be led to believe that the next day everybody turned up in torn Levi's, spitting at the nearest authority figure.

Misting over obvious facts of our common history like this are important to explain our common national narrative. We love to love myths — and need them and create them. Which is exactly how revolutions are remembered, in shorthand with only the key joyous/boo-hiss moments featured, it's very dramatic in fact. But I've never understood the *Look Back in Anger* cult. But if you want to look at great theatre pieces that have come from the last few decades when you can't use the mists of time as a filter, then I think there is a playwright who has the chops to do it and that's Mike Bartlett *[from Oxford]*. If you look at his body of work in the last ten years, he is asking all the right questions.

Okay. I could be convinced. Certainly he's consistent.

The problem is that people are being entertained by them and not moved by them. They're falling into Brecht's old critique of the dramatic theatre. They're crying when the characters cry, and they're laughing when the characters laugh. Whereas to me, you should watch a Bartlett piece or even a Moira Buffini *[from Cheshire]* piece and you should do the opposite. When you watch Bartlett's *Love Love Love*, at the end you should be going out into the street and shaking anybody under the age of 40 and burning down the house of anyone over — and *then* go to the bar. But the reality is that people are doing exactly the thing that Brecht told them not to. *[laughs]*

How can we take it in a positive direction for people to feel invigorated to go along and pick up a Mike Bartlett play and take it all in to see whether they can come up with something to counter it, parallel it or come up with something entirely in their own direction, a local response to something that needs it? Obviously this is coming in the immediate aftermath of an election *[the 2019 landslide victory by the Conservative Party on a Brexit ticket]*, and these problems feel more permanent than anything we've seen in recent decades.

As an activist, it was the first election campaign I've ever done where the split feels generational, the first one where the old class arguments didn't work. They didn't get through, because nobody believed them. Nobody wanted to believe them. They wanted to believe in some kind of abstract notion of national identity as far as I could tell. And that generational split . . . people are assuming that the old thing of 'Conservatism as you age' is going to hold. We'll I'm not convinced it will, but neither am I convinced that it will become socialism either.

I hope to be proved wrong but there's something else coming instead which looks like a very narrow parochial flag-waving nationalism. But in terms of what can we do about it, I'm not sure. I'm saying yes, you could challenge things on a local basis. I think any kind of response is going to have to be local, whether this be a political or an artistic response. But at the moment it's that question: is anybody going to listen?

In the short term we're going to have to keep challenging, keep asking questions and try and see if people start to listen. We have to bear in mind the fact that we are living in an alternative facts era, the irony being that people have access to the greatest repository of knowledge in human history, which means they are able choose their own narratives. That is going to be a very hard thing to break. As John McGrath *[Northern founder of Glasgow-based 7:84 agitprop theatre company, the name coined from data at the time that 7% of the nation owned 84% of the country's wealth]* said, there is a need for a sharp critical theatre to contest the borders of our democracy. Such things only work if people are prepared to listen.

And to start people listening, it needs to happen through education. But then you hit the thing of education being marketised, where everything is being taught to right or wrong answers. We need to rip it up and start again, but I can't see any appetite coming to do that for our future students.

What I see happening onstage nowadays is maybe technically interesting, maybe pioneering and all the rest of it, maybe a lot of politics and stuff like that. It's very worthwhile. But to me none of it in practice is saying anything, because as you say people aren't listening. It seems that we have a country now of theatremakers (and not just British because we have so many people from all over the world making theatre here) whose opinions are far more interesting and have far more influence than the work that they actually make, which doesn't seem to be much unfortunately. At least they're trying to make the case for theatre as a positive force, something seriously absent from stand-up, no matter how cuddly and enlightened the comics might seem.

Stand-up and theatre share the issue that lots of people use them as stepping stones to 'something better'. Are you doing stand-up because that's the best medium for you to say what you have to say? Or are you using stand-up as a route to the panel shows? Or to the Netflix special? It's the court jesters again. Is theatre its own reward or is theatre a way to get a sitcom? It's just another symptom of the marketisation of theatre.

Take our mainstream theatre. They have all the challenges of an individual practitioner but on a grand scale. Do you take a risk for your art or do you take the safe option and make sure that you can pay the rent next month? Yes, they can still run the youth projects and the outreach, but the product in the main house wouldn't have looked out of place 20 years ago. There are some companies that break away from this (Red Ladder for example) but the day of the producing house is passing.

Increasingly too, the theatre, even in the West End, is the place where 'screen' actors go to prove they 'still have it'. Often these are good performers in their own right no doubt, but if *[American screen actor]* Lindsay Lohan is appearing in a David Mamet revival for 'credibility' or yet another thirtysomething actor is playing the Dane (because you do) then that is one fewer opportunity for an up and coming actor.

> *I started a book on UK critics at a point when I realised that the profession was finally at tipping point and the erosion of professional critics as we knew them had reduced us to zero even before The Guardian's sacking of [critic & commentator] Lyn Gardner. I was wondering should I give it a mind-numbing academic title or a snappy one that might attract people to read it? Or why not just give it a title that says what I actually want to say? One of the suggestions I came up with for the latter that's stuck with me is 'Can You Be a Theatre Critic and Vote Tory'? But of course you can vote Tory and be a theatre critic, and there are tons of people who aren't Labour but would never vote Tory because they can see it kills what they love. So then I thought, stepping out of the party politics, that a better title might be 'Can You Be a Theatre Critic and Not Be Progressive'?*

But in this political and economic climate, what does 'progressive' mean? If you're progressive, you can 'progressively' fall down a flight of stairs. It doesn't mean it's a good thing to do. So I think your first original title is a great title! And if there is an energy, now, within this malaise, it is in this culture war that people keep trying to make happen. And people tried to make to make happen over the EU Referendum.

> *Define 'culture war' then.*

How you voted in the Brexit Referendum. People tried to make an identity, and through that whole discussion you defined yourself. And again, I saw this on the doorsteps a lot in the election, people defining themselves first and foremost as "I am a Leaver" or "I am a Remainer". There's a will to fight, but I'm not sure that people are fighting the right things, or fighting for the right causes.

As much as I campaigned for Remain, I never considered myself a 'Remainer'. Because that was something that seemed to be a sideshow to the actual causes of the vote to leave in the first place. And had the people fought with as much energy and as much passion for the reasons why people voted to leave because any change was better than nothing, then ironically, it probably wouldn't have happened in the first place. Very strange.

But you did put me in mind of something when you were talking about the erosion of the critics — well, of the professional critics anyway. In *Road*, the

Jim Cartwright play, there's a line at the end of Act One where the couple who are starving themselves to death as a protest, one of them has the line where she says something along the lines of "When the last person loses their job, I wonder will there be any kind of ceremony, will people turn out to what's the last person be sacked or made redundant? Or will it just happen without comment?" And it struck me as beyond a little bit of hoopla on Twitter about Lyn Gardner's sacking from *The Guardian*, very little else was made of that. Her loss wasn't heavily remarked upon, and I thought it would be made of it more than it was. But instead it felt like something that was just "Well, yes, that's just typical of where we are now."

Theatre criticism is not seen as something that creates revenue — therefore it is, if anything, a random practice. What was once a profession in itself has now become something that in the mind of the media any hack can turn their hand to. Or it should now be for spirited amateurs or just what people do as ancillary to something else. It's a symptom of that Cameronesque 'Big Society' thing, that fundamental rights and services should be provided by volunteers. And that's one of the things that are stifling our talent today. What were professions are now hobbies, they're not something you can build a life on.

*

27

Gbolahan Obisesan

'Without visibility there will be no evolution of ideas or work'

Gbolahan Obisesan is a writer, director & artistic director of Brixton House (formerly Ovalhouse) Theatre, London. Based in South East London, he was born in Ibadan, Nigeria, & raised in Ibadan & South East London. • *brixtonhouse.co.uk, @GreatObisesan*

Photo: David Sandison

You come from a bilingual background, don't you?

I was born in Nigeria in Ibadan. I learnt English at nursery school and primary school and also spoke Yoruba predominately. So yes that's how I grew up.

When you were a kid in Ibadan, were there any differences in access to the performing arts to the way it's done here in the UK?

Cinema was the primary medium of entertainment that I was aware of as a child. My parents had been students who travelled for education and when they returned home to Ibadan, they felt like a VCR was a window out into the rest of the world. So we had a video-player and a TV that we'd sit around and watch Nollywood and Bollywood films — and a lot of martial arts films!

Film is a very specific artistic visual medium, but it also offers you subtitled films that inform you differently about things like literacy, so it encouraged my reading. As for other art forms in Nigeria, I can't remember ever going to the theatre or performing in anything at school, but I was very precocious in some ways so I would always go out after I had seen a great film and try to create a version of it with my friends in the compound where we lived in

Ibadan. So, for the most part, films were definitely my only primary source of visual or artistic stimulation.

Why did you come to the UK? How did that come about?

We had a tragedy in my family, an accident happened and we lost my brother. My Mum was working as a nurse in Guy's Hospital here in London. She had lost a son and so, rightly quite anxious about any other unfortunate events happening to us, she demanded that we come and live with her in Bermondsey. My two sisters went ahead of me and then I followed, which was almost a year later because visas were very tricky. When I arrived, my sisters had already settled in London, but when we nostalgically look back on those early years there they remember living somewhere much less comfortable or desirable with my Mum. My sisters were at Camelot primary school in Peckham, and due to lack of space there I went to Ilderton primary school in South Bermondsey.

So how was the culture shock? Suddenly swapping a big compound in sunny Ibadan for a cramped flat in grey South London must have been a weird contrast.

I was nine when I moved — I'm the eldest. I remember when I flew over, there had been some confusion about when I was arriving and my Dad couldn't get information to my Mum so she wasn't there to meet me. My chaperone just left me at the airport *[laughs at the memory]* and then one of the Nigerian air stewardesses on my flight noticed that I was a little bit lost, and she took me home with her boyfriend. I stayed with them for a day or two in a room mostly staring out of the window. I think it was snowing at the time. Eventually my Mum came to collect me, so yeah it was bizarre. And then we ended up on an estate in Bermondsey and it was cold and still snowing.

It seems strange now, but one of my first memories of Bermondsey was that of people smiling at you. It seemed really peculiar to me because I'd never met those people before, I didn't know who they were. Maybe it was just curious English people in general, but it was most probably just because we were cute black children. I mean, now that I'm an adult and I have a child, I understand there's a genuine innocence in children that we find endearing, and now that I'm a parent, I can honestly say I myself might occasionally smile at the children of strangers because they're endearing and we share funny faces to make each other smile or chuckle.

But growing up in Bermondsey, at the time when you moved there, it was very white and very . . .

It was very white, quite narrow-minded and very racist.

But I'm guessing that it was complicated for you, by the fact that it was rough for people if they're not from there but not rough if they know you're from there. No drug gangs at the time either — well, to begin with.

Yes, exactly like that. But there was nothing rough that I knew of in South Bermondsey where we first lived. But we did find those problems due to regeneration when were moved down the road to what is kind of central Bermondsey near Surrey Quays. We used to live near where the New Den is *[stadium for Millwall Football Club]*, which was in a wasteland of just nothingness and there was an Irish Gypsy community near the train station who kept their horses and carts and carriages and discarded caravans on the wasteland.

So we moved to Silwood Estate in Surrey Quays which was a little bit rougher because although it was a real hotspot of cultures, it was still predominately white working class. There were strong racist attitudes and drug abuse on the estate in needles frequently in our block or me and my sisters would regularly see children of our white neighbours shooting heroin on the stairs to the point where for the most part, we just stayed in because it was safer to be indoors. We moved there not long after Stephen Lawrence was murdered in Eltham as well *[Stephen was a black British teenager from Plumstead, South East London, who was murdered in a racist attack by white youths while waiting for a bus in nearby Eltham in 1993]*, and once that happened the social rules became very defined, either you stay in, or you learn to frighten those who want to torment you with racial abuse and hope that other immigrant black boys on the estate will have your back.

The Bonamy Estate in South Bermondsey was a little bit more mixed and it was also a bit of a warren and I remember that whenever you watched *The Bill [ITV police series]* back in the day, whilst we were at school they had been shooting scenes on the estate. The garages underneath the estate were always on *The Bill*. Most criminals on *The Bill* were either chased or arrested on the Bonamy Estate. It was ridiculous! More frustrating because I could never get on that TV show as an actor, when I could have easily walked onto the set as a child. Very irritating to say the least.

My primary school was a walk up the road from Silwood Estate and that was a very multi-ethnic sort of school, but you know I had racial prejudice again, funnily enough not from white children in the school but the black Caribbean children who wanted to distinguish themselves from me being African, Nigerian. I don't think it was even that nuanced — I didn't come from a country, I just came from the continent. So all the kinds of racial abuse that I endured were pretty much encapsulated around derogatory ideas of the continent being backward and uncivilised. Funnily enough, it was never violent or threatening, and some of those boys I still see now in our barber shop or Deptford market and I believe they know they were a bit misguided back then in terms of their attitudes. We are casual friends now and trust each other and we understand that the environment we occupy was designed against us.

Growing up on Silwood Estate was, like you say, was quite dangerous if you weren't from there. But once you were known as being from there, that you lived there, then you became subjected to less daily threats, although that's not to say you still didn't have to endure racist language and the random physical assault for no reason. And yet whenever we went to the church on Sunday, near the New Den, we'd walk past Millwall supporters *[known for their racism & violence]* it never felt life-threatening! Maybe it was because as children we had the cloak of innocence and God on us that that meant these grown men or even some of the young men that went to the football matches felt they didn't need to threaten us or attack us.

I can imagine that if you weren't from there and if you clearly showed signs of fear in that sort of situation, that could be pretty much it for you. But for us, it was just like, "I've heard everything about you lot but this is my roots now, my home now, I'm not going to be scared." For the most part, however, I'm also not staring in people's faces to challenge them on their identity or their reputation for racial hatred or violence. Maybe you just have spiritual guides protecting you in those sort of circumstances, because certainly for some of those encounters I had looked back, and thought, yeah that could have gone left, it could have been a lot worse.

So a flashpoint on every corner and a guaranteed one every Wednesday night and Saturday afternoon?

Yes.

My family moved to this country when I was 14 and it was hard to miss the constant stories about Millwall supporters. To this day I still can't help thinking they're an invention out of Viz Magazine or The Beano. I could never believe that they were real and tolerated because they made such predictable, even self-affirming newsfodder. It just seemed to be such a bizarre thing, a construct that people had made up to sum up the white side of life. But Millwall is real, and it hasn't changed, certainly in terms of racism.

I'm not going to lie, there were clashes. There were definitely clashes we were aware of that happened literally on the end of our road. But then those were the sort of days where you were drawn to the spectacle of violence but you didn't want to be caught up in it. You didn't want to be down on the road, but you could certainly watch it from the landing of the flats or the balconies at the back.

Could that have been an introduction to theatre?

There is that, I hear what you're saying. But it's not the same. Actually my first introduction to theatre was at that Ilderton primary school, when we did *[laughs]* a play about George and the Dragon and I wanted to be George strangely enough. I felt as if I had theatrical bones in my body — I think this was from Nigeria, jumping around and acting with my friends there after watching films. I felt I was exuberant enough and had the capacity to deliver what was required. And I was cast as the Dragon *[laughs]* — no no, I was cast as a guard I think. Some other poor soul got cast as the Dragon because I remember they had to wear a Chinese dragon costume. So that was what I remember as my first introduction to theatre in a primary school context. And I didn't really do any acting again until I was 14 when I went to secondary school.

What was the opportunity there? Was it a drama course or there was a class or afterschool project going on?

It was just a class. My drama teacher was the first person to do drama at my school in something like ten years.

Okay so that's quite significant then, that little gap in the door.

Funnily enough I didn't initially go to that school. I first went to an all-boys school in Dulwich, William Penn, which was genuinely full of delinquents. It's closed down now, it's now called the Charter School, but at the time it was literally fully outfitted with young gang members who lived that life. Every other day it was CS gas on the train, hammers being taken off the trains, people being attacked. One of the first things I saw when I went there was a guy standing in front the canteen to collect money from the Year 7s and Year 8s. Someone stabbed him with a metal compass and he dropped to the floor, and everyone just stepped over his bleeding stomach. So it was a bit rough, to say the least.

I ended up fighting too much in that school, so my Mum was like, "This is not the right environment." *[laughs]* Basically her deduction was, "There's too much testosterone in that school, so you need to go to a mixed comprehensive because being around girls and being in that sort of environment will *mellow* you." Essentially her plan worked, but then there was a lot of gang culture in the 1990s around the schools in any case, there were a lot of rivalries and street gangs.

I don't know how much of that my Mum knew, but there were loads of 'visits' to my school by gangs pretty much every other day and to this day I don't know how I was never in a gang. Well, I kind of do — I think it was probably my sense of the traumatic reason why I ended up in this country and the fact I didn't want to stress or disappointment my Mum and Dad. That certainly motivated my air of caution and lone wolf mentality. She did warn me. She just said, "You know, in this country they're going to try and pull you into gangs, and only the weak end up joining the gangs. So whatever you do, what you have to do, however you mean to do it, just avoid it at all costs, because once you're in, you won't get out." Growing up watching a lot of films about exactly that sort of thing, you have to go, "She's right." Once you're in, the repercussions are much greater and the consequences are much greater than not joining.

Good at that age to be able to rationalise it that way.

Yes, it was weird. Luckily I was able to look at the consequences and repercussions of certain actions before taking the decision. And more fortunately, I was a likeable person which helped in the first scenario of being pressured in that sort of situation. I'd moved to my second secondary school and a gang member was about to rob me on school premises. At my previous school William Penn, I had got into a lot of fights and got a name for myself and a boy in the gang, who was a couple of years older than me, suddenly recognised me and was like, "Oh I didn't even know you'd left William Penn, when did you start here?" But even though I was literally about to get robbed, I had a new group of friends, class mates whose money I was holding to buy from the shops, so I had to tell him, "Look, I'm going to the shop and also buying food for my friends and I can't let go of the money I've got, so . . . can you talk to your boys?" And he was like, "Yeah man. Allow him, allow him, he's cool."

And I literally got to walk to the shops and come back into the school without getting touched. That happened a few times because I could always see my guy, and I worried for the day that he wasn't there or had been arrested or something like that. Sometimes if the gang wants you, you'll either get stalked, jumped regularly and eventually pressured into joining. That definitely happened with a couple of other friends of mine who were in gangs — you get talked to. But when I got moved to the new school, it was always respectful, I guess — "Do you want to join? You don't want to join? Oh alright cool, whenever you change your mind, come to us!" sort of thing.

Sounds like they were coming to you on an equal level as opposed to trying to manipulate you into it.

Yes, because a lot of the time you do get into scenarios where you have to prove your strength or get a reputation somehow. That's why from 11 to 14 years old I fought and got a reputation that went from one school to the other school. At the new one I had a couple of scraps there, well more than a couple, and got a reputation that I actually needed to be left alone, so drama classes definitely became an outlet.

Mr Camplin was the first person to do drama at our school and I started in Year 9. I chose it for GCSEs, because I enjoyed it. It was either that or history, and at the time my history teacher couldn't justify the importance of history to me because I saw it as a syllabus of Eurocentric and colonial narratives. I was like, I'm not really interested in that, I'd rather do drama — plus all my favorite people were also doing drama at the time!

My drama teacher then said, "There's this thing called the National Youth Theatre. I did it when I was your age. You can go and audition, then see how you get on." I wasn't quite sure but three other people from my class also applied but I was the only one that got in. I was very shocked at that, but also elated that I basically get to do drama for nearly the whole summer. I went to North London, travel from south to north, to do the NYT drama course on Holloway Road, where it was survive and prove yourself on the course, show your enthusiasm for acting for three weeks, and then you get your certificate.

I got my certificate that said I was an NYT member. And from then on, I could audition for productions. For the following year, because I'd left school by then, I'd go back to my drama teacher and he'd work with me on my speeches, and I did *Oedipus the King*. After that I got a job at the Barbican working in the Coffee Point — they've got a library upstairs, I'd go there in my breaks and find speeches and work on them myself. I auditioned and got into the NYT again, and so that continued for a few years. I had made friends in the NYT and we'd encourage each other to go see plays at the National Theatre and write poetry, and stuff like that, so I started doing poetry. Then at college I got interested in film so I started writing short films and incorporating poetry, and that carried on until I went to university.

When I went to university, I didn't go to drama school or anything — I wanted to study film, but I didn't get into the film schools like Ravensbourne University London. It was Ravensbourne that I really wanted to go to and I was a little bit impatient, but I felt I didn't have the time to wait another year to re-apply, so I went and did a broad communications course at London Guildhall University, which is now London Met. When I got there I wanted to do a specifically film focused course, but at the time I think they were in debt so they literally packed any course that had an appeal for international students with international students fees, so I opted to just do the general communications course.

That was really helpful because I'm was quite eclectic designed for students to be stimulated by different ideas and thoughts, and that definitely contributed to me becoming a theatremaker. It was essentially just being able to see things from a different perspective, to consider different approaches and also utilise different modules of my own knowledge alongside other people's knowledge to inform my work.

Alongside that I was still doing plays at the NYT while I was at uni and one summer I went to audition for Lamda — it was the only school I wanted to get into. I got through to the third round and then realised that I was in a bit of a conundrum because I'd just finished my second year at university and if I got a place at Lamda I would be in a conundrum about going into my third year, but — I could finish the course, get a degree and make sure my parents knew that. But to throw all of that away and still have the debt and then be picking up more debt from drama school? I'd like to think that Lamda were also thinking the same thing. Anyway I got the letter and I didn't get in. I think I was just trying to prove to myself that I could get in, because I knew and felt I'd smashed my audition!

Your parents. Did they have reservations about you going into the performing arts? I mean we're not going for stereotypes but surely they would have wanted you to become an accountant or an engineer?

My Dad was an accountant! And for a while I was actually good at maths until I got to GCSEs and thought it was all gibberish. I think my Dad struggled with his own choice. He would have liked to have studied in Britain properly and perhaps found a different career for himself, but I think he met with a lot of racist attitudes and also financial challenges and getting a student visa. It felt like he settled for accountancy, but he did the job with care and pride. I found out my Mum wanted to be a fashion designer, but again as a Nigerian that wasn't a stable career to pursue and so it meant that she went into nursing, eventually specialising in endoscopy. We definitely didn't live a lavish lifestyle from their wages or anything because they weren't in that sort of position.

So if the family had stayed in Nigeria, your family would have probably seen quite a different career path for you. Whereas in the UK they could see that there were other avenues and opportunities.

I think I had proven myself that I was not very academic. *[laughs]*

But you'd done things like getting a GCSE in drama, getting into NYT, uni.

It was clear that I thrived through leaning towards artistic expression and creative language, so it just meant that they probably had a quiet conversation and agreed, "He'll work it out." If at any time I was behaving foolishly, they would pull me back and explicitly tell me, "You know you're black, right? And you're black in a predominately white country and no one is out to help you, so don't mess up your future." They definitely meant that, so I just needed to push for the stuff that made sense to me, the stuff that I could do, areas I excelled in.

Part of that for them was me getting into the NYT, regardless of not seeing that many black people or black representation on TV at the time — and there wasn't really any in theatre. There were the obvious few — shows like the *[Channel 4 sitcom] Desmond's* and the family on *EastEnders* — but for my parents it was mostly other people saying to them, "He's good at this thing and he seems to enjoy it and to be finding a way of expressing himself, so perhaps just let him carry on doing that and see where it goes." So that's kind of what happened, they just let me pursue what I wanted to pursue.

Can you say no to a Nigerian parent?

Yes of course you can! They're all different aren't they? Obviously most are bound up or conditioned by their own upbringing and that cultural impetus towards making sure that you don't embarrass the family, that you pursue a notable career, that you do it well, and you are able to provide for you family or contribute to the general upkeep of the household, whether that's your immediate household or even your extended family. That's incredibly important. I believe it's a hang-up from the Yoruba feudal systems and other Nigerian communities are built on. That is where our motivation and aspirations towards academic route comes from, to follow respected career paths that offers consistent intellectual and economic growth.

But also there will never be a dearth of need for lawyers, doctors, accountants, engineers, will there? Highly sought-after careers like that are always going to be there for you, whereas 'artists'? *[laughs]* Artists have an enigma that makes Nigerians go, "I don't know what that is. I don't know how they make money and who pays them." Being a pure artist like a painter is probably even more precarious as a career than theatre, but if you're going to do it you have to be incredibly brave or incredibly stubborn and thick-skinned to go down that route. *[Nigerian]* Fela Kuti was famously allowed to come to England to study medicine but decided to turn his attention to music, and thank God he made that decision for himself. I'm grateful for pioneers like him because my parents knew his story and enjoyed his music. I feel my parents saw evidence of me somehow making progress within theatre as well. It was slow, and at times really uncertain, but it was what I'd chosen.

You've explained why you were stubborn and thick-skinned enough to embark on making theatre your career, but how did the challenges change once you started working professionally in the business as a director and writer?

There was a pivotal point in terms of me asserting that I was a director. I won an award to direct a production of *Sus [2010]* at the Young Vic. It was very well received critically and by audiences. It was picked up for a tour, did very well on tour, and then after that . . . nothing happened. Literally nothing happened. Like no one cared, no one offered me a job, no one asked to meet with me, do you know what I'm saying?

So even now, if I get to direct a show every two years, those are my stats as a director. A show every two years. I can't live on that. I literally can't live on that. That's not sustainable, that's not fair at all. When I look at other people in terms of how they are lauded by critics for one show and then institutional leaders seek them out and everyone says, "Oh it's about ideas, it's about ideas!" No it's not, not always. It's about you going, "Ah, here's this bright young thing who I *like*, who sounds like me, or laughs at my jokes. I want to push them forward as a protegé of mine and therefore I'm going to give them an opportunity to direct something in my building."

That's what happens. Don't tell yourself that's not what happens, because that's exactly what you do. And that system of 'meritocracy' was not something that I have benefited from. My meritocracy was being black enough to assist on your black production or when you wanted to fill out an Arts Council diversity quota form to get more funding to keep minority ethnic creatives in training roles or assistant director jobs but not to be visibly seen as a stand-alone or even outstanding artist trying to build a career.

Because it's not a meritocracy.

It's not. It's biased. It's biased in ways that people don't want to admit to themselves or to the wider sector, industry, community, whatever. It's *incredibly* biased. Also, I'm a black guy with an African name, which already suggests that my lineage doesn't glorify the privileges of colonialism, so that doesn't make me any more palatable as an idea or an entity to European artistic leaders. So again it Others me in a way that they might not conceive of, even if I make that leap for them and go, "Actually, you've probably done that as well: how do we sell a show on Gbolahan's name, will people be able to read Gbolahan's name and go, 'I want to see a show by this guy', or if they find out he's a black African man, is that a selling point for them as an artist, as a theatremaker?" But I simply go, "It doesn't matter. Just show me the same level of respect and the same level of opportunity that you show other people, that you give other people. That's what you've got to do because I like what I do so I'm going to pour my all into it and try to get the best result out of the process, out of my collaborators and out of the work that we make."

But then what we don't take into account is the fact that however liberal *[theatre critic & commentator]* Lyn Gardner says she is or however liberal *[theatre critic]* Michael Billington says he is, or anyone else for that matter, they still have biases of their own as to how they review people. And those biases certainly influence how people that look like me are perceived, how our work is valued or devalued and ultimately how it affects the longevity of our careers.

With something like that it's difficult for me not to add my own thoughts and agendas, because that's not my role here . . .

So ask me the question.

Do they honestly know they have those biases? We're talking about white people who believe they're liberal and woke but offer no real sustainability in supporting the inequality that's actually around them — professionally at least. If they're standing up for Black Lives Matter, they're doing it on one level because it's flavour of the month and they need to professionally (and morally of course) address it before moving on to the next issue in line, because they don't have enough room to keep the things that need to be addressed and changed on the same table at the same time. It's not to question their desire for equity or sense of it, but the reality is not only do they not live it, they don't see others living it, and you can't help but wonder about the securely bubbled white middle class homes they go back to at the end of the day.

And I get it. I think sometimes it is about capacity, but then there's also the fact that once upon a time I got told to 'tell my story'. To make my story part of the narrative when people are considering me for the role. And I'm like no, the story is in the work that I do. The story is in the work that I've made and want to make. That's how it is for everybody 'white'. That's all you need to encounter or draw upon, so whether you read reviews or you phone up one of your mates and go, "Oh you know Gbolahan? What's he like and do you think he's the artist that everyone says he is?" And hopefully they say good things that make you go, "All right, thank you, because I missed the last show that he did" — and therefore you give me that opportunity in the same way as everyone else, which allows you room to imagine and to maybe call me up and ask me about someone else that you want to give an opportunity to that you don't know very well, right? But then what seems to be the default is that my story never mattered at all, and neither does what I've done or anything positive anyone has to say. Your precedence is the belief that you have autonomy over all stories and only those who fit your narrative and uphold your status quo and continue to benefit regardless of efforts towards social justice and equality.

I can't say all of that without acknowledging that resources play a factor and the fact that buildings have associates and they have to justify the reasons why they're on payroll and stuff like that, but then I don't know how you can basically do that season by season and still invite the same people back for successive seasons. That doesn't look like there's a window for broad representation or anyone new for that matter, to surprise or add to the narrative of what the work is being put out by your building — nor showing how you're trying to support a broad spectrum of artists from all different backgrounds and experiences. So that's incredibly disappointing and it's incredibly egotistical of certain institutional leaders to think that we can't suss that out, that we've haven't sussed you out.

They'll also blame their audience for it: "I'd love to . . . but our audience won't get it."

They either blame audiences or they don't even admit a lack of insight into the absent or those underrepresented in their programming. Because by exposing that reality you are ultimately admitting your own negative assumptions about people's capabilities, your negative assumptions of what people can do by not employing them. But all you have to do for the most part is say "have a read of this play, say what you think of it, ask would you like to do it?" That goes for directors of diverse backgrounds and prominent actors/performers from minority communities. Of course, artists will accept stuff because we're desperate to eat and we know that if it does well, *when* it does well, we hope to get other jobs. *[laughs]* Because you should learn to trust us. We don't want to fail, we don't want to just come in and muck it up.

I've not had too much at the top level myself. I did *The Last King of Scotland* last year *[2019]* on the main stage at Sheffield Crucible, and it was a risky production — risky because of the title, risky because of the legacy of its previous incarnation as an Oscar-winning film attached to it, and risky because the central protagonist was a deplorable manic, a sad spawn of colonialism. But I wanted that challenge and I also wanted to see how I could collaborate and be a creatively visionary at that level without feeling like a fish out of water. And again, on a mid-scale level I don't think I've had that much experience either . . .

Well that's still a career by theatre's standard.

But the point I was trying to make is that part of the psychosis and ego lies in the fact that theatre is still seen as a Eurocentric medium of expression. People haven't quite admitted to themselves that anyone else who isn't white can contribute to that narrative of innovation and excellence in theatre.

That's where some of the resistance and that unspoken desire to not promote, not encourage theatremakers from minority communities to make work at a prominent level comes from; because it stops being a eurocentric medium if you let someone who's Black or South Asian or East Asian, bring a different aesthetic or way of making work. You'd go, "Oh shit, we don't know where this person has come from. We don't know where their lineage of making work comes from or what's informed it. We have to be able to trace who they were an apprentice to, then attribute that aesthetic to that white individual, and so we can say they learned it off that white person." It's something that British theatre is trying not to admit to itself. But instead it should be going, "Oh shit, that's part of the psychology of where and why we don't want to give opportunities to people of minority background, because then they develop their own voice and their own forms of education within this industry that my grandad and my parents have invested in and I've invested in for so long, and then it stops being ours any more. We can no longer call it European theatre. We now have to share it."

Is there a thread in the way you work that conveys what you believe?

One thing I've always said to myself is that whether it's directing or writing — because I've committed myself to those areas — I have always tried to make sure that what I do is valuable and that it contributes to a wider narrative regarding representation. My main focus therefore has always been about visibility. I need to be visible so that other people who are upcoming can look at me and go, "If he's there and looks like me, then I should be able to do it, or I *can* do it and there's room for me to thrive there." The industry needs to understand that's the most important thing.

Otherwise, in terms of visibility, in terms of broad representation and inclusivity, you just need to understand that in this industry there will be no evolution of ideas or of the work that's being made. If you go to Germany and copy what they're doing there, you need to know that Germany has its own reasons for why they have a particular theatre aesthetic or theatrical response to the work that they put on. You need to know that part of it is because there is a big influx of Europeans from multiple European countries flooding to Germany to make work. They might all look white but they're all coming from different countries with different impulses and ideas about what theatre is. What you've got in Britain is a situation where we are still saying, you should be celebrating the multiple cultural representation of people, ideas and perspectives and how they respond to a piece of work and how they want to share that with other people.

So if you remove the resistance and instead celebrate and embrace that multiple cultural representation, then you're going to naturally evolve, based on the ecology of what's around you and how people want to represent humanity.

*

28

Miguel Oyarzun

'Theatre needs more than location, it also needs a community'

Miguel Oyarzun is a director, actor & co-director/founder with Isla Aguilar of BE Festival (UK) & Mirage Teatro (Spain). Based in Madrid, Spain, after living in London & Birmingham, he was born & raised in Madrid. • befestival.org

As Spaniards working both in the UK and Spain year-round, you and co-director Isla must have an amazing perspective on the workings of the performing arts in the UK. But in Spain itself, how do people get into theatre?

When I was 14, my parents took me to see a show called *La Vida es sueño ['Life Is a Dream']* at the Almagro Festival and that was when I knew I wanted to tell stories. I started theatre at school and then auditioned for RESAD, the equivalent of RADA in Spain. I got through and did four years of what was fairly traditional 'conservatoire' acting, and after graduating I worked as an actor in Madrid. I then got a grant to go abroad to continue my studies at LISPA *[London International School of Performing Arts]* in East London. I did a course in Lecoq technique there and that's how I discovered theatre was not only theatre where there's a director and actors, but there are also different ways of creating and devising. And not just theatre but performance and all the hybrids that exist.

I went to London with Isla, who is my partner in real life. When I finished my course, Isla had started a course in curating at Goldsmiths *[South London, part of University of London]* — she had previously worked more in the visual arts like at the Prado, at other museums in Spain and publishers of art books. So we started thinking of collaborating on projects and creating a company together.

At that time we met Mike Tweddle, a theatre director, through work we did together in CASA Festival in London, and we went to Birmingham to discover the city and see what the scene was like there. We had the idea of maybe establishing a company there, because London was a more difficult place to live. We had thought why don't we see what's going on outside, not just beyond the centre of London but beyond the outskirts of London?

We ended up on Birmingham in the context of a two-day conference held by the Arts Council, an open space run by Improbable to discuss how to improve the Midlands arts scene. To our surprise, they said there was a big need for international work from the sector. Everyone was saying that there wasn't enough international presence. So of course we were pleased with that, because we thought, well, we are both foreigners and in the city they might want work by international makers.

Suddenly that was an exciting prospect for us. Well, you know how these conferences work, they invite you to make suggestions and throw ideas into the ring, and so we asked, "When is the international theatre festival taking place in the city?" And again to our surprise, they said, "It isn't. There is no festival." There's a festival of performance Fierce Festival, and a festival of cinema Flatpack, a few music festivals, and there's a biennial festival of dance, IDFB. But there was no theatre festival as such.

And so we proposed the idea that there was a need for an international theatre festival in the region. We threw that in, not thinking we would be doing it but thinking that the city needed it. The idea was very well received by a lot of people in the room. Some even suggested that since we had already been travelling around with a few projects and taking part in festivals abroad — we had shared our experience with them — they thought it would be great having us do a new festival!

Perhaps it was a language thing, you know we had made our proposal in such a way that it sounded as if we wanted to do it — which wasn't on our mind — but anyway that day people thought that we were actually creating a theatre festival. Stan's Cafe [theatre company] instantly said that we could use the space they were using for rehearsal which was at the @AE Harris factory theatre.

So we went to visit the building, and within a day suddenly we had a space to create a festival — and a sector excited by us making a festival. So right then we thought, well, let's just write down what us as audience and us as artists would like this festival to be within the context of this city and what this city needs. And from that moment on, we knew that we needed to do two main things. Firstly to create a context to support emerging international artists in entering the UK market — because of the way things work with funding and so on, that is a massive challenge.

Especially via the portal of London of course.

Especially via London. So that was the first thing, knowing that it had to be international because that's what the city was demanding. Secondly, we needed to place ourselves within a space that was not already provided by the city, in other words that hybrid space found in the overlap of theatre, dance, performance — everything between those areas, because traditional theatre in Birmingham is covered by the existing theatres it has, but there was not an offer of contemporary international theatre. So we thought that the philosophy or ethos of the new festival would be to present work that crosses borders — cultural borders, work that crosses or is found in between international disciplines and linguistic borders.

And so we started BE Festival (shortened from 'Birmingham European Festival') which takes place every June/July now. In the first years, we were very careful to programme a lot of work that was non-verbal and/or physical. And when it was verbal, the text was not the only form present in the work. We also wanted work that crossed the border between audience and artist, more immersive, speaking to the audience in different formats like promenade, interactive and so on.

Another important element we decided to have was to create a space for encounter. We not only wanted to present work that speaks to every audience, but also to create spaces where the audiences can encounter the artists with the purpose of breaking down the border that sometimes exists between the general audience and the contemporary work.

One of the things we first encountered outside London was when you talk about European theatre for the general audience, people think this sort of work is not accessible. Of course there is work that is not accessible, but obviously that's not all there is. So when we programme, we try to present a combination of work that is challenging and work that is accessible and that is why we came up with the format that drives the festival. We are now starting to change it, but for the first ten years we have presented four shows a night of 30 minutes each, which give us the opportunity to in a single night to offer the audience a package in which they would see four different ways of working.

So on any one night you'll find what you would call audience-pleasers — circus-based, for example — along with shows more challenging both in content or in form. So that was the format we created, with an interval dinner in which audiences and artists would sit together to discuss the work they had just seen and then an evening with a DJ or party or concerts to mingle and again have the space to speak. So that's what the festival is, sharing that diversity from the beginning, having international work in a place where there's not so much international work.

From the first year we created a project along with the festival year that was just at the festival but then it grew to be an annual project for young people aged 14-19, a youth theatre programme aimed at young people who don't speak English as a first language or they speak another language at home.

Since Birmingham is one of the youngest cities in the UK and one of the most diverse, we knew we needed to acknowledge this in the programme and in the work we were doing. So we created a lab project we call BE Next. Depending on funding, three to five times a year we work in intensive periods for about ten days coinciding with the half-term and main school holidays. We put two artists who haven't worked together before and at least one of them doesn't have English as a first language. That way they establish a common ground with the teenagers who don't speak English as a first language either, and they work together to facilitate the process of creation for the young people to present a piece at the end of the project.

BE Next has enabled hundreds of young people over the last ten years to engage with performing arts for long periods with free access and the possibility to see international work that might talk to them because it's more diverse and more international. Some of the participants in this lab project have gone on to become performers, creators, directors, or they've actively used the tools they've acquired over the years for their own work. It has included a lot of refugees, asylum-seekers, people from neighbourhoods, from deprived areas in Birmingham, and it's working with ethnic diversities in a depth of ways.

You've also been building up a network of European theatre festivals?

Yes, it's aimed at emerging and mid-scale companies. The current network is formed with Amsterdam's Its Festival, Sarajevo's Mess Festival, Rome's Short Festival and Bilbao's Act Festival. In parallel to doing the festival and the network, Isla and I also started working as an independent theatre company. Something we've criticised in the past is that there are people who become directors of a festival and then they put on their own shows in the same festival. Of course we understand that, but, depending on how it's done, it might produce an ethical conflict of interest.

So we decided for our own ethics' sake to make our work very separate from BE, so we made the decision to work with our theatre company in Spain and have the festival in the UK. Also that way I could write in Spanish and wouldn't have English as a barrier. As a result we have been travelling many years back and forth between the two countries. The Spanish company, Mirage Teatro, specialises in community work — something that we've learned in the UK because it's very developed there compared to places like Spain. In the UK you have a long tradition of community work but in Spain there's very very little. Everything that we learned from the work that is created in the UK we've been able to transpose to Spain, and we created a sequence of community-based projects.

One of the shows was *Quijotadas ['Quixotics' in Spanish]*, which toured over a three-year period, working with Africans who had travelled to Spain via different routes and who basically at the time had no papers *['sin papeles', the equivalent of 'illegal immigrant']*. The show took their journeys from Africa to Spain and linked them to that of Don Quijote *[Miguel Cervantes' novel is a national classic studied at school by everyone in Spain]*, where the main character thinks the world is one way but encounters a reality that is very different to how he imagines it. We put that in parallel to the life of migrants from Africa to Europe, working with communities for three years and touring to Teatro Español, Spain's equivalent of the Barbican, and other venues around the country.

In Madrid you and Isla used that radical programming to make an overnight transformation of the prominent but underused, undervalued and directionless Conde Duque municipal cultural centre in the heart of Madrid. And then they sacked you for achieving precisely that transformation [in November 2019]?

Yes, it's unfortunate to say the least. Madrid's *[right-wing populist, recently elected at the time]* city council is intervening in culture, and that's the situation in the whole country. Culture is not independent from politics, at least not to the level it is in the UK.

Conde Duque is a massive old edifice in the centre of the city where nothing much was happening, and your appointment there to oversee its revamp was a key part of Madrid City Council's plan under the leftwing mayor Manuela Carmena to create a 'cultural spring'. The rightwing then got voted in, like everywhere else in the world it seems, and her plan was promptly demolished.

Manuela Carmena's vision was to attract practitioners with experience in cultural management of festivals and organisations elsewhere in Spain and beyond. In 2018, after an open application process, the council appointed Isla and me as joint-artistic directors — we job-shared — of Conde Duque, which, as you say, lacked direction and was underused. It's an 18th century building, a former royal barracks with 58,777 square metres of infrastructures used for cultural purposes. *[Also home to the Archivo de la Villa, the Historical Library, the Municipal Library and the Biblioteca Digital Memoria of Madrid.]*

We transformed a centre dedicated to mere exhibition into a centre for creation. In less than two years, we maximised our capacity for R&D and supported more than 40 projects, including national and international co-productions. In just one year of programming, and despite all the difficulties, the centre improved its income, diversity and audience with an increase of more than 35 per cent. In short, we carried out the artistic remit that we were contracted to do.

Since 2019 was a year of particular political turmoil for Spain when culture came very visibly under relentless attack by the right, it can't have come as much of a surprise to find yourselves a target.

The reasons offered by the new city council were based on unfounded accusations of management issues — which were cleared by an internal investigation as a historic problem linked to Madrid Destino, the already existing company that formally runs the venue and which we weren't a part of — and they also tried to show that there was a conflict with our roles as artistic directors of BE Festival, despite having signed a contract with a clause that specifically allowed us to maintain that pre-existing position.

But the reality is that we inherited a system that didn't work and already had all those problems. When we started with our own programming in September 2018, we already had a decimated team from months before. As artistic directors we were not part of the official corporate hierarchy of Madrid Destino. As such, we had no say in anything related to the pre-existing team or new positions. We weren't able to modify staff duties for new projects, not even be part of the selection process for new staff.

I've seen that Spain's artistic sector nationally have made it very clear that the dismissal is a purely political act and they have very vocally supported you. And yet many of them too are facing exactly the same threat to their positions.

Yes, in Madrid alone, the artistic directors of M21 Radio, CentroCentro arts centre and Fernán Gómez Theatre, all appointed by open public competitions, have also come under attack. It's not hard to see the connection. Our programme in the last months addressed topics such as the refugee and climate crises, the revision of historical memory. Many of the artists involved in our programmes aim to provoke thought and to question our preconceptions.

The new party in power on the council, Partido Popular, is there with the support of the extreme right and such topics are not well received. Our sacking is an attack on artistic freedom. Of course we're open to starting new projects in Spain but we are also open to moving elsewhere if the right project appears. After all, we belong to a generation that is now so often forced to migrate in search of opportunities.

Politicians having that sort of interference in culture in the UK is uncommon, whereas in Spain it's unfortunately very common. It happens, but it's such a shame because the problem is that culture, especially driven by political issues, cannot thrive because politicians intervene and don't let the projects happen. For a cultural project to happen properly, you need to provide time and resources so you can thrive. And when the projects start to happen, then political change starts to happen — the politicians want to have their say and put people they trust in positions of influence. They don't respect the public open calls for work or transparent processes of selection of artistic directors and other positions in the sector. It's a very sad situation. And after working from the UK where it's all very different, the shock is even greater for us.

What is that difference?

To start with, in the UK the Arts Council is a model which of course has its flaws, but it's still a great model because it puts the art and the artists and the audience at the centre. The people who run and guide the Arts Council are professionals from the sector, so in general there's very little political involvement in how it operates — other than, effectively, its budget. Actual policy is very much decided by professionals, with some guidelines and criteria that obviously need to have some sort of connection with the politicians in government, but they are still very much independent in a vast majority of the decisions. That therefore has an impact on the whole cultural sector in the UK because the Arts Council is the main body of support for the arts. So this provides support, steady support that has little or no connection with the changes of politics of whether there's a Conservative or Labour government in power. There are political implications of course in the levels of funding available, but that's something else.

Of course these are times when the Arts Council is less involved because of lack of funds and so on, but its level of involvement in the arts compared to a country like Spain is massive. The Arts Council in the UK has an independence that provides the arts with a solidity, a base on which artists can attract and build other sorts of support. Importantly, it also gives the artists the independence to say whatever they want.

However, in Spain culture is politicised and therefore the support is politicised. That particularly affects the position of artistic directors. There's a few exceptions, like when we were selected for Conde Duque it was by an open call and so it had nothing to do with any political party, but in most cases it's done purely by designation. The directors of the main public venues and centres are chosen by the politicians in the government — local or regional or at state level. And that brings politics directly into culture, because if you are selected by a political government or political party, then work you are going to present will be of a certain kind. You can say it won't be, but it will be.

The artist programmed within that project will be associated with a particular party and so on. And so culture becomes a political question. This is a huge barrier if you are an artist who understands that, regardless of what party you belong to, we are confronting problems in the world that affect all of society. But that point of view which you take on those issues as an artist will be questioned and opposed by the political side. And therefore culture becomes a political asset.

So for example, if an artistic director manages to improve audience levels at a theatre, it is taken as a positive political achievement by the government. It shouldn't be like that because it's down to the artistic director, their team and everyone at the theatre. If we create a good programme or a good project, it has nothing to do with the politicians. If it's politicised it's used as a political weapon, so culture is being used as a political weapon. So when you hold a public cultural position in Spain like the one we held, you are in the middle of a political situation.

Obviously it shouldn't be like that. Any funder in that position of control should seek to be independent and focused on supporting the arts, supporting the artists who work for the audiences, getting society to participate in the projects you create and make happen. That's the main difference from the political approach to culture, and it's a huge difference. The situation is similar in other countries such as Italy, and it's one that should change and needs to change so that both artists and audiences can take more risks in the work and experiencing the work. Otherwise, your artists and audiences are contained and limited within a political fight.

But culture in general and theatre in particular have always been vulnerable as an art form to this sort of thing.

To political interference? Oh yes. The direction I'm coming from is that it's like having a kid. You have to send the kid to school, so you have to pick the school that's near you. Maybe you can go to another town or even country if you think it's better there, but if you live where you live, you have to pick that school near you. So your choice is limited. It's the same thing with theatre. If you want to make theatre, it's something that's very time and people intensive but, because of its nature, it's not a negative thing. So you have to make the commitment and if you find the funding from somewhere, then you have to go with it.

But then you have to deal with the problems that come with that funding. Perhaps you have already recognised from the start that you are vulnerable to making that commitment but you're not flexible enough to move to another town or region or another country. Well you can. You can make a film anywhere, can't you? You can paint pictures anywhere and exhibit them anywhere. But with theatre you can't do that. You need more than location to do it, you also need a community. You need a theatre, a space, and all the rest of it. You need a season, then similar spaces if you're doing a tour, all of which requires fixed defined spaces.

In fact each art form has its particular difficulties. The budget and time required, for example, to create a single film is much much greater than a theatre play. So one could say that cinema is even more difficult than theatre in that regard, because a film involves many more people to make it than a play and far more money. A writer has different problems, and so on. So every art form has its problems, and what is at stake overall at the moment is the kind of system we want to put in place to support the arts. Because ultimately, entertainment is one big thing, which is fantastic and which is why there is a private sector that thrives in many countries and then can support artists that are involved in that area of the arts.

That's absolutely fine and valuable both for audiences and artists — and also for the business people involved in the private sector. Of course it's important that places like the West End are thriving. This is something that *[theatre critic & commentator]* Lyn Gardner was saying in an article a few months ago: if you want a new Shakespeare-literate generation to happen and for them to write the new plays that in a few centuries we'll be discussing at school because they depict our society, and they'll really be putting those problems out there, then you need to support the art for that to happen.

So why, for example, is dance thriving in Belgium, and why now? Why are so many of the choreographers currently turning international dance upside-down based in Belgium at the moment? There's a simple reason for that: in Belgium they decided to bet on that and they have invested, from the government downwards, the support for this to happen. They have the 'statut de l'artiste' system *[French for 'artist status', in Dutch 'statuut van kunstenaar']* which guarantees artists unemployment support when they are not performing, allowing them to generate new work and do R&D. So this is like supporting scientists in the labs. You try out things, most of the time they don't work but if you keep on trying, sometimes you arrive at something fantastic. Otherwise you end up doing things that you know, which is also fine but it won't change the sector, it won't change the art form, it won't evolve the art form.

You know, it comes down to very basic questions like what is it that needs support from the public sector, from the Arts Council, from the governments? Do we need to support the fact that there is just art, entertainment, culture, or do we need to support the fact that we allow artists to investigate, go out there and discover new ways of confronting stories and creating forms? This is why it's so important that bodies such as the Arts Council or the 'artist status' schemes in Belgium or in France happen and are not cut. They need to be independent and to have adequate resources for the cultural sector to enable the particularity of theatre to thrive along with sectors such as the visual arts or writing. It needs to be collaboratory work that also needs the audience to be in on it, and therefore demands that not only the process of creation be supported, but also the process of exhibiting and distributing the work. It needs to support people so they understand the value of that support and of making the work accessible through research, innovation, development of new ways of telling stories.

But obviously this needs to be developed through a large structure so the distribution and exhibition accompanying the processes of contemporary work can be understood and not rejected by audiences. Because in the end, contemporary work is contemporary, meaning relevant to now, so it should be for people who live now. But sometimes it happens that there's a rejection of contemporary work because it's either less accessible or because we are not giving the tools to audiences to access this work. If I had seen some of the work that I see now 15 years ago, I probably wouldn't have liked it or understood it in the way I do now. But the reason that I access that differently is because I am now able to see a lot of work and a wide range. That's how you develop a taste, how you develop some criteria. It's a process that takes time and also people around you to help you do that. And that's what I think the structures, both theatre and governmental, need to do — to completely get behind supporting contemporary art and making it more accessible.

The UK is a good place to do that, given the interplay between the commercial work and the funded sector, which within the global context is definitely a unique ecosystem. Do you have any insights from observing the commercial way of doing theatre as it weaves in and out of the funded stuff?

I think that the big difference between the UK and other countries in terms of what is commercial is that in the UK there is a such a huge industry. It's the extensive structure, not only in London but in the rest of the country, that makes commercial work thrive. Plus there's the fact that English as a language helps as a common interface. The West End works profitably because it represents top quality, and that's undeniable. The work there has a standard that is done to the levels of professionalisation of the culture scene as an industry. That's the real difference between the UK and a country like in Spain where the industry is yet to be fully professionalised, although of course there is very successful work in the Spanish commercial area.

Standards are growing more and more, and there will be a point where all the actors will come from conservatoires with training to the high level that's currently found in the UK's drama schools and so on. But that takes time and of course in the UK this has been happening for a long time. In other countries you have to realise that it's yet to be developed or is in development.

In terms of the funding structures connecting with the commercial sector, that's a huge debate, i.e. where do you draw the line, which has huge implications for the future of culture. I don't exactly know where that line is in the UK for the simple reason that I haven't been involved in projects that merge the commercial and the public sides.

The commercial aspect that works in the UK can work too in Spain if it's done properly and professionally, with the right support and without interference. The difference is just how big that cultural industry can grow. But we do need to be aware that there is a difference between 'cultural industry' and 'culture', they're not the same. If we are in a cultural industry then we are costifying, we are reifying, we are making products. We know what works, what doesn't work. We do it with the purpose of selling tickets. I think that's perfectly fine. But culture shouldn't be just about selling tickets. Of course we do the work for audiences to see it, but ultimately many artists do work for something beyond that, work that has social value, a value that has to do with social cohesion, with ethics that don't necessarily have their place within a commercial structure.

In the public sector, we should be supporting those ethics. And that's why when it comes to the Arts Council you need to tickbox certain things. Of course it's perverse the way some people tick the boxes just to get the funding. Of course that happens and that's not right. But you should always find a way that allows you to describe how the work you're doing with public money will have a value that goes beyond the cultural industry, work that has research value, social value and all the things that reflect us in art and culture.

And if we're talking about bringing extra value to something, food seems to perfectly sum up bringing people together. Without wishing to impose any cultural stereotype, I'm still guessing that the fact that you're Spanish allows you to bring a extra sensitivity for the idea of food to link up with art. Did BE Festival's concept of eating evolve over time or was it integral from the beginning?

What came first was that idea of crossing the border, the gap between artists and audiences. In the programme obviously we do that, but we also set out to cross borders in what's *around* the programme and therefore we looked at what we could do during the day or outside the black box that provides the encounter with theatre. We realised that food could be a perfect moment to break that barrier. In Latin cultures, in Mediterranean cultures — just like you've seen in the movies — people really do gather to eat on the terraces in the villages with their long tables. You sit, you eat and drink, and you meet strangers and start conversations with people you might not know but you're sharing that time where there's not the pressure of doing anything else but to eat, drink and talk. So we thought, why don't we do that, and provide a space for people to encounter, relax, have a glass of wine and food. We started doing it, and it's one of the key elements that has stayed from year one. It's something that has been most valued by both audiences and professionals who come to the festival.

You can have a programmer sitting side by side with an audience member for whom it's the first time they've seen contemporary work like this. Of course, after a couple of shows the first thing you are going to be talking about with people you don't know is the shows you've just seen. And then over dinner that can lead all into, say, a debate about the art in those shows. That's valuable because it makes you acknowledge that there are so many things that unite us, despite someone having more knowledge about something or coming from a different background. In the end, you have all experienced the same thing and you're now all experiencing the same thing.

We started with a London catering company Blanch & Shock, who have worked with artists and companies in combining theatre and food. Now we're working with the local caterers of the theatre building itself — it's a different experience, but everything's all in one place! Before, we had to create a kitchen and all the logistical aspects to make the catering happen. Now the kitchen is on site and it's a far simpler process. When we've gone on tour, we've replicated the model. In some places we've had tapas and it's worked really well. In other places we've had dinner, like at the Barbican Centre [in Central London] and the Traverse Theatre [in Edinburgh]. It's always been one of the elements, and the audience has always valued the fact that you can sit with the artists, have dinner and exchange with other audience members your thoughts about the work. It's a relaxed environment, not a Q&A session in an auditorium where there's pressure to answer a question with a smart answer. Around the table, you can just say, "I liked it" or "I didn't like it" and then the conversation starts and it's from another point of view. It's not where your question or your comment is heard by all the people around, but by your neighbour.

That's the value of theatre. To expand that ritualistic aspect of all being together in the same room, watching something together, to expand beyond that moment and create spaces where that moment can flourish. And from our experience, over food it really really works!

*

29
Francesca Peschier

'What can I do with the building,
how can I make that useful?'

*Francesca Peschier, dramaturg, writer,
lecturer & head of new works at the
Liverpool Everyman & Playhouse
theatres. Based in Liverpool, she was born
in London & raised in Croydon.*
• *everymanplayhouse.com, @FrankPeschier*

*Funding must be something of an all-consuming distraction particularly for a
theatre — as a building, you literally can't run away from it.*

We are gruesomely underfunded, though obviously I can't speak for all of the
North. I did go to Venues North yesterday *[a network of venues from across the
North of England committed to supporting artists to create new work]* and it's funny
listening across the venues to find that everyone has the same problem. It's not
helped by this cherrypicking exoticism of the North that still exists. There's
still the image that everyone has whippets and flat caps, that every single piece
of work that has to come out is *Educating Rita*, that the place hasn't moved on,
which is just not true. If you live here, you know that's not true. But it's really
hard to fight against that assumption of what a Northern show looks like.

The problems are obvious. The first is money and underfunding. The
second is reputation. Particularly in Liverpool where we have a changed
theatre ecology today, meaning that we have a relatively large amount of
theatres in a small space and very low disposable income. If you're, say, Story
House in Chester *[Cheshire]*, you just don't have that sort of problem: you are
the theatre to give money to, compared to Liverpool at least. And then there's
the thing of people thinking of the North West as a big homogenous blob,
that all of the North is the same. The difference between the identity of

Newcastle and Liverpool is *huge* and it always really annoys me because people don't do that with the South. They don't expect somebody from Kent to represent somebody from Bristol, do they? That drives me absolutely up the wall.

The problem with the North as well is that Liverpool isn't London. Now, I don't actually particularly like the word 'diverse', I don't tend to use it because I think it's a bit nonsensical. I like 'representative'. Is your theatre *representative* of modern Britain? Is it *representative* of modern Liverpool?

It's the way that we're representative that is interesting. Looking at playwrights, for example, and breaking that down of we are, is really really representative in terms of LGBTQ+ and class representation. But for in terms of representation of black and minority groups, there's myriad reasons why we're still not fully representative, but so much of that comes down to not having the resources. I've just made the point that Northern theatres are often expected to answer as the servant to a lot of masters whilst not having the resources or the privileges London theatres to do the same thing. One of the best conversations I had in that line was at a theatre in London where someone made the comment, "Oh, we'll just ask our legal department about that." All I could think was that the person who looks at anything legal in our theatre is the same person who does the payroll, does the admin, and even orders the stationery, we just don't have that kind of team. Our 'new works department' is *me*. I'm not a department. I'm one person with a plastic rat on my desk.

We can't do everything. We have to choose what we *can* do and accept that we'll still get a lot of stick for not doing everything. The problem with London is that there are London theatres that actually have the resources to do everything, or what they should be doing, but they aren't doing it — and there's a relatively small amount of people competing for the same thing. There's also things like when I go to literary managers' meetings, everybody's like me, nearly everyone is middle class and white and mostly female. I'm very conscious and aware of that because I fear it means that you're only going to get one type of 'product'.

London in particular — I'm not going to say the South — is where the commercial theatres take up so much space because they can afford to fail. So space is at a premium there, just getting rehearsal space and things for small companies is getting increasingly hard because the high cost and availability of everything is such a squeeze. There is too much of what I think of as coach party theatre and you just think, this is taking up so much space, where's the space for new writing or something truly innovative? And it makes me question whether that really is what people want to see?

Well that also highlights who can and can't risk a long run for a show that deserves it. In London, you can put on a lucrative show for months or even years, which just couldn't possibly happen in Liverpool or most other places to be honest. Your main option I suppose, if you work on it, is to extend your panto by a month, but the idea of spinning it off elsewhere afterwards, well, it's just not going to happen.

Because we can't afford it. That's the number one thing. It's not that the will isn't here, and it's *not* that the talent isn't here. You'll find the will and talent all across the North. Actually in Liverpool our talent development is very strong, and it's not just us, you'll find the same everywhere in Liverpool. For example, the Unity Theatre has a great creative development programme, 20 Stories High are doing amazing work. We're a major university city, and of course we've got really great grassroots artists, groups like the Lantern Writers, Kazamia, Take Stock, Black Fest — it's really happening here. There *are* those voices, there *are* people making, there *are* people getting through. What we don't have after this point is an opportunity to put on that as mid-scale work. So you've written your first script, you've been through a writers' programme, done a couple of scratches. What next? That's the bit that's missing, and it needs funding for theatres to take chances on those first-time writers and artists and creatives who haven't been out there before.

And it's true you need to do that, because you'll see it proved when something does manage to get to London and it'll be like, "This 'unknown' writer!" You go, "Yeah, they're *not* 'unknown'. They had a full run at the Studio at Sheffield Theatres." It can be very frustrating if it happens that you're known as an artist, you've taken your time for development, but there isn't the money to do that first play. And then it goes on in London. For example, Sunderland, they just haven't had the theatres or the arts centres or the accessible training experience trying things out, having the space to fail.

I was speaking to Helen Hallenby, who runs the Sunderland Arts Centre *[in Tyne & Wear]*, and she was saying that the area has loads of people who have never been in a theatre before and are keen to go, and they're starting from absolute scratch as opposed to if they opened up somewhere in, say, Finsbury Park *[North London]* where half the people would have already had a reading of their play at the Park Theatre. You know, there isn't the theatre ecology in a place like Sunderland.

Which identifies a fairly key feature of the theatre business — if you don't have access to it, audience and practitioner alike need to move. And obviously if you don't have the wherewithal to move socially or financially, you just stay where you are and work with what you're given. But in the case of Liverpool we're talking about a city that is well connected, has its own international airport, a big university like you said, and a constantly vibrant network of communities. I know a lot of Nordics, for example, who say that Liverpool's cool and accessible. They prefer to go there than London. And yet the gulfs remain, and those who can, leave.

Definitely. There's great essay somewhere that's called something like 'The Great Migration' about basically just how many people finish their skills training, not just in the arts but across all the subjects in the North, and then they move. So then you get a skills vacuum. It's that incredibly shortsighted funding thing that if you don't provide the opportunities and the routes for progression for those people, then they'll leave.

Down South, not everyone understands those gulfs because we're not talking about a smaller pool of resources, we're also talking about the more limited vistas for work that has a commercial rationale. A far higher percentage of mainstage work for example needs funding, and that's a problem because there's the attitude of 'let the market dictate'. But that raises the spectre of the word 'sustainability'. So what is sustainable in Liverpool in particular, in the North, in general?

Before looking at what's sustainable, a really interesting conversation I had once was with someone who was on a theatre board, not ours. And they said, "I don't understand why you can't have something like a *[American musical]* Hamilton that's modern and contemporary but also really commercial!" But do they seriously think *Hamilton* just rocked up fully formed? Is that what they think happened? *Hamilton* was developed at the Public Theater in New York over the course of a couple of years. If you haven't got the money for that R&D, that training to put 20 actors in the room with a proper choreographer and to pay Lin-Manuel *[Miranda, creator of the American musical]*, well you don't get *Hamilton*.

I don't understand how people think you just pay up straightaway and the product's finished. There's no consideration of time in that attitude — the timeline of theatre is completely different to other industries. Again there's the attitude that you don't need time to develop anything that isn't funded, trusting in the fact that it's a commercial product. Now I'm not anti-mainstream product, but how many shows have we seen close in the West End because somebody had a commercial idea but didn't spend the time to do it well?

So . . . what's sustainable in Liverpool? Before I joined the theatre, I did my PhD on the Everyman *['Theatre Design in Regional Theatre: Realising the Visual at The Liverpool Everyman and Playhouse 2003-2015'],* so I've had a longstanding relationship here and looked at its peaks and troughs ever since its inception — and in fact we don't really know what's sustainable because the city's changing all the time. You need to make work that develops your artistic community, provides those opportunities for them and builds up that sense in the city of theatre as a cultural hub but also as a social place to hang out. I'm not sure if theatre anywhere outside the West End can survive by what's on the stages alone.

So it's everything around it. We've turned the Playhouse into a 'life room' on Mondays and Tuesdays — it's an initiative with Mersey Care and is a mental health supported space. That to me is firstly what theatre should be, but it's also thinking more widely, if one of the biggest assets we've got is buildings, what else do we do with buildings? I'm fascinated by a stage manager from the 1940s at the Playhouse called Maud Carpenter. She used to keep this really anally retentive log of every ice cream and chocolate sold and how popular they were. You can tell a hell of a lot about who's coming to your theatre by what chocolate they buy. So it's everything, it's having a buzzing cafe, it's having a restaurant. If I have my own theatre, if somebody gave me a load of money and said, right, okay, you're going to run your theatre, do you know what the first thing I'd put in is?

Chocolate?

No, a creche. Apart from a stage, of course. I don't understand why there isn't a creche in every business, because you're missing out on a whole generation, particularly of women, who can't bring their kids to work. That's the question that is always brought up by Parents in Performing Arts *[PiPA]*, who are amazing and do incredible work, why don't we just build a creche? It's about changing the whole ethos of how we work as buildings, not just what's on the stage, and that's how you become sustainable.

So sustainability is in the proof of what you do, not what you set out to do?

It's in the proof of what you do and that proof of everything is across the whole building. It's not just 'this is what we're going to programme', it's — and I hate this expression, it's so corporate — 'thinking 360'. It's also what you set out to do, but what do you set out to do in your *cafe?* That's to me what sustainability is. It's funny when you do forecasting for shows and people go, "But that sold so well in 2014, right?" Yeah, but that was a different time. I don't know if that would sell now. People's hearts and minds change so quickly, and a theatre has to know that.

But on the other hand, we do have to live in that changing world and it's hard to keep up, even with the right backing. We've seen it with the Arts Council revamping the museums and libraries to hand them over to the people — the ones that haven't closed down, that is.

It's interesting that Mersey Care Life Rooms started in libraries and it was one of the biggest things they had with the council coming in and going, "We have to do this, so we're going to put in loads of tech and screens." And Mersey Care were going, "Cool. You need more chairs. There's nowhere for anyone to sit. If you want people to stay in the space. You need somewhere for them to sit down. You haven't got any *chairs*." And they kept the library, they put free wifi in, they put some computers in, but also people who would show you how to do your benefits forms, an affordable cafe, a stitch and bitch circle, like *that's* the stuff that makes the building work. You know, it's not always big and flashy.

Theatre as social service really. A town doesn't need an opera house, but it does need a theatre, and actually do most people care what it does? So long as it just does.

I agree. It's supposed to be only football and theatre where people's heartbeats synchronise when they're watching it. And I know it's really cheesy, but there's something important about theatre being somewhere that people can come and, like football, laugh together and be *angry* together. I quite like theatre that makes you angry, but that will only get people to come and watch that if it's in a space where they feel comfortable, where they feel welcome. We're called the 'Everyman' for fuck's sake. We belong to Liverpool. Liverpool doesn't owe us anything.

So is there any particular quirk, trick or secret that the Everyman has to bring everyone in?

No, I don't think so. I'm not holding Everyman up as a paragon of brilliance, but what we *are* doing now — which maybe wasn't our priority when we have focused on other things like doing company and stuff — is listening. I think we're getting a lot better at that.

Someone who really listens is Chris Sonnex at the Bunker Theatre *[in London, now closed]* — he just does what he hears. To then turn your theatre over to the artists and have those takeovers and do what he's doing on *minuscule* money is incredible. I am such a fan. So I don't think there's any secret, all you can do is try and listen and also to be out there in your city. I know of people in engagement-type roles or artistic-type roles who don't know the place they live. They don't *know*, I don't even like the word, their 'community'.

If you read *Mouthpiece* by Kieran Hurley *[based in Glasgow]*, there's a bit in it where a woman meets a young lad. She's a playwright, his mum's a heroin addict, and she says to him, you know, people like you, it's your voices that are what we need on stage, I just want to help represent you and your community. He says, oh so you're one of those cunts! And I love that so much. I've stuck it above my desk, like don't be one of those cunts, because it shouldn't be the 'community' of Bradford, the 'community' of Leeds. If you work there, that should be *your* community. You should know those people you should bump into them in the pub and feel friends with them. And if you don't do that, then I think it's insincere bullshit.

All theatres like ours have to be very aware that having a building is a massive privilege. So you've got the building, okay, but I can't afford to do anything on stage. Well what can I do with the building, how can I make that useful? I started the Spare Rooms Scheme here, which basically gives away rehearsal space for free, so it's brought a whole group people in who wouldn't normally use it.

So a theatre building brings a whole other level of demand on top of an already strained budget. But unlike an office block, it really is a living organism and needs to be treated as such. But it's money again, literally the life blood.

There's a difference between how you take risks and how you consider risk-taking. What I mean is that at the National or even to a lesser extent like the Soho *[theatre in Central London]* is that you have access to an increased R&D budget that allows you to muck about with stuff. This idea of filling the hopper with work that's ready to go relies on allowing that a certain percentage of that work will never happen.

This is true of any theatre, but I think at the Everyman our pastoral care management is bit more complex, which means it's important not to pay lip service to having writers' programmes or unsolicited submissions which then never lead to anything. I heard the other day how many applications a major national playwriting prize, which I won't name, received and it was a thousand more than they were expecting. There are a lot of writers out there, there are a lot of people wanting to get their work on, and it's no good saying oh yes you'll listen to everyone and read everything if you can't actually offer anything.

So what we try and do here is to have a multi-stranded pathway for talent development. So you can be on the writers' programme, you can be in a scratch studio, you might get a seed commission, you might do a short form or short studio show. The studio is only for local artists and it's a launchpad for them. But there are lots of other ways you can do work that aren't necessarily a full commission. Another word I've never liked is 'emerging', but for companies who haven't had their first full professional run it's particularly difficult for them to understand how that works. I get a lot of people asking, "Why can't you just put the show on?" Well, because an actor is £450 a week. So you have to find ways that are not asking people to work for free and that aren't exploitative, where everybody is still getting something out of it.

In terms of the type of work, there is one show called *YMAM* by Majid Mehdizadeh which is a good example of someone who did the playwright's programme. He finished it in 2018 and then shared a ten-minute short piece of work in a writers' showcase that we did in the Playhouse Studio. It was a good piece of work, we really liked his voice, but we didn't think it was the right piece of work. And then he came to us with another idea, we gave him a seed commission to develop that, he then got match funding from the Arts Council for that and he developed a piece of work. It's about anger and masculinity, and it mixes grime and spoken word, rap, and projection. And he'll come back and do development on that and then he's having a two-night run in the Ev1 space which is our Young Everyman space.

So he can do it in there because he has young actors involved in helping him make it, it's being teched and designed by our young technicians, so they benefit from it, he gets to show his show, he does one sold night and he does one industry invitation night. So it's not just "we're going to put on your show", it's "this is a fully mentored thing that benefits you, benefits us that we've invested in an artist that we think is very good, who's got a good idea, and it's also benefited the young people at the theatres as well." So if you haven't got all the resources for being able to pick the projects, even if that show never ends up on the mainstage or it never ends up in a full run, still something useful has come out of it for the artist and something useful has come out of it for the theatre.

It's the rising costs that are affecting a big block to access from a creative point of view but also from the audience's point of view and therefore it's also a block to the venues themselves putting on stuff. It's like composers who write symphonies but there's no way to get an orchestra to play them. I think it was the BBC that came up with the idea of picking up an emerging composer's work, getting it properly scored out and then they might just get one concert out of it, which from the creator's point of view is amazing. In your case it must be heartbreaking to see a steady stream of proposals but not have the capacity to give them a chance. You don't know what talent you're losing, do you? And you must have to say no a lot.

There was a big gathering at Venues North a couple of weeks ago about how we say no to artists and how do we say no in a way that is not crushing and not bad for people's mental health, but also is a clear no? It's a bit like casting, where people don't hear back a no and then they hear that someone else got it, and then that's really hard for them but also it takes a lot of time. And then there's some people where it's a no to this, but we like you and there's some people where it's a never. And how can you be honest about that and not give people false hope, or signpost something that might be better, something that's more right for them?

So rejection is part of the creative process, in a way.

But how do you know if you've said something that might then go on to have a life elsewhere? It's funny, we actually had someone come through the other day who was like, "You said no to my show and then it went on to have a great run somewhere else." Good! I'm not sad, I'm happy for you. It wouldn't necessarily have had that great life with us. There was a *reason* I said no.

The interrelationship of your twin theatres, the Everyman and Playhouse, means that you're also open to picking up work that is already perfectly formed, not just touring stuff from elsewhere but also work that comes from within your 'community' — which just happens to be extraordinarily vibrant.

Definitely, and yes we do get stuff that's fully formed, but then that wouldn't tend to go through me so much. Because my role is much more about current development and new work and stages. If things that come from the community are ready to go then they would go to Programming.

If you hear of work in the community that's bubbling away and getting audiences, and you realise that it may work in a street or in a community centre but might not work as well within a more formal theatre setting, do you get involved in projects at that sort of level?

That tends to come out of the triangulation in what we do between artistic and what we in this department call 'creativity and social change'. So there are projects that sit in between there. For example, there was a project with sex workers called *Jewels* — they created a show which was basically a Nativity and it was performed in the community. That's an example of something that wouldn't be a mainstage show, so we go out and do it in the community. In terms of picking shows that are already happening elsewhere, I just think because it's already perfectly formed and existing well in that environment, why would you try and make it into something it isn't? So what I would do is approach that company and see what other ideas they have.

Tell me a bit more about that triangulation process.

For a lot of theatres, the engagement with the community either sits in either an engagement type of activity or education programme, which tend to be outside the main programme. We made a really conscious decision last year that if it comes under artistic, it comes under artistic, so that's everything. And whilst things have different financial weightings and resource weightings, in terms of the ethos of us as a building, everything is valued equally. So that means if it's a choice between us doing something that's (a) very promotional or (b) something which is in our community, and we're not sure that way, we might well go with (b). Sometimes that means making a choice on something that isn't profitable but we'll do it anyway.

We also have a role that's quite unique, I think, which is called the Community Catalyst. She works as part of the creative and social change team and one of her main responsibilities is to feed back ideas and concerns but also stories of interest that are coming from the community. So for example, we did a play in 2006 called *Unprotected* about the legislation of the red light district in Merseyside. There's been a growing concern in the community about how that red light district is functioning over ten years on, so we're looking at what sort of work we could do to respond to that, which also involves those people that are concerned. So it's not story-mining, it's not nicking people's experiences and co-opting them into theatre, but it is having a direct joined-up approach to how we try and make theatre that is led by, not just for, in a patronising way, the community.

You say that this is unusual practice and it was only last year you decided to do that, so how did it come about? Is this a natural product of the constant evolution of your theatres or are there specific circumstances that create opportunities like this, such as being linked to a funding remit?

It's no secret that the theatre had to come out of the NPO [*Arts Council long-term funding as a 'national portfolio organisation'*], and in order go back into the NPO we had to be much more explicit about our values. It's not that the theatre hasn't been doing those things, it always has been, but we were not very good at talking about it. I was telling someone from London the other day about our youth theatre and I don't think there is another youth theatre that has six strands in the work we do — it has actors, directors, but also producers, marketers, technicians, writers. I don't think that's standard. And it's free, they put on full shows on the mainstage and they're good shows. So we've always been doing it, we just don't really speak about it so we decided to make it a really explicit part of what our business plan is and our API is — 'this is how we work'.

Tell us more about the youth theatre.

Of the six strands, the actors have a much wider remit because they can start from drama club level, so you can get quite little ones in there. But most of the strands are 18-25, and they vary. It launched in 2012. We had a youth theatre before then, but the YEP *[Young Everyman Playhouse]* model started in 2012. The actors can start quite young and some of them stay in YEP for five years, and they come to do one largescale scripted show, and one largescale devised show in a year, but they also do loads of other things during the year as well. So that's the two big built-in stuff.

And then we have YEP directors as a two-year course, and they get to direct their own play with using the YEP actors. YEP writers is a two-year course as well, which is a bit different — in the first year it's a weekly taught course with the writer Joe Ward Munrow and then in the second year they get mentored by me. So that's interesting as it gets a bit self-selecting as to who carries on and who doesn't. So we've only operated the writers under that model since 2019 and so out of the six we had last year there's two who really stuck with it, and that's good because YEP writers is meant to be very entry level where some people do it and then come out the end and go, "Doing a play's not for me." And that's fine. What it's meant to be is, "You've got an interesting voice and you think you'd like to write for the stage, so this is where you start to find out."

YEP producers produce a big final piece, and they've done some really exciting things in the past, things like *Light Night*, which is a big charity open event in Liverpool. YEP producers have gone to do lots of good stuff as well, it's got a really good success rate at putting people into the industry. YEP marketers create all the multimedia content for all of the YEP shows, and the YEP techs basically run Ev1, which is our YEP space. Along with the YEP techs we also have base techs which is for young people outside of education, from 17 years old. And that's great because technical theatre is a great skill to have.

Nothing you're doing there seems like it's operating on levels of shoestring quality — quite the opposite. Based on that sort of creative activity in general, could you be geared towards regularly taking anything beyond Liverpool?

We are very up for taking things beyond. But there's this false idea that a theatre needs to be looking towards London. I am personally more interested at the moment in Northern touring, and I also think there's no reason you can't make a show about anything massively global from a Liverpool perspective — it brings something unique and interesting to it, and for me it isn't parochial in any way.

There's a lot of talk about finding voices for people and all that it entails, but it's people like yourself who are making the case that in fact everyone has a voice, it's always there, it's just a question of giving it the platform it deserves. Do you think that this is something people are beginning to cotton on to? Or have we got a long way to go? It certainly sounds as if the Everyman's providing a platform for voices that doesn't judge.

Hundred per cent. We are definitely trying to do that. I think the industry is cottoning on to that but it's still an industry that spits people out, it goes, "Oh, you're an underrepresented voice, let's put you on, let's do the show, oh wait it didn't sell very well, oh well you can't . . ." and then spits people out and doesn't have them back. I wouldn't call it tokenistic, but I would say there's a thinking that it's all going to happen overnight. And there's still the myth of everyone's still looking a bit for another Andrea Dunbar *[playwright from Bradford, Yorkshire]* and the whole mythology of genius in the slums, which I think is deeply deeply problematic. That doesn't help anybody in the long term. There should be interest in that voice — not in a way that you come and gawk at it, but because it's an interesting story, it has a platform, it knows who it wants to speak to.

*

30

Tim Renkow

'There'll always be an audience wanting that conversation'

Tim Renkow is a comedian, actor & writer. Based in South London, he was born in Mexico City, Mexico, & raised in North Carolina.
@timrenkowcomedy

How did you get into all of this?

I started doing comedy because there was a bar next to where I lived in Memphis, Tennessee — I was at art school there. It had a comedy competition, I joined it and then I got hooked. Then I kind of bounced around, ended up in New York City, and I hated that, so eight years ago I came to London to study fine art — and started comedy here.

Ending up in New York and London, did that just happen? Were you dragged in by their centrifugal cultural forces or were there any more specific reasons that got you there — professional, personal, social, financial?

New York just seemed right for me. In the States, NYC is the only place where you can be a comic where you don't have to drive *[Tim has cerebral palsy]*. So it was kind of the only option for me. And my parents have always been super supportive, they come to every one of my shows when they can. They're performers too, not professionally, so they understand what I'm doing.

Mind you, New York doesn't strike me as a particularly accessible city.

No it's not that accessible. But in terms of all of America it's the best, I think. That and Chicago. But Chicago's *cold [laughs]* — North Carolina where I was raised is much warmer.

If I'd stayed in the States, I don't know how it would have gone for my career. The reason I came here was that you don't need to drive, and you do need to drive in America. I would have had to move more to the writing side of it. I always liked writing really, it's the funnest part of comedy, and I always wanted to be a writer. But I like everything about writing except the physical writing part, so I did stand-up because I didn't need to get the physical writing stuff down.

In terms of coming to the UK, it was London that got you over and not the Edinburgh Festival Fringe?

It wasn't Edinburgh. I always liked London and I was a big Bill Hicks fan and a big Patrick O'Neal fan and they both came here first *[both were American stand-ups, O'Neal was brought over by UK stand-up & actor John Simmit, aka Dipsy in Teletubbies]*, so the city was on my radar and I thought I'd try it. And the money's better! I came over, just like that.

With no family or friends already here?

No family. I figured I'd come over here to study, so I looked at a map of London and looked at what university was in the middle of the city, I found London South Bank University — famous alumni include an architect, a painter and one of the planners of 9/11. That was good enough for me. Now I'd like to be one of the most famous alumni too, but I'll never be more famous than the architect of 9/11, right?

So how are you doing on the visas — that's a whole different area of exclusion, isn't it?

Visas are a pain in the ass. But I just got a German passport. My grandparents were German Jews so you go up to the German embassy and say, "You tried to kill my grandpa," and they go, "Yeah we did, we're sorry, here's a passport." And now my worry's moved on to what happens next depending on where Brexit goes. But the idea was always to follow a stand-up career. I set out to do that because it was something I could do for myself, and that's why I ended up studying fine art in London. The problem is that I'm not a fine artist, but the reason I chose fine art was because I could make my own decisions. I changed to creative writing and at the same time I got on to the stand-up circuit. Thinking about it, if I wasn't disabled I would probably have been a veterinarian or something.

So you're saying that stand-up is a particularly empowering art form?

Yeah, I guess so. If you want to be a douche-bag about it you could say that. It's not so much that, although I guess it is empowering in that it suggests a clear option of what is possible.

You came over in 2012 and I'd say your trajectory since then has mapped the bottom falling out of many of the circuits for the various arts sectors. The theatres were already facing an economic crisis around that time and they had to reinvent themselves as things like cafes, while the comedy and music clubs were being simply decimated — and still are, even if this has been offset by the rise of the festivals.

Sure. For example, a couple of years after I got here, [chain of comedy clubs] Jongleurs was already in trouble and eventually folded. Everyone was complaining about things weren't the same and telling me how I'd missed the good years on the circuits and how much easier it had been in the years before I got here to make a living from stand-up. So I think that wave of transformation changed the idea of what performance was and how to sell yourself. I feel like now it's harder on the club circuit, but on the other hand it's much easier to promote yourself than it was before.

Even though it's not that long ago, the point when you came over was when huge changes were also being made in the way diversity was reflected in comedy and the rest of the performing arts. When you were in the States, were you aware of that growth in awareness here for everyone's right to an equal space on those stages?

Well I knew of [comedian, actor, broadcaster & disability rights activist] Liz Carr from before because she had a podcast, and so she's one of the reasons I came. The same year I came, Lost Voice Guy [comedian & actor Lee Ridley, who has a neurological form of cerebral palsy] started on the circuit, so I basically arrived at a particularly interesting time. Of course there were other people around before, but the changes in what comedy looked like were definitely different and I was curious. And because that was all starting at the same time as I was starting out, it didn't feel like I was just jumping into something that was already established.

I could be wrong but I feel like I was doing this disabled thing before it was cool. Though me and Lost Voice Guy started at about the same time, we kind of went in opposite directions tonally. There's also Josh Blue *[comic with cerebral palsy]* in America who is good and started way before I did. I would watch him but also think that guy doesn't talk for me. So I kind of began developing my voice not to be Josh and then I just loved Liz Carr who also was doing that. Disability now includes all those stand-ups and lets us do bigger things in comedy, and I'd say that's really only happened in the last five years.

Why do you think that has happened?

I don't know exactly. I don't think it's anything in the business that made it that way. I could be wrong, but I feel that people saw comics like Liz as a disabled person onstage and then they just got inspired. That was the case for me when I saw her doing it, and I thought I should be doing that too.

Critical mass then.

Yes. As soon as you've done the hardest part of figuring out how you're going to do it, of course — like coming up with those initial ideas of what you're going to say. And once those ideas are out there, more and more people are likely to do it, and that creates a bunch of people who do something that is similar and supportive of what it is. And I hope there's a bunch of people that want to listen to us, even if it's audiences out there who don't agree with how I get my point of view across.

Mind you, from day one you've been pretty uncompromising in your point of view, and not giving an inch on grabbing that level playing-field.

When I started stuff in New York I was, like, I'm not going to mention disability at all. So I did that and, you know what, I realised it's still letting people control my life, if I'm doing the complete opposite of what they tell me to do. But I don't know that I've been put in a good place to always be able to talk about disability when it comes up — or *not* having to talk about it. Like I just did a set on TV where I was talking about being a wheelchair, but that was just to explain why I was in the place I was in, whereas the actual story had nothing to do with being in the wheelchair except that I wouldn't have been in the situation that I ended up in.

I don't think that disability is really that essential a subject. Comedians still have so many other problems to talk about, disabled people have so many other problems to talk about. I would say disability is like salt, it definitely adds flavour to the story but it's not essential. What's actually funny is how people treat me — they treat me the way they do because I'm disabled, but that's not what's funny, the funny thing is the weird things they say and do.

So it's 'other people'?

Yeah. I'm not the problem. They are. It's like people come up to you and starting talking about their life-threatening problems, like, "I know how you feel, oh yeah, my niece died of malaria." Like, *why* do I need to know that?!

Do you feel there's any pressure on you to be aspirational?

I feel the need *not* to be aspirational because I really do meet the craziest people who think I've been sent to them by God to make their lives better. I had to sincerely tell a guy, "Buddy I'm not the Second Coming of Jesus, stop bothering me" — because he was following me with all this Redeemer stuff. It can be super funny but it also gets scary when somebody thinks you're Jesus and at the same time finds out that you're not Jesus and they get mad at you when I try to walk on water but just can't do it.

Part of that reaction to me is the stereotype of Tiny Tim and the Holy Disabled Person. I suppose that projected persona makes up for the lack of physicality, because human nature wants that, but to take that away from you, to take the ability to be flawed away from people, it never works out because people are just idiots, and people with no flaws always turn out to be creeps. We are disabled, we are not disabled, we are all flawed. I even have pretended to be retarded to stop people — I don't want your respect, I want the opportunity to *earn* your respect.

But exuding integrity isn't a common USP for a stand-up, is it?

I'm sure you'll find people who will totally run away from that, yeah. But you know, integrity's a good word, it's important to have it around. It's something that can be taken away by accident from people with good intentions, like when they think they have it but they're not actually helping, like when people help me cross the street — the street that I don't want to cross. That actually happens. But the intention is good, it's not like they're evil, or they're malicious, it's just the act isn't particularly good because they haven't thought of who you are.

All that tickboxing on both sides got you the TV series [Jerk, BBC sitcom starring and co-written by Tim about a guy with cerebral palsy who tries to use his condition to his advantage, it builds on his previous BBC production, A Brief History of Tim]—

It did get me the TV series! *[laughs]* I'm part of a quota system . . .

But on the other hand Jerk defies being quota fodder because it's quality — and disturbingly funny with its treatment of cerebral palsy and immigration in the UK, which must have surprised a lot of people expecting to happily tune into the tokenism and political correctness they may have assumed you'd deliver.

I think it's good to have a unique voice because not even politically correct statements are straight-up any more. You just get tired of seeing middle class white people being middle class white people who you know are being watched by middle class white people. Because then you get to the point where you're like, "Okay, I want, I *need* another type of story." But then that's the part that gets tricky, because there's less of a pool to pick from. If you're not represented by a top comedy agent, if you didn't go to Oxford or Cambridge, if you just don't have those connections you're not likely to get your voice heard. But I'm a disabled redneck Mexican Jew, that's my voice, I can make fun of anyone.

Back to the club circuit and stand-up, when you're onstage do you find yourself thinking God I've really hit something here, let's follow this because it's doing more than make people laugh. Or do you discard it — sometimes deep stuff happens and sometimes it doesn't?

I never discard anything on stage that's working. I did improv so I'm pretty comfortable going on the uptake if something fun comes up — whether it's deep or not. There's the idea that if something interesting comes up, I can store it and instantly use it. That comes from high school, where I was on the improv high school team for four years. A lot of schools there have improv clubs, it's not mandatory or across the board but it's not totally uncommon, and it was certainly enough to give me a lot of grounding for what I'm doing now.

You cut your teeth at the Edinburgh fringe, how does it fit in with your year now?

I don't know, because I have a hard time at Edinburgh. I don't quite love the culture there. The Comedy Awards there reward stage comedy like the one-man shows, which is fine but it's just not the same thing as what I do. I always get attention in Edinburgh but then I do something that somebody's not going to like it. Like last year *[2019]* I decided to injure myself with the press in my show *Tim Renkow Tries to Punch Down*. Fuck the Jews. Because I used to say fuck every other people but not the Jews. That sets off a reaction and makes a little more traction.

At Edinburgh my show's been at Heroes and that's why I owe *[Heroes director/founder]* Bob Slayer. He's so good about the money, and like a lot of other people in Edinburgh I owe him quite a bit. He's even let me stay at his flat when I lost my place and had nowhere else to go. The important thing about Bob is that the venue is supporting the artist, that's the most important thing to him. It's kind of like Don Quixote, everyone says they want what he wants but he's the only guy actually crazy enough to do it. And not only does he do it, but he makes it work.

I want my work to make me self-sustainable but I still had to go up to Edinburgh every year. I know I would have never done that without Bob because I don't like being in debt, I just don't go in debt. So if somebody tells me to make a show but I'd have to pay them ten grand — which is what happens at Edinburgh — I'd just be like no. But Bob doesn't do that, he supports the acts and I like that.

Edinburgh is useful. It's important but for me it's so physically exhausting that after just a week of it I don't have the energy to spare for anything except my performances, so I hope I'm past it in a way, on the physical side of it at least. I think for a comedian, no matter how progressed you are in your career, doing 30 shows-plus in 30 days will always be a hurdle — and that's not even including all the spots and other appearances you do.

Like New York, Edinburgh as a city presents obstacles to physical accessibility. More than a few in fact, and I'd say one of the enduring sights for me of the festival every August is of you barefoot with a battered walking frame tackling the most inadvertently inaccessible streets and still managing to negotiate them. Even when pissed out of your head. How do you manage that?

Well being pissed out of your head helps. Edinburgh is the perfect city — except for the fact that I cannot get around it. I kind of do it and being drunk does help and I do sleep a lot for energy. But yeah, you just kind of have to remind yourself that every time that if there's an uphill, there will be a downhill at some point. Which is usually right, except in Edinburgh. Sometimes it's only uphill.

You've got cobbles everywhere too and other drunk people in the way. And there's all the winding venues . . .

I guess I'm not really thinking about it because I've never lived on the ground floor in any case. *[chuckles]* I know a lot of people who want accessibility to change at Edinburgh, but it's an 800 year old city, and it's not the responsibility of the Fringe Society *[the charity that supports the running of the fringe]*. A report's just said that only 40 per cent of fringe venues are accessible, and my thought was hey, that's not bad! There are buildings that are literally made out of stairs, like an Escher painting. Buildings are diverse too.

Can we talk about the comedy circuit in terms of prejudice, accessibility, non-bookers, hostile audiences even? Is there anything in particular where you've seen major changes in attitudes?

Some people don't book me, and that's fine. There's two types of people that don't book me. The first, and I hope this is the more common part, they just don't like my humour. I've got no problem with that. But there are a few bookers who I know of who never book me because of the disability, and that's not cool.

I mean, my sense of humour is dark, so it's not great for political shows for example. In fact there's multiple types of shows I'm not suited for. Like, I could be if I made the effort but I don't. But if comedians need to respect the crowd, then the bookers also need to respect the crowd — and that goes for when people don't book me because I'm disabled. It's not because they have anything against me, it's because they don't respect their crowd enough, they don't *trust* their crowd enough to accept me, and that's why I also think that shows no respect for me as a comedian.

And for every one person I've had that has a problem with the disability, there's like 10 or 20 that have a problem because they think I'm *pretending* to be disabled. That happens a lot, like on my Twitter page where there's people always complaining about that. When I started out there was a lot of prejudice and certainly there still probably is a lot around today. But I never minded — I mean, I minded on an ethical level but I never did on a professional level because I want to be better than you are.

For Jerk, was there a big difference in terms of writing, or was it just the same thing as you onstage but with more people?

There wasn't really a difference, and when I moved to TV writing I got paired with an actual writer, so obviously that's different. The producers were happy because they knew they had someone there who knew what they were doing. There were tons of battles, but things like staging aren't really an argument, because they go, "We can't afford to do that", and you go, "Okay. If you can't do it, you just can't." So in that respect it was very instructional. It's the same with being allowed to cast people *[Tim cast Sopranos star Lorraine Bracco, who's American, as his screen character's mother]*. The way I see it is, I didn't always get the kind of yes I wanted, but I could have said no.

So if they gave you wall-to-wall TV work, would you still carry on with club comedy?

That's interesting. Mentally yes. Definitely. Club comedy is just a different thing from TV. It's like saying now that you're eating breakfast, would you go for a jog? They're great but just two different things. The reason I like club comedy is you're not just chatting to people in the pub. I'm just an asshole who likes contributing to the discussion and I'm more comfortable talking to people in a live audience in a live venue rather than stealing my own TV special where I know everyone likes it. Club comedy is a different thing and I don't think it will go away because there'll always be an audience wanting that conversation. There is something sad if we ever lost it, we'd be losing the necessity to talk to people who don't agree with you.

It's back to that idea of trust the crowd.

It's fun when people disagree with you. I know this is harsh, but I don't think the human experience is as unique as people want it to be. I think it's easy to see 'disabled' as something heroic — and if I'm your hero then you've seriously made a mistake — but whatever you're talking about, we've all experienced stuff, we all have stuff that we don't want to deal with. It's like the colour wheel in that there are very few base emotions and there's an infinite amount of possibilities around those basic things. There's just not that many basic things in everyone's lives, it all comes from the same place — your family, your work, your health.

I think I just like stories — there's the audience, there they are, tell them a story. I just always admired anyone being able to tell a story, and it can be a nice way to cover all those basics.

So what's the function of comedy for you? What's the reason you're up there doing it?

The main function is to make people laugh. I'm not fooling myself. Despite the trendy claims, comedy is not a luxury item, but I would say that if you want to get deep about it and claim it's a social mover, which I'm not sure I'm a believer in, then the function is to point out problems not just solutions. Most of the time I just do it for the hell of it. Like I said, I do it pretty much as the only thing I can do, and if you're looking for a message, that's not always what you'll get.

*

31
Paul Ricketts

'Are you a better act if you just perform to people like you?'

Paul Ricketts is a comedian, writer & musician. Based in South East London, he was born in Yorkshire & raised in Bedford, Bedfordshire.
• *paulrickettscomedian.com, @paulricketts10*

Tell us about your Mum, what she told you in the 1980s.

I'll you about my Mum . . . My Mum used to say to me, "Ya kno Paal, white people dey *never* change." And I'd say, "Oh no it'll be different, Mum, it'll be different. Our generation will change it all. You know, it won't be the same as you've had it."

But of course she's right. She's 80 now and the other day I said, "You were right, you know." And she says, "Ah me *kno* dat!" So all it took me was 30 years to work it out. She was spot on. Especially given that my generation, unfortunately it turns out, that we're Brexit, we're that generation, we're the one who turned out to have exactly the same racisms and prejudices of our parents. Because when life happens to us we react, strangely enough, in exactly the same way as they did. We've all gone back to our little tribes.

I thought my generation would change things. We didn't change anything. The white working class community I grew up in has turned into a right bunch of arseholes who have pulled the ladder up. You know: buy their own council house, become as racist and as small-minded as their parents were, hopefully retire to Spain in their 50s because they can't stand foreigners coming into this country. Fuck one country up and then move abroad and fuck up another and, while they're there, say, "This place would great if it weren't for the Spanish." "Well it's their country isn't it?" "Well no. Spain is *wasted* on the Spanish!"

I meet them every night doing comedy. I was in Billericay *[in Essex]* last Saturday night — it wasn't even a proper comedy night, but one in aid of some charity like 'Suntan Abuse'. It was weird because there's them looking at me: aspiring white working class people who think they're now middle class. In the counties like that you can go to one village and everyone's posh, go back the next night to the same village and everyone's going "awrright?!" You just don't know.

So in Billericay I checked and asked the audience, who was "oi!" *[very self-assertively working class, especially associated with Estuary England]*? They were all "oi" but I saw them looking at me going, "Oooh, I dunno . . . I mean, you don't *look* like us. But you *do* sound like us . . . I just don't get it. What you about, man?" I been doing this long enough so I know that you're supposed to explain who you are to the audience, but at that gig I started the other way round because I'm getting fed up of having to start of my set to explaining who the fuck am I. So no, let's not do that, let's instead start off with material about things I want to talk about and *then* explain who I am halfway through. By this point the audience will already have an idea of who I am. And when you don't explain yourself, there's more resonance somehow, you get better laughs.

And I also think it shows confidence as a comic not to do all that, when you start off with all that "hello-my-name's-bla-bla-bla, I-come-from-bla-bla-bla". But for Billericay I really should have gone back to that traditional introduction and explained myself first, because they were simply going, "I can't work out this black guy who doesn't sound 'urban', but sounds a bit like us."

We should perhaps point out that not only did this gig take place in the 21st century but also in a settlement within spitting distance of London, a place from where half the people commute to the capital every day.

At the risk of repeating myself in terms of previous conversations and interviews, the black voice is such a narrow thing in the UK and even amongst the black community the idea of what is a black voice is narrow. The London 'urban' voice dominates throughout the country and to be clear I've got nothing against that voice. But in the Asian community that does not apply. There's a comedian from Birmingham, Guz Khan, and I've just seen the new trailer for his *Man Like Mobeen* series where his Mobeen character speaks with a mix of Jamaican Patois with a Brummie accent. But in the trailer he's also dressed as an old English gentleman . . . So he's a Brummie Asian dressed as an Englishman doing a Jamaican Patois.

Pretty much sums up a version of modern Britain and the mainstream will buy into this because, of course, "Oh he's Asian, he's urban, he's from a city. He sounds authentic." And Guz does talk like that, so *that's* not a problem. But there are other Asian comics on TV like Nish Kumar and Romesh Ranganathan who have completely different voices. Nish's is a totally English middle class accent and Romesh has a Thames Estuary voice similar to mine. Both these voices are also seen as authentic whereas a black man having a similar voice is seen as suspicious and inauthentic. I find it's strange that a black male voice can't do that, but the idea of a black male non-urban voice isn't supposed to exist in the mainstream — although it does with black women. But this is a restriction projected on us and also partly our fault . . . well, it's not our fault. Fault's not the right word. 'Choice' is a better word.

'Fate' maybe?

No, not fate, because I think there's some choice in it. Black culture isn't passive and there's always the ghettoisation thing, it's ghettocentricity, and that *is* partly a choice, cos it gives you certain sort of power. Now of course I'm not denying all the stuff that's projected on you, but some of it *is* a community choice to define ourselves against white culture. And you get power by defining yourself against a dominant culture. You get tons of power by doing that, I totally get it.

I've lived through it, being part of the start of *[urban black accent]* "talkin' like dis yeah?" At some point in the early 1970s in every school black kids decided, "Well we can go on talking like *this*. Or we can change it slightly and make this amalgam of fake Jamaicanness/fake Black Americanness and come up with this *new* accent." And suddenly people got "well wicked" and it all got a bit "like dis", and everyone started taking "like dis yeah?" And it hasn't gone away — and over the years it's also morphed and took words from many cultures and becoming this evolving urban voice. Because like all languages, it develops.

Especially developing as a way of keeping one step ahead of the white and Asian kids who start imitating you.

Ah . . . but the white kids almost straightaway were going, "We want to talk like that!" *[laughs]* And that's where you can see the *power*. As soon as we started doing that, I was actually going, "I'm too lazy to change how I talk." But everyone else was going for it but I'm a product of where I was brought up — a majority white working class housing estate in a Home Counties town. But as soon as we started using *[Jamaican]* Patois to each other, there'd be the kids whose Caribbean parents would be ashamed to hear their children using it. The parents would go, "Ohhh, *why* you do dat?" — because not every Caribbean family is from Jamaica and they certainly don't want to hear their kids speaking like that. It was *distressing* to them. They didn't come all the way over to England for their children to sound like Jamaicans!

As background for those who are unaware, we need to point out that people from the 'Small Islands' of the Caribbean stood out when they came to the UK because they were noticeably better spoken — and educated — than many of our nation's existing white population.

Too true. But anyway the choice was made to do the 'voice' and it was part of asserting a confident identity. As soon as we started doing it and adding Patois and kissing our teeth and everything like that, you could see white kids going, "What're you doing? What do these words mean?" "Well I'm not telling you." "Oh go on . . . what does 'bludclart' mean?" And as soon as the first finger flick came, which was about 1973, which I still can't bloody do—

[White interviewer flicks fingers.]

—bastard . . . A lot of it was culturally tied to the cricket tours of the UK by the West Indies in 1973, 76. I was with relatives in Peckham at the time for those two summers and there was a *strut* growing within us because it was about us taking on the English. And in 1973 there was Tony Gregg, the *[white]* South African England captain who went into that tour saying, *[South African accent]* "The West Indies don't like playing so hard, well we're going to make sure they grovel." And to hear that voice on the TV saying that, every West Indian in Britain was determined to see us beat them.

And of course we did, and there was a lot of strut coming from that. West Indian sporting heroes dominating the English at that particular point was also when there was still a great love of cricket within the West Indian community in Britain — which there isn't now. People turned up to the matches, everyone played, all my parents' generation played cricket — and that was gone in a generation.

1973 and 76, that was the start, and we also dominated cricket in the 1980s. That sense of domination had an impact on *all* the people growing up in this country, so that Caribbean language and identity was projected at the same time and young white people wanted a part of it. Of course they did. Later on I realised how there's power in moving yourself away, not assimilating, doing the opposite. I now also realise that there is also power being taken from us by always being seen as 'ghetto'.

That's why I'm not even sure about the use of the term BAME. It reduces down a great and diverse group of people. Just think of all the differences within the Asian community. You've got Indians, Pakistanis, Bengalis, Sri Lankans, Indians from Uganda and the West Indies and loads more with cultural differences and everyone goes, "Oh, it's just the same thing." No it isn't, so no it's *not* the same thing. There's differences between the kids from a Caribbean background and kids from an African one. We've had different life experiences within this country and from outside it. A completely different mental attitude too, and that's a huge thing. Nigerians, for example, seem to have higher expectations in what they can achieve in life.

I was reading an article with this black English sportsman, and he was going, "Oh, I was brought up in South London, I'm lucky I've got sport because I've got a lot of anger in me, Dad's not here, everybody was telling me I'm not going to be much. Well, now I've done this in sports, I've learned to be a man." Ok, some of this definitely came from substandard schooling and teachers. But I also think wait a minute, you're from a Caribbean background and going for the baby mother *[single-mother families]* phenomenon, all that bullshit. Things that used to work in the West Indies, in Jamaica in particular, don't work here. You can't transplant not having a father around and being raised by baby mothers here from Jamaica. It's not the same thing. In Jamaica, the *[single]* mothers would all congregate in the same parish, they would all come together and help to bring up their kids mutually. But it doesn't work over here — one mother lives on that estate and the other mother lives over here, they're not going to get together to help to bring up somebody else's kids.

And then the fathers? The whole thing about a Jamaican man spreading his seed as far as possible with as many different mothers is a *slave mentality* — it's a terrible slave mentality hangover. You wouldn't take ownership for your kids because in essence you don't own them, someone else does. That's an awful thing to have here in the UK. Whereas you don't get that in a Nigerian community. My point is we are different. You can't just put B-A-M-E and go, "Well any one of them will do." No it won't, we're different.

And at the moment we seem to be at the lowest level of that. It's almost like because we're the black originals, *[Luton accent]* "Oh you know the West Indians come over I've been here since the 1950s, nah they've never done that well have they?" *[posh accent]* "Whereas your Nigerians . . . they're really good businessmen, the Nigerians. Stormzy's wonderful isn't he? I like Stormzy. Do you like Stormzy? We all like Stormzy." *[intellectual accent]* "And Nish, and all the wonderful Asians, wonderful. So many of them are Doctors or Dentists . . ."

We're at the bottom. We are totally at the bottom. But in terms of post-war immigration we've been here the longest! *[laughs long and hard]* It's like first in, first dismissed. And it's weird that we seem to accept it. That's the thing that gets me. We watch the Nigerians come in and achieve educationally and businesswise, we've seen Asians come in and achieve educationally, professionally and businesswise, and we just seem to stay in the same place. Why is that? Because we can't even blame education any more. We can't even blame comprehensive education. They went to the same schools as us!

I wish the Caribbean community would move out of London, Manchester and Birmingham where 70 per cent of us still live. Which is what the Asian community and the African community have already done — they've moved to suburban areas and then their children go to better schools and they've had more prosperity. I hope this generation will get out of, say, London and go into the Home Counties. So there would be no shame in black people making it in non-ghetto ways. I'm partly joking here but I'd love to see black accountants, for example, getting a reputation as the best you can get. But it doesn't ever seem to happen to the Caribbean community.

Well it does, but you just don't hear about it.

Obviously there's going to be people who do well. And you're right, we don't hear about it.

But it's not a community that gets credit for that progression or is able to celebrate it in the national eye.

I find that really sad. I'm sorry. I find that heartbreaking.

If we go back to the 1980s when you were talking to your Mum, you could pick any one of those years in the decade and it would have been a watershed for people identifying issues, tackling them and making cash and legislation available, despite the simultaneous downward dismantling of society by the Thatcher government. The terminology they came up with wasn't always a bad thing, because it kept pace with the changes, gave it a name and educated us. Terminology generated more often than not by the actual groups fighting for their rights to be equal in British society. As the idea of equality and change in society became more and more formalised, we got landed with the idea of tickbox culture which became self-fulfilling as our academics, institutes, ministries, thinktanks, spads and consultations decided that things like BAME should exist. It's social engineering weirdly, where people get *included* by being defined by someone else — "We have a name for you, therefore you exist." Has that changed anything?

I don't think *anything's* changed. You used to go for the job and if you're lucky to get the interview, they'd be looking at you even as you came through the door. "Are you sure you're in the right place?" *[wearily]* "Yes, I've come for the interview." Then what changed was they'd give you this sheet before you do the interview, the 'ethnic monitoring form'. And you'd tick all the stuff on the ethnic monitoring form, and after about a decade of this I suddenly realised that nobody's ever got a job through ethnic monitoring forms. Ethnic monitoring forms don't change anything. They just tell you how many people didn't get the job but have applied for it.

I remember them at the National Theatre in the early 2000s. They're constantly going on about what they're doing for diversity by telling you how BAME people applied for jobs and didn't get them. But the National Theatre was an organisation with racist people working there and some of them still do. I worked there with some sneaky snidey ones, which is your traditional racist, and then some quite brazenly racist ones. It's actually quite refreshing to have someone who just says to you, "Yeah, I'm a bit racist. I just think you're alright, Paul. I've just got to say I'm a bit racist." And you're thinking, "Well thank fuck you're being honest." I don't know about the "you're alright" bullshit but at least you knew where you were. You never knew with the rest of them sneaky snidey arseholes. But that's a place full of ethnic monitoring. Full of it.

The audience too . . .

And yet there it is. Well, I'm only referring to people who worked backstage when I was there. You could argue it's changed or it's *changing*. Yeah right. Remember it's the intelligent ones who tend to be the snidier ones, the ones you can't quite pin down. Obviously the stupid ones are stupid enough to tell you, "I'm a bit racist."

Let's look at the business of being a stand-up. Although it's likely to change nothing, the last Edinburgh Festival Fringe [2019] was significant for putting racial diversity in the frame in several ways, including the Fringe of Colour scheme that was set up by the Fringe Society [the charity that supports the running of the fringe] to 'spotlight black and brown performers', 'get black audiences in', and thus 'counter the overwhelming whiteness' of the festival.

So you could instantly find the black performer because it's got 'FoC' written on the top of the programme entry . . . so why not a little Sambo emoji? I mean, it's basically an ethnic monitoring form but for a festival.

Well the question is: is an initiative like this good in itself, or does it need to have

a 'commercial' effect? Is it enough to just create a talking point? There'll be a
glowing report of course from the fringe. With figures, data and . . . outcomes.

I've got nothing against the idea, but the terminology's always the bullshit thing. They went with 'Fringe of Colour' this time — and 'of Colour' means you can be broader. So you can get all sorts of weird people in there and it gives you some figures which makes it look like you're doing something. "He's Maltese, he looks a bit black, we'll get him in . . . So how many shows now? . . . 22?! We only started off with two this morning . . . And now we've got this Welsh bloke in and he also looks a bit 'of colour' . . . whatever."

But is that going to change Edinburgh? If you can't even change the basic things that make it unattractive for everyone, white or black? I was talking to Ninia Benjamin about why she's never done the festival. I think she's brilliant, but she was saying, "Why should I go up to Edinburgh and spend £5000 when that can buy me a new kitchen? What am I going up there for? I'll get four stars — which ain't going to cook my dinner." And so she's just thinking what's the point? So she's never been up there. Levelling the playing-field isn't putting 'FoC' on your poster, if you can't afford to lose the money.

I know a lot of other black comics who may have been up there in their early days but now would never go up there for the same reason. And then there's the question of what your act is. I've seen black comics go up there from the urban circuit and totally misjudge what they're doing. One of them went up and did a late-night gig with all his homophobic 'batty bwoy' material and got booed offstage, *[laughs]* and then the *[white]* MC came out afterwards and "I apologise to everyone here . . ." Of course this urban comic thought, "I'll come up here and do my black urban Saturday night stuff to this mainly white middle class audience in Scotland" — and of course they booed him off.

So to come back to the original question, is an initiative like Fringe of Colour a good thing? From a performer's point of view, if it adds numbers, it's a good thing. From a publicity point of view, it depends what the audience think of it. As a performer, it's not going to hurt me. It *is* ghettoey? of course it is — but then all these sorts of things are ghettoey.

And you also need to factor in that whole other level of prejudice, not just at
Edinburgh, where the economic barrier excludes people of all types and dictates
what you see and don't see. Still, it's remarkable how something as massive as
Edinburgh can still stay resolutely white, defying the level playing-field
philosophy (well, it's a brand now) it espouses. But again Edinburgh is a
'domain', a platform earmarked for the aspirational middle classes and above.
It's like not everyone gets to go grouse shooting. So why should we (a) be shocked

and (b) feel tempted to join in — or indeed criticise? It's never going to change, for all the good works of something like FoC.

Of course it isn't going to change. And it's become even more and more clear over the last ten years. For these acts that dismiss the comedy circuits, there's now an alternative comedy circuit for acts who don't want to play to any old audience. We live in the era of audience targeting — "we know what we want" — and these are the performers saying, "I want my audience to be *this*. I don't want to perform to all and sundry." Does it really show you to be a much better act if you just perform to people who look and sound exactly like you? Let's face it, that's what the urban circuit is about and that's the strength and weakness of it. In the North there's a club full of young Scouse comics just talking about relationships and then in London here there's comedy clubs where it's just *[hipster voice]* "How we doing guys?"

Those Islington and Camden comics who don't want to do the national circuit to ascend and learn. They'd rather just do is to do Camden and Islington only in London, hopefully get successful there, taken up by an agent and go straight to the posher gigs without having to do the nasty gigs. The end of that process is to do an Edinburgh show and jump straight from there — because no one is 'discovered' in Edinburgh, they're anointed. The industry have chosen you before the fringe starts and afterwards they make your bid for a TV spot with a run in the Soho Theatre *[in Central London]*.

At Edinburgh, despite all that ever-expanding variety on offer, the right venue will give them exactly the audience they want who are just like them.

A Big Four *[venues]* room, at the right time with the right agent, of course. And if you're going well, you'll get force-fed into a BBC free show or, if you're a little bit older, perhaps you might get Channel 4 — they still do the odd comic thing. They want to go straight to telly, miss out travelling the country playing to everybody. They want to 'find' their audience instead. So some of these comics get forced through onto TV too early. These aren't mass or even mainstream comedians, so they throw them at the wall and some fall off and the UK TV audience says to itself, "Oh they're all shit" — which of course isn't the case, it's just that perhaps not all the best ones are being chosen.

So for any diversity initiative, it's not even that it's going to make a difference, it's just not relevant.

With Edinburgh it's not relevant. I mean look, it's mainly white, it's mainly middle class. That's what it is. The majority of the shows are people doing shows about them bloody selves. It's like *[American comedy-drama TV series] The Wonder Years*, 40 minutes in everybody's going to say "and what did I learn about this? Well of course, when Dad died, . . ." It's essentially a very middle class activity and the fringe is very middle class. It doesn't even include Scottish people half the time, not even from the people from Edinburgh. The most ridiculous thing is to see when you go to Edinburgh that Scottish comedy is ghettoised into one night. There's one dedicated venue to Scottish comedians in the Grassmarket . . . this is Scotland and they've got you all in this one building: "This is the Scotch Comedy Building here."

But they are trying for diversity against the odds. It certainly wasn't a surprise that in this year's [2019] Comedy Awards at Edinburgh the presence of black nominees reflected that. And you could feel the (all white?) judges and organisations feel very good about this, but really will it make any difference even if there's a black winner?

No. Anyway . . . the best show for me by miles *[at Edinburgh 2019]* was Marlon Davis. I went to see his show, *Emotional Black Male*, and I left it completely and angry at the experience of being in that show — for several reasons.

I already knew what was going to be in the show because I'd done some gigs with Marlon. This year he was in the Gilded Balloon, a Big Four venue, lovely room. He had had a car crash a couple of years ago and was in a coma for some time. When he came out of the coma, he couldn't remember anything but the one thing he knew was that he was a comedian. Now before he had the accident, he was playing a bit fast and loose with comedy and then he had the accident. And so the whole story of the show is how comedy saved his life.

One of the most beautiful bits was him describing how he comes of the coma and he's trying to remember who he is. He says to the bloke in the bed next to him, who also has brain damage and asks, "Who am I?" And the guy goes, "You're a comedian mate, that's who you are." And Marlon realises, "Yeah, you're right, I'm a *comedian*. What's my name?" The other patient says, "*Bill Cosby!*" And Marlon thought he was Bill Cosby for a bit . . . but at least it reaffirmed that he was a comedian.

Now Marlon's back on the circuit, he's a different sort of comic because now it's *him* — there is no artifice there any more, there's no pretending to be black American, which was understandable before as all his comic heroes were black American. That's all gone now, you just get Marlon being himself in what's a beautifully written show.

So I'm watching the show, and already one of the things that annoyed me was that his agent had forced him to take out the Bill Cosby line because they thought it was too, you know . . . The second thing was the experience of being in the show itself. I was sat next a stag party group of white guys who had decided to buy tickets to Marlon's show because they saw this black smiley face on the flier and from that alone they thought he would be a "let's talk about the pussy" comic. All these expectations were projected onto a picture of Marlon's face. When the show started and they watched Marlon talking about his accident and being in hospital, they were going, "We haven't come here to see this sort of show . . . We thought this was going to be another sort of show . . ." And they just kept on talking to each other throughout the show and taking the piss.

I was thinking, "What am I going to do here? If I start having a massive argument with them—" which I really wanted to have, "—I'm going to ruin Marlon's show." So at one point I just got up and went and sat in another row — because otherwise I knew I was going to kick off on them. I sat behind young white couple and *they* too were whispering to each other saying, "I didn't think it was going to be like this . . . I thought it was going to be, you know . . ." A few of the stag group walked out and then, just before the end, the remaining five got up and walked out. My partner Verity was going mental at them . . . but the worst thing was I was one of six black people in there and we all looked at each other and asked, "What could we do?"

What angered me was the assumption the stag group made on just seeing a black face on a poster. They just thought he must be *this* sort of comic, when he *isn't* that sort of comic, and then they just dismissed what he was doing — "Well if he can't be arsed to do that for us, give us what we expect, then well fuck it then." And they were actually posh. Rugger-buggers. Arseholes. The point is they'd paid 15 quid each to see the show but it's done with "this is what we expect because he's *black*." That's the assumption and when they didn't get what they assumed, there's a complete lack of respect to even to listen to what Marlon's doing, ooh I was so angry.

But I talked to Marlon afterwards and he was going, "No, no, if they don't like it, they don't like it. If they walk out, then that's my fault." *[laughs]* But he's like that now, he's very chilled out.

Can you change a monster like Edinburgh? It would be easier to try to change the entire rest of the UK circuit.

I think the circuit will have to change before we change Edinburgh. Let's face it, British comedy would have to change. That will have to happen first, because I can't see Edinburgh changing, it isn't welcoming. But then I don't think the circuit is welcoming to black comics. Not really. When I think about some of the things I've been involved in, the promoters who've done terrible things to black comics and I tried to take them on and get a better deal, well no white comic's ever come and supported me. Ever. And when I've even written stuff about it online occasionally I'll go, "Do you know this person?" And the answer always comes, "Well, he's always been nice to me, he even sent me a message of support . . ."

One promoter was paying me and a lot of really good black comedians badly, and he asked to see me after we did a sort of revolt. He admitted that what he was paying us was embarrassing . . . and then he actually admitted that the only reason the night was on was because he had a *quota* to meet. He needed so many black comics a week and he thought, "It's a lot easier to do it all in one night . . ." *So our night was just set up for him to hit his weekly quota of black comics.* To which I said, "Why don't you put us all on at the weekends?" Now I knew someone else had already asked him that, and he'd said to them, "No, we can't have two of you on the night . . . it *frightens* the audience." But of course that's bollocks — and he did say he was joking, and I'm sure he was . . . a little bit.

I'm not saying he's racist though, but he's also reflecting the audience's racism, and he's not the only comedy promoter to do this. That's exactly why I seldom get to work with the other black comics that work on the mainstream circuit, because two of us never get booked on the same night. If it does occasionally happen, then one of us will be an MC. And in that case, I'm more likely to work with black female comics than black male comics — "Why have two of the male comics? They're all talking about the same shit anyway." I'm sorry to say that is true of the majority of mainstream promoters in this country. Of course they all go, "No, of course I'm not racist!" Yeah, but you don't book two black male comics. So you're pandering a little bit to your audience's prejudice. Of course you are . . . You're making some sort of assumption here for your audience. You are involved in this shit.

Most of us have never gone back to that particular promoter. Everyone else goes, "Oh, what a great club it is, why don't you go and do it, Paul?" "Erm, I don't want to tell you the reasons . . ." Well, I do tell them the reasons but that's never stopped any white comic from playing there. When I posted about it afterwards, no white comic supported us on it, nobody. Instead it was, "No, I've never had a problem with him . . ." "But I've just told you this. All of it's true." "But he's been fine with me though" So I'd never expect any white comic to do fuck all to support. I'm not saying all of them, but as a group en masse they don't and won't.

Are there any black comedy promoters on the mainstream circuit?

On the urban circuit, yes. But mainstream there aren't any. When I started there was one. He did the world's most racist black joke. I can't remember his name now but he was from a Caribbean background. He's sort of gone now . . .

So theatre and dance are clearly faring better than comedy in terms of diversity and equality.

Do you remember the *[pioneering black-led]* Push festivals that used to be at the Young Vic with *[director, actor & activist]* Josette Bushell-Mingo?

Yes. She used them to open up a serious amount of doors for people.

Well I ended up working on them because there weren't any black theatre technicians about. I ended up doing video and follow-spotting, and also having a really bad time with the Young Vic people who worked backstage. It's different now, I'm sure, but at that time there was a bunch of racists there. I came in and they gave me the worst possible jobs they could think of.

Maybe it can't be held against the theatres for the racism, historically at least, since backstagers at the big theatres anywhere in the world were anti anyone trying to break into their world. They were a closed shop, notoriously closed ranks and the London theatre system itself traditionally drew from the white working class areas around the buildings and all the attitudes that that entailed.

Sure, that was then. That was the 1990s. There was also that defensive closed-shop attitude of "we don't like the fact that you're here". Anyway I did my thing on the festivals, which were a bit ghettoised though there were some great things in them. I was chatting to Mingo at one point and saying. "I've got plays I'd like to bring in." And she said, "What are they about?" I told her about one I had at the time which was about a bloke who sticks up prostitute cards — a mate of mine had that as a job and even I did that for a little bit. She goes, "Oh . . . it's got to be a bit more . . ." You know: black, pretty, relevant. So obviously I never did send anything to her. But the Push festivals were definitely a worthwhile experience. Some of the technicians that Mingo brought in ended up getting proper work out of it.

As people like to say, things were different then.

Well, thinking about it now, no they weren't. In a funny sort of way they were better. Because there wasn't the social media to encourage racists and make them realise, "Wait a minute there's loads of people like me." Before you had to go to the right pub or work in the right place, and it's a nod and a wink — "Okay you think the same as me thank God for that. We'll all talk about it in the pub together and as soon as other people turn up we'll stop." Now you just go online and find thousands, hundreds of thousands, millions of people who will agree with you on the forums and makes you feel, "Yeah why the fuck should I shut up? It's freedom of speech." The amazing thing about freedom of speech today is that the more people bang on about freedom of speech, the more they finish and then go, "Yeah Hitler what a lovely bloke."

Moving on. Race and class tend to get conflated in a lazy way. Obviously they're linked but you can also see there's a lot of issues being addressed concerning race that are really class and vice-versa. And you're very much about that. Because it's a white country, it's very easy to look at you and go yeah angry black man, but it's also angry working class man. And yet you're also highly educated, your Mum bought you up to think for yourself and rise above the white working class community you grew up in. And it's not that you escaped, but you used the same basic ladder upwards that society offered all of those others. And that's a ladder with hurdles that are based on class divisions as well as race. You've progressed, and in the meantime the whole idea at least of what working class is has changed.

We get hung up on terminology. And the very idea of working? A lot of them don't work. How can they be *working* class? Everyone knows what that means, because everyone knows what middle class is. And everyone knows what upper class is. Of course because this is Britain we'd rather pretend they didn't exist. And politically, Margaret Thatcher through David Cameron to today, the Tories have been, "Do the working class really exist? Can't we split and divide them like the Victorians? The more we make them smaller and smaller and smaller, the less people will care. In fact if we can dehumanise them and give them a really good name such as the 'underclass' then the better for us."

Go to any comedy club in this country and ask them, "Who here is middle class?" I did that in Highgate *[posh part of North London]* the other night. They all kept their hands down. Because they're ashamed to admit it. "Who here is working class?" They all kept their hands down because they weren't. *[laughs]* "Who here is upper class?" And they all kept their hands down because some of them were of course — this was a private school which costs £20,000 a term. They were going, "Is he taking the piss?" And yeah I was. But the *fear*, we all know it exists, where people won't even admit to the class they're in because they don't want to.

Perhaps because by admitting their own class they have to acknowledge the unpalatable reality that other people exist and that we're all defined by each other? And any mobility involving other people encroaches on their own bubbles — it's as cultural as it is economic.

Well, most of the time if you ask any audience who are really middle class and they won't answer and if you say, "Well are you working class then?" — a lot of them go "Ye-es . . ." No you're not. But you do feel safer identifying like that. It's a weird one. We're fucked up by class, and I think we always will be.

We've been chipping away at the class system since the World Wars but somehow we've ended up with more and more Old Etonians in the government and more and more private school-educated people in the performing arts who are squeezing everyone else out. Somehow it's all getting less representative the more it's officially getting representative. So tackling class head-on in the UK gets sidelined into areas like race, regions and other excluded groups.

But a lot of your agenda is how closely connected you are to excluded people who actually matter to you — and so have power. It helps you concentrate on that X per cent of the population if it includes nice middle class people. There's a lot of that moving issues forward and shunting them up the agenda because some of these people could be middle class, some of them could be our friends or even family. And so we can associate more with them, we might know them, whereas some of the other people we don't know them, we haven't met them, they are really Other, whereas this lot aren't so Other, so we'll pull them in.

And so the chance for change boils down to the whims of class.

In this country I think that's definitely the case. In other countries not so much so. There it could just be money. The other thing is in terms of the conversations we've had about the 1960s and 70s and even the 80s about working class culture is music, which was driving class awareness and change. They've looked at the charts at the start of this year *[2019]* and compared them to the charts in 1979, looking at the class origins of the British acts in the Top 20. In 1979, it was something 70 per cent working class, and today it's 70 per cent upper and middle class. Even the boy bands today are posh boy bands. And the reason why, is that these people don't tend to fuck it up. They don't have drug problems, well some of them might do—

—but they end up with the support network not of social services but of Mummy

and Daddy and their connections. Who are busy investing their money sensibly for them while they're in rehab.

Exactly. They're not going to go mental and blow all their advance by buying a big house for their mum out of working class guilt — because their mum's already got quite a nice six-bedroom house. They're not going to do that. They're going to stay sane. And they'll have extended and long careers. Without having to go to rehab half as often and lose it quite as terribly. And also they can talk to the management and 'do as they're told'. Because they know what the game is.

Thinking of those charts, it wasn't just a question of class, it was an explosion of diversity that opened up gender, race, region, immigrant culture, and every genre under the sun. If only for The Selecter! I'm not sure that the word multiculturalism had been introduced by then. Everyone just took everything as it was and the government carried on blithely.

As an example we talk about people like Jerry Dammers *[keyboardist in the Specials & founder of 2 Tone Records]* who looked like one thing but actually is another thing classwise. As much as Joe Strummer *[vocalist/guitarist in the Clash]* was like one thing but he was another thing too. But I don't mind that.

Because no one can question the contribution they've made to society through their art. Our generation's class-based sneering aside, that's diversity to be applauded. We shouldn't deny what they meant and what they did.

It was open to the fact that these lucky private school kids could be here with these working class comprehensive kids and create this band and do this politically aware music.

But that does explain their instant and enduring success because they had the confidence to resonate with both working and middle classes and we're aspirational with it, if that's the right word here.

Yeah and they got funky bursts in there. Well tried to anyway. But you didn't mind that because at least it was a mix. You didn't have to be all of one thing. Especially not in 1979/80. That was the whole point. That was the first UK youth movement that I could associate with . . . the bands were mixed the music was mixed.

The audiences were mixed.

Definitely. I felt I could be part of it. I didn't think I wasn't part of it. I thought it was done by people like me. For people like me. But it was also pop, inclusive and accessible to the mainstream. That used to be an important part of British popular culture. So that's why you end up with Boris Johnson claiming, without any sense of irony, that his favourite band is The Clash.

It was an interesting time: black people could rock, white people could skank.

And it was *British*. It wasn't copycat Jamaican. It was ska but it got punked up till it was so much faster. And it wasn't even London, it was Coventry!

And Handsworth Revolution next door.

All that stuff and you're thinking it's all the stuff you want! We probably have it going on now but I'm too old to hear it.

Well you sort of do, it's all there and available for you to pick up whenever, but it's not the same thing is it? That sort of off-the-shelf cultural diversity today is passive in some ways. There's not much in Little Mix to set your soul on fire forever in quite the same way. That pool of amazing spontaneous diversity happened as a result of people doing for themselves — no multicultural initiatives, no social change movements, no government programmes — and anyway the government followed, not initiated. But since that period, the government and the powers that be became engaged by launching their own bit of social engineering in the name of equal rights, and ended us up with this contemporary notion of diversity and inclusion, summed up by the anti-diverse, isolating, clumping-together of BAME. The further you delve into those policy units, the backroom decision-makers get whiter and whiter and the performing arts are no exception. Empowerment doesn't really mean the same thing as it used to.

Empowerment! At that time, the people who controlled the product were the bands themselves because of organisations like The Cartel, where a whole do-it-yourself philosophy was turned into a national industry. You could make your product in Coventry, send it out to The Cartel and you'd be in shops all over the country the same week. You didn't have to deal with the big chains to get your record out. Anyone could still buy it. That was an alternative set-up that was genuinely national, created to get round big business. We can't do that now. There's nothing like that now.

The irony being that we have tools that empower that never existed before. Thanks to the digital age, everyone's opinions, creativity, products have access to the whole world at every level, and yet 'access' is another thing that doesn't quite mean what it should.

As we all know, you can just stick it on the internet . . . then watch it disappear. There's too much content. How do you get through all that content? Everyone's knocking product out. Everyone's putting content on platforms and sinking into the morass.

I suppose that's where the illusion of access gains reality only when serious corporate-level money seems to be the key to giving you a voice or getting that product into hands. And what's also changed is what you said about the racists in the old days having to shut up and get on with it. Now they can get their views out there not only on social media but entire media outlets. Rather than entering the promised land of unity through diversity, we've ended up in a diversity of ghettos. So where do you think you've got to at this point?

I'm a bit like yourself. I'm in the space where I can do what I want and I've not given up on artistic expression and following my instincts while responding to reality of the world out there. So there may be a few nasty bits in the bread and butter work I have to do now and again — *proper work* — but most of it isn't nasty. So it's a nice space to be in.

I was talking to a comedian mate and he was saying, "I'm going to be doing what we're doing till we're 70 or more. But I'm quite happy to do that. I've got my two houses, that's my pension so I'll keep doing it until they tell me to stop." In a strange sort of way that's why he does gigs against the advice of his agent and the effect the trajectory of his career because he's just so happy to get out there. He will do Bedford for £170 and he shouldn't be doing that, but he just loves performing. I see myself doing exactly the same thing and being creative as long as I've got the ability to do it. You've got to use it before you lose it.

Yeah, but are you making a difference?

I don't know if I am . . . I occasionally meet up with other people who say "You were very important to me, Paul, when I started." *[cackles]* "Oh really?!" Even the occasional white ones will come up and go the same. Comics from Bedford that came up and saw me in Edinburgh and years later they said, "When we saw you, we said if he can do it we can do it!" Now I'm not sure that's a compliment.

But I feel lucky. I don't know if in previous decades this wouldn't have been possible. Because all because the technology has made a huge terrible difference. Still, I can now do things across different genres. If I want to make a film I can make a film, if I want to make an album I can make an album, artwork, a play. I can do anything I fancy doing. Put it out there, stick it in a frame and sell it. Make a website and sell it. It's hard work, but you can make the web work for you. I can self-publish a book even as a vanity project, it doesn't stop you getting that stuff out there, whether anyone reads it or not. But with certain things you still need the objects. Like live performance. Like going on stage and wrangling about class and race and identity with a bunch of people in Highgate or Billericay.

Nowadays it's hard to evaluate whether you're making any difference or not . . .

And in the end there's a point where you think do I care? I mean I just want people to see it. Listen to it. And read it. Does any of that makes a difference? Is it up to me to make the difference?

When you hear people of our age moaning about young people, you know: "Oh, they're not as radical as we were!" and bla bla bla. Well yes they are. They're just radical about different things. Extinction Rebellion, that's the most middle class of all the rebellions I've ever seen but it's still a rebellion. These are people at their first demos. It's heartwarming to see them go, "Oooh, I'm going to get arrested!"

And they get arrested in a very nice middle class way. My 15 year old's out there with a loudhailer in one hand and his XR arrest advice sheet in the other. I can see Gen Z and the Boomers linking up — after all, we were there during the Thatcher years.

Totally and I've no problem with that at all. And before they've been arrested they're passing around nice baked cakes and stuff like that.

And they don't get kettled any more.

Well if they do, they assume yoga positions and wait for it to be over. And I must admit, there's something really nice about that. In our day you'd just get truncheoned. I was involved one of the first bits of kettling and what a boring activity that is. That was the infamous May Day protests in 2001 when they kettled us along with a load of shoppers into Oxford Circus. We finally got out down the side of the Palladium. And so the kettle was born. Funnily enough, we were working in the theatre that night.

But young people, of course they want to change the world. They might not be as countercultural as us, but everybody looks at things differently, don't they?

*

32
Barrie Rutter

'With core funding, we were never in the red. We couldn't be'

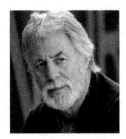

Barrie Rutter is an actor, director, producer & former artistic director/ founder of Northern Broadsides. Based in Halifax, he was born & raised in Hull, Yorkshire.
• *@BarrieRutter*

Funding in the UK is still more focused than mere postcode lottery, isn't it?

Funding for the North as opposed to the South is a proven fiscal fact. Nobody needs to go over that again. It just *is*. We get far less. The so-called centres of excellence are all in the South. It doesn't need to be amplified by me because there's enough material out there on the subject. *Parity* would be a rather a nice way of going about it. But the powers that be, they don't care. Like *[proposed high-speed rail link from London]* HS2, they don't care what happens above Birmingham. Oh, it's too costly to put in a branch line to Sheffield or Hull. It's that sort of attitude, and I get fed up of defending the North when I'm in London, and attacking the South when I'm in the North. I wish it wasn't the case.

Those sentiments were there for all to see when you started Northern Broadsides, but the company didn't come out of nowhere did it?

No, it didn't. It came out of Tony Harrison writing in classical language for my voice, because it sounded like it did. And the road to Damascus was that performance of *The Trackers of Oxyrhynchus* in 1992 at Salts Mill *[Saltaire, Bradford, Yorkshire]* where the natural voice of the play met its natural sounding audience in an old mill room — as I christened it, a 'non velvet space' and that was my sort of mantra for starting up Northern Broadsides. A *Guardian* review said "this is a broadside against gentility" or something like that. So I just put 'Northern' in front of 'Broadsides'. I just thought I had one good idea to be honest with you, and from then on it became obvious that I'd started something and by then Year Two was already in hand. And then I finished after 25 years — and it's still going.

There was a need, wasn't there? I know that's really obvious, but . . .

In 1992, Northern Broadsides proved to be a big impact. You couldn't start up something like that today because society is different. If somebody came up to me and said, "Oh, I've got this great idea", and described what became my own ethos, I'd just turn around and say, "Sod off, because it's been done." But it hadn't really been done in 92 like that, so I was able to made a mark and that got supported by audiences, by fellow professionals and by the Arts Council in a slightly grudging way at first. And then with proper funding from 2000 onwards, the success of the company is there in the annals of British drama.

It seems to be a very sort of British revolution where major situations requiring a simple and obvious solution are very often resolved or opened up by a single individual. So often it doesn't take a critical mass of people to make the breakthrough. And generally it almost seems haphazard, the way it happens.

I think you're right. People are always commenting on what *they* are doing. There's always a mysterious 'they', but there isn't a 'they'. You're quite right. It's an individual, in a positive way. I got a burning idea — burning to me anyway — and I managed to get it off the ground. But it was me doggedly saying this is worth doing, and getting enough people around me to support the idea and give it some oxygen.

What was it in your background, your training, your formation that gave you not just the wherewithal to leap into action but also the perspective to realise that this was actually fulfilling a need?

It was a combination of my own bloody-mindedness and, as I've mentioned, the dignity which Tony Harrison bestowed on the sound of my voice by writing for it in a classical form. At the time of his poem 'V' for instance, when there was that great furore in Parliament *[plans by Channel 4 in 1987 to screen the poem written after his parents' grave was vandalised led to outrage and a debate in Parliament]*, he was the president of the Classical Society of Great Britain.

And people in Parliament, these idiots who demanded to know who was this unknown poet, it was them that were fucking unknown. Not Tony Harrison. And so you had a man with a voice, like he has, the voice of the North writing in a classical form. And the juxtaposition . . . in a way it's as if the Establishment couldn't believe that he'd got inside the castle keep of education and could write in Latin and Ancient Greek and yet come out with this popular form of theatre. And then there was a bit of revenge that I got off Tony with his Seminal Sonnets 'Them' and 'Uz' — look them up because they're two poems that go together and they encapsulate everything. So I picked all that up off Tony, that getting inside the castle keep as it were.

For today's audiences, could you expand on that idea of Northern theatre?

Well, you can stand onstage and use classical-form language, like rhyming couplets and all like that in the regional accents without the sort of dialects of the accent coming through necessarily. It's the sound and the rhythm and the music — the *music*, you know, areas of different sounds have different musics. Of course, you need skill and delivery, you have to be able to reach the back row, to know who you are talking to and the situation, but sometimes it's just meat and two veg. Just say the bugger. When Tony was writing that stuff right through the 1980s, when I was at the National Theatre, I was in *The Mysteries [based largely on the Wakefield & York cycle of mystery plays]*. I did something for him on television in the same vein and then came *The Trackers of Oxyrhynchus* which he wrote for my voice. Well, you couldn't help but be thrilled. And that was my launchpad into the thinking that created Northern Broadsides.

Northern Broadsides' first production was Richard III with you as Richard and fellow Yorkshireman Brian Glover as Buckingham, and that was the first time you'd directed anything on this scale, wasn't it?

It were only me who had the vision. Before that I had directed a Ken Campbell play at the Shaw Theatre *[Euston, in North Central London]* and little things at the National as an assistant director. There was a bit of resistance to *Richard III*. One or two called it "*Coronation Street* Shakespeare" *[BBC Northern soap opera]*, things like that. Well, if you want everything in RP *[Received Pronunciation, a 'standard' (Southern) English that in practice is used to impose undeserved social privilege]* and stiff upper-lip and tight-arsed stiff-neck production, then you will look for that. I can't help thinking how I started Northern Broadsides in 1992 and one year later in 1993, there was the birth of what is now English Touring Theatre, or English Tour. And their promise was to build classical drama in proper costumes, their HQ was in Crewe *[in*

Cheshire, North West England, and now based in London], and they got funding straight off. Now I can't prove it, but don't tell me that somebody didn't think of an antidote to Rutter over in Yorkshire doing what he was doing. In a mill. It's that sort of a half-Establishment reaction. The thing about the arts is that they can't corral us. You can't corral the imagination and that's what they don't like. Because we ask them for money to subsidy, and then we lampoon them and they don't like that. And it don't matter what bloody party is in.

It's pathetic the way the arts are subsidised in this country, because in fact every fiscal argument they can raise against doing that is won. If it's just the arts alone, then anything between four and seven pounds goes back to the coffers for every pound given in subsidy. It's a proven fact. What *[Tory prime minister John]* Major did is he put us in *[the ministry of]* media and sports, so the big portfolio loses money. We, the arts, don't.

Which is highly relevant to the history of Northern Broadsides, which filled a void that could only be done with funding since that was why the void was there in the first place. If you are actually fulfilling a need, if there is actually a whole area of people out there who aren't being catered for, the mere fact that they're not being catered for means that after two years you're hardly going to be up on your own feet self-sustaining in a commercial sense.

Of course. It just doesn't work like that, you need the core funding and the money to set it up in the first place because there's nothing behind you. You can't set it up if there's nothing behind you. That's what subsidy does. And it very quickly comes back indirectly, like in petrol tax, like in food tax, restaurants, cafes, travel, all of that. That's the other way it all comes back to the coffers of the government. With that core funding, the commercial side of it is actually that in 25 years we were never ever in the red as a touring company. We couldn't be.

Why?

Because there was nothing to underpin us being in the red. We didn't have a building. The number of buildings that have been bailed out in my time that I've taken plays to are legion, and I do know that because I've been touring into them for 25 years. If you've got a building and it's going belly up, then there will be Arts Council strategies to call it something else and bail the bloody building out, time after time after time. Now, I quite agree with that bailing out. But you know, don't use it to beat other companies like a touring company that doesn't have a building and that can't call upon an overdraft — which a touring company cannot.

I'm not browbeating the Arts Council here, I'm just saying for one or two of the tactics, it's much easier if you've got four walls than it is if you're a touring company. You can always go into gentle artistic blackmail if you've got a building — "Well? Do you want to see it closed?" You know what I mean? It goes on, and with cuts in local funding also having a big impact, that sort of thing has to have gone on in the past.

And pertinently the reason you both started and left Northern Broadsides was funding, wasn't it?

We asked for £400,000 over four years to give some sort of parity. We didn't get it and were told that our 25 years of work didn't matter. That was 2017. It was the way they did it: they didn't want to fund our proposal but they would fund something far less than that, but also there was a big accusation of neglect about diversity. And that left me furious because diversity, when we finally collared the person at the Arts Council, was about colour of skin or physical disability, in a year when Mat Fraser, an actor with phocomelia *[caused by the drug thalidomide]*, played *Richard III [production at Hull Truck Theatre as part of Hull UK City of Culture 2017]* — there was none of what we actually do, who we actually represent, it's coming up now more and more socioeconomics.

But I set Northern Broadsides up based on diversity, the diversity of sound, of geography, of attitude, of all of those things. And we did what we did. And one of the proudest boasts of Northern Broadsides was the amount of people we employed over the years on the lowest grants in our group — over 700 actors and crew. It's a phenomenal record of employment, and look how much NI and Schedule E and Schedule D and VAT goes back into the system because of that. So that was the reason I don't want to fight this battle anymore. I saw what the Arts Council wanted us to become and I didn't like it, so I just got out.

Creating employment on that scale takes the remit beyond 'value added', as was reaching out to audiences beyond the Yorkshire Sprachbund, which you did.

We did! As soon as we began to be established, we had to change from being a summer touring company to a spring and autumn one because we were in demand. We went anywhere we were asked, and I very soon dropped the 'non velvet' thing. But it sort of lingered on me — people are still using it today, and there's no reason why they shouldn't, but still it's a bit moribund now. It's a bit like Muhammad Ali when he first started out saying, "What's my name? What's my name?", punching anyone to the ground who called him

'Cassius Clay', it was a bit like me saying, "Where's your passport? Where's your Yorkshire passport? Where's your *Yorkshire* passport?"

But we soon became national and *international*. In 1993 in our second year we did a whole tour of India with *The Merry Wives of Windsor*, a play that had never been taken over there on that scale. I made choices of plays where I never chose a set book *[on the national schools curriculum]*, and if it was a set book, it was completely by accident. But equally you can't choose, let's say, *All's Well That Ends Well* at a time like 1992 when there was a major recession and expect to sell a 14-week national tour. You just have to be shrewd about it — places like Stratford can do those plays and things, but we couldn't, not with only one or two slots a year. You have to choose, you have to have a semi-commercial mind on your shoulders.

But we had. And we did it. We did things like *Samson Agonistes* by Milton, things like *The Mysteries* and we did new translations by Blake Morrison of Kleist *[The Cracked Pot, adaptation of Heinrich von Kleist's Der Zerbrochene Krug]*. And made them great plays. Really great plays. I think every ancient play that I chose that wasn't Shakespeare, we always did a new version of it. Blake has done seven plays for us: *Oedipus*, *Antigone*, *The Cracked Pot*, *Lysistrata*, the list goes on. Seven brand-new textual versions of ancient classic plays.

And that aren't dictated to by the constraints of RP, RSC and all the rest of our linguistic baggage.

Exactly. And the words changed too. I remember in *Oedipus* when that servant comes on to describe the blood running down Oedipus, she says it was like a 'beck in spate' *['a stream in flood']*, a wonderful wonderful phrase. In *The Cracked Pot*, for 'pull wool over your eyes', all Blake did was change 'wool' to 'fleece' and it becomes a brand new phrase, 'pull fleece over your eyes'. It's the little things as well as the big things, it's that sort of musical magic, in the music of an area where we've had a lot of our great glories. We certainly showed what could be done.

You founded Northern Broadsides at a time when there was the almost religious vision passed over from the 1980s of the business model of expand expand expand, and then that morphed into concepts of sustainability and commercial returns. You must have faced immense pressure to grow ever bigger, to create spaces, different touring units, a bigger office even. How did you keep all that in perspective — and in control?

In terms of expanding to venues, that happened. We could put together a 14-week tour in the spring, with a slightly shorter autumn, and go as far south as Southampton, Portsmouth, and then up north to Glasgow. It was nationwide, Liverpool to Scarborough, to Bristol, all over the shop. So we weren't backward in coming forward. And we did play in some really really odd-sods, with the actors going, "Oh bloody hell, Barrie, what a f'cking awful place this is!" And I'd have to tell them, "I know, but it was the only thing we could get for this week and a week out is a fairly expensive venture." So we took rough with the smooth, but we expanded geography, certainly.

You have to have a commercial heart. You also need to have the bureaucracy of the company, and my longterm chief exec Sue Andrews, who was with me for 24 out of the 25 years, was wonderful for that. Just sit down and pick a title, and the rest was done for me while I got on with it in the rehearsal room. The expansion in that way was down to Sue in a way, because nobody likes dealing with the artist.

They always want to deal with a bureaucrat, like in the last 25 years there's been this thing of having a dual head at the top of the big organisations because they don't want to deal with the artists. They're somehow terrified, and sometimes the artists are quite right to terrify them because often the artists are the only ones who they want to talk about. But all big companies need to be art led. There are twosomes all over the place in the commercial world as well as in the subsidised world, with two people running the building. Whereas I was very firmly of the opinion that although a chief executive would do all the bureaucratic work, I would remain its figurehead because it had to be art led. If it was going to go down, it was going to go down through art, not through business.

There's been much more emphasis on the business side of things recently, but it still remains that this is the most creative country in the world across all the arts. Of course there are countries that have individual superiority over the bunch of artists that we have, but I do think that as a country taken as a whole there is nowhere more creative than Britain.

Why do you think that is?

Maybe because of our length of time of being a country, as it were. Maybe because the English language is such a wonderful language to write in. I think our greater glories are linguistic. Dance of course is an international language and there are wonderful companies all over the world. But the English language as our bedrock of the springboard of creativity is probably the best answer. I suppose there's people could probably disagree with me there or add to what I've said, but even in things like art where spoken language doesn't come into it, there's still a bedrock of language in terms of the communication of the work.

Well there's a lot of people across the country who are deprived of the right to express that creativity in their own way of speaking still to this day. When you were growing up, what was the block to you yourself getting on?

It wasn't a block, it just simply wasn't there. I mean, there wasn't a book in my house. I'm a fish dock kid, the only written material in my house was a daily newspaper and the *News of the World* on a Sunday. It was only when I got into sixth form that there was a teacher who backed me in terms of National Youth Theatre and drama school, and I could start to swim in that world. So I started to read. I read *The Times* because I wanted to see the review of the National Youth Theatre production. So you pick up the newspaper to read the review and by extension, by osmosis, you start to read the newspapers. And I then switched to *The Guardian*. And that's my choice of paper now.

So you read across the board because of other things and then they affect you. The bigger the newspaper, as it were, the more it affects you. But though I became an avid reader, I'm a classicist by experience, not by education at all but by experience on stage. What I glean and pick up and remember or try to remember and try to pass on, all that comes from a sponge-like attitude to wanting to learn about things that were never there in my first 16 years.

That opening up of your horizons, was it your school or just that one teacher?

It was one teacher. It was a technical grammar school but I passed the 11-plus to get there. When I scraped the five O-levels that you had to get to go on to do A-levels, because I was a bit of a tear-arse — I mean I wasn't a bad lad but I was a bit of a tear-arse — there were many a teacher who said, "Oh fucking hell, Rutter's come back for A-level?!" Actually it was the making of me! There was the added responsibility just at school level for being a prefect and being backed by the very enthusiastic Mr Siddle, who really was the main guy who led me in all the paperwork for the National Youth Theatre and looked out for drama schools and things. Because there was a teacher who believed in me, and you know, it was a whole world I never knew.

But the National Youth Theatre was a world that I really enjoyed because it was like, you know, going to London and meeting up with . . . well, I remember in my first year I was so excited, this kid a young dustman from Plymouth had got into the National Youth Theatre, they'd paid all his money and fare and living expenses. It was that sort of world. I just fell in love with it. I've always been happy on a stage. What I mean by that is I just knew what to do. I'm not talking about talent. I leave that to other people, but I'd always been comfortable. I was good with props. I was good at staging myself if you like. I felt very comfortable on a stage and knew that I wanted to do more and more of it.

So what's the logical next step? You do your National Youth Theatre, you find out you've got the backing of your community as well on that, which is really important, you had that Billy Elliot experience. You go to London and people think, "Oh okay . . . that's all right!" which actually shows the positive side of London, where Northern becomes an imprimatur for stepping into culture as a cool thing, doesn't it?

Just by recognising what I could do, it got me out of Hull because my background as a kid was very unhappy. So once I got out, I rarely went back. I got out for family reasons, which I won't bore you with, but I was on the road to Samarkand. There's no two ways about it and I embraced it.

If you'd left school at 15-16 and had not gone on to do your A-levels, what were you supposed to have become?

I had no idea whatsoever. Let's see, 15 and a half, 16, I was just desperately waiting on that August and the appearance of the O-level results. I didn't know what to do. My Dad didn't want me to go on the fish dock like every other one of my peers who I grew up with down the same street. But apart from that, I wouldn't have known what the hell to do. There was one point when I first got back into the sixth form, there was an idea of being a geography teacher because that was my favourite subject. But it soon became obvious, or was always made obvious to me, by my English teacher Mr Siddle that I really should try and follow the stage career.

That was quite a cut across the expectations of where you came from, wasn't it?

Yes. I mean, that was 1964.

So you're something of a rough diamond.

And you're not the first to say that!

Who's not going back to Hull. And you're in London now, you've got to assimilate, haven't you in terms of onstage, the way that you speak and deport yourself?

Well no. I was encouraged to use my own voice by Michael Croft, the founder and then director of the National Youth Theatre. He wanted regional voices, but *clarity* was paramount. We're not talking sloppy pavement chat from Hull here. We're talking projected normal voices using whatever skills an older generation can give us at 17 and a half, 18 in the National Youth Theatre and performing onstage at the Queen's Theatre, Shaftesbury Avenue *[West End of London]*, in 1964, which is what I did. He couldn't abide sloppiness. It wasn't a case of any voice will do.

What was your next step on from there?

My next step was the Royal Scottish Academy of Music & Drama in Glasgow. I was the only Englishman in a class of Scots and they told me I talked funny. So I always had a bit of chip on my shoulder up there. Because I was also, by the time of end of year one, playing leads in the National Youth Theatre. I was getting star reviews in national newspapers and they're still putting the brakes on me. So I left early and they've never acknowledged me as an alumnus of the college because I left early. *[chuckles]*

Did you go straight to work?

Straight to work, a full year at Nottingham Playhouse. But again, I had a great springboard. The year 1966 saw the first modern play by the NYT, David Halliwell's *Little Malcolm and His Struggle Against the Eunuchs* at the Royal Court, in which I played Nipple. 1967 saw the beginning of the era of Peter Terson with *Zigger Zagger* which became a world-famous sensation, and in 1968 Peter's *The Apprentices* which was written totally around me. Totally. My launch into the profession in September 1968 when it opened was massive, and I suppose I could have really played up to that at the time. But I liked the stage, so I went away for a year to Nottingham Playhouse and didn't follow any fame. And I was doing okay. I joined the RSC in 1975 and stayed there for a few years. And then in 1980, I went to the National Theatre and there it was Tony Harrison who said, "You know, I've just been spending ten years translating *The Orestaia* for voices like yours." Well . . . you know, how wonderful is that? *[laughs]*

You can't say no.

You can't say *better*, can you?

But it's not just about dialect, it's far more than that, isn't it? It's about identity, community, belonging.

Yes, it is, It's the granite and millstone grit of the West Riding, and the chalk and the clay of the East Riding where I were born. It's fundamental. It's basic.

Well I think so, anyway! Everyone, whether they're a nurse or a writer, works in the blood, sweat and tears of their own particular choice or profession, but everyone hopefully works at or near the top of their own integrity as well. And when that's very muscular — I mean muscular in language combined with a great education, like Tony Harrison introduced me to — then of course it opens up the world of something like Shakespeare in a different way. Of course it had been discovered before, but Tony opened it up in an enlightened way for me which I then wanted to embrace and to pass on. So that's what I did.

Things like Northern Broadsides and regional accents in broadcasting have made the case for diversity of speech, and yet we're still living all over the UK with the very calculated legacy of the destruction of how people speak, made in the name of standardisation. It was done with our indigenous languages, and in the same way people's 'regional' speech has been used against them as a class and regional blocker to keep the population in their place. Just from the way you speak. It's ironic how the UK was giving language rights to populations across the British Empire while perpetuating the death of our own languages and dialects at home. The last few decades have delivered the death knell to our dialects, our accents and 'deviant' grammar are still looked down on, and yet there isn't even a single name for the English they want everyone to aspire to — RP, Queen's English, Oxford English, Public School English, BBC English, it's anyone's guess. It's region, it's class . . .

And it's socioeconomic as well.

Well, there you go. That sums it up, doesn't it?

I agree. Totally. Everything you've just said. And there is this idea of the glee that comes with revenge against that. The attack again, to get inside the castle keep of that. It's a real pleasure when you win against that language that's based on privileged Southern English public schools *[elite private schools]*. And Daniel Jones, book of language etiquette *[The Pronunciation of English, 1909 and following revised editions]*, he'd say things like 97 per cent of the people are wrong because they say this, and you say, piss off, you pompous sod, if it's 97 per cent, they must be right.

In a way, the intellectual side of that has been won hands down, like you're saying, and people know that. But the practical battle is still going on. I get young people writing to me still saying, "They're trying to rip out my natural voice at drama school, what do I do?" My advice is always to fight back. I was never very good at RP, you see, this is the point. I didn't spurn it, it spurned me. I could never bloody do it. I mean, I tried. I'd sound terrible, and even now my attempts at it, if I've had to put it into say a bit of reported speech on the stage, I'm still terrible at it. Awful. I was just never comfortable with RP and I thought, why am I perpetuating this bloody thing which I cannot get? I tried. Of course I tried. When I was at a college, I had to try. But I just couldn't get it. So it spurned me.

I've never quite thought of it this way, but we all know an actor has to go onstage and be certain things. The words come from the writer who has to write in different voices, but if it's different voices for a woman, for a man, for a child, for a dog maybe, if they're all in Yorkshire speech then you do have that common voice, don't you? But that point of reference is very often taken away from you, isn't it? At the same time I don't think it's any actor's job to *be* anybody. I think it's an actor's job to *convince* an audience that you're somebody. You can't be a mass murderer eight shows a week because you're playing Macbeth. You cannot, it's just psychologically impossible.

It's a model that worked for Midlander Lenny Henry [comedian, actor, writer & TV presenter from Dudley, West Midlands].

Yes, it did, in a big way. When Lenny Henry was doing his Shakespeare radio programme called *Lenny and Will [BBC Radio 4]*, it was made from the premise that when he was at school, Shakespeare was just a foreign language, it was all 'thees' and 'thous'. They got in touch with me because of that, and that was the birth of me directing Lenny as Othello *[a Northern Broadsides production in 2009]*, a real change in his life, and he always credits me as helping him find his sixth gear. So that was a case of a man finding something which he thought had spurned him or he'd spurned at age 15 and then at age 49, 50, he found Othello.

And what did you get out of that?

There were other people asking could I do something like that with them and have me change their career. That was very pleasant. But what did I really get out of it? I'll tell you what I got out of it — first, a lifelong friend in Lenny, and obviously the company got publicity from it.

What I also got out of it is that I'm actually a very good teacher and I enjoy it too. You can call me a director, but I can teach as well, the way I want the Shakespeare to appear. You know, that side of it in the rehearsal room of asking actors not to hit pronouns, not to hit the word 'and', not to elide the word 'but'. You know, they often say, "I love you but Dot, dot, dot, dot, dot. Not on a Tuesday." Whereas the sentence is, "I love you. Dot, dot, dot. But not on a Tuesday." And you listen, you watch television, you watch films, everybody elides 'buts'. So that's the sort of thing I try to bring in, you know, it's English, it's all English. It's not mystery, it's not robbing them of acting skills, just observe the English.

But that English is still being used as a social weapon against people in the UK.

But I've never mentioned the word 'accent' or 'dialect' — it's others that have — "Oh, you're the one that does Shakespeare with Northern accents." No, I don't. I use the 'Northern voice' with its alacrity, with its limestone grit consonants and short vowels. And where does the North start and end? I use everyone from Geordies to people from Nottingham. But it's still being used against us, the battle isn't over.

It isn't. I did a show on Friday night in Hull with my great friend Eliza Carthy, the folksinger *[from Yorkshire]*, just the two of us onstage entertaining. And what a pleasure it is to stand in Hull and perform Andrew Marvell's 'To His Coy Mistress' *[poem by the 17th-century Yorkshire poet]* in my own Hull voice, it's just wonderful. And that's a classic poem of our time. You know, Marvell, he might have had a different syntax but it sounded as he sounded, he didn't have an RP, nor did kings. And that was my point originally, going back to forming Northern Broadsides, the rulers probably had a different syntax but the sound of the way they spoke was very very similar to the working population.

You and Northern Broadsides have been all about fighting for a place in the arts funding landscape of the UK. Did that wear you out?

It didn't wear me out at all. What wore me out was I didn't like what the Arts Council said about me and mine, and I didn't like that their plan for what the future was going to be for the company. Because there was far more diktat and I was eschewing their diktat.

I suppose that sort of thing is inevitable. I mean, some people feel lucky to get two and a half years let alone 25 years.

And it fell on the 25th year. So I thought, yeah, enough's enough of that — of that particular thing, anyway.

But then again, it comes down to what we were saying about how sometimes it's weirdly just one person who shows how to make a difference.

Well they're everywhere, but they're in different arts. This is what I mean about the depths of creativity, there must be thousands of individuals like that in this country. One of the great pleasures is how many there are in the young people.

But a lot of the rewriting and reorganising that we've done of the classics just goes by. Sometimes it shows up on a nice site or something and then people will say, "Well, it *is* about the modern age." But more often people say, "It's just theatre." Well, I can take that with a big bushel of salt, and that's because I'm an old dinosaur who loves rhyming couplets and not eliding 'buts'. But there are so many other people out there being wonderfully creative and who are desperate to get their ideas off the ground but not getting the wherewithal to do that. Now I'm not blaming the Arts Council on this because they're shat upon from above, but for this country of all countries to give an art portfolio of less than £500 million for all the glories that we've got in every region is just awful. It stinks. And we're not asking for a lot of money. Because this is the myth about the arts. We've never ever asked for a lot of money. We've only ever asked for enough.

*

33
Faz Shah

'We're missing safe spaces for the arts, to be honest'

Faz Shah is a musician, actor & composer. He is based in Oldham, Greater Manchester, where he was born & raised.
• *@faz_shah_music*

Born, raised, educated, based in the North of England — that must give you quite an appreciation of the language and identity that people in the rest of the country, for no fault of their own, might not necessarily get.

The fact is that I'm a product of all the collaborative social angsts that meet in the town where I'm from. Oldham is a very different place now than when I was growing up. When I was growing up, it was heavily racially segregated. It's still racially segregated, but there is an unspoken acceptance today that this is the make-up of those who live in Oldham, this is what Oldham looks like now — rather than when I was growing up, where it was more like Oldham *should* look a certain way and that these people coming to live here are not welcome.

So there's a general acceptance now. But I grew up in the heart of that mixed feeling when it was not so much the 'Muslim' narrative that was propagated in the media as it was the 'Asian' narrative. So from the beginning of the 1990s it was definitely the Asian narrative that the media was against, and so that was the environment I grew up in. I learned very quickly that how you *look* matters — it really does matter. Depending on who you speak to, it can work for you or against you. I'm still fighting with that, I guess, in various different ways and I'll get onto that a bit later.

I started the violin because my parents were in a financial position where they could choose between a state school and a private school. I would say we were one of the few mixed or Asian families that were able to do that. They'd chosen a private education for me, and through that private education I was able to start the violin. So that already speaks volumes, because in terms of opportunities and accessibility within the area generally, there is an unspoken rule in the Asian community about music not being widely accepted. Many from the Asian community would say it's a cultural thing. But I can say with full conviction it's not. The culture story is a bit of a cover-up for the religious [Islamic] one. It's a religious obligation, but most of the community don't know the rulings on it. So we'll just say it's a cultural one. It avoids all that questioning and the awkward long answers and it covers up a lot of insecurity about what people actually know about their own religion.

So I was rubbing the community up the wrong way just by playing the violin. But it came as part of the private education where it was perfectly normal and I didn't know any different. So that's my beginning on the violin. But I quickly did know different, after I was kicked out of that private education. I went straight to the state school where they couldn't afford a uniform and was majority Asian kids. It was a stark contrast. It was a big learning curve for me that — oh my gosh, I couldn't believe that this school was literally metres away from the junior grammar school yet there were no opportunities here. The actual local aspiration was well, whoever was *flaunting* success in the area — and that was the guy with a big chain and a nice car outside the school gates. Whatever they're doing, they must be doing something right, otherwise they wouldn't be so bold and flaunting this cash about. So the seeds of crime were inspired from that period really in the area. I've got a lot of friends who went that way, and if I hadn't had things like theatre or music or the arts, I definitely would have also fallen into it, without a shadow of a doubt, because it was such a strong narrative.

I was lucky I had an alternative to that. But in terms of opportunities and diversity in the arts, I didn't know any different until I started doing things outside of Oldham. My engagement with the arts as a young person was going into the studio and helping the local rappers with their instrumental beats so that they could rap over something. From the age of nine, ten, I was already on various projects, local Bangladeshi community, local Pakistani community, you know, they were rapping, they were doing this Bhangra-garage-mixed-rap thing. It was really popular . . . people like RDB *[Rhythm Dhol Bass]*, Stereo Nation, Metz and Trix, you know, these people were really *hot* on the underground Asian garage scene and everybody in the community wanted to be like them.

So I was exposed to all that from an early age. But my exposure was also learning classical music, getting it from my private education. But now I wasn't in that environment but at the state school I had to hold onto it. And then I realised that I could actually offer something even at that early age. In hindsight I wasn't thinking this at the time, but I realised that I was the only one playing the violin and being with these rappers. You know, if you need a good violinist in the studio to record something decent, well I can provide that. So that was pretty cool. So yes, diversity in the arts!

My theatre background started a bit after this, when I was like eleven, twelve. I joined a group called Peshkar [formed in 1991 as a community theatre project for Oldham's Asian community, now the UK's leading participatory arts organisation targeting young people deemed hard to reach or socially disadvantaged]. They don't do this now, but Peshkar at the time were focused on telling the stories of Southeast Asian arts and sort of storytelling through theatre, so things like A Thousand and One Nights, Arabian Nights, Shaherazade, and refugee stories. It was in stark contrast with the alternative, which was the local amateur dramatics society, what you could call all-singing, all-dancing, all-acting musical training. It pulled in the white kids with nice haircuts from outside the neighbourhood who used to come into Oldham and be part of that, but I was always intimidated by that group and never joined when I was a youth.

I couldn't even articulate it, but I knew straight off that I just would not fit at all. It's not what I knew. It was so alien to me and I'd feel uncomfortable in that environment. So I started with Peshkar, where it was majority Asian participants — Bangladeshi, Pakistani, with one boy of African heritage. We collaborated extensively on telling these mythical Southeast Asian and Arab stories in interesting ways, and them are some of the best times I've had with this group because it was so real, it was so close to home — and those who were leading the workshop sessions really cared about it.

We had Asian workshop leaders from that demographic, so I would say I was exposed to brown faces leading brown artistic development. It's funny because in the same industry there's two different narratives: you can either fall in with the going white mainstream narrative, which would be the Stagecoach type of schooling, amateur dramatics, or it would be the alternative which was offered, which was the little groups like Peshkar who were available. And you know, there was no comparison for me, I'd go straight for the brown line. It was awesome. It was brilliant.

The main reason I then started beatboxing was because there was so much racial tension in my secondary school. Beatboxing was a response to just make life a bit easier. Here I'll be honest and say that being mixed race, there were all the things that people called me and my family because of my English side. And then from the other side there was being called all kinds of things because of my Asian side. It was a very confusing time and it was beatboxing that helped me build a name for myself away from that hostility. That genuinely is the reason why I started, because the violin wasn't resonating, as you can imagine. *[laughs]*

But working in the arts, I'm facing a very different problem at the moment in that I don't know whether I am employed for my background and demographic or my skill. I'm very aware of this, I don't want to be lured into a false sense of security where I believe myself to be better than I am. That's always a fear of being called to account for representation on a community that spat me out a long time ago. So there's a bit of internal conflict happening there.

In terms of my identity of being from the North, there's things like the new high-speed train line being built, HS2 *[from London to parts of the North]*. To be honest with you, it's very simple for everyone up here. They know what it means, it's just all roads lead to Rome — and London is basically Rome. It's another subliminal message: "Everyone, you can get to London faster now. You can be successful, faster, in quicker time." That's all it feeds.

But also there's a bit of a superiority complex from London realising that places like Manchester have got a lot to offer — *[BBC]* Media City's up here for a start. They're trying to connect the two cities as if trying to measure success rates, and also if Manchester is part of London then it will be more widely accepted. It's this whole London economic, its own bubble. Don't get me wrong, I love London. I love going there. It's bursting at the seams full of opportunity and talent. In fact I am not the best person to speak to about London because I believe it to be far more accepting of diverse backgrounds and skills than any other part of country. It's purely because it's the capital that it's always going to be a few steps ahead. In the North, I think the arts are heavily influenced by racial segregation and the inferiority of being forgotten — the forgotten masses, the forgotten areas, the forgotten voice constantly being propagated through the arts.

It sounds like you're constantly evolving the projects that you're involved with — working on that crossover between music and theatre, and then actively applying it further to include marginalised groups.

I guess the story of the local presence of the arts within these communities is fast diminishing, especially in Oldham, Rochdale and Bury. Apart from things like Bolton and Oldham Music Services provided by the councils, they're all what you could call weathering the storm. From an austerity that's been long imposed. I think that the highly polarised politics is both feeding the arts and taking away from it. In fact we're identity obsessed at the moment — you know, if it's identity, you've got to tell the story, but what actually is identity, what does life mean for *you*? And that can be quite divisive.

So in terms of 'identity', I'm very careful how I use the word because my identity changes every day. Like the times when I enter a majority white arts environment, a pristine glossy white culture but there's the presence of people like myself. For example, I'm very conscious of praying openly in an environment like that as a Muslim, because either I'm completely on my own or there's only one or two other Muslims that I can count in the building.

Now that's not a reflection on places like that not being open to other people working there. It's more of a reflection on identity actually mattering: how do I fit in here, how does my identity pertain? But actually in the arts it's less about identity and more about what is inclusive for *everyone*. Whether or not I'm a Muslim, whether or not I have this culture or identity, another Muslim could walk through the door and they could have a different identity. They could be coming from Birmingham or from London. It's identity in the arts that is a tool for forging voices. But it can be quite divisive as well — it's almost like holding a mirror up to the industry. The mirror helps us get onto the platform, but . . .

> *It's a complex thing, like you say, where you see that idea of your identity changing on a day-to-day basis as a religious thing, a cultural thing, an ethnic thing but also a class thing which cuts across the segregation and the other divisions. Because of your background, you have an inbuilt perspective that you can't cook up in a policy workshop — and, as you say, nothing is clear-cut in any case — so are you in a position that you don't have to take sides?*

The biggest problem that we have is not just in the arts but everywhere else. You see it in the people in families who are breaking up over the whole Brexit thing, disagreeing with each other. It just comes from the notion that my opinion trumps your opinion, my identity and my belief and my perspective is right and yours is wrong and that's because we can't hold different views and stay in the same room. *[laughs]* You know, it's like we've got this really, I dunno, *selfish* environment where everyone is being separated from people that they once held close and dear, just in the name of opinion — and identity comes into that. No one's thinking about anyone else but themselves but, moving forward as a country, you should think collectively — and no one is doing that.

This mindset is heavily saturating everyone, people are scared to speak their mind, and that feeds into the arts as well. You know, how can you have an honest conversation when people are scared, wondering whether there's a fake oppressive censoring that's going on, where you don't say the wrong thing because it could be used against you. It makes functioning in society very difficult. And the arts are not exempt from that. In fact, I would say the arts are trying to coin it, in the way that the arts do, to tell the story of that mindset, which is holding a mirror up to the arts, feeding the arts' own story.

*How do you transfer that over to the wider sense of community in your work,
such as the workshops that you do with marginalised groups?*

I think the performing arts is a way of expressing opinion, the hidden
perspective, the underdog. But the arts can't just champion that, they need to
also champion a collective effort. That's a collective effort in the sense of where
everyone reaches a consensus, everyone is in agreement that there is an injustice
in the country, and once everyone establishes it then this agreement can be
formulated into something productive. At the moment, I have friends who
believe, for example, that white privilege is not a thing. There was something
recently about that on *Question Time [BBC One topical debate show]* when a *[white]*
actor Laurence Someone-or-Other said that "playing the race card" was getting
"boring", and people were messaging everyone about it saying, "Do you believe
what he said? Can you believe what he said?" And I'm like, "Yeah, I *can* believe
what he said. Because there's many people who think like him."

The shock of all the friends who were messaging me is only because they've
been telling me they've unfriended everyone on Facebook or whatever
because they hold different views or opinions. I'm thinking, "No wonder
you're shocked by that interview, you've shot the debate down even before
you even got to the table." So someone like Laurence Fox, it might be a shock
to you, but it's not a shock to me, because I know there are people who hold
different views on what needs to be changed and what doesn't, and that's fine.

So when we talk about refugees, when the media bandies the word 'refugee'
around, they have no idea what they're talking about. In 2015-16, when they were
saying that "all the refugees are coming over the border", well a 'refugee' is an
official status that the Home Office has to give someone. So how do you know
that they're refugees coming over the border when none of them have got any
status yet? We don't know who they are. They could be migrants, they could be
asylum-seekers, they could be refugees. They could be migrants for different
reasons like economic migrants. It could be also all sorts of different reasons.

So the media latched on to this word 'refugee' and that community was
really penalised for it. I work now with asylum-seekers and refugees, I spread
their stories and it's horrifying what refugees have been through. Basically, if
they have been granted refugee status, it means the Home Office have had to
admit this, that the grey area of the Home Office, as dodgy as they are, have
had to admit that "Yeah, your life is in danger. If we send you back to your
home country, it's most likely you're going to be in mortal danger. You're
going to get killed."

So these are the most vulnerable of the most vulnerable of the most
vulnerable in our society. These are the people who we should try to be
helping, but they're at the butt of every joke at the moment. Only the other

day, I was speaking to someone who does similar work to me helping refugees, who said their sister was telling them, "Oh yeah, well we've voted Out *[in favour of Brexit]*. So you don't need to work with them refugees anymore. They're going to go home. We don't need to do that anymore and you don't need to do that anymore. We voted Out, you know." It's a sad state of affairs that the most vulnerable are the most marginalised. That's why I'm focused on sharing their stories because their perspective, their story needs to be heard, because it's actually a big vilification, a big tarnish on that name.

The asylum-seekers and refugees obviously represent a heavily racialised area as well, and this doesn't do anything for the existing problem of segregated race communities within the UK, especially in the North. London has its own problem but in the North it's definitely heavily racially segregated. But you can throw up a mirror to that through the arts, you can share stories like the asylum-seekers and refugees and put their story to the masses. And if you're in the position to be able to do that, it's your duty to do it and you also define your own identity by doing it. For example, myself, I have my own following, I've got a certain set of skills, I've been gifted with privilege. I'm under no illusion that I started off with a financial advantage over many other people in Oldham, my community. I'm not hiding away from that. But the moment I reject it, I reject the issue of the disparity and the financial implications of forwarding yourself in the arts in a certain field or going down another field in the arts. Then it becomes a problem.

We're not helped by the coding of language in society, which I also reject. For example, 'urban' is a code word for 'black'. If you say someone's playing 'very urban music' you mean 'very black music'. Or you're looking 'very urban'. 'Economically vibrant' is popular. Why don't you tell your 'story'? It's very . . . 'different', meaning for every person of colour that your story is 'non-white'. Here's all this subliminal phrase-coining which is why we're scared to say what we need to say. But the arts is a great way to lift the lid on these issues and have an honest conversation.

What are the things we're missing for empowering the talent of the communities that aren't getting through the 'system' in areas like the North West?

We're missing safe spaces for the arts, to be honest. Safe spaces for the marginalised communities, for the vulnerable who are able to engage, for the financially deprived, for the segregated, for the disadvantaged. There's no safe space to engage with the arts because the people who hold the keys are those who are looking for a token representation first. For example, they'll only be looking into the Muslim or the Asian community, because they're a Muslim or Asian community first before anything else. And if you are being given a space to learn about or explore the arts, there should be no limit on that. It could be rapping, it could be theatre, it could be spoken word, it could be violin, it could be music.

If you're only given opportunities because of your identity, that is *not* a safe space. It's exploitation. That's not a safe space that caters for everyone, a space where basically you can count on everyone to support you, because it's heavily biased. We are missing these open neutral spaces for everyone, that are open to everyone to engage with. It's something that's definitely lacking in the arts. There's also the fact that a lot of charities have become more business-minded now because it's become a bit of a competition as the funding pots are drying up for the arts. But as long as there is an arts sector, you can weather such storms because you're not afraid to put something on when you've only been given a shoestring.

I don't actually know any other area like the performing arts that could *thrive* on that. Hip hop for example was born out of economic depression and necessity in the most marginalised communities. The little beatbox machine that was popular, that played the James Brown drum fills over and over, it was one of the pioneering elements of hip hop. Then those who couldn't even afford that beatbox machine would emulate the sounds with their mouth so they became known as human beatboxes. So beatboxing as we know it today started from having nothing.

We are lacking that sort of creativity, that open space, a stand against the hostile environment. These neutral spaces are really important and I can count on one hand the organisations I've worked with that can actually claim to be as 'open' as they claim to be. That's really sad because it's not the world I knew, that's not how I experienced the arts growing up, when it was led by the community, delivered by the community and performed by the community. And that doesn't happen anymore.

What's your role in all of this — looking back, looking forward, looking at where you are at the moment?

My role? I'm under no illusion that I'm in a position where I am representative of a certain faith, a certain background and a certain geographical position in the UK. You can't get away from that because we are so obsessed with representation and identity. That you're just a speaker for hundreds of thousands of others. So you've got to be very careful what you say, how you say it and what you do. But I actually like it, in the sense that it forces you to take seriously what you say — don't squander your words and the actions that you take.

I've just delivered a talk in Leicester where I was talking about my story, similar as what I'm saying here, but also about Islam and music and why there's such friction between music educators and facilitators and the Muslim community in the UK. I talked about how to tackle that and then what we can do to solve that as a country. So anyway, I'm doing that and I'm doing more things like that. At the same time I'm not neglecting my craft. I'm giving workshops but also going for auditions and trying to raise my level and personal development. If you stop trying to develop yourself, you flatline — which basically means dead.

My role, I guess, is to just continue what I'm doing. I'm not putting myself under any pressure to be bigger or speak beyond my means. But I'm also aware that there are communities who are calling for representation from me as well. So I've got to take both into account. You know, when you take all the people away from the country, what you're left with is useless really. We are human beings, we only have our actions between each other as something of worth. I just hope that my actions can be of benefit, that mine are positive, and if I can offer something to a community that they otherwise would not be able to receive such a representation without me, then I'm happy to say I will do a good job, you know?

Any thoughts on the connection between music and theatre and the way that you're able to knock them up together onstage and hit audiences, communities and participants in a very different way to just theatre or just music?

Music and theatre are always two lights from the same flame. They're just different forms of expressing the same thing that aid each other. They just expand the storytelling really. What I really like about theatre, which music doesn't really offer, is that you literally create a space and a world. You can create a world that can be fictional or it can be very uncomfortably real, and music can serve that space in the best possible way. And likewise, something that music offers that theatre doesn't is that you can just play a few notes and it transports you to a different country, culture — a different place, a different time.

These elements are absolutely invaluable, which is why I would like more young people from different communities to be trained not only in the way to learn classical music via the formal route but also to taproot into their own culture, into their own sound and the sounds that they grew up on, into not letting them things go. And bringing all that into the space. That's really what we need. I mean, do we honestly need to be *forced* to do that?

*

34
Bob Slayer

'It's about letting money pass through to the benefit of all'

Bob Slayer is a comedian & founder/ co-director of fringe venue Heroes & the BlundaBus doubledecker pop-up venue. Based in Worcestershire, he was raised in Shropshire.
• heroesoffringe.com

What are the challenges for Heroes?

I often find it difficult to nail down what we do and why. In many ways I go on my feeling and follow my nose, then people say that we're doing something interesting. Which I am very proud of. But when I focus too much on trying to define what that is, it can get away from the heart of it.

One of the biggest challenges we all face at the moment are the systems of global business. Business is a psychopath but we allow a corporation to have the same rights as a person and all that — like the 2003 documentary *The Corporation*. In all of the industries I've moved through — and there have been a fair few — I've seen it again and again. The music industry, festivals, comedy, Edinburgh fringe, horseracing, funeral business, chicken factories, the City, oh yeah definitely the City . . . it's always the same problem — even when it is not understood as such or in deep denial — which is basically self-interest defending the broken system that props up its existence. And I've never been good with authority, ever since Mrs James, my Seventh Day Adventist primary school teacher, tried to tell me that dinosaurs did not exist and that their bones were put in the ground to test us. Well Mrs James, that was a test that I was happy to fail, you weren't going to take dinosaurs away from seven year old me and I've gone my own way ever since.

So Heroes started as a passion project really. I got into music and then comedy and was just trying to avoid having a real job. But then I worked harder than I had in any previous so-called 'proper' jobs. Which is probably why I was fired from every job I have ever had. Then, somehow, I landed a supposed really 'proper job' in the city in my late 20s. And to my surprise I was quite good at it. But the more successful I became, the more I could see it for the bullshit it was. I was just part of the corporate world, moving money around, exploiting people, and I was soon thinking, "What's the point?"

So I quit that, my last ever salaried job, in 2001 — and by 2003 I was on tour with Japanese rock band Electric Eel Shock. I managed them for six years. I had effectively run away with the circus. I was skint but I loved what we were doing. The thing I enjoyed most was the creativity of making our own path and working with an interesting and exciting band who felt the same way.

Precarious and dog-eat-dog as it is, the music business always seems to be ahead of the rest of the live performing arts pack, often by a good decade.

Yes totally. A good example of innovation filtering from the music industry into performing arts is the influence punk in the 1970s had on alternative comedy in the 1980s. And the corporate side of music is more established, that's the thing that has led to a more developed resistance — there's a pushback from artists and that generates an alternative side and counter-culture. Innovation comes from the oppressed and is appropriated by the oppressor, necessity is the mother of invention. Did Karl Marx say that?

Around 2002, just before I met Electric Eel Shock, I went to a music managers' conference for junior wannabee managers like me. There were talks from the expected range of industry folks, agents, promoters, producers, PRs, and they were all talking about the same thing in different ways. And I realised that most of the people there were only really interested in impressing upon the room their ranking on the conveyor belt industry of producing massive hits, and letting everybody else know how important a gatekeeper they were. Then *[vocalist]* Steve Hogarth of Marillion — habitually uncool prog-rockers who had been successful in the 1980s — was on a panel. He was talking about their 2001 album *Anoraknophobia*, which they had funded through fans, and it became the most successful album they'd had in years.

This was fascinating to me. Here was someone sharing how they had successfully circumvented these gatekeepers and dealt directly with the fans. You have to think this was eight or nine years before Kickstarter, the term 'crowdfunding' hadn't even been coined. I hung on his every word, and stuck around to ask questions at the end. I expected everyone would want to ask questions, but no one else was interested. They were all off to speak to the agents and other 'old industry' folk. I genuinely believed that fan-funding could change the way music was made and be a real viable alternative to the failing industry model. But the general music industry feeling was that it was a quirky little thing that suited Marillion, and wasn't really relevant elsewhere. But then they would think that, wouldn't they? Because even if they wouldn't admit it, they feared a model like that would make them redundant. And they were all already shitting themselves over the death knell that Napster *[pioneering peer-to-peer file sharing web software that kicked off the digital revolution before being shut down by the music industry in a huge major lawsuit]* had rung for their idea of the traditional music industry a year or so before.

All of those people were upholding a clearly broken system and their only reason was "that's just the way it is" or perhaps "we can't change it". It made me feel so angry that they continued to position themselves for their own self-interest whilst actively marginalising and undermining the people who sought to improve things for artists. Many acts were consciously choosing to not sign to big record labels and put out their own records instead. Electric Eel Shock, who I was to meet shortly afterwards, operated like that. During the time we worked together I would promote them as a strong independent band, but they were often described as 'unsigned' in the press — i.e. not legitimate.

Then in 2007 Radiohead became headline news when they elected not to renew their contract with EMI and self-release their seventh album *In Rainbows* as a 'pay-what-you-want' download. All of a sudden independent was cool again and finally Electric Eel Shock got some recognition. Of course the industry soon appropriated the cool, and major labels would slap a thin veneer of independence on their own releases in an effort to boost credibility until the whole notion became worthless again. But the territory is constantly shifting, that's why we need new folks and new ideas coming in all the time.

I suppose that's where my "fuck it" attitude comes from. Later, as I gained more experience I was able to develop the nihilistic "fuck this" into "sorry no really fuck this and these are the reasons why . . ." It is a subtle and important difference that says, "Hello, I'm passionate about all of this and would like to be part of it, but not part of it how you are making it at the moment, so shall we make it better?" *[laughs]*

A year after this conference I had met and was managing Electric Eel Shock. Up until then, the band had always independently self-recorded their albums. But then, in a fortunate turn of events, we met Grammy-nominated Dutch producer Attie Bauw at one of their gigs at the Melkweg in Amsterdam. Attie loved the band and had proposed recording them in the prestigious Wisseloord Studios in Hilversum. We were getting a knockdown deal on all of this but it was still beyond our budget so we presented it to a small record label. They jumped at the opportunity of being involved. But as we approached the recording date, predictably, the label got greedy. They tried to renegotiate the contract to include control over the band's back catalogue, which we were quite happily releasing ourselves. They thought that if they made it difficult to access the money needed for this upcoming recording, we would either be forced to renegotiate and give them what they wanted or have to pass over this chance to record. As they knew we were desperate to complete this project, they thought they had us over a barrel.

What they didn't expect was that this was just the push we needed to try the third option of telling them to stick it and then going direct to the band's fans. I then engaged a lawyer who I'd gotten wasted with after a gig to get us out of that contract in return for a credit on the album for her. And then hit up the band's emailing list — this was 2003, very few bands were collecting email addresses, it was even before Myspace was widely used. But for a couple of years Electric Eel Shock had been shouting from the stages, "We want your Sex, Drugs & Email. . ." So we had a pile of emails all written on A4 bits of paper and we had never used them. Now was the time to type them up and send out an email to these fans that told them about the shit the label was dropping on us and gave them a link to a PayPal account. Anyone who chipped in £100 got to be on the 'guestlist for life' at any future Electric Eel Shock gig.

We raised the money in a week and the band recorded the album *Beat Me* themselves. We licensed it to different record labels for each territory and toured worldwide to promote it for the next two years. Incidentally the email we sent out to fans stipulated that it was to be for my life not theirs, so there are 100 Electric Eel Shock fans out there who want to keep me alive. Again, this was five years before Kickstarter started, and I'm also happy to report that 17 years later the band, who remain good friends, are still going strong and the record label has been toast for years.

I learnt a hell of a lot from Electric Eel Shock. We were all, from experience, very wary of corporate bullshit and all actively shied away from it. So many artists go through the commercial system and then say there must be a different way. We spent the next six years looking for this way together, and I think we all learnt a lot from each other.

As you gain experience opportunities present themselves, but when you're skint sometimes you're pulled to make choices that aren't in your own best interests. Electric Eel Shock wanted to play live and tour as much as possible without any creative compromises. I loved the creativity of making things happen on our own terms and the connections of the community that we were building. These things were much more important to us than courting an industry who sought to impose their vision on any project — a vision dictated by producing marketable product and financial return for them.

So we decided that the money-making element had to come second in our decision making processes. Of course we still needed to make money, we didn't have any other sources of income. But we decided to direct our energies towards keeping our costs as low as possible so that the amount of money we could generate from the gigs and tours we wanted to do was enough to keep things viable. Even if it was very tight at times, this approach really worked for Electric Eel Shock. We learnt that if money was the main driver then it was probably the wrong path. We have to think about money to continue doing what we do, but how we think about money is up to us. We found that things can really change when you view money as a tool, not the goal.

When I was managing the band I was always wrestling with the notion of making it. You often hear in creative circles about the 'Big Break' — the tantalising idea that a significant success is just around the corner. I used to kick myself as the band's manager if they weren't getting bigger all the time. I would consider that I was doing something wrong, they should be moving into bigger venues, they should be growing, but I think that's just inherited capitalist thinking, pure and simple. Big Break thinking results in an attitude that whatever you have achieved isn't enough, so keep growing, produce more than you did last year — but in reality, as long as you can do what you love and make a living out of it, well, then you have made it. As artists we should be aiming for that, to carry on doing, of course not just the same old thing, but to carry on creating, learning, taking risks and growing creatively and that's the beauty of it.

[Comedian] Stewart Lee writes about it brilliantly in his book *How I Escaped My Certain Fate*, which I wholeheartedly recommend. It's his in-depth journey through similar realisations written in the extended footnotes to the three full-length shows he wrote and performed after he left the big comedy agent Avalon and went his own way.

Once you'd got to that realisation as a result of managing other people's creativity, the next step presumably was to step forward yourself as a creative individual — and take the responsibility for that too?

The responsibility of managing other people's creativity is tough. The music industry and the Edinburgh Festival Fringe — or certainly the comedy industry side of the fringe, which I worked in later, and still do — have a lot in common in how they take this on. Generally they both adopt a model which has individual agents, managers, PRs, etc working with multiple acts, and the model works if a few of these acts do well, which justifies the investment in the ones that won't do so well. And by 'well', we're talking about financial return again. So there's a degree of gambling on the part of the labels or venues, agents etc, and they all use that to justify giving bad deals to the artists. Artists that they are openly gambling with. If an album or a show or other creative project is not a success and it loses money then the act will be considered a failure. But it is just as likely that it was the marketing spend that has failed, or even the industry model itself. And look, anyway, in the creative process there has to be room for failure. It's part of the territory.

When I worked with Electric Eel Shock, whether it was going well or not, I was spending 100 per cent of my time on it. And it was through the experience of living that creative process with them that I came to the realisation that there are actually different ways to measure success, and the key thing is just to keep going. Keep finding the way that makes it a success for you.

However inevitably we came to a point where the direction Electric Eel Shock wanted to take and the one I wanted to take were no longer running in parallel. We were all still in agreement about steering clear of corporate bullshit but now the things we wanted were different. I'd started to get onstage myself doing comedy and I was really enjoying that. I came to the Edinburgh fringe for the first time in 2008, as a holiday really, with no responsibility for anyone. I'd also started working with other bands and I'd had a role in the production team on two Snoop Dogg tours. Yeah I know, right? How did that happen? Me and Snoop Doggy Dog? So anyway my first couple of years at the fringe were funded by the Bank of Snoop Dogg which enabled me to see what Edinburgh was about while having a wild carefree time.

When I first started performing I promoted myself as the Wild Man of Comedy, Iggy Pop & GG Allin meets *Jackass*, a wildly transgressive, boundary pushing artist both on and off stage. The shows I did were a mash-up of exaggerated drunken stories, improvised happenings and daft props. I set out to provoke — sometimes this led to a really fun show and sometimes it was a mess. Unlike most performers who want the approval of the industry, at the time I was just on holiday from the music industry, and anyway my wild shows were so far away from anything that could be obviously commodified. I had nothing to lose. Which meant I had total freedom to call out what I could see. It became quite a part of my act. Looking for ways to call it out with humour and from a different perspective, and with some actual experience.

I was surprised and not surprised to find that the Edinburgh fringe shared the same problems as the supposedly evil music industry. I'd arrived there by steering away from the corporate world and into music, then steering away from the corporate side of music and ultimately into comedy. I then realised ah shit, it's here as well, this is all the same. But I liked the fringe. And my experience with Eel Shock had given me insight into the workings of a creative industry. The development of the internet had made it possible for me to manage a band, set up international tours, a label, a production company all completely independently. I saw no reason why I couldn't do my own thing at the fringe. That's making me sound like I knew what I was doing but I definitely didn't.

I had a conversation with comedian Phil Kay in early 2011. I was doing some gigs with him and I asked him what he was going to do at the next fringe because I always went and saw his shows there. He said that he possibly wasn't going to do Edinburgh again as he'd fallen out of love with it. For years he'd always done various paid venues but he was enjoying it less and less. So I suggested, "Why don't you come and do a free show in this venue that I'm in?" The promoter Alex Petty of Laughing Horse Free Festival was only too happy to have him and also asked me if I wanted to book anyone else. Which I did, mostly so that I could perform alongside and hang out with friends all month. This accidentally became the very start of Heroes, the group of venues where I programme comedy *[and alternative/avant-garde acts]* each year at the fringe.

I totally remember Phil Kay's first show at the Hive *[Edinburgh pub/club]*. He had got quite excited about not having to worry about ticket sales and just letting people turn up. And they turned up alright, we crammed over 160 people into a 130-capacity room and it was one of the greatest shows I've seen. Seriously. He'd found something, they found something, and at the end of the show he was getting this standing ovation and he's waving goodbye and I had to shout out to him from the back of the room: "Remember the bucket! Remember to ask them for some money!" Because money's not the problem, it's money calling the shots that's the problem. And here was Phil so free from it, he'd forgotten about it entirely. *[laughs]* I held the bucket at the back — which was actually a hastily grabbed pint glass — I remember people just shoving in tenners and 20 quids, whatever they had, I don't know how much it was. But they knew that this money was going directly to Phil. They totally filled one glass and then I grabbed somebody else's on the way out, filled that as well and then pushed it all into Phil's pockets.

We've worked with Phil ever since. Any time we do a new venue Phil usually does his show in there because he likes to keep changing and doing something different. Phil's been a sort of litmus paper for what we've been doing as well. He's been around the fringe since the early 1990s, his style of follow-your-nose in-the-moment storytelling comedy has influenced all sorts of people like Russell Howard, Stewart Lee and, most notably, Ross Noble. He's done national tours and he's had his own TV show, been on *[BBC/Dave comedy panel quiz show]* QI, all that malarkey. Yet he's always followed his own path and I've learned that the best way for us to work together is to simply ask him what he wants to do and then find the best way to do that. I sometimes will suggest advice but if I decide that I know what Phil should do and then try to steer him too much or worse still persuade him to do it — it invariably doesn't work out very well. I think he's probably taught me a valuable lesson there.

For any artist, your career should be about finding the right path for you, the right way to let your creativity shine, the way you can really work. That's at the heart of Heroes — because I think so much of the industry is about telling the acts what the right way is, that there's one particular way, this is how you get on. Take comedy: they tell you to do this gig, do that gig, get in one of the finals of the comedy competitions, get on a TV show, [BBC topical satirical celebrity panel show] Mock the Week or whatever is the favoured stepping stone at the moment, get the right agent, etc. This is the path where you will grow . . . But it's not treating performers as individuals and it's that growing as a commercial product thing again. And that isn't for everyone, it really isn't. Having the financial pressure of constant growth is bullshit for creativity and apart from anything else we can't sustain everything growing forever. We just cannot.

In one way your currency is trust working in both directions, like with Phil Kay.

Yes absolutely. And that was another thing that came from working with Electric Eel Shock. We didn't want to tie each other into a contract, but we did want to respect the time and effort we all put into the band. We had a very simple one-page agreement, basically "I'll do this, you do that . . ." We were clear about our expectations and we could look at it when we needed to: "That's what we're doing, let's go forward with that, and if it's not working or we decide that either side wants to do something different, well let's just stop." I think the performers at Heroes feel comfortable because it's a very clear and simple model which can be written down in a few sentences.

This would be a good point to note that when you started the seeds of Heroes and built that community around you, it was when all the venues were being sucked up into the escalating pay-to-play ethos, the contracts were all about getting every last penny out of artists and it skewed the entire physical shape of the fringe. Before, you could have stayed out of that simply by avoiding the Big Four (and later Five) venues since all the other venues offered you a lot more leeway, but they also got sucked up into the economics and jettisoned the spirit of what fringe is about, i.e. nurturing creativity, and that shift affected the audiences as well. It was logical to see a new parallel fringe spring up in real time to reclaim the original spirit, and so then there came—

—the Free Fringe and the Free Festival of course! The pair of them were already there with their simple model when I turned up and I naturally gravitated towards them, because I went, "Oh, this makes sense, I like this." But I had no idea about how the rest of the fringe worked, that all the posters plastered around town, mostly for shows in the paid venues, are paid for by the actual performers themselves. I also didn't realise that paid venues charge shows four-figure sums to perform in their rooms, payable before the fringe even starts — and that performers have to try and make that outlay back from ticket sales, or more accurately 60 per cent of ticket sales, less deductions, quite a lot of deductions actually. And I didn't know what producers, PRs and marketing folk do. I often still don't, other than push their 'essential' services onto performers. Then there are the increasingly ridiculous accommodation costs that all of us have to deal with.

It is no wonder that the majority of shows do not recoup these up-front costs through ticket sales. Such is the economic skew of Edinburgh deals that even shows that are selling out every night are not guaranteed to cover costs. And the result for the punter is higher ticket prices of which very little will reach the performer.

I totally love the Edinburgh fringe and its explosion of creativity throughout August. The festival's success has a lot to do with its open access nature. If a performer can find a place to perform then they can be part of it. However the financial models that lump the burden and pressure onto performers means that large parts of the fringe are only open access if you have the financial means to afford it.

There was a newspaper piece Stewart wrote in 2012 entitled 'The Slow Death of the Edinburgh Fringe' but it's still relevant today, certainly in comedy. Other disciplines such as theatre, dance, performance art etc will all have their own experiences: different production requirements, different venues, different commercial pressures. But when you scratch beneath the surface I suspect that they have similar problems.

[Writing in The Guardian (July 30, 2012), Lee said: "For decades, the fringe has been a utopia for artists and performers — but now profit-obsessed promoters are tearing it to pieces. It can cost so much to perform in the Edinburgh Fringe now, and the very people being deterred by these costs are just the sort of independent minds we used to value as a society; the same people now, demonstrably, priced out of further education. It's another example of the erosion of access, the reversal of social mobility, the entrenchment of privilege, and the gradual silencing of diverse voices. British comedy is much healthier than TV and radio output suggests. But more interesting talents desert its traditional spawning ground, broke, as promoters and performers replicate familiar marketable models. ... The comedy industry is complicit in supporting a broken system."]

This was back when a number of big comedy agents would act as producers at the fringe and tie their acts into contracts that would almost certainly lose them ten grand. The comedy agent would kindly front that ten grand but then the acts would be tied into staying with them to work that debt off the rest of the year. There was a strange complicity in this on the part of the Big Four venues, to the point of codependency.

Yes, which means you have less choice over which projects you do, you've got to do an advert for something you don't believe in or a gig you know you won't enjoy, because your agent has rigged it so that you owe them money and is now calling the shots. Of course the potential upside to all this risk for the few that Make It can be huge. Which is sold to performers under the industry's twisted Big Break notion. Like this is the only way that it can be.

During my first fringe, just having fun in a free venue, I would meet up with friends who were performing in the paid rooms and see the stress that they were under. Why? Why put yourself through that? But at the time there were two ways to do the fringe, free venue or paid venue, they were poles apart and they were moving further away from each other. This gave any performer two choices as I saw it. The first was to risk a lot of money — a lot of it on marketing — by tying yourself into a contract either with one of the big venues or with your producer, for a chance to Make It. And I thought that was total bullshit. More than that, I thought it was wrong. It didn't need to be like that. And I encountered the same frustrations that I'd felt in the music industry. Exploitation does not need to be built into the fringe model and to claim that it is an inevitability or a choice for individuals rather than something that works to the advantage of business is just not true. So there.

The alternative was to go to one of the free rooms *[free festival venues]*. Which was a much less pressured Shit or Bust route, but at that time by taking this route you risked being ignored by press, awards and industry. And it could be hard. Especially as the industry promotes a culture that strongly implies that if you don't follow their suggestions then you're responsible for your own marginalisation. They cite the big success stories as examples, but what they are less keen to discuss are the disproportionate number of shows that fall through the cracks and neither are they prepared to recognise and address that many individuals do not have the financial means to make those choices.

There was and is also a perception that the level of production was considerably lower in the free rooms. Which can be true, because free venues are making things work on a tight budget, however there are free rooms that are better than paid rooms and many paid rooms that are appalling.

What I found back then, was that there was nothing in between these two models. They were being increasingly seen as opposing, rather than alternative, choices. So if a performer had done well in one of the free venues, it felt like a huge leap to go from there — where you're doing it on your terms, passing a bucket round and it's going well, then wanting to build on that the following year and be a bit more visible, have better production — to suddenly having to find several grand before you can even start thinking about doing your show.

It came to the point when that gap between the free festival and the paid had become too huge, and that's where we came in with 'pay-what-you-want' in 2013. It of course wasn't a new model, it's been used all over the place but we made it work in the context of the fringe for the first time. It takes the best of both the paid and free models. Audiences got the hang of it and it worked, because — and a lot of people misunderstand this — the actual mechanics of pay-what-you-want are in line with how paid shows work but the ethos is that of the free model. As 'bonkers' radio DJ Ivan Brackenbury *[character created by comedian Tom Binns]* consistently pointed out, "It's like free only better. Because it's not free."

Paid shows are 'papered' all the time, that's when tickets are given away free to get bums on seats, which it succeeds in doing but there's no chance for the artist to gather payment at the end, or for punters to say thank you for a show that they have enjoyed, and it's a bit of a trick, to make the show look more successful than it actually is. Whereas pay-what-you-want shows are honest. It's saying, if this show isn't sold out, you can come in and pay after. The audience also gets a guide for how much to put in the bucket so it takes away that anxiety at the end.

It's worked for so many reasons, and in so many ways, the model is particularly successful at harnessing word of mouth for good shows, which is the only true promotion. Hot shows soon have people queuing out the door, *Adrienne Truscott's Asking for It: A One-Lady Rape about Comedy Starring Her Pussy and Little Else* was in a small venue so after the first few days if you didn't buy a ticket simply you weren't going to get in. Adrienne had a fantastic year that year, winning the Comedy Award Panel Prize as well as the Malcolm Hardee Award for Comic Originality. And it was all achieved with practically no marketing. Lots of other shows and venues adopt the model now. Pay-what-you-want shows have become ten per cent of the fringe now and I'm very proud of that. Incidentally that is the same percentage that free shows were ten years ago, however they have now become 20 per cent of the fringe. It shows that the independent share of the fringe has really grown, but there remains still much to do to balance the fringe.

Something we thought about a lot was how and if at all to take a cut of those ticket sales. Because that's slippery territory. So the first year, when it was an experiment, all of the acts kept 100 per cent of the money while we found out if the model would work. At the end of that fringe we could see that at the very least acts made ten per cent more in ticket sales than they would have if the shows were 'free', so we decided a fair cut to take would be ten per cent — that way we wouldn't be taking anything away. And it's been that way ever since. In fact we only take our cut from shows that have sold over £1000 of tickets in advance. And all shows keep 100 per cent of the bucket. It just isn't right for the house to put their hand in the tip jar.

So we're only taking money off the shows as they do better and audiences start reserving online to make sure they'll get a seat. That's great. If they're not selling enough tickets and it's just people wandering in, they're not quite in a position for us to take any money yet. It goes back to that industry problem where venues, PR, marketing, producers taking money off acts as a guarantee against potential in the future while telling them the lie, with no hint of irony that "no one makes money at the fringe . . ."

We thought we should only take money off what is actually happening. Over three million tickets are sold at the fringe and we think it's only right that the system is shaken up so that performers start seeing a chunk of that income. So Heroes came in with pay-what-you-want and occupied that gap — there was a real need for it and it caught on. Now it seems independent spirit is growing again, there are an increasing number of ways and models to do the fringe, all bridging that big divide between those two distinct ways of doing the fringe. Heroes recognised that, occupied that space and grew, but then that brought me face to face with that notion of success equals growth again.

We had been so preoccupied with supporting performers that we had not stepped back and looked at the bigger picture. Then our staff quite rightly raised the question, "What about us?" Initially I thought, "But we're paying better than most venues at the fringe." But fortunately I was able to hear them. We reviewed what we were doing and realised that our pay had not grown in line with Heroes' growth. We had been struggling to make everything work for so long that when our finances started getting healthier we were enjoying the relief, without checking to see if that relief was being shared by all. We needed to be setting our own standards on how we're paying people, and how we operate during fringe. We went from paying what we could in the early days to paying by the hour — minimum wage to living wage — and we're always looking to improve that.

As the Heroes model has become more successful we have looked to improve and evolve from our start point of giving the best deals to acts, to trying to find the way to best support everyone involved. It's about finding other ways to grow, creatively rather than in numbers, from negotiating creative environments where the terms are set by others to growing one for everyone to be in, where the performers have more control over the terms. We have established a fairer model for artists, punters and all involved. The focus is not purely about generating money, rather it's about letting money pass through to the benefit of all. There's still a lot to learn and improve.

The shiny venues, the Big Four, made themselves unassailable because they made comedy their cash cow which totally changed the face of the fringe and skewed the financial model to create the landscape as we know it today — and which has had an impact on fringes worldwide. They created that aspirational, or rather pressurised, hierarchy that divided the venues and crushed the holistic ecosystem where smaller and bigger venues complemented each other. The smaller venues have seen their offer become defined by what the Big Four does, and that codependency created the void into which something logically had to step, which turned out to be the frees — as we've seen. We talk of comedy then hitting its own crisis, but theatre had had one previously after the shock of finding it had become outnumbered and out-boxofficed by comedy, and it became hard to find a home for the acts who slipped in between the genres. There's a good argument that the Australians singlehandedly opened it all up again with alternative cabaret, along with (linked) venue rethinks like the Spiegeltent, and, latterly, like Heroes which has found a home for the avant-garde and whatever's coming next in theatre-comedy, alternative performance and, of course, comedians. The spirit of Edinburgh has become interesting again, especially now that it's spilling into London via the Vault Festival — and you can see that the somewhat stale Big Four are somewhat threatened.

I don't know if they really are threatened. And people are very nice to me on the whole. If I go back to our earliest of potential clashes, we were involved with Cockgate where when K*nt and the Gang was doing his badly drawn cock sticker, dishing them out to his audiences and encouraging them to stick it on the faces on people's posters. The Underbelly threatened to sue us and that got picked up by the press. It was something we were happy to play along with in a trickstery way, but I knew all along that it wasn't *[Big Four venue Underbelly founders/directors]* Ed Bartlam and Charlie Wood who threatened us with court, it was somebody lower down in their organisation, and when they found out they realised that it wasn't not a good PR move — and also I don't think they would have ever wanted to have that attitude. I don't think people like Ed and Charlie ever have been threatened by people like us. You know, the next year I was at an event talking to them right at the beginning of the fringe and I mentioned that our venue still needed stuff.

Like chairs?

They instantly offered to lend us some chairs, you know that?

Well I did help you carry them.

Of course! Well it's exactly that sort of helping each other, the little things. I think people in the position of Ed and Charlie, Anthony Alderson *[director of the Pleasance, Big Four venue with a permanent theatre in North London]* and Ryan Taylor *[Pleasance head of comedy]* are very secure in that they know exactly what they're doing and they know they can weather anything and go with any changes big or small. But what I hope is that we can all encourage people who are doing well out of the system to question more. Including questioning everything that makes their position so comfortable. Get them to question why there are other people who are not doing so well and get them to engage in ways that it can be improved as opposed to looking to pass the buck.

There's a lot of confusion over the role of the Fringe Society [the charity that supports the running of the fringe] in all of this, isn't there?

Well yes. The big problem that I see is that the Fringe Society doesn't really know who it represents. This is quite an important oversight. We have had all these positive developments in the last ten years to readjust and commit to a more level playing-field and yet the Fringe Society, the body that oversees the fringe, has refused to get involved with this much needed change.

Their reasoning they give is that they are a neutral body that are there to "support, advise and encourage everyone who wants to participate in the fringe". This is all fine when representing the fringe as a whole externally, something it does very well, but with so many conflicting interests internally it is impossible to represent all participants all of the time.

For example, when it comes to a conflict between the commercial interests of venues versus the creative interests of performers. The venues and other commercial interests are in a position of strength which allows them to dictate terms to the performers. Not getting involved in this conflict due to a desire to support both parties is in fact supporting the power imbalance and not a neutral position.

Fringe performers pay the Fringe Society £300 to £400 to register their show, which makes up a sizable chunk of the society income, and yet these performers are not automatically made members of the Fringe Society as part of that show registration. Instead, anyone with £10 can be a member and have more rights than the performers who actually make up the fringe. This seems constitutionally corrupt and contradictory to the fringe blueprint that states the Fringe Society is a charity established by participants.

Also while the Fringe Society will consult with the various venues that make up the fringe it no longer has a direct relationship with the majority of performers. At some stage in the evolution of the fringe, the Big Four and other venues were given the ability to register their shows in bulk. Which of course seems a move for convenience, but the result is that the Fringe Society does not get direct contact details for shows. The only way to communicate with these performers is through the venue. For a member organisation to allow a third party to manage the relationship with their participants feels like a corporate corruption of a system that should be equitable.

The Fringe Office *[the physical admin interface of the Fringe Society]* does an enormous amount of good work behind the scenes running all sorts of interesting projects to improve access and community engagement etc. However without addressing the fundamentals, to me this seems like treating the symptoms not the cause, and not an efficient use of resources.

Whenever we have worked with an act but haven't had a direct communication with them, maybe an agent or a producer is involved, that is when misunderstandings have been more likely to creep in. I think it's vital to be in touch directly with the acts and I can really see how the Fringe Society has lost touch with the very people that make the fringe happen.

Without performers automatically becoming members of the Fringe Society, without that direct communication and a duty of care to protect performers from commercial interests being expressly stated anywhere in the constitution, this remains a considerable barrier for the improvement of their lot for performers and an undermining of the spirit of the fringe. I think the answers are in the system. Get the system right and the whole thing will flow better, especially for those easily maginalised by the corporate system.

The important thing to note as well here is that the Heroes model has continued to evolve around all of this. Another hugely disruptive factor that the Fringe Society ran away from was the greed, and that really is the word, of the landlords in Edinburgh. We've just seen the latest instalment recently with the change in rent laws in the city which has affected acts and audiences alike, we've seen the university playing the venues off against each other, the council giving George Square to some corporation and shitting on everything that [venue] The Stand had done to reclaim it. It was handy that you came up with not only a venue that wasn't subject to those financial and creative black holes but was also mobile so it wasn't even confined to August or indeed Edinburgh.

Yes, the BlundaBus. That all started with a very fortuitous conversation with a man in a pub in Croydon. He wanted us to do a pop-up venue in Croydon but the venue he was looking at was very large. And if you want to fill a large venue, you need a large name, and you're back in that money game again. Don't get me wrong, I'm fine with making money, it's just everything gets boring really fast when it's not as the main focus, too booooring. So we had to find a solution for a small venue. At some point during the conversation in an aside he mentioned buses, that he liked buses. And I thought a bus is exactly the right size, and then of course afterwards we could take it up to Edinburgh. We'd done two pop-up venues in Edinburgh the two years previously and the second year it really was an amazing piece of luck we found somewhere at all, and then it wasn't cheap, and if the cost of the venue was going to compromise our model then it wouldn't be worth doing at all. As it turned out, finding somewhere to park a bus in Edinburgh was much easier than finding an empty building. The BlundaBus also frees us up to go to summer festivals and tour outside of Edinburgh.

We're always exploring new possibilities. Something we've found works really well for fringe are the smaller venues, 45-50 capacity, that's a really good size for our model and means we don't have to pander too much to marketing. We've found that it works really well for all types of acts — even bigger acts can make better money than they would in bigger venues simply because their costs are much lower and they don't need to do the marketing. As a result, we've added the SpiegelYurt to the BlundaBus and now we're planning to add a black box with raked seating, called the BlundaBox.

Three mobile venues in one. And why not? We should also add that you've taken the BlundaBus over to the Continent as far north as Norway. Right from the very beginning you've displayed that poverty-centric modus operandi based around a comedy core, but it never strays far from the music biz lessons you learned. Either way, it ended up with the Heroes umbrella-venue which blurs the lines to create a broader church of genres that doesn't judge, but reaches out to other genres through comedy, which it couldn't have done if you came from theatre. You've taken more of the circus approach, a ringmaster for alternative performance, which is really at the heart of what you do — well, at least it's not comedy as the shiny venues know it, unless they nicked it off you obviously.

Well comedy itself has been going in an interesting direction. Ten, eleven, twelve years ago when we started there was that division in the fringe but there was also a division in comedy. It's difficult to explain because I have a much better view of everything now so I don't really know how much it's that comedy has changed or it's my understanding of it, but it does seem that a decade ago comedy was all about shiny stand-ups. I think it has now got more interesting with people like Spencer Jones, who may have been the first prop act to be on *[BBC TV comedy series] Live at the Apollo* — he follows in a line of people like Vic & Bob and Harry Hill who are out there and different but still able to hold mainstream appeal.

I reckon Heroes proved it could put on anything when you did Chilcot [in 2016 1,500 comedians and members of the public read the entirety of the 2.6 million word Chilcot Report on the War in Iraq for 24 hours a day over 13 days, winning the Edinburgh Comedy Awards Panel Prize for Spirit of the Fringe].

Oh yes and what an amazing project that was. It was wonderful how so many people came together to get behind such a particular piece of performance art. But the fringe has always been like that. There have been all sorts of interesting political acts of performance art at the fringe. We just happened to be in a space where there was a bit of a void, where all of that wasn't being done at the time, and we brought it back to the centre which tipped things off their axis a bit. Us and a load of others, we were part of a wave that shook up certain parts of the fringe at that time.

I definitely thought at one point, "Oh we've cracked this, now the fringe is going to be totally changed in an amazing way." We'd got some attention with the Chilcot reading and I really hoped that once we showed that it is commercially viable to do the fringe without putting performers in debt, this would become a new normal. But I realise that all we'd done was kick the table, it wobbled it a bit and got interesting then things were appropriated by commercial interests again. If we want to keep things interesting that table needs to keep being kicked. And slowly things will change, the table never quite settles back into the same place.

The fringe after we read the Chilcot Report was in some terms our most successful so far with four of our shows being nominated for the main Edinburgh Comedy awards. But this led me to having a minor crisis of what we were going to do next? How would we top the previous two years? Maybe Heroes could keep adding venues and become the alternative that would put the fringe in balance? Fortunately Lucy Hopkins got involved with Heroes at that time and brought some much needed sanity and perspective. She is not only a great performer, she also has great feeling and vision and has really helped me see what Heroes does best. We have really looked at how we can work on improving that not by getting bigger but by doing it better and more sustainably. And if we want to influence the wider ecology then we need to keep encouraging and supporting other voices. And of course keep kicking giving the table the odd kick.

The kicks are the questions, really. Why is it done like that? Is there a better or fairer way? That includes questioning ourselves. Kicking your own table. I'd argue actually that questioning should be at the heart of all creative endeavours. We need more sense of wonder. Things have improved from ten years ago. Yes there are still a lot of the same issues and it's easy to get frustrated, but let's take comfort that there has been improvement.

Is this a cop-out? Maybe I'm losing my edge? Maybe it's just that we are sitting at the table now . . . On a wobbly chair probably . . . Hopefully listening to all the ways everybody's talking about the table. Feckin' table. But just as we need an ecology at the fringe, so we need an ecology of ideas and dissent. I welcome criticism, I hope people always feel able to question or call us — and me — out. This is how things change and evolve.

Also the territory shifts doesn't it? I felt like I was fighting a battle for years. But the battle's moved on. I can chase it, or try to do something really good with the territory that has been won. There's no good denying that as time passes, and we continue to exist, so we unavoidably become established. So let's make sure that the part of the establishment that we occupy embodies all the things we've fought for. Namely, questioning everything. And defending those who need it, supporting individuals. And especially challenging the attitude that things cannot be changed. As we are seeing, change is needed everywhere, in all of our systems and in ourselves. Why would the fringe be above the system that controls the whole planet? Everything will change.

Lucy and I saw this great film *2040* the other day and in it Kate Raworth, renegade economist, makes the simple observation that "instead of having governments and companies that are reacting to disasters we need governments and companies to take us off in a new direction". For me the point of Heroes is to provide a space where we and acts can do that. Take us all off in new directions. Develop their own voices, build skills to negotiate and renegotiate the commercial world, learn how to better exist independently, expand their audience, enjoy fringe, enjoy life. What's not to like? Let's just make sure we keep questioning everything.

*

35

Chris Sonnex

'If we're talking about activism, the key word there is *active*'

Chris Sonnex is a director & former artistic director of the Bunker Theatre. Based in South East London, he was born & raised in Pimlico, Central/South London.
• *@ChrisSonnex*

The Bunker Theatre is the sort of venue you'd expect to be run by someone who's Oxbridge and with an independent income. But you're not, are you?

No I'm not. I'm from Pimlico, South West London.

One of the posh council estates.

Yeah, one of the posh estates.

The flats are all worth a million now, aren't they, regardless of occupants' income?

Well, the really interesting thing is that Pimlico is so affluent and so deprived at the same time.

But that's London everywhere, isn't it?

Yeah, but Pimlico's so small, it becomes this microcosm of what London actually is. If you go down Lupus Street you've got all the million pound houses on one side and then you've got one of the biggest council estates in Europe on the other side where you're literally looking over at the wealth.

And the wealth are looking over at the poverty. But the poverty has now been shined up and it looks pretty enough to be looked at.

Spruced up with nice shiny flammable cladding presumably?

Exactly. That's why Grenfell *[a fire broke out on June 14, 2017 in Grenfell Tower, a council housing 24-storey block of flats in West London, causing 72 deaths, the worst UK residential fire since the Second World War, caused by the building's inflammable cladding]* really hit home and why it still angers me, but there's nothing I can actually do or put into words. I'm normally really good at words, at putting things together and say something about it but all I can say is like fuck you. You know you let these poor people die and then you've done the massive trick of convincing other poor people to hate the people that were affected. These sorts of council housing are funny because there's an optics to them. It's changing now, but whenever I met anybody and told them that I grew up in Pimlico, they would say, "Pimlico? Oh that accent must be fake then." Or, "What you talking about working class? They're million pound houses!" And that's the optics of what Pimlico is because they've never fucking been there, so they wouldn't know. So every time I had to go, "Yes, Pimlico, but in a council estate in Pimlico." Which seems nonsense to have to say it or justify it or quantify it.

   The other thing is that because of those geographics, I support Chelsea. *[laughs]* So there you've got two things that are weirdly linked in to coming from Pimlico. It's quite depressing when you grow up on Churchill Gardens, but they can't get rid of it because it's got cultural significance, it's listed for one mad reason.

Which is?

When Battersea power station was operating *[on the opposite bank of the River Thames]*, they built a tunnel that goes from the power station right underneath the river all the way across for the unused steam from the turbines to give power to Churchill Gardens. It doesn't work now obviously but because it's there, because it exists, and the system exists, they can't get rid of it. There's another estate which has been bought up because of the Thatcher shit, but it was also built by the guys who built the Barbican and it's built so that each flat is different to everybody else's flat and each one has an outside area. It all looks in towards a pond and you can't hear anything even though it's literally on Vauxhall Bridge Road, it just feels like this lovely little social utopia. Everything's been bought up now of course, but it was all one big council estate and there's still some social housing there. Prime real estate and that's funny because Pimlico used to be shit, it used to be a working class area.

Growing up in all that, were the schools really shit or were they sort of okay?
Were they bolstered by having mixed catchment areas or just from the single
proud community that you grew up in even though you lived on the poor side?

The weird thing is, because I was brought up Catholic, my primary school was just behind Sloane Square *[very posh area up the road, where the Royal Court Theatre is]*. So when I went to secondary school that's when it was a real change because I went to Pimlico School *[in Lupus Street]*. It used to be a big Brutalist greenhouse made of concrete and glass that was in special measures. It was a feeder school for all of the people that couldn't get into the decent schools in other parts of London like Bermondsey, Peckham, Brixton. So they had to go halfway across the city to get there. My friend from Rotherhithe, he used to have to take two buses and pay, and now you can get one bus and don't have to pay because you're school age.

In Pimlico, because you've got that massive divide between wealth and not, there was a strong community on the estate but it was in the pubs really. It did feel in those pubs like there was a community with all the drama and all the love that you get — or at least you used to get. But then when I went to secondary school I suddenly found another community where it felt like I belonged too. All my friends were from South East London, which has weirdly influenced my accent — a lot of people think I'm from South East London when they talk to me, which is great but technically I am *South* London. But anyway, the school community became the thing for me, which is not to say that everybody got on and there wasn't bullying and all of that stuff going on — although I actually escaped that really brilliantly, I don't know how. Maybe it's because I was quite big, six foot one. But then maybe it's also because you used to bunk off all the time, is the truth of the matter.

So school became my community. I guess that's just a generational thing, but I didn't hang out with many people that were from Pimlico then. Mind you, I was quite a loner when I was young, and I don't want to go too much into home life, but it wasn't nice, so it does make you cut off from a lot of people — and I'm an only child, so there was that. So community became a thing and then art became a thing, and music too was a massive thing.

Pimlico School is now an academy and apparently much better with a new building because they knocked it down and they made it lovely whatever, but back then it was in special measures *[government controls imposed to revive failing schools]*. There were police meat wagons outside every day and mostly it was because a lot of the time there would be rucks between schools. There's a conspiracy theory here, but I sometimes think that some of the boys use to go and rob the *[private]* Westminster School boys, *[laughs]* which I think is fair game because it's only round the corner. I think that's why the police were there, mostly to protect the rich boys. One of my friends who works in theatre now, he went to that school and he always makes the joke when we worked together that I used to beat him up, that's how common it was. But having said all of that, Pimlico School was a special school for music and drama, which is interesting.

Was that part of its origins or was it was just imposed on the school as local education authority window-dressing?

I think it had always been good for music and drama. Some of the alumni of that school are footballers obviously, because that's how the class system works apparently, that's how you get out of the shit. Musicians as well, like La Roux, she went there, Asher D/Ashley Waters went there too. There's quite famousy arty people that went there and there's definitely a correlation between class and looking for a way out. When I was growing up it used to be the only way that you could get out was to be an actor or to be a footballer. It's changed now. It's indicative of theatre that nobody gives a shit about being an actor, they don't think you can do it anything with it any more. So it's rap now because you can make rap in your bedroom, like punk I guess. So it's rapper or footballer nowadays, but when I was growing up it was acting.

And did you?

Yeah. I was good at it. I mean I didn't know there was anything else. Again talking about the class system and it keeping you down, I didn't know that there was anything other than acting, I just thought it just appeared as a sort of thing, I didn't know there were writers or directors or everything. Just watching *EastEnders* and seeing there's actors in it, I didn't think about the credits all over it. And then you start to get a little bit aware of what was going on. I was aware that directors existed and I was aware that writers existed but everything else in theatre I still didn't know.

I liked acting but there was always a sense in myself that I felt like I was just going through the motions. Not that I wasn't good at it. When I was little I was in *Cavalcade* at Sadler's Wells.

So basically you had a good drama department that set up those industry connections for you if you wanted to step out in that direction after you left school.

I ended up doing my work experience in Regent's Park Open Air Theatre *[Central London]*, which is completely opposite to everything that I give a shit about nowadays, but then it was cool, wicked. But there was always something niggling me, so I also went quite heavily into GCSE and A-level drama where I was always going, "Oh let's devise, let's come up with weird ideas and stage it!" But nowadays you probably couldn't do that so easily — I was in drama in that school from Year 7, but even if it's on the curriculum you don't get to choose it until you're in Year 9.

Well they're killing it now in the schools. I want my kids to do drama, not to work in theatre but for the creative insights and the self-confidence it gives them, the modern equivalent of boxing at school or whatever. But the opportunity to do it at GCSE has just been snatched away from them by the social engineering of the new curriculum. It's gutting to see that everything their drama teacher stands for and has built up was literally taken away overnight from under him by the government. No back-up for him or the kids.

Because they don't quantify it as of interest or significant and — I'll bang on about it — the class divide comes into it. At Westminster School you get trained for public speaking, they do lessons in public speaking. What do you think drama's doing for the rest of us? *[laughs]* Training you to be able to be able to communicate with people by articulating, pronouncing, projecting your voice?

And confidence to hold your own in front of other people, whoever they may be. It's handy, isn't it, if they take drama out, because that's helping to deprive a generation of a voice.

So don't take it out! Again, what's really brilliant and lucky with that school (and I was not the ideal student to be fair) is that they realised that I was shit at quite a lot of things because I wasn't engaged in it. You know, one of those classic under-achievers basically, because I was marked in Year 7 as a child of excellence but I didn't care about maths, I didn't care about English or IT, because the teacher was shit. I really liked food technology, so I excelled at that, *[laughs]* because I liked cooking.

When it came down to picking GCSEs the rule was that you could only take one of the arts subjects. They wanted me to do music a year early but I was 15 and was like, "Whatever, I don't care, but I want to do music and drama together." Now normally that wouldn't be allowed, but they also allowed me not to do a *[foreign]* language for GCSE so that I could do art.

In fact, I was really good at English but again you need a teacher to believe in you. I remember coming up against this one particular English teacher whose attitude was that because of the way I sounded and because of the school I was in, I couldn't possibly have an opinion on something — "You can't ask this question but you must now say that *Of Mice and Men* is really really great." But that would never have happened if I was from a different social economic class or if I went to a different school. It would be something else, the idea of challenging or questioning would be encouraged. It took me so long to get out of that mindset, especially when I was at university where I was just like, "Must take everything as gospel, duh duh duh." But then I went, "Do you know what, actually I'm paying you for this shit, I should be able to question and you should encourage it." I also saw the posher kids at university asking questions and challenging things and having their opinions and having a conviction of their opinions, and I was like, this is weird, the rest of us are just meant to follow orders. And that's why I think I've got a problem with authority, and that's inherent in me regardless of what that authority it.

> *However it does sound that the course of what you've been doing, maybe it's patronising to say, is to channel that 'problem' through your theatre career. You're challenging authority but from a positive platform, so you get a tangible result out of it as opposed to just mouthing off. Which is what so many other people end up doing, like The Guardian readers who are always shouting how terrible Brexit is or Boris Johnson and the Tories are — or worrying about the well-being of the refugees just so long as they're in France and not here. Yeah, but what are you doing about it? Do you even bother to see how other people live, to see with your own eyes why they don't do the things that you demand of them to do. They don't live like you, because they're not you. Go up North and see for yourself why Labour voters now vote Tory. It'll make sense if you go and look. But not sitting in London and the Home Counties it won't.*

Hey listen, the mad thing is it doesn't matter. Well of course it matters. If we want a better world, we need to have better leaders, yes we need to vote those better leaders in, and we need not to be duped by people in power. But the problem that we have now in society and that we've had for the last five or six years, maybe even longer, is that the left absolutely think they're right, and the right think they're absolutely right. And I'm not centrist in any way whatsoever, but there is nobody going, "Oh I understand that we have to do something about our problems." They don't want to understand.

Everything's binary, it's the footballification of everything, isn't it? It's like I support Chelsea. Now I don't know if you watch football, but when I watch a game and Chelsea foul someone really really badly and it should be a red card, I'm like, *"What you talking about ref?!"* It's there, right in your vision but you just go, "Well that's my team, so I'm going to back them regardless." And that's exactly what's happening. It's like bad people are only bad and good people are only good. And that is not helpful narrative. People make mistakes, people are human.

I had this when I was in the refugee camps in Calais. A lot of trustafarians were there being, "Oh isn't it sad that these refugees are here, and look we must do the great thing that we're doing, it's God's work, we're brilliant and we're saviours . . ." and all of that shit, which is all problematic in many cases anyway, but what they particularly perpetuated is the idea that every refugee was an angel. But what refugees are actually doing is to run away from the terror and horror of conflict. So the constant narrative in the newspapers or from those people is look at these angels who are victims, which is wrong. because some of them are dickheads. And it's okay that they are dickheads, because people are human.

Now if you go down to your local Wetherspoons in South East London or wherever and you start talking about these angel refugees to a UKIP supporter, they don't know any fucking angels. They live in a world where angels don't exist, so what are you talking about angels? It just becomes Othering to them and they go, "What you talking about? This is nonsense. They're all terrorists." And so they go the other fucking way. Or there's the people who'll be proud of the people who work with refugees but at the same time still use a racial slur to describe the refugees.

So I had people asking me, "What's it like in the refugee camp? What are the refugees like?" Now the normal narrative was to go, "Oh it's amazing they're here, some of them are structural engineers and they're running away from great horrors." I could say that and it is true, but my first instinct was to say instead, "Yeah some of them are dickheads, some of them are rude, some of them are outrageous, but they shouldn't be in this situation and this institution is being perpetuated by us with our foreign policies and all of that stuff — and also they want to come here because of the way we sell Britain so for them Britain is fucking Mr Bean and *Downton Abbey* and whatever, do you know what I mean? It looks great, James Bond, it's amazing!" That's what we're selling, the things you're proud of they're proud of too, so they want to come.

You have to talk to people like that with the nuance and understanding of that and everything else. If you don't take the effort to talk to the mad staunch Tory person that thinks Boris is the Second Coming, if you don't understand where they're coming from, how are you meant to fight that person? How are you meant to have an argument with that person? It's like you're playing chess and they're playing checkers, there's no fucking point, you might as well just walk away and carry on in your bubble. It simply annoys me that people don't want to dig a little bit deeper. Especially when those people are in theatre, which is a whole world of digging deeper. It's your job isn't it?

They shouldn't have to be reminded, should they?

Well I was talking to the Bunker's executive director David Ralf the other day about how there's been a lot of miscasting and silencing of voices in some very high-profile cases recently, be that Jewish, be that trans, be that whatever. I was annoyed with it — well I'm annoyed with it generally — because I was trying to understand the thought process more than anything. Objectively, I know that you've done wrong by that miscasting and silencing of voices, but what I want to know is *how* you've got to that fucking point? So I'm sitting there in that office and I'm like, well I just don't understand, where did they think it would be a good idea? Why did they think they were going to get away with that in 2020? Why? And David says to me, "It's because not everybody thinks like you. You think theatre is a moral obligation and everybody else thinks that theatre's a commercial thing."

However . . . that doesn't put me on top of some weird pedestal above everybody else just because I've got a 'moral compass'. There's a direct correlation between the class of the people making the decisions and the decisions they're making. When I grew up in that council estate, I grew up with Muslims, Jamaicans, Africans, I grew up with sex workers across the road, our neighbours were gay, my Mum's friends were gay. There is so much diversity around you in those council estates, which isn't to say that racism wasn't rife in those communities either, or sexism or misogyny or homophobia or Islamophobia. But there was something in me that's always said, this is incredible, look at all of these melting pot of people that are here and they've got all these brilliant stories, they've got different cultures and they cook different food and they do different things and they party and they don't party and they drink and they don't drink. I thought, fuck man that's incredible, and instead of turning to say, "These immigrants are taking over the houses", I was more like, "Oh cool, let's talk to the immigrants!"

That's so ingrained in me from my upbringing, it's always in my thought processes, that representation of what I grew up in and the presentation of how it's made up on the Tube or on the bus or who's around you at any given point. And shocking as it might seem, I grew with middle class people too — the white middle class men that people might consider that I've historically pushed out of this theatre building. Except I haven't. Their stories aren't good enough, is the truth of the matter. There is no representation of white middle class men in this theatre apart from people like my executive director, at least since I've taken over. The people that set the Bunker up are, but the artists and the people that are working here aren't.

How's that come about?

The programming?

Well, it's a good point to look at that, since at the time of this chat we're a matter of days away from all this turning into 'legacy', aren't we, when the Bunker closes down?

[sighs] Yeah. "Legacy soon to be legendary", I think somebody said in an article. Well, the programming came about because I started with the writers mostly, the plays. I came to the Bunker from the Royal Court where I was an artistic associate, which is how I know how to do things, because that was a massive training ground for me. Always start with the writer, always start with the play. But I knew that it had to be the voices I wanted to hear and the voices that I found interesting. That's taking the activism and all of that shit out of the way and not putting on the voices that you find in a lot of the London new writing theatres. That's not me having a go, but those places have a very specific demographic. So I wanted to find and platform those voices I did want to hear — and while I've done a massively diverse couple of seasons that are representative and mostly female, and the stories are brilliant, I could have replaced all of those seasons with even more people that were from those demographics. It wasn't like I had a small group of people that was all I had to choose — I was making albums in my head!

So there is tons of stuff out there, you had a choice.

I had a choice, I have a massive choice. And the reason that I have a massive choice is also because I did a lot of the groundwork when I was at the Royal Court, like *Funeral Flowers [by Emma Dennis-Edwards]*, and Monsay Whitney *[Box Clever]* who I met in Tottenham when I was doing work at the Royal Court, Rachel De-Lahay *My White Best Friend]*. *Funeral Flowers* — in fact I commissioned and directed the first iteration of it in Tottenham on the High Road before it went up to Edinburgh and won all those awards. So plays and writers like that were knocking all around me anyway.

All of those people are doing loads of things now, but they were already there and I'd done all the groundwork. So it was really easy for me to programme at the Bunker from that grassroots level. And then, of course, if you programme someone like Emma Dennis-Edwards as a writer, what she is going to do is then platform people that *she* gives a shit about. So Rachel Nwokoro, the director was young, first time round, black, and the producers are black. And it continues to escalate once you make that one big decision, because it's top down, it starts to trickle down everywhere.

But it has to be a decision from the top, doesn't it? Which means it has be me saying, "I'm going to make this decision, and if all is good, we will start to get more and more people that are not Oxbridge, right?" Hopefully in those creative teams but also with who is onstage. Because for too long now, what we have is somebody just throwing a black face onstage and saying, "Look at our representation!" But you go, "Hang on a minute, let me look at that guy, he's from Surrey and went to Oxford, is that representation really?" Maybe not. It's just gloss, it doesn't mean anything. What I'm more concerned about is everything underneath it.

Keep going . . .

I want the sound designer to be a young black grime artist, I want the set designer to be a young Asian female. You know, if we look at just light designers, how many are women? Not fucking many. How many are black? Not fucking many. And so that's the real fucking problem and also they're the people that have the work far more consistently than actors and directors. So do it, give them the fucking money, what are you waiting for?

It's even things like crew in a production department in the bigger theatres. That's how I started, and you can make a decent amount of money. In fact I may have made more money in crew than I've ever done. And that's a legitimate career, so if we're going to talk about getting people that aren't normally into theatre into theatre, there's so many jobs for that to happen that don't have to be acting, that don't have to be directing or writing. There could be loads of different things, and that's my biggest bugbear.

It does annoy me when there's an all-white cast, don't get me wrong. And actually when we did *We Anchor in Hope [by Anna Jordan]* that was five people set in a pub. It's never really stated, but I know that to a lot of other people it would have staged as an all-white cast because of the area it's set in — or what they assume the area is. But luckily because it's set in Pimlico, I obviously know that it's somewhere where there are people of colour around, so what we ended up doing was, instead of having five white actors onstage, we had two people of colour and three white people. It's a male-heavy show because it's written as a male-heavy show, but that's okay, there's four men and one woman, great, and me directing it, it's a female writer. What should I do then? Oh, I should offset that by making the whole rest of the creative team female, which I did, because there were too many male voices in the room.

That might not be important to anybody else, but it's important to me. And if you look at the reaction and the reception of that play, people were really very happy with it, and it's that way because of all of the female voices that were there in it. Because it wasn't as heavy as you would have made it if it was male-heavy on the creative side. You would have gone, "Oh, I know a pub like that, oh this is what a pub should be like, it should be grizzly and rank and all of that stuff." But no, of course it shouldn't have to be like that. Everybody behind the scenes should also be diverse, and we should stop talking about who's on the fucking stage — because that should just be a given.

Having the bricks and mortar though lets you do that.

Massively important.

It's always challenging to push that diversity through stage work and make it stick. Having the solid base of a building in the shape of the Bunker has allowed you to achieve that consistency, to be able to do it and not just to breeze into a pub theatre production and say everyone's going to be diverse and then when you finish and leave you have no impact on what that venue puts on next or the future presence of the people that you've brought together for the play. A building for the shows means they'll be reflected in a positive way in their audience, who will be confident to go back knowing they'll find what attracted them again — so it's empowerment of the group and confidence to infect others. It's interesting how people articulate the Bunker in different ways but ultimately it all leads to the same lode, which is what you've been saying: if it's got a voice, if it's relevant and if you want to have a chance, then here it is, this is your space. Plus you've been democratic in terms of handing the building over to artist take-overs. I figure that's done a good job of infecting the industry and bits of society by extension, which I suppose is the whole point of theatre. It's a door they can't close, plus the Bunker represents the benchmark for a quality and breadth of work that we haven't seen much of recently.

And you have to start with the art. You have to start with the artist. So if you believe in the artist you know that they could make something somewhere that will have an impact.

But isn't that a load of wanky shit?

It sounds like it. I would be sitting in your position going, oh yeah that *is* wanky.

But I believe it, I just need you to tell us why you believe it.

I genuinely would be sitting in your position going, "Errrr, are you really saying that . . . ?" But it is true! I remember when I first got this job, a mate said, "Just do what you do best and concentrate on the artist and don't worry about it. Concentrate on the art and everything else will fall in place." And I thought *that's* wanky. *[laughs]* But he is a man from Leeds, and from a council estate, so it's slightly different coming from someone like him. However I was like, actually yes I have been doing that with artists consistently. And if the artist isn't good or if I've worked with somebody because I've been told to work with them and they are just not serious (which has happened on occasion on a couple of projects, but not The Bunker), everything falls apart because the vision isn't there.

It's vision that helps good theatre stand above it all, I suppose. Which brings us back to bricks and mortar.

It's clear we're obsessed with real estate as a country. And in theatre it's used as a source of power that's hard to work without. And one of the things that I find really difficult, and will find difficult when I leave, is freelancing — because it feels that as one person you can't do anything because you don't have a building behind you. So at the Royal Court I could change loads of things and find loads of people, but when I was in that in-between gap between the Royal Court and the Bunker, I couldn't do anything, I couldn't really *change* anything. All that I could do was go, "I think this writer should be of colour or whatever", but beyond that I couldn't do anything that changed anything. That's what I've find the hardest.

But being part of a building, like at the Bunker, there's the ethos that comes with it, where you can go, "Yes the art is great, the work is brilliant, I believe in that, let's do it!" And of course it's not just about the script, it's about the artists themselves.

That bricks and mortar confidence has meant there has even been an occasion when I've programmed a play that I hadn't read. Basically I had put out a call to that said, "What the fuck are we meant to do with this working class thing? Because all I can see is you moaning about shit" — in a much more polite way — "and it's not really helping. So if we're talking about activism, the key word there is 'active'. *[cackles]* And what are you fucking doing? You're sitting there doing nothing and moaning on a keyboard, or you're on a panel moaning, 'What do we do?' Well, Sabrina Mahfouz *[writer & performer from South London]* has stopped going on panels to just talk about it and instead she's saying, 'If you want me to do it, I'm going to do workshops that are free for working class kids. That's what I'm going to do.' You see that's *active*, that's doing something, so what are we doing?"

So anyway, a few people got in touch with me and said, "Oh I think I've got a couple of ideas, duh duh duh . . ." One writer Natalie Mitchell came to me and said loads of brilliant ideas, but I wanted to know about her as well. She said that she's working class from Medway *[in Kent]*, she lives in Bermondsey *[in South East London]*, she'd done all the writing groups and she writes for *EastEnders* — great, she makes a living out of it but nobody will put her plays on for some reason. Don't know why.

And we were talking about what we could do, and I sat there and thought, "Do you know what I've a two-week slot. What am I doing? This is the real playing it forward here, isn't it? You're working class from Medway and your voice is being stifled and not heard, I'm going to give you that slot if you want it." Which was a mad mental thing to do as an artistic director but it was basically, "I have power, I'm going to give you some, here you go."

There was also a sort of mad confidence in myself that was going, "It doesn't really matter whether the script's shit, I know I can fix the script." I mean, it wasn't as easy as me just going, "Oh well, I'll programme you and that's it and then never read the script until opening day." I did read it immediately and went, "Okay . . . thank God it's good!" But I *knew* it was going to be good because I'd met Natalie, I just had a feeling, it was that leap of faith.

So in a building like this the art is happening — but there's also the ethos saying you are welcome, and also you are welcome *not* to come. That's also important. Stop trying to get people to come and sit for something that they don't want to come to. If we're talking about true diversity, true representation, 'true' means opening up the doors and saying, "You have a choice", because everybody has a choice. Why are we trying to make people come and see *Hamlet* when they're 14 years old from a council estate in South East London? They couldn't give a fuck about Shakespeare. Just give them the option: if they want to come, they can come. But don't try to make them come, because they'll fucking hate it.

Just do it. Like there's lots of people talking about this gender neutral toilet thing, making it into an issue. The Bunker had gender neutral toilets from day one, we just never said anything about it, so all of a sudden we don't have a massive thing about it. Nobody's moaning about it. Nobody's coming out and saying stuff about it. Nobody gives a shit because we never said anything about it. We just did it, do you know what I mean? We didn't want the kudos for it. In the same way in those toilets we've got toilet paper and soap, so why don't we just provide free sanitary products? And if we can do that in an unfunded theatre, then why isn't everyone doing it?

We've got a room that is really shit and dank and horrible, and we can make it look a little bit prettier and allow writers to come in and use it instead of going into the cafes and paying three pound every hour for a coffee or whatever. They can sit here. Let them come in here in the relative warmth with shit wifi, but at least they can sit down and write. And that systemically comes from that boy in that council estate looking at everybody and going,

"It's shit that you have to pay money to go and write somewhere when you don't have any money. It's shit that you have to pay for period products when you don't have any money." If we're a civic/theatre space, we can offer stuff like that which is actually useful.

> *I don't want to jump into the territory of venues and companies giving all their sob stories about no one giving them any money and bashing the funders. But how do we make it relevant that you are resolutely unfunded and it's something that has actually made you such an epicentre of influence today? I suppose a lot of other people can say they're proud to be unfunded, but in your case the actual concept of making money just doesn't seem to be in your vocabulary in the first place.*

There's a couple of reasons why this works. The Bunker is unfunded and we don't have to report to a board because we're not a charity, we're a community interest company, which also that means that I can do whatever the fuck I want. It also means that I'm not tied to the sort of gagging order that comes with funding that says you can't be overtly political. The Bunker can say "Don't vote for Boris Fucking Johnson", right? The Royal Court, the National, the Bush, they can't do that because they're NPOs *[national portfolio organisations]*, they can't do that because they're charities. They simply cannot do that because their status and funding simply doesn't allow it. So the fact that I can do and say things like "Don't vote for Boris Fucking Johnson" means that identity becomes quite defined by exactly the fact that we don't have any funding nor are we a charity, which is really lovely.

There are things that we can do when we're being not funded that people who get lots and lots of money can't do. You get to do these little tiny things that really help society, that don't actually cost that much money. On a bigger level, the biggest successes of the Bunker in my period are the black-centric work because black audiences come to support their artists and their culture. So if we're looking at something to say to the funded theatres, we'd say, "This makes money and, if we're being really really fucking capitalist about it, put black work on because black audiences come to black work. And that means you're diversifying your audiences which is great, but also you're getting people paying money to come to shows. Happy days!"

I have an argument that says that the only time that I've ever really had any trouble with artist is when they've been white middle class. I could turn around to the Almeida and Rupert Goold *[artistic director of the North London theatre]* and go, "Maybe you should start programming some working class queers, because it's a pure joy to work with them." I mean that sort of thing isn't completely true, it's a sweeping statement, but you can make these cases, saying, "In my experience, when we have no money, this is how you can change theatre." But theatres are obsessed with the idea of how they need to keep running and I do understand why an establishment like the National Theatre takes so long to move and change. It's too big, a hundred staff, and it's got three spaces, it's massive. I don't necessarily agree with the National as a thing — I don't know how you can be a national theatre based in London — but I do know why it can't be as good as everybody wants it to be.

We can't knock it for that, sure.

And likewise if somebody knocks the Almeida for their programming — well, it works for them, it's consistently getting West End transfers and getting audiences. That's why we can't always knock the people that are in power. We just have to understand why it works like that and to also understand how the entire theatre system works. Like, I may not agree with the Almeida's programming or I might not agree with their vision, but I can seek to understand at least in a way *why* it works. And then, because I'm unfunded and because the Bunker is underfunded, we can tell everyone that these are the real ways you can make things better when you don't actually have to pay out the money.

I've had a few interviews for other artistic director jobs and there's been a very sceptical notion about me being a CEO because of my accent, which is classism. Whatever. And then in one of those interviews somebody asked me, "How do you manage these budgets?" Not to mention first that I've managed massive budgets at the Royal Court, my argument always is. "You're looking at it the wrong way. The question is, have *you* ever lived on benefits of 70 pound every fortnight? Cos I have and I knew how to budget that." *[laughs]* So if we're talking about budgeting, then let me tell you something about budgeting. But people don't think that way, do they? And so they think I can't run a business.

I do understand that attitude innately. But I just don't care. I just care about the art and the politics of what we're making, and it's a question of numbers again, innit? But my point is that lived experience benefits everybody. If your organisation doesn't have somebody like me in it or it doesn't have Emma Dennis-Edwards, Kat Woods or any of these brilliant writers that are from benefit classes or are of colour or whatever, if you don't have any of those people in your organisation, something is *wrong*! Something is inherently wrong. Because who are you talking to? The same people? The same Oxbridge-educated people? And why? Because they're a safe bet to you?

And a safe bet to your audience, who you want to be like you.

Yeah. Are you actually working? Are you doing any work here? Get your fucking finger out and get some brilliant people in!

It doesn't work that way practically speaking, as we both know, but rather than go down that self-congratulatory virtue-signalling attack on them — much as I think we'd like to — we can flip that and ask instead why isn't there a Bunker on every corner? Certainly with what we all know now. None of the problems have gone away, none of the challenges or barriers in UK society. What you've done is apply a top bar of quality to a punk ethic that defies the economics of running a theatre and producing work — just open the space and the artists and audience alike will come in. However, we do have to be realistic about location. The Bunker may be a concrete carpark slated for redevelopment, but it's a concrete carpark smack bang in the centre of London. It's not stuck in a housing estate in Leeds or a moor in Scotland, although of course there are Bunkers in their own way all over the country trying to do the same thing, where they seek to honestly reflect the local equivalent of that representative cross-section of 'people on the Tube'. Still — not to put you back up on that pedestal — but you are getting a lot of well-deserved credit for having pulled off something near impossible to do in Central London.

I think ultimately it works because of the leadership. It has to go top down, doesn't it? If you want to make something happen, you need to make it happen, and if you want to do it, it's really simple. In our first season especially I wanted to programme all women. I didn't want to shout about it, I just did it. Done, sorted, easy. But that's the vision. If you look at the economics of the situation, I can't afford to do this job. Like I just can't do it. I'm in debt because of doing this job, so it's almost like I've *bought* the awards we've got, because I'm 10-15 grand in debt from doing this for two years.

So little . . .

So is anybody like me really going to do that? No, not really. I wish I fucking hadn't, actually. Because now I'm out of a job at the end of March *[2020]* and I don't have any savings and I'm in debt. I don't know how I'm going to pay the bills next month. So if the people that are in charge can't afford to do it, the people like me, it's hard to keep going. The people who can keep going are the ones that can afford to do it, and sometimes they're really well-meaning with what they're doing — but they're not surrounded necessarily by the people that can make it genuine, and that's the real problem.

But they often move in different social/class circles and can't break out of that.

How many times I heard somebody wanting to put a Grenfell play on is the truth of the matter. And they're always white and they're always middle class. It's the worst idea ever — and also, don't manipulate somebody's grief. We're not ready for a Grenfell play. It seems awful to do that, and also theatre's better than that actually, it doesn't need to make a Grenfell play, it can just make a dystopian fucking whatever play that is obviously about Grenfell. They want to do it because they have well-meaning intentions and they want to help and they want to put it out there in the world, but they're not surrounded by the people from that world.

There's also their thought patterns. For me, there's a moral obligation for anyone people wanting to make art, but their thought processes don't work like that. I've had a couple of black writers who want me to direct their shows about racism and I've said, "I don't think I have any right to direct that show", so I put myself out of competition. But that puts me out of money. Morals cost money — but that's the way I think. I've said no to those plays and said instead, "Here's a load of black directors who can do it." And in some of those cases it's actually ended up being a white middle class man who's directed it.

Do you think the Catholic thing comes into it? The values, the minority status, the weirdness of British Catholicism — it's hard for those of us afflicted to explain how our culture is completely different to the Catholicism in the rest of the world. We're ready to stand up for the rights of the oppressed, yet are prepared to let people walk all over us. I think a lot of British Jews are a bit like that too.

[chuckles long & hard] There's definitely parallels between Catholicism and Judaism, the guilt and the fieriness. I think the values in most religions always tend to be the same, playing it forward with love, respect and community, but what I do have from Catholicism is *theatricality*. It is nothing if not theatrical. And I would be interested in how many theatre directors were brought up Roman Catholic. Because there has to be quite a lot of them . . . and a load of them already come to mind.

It is just consistently theatrical isn't it? As a kid — I was a weird kid — at one point I definitely wanted to be a priest. It's the storytelling, the being up onstage saying something. So I'm sure there's a link. For the record I am staunchly atheist but I've still got all of the Catholic guilt and the ritual coded into me. There's definitely a link.

It also explains the bit about not paying yourself.

It's that world of being Jesus — slightly. But what it really is, is "I'm going to do this for the greater good but I have no expectation of benefiting from it in any way!"

*

36

Cleo Sylvestre

'There was something always inside of me to go out and help'

Cleo Sylvestre is an actor, writer & musician. Based in North London, she was born in Hertfordshire & raised in Camden, North Central London.
• @CleoSylvestre, @HoneybmamaF

There've been immense strides in terms of representation, diversity, voices getting out there. But though everything's on the table, there are still closed doors and ceilings of every type if you're black and starting out in the UK performing arts.

That's right but it has improved. I went to see *Emilia [by Morgan Lloyd Malcolm]* the other week and I thought my God, this would never have happened ten years ago! And I had exactly the same reaction when I saw *Sylvia [by Kate Prince & Priya Parmar, music by Josh Cohen & DJ Walde]* at the Old Vic *[in Central South London]*. So strides have been made and I do think that things are easier now.

It makes me remember when I was at the National Theatre, in *The National Health [1969, by Peter Nichols]*. Because I hadn't formally had any training and I had suddenly ended up there in this role, I wrote to every single rep company I could think of, saying, "Currently playing the lead at the National, blah de blah . . . I'd love to . . . Great reviews and everything . . . Would you . . . ?" And only about three of them bothered to reply, who all said, "If we're doing *The Crucible*, we will bear you in mind." Admittedly this was 'all those years ago', but I would hope that things have changed since then and that people in that position would find it slightly . . . well a lot easier!

Should black performers feel confident to go into the business as individuals, or should they still be aware that they might need to clump in order to share resources and create a single voice that can be heard.

That's interesting question. Because . . .

It's a divisive question too.

It is. I've always been someone who's thought of myself as an individual, and not as part of a group. And again, I'm sorry to harp back to this, but having been brought up in a very working class, *white* working class environment, I first of all thought of myself as working class. I identified as working class before I identified myself as being mixed race, black, whatever.

I feel the same with feminism in a way, because at the end of the day, although I am a feminist there's the bigger picture. It's about the whole of humanity. What we're trying to achieve, or what *I'm* trying to achieve on the stage, is to bring thoughts and intelligence, to try and show people that we are here, that there is another world. And to *represent that*. I don't just stand up on stage and be me as a black woman. I want to represent me as a human being. But obviously there are still huge barriers to me being in a position to do that.

I think the first major barrier was when I went to school, the Camden School for Girls *[a single-sex grammar school at the time, long associated with the advancement of women's education]*. And when I was leaving, I went for the talk with the head teacher, and she said, "What do you want to do, Cleopatra?" And I said, "I want to be an actress." "There are no parts for coloured actresses in Britain." That's what she said and, in fact, she was correct. There were no parts in those days.

She was telling it like it was, I suppose.

Yes. But she was obviously trying to dissuade me in any case. And that made me think the other way: "Well, if there aren't any parts, then I'm going to make sure that they bloody well are!" So her advice had the reverse effect on me, it made me even more determined to do something which I was passionate about.

It was a struggle, but then again I was fortunate in meeting people like *[filmmaker]* Ken Loach. He used me as not to prove a point but as part of the representation of London *[in BBC TV plays Up the Junction (1965), Cathy Come Home (1966) and his first feature film Poor Cow (1967)]*. He saw that there were people like myself who'd been born and brought up in London, who belonged to London. So yeah, I was fortunate then. But at the same time, of course, I always wanted to do Restoration comedy — I was passionate about it.

Where did that come from?

I don't know, I just loved the language, wit and extreme characters. But it never happened. I think now, if I was starting out and had a passion like that, even though Restoration isn't often done nowadays, I would have a much bigger chance of actually achieving that.

But if you went back to your sixth form self, walking out from that headmistress's office, what would you say to yourself, now you've got to where you've got and done what you've done?

I would say to myself, you've got to do what you passionately believe in. And don't do things to please other people. If you feel that you've got to do something, then do it. Don't be afraid of failing. *Don't be afraid of failing.* Things don't always work out but you've got to take that risk. Because I don't want to be lying on my deathbed, thinking, "If only, if only."

What do you see as your first break working in the performing arts?

I would say it was *Wise Child* in 1967. It was Simon Gray's first West End play, with an amazing cast. It had Alec Guinness in it, Simon Ward, Gordon Jackson and little old me. Little *young* me!

And how did that come about? Because that that's an extraordinary role to land for any actress, and you landed it.

It came about because I was swapping over from doing French to Drama at college. I was at Gipsy Hill Teachers Training College (later Kingston Poly), it's now a uni, doing a BEd *[Bachelor of Education degree]* there.

You decided to go from French to Drama. Okay. As one does.

Well I love French. But I was pressurised into going off to train to be a teacher, just to keep the headmistress happy.

But you finished the course?

No, I didn't. I suddenly thought after a year, "Why am I doing this? I love French, but I really don't want to be a teacher. I want to act." And then, because it was those days, I was lucky — it was ILEA *[Inner London Education Authority]* and no student loans, I mean you had a grant to live off, for heaven's sake! So I wrote to the educational grant authority and said, "I'm thinking of changing over." And they said, "Well, fine. You get accepted by drama school and we'll swap your grant over."

In the meantime, because I had acted as a kid, I went to an agent's and said, "Oh is there any work going, just in the holidays, while I'm looking around for auditioning for drama schools?" They came up with this audition, which I got. So it was all quite sort of random, really. And that's why I never went back to my studies.

Blimey. That's quite a leap, isn't it? And great that the producers did what all producers should be doing, taking a punt on new talent.

I suppose. Michael Codron was producer and John Dexter was director. I remember all my friends phoning me up and saying, "Oh my God, *John Dexter!*" because he had a reputation about having whipping boys or girls in his productions and he apparently wasn't supposed to be especially kind to actresses. But I got on really well. I was obviously petrified, but got on really well with him.

And the rest of the cast were good with you as well?

Oh fantastic. They really were. Alec couldn't have been nicer and I learned so much from him. Well, all of them in fact. I used to sit there in the rehearsal room just watching and watching and watching. And I also learned a lot from Doreen Cannon, who a whole bunch of us younger actors used to go to. People like Warren Mitchell also used to go to her courses — she was very much Stanislavski Actors' Studio *[method acting]*. So I used to go to Doreen and she was amazing for us all as well, this American woman who wouldn't let you get away with anything.

You got a most promising new actress nomination, moved on to the National Theatre where you were the first black actress in a leading role at the National Theatre in The National Health in 1969, and then several seasons with the Young Vic Company, which had only just started up. A brilliant time to be getting into the business.

I was on the board of the Young Vic which was started by Frank Dunlop, who I adore. He and Joan Littlewood *[who started Theatre Workshop in East London]*, both believed in and championed theatre for the people and not for the privileged few. And he made sure that it was. The whole ethos behind the Young Vic in those days was that everybody was equal. From the cleaner upwards, there was no division whatsoever. And this is right from the moment it was founded *[1970]*. Frank also wanted people who weren't traditional theatregoers to go along there, and have that experience. And it does worry me and upset me now because I go to shows in the West End and sometimes I'm still the only black person in the audience. You think God, this is 2020 or whatever? What's happening? Why do people feel this is okay?

When you were little did you go to the theatre?

I did. When my mum could afford it she would take me. She had worked in cabaret, but not when I was growing up. This was prior to when she had me. She was a tap dancer and she used to tour in what were called 'coloured shows'. They were shows which came over from America and needed chorus members. I've got pictures of her in different shows and things. She was a dancer during the War and also worked in the fire service. And then I was born just at the end of the War and she did a variety of jobs after that but she didn't really dance at all after she had me.

I lived in Camden, on Regent's Park Estate, off Hampstead road. We were originally in two rooms down the road in Drummond Street. My Mum divorced from my Dad when I was about nine or ten and she put her name down for a council flat. I remember the guy came round from the council to look at our two rooms and the outside loo. And then eventually we got a council flat. So we initially got the one bedroom room in *[housing block]* Langdale — Mum was sleeping in the sitting room and I had the bedroom. When I was about 16, she went to the council and said, "Come on" and so we got two bedroom flat in Derwent. But even though she had that theatre background, we didn't go very often, simply because we didn't have much money. We'd go and see things like pantomime. One of my godfathers was a conductor at the Sadler's Wells, so I'd go to the ballet quite a lot. But there again, I would never tell my friends or classmates.

Because?

Because working class kids didn't go to the ballet. So that was a Big Secret.

And then as you got older? Camden School for Girls has always been one of the best schools — in the whole country not just London. So did they have a good drama department? Was that important?

They did. But I was never cast in anything major. I would just do tiny little things there. And then I went straight to college to do French.

So you weren't having to do roles in The Crucible at drama school or anything like that but made a direct leap into professional acting that was obviously a measure of your capabilities. So do you think theatre has the power to change people's way of thinking? Certainly after your Young Vic experience?

It can have. Provided the right people go and see it. Because if you're doing agitprop, then obviously you're not going to access everyone, people will go, "Oh no, that's not for me." Theatre that makes a difference has to be done in a very sort of subtle way. So that people think they're going along to see one thing, and actually at the end of the night, they think. "Oh my God, that's really made me think . . ." It does have a power.

Film and TV have a different power?

They have a different power. Yeah. But they still have a power.

Though you've done both, you've always been drawn to theatre — and music.

It's the communication thing. I love that feeling that you can connect with an audience. Whereas with television and film, it is a more technical thing. A lot depends on what happens in the editing room, whereas with theatre, if something doesn't work one night, you can go out the next night and rectify it. Or hopefully rectify it. I'm never happy with a theatre performance because it's a constant work — plus a lot depends on the audience and also a lot depends on just maybe what you've taken onto the stage from that particular day.

The whole business today seems to be a more complicated process with things like showreels and media presence adding to the pressures of finding work. It's a weird flip on access really.

I don't know whether it's an age thing but all the younger actors that I work with seem to be totally at ease doing it and they've got all the equipment and technical stuff. But I find it worrying, because I like to go along, chat to the director or the casting director, and you know, try things and then maybe try it another way and eventually you hopefully do what they want. Whereas with a self-tape, there's none of that. Sometimes you won't be even sent the whole script so you don't know the context. Or you might be sent a script and it's got your name printed all over it. So it's quite difficult to read.

My agent said to me, "You've got to learn to love self-tapes" — and I think I have actually, but I still don't like doing them. I think it excludes a lot of people too. It is a question of accessibility because you're not dealing ultimately with human beings, you're basically dealing with a machine.

Almost 'the computer says no' sort of process. There are so many people out there now in the business that it's very difficult for producers to actually to have access to the range of performers they're looking for. And so filters like class and education start to creep back in, which in turn locks out people who don't have access to either.

Working class nowadays has got a slightly different meaning from when I grew up. Because there was definitely a working class, then. Growing up in the 1950s, there were more factories, there were the miners, there was lots of industry and people that worked in it. The bulk of the people who worked in the world were working class and would identify as such. Nowadays it's far more difficult. Although I'm not now so-called working class, I still identify as being working class, inasmuch as I identify with people who I feel are put down, suppressed, exploited, which you're bound to get in a society where you have an elite that rules society, and where the division has got even greater.

Here in the UK it's visible. You just walk five yards out of here *[the Arts Theatre Café in London's West End]*, there'll be a homeless person, and the amounts of poverty, and the amount of people that go without. Ken Loach's films *Cathy Come Home* and more recently *Sorry We Missed You* both say this: the people who are actually working but can't afford to exist properly, it's because of the fact that they're not working for much money or they're having to work all hours God sends them, and their family suffers as a result. Things are really bad at the moment, and we've reached this position because we're governed by people who have never known poverty, having to worry where the next week's rent or food is coming from. We're governed by these people who live such a privileged existence, and until that changes, the situation is just going to get worse.

I really miss, for example, TIE *[Theatre in Education]*, which was a really fantastic system. Theatre companies would go into schools, particularly disadvantaged schools and give them a theatre production. Nowadays there doesn't seem to be the same opportunities, it's like a postcode lottery. I see that through my son's experience — he's a primary school teacher and it's so difficult taking kids out to see a show. I mean it's difficult teaching anyway today, but to go and see a show there's a cost, plus you have to get enough responsible adults to go with you. They all have to be checked. So it's a whole business to do that, whereas TIE provided a much-needed introduction to working class kids who probably never had that experience of seeing something live on the stage and engaging with it.

It's no surprise that you've always mixed theatre with politics — or, a better word, activism.

I've always had the passion for both, I suppose. When I first started out, I thought I would just change the world in a rather Brechtian way. But that developed into wanting to feel that you're contributing to something — a play, a film or whatever — that entertains people in a way that they'll maybe learn from it, get angry about it, some sort of reaction. I quickly realised that was really what I wanted to do and I was determined to do it.

Where does that come from?

A lot of it was to do with growing up on the council estate, because when I went to Camden School for Girls, the attitude of all my friends on the estate changed. I could see it was because my world would be quite different from theirs, because they all went to the secondary modern and I was going to grammar school. That really upset me. Some of them would say snide comments, you know, like, "Oh, you're going to be a snob, only snobs go there" — things like that. I thought that this shouldn't be like this, people should be able to have a good education even if they were living in a council estate. I felt saddened and I just wanted to help them to see there are other things beyond that narrow existence in that sense of looking after those who are left behind.

Do you think you were successful in making them see that?

[laughs] I don't know. When I was doing *Crossroads [longrunning ITV soap]* and things, they were all thrilled. So in a way it showed them that somebody like me could get on to national telly. There was never any animosity towards me, and they were all very proud of the fact, which was great. But at the same time . . . I was at the National, went into *Crossroads* and then I went back to the National. The caretaker on our estate said to my Mum, "Oh, hold on, we haven't seen Cleo on telly recently, Mrs Sylvestre!" My Mum said, very proudly, "Oh no, she's gone back to the National Theatre." And he said, "Oh . . . *never mind!*"

Your sense of activism is a notable extra level to your career, like working with Equity for equality. Were you always like that?

There was something always inside of me to go out and help. I've always done that. Tomorrow, I've got independent custody visiting, and I do the homeless

506   Equal Stages

night shelter. I've always felt that I must put something back into society.
That's why I've always been a passionate believer in unions and I joined
Equity as soon as I could. I used to go along to the meetings and I think
somebody said to me, "I think you should stand for council." I was still quite
young, I can't remember exactly what year it was, but I didn't expect to get on
because there were lots of big names standing in those days. But I did get on
and joined what was then called the Coloured Artists Committee, formed by
Tommy Baptiste and Louis Mahoney.

It then became the Afro-Asian Artists Committee, now it's the BAME —
it's gone through various incarnations. Who knows what they'll call it next! I
was there with Tommy, who was from Guyana, Louis, from Gambia, David
Yip from Liverpool, Isabelle Lucas she was Canadian and Burt Kwouk *[born
in Warrington, raised in Shanghai]*.

*Did you know Tommy before? Had you come into contact with him before you
went on the committee?*

I'd worked with him once, we did a double bill at the ICA and he had a play
on, *Talk Shop*, which he always said was the basis for *[Channel 4 sitcom]
Desmond's* — it was set in a barber shop and basically the plot of *Desmond's*.

Where did he get his fire from, in terms of activism and stuff like that?

Probably from his upbringing, He came from Guyana to England to train as
an opera singer. He did concerts at places like Wigmore Hall but realised that
no way was he going to make it as a black opera singer. He knew he wouldn't
even get to do *[Verdi's] Otello*, so he switched to stage acting and, as it was in
those days, a bit of radio, TV and film as well.

*Presumably Equity at the time was the safest place to find a platform for Tommy
to work to change that.*

Yes. And that's reflected in his writing, because he was a writer too. Since he
died, I discovered loads of plays that he wrote, a short film. Oh God, it was all
to do with unions! So he was obviously quite involved and quite political.

Would you say he was fearless?

Definitely. And though he could be quite imperious, he was great because he
always encouraged younger actors. Victor Richards, who does a one-man show
about Windrush, *Streets of Gold*, always said it was Tommy who encouraged

him, told him to go to drama school and supported his work. It's very sad that Tommy wasn't recognised more when he was alive, even though he got a posthumous award.

Especially for the huge strides you collectively made via Equity . . .

The vision then was to get greater representation, to have colour-blind casting, and we were very active. It was quite daunting in a way, being on the council itself because (a) there weren't that many women, and (b) there certainly weren't any other with *my* colour. There were also a lot of old school actors, *really* old school actors, who tended to be very dismissive if you squeaked up in a similar way to them. Even when I was first on the board of the Young Vic, I was one of just two women, although more then came along. And even when there were more women, then there was always that thing of whether the men were listening to you. I remember once at a meeting suggesting something and it wasn't taken up. And then about two or three meetings later, one of the men suggested exactly the same thing and everybody said, "Oh yes, what a good idea!" You know, you just think, hang on a minute . . . But I just kept quiet and thought, well, at least it's been done, you know?

How did the union thing actually work beyond the AGMs and public proclamations?

We did press, for example, when Americans were bringing productions over with black American actors or a cast, and saying that there weren't any black actors in Britain to take the roles. They would have just brought over the whole thing, and not done a full casting for it over here. Initially there was resistance but we persevered and it gradually it became accepted that there were and there are actors in Britain who could do that. It's more fluid today, so people can go and from both countries to work. But there's so many other ways how things get controlled without actually being seen by producers.

Responding on a regular basis to inequalities was a given, really. When I was Equity rep at the Young Vic, representation wasn't such a problem, but there was always something to think about. Performance fees, for example, where they tried to pay less for children's shows than for a regular show because they were shorter. At one point we were doing a children's show, which just was one hour, and Othello, which was about three hours and getting paid different rates. Most shows averaged two hours, so I said, "If that's the case, that you're paying less for the children's show because shows are usually two hours, then we should get paid more for Othello." It was all resolved and we got our money.

And there was fringe theatre too. When I ran the Rosemary Branch *[pub theatre in North London]* for example, we always paid. We wouldn't produce shows unless the actors were paid. Well I was lucky inasmuch as the woman I ran it with — Cecilia Darker and her husband owned the pub — and they more or less subsidised the theatre. At one stage I was doing a show at the Almeida Theatre *[in North London nearby]* while I was still running the Rosie. The leading actor at the show that we had at the Rosie was getting paid more than what we were being paid at the Almeida! It was a drag show, a version of *Dracula* called *Dragula,* and the director had insisted they wanted this particular artist who was very well known. They insisted on his fee and he got it. We're proud of the stuff that we did like that.

But there's always other challenges. Like with the drama schools and the student loan system. This is having a hugely negative effect because it gets back to the class thing whereby lots of drama students come from fairly well-off, affluent parents who can afford to subsidise them. It has to create an imbalance that disadvantages those whose families can't afford that sort of support. It's similar to the situation when I started. But there is a slight shift in attitude now, where lots of working class people are able to think, "Yes, I want to be an actor, I'd love to be an actor, I'm going to be an actor." Whereas when I was starting out, lots of working class people were like, "Oh no, that's not something I can do, that's something I'm not *allowed* to do, it's not or me."

At Equity we always had that in mind as we pushed our core aims for integrated casting, more opportunities all round, and basically to support British black actors. There are still so many other areas — you don't see many black make-up artists, or indeed directors, camera operators, casting directors. The list just goes on and on. Producers . . . Like I've said, it's slightly improved, but while it's so good to see more and more plays with black people in them or by them at theatres like the National, you'll still often go there and find you're the only black person sitting there in the whole auditorium.

Does that made you angry or you think that it's just the way it is — and change will come, so you concentrate on the challenge that's right in front of you?

I try not to get angry. I suppose it's frustrating, but it is improving. The first time I went to the BBC to do a telly, the make-up room was in a panic because they didn't know, they didn't have any sort of darker make-up at all. They had to mix up stuff. Even when I was at the National, I went to Lichner to get my stage makeup. There was 'Light Egyptian', 'Dark Egyptian', 'Negro 1', Negro 2'. I came across my old make-up book the other day and those were the names. It's got things like what make-up you need to use for 'Jew' and . . .

[laughs] It beggars belief, but it goes with the times and we have moved on in that respect.

> *It's a business, so when people say those were different times, in a way there's a sort of justification because it was supply and demand. You have to hit a critical point to prove there's a viable market for change and then suddenly the market is permitted to create itself, like the way black hair products took off in the United States.*

Like what's just happened in ballet — dancer Precious Adams gets supported by English National Ballet to wear tights and shoes that match her flesh tone, and Ballet Black and shoemakers Freed of London collaborating on pointed shoes for all skins. It's all been pink since the 19th century, but there again there probably weren't that many black ballet dancers around in the 19th century!

> *Back at the Young Vic, even the smallest changes in attitudes like that must have been amazing to witness. Or was it still too early for that?*

Frank had me there and, later, actors like Tony Osoba and David Yip. That was way before people in general had even begun to discuss making changes. Yes, we were discussing integrated casting at Equity, but people weren't *practising* it. Frank was one of the first companies to do it, and what was great was that he also used people of different shapes and sizes, and Joan Littlewood's Theatre Workshop was also doing it. If you think about, in those days you'd go along and see all of styles and genres of drama at the theatres but the actors would all be this sort of regular regulation size. You wouldn't really get somebody very big on stage or somebody very short, but Frank had everybody. Like Joan, to him theatre was a reflection of life. I remember the wardrobe mistress at the Young Vic was deaf. It was all very inclusive there.

> *How do you think that was permitted to happen?*

That was purely through the likes of Frank.

> *So where did he get it from?*

Oh, he just had it.

> *Did other people pick up on it at the time?*

I'm not sure how other people thought about the Young Vic. They probably just thought, "Oh, it's that strange little theatre, you know, the one in The Cut that's not going to last very long." And now look at it! Fifty years later, it's still pushing boundaries.

Why didn't the National become something like that? It's the Young Vic, just down the road from it, that's actually taken the role of our real nation's theatre.

I agree. The National took a long long time to catch up with inclusivity and it seems as if they've only just begun to really go for it. Not just colour but women playwrights and so on. Getting black faces in the audience has taken a long time, and as for class and age, you can see what sorts of audiences there are at the National. Not that one can or should judge class by their clothes or anything. But one has a pretty good idea of who's in those audiences.

You've also moved into music, which is a bit of a statement as well.

I've moved into music partly because I've become disillusioned with the whole process of auditioning, and also partly because there's not that many parts for women of my age. At the moment I'm not doing original staff material but I do blues songs which I reference and update. A lots of blues, especially male blues, for example, can be quite misogynistic, but I change that by writing in references to issues like student loans, the destruction of the National Health Service and Grenfell *[a fire broke out on June 14, 2017, in Grenfell Tower, a council housing 24-storey block of flats in West London, causing 72 deaths, the worst UK residential fire since the Second World War & caused by the building's inflammable cladding].* So that's continuing my liberal protest, to make anybody in the audience maybe think about things that matter if they're not really thinking about them already.

But I haven't given up on theatre and theatre hasn't given up on me. Recently I've done debbie tucker green's *Generations* at Chichester, *[the world premiere of]* Alan Bennett's *Allelujah!* at the Bridge Theatre and then Thornton Wilder's *Our Town* at the Regent's Park Open Air Theatre. So I haven't given up completely!

In terms of the protest work, why did you drop out of Equity? Did you feel it was going in a different direction or simply that you'd done your job and it was time for someone else to take over?

I was on the Women's Committee as well as the Afro-Asian Artists Committee by the end. Although I didn't have the kids at that point, I did think it was time for somebody else to carry on. I'm still passionate supporter of Equity.

When the kids came along, did the responsibilities of a young family add pressure to you as a woman working in the business?

Again, I was very lucky. My husband was great and very supportive, but still I decided not to go away on tour or a theatre out of town. Then, I was offered a season at Oxford Playhouse and the temptation was too great to resist. We rehearsed in London so my mother babysat my two daughters who are ten months apart. When playing in Oxford we rented a cottage, my husband would come up from working in London at the weekend and my mum came with me to look after the girls. Later, not long after my youngest was born, I was asked to return. So said to the director Gordon McDougall, "Look, I've just had another baby and Gordon said to me, "That's fine. You can bring the baby to rehearsals." So I took the job.

Beforehand, the very first rehearsal, the read-through, was in London at the London Welsh Centre in Gray's Inn Road. I went and there, there were some gardens opposite so I went with my Mum to play with the kids while I fed the baby. I took changed him and everything, put him in the Moses basket, and took him to the rehearsal. I got to the room very early and put him under a big long table. One of the actors, Bob had brought along his dog, which he always used to do, but at the end of the read-through there was this little "eeerh eeerh", and somebody said, "What's that noise?" And somebody said, "Oh, it's Bob's dog." But no, it was Cleo's *baby*!

No one had a problem with him being there, and he was bought up until he was eight months old in the dressing room at Oxford Playhouse. But Gordon really wanted me to do the part. And I want really wanted to do it. And I thought, well, you know, I wouldn't have it done it had my Mum not been there. I wouldn't have palmed them off on anybody or a nanny.

Currently there's a discussion about making provision for childcare during rehearsals. I was lucky to have support. It meant I had the confidence to say, "Well, it is a challenge but I'll do it!"

*

37

David K S Tse

'I'm driven to be an activist but I also want to entertain'

David K S Tse is a director, writer & actor, former artistic director of Yellow Earth Theatre & former creative director of Chinese Arts Space. Based in Central London, he was born in Hong Kong & raised in Herefordshire. • @dtks888

Photo: Sharon Sephton

You've been doing radio recently?

I've recently directed two dramas for BBC Radio 4. The first was *The Disappearance of Mr Chan*, inspired by the Hong Kong struggle for democracy, and the second was part of *This Is Your Country Now, Too*, seven stories which looked at the global history of child refugees entering British administrations around the world and how they were treated.

The episode I directed, *Chung-yun and So-ling*, is about a couple of mainland Chinese teenagers fleeing mass starvation in China in 1962, after Mao's disastrous Great Leap Forward and the resulting famine which killed 40 million people. They swim to Hong Kong for their survival and are eventually adopted by Chinese families in America and Hong Kong.

Directing a story like that makes you think, there but for the grace of God . . . If you're unlucky to be born into poverty or during a turbulent time, of course you'd try to change that, you'd want to improve your life or go elsewhere to survive and be safe. That's the story of humanity, ever since the first human beings walked the earth in Africa. We're all global migrants, our ancestors have always travelled in search of better opportunities. That's the best response to those on the far right who disparage and mock migrants or refugees, saying they're a threat. In fact, migrants usually come to work hard and make a living — like my parents, who came to the UK with very little except their dreams, their hard work and entrepreneurialism. They were part of that first generation of Hong Kong economic immigrants who set up fish & chip shops/Chinese takeaways and restaurants all over the UK. The whole family worked incredibly long hours to make the business a success.

Doing the work that a lot of white British people wouldn't contemplate doing . . .

Yes, that's what the Windrush generation did after the Second World War, they helped to rebuild post-war Britain. By the 1960s, the British had more money to spend on eating out. My father emigrated to the UK to work initially as a waiter, and later, when my mother joined him, he started a takeaway and, when they had enough resources, they expanded to two takeaways.

My family moved from Hong Kong *[colony & British Dependent Territory of the UK from 1841 to 1997]* to the UK in 1970. Dad had come here earlier. My parents were working class Cantonese who'd had little education due to poverty and the Japanese occupation of Hong Kong during the Second World War. What they brought was their culture and family values — and spiritual outlook — a combination of Confucianism in terms of their ethics and ancestor worship, Taoism and Buddhism, in a non-strict, secular way. They were armed with a strong pragmatic work ethic, where they never asked for hand-outs. Self-reliant and very entrepreneurial, they got the whole family to work in the takeaway.

I was the youngest of five kids. On Fridays and Saturdays, when it was the busiest in the shop, I'd be fed my tea at home and then the rest of my siblings would go and work in the takeaway. I was a bit of a latchkey kid, but I didn't go crazy — I was very Confucian, taught to behave and to respect my parents. And then when I was ten years old, the local bank manager asked, "How's David doing at school?" Even though Dad said I was doing well, the manager said, "Oh, I'm sure he'll get a better education if he's sent to private school."

Which is nonsense. But because my parents were initially working seven nights a week, they worried that they weren't looking after me sufficiently — one of my older siblings usually did that. By that stage, my parents had saved up enough to send one of their children to a local boarding school in Shropshire, so I was packed off when I was eleven years old. I boarded full-time and you were allowed two weekends each term to go home.

At the beginning it was exciting, but when the hormones started to kick in at twelve or thirteen years old, boys got very competitive over girls. Like animals, alpha males tried to bully and control others around them to be popular. Gradually, life became hell on earth, because I was trapped in this prison-like environment full of racists. There were other international kids and my best friend was half-black British, so it wasn't all parochial, but there were lots of kids from local wealthy farmers in the area, who had seen little of the world. If you were bright, they would pull you down — that seemed to be the school culture of the UK in the 1970s. There was a lot of jealousy and racism as a result. While Confucianism celebrates hard work and academic success, it was considered uncool in the UK to be a swot. You had to keep your light under a bushel, so culturally that was quite bizarre.

At the age of thirteen, I was cast in my first school play and suddenly I rediscovered myself again, having endured a year of non-stop racism that had whittled away at my self-esteem. Acting allowed me to show my humanity again, to hide my vulnerabilities with a superficial confidence onstage that said I was more than just 'Chinese'. Racism at school was combined with serving drunken racist customers in the takeaway during the holidays. It seemed that one could rarely escape racism in the UK during the 1970s and 80s, when even television programmes were racist, like *Love Thy Neighbour*, *Mind Your Language*, *It Ain't Half Hot Mum* and *The Black & White Minstrel Show*.

We lived in a small market town, Leominster in Herefordshire — the only Chinese family in a population of 10,000 people, where there was very little for the locals to do at the weekends, except go to the pub. Very similar in fact to rural life in *[long-running BBC Radio 4 soap opera]* *The Archers*, which begs the question why there are no regular British Chinese characters there or in any of the TV soap operas or medical dramas in the UK? Why has my community been rendered 'culturally invisible' for more than half a century, despite East Asians being the third largest ethnic minority in the UK?

Compare the character of Usha Gupta, the South Asian lawyer in *The Archers* for 30 years, or the character of Ric Griffin, the black surgeon on *[BBC hospital drama]* *Holby City* for 19 years. British East Asian *[BEA, which includes Southeast Asian]* doctors, nurses and social care workers populate the National Health Service — consultant anaesthetist Dr Kevin Fong is a BBC presenter — but we don't see any regular BEA characters on *Casualty* or *Call the Midwife* *[both BBC medical dramas]*. So why is this British history constantly being 'whitewashed' and the BEA contribution ignored and erased from history?

EastEnders has been broadcasting for 35 years, during which there have been five different South Asian families, various black families, LGBTQI+ and disabled characters. London has the highest concentrations of British Chinese, Vietnamese, Filipino, Korean, Japanese families and so on, Limehouse in the East End was the original Chinatown, and yet there has never been a 'normal' British East Asian family on the series. Why? Sadly, one can only conclude that it's institutional racism, which is shameful for a public broadcaster like the BBC, which is currently being subsidised by British

East Asian communities who get very little representation compared to other BAME groups.

So this is clearly more than a wake-up call?

Well they had better start doing something — otherwise British East Asians should start withholding their licence fee payments!

Those racist shows on TV when you were growing up, let's remember there were only up to four channels for the whole country during that period, so those attitudes would have immensely reflected some of the clientele of the takeaways.

A lot of people seemed stuck in dead-end jobs in Leominster, so weekends were the chance to get trashed in the pub followed by a takeaway, which was either Indian or Chinese. It's like the *Goodness Gracious Me* comedy skit *[1990s satirical British South Asian sketch show on BBC radio/TV]* 'Going for an English'. A white waiter in a 'typically bland' English restaurant is satirically made the butt of jokes by a bunch of drunken South Asian customers. It really showed the level of abuse — wittily in reverse — that South Asians historically received in the UK, while working in catering. The same is sadly true of the British Chinese experience.

It was a shock to me as a teenager, seeing that level of abuse from some British people who, as adults, were supposed to be more mature. As a child you're playful, you're open, you want to be friendly to everybody. I had an idyllic sunny childhood in Hong Kong. I grew up on a little island called Cheung Chau where there were no cars, kids could play freely on the streets and swim in the sea. Even though we were poor, we were happy, with lots of extended family and friends.

Then we moved to this cold grey country and gradually I saw the bleakness of some adult British lives. The unwelcome hostility from some ignorant racists, plus the difficulties of cultural dislocation for some of my older siblings, affected the family in profound ways. We went from living as part of a healthy open community to being extremely isolated and inward-looking, cut off from the rest of our large extended family in Hong Kong. Don't forget, this was pre-internet days so you only had letters or very expensive long-distance phone calls to keep in touch.

Racism at school, relentless work in the takeaway and family pressures caused huge dysfunction for a couple of my siblings. It's taken the family about 20 years to heal. I became an actor because I needed to process this emotional rollercoaster. I turned to spiritual questions at school, as I needed the lifeline of possible utopian alternatives to the racist hell that I endured as a teenager in the UK.

> *Those were the days when everything closed down at 5pm, just as the pubs opened. Plus the tradition of 'half-day closing', the weekends shutting down halfway through Saturday and totally closed on Sunday. If you didn't have a cinema, the pub and the off-licence would be the only places actually open in the afternoon or evening at the weekends — and of course, takeaways.*

Exactly! A lot of British food in the 1970s was incredibly bland, so immigrants brought exciting flavours from the Caribbean, India and Hong Kong, which made a huge difference to the enjoyment of life in the UK for everyone.

When I talk to British Born Chinese *[BBC]* friends of my age, it's shocking to learn the levels of racism that many suffered during their teenage years. I've always wondered why we don't hear more about these appalling events in mainstream discourse. You hear about the racism that black and South Asian communities have suffered, eg. Lenny Henry *[Danny & the Human Zoo]* and Meera Syal's *[Anita & Me]* life stories were turned into TV movies, but you rarely hear it from the British Chinese perspective. It's been wonderful to see the recent success of Sue Cheung's *Chinglish* novel for young adults *[2019]* — finally someone from a British Chinese catering family *[in the Midlands]* was allowed to tell her story to a mainstream audience. But Sue is an exception to the rule.

Is it systemic racism from producers and commissioning editors that has historically kept most British Chinese, East and Southeast Asian voices silent? Is it because of what many of our families taught us about Confucian stoicism, not to cause trouble or get involved in politics because of China's turbulent 20th century? A lot of my male BBC peers learnt martial arts as teenagers so they could fight back. It seemed like there were two choices growing up in the UK as a BBC: you either fought back at school with your intellect or in fights.

It's not surprising that in every poll, most British Chinese kids top the academic charts and go on to become professionals. Confucianism and the emphasis on education, plus the desire to escape catering and find a lifeboat of self-worth in a sea of racist bullying, drove many beyond their own potential. Of course, for those who couldn't find a lifejacket in terms of family or friends' support, mental health problems ensued.

For most BBCs in the 1970s and 80s, you dealt with the problem of racism yourself rather than constantly moaning about it. Besides, parents were often too busy working or might not fully comprehend, since they didn't attend school in the UK or experience racism in quite the same way. I want to let people know these BBC stories because I'm an artist. I want the British public to hear this bleak history and see the mirror held up to its own culture.

You started very early — in the 1990s.

Most of my early work in Yellow Earth Theatre, where I was artistic director between 1995-2008, has already covered these stories, notably *New Territories* and *Play to Win*. I was writing and directing, trying to process and understand where this bleakness came from, what were the roots of violence? It's like King Lear asking, "Is there any cause in nature that makes these hard hearts?"

That's a universal question that all artists and philosophers have grappled with over the centuries, but when you've experienced it for yourself in such a visceral way . . . When you watch *King Lear*, you realise that Shakespeare understood this bleakness, this coldness and cruelty. But where does it come from and how do we process or understand it?

My English teacher Ernest became my surrogate father at school. He inspired my love of Shakespeare. He taught me to play tennis and he directed the annual school play — he was a salt-of-the-earth Christian who had tragically lost his entire family, his wife and kids, in a terrible car accident. Consequently other staff and kids at school became his family. He became firm friends with my parents, we used to treat him to dim sum lunch in Birmingham during the holidays.

There were six pupils in my year that gave so much back to him, constantly vying to come top of the class to win the form prize. He told me, many years after I left Bedstone College, that in all his years of teaching, the six of us had brought him the most joy as a teacher. There were four white kids (three girls, one boy), me and my best friend Michael, who was like my twin brother — he and I helped each other through school, since he was bullied because he was mixed-race. If you were bright, you were bullied, so two of the white kids also got bullied. Two of the girls had been there longer, since prep school, they were sporty and popular so they weren't such targets.

Familiar school dynamics . . .

Right. But Michael and I were bullied the most, because we weren't white. They could bully the others with a nasty remark, but with us, they used our ethnicities. That's incredibly hurtful because they were insulting our core beings, something we couldn't change, our families and our cultures. You try to be as friendly as possible to everyone, but you can't stop people's prejudices. You can't stop their jealousy or resentments.

I wish now I'd been more streetwise, savvier and wittier, more charming or had learnt to just hang out rather than always striving for success, but instead I withdrew to study. My working class family sacrificed a lot to send me to boarding school — thank goodness I won a scholarship that reduced the financial burden on them — so I had to succeed and 'pay them back'. And when people are unkind, you can either spend lots of energy challenging that or focus instead on being constructive. I withdrew to somewhere safe to concentrate on why I was actually there, which was to study. I worked hard and my English teacher, like a surrogate dad, encouraged me by letting me use his study. I became that archetypal Confucian swot! I'm an average person, so my ability to come top of the class was through sheer hard work. I had to prove to the racists that I could succeed at something, despite their constant attempts to bring me down.

When the host community treats you as an outsider, even if you're BBC and you're completely British, if you don't get any positive role models in the media, you need to react. That's why I became an artist — actor, writer, director — because the British East Asian community was culturally invisible. Any time that a Chinese character(s) appeared on British television, film, theatre or radio, they were usually criminals portrayed in a negative way — like in *Sherlock: The Blind Banker* — or they were the butt of racist jokes, foreigners made to feel unwelcome.

Part of the reaction against being forced to be an outsider, even when you're BBC, is wanting to prove to yourself and your family that you can say to the bullies trying to silence you, "No, I can be just as good as you. If not better." And that's why this drive to succeed amongst some of us is incredibly strong. It can seem arrogant, but actually it was a form of self-defence.

Of my five siblings, I'm the only one that went to university. The others sacrificed so much for the family, working in the shop. Amongst the next generation, four of my five nephews and nieces graduated from university. My older siblings can read and write Chinese, but I'm illiterate because of the age that I left Hong Kong. I speak intermediate Chinese, thank goodness, so I could still communicate on some level with my parents. Dad was charmingly bilingual — he used to sign off his letters "Daddy love you forever" — but Mum spoke limited English, forcing me to practise my Cantonese. But it's my older siblings who have real access to mother culture, writing to one WhatsApp group of Hong Kong cousins in Chinese, while I write in English to another group of HK cousins.

But that also implies reduced access to British culture for some of your family.

It doesn't matter, as long as they're happy. All of my siblings can communicate in English. It's no loss that they might not appreciate *Wolf Hall [novel by Hilary*

Mantel], that's not their history. How many people in the UK know about the nefarious British Opium Wars, the sensuous beauty of Tang poetry or the insight into human nature in the Taoist poetry of the *Tao Te Ching* (I'm particularly fond of Chapter 54)? Although my siblings did other jobs, they mostly worked in catering and have created comfortable suburban lives for themselves. I'm the only one who escaped the catering world, because of the educational opportunities I received and being encouraged to act at school.

The first play I did was *A Midsummer Night's Dream*, when I played Tom Snout the tinker. I did it in a West Country accent *[laughs]* but I was embarrassed to say, "And such a wall, as I would have you think / That had in it a crannied hole or c***k."

Despite that unfortunate C-word, acting gave me such confidence and I thought, "Well, that's the way to bridge this kind of ignorance and prejudice: to be an actor, to play different roles, show what the Chinese community really is to the people who misunderstand and mistreat us, up and down the country." Because I knew that it wasn't just me, I knew racist bullying was happening to other BBCs and of course, to other ethnic minorities. So to anyone who's ever been bullied because of their ethnicity, I want to say, "Nobody is entitled to do that to you." Indeed, under the Equality Act and the police's definition of hate crime today, it's illegal to do so. At least in law, the UK has become more civilised.

As an artist, it's good to find ways to explore your cultural background and process some of these prejudices, but it's best not to be too didactic or obvious. That may sometimes work for street theatre but not in mainstream theatres, where audiences generally want to think more for themselves.

Artistically that must cause problems, if you think, "Oh, but this really does say what I want it to say."

You can't be preachy or self-absorbed at the expense of your audience. That's why with any good performance art, you have to work in a team and you have to listen to others. By all means have a strong vision, but also the humility to listen to constructive feedback. As an artist, you want to communicate your story to the widest possible audience, rather than lecture, patronise or alienate them.

Perhaps for some, their activism eclipses their artistry. But for you, does activism inspire your art?

Yes, people calling out injustice inspire me, but I'm always conscious that quality and good dramaturgy has to be there, when it comes to telling an interesting story that engages others. Whether I'm acting, writing or directing, work has to be nuanced rather than didactic. So while I'm driven by an activist's need to inform and educate, I also want to entertain. I have that within my DNA and my life experiences.

That's an important obvious point: it's not just that you aspire to it, but you actually embody all those things — whether you like it or not, if we're honest.

Indeed! I embody it, because I've lived it. But when it comes to being allowed to share some of those stories in the mainstream sector, let me relate this experience of British censorship. As I'm also moving into filmmaking/ screenwriting, I send scripts out. One short screenplay landed me a meeting with a significant public broadcasting gatekeeper. After we discussed some of the stories that I wanted to tell, she said, "Oh, we don't really want to hear more stories about racism, we've heard that so often already." I was shocked, thinking that she had never given any British East Asian artist the chance to create mainstream work — and here she was, trying to censor me?

It was incredibly arrogant, this middle class white woman was dismissing the lived visceral experience of an entire generation of BBCs, whose working class parents had migrated to the UK. Just before that meeting, a prospective UKIP parliamentary candidate had compounded my anger by using the C-word, which is as offensive to the Chinese community as the P-word for South Asians or the N-word for the black community. *[UKIP former leader]* Nigel Farage had the cheek to defend the former candidate: "If you and your mates were going out for a Chinese, what do you say you're going for?"

I remember at university in the 1980s, some Christian friends made the same mistake: "We're going for a c***ky." When I questioned their language, they said "Oh, it's just shorthand for a takeaway, like saying 'chippy'." I explained that no white kid growing up in a fish & chip shop had ever been taunted relentlessly with the words "chippy, chippy, chippy!" so as Christians, they should be mindful of offensive language. My friends duly apologised.

Farage, the leading anti-immigrant Brexiteer, condoned racist language in December 2014 to describe the Chinese, so BBC Newsbeat interviewed young adult BBCs in January 2015 to hear about their experiences. Their stories of ongoing racism in the UK were truly shocking. One young woman described her mother being horrifically kicked unconscious by a gang of young men outside their takeaway, as well as their shop windows being regularly pelted with stones. Most BBCs felt ignored and unprotected by the police. Anti-immigrant rhetoric in the run-up to Brexit — coupled with broadcasters' failure to normalise British East Asian lives, due to lack of regular representation in any of the TV soaps — clearly played a huge part in

Othering, dehumanising and increasing hate crime against BBCs, especially those who worked in restaurants or takeaways at the coalface of racism.

In January 2020, *[presenter]* Piers Morgan's offensive mocking of the Chinese language on *[ITV breakfast show] Good Morning Britain*, shows that we haven't really moved on. Despite more than 1,600 complaints, *[UK communications regulator]* Ofcom's subsequent warning to ITV has been ineffectual and sends a signal that high-profile racists can get away with it, because the UK is institutionally racist towards British East Asians and is culturally Sinophobic.

It's testament to the strength of the British Chinese that we've been able to survive all this time, getting on and improving our lives, but at the same time, how much are we glossing over if cultural gatekeepers keep censoring us? What kind of a life can British East Asians living in the world's sixth richest economy reasonably expect — one in which the Equality Act is enforced, or one in which hate crime against us continues to rise?

That sort of problem aside, do you think that something like live theatre — not radio or film because they're quite different — is a good vehicle to allow that spirit to shine through? With Yellow Earth Theatre, just the mere fact of bringing it into existence in 1995 was a major political act. But sustaining that in the years that followed hasn't been an easy task, has it?

Yellow Earth Theatre grew and developed over the course of my thirteen years' tenure as artistic director from 1995-2008, from project-funded touring in fringe venues to revenue-funded touring on the middle scale. Unfortunately, the early resignation of the two new co-artistic directors in 2010 coincided with the global financial crisis in 2008 and Arts Council England's decision to cut certain companies completely in 2011. The shock announcement that Yellow Earth had lost its funding, soon after Kumiko Mendl was appointed the new artistic director, sent the company into the wilderness for seven years. It's testament to the tenacity and vision of Kumiko and the former general manager Chris Corner that they persevered on project funding, until they finally secured NPO *[national portfolio organisation]* funding again in 2018, securing the company's future until 2022.

I just assumed at the time that the company had disappeared.

No. But during that period it really struggled. If it got funding, a project went ahead but if it didn't, then the work wasn't created and British East Asian artists were deprived of opportunities. I think that the Arts Council was incredibly shortsighted, potentially throwing away 16 years of company history, development and support for the sector. While black and South Asian companies had their funding reduced, most of them were allowed to continue. Cutting Yellow Earth completely — the only British East Asian company in the UK at that time — was a political act and the Arts Council could be accused of systemic racism against the British East Asian sector. The Arts Council seemed to have ignored its own 2001 Eclipse Report on institutional racism in theatre — in which I gave a keynote speech, for crying out loud!

There must have been times when things became so difficult during those seven years in the wilderness, that Kumiko might have considered giving up, and I'm so grateful that she didn't. Now they've regained their NPO revenue funding, Yellow Earth is empowering even more British East Asian writers, actors, directors and designers. When I was with the company, we ran a new writers' scheme called Yellow Ink in collaboration with Soho Theatre *[Central London]*, and a new directors' scheme Yellow Stages in collaboration with the Young Vic. From the beginning, it was clear that while there were a lot of British East Asian actors in the 1990s, there was a dearth of the other creatives that you needed to make shows happen — BEA writers, directors, producers, designers, etc.

Yellow Earth at the beginning, like most new theatre companies starting out, failed to attract any funding between 1993-95. It got its first small project grant in 1995, then more annual project-funding, and after a lot of hard work, successfully secured revenue-funding from 2002 to produce one show a year and tour it across England. When revenue-funding started, I said to the board of trustees that I wanted the freedom to continue acting occasionally on short TV or film contracts, so I was only paid three days a week for my full-time job as artistic director.

In a sense, I was exploiting myself, being underpaid for the hours I was actually doing at Yellow Earth. However, this was balanced by the luxury of being able to do the odd filming job, which brought in a much better income. When I was away, I continued working remotely for Yellow Earth. By underpaying me as artistic director, Yellow Earth had more resources to invest in its training schemes, as well as an annual East Asian playreading festival, Typhoon. None of these additional activities were initially funded by ACE, but they occurred due to the prudent management of our limited resources.

Today, there's a whole new generation of British East Asian artists coming forward and Kumiko's priorities are finding and giving opportunities to new BEA talent, as well as supporting and commissioning new BEA writers. In the early days of Yellow Ink, Benjamin Yeoh wrote the play *Yellow Gentleman* through the scheme. Unfortunately, there wasn't additional funding to produce his play, since our annual tour had already been planned two years ahead. So Ben found a director in Bronwyn Lim, an actress-turned-director who'd developed through Yellow Stages. He then found a freelance producer and set up a company, Sirius Arts, to produce the show. When they applied for Arts Council project funding, Yellow Earth supported their application and marketing. We wanted to empower and encourage other British East Asian companies to develop, instead of everybody just relying on one company to provide all their opportunities.

Ben joined Yellow Ink alongside others, including a young British Japanese female writer Kumiko Toda. I ran the first workshop and asked what stories or characters they'd written before, and what stories they wanted to tell? While Ben and Kumiko had already written many stories, neither had ever written one featuring East Asian characters. I said that this reflected the Eurocentric education we'd received in this country, where white or other BAME characters, except from our own cultural backgrounds, had populated almost everything we'd read. And since much of the greatest work by writers drew from their own family backgrounds or life experiences, why wouldn't a British East Asian story be equally engaging? Some of us may consider personal history as baggage and want to move on, but historically many writers have transformed aspects of their lives into great art.

And one is praised and rewarded for bringing all that to the fore.

Exactly . . . if you do it well and it's honest and touches on something that's universal. It can be very culturally specific but if it's truthful, it becomes universal. I can laugh or cry at a Woody Allen film, which is usually located in an urban white Jewish New York environment, but I get as much out of that as anybody. I relate to it because it speaks to our common humanity, our fears of illness and mortality, our need for love and the comic absurdities we go to, in order to find it.

And you don't mock it or knock it for that. You don't bring your prejudice to it.

Not at all. Obviously, I wish Allen had more diversity in his casting. Some of his later films were set in Europe, so at least he started working with European actors, but the sensibility and humour were much the same.

The theatre show you directed in 2019, From Shore to Shore [produced by On the Wire Productions] makes me think of our local Chinese takeaway in Morecambe. It's reputed to be one of the best around, but it closes just before 10pm each night because of the pubs. They could make extra money from the people coming in drunk, but they also know that closing early removes having to confront that aggression. Of course, that doesn't mean it doesn't happen during the rest of the day. Recent things like From Shore to Shore and the BBC Newsbeat reports on the British Chinese have helped give a voice to the community. It was shocking to hear about the mother being kicked unconscious. Yet it was intriguing when they went around a group of twentysomethings asking them what 'Number 26' was on their family takeaway or restaurant's menu. Every one of them instantly recalled the name of whatever dish it was that tallied with the number. They laughed at this strange commonality, but it was poignantly symbolic of the succession of generations for whom a huge part of their childhood and teenage years was working after school and at weekends in catering. I found myself asking what had they lost or gained through growing up that way? That's very much part of From Shore to Shore, with the added genius of setting it in a Chinese restaurant — how did that come about?

From Shore to Shore came about because playwright Mary Cooper, working for the University of Bolton *[in Greater Manchester]*, was invited by the former Chinese Arts Centre in Manchester (now rebranded the Centre for Contemporary Chinese Art) to run a 12-week writing course. Like Yellow Ink's aim of encouraging British East Asian writing for theatre, they wanted to engage British Chinese people to write poetry, fiction or plays.

The course went well and I was asked to act in some of the playreadings that they presented at the Octagon Theatre in Bolton. One of the Chinese writers taking part was Mimi Webster *[pen name, M W Sun]*. Mimi and Mary wanted to unearth hidden British Chinese stories, particularly those of older Chinese people in Northern England. They started to collaborate on a period of research over two years, interviewing members of the British Chinese community, mainly in Leeds and Manchester. The interviewees spoke English or Chinese *[Cantonese from Hong Kong/Southeast China, occasionally Hakka from rural Hong Kong/Southeast China, some other regional dialects or Mandarin from the rest of China]*. Mimi translated the Chinese interviews into English where possible, and worked within the community to translate the lesser-known dialects.

The process unearthed a lot of rich material from different generations of British Chinese. From this, Mary and Mimi decided to write a play, where Mimi dealt with cultural and linguistic elements in the story, incorporating occasional words and phrases in Cantonese and Mandarin to honour the interviewees. During rehearsals for the revival in 2019, we also included some Hakka phrases for one of the rural characters.

When they had a first draft in 2017, Mary and producer Deborah Dickinson approached me and asked if I was interested to direct. I read it and loved the material — much of it resonated with British East Asian lives including my own — so I agreed. We did a week's rehearsal and presented a workshop performance in a Chinese restaurant in Leeds. The five versatile British East Asian actors worked very hard to play a variety of characters and incredibly, managed to be off-book *[i.e. having memorised your lines from the script]* after only one week — the producer requested that so I had asked them to prepare well in advance. Everyone was keen to do this in a site-specific way in Chinese restaurants, to attract people who regularly eat there but don't normally go to the theatre.

Minority untold stories, that Northern spirit, new audiences and a non-conventional theatre space — you can't go wrong. Food was incorporated as well! That's exactly my type of theatre — all you're missing is a song or two.

[laughs] We had songs in the pre-show cabaret, if you remember? And a few during the show — but it wasn't a musical. People might regularly eat in their local Chinese restaurant but actually know nothing about the people who were serving them. It was the same when my family ran the takeaway. Customers would rarely have a proper conversation, unless they were particularly friendly. Most of the time they were in and out of the shop. They'd get their food and that was all their experience of us — they knew nothing of the conditions of living and working as a family 24-7.

So I was keen to direct and develop the piece. The audiences were very diverse, many British Chinese watched theatre for the first time and audience responses were very positive indeed. They laughed and cried, so we knew we were on to a winner. The company On the Wire produced a nine-city restaurant tour in 2017 where food was integral to the production, because within most traditional Chinese families of a certain generation, love was expressed more through feeding your family and your children, rather than through words or being overly tactile. It was a running motif through all the stories — part of the site-specific experience included a bowl of soup on arrival, because mother's soup was highly symbolic within the story of the oldest character Cheung Wing. By the end of the play, the audience, who are sat around circular tables throughout, were served a full Chinese dinner.

This allowed audiences to discuss the play with complete strangers eating with them, and also to celebrate the good food and sense of community engendered by the show. They were enjoying something that had come directly from the story, since two of the main characters were involved with catering. So audiences experienced in a very visceral way the benefits of immigration.

The show was a sell-out success. Mary and Deborah organised a second tour in 2019 with support from Arts Council England's Strategic Touring funding and the Confucius Institutes in Leeds, Manchester, Newcastle, Lancaster and Liverpool. *From Shore to Shore* toured to five cities and had a closer working relationship with the regional repertory theatres it partnered with, because they were keen to develop new audiences and were conscious that this piece really tapped into the local British Chinese community.

On the Wire and the reps *[repertory theatres]* teamed up with local Chinese community organisations, Chinese churches, Chinese schools, universities and Confucius Institutes, even a casino, and they did a lot of outreach, running workshops and encouraging them to come to the show. Hopefully, it has left a legacy of people who, having enjoyed *From Shore to Shore*, might continue to attend the reps — so long as they programme something that's relevant to those communities. Gradually, through developing their appreciation of theatre, these communities might then try other productions. That's the hope and dream of all theatres in reaching new audiences. In fact, 26 per cent of audiences for *From Shore to Shore* were new to the reps.

I left a similar legacy when I first trained as a director at the Leicester Haymarket Theatre in 1996. I ran a six-month community theatre outreach programme to the South Asian community there, where 45 young people ranging from five year olds to early 20s took part. Eventually they performed on the main stage of the Haymarket. It was packed to the gills with the South Asian community and their friends — the first time ever in the history of that theatre. And from that day onwards, the Peacock Theatre was created, a South Asian youth theatre group attached to the Haymarket, which has now become the Curve theatre.

This type of theatre isn't playing to ghettoised communities. What *From Shore to Shore* did was bring culturally specific work of particular interest to British East Asians and share familial stories of love and dysfunction, which are universally relevant to anyone who saw the show. By building intercultural bridges, we better understand our common humanity and build social cohesion. Through entertainment, audiences are moved to empathise and think about the 'invisible lives' of people living amongst them, because these previously hidden stories are all authentic. BBCs are 'normalised' and their humanity is writ large.

The three main characters of *From Shore to Shore* are composite creations drawn from oral history. One of them was old Cheung Wing. In his 80s, he was a Chinese pensioner in Leeds, who'd had an incredibly epic journey from China. He was separated from his mother when he was seven, sold into child labour on a remote farm during the Japanese occupation of China, and was finally reunited with his mother ten years later in colonial Hong Kong. There wasn't a dry eye in the house when they played that scene. Whatever your racial background, people understand that sort of family loss and reunion. The heartache involved was incredibly moving and beautifully captured by Mary Cooper and M W Sun's script and research.

Cheung Wing worked with his wife in British Chinese restaurant kitchens, to save up enough to invest in his own takeaway and make a success of it. Like my parents (who did their best), he made sure that all his kids were educated, and in the play his son was a university lecturer.

The real person who mostly inspired Cheung Wing's character is happily retired and very grateful to this country for everything that Leeds gave him, which were a productive life and security. His children are educated and integrated — none of them followed him into catering, they're all working as successful professionals.

The middle story was about Mei Lan, who was born in Leeds but sent back to Hong Kong as a baby, because her parents had to work in the takeaway. Her maternal grandmother brought her up along with her cousins, whose parents also worked in British takeaways. Mei Lan and her brother came back to the UK when they were children and started helping in their parents' takeaway (like me and my siblings). Mei Lan's father is an alcoholic who beats his wife, and Mei Lan's mother is so unhappy that she becomes a gambler, playing mahjong or going to the local casino.

For that generation, if they didn't have much English language, there were few options for entertainment. Casinos closed very late so it was suitable for late-night workers, and on any given weekday you usually found fellow catering staff there, so you could talk to each other in Chinese. Soft drinks and snacks were free, so casinos became an informal social club for many working in catering, and the only source of entertainment before the advent of Hong Kong soap operas on rented videos in the 1980s.

Once my siblings were old enough to run the shop by themselves, my parents would take one day off a week to go to Birmingham and I would go with them. We'd have dim sum lunch, followed by shopping in the Chinese supermarket (dry goods only) for the takeaway. In the evening after dinner, I would head off to the theatre or cinema as part of my growing interest in drama. But since my mother spoke little English, they had nowhere to go except the casino.

I remember expressing my concern about that, but Dad reassured me: "David, we know how much we earn. We give ourselves a budget to have a flutter and meet our friends. Just as you spend your pocket money on the arts, we spend our money carefully on entertainment in the casino. But we'd never go over our budget and we're not addictive types." They were true to their word, so I didn't worry after that.

Mei Lan's family reflected some of the darker stories that Mary had heard and amalgamated together. The racism that Mei Lan is subjected to at school, is symptomatic of everything I've described already. When she suddenly explodes and punches a persistently racist girl, shouting "Don't you ever. . . use that word again!", the anger and hurt from the British East Asian actress playing her and from others in the audience who'd experienced bullying was palpable and painful.

The very last character featured in *From Shore to Shore* had nothing to do with catering. Yi Di is a young very bright girl, part of China's one-child generation. Her patriarchal father is massively disappointed that she wasn't a boy and exerts 'tiger parenting' on her always to come top of the class (and make up for the loss of his own education during the Cultural Revolution). By the time she reaches 28, both her parents are pressurising her to get married because in China, an unmarried 29 year old is regarded as a 'leftover woman'. So Yi Di leaves home and takes up a PhD at Leeds University, where she meets and falls in love with Cheung Wing's son, the lecturer. They marry and start a family, and her dilemma in the play is about both hers and her young son's sense of cultural identity, growing up in the UK.

Old Cheung Wing ends the play reflecting on his interview and the importance of telling one's own stories: "Otherwise, how will they *[his children and grandchildren]* understand where they come from?" Everyone who watched the play was deeply moved by the heartfelt gravitas and agreed with the humane internationalist sentiments expressed, that all of us have travelled 'from shore to shore' literally or metaphorically to overcome hardship and trauma.

No matter where people come from — UK, Hong Kong, mainland China and so on — British East Asian people and characters are all entitled to be represented on our stages. Their experience of life is shaped by this country and sometimes in others — you can't suddenly wipe out their personal histories just because they're living here now.

And we should celebrate it.

Absolutely! We're legitimately here and we're part of the fabric of British life. Everybody is entitled to a space and a place on our stages. There's room for everybody's stories and we need to make sure they're heard, especially with the current pernicious drift towards nationalism and fascism around the world, including the anti-immigrant rhetoric of Brexit.

Systemic racism sadly still exists within British culture. The need for British East Asian artists to speak out is stronger than ever. We also need cultural gatekeepers and mainstream media to support British East Asian artists' efforts to communicate their humanity to as wide an audience as possible (I've been saying that since the Arts Council's Eclipse Report).

So for me, 'Equal Stages' doesn't just apply to theatre, it's about all forms of British East Asian artistic expression in the UK. There's the rolling petition I started ten years ago, 'Let's Get More British Chinese/East Asians on TV, film, theatre & radio' (there's also a Facebook group with the same name) which is lobbying broadcasters and cultural gatekeepers to respond positively to the demands for equality in the British East Asian sector.

Between 2006 and 2017, I was founder and part-time creative director of Chinese Arts Space [originally Chinatown Arts Space, then CAS, now rebranded Chinese Arts Now or CAN] which commissioned a wide variety of British East Asian artists in music, dance, visual arts and cross-artforms, staging works across London and also the British Council's UK Now! festival in Beijing. A contemporary sculpture, Flowing by Chua Boon-Kee, was unveiled in the West End after a CAS global competition to commission a public artwork in response to the theme of sustainability. After securing NPO revenue funding for CAN for the first time from 2018, I left in the summer of 2017. Unfortunately, the CAS website no longer exists, so much of the documentation for that groundbreaking work and British East Asian talent has been lost.

It's a logical extension to the theatre you've created.

Most of my theatre work has been for Yellow Earth, because I was there for so long. I wrote a story called Play to Win [2000] about a multiracial, predominantly British Filipino gang, inspired by the real story of some British East Asian teenagers involved in the murder of headmaster Philip Lawrence [school headmaster who was stabbed to death in 1995 outside the gates of his school in Maida Vale, London, when he went to the aid of a pupil who was being attacked by the gang]. It was the story of a few disenfranchised angry and immature BEA teenagers who had empowered themselves by creating a sub-culture of misunderstanding: notions of 'tough' triads, 'manly' martial arts and East Asian forms of masculinity expressed through action movies or violent video games. Why did British East Asian teenagers, 14-17 years old, who were so young, become so violent? Why were they so angry and marginalised? In my research about gangs, I saw it had something to do with missing British East Asian role models in mainstream UK culture, absent protective father figures and bad experiences of racism at school.

Any production of Play to Win would be an interesting casting opportunity.

It was a challenge, casting Play to Win. The multiracial cast had to be versatile and talented, playing a wide variety of characters, but also physically able to perform some of the rigorous martial arts training sequences in the fantasy computer game sequences. Only actor Tom Wu with his high level of martial arts training, was capable of playing the bullied youngster Paul de la Cruz, who gradually learns to fight back. Kumiko Mendl jokes that she also got incredibly fit, playing one of the Shoalin computer game characters. The script eschewed typical naturalistic narratives such as calling Childline *[national telephone helpline for children & teenagers]* for a more theatrical leap, creating a contemporary fable that explored the growing pains of a new gang member and the possible choices still open to him to escape a life of crime.

Bullying is a running theme in my productions — I focus on the abuse of power because of my own teenage experiences of racism. But we can see that even in the adult world these traits continue, with Donald Trump the world's global bully — there isn't any minority group he hasn't attacked — followed by his racist poodle Boris Johnson. Trump and Johnson have regularly spouted racist anti-immigrant propaganda. Othering, bullying, scapegoating and eventually 'exterminating them' are the stock-in-trade of all tyrannies seen throughout history.

The very first play I wrote for Yellow Earth was *New Territories [1995, developed further in 1996 & toured 1997]*, in which the contemporary scenes were performed naturalistically, while the mythic storytelling sequences used Beijing Opera movement. It was a coming-of-age story about a teenager from Hong Kong's New Territories, who travels from East to West on a scholarship to a British boarding school. Echoing his journey are the four mythic heroes from *Journey to the West* on their legendary pilgrimage to India, to obtain Buddhist sacred texts. Amidst the competitiveness of school life and rampant racism, the play explored both the teenager's spiritual and sexual awakening. As he makes these personal discoveries, the teenager realises that his experiences along the journey, like the mythic heroes, are more important than the end result (securing the form prize for him, or the Buddhist sacred texts in the fable).

My last show for Yellow Earth returned full circle with *Running the Silk Road [2008]* at the Barbican — I conceived and directed the piece, while Paul Sirett wrote the text. A contemporary intercultural love story follows a young BBC man, who sets off on an epic 'journey to the East' supported by three London friends. He runs 5,000 miles along the ancient Silk Road to fundraise for environmental causes, arriving in time to catch global media attention at the start of the Beijing Olympics, in order to win back his environmentalist girlfriend in China. Along the way, he has nightmares about floods and droughts — these mythic sequences were brought vividly to life through puppetry and the spectacular physical theatre skills of Beijing Opera actors from China.

Two other international Yellow Earth collaborations were my adaptation of

The Nightingale [2005] for the HK Arts Festival, to commemorate the bicentenary of Hans Christian Andersen, performed in English and Cantonese with a transnational cast. And also my futuristic adaptation of *King Lear [2006]* performed in English and Mandarin with a transnational cast at the Shanghai Dramatic Arts Centre and the RSC. My old drama school, Rose Bruford College, generously granted me a Fellowship Award after the *King Lear* production.

British East Asian artists continually need to guard against and speak up about the discrimination, lack of opportunities or shameless 'yellow face' casting and 'whitewashing' that occasionally still occurs in the industry. We've been living in a Eurocentric world for too long. The push for 'Equal Stages' sits alongside other social justice campaigns such as #BlackLivesMatter, #MeToo, #OscarsSoWhite, #AgainstDisablism and calling out #Islamophobia, #Homophobia, #AntiSemitism, #Ageism and #Sinophobia

Social media continues to polarise people into aggressive positions. Perhaps we need kinder, gentler and calmer Buddhist or Taoist values that advocate the 'middle way' and of letting go — harmony with nature and simplicity, the opposite of having extreme opinions, collective cooperation rather than singular polarisation. What's missing in our global discourse, be it cultural, religious, political or economic, is exactly this kind of East Asian perspective.

*

38

Lola Williams

'If we keep chipping away, then we can open it up for everyone'

Lola Williams is an agent & director of New Wonder Management Talent Agency. Based in Hertfordshire, she was born in Manchester & raised both there & in Lagos, Nigeria.
• newwondermanagement.co.uk

Photo: Kirsten Reddington

The digital age is quite a gamechanger in your sector, and it has also brought its challenges, hasn't it?

From an agent's point of view, everything's online now. If you're not part of that, that's risky. Even if it doesn't come naturally, you have put yourself out there on social media. The days of picking up the phone and introducing yourself-cold calling-don't really exist anymore. Now you send a link to your website if you want to create interaction, or you send a self-tape. That 'face-to-face' connection has vanished to a certain degree. It can involve a bit of tough love to say to actors that you've got to change, but on the other hand, with all the different avenues of social media and tech opening up, you can make that move a gradual thing without too much pain.

It's still revolutionary that you can be anywhere in this country and be able to make contact with people in the industry thanks to the tech. But the idea still lingers that you have to be in London regardless, which is pretty exclusionary for the rest of the country.

I agree with that. You can't deny the fact of location and obviously if you're in London, you pick up on things quicker and you're closer to the trends. If you are further away from London and the South East, you will often feel at a disadvantage, but that has been somewhat helped by the fact that internet connectivity is getting better in most parts of the country. There's an increasing number of casting directors and meetings that happen via Skype or Zoom. So if you're in the village it's not necessarily as big a disadvantage as it once was, because they can say, "Well, let's Skype. I don't expect you to come all the way down from wherever to come to London."

Casting is quite a particular minefield for equality, though.

From my point of view, when we talk about diversity and inclusion, you have to take it beyond just the individual performer. We're in such a huge sector and there's always discussion about diversity and inclusion in the arts. But practically what does that mean? You have performers, for example, saying that they don't get a look in progressing their careers because they feel there aren't enough opportunities for them because of their background. On the other side, you have organisations bringing in initiatives to try to encourage more doors to be opened more in terms of diversity and inclusion.

As a result we're now seeing a drip-drip effect. For instance, I've noticed a subtle change in the casting briefs from Spotlight *[the UK's main casting platform, connecting performers, agents and casting directors platform for acting jobs, auditions and casting calls for theatre, TV & film, TV]* — we're now getting briefs where they're actually saying, "We want to see nonbinary actors, we want to see transgender actors." They're more specific about trying to include actors of all types and backgrounds. Even five years ago, that just didn't happen.

But what that also suggests to me is that there are more people behind the scenes, such as writers and producers who understand those differences, are now writing about situations that involve those differences, writing roles that reflect them and also accepting that there are also roles they can write to played by anyone, rather than just the usual stereotypes. It has something many of us in the industry have been talking about for a long time, but the major reason why that gradual change has started to take hold is probably because celebrities with higher profiles have been banging the drum.

Even though diversity and inclusion covers a broad of topics, for me, one key word is 'acceptance'. If we all accept it as a positive thing, all of us individually, then collectively it just falls into place. And with that comes the genuine acceptance of the fact that everybody's different and that is how it should be. If we can accept that, then there won't be the barriers. They are only there because if we don't understand something then often reject it — that sense of 'if we don't understand it, it can't be right'. No, acceptance has to be the baseline. And then you build knowledge. That's why we always say ignorance is not an excuse because lack of knowledge doesn't mean you have to always take the default position of rejection.

When you include someone, you accept them as they are. Even though that might seem very simple, it's not always the case — as human beings we all have our own little prejudices and we don't understand everything. That's fine-we're not supposed to understand everything. What we do need to know is *how* to accept, even if we don't always understand why we're doing it. Now, there is a fine line because you want people to be able to hold on to what they have in terms of their own beliefs too. So how do you marry that and get a level playing-field, where they don't feel something's being imposed on them by others and they can hold onto the effort that's their right.

I know people keep asking why is it that there are so many failed initiatives about inclusion. There are all these wonderful strategies, but it all goes back to being about the human being. Without accepting that, an inclusion policy is not a living thing. It's just a document. And if I just read it, it's not really going to change my life, to be honest. I may agree with some of it, but then I'll put it down and do something else . . . usually the thing I have always done. So it needs to more than just something on paper, it has to be more about interaction, about understanding and creating lasting awareness.

How do you take that general attitude and place it within the specifics of casting?

We represent artists in theatre, TV and film, and every day I have emails coming from actors saying, "I want to be on your books." Now a good agent will say, "Okay, first of all, I just need to check that I haven't got someone who is very similar to this person on the books already." That doesn't — or shouldn't — mean you only want one black actor, one Asian actor, one mixed-race actor, it's just that casting being often based on types, you want to make sure you don't have two actors who look so similar that they are constantly going up against each other for the same roles.

If one of them gets the job, the agency wins either way, so not every agency operates the same policy, but to me that just isn't fair to individual actors or good for team spirit. Once you've established that this isn't the case — and this is where the diverse and inclusion comes in — you have to be careful not to allow your own personal prejudice start to dictate. You now need to ask what are the skill sets? Because it's all about the skill set. Yes, past credits are important but for example, if somebody who is blind or partially sighted is working in the industry, in theatre and they haven't got many credits because a lot of casting directors haven't called them in, that's no reason not to take on that actor because maybe as their agent, you can be the one to help them get beyond that prejudice.

Your job as an agent is to go looking, to break down the door to say, "I have someone who is blind who is a fantastic actor and I want to see people see them." There are lots of actors who are wheelchair-users who I see on Twitter, for example, saying that the door is closed to them because castings are so prescriptive that the only reason you can get considered for a role has to be *because* you're in a wheelchair. We need to flip that narrative and say, well, actually, why? Why can't a person who is in a wheelchair get a role simply because it's a role? So it's like changing the narrative and that's what we're trying to say to producers that a disabled person is a person, is an actor, just hire the person for the skill set and you do your bit around the set to make sure they have an equal chance to do their job.

But that lack of opportunity makes it easy for some agents to say, well I won't put this person on my books. If we all decided as agents to open it up and start knocking harder on the doors of producers, then it would make a difference. But that collective choice has to come out of everyone's individual choice to say, let's do this.

That's not an easy choice to make because those doors are still often closed but I believe if we keep chipping away, then eventually we can open it up for everyone, and address those tokenistic gestures and tickbox exercises. We can help them to see that it doesn't work if all you want is to do is be seen to be 'right on' so that people might nod approvingly and go, oh yeah, they've got one actor of colour, they've got one actor who has a disability. We've got to get past all that. It should be just about the person and the skill set and what they want to do, their vision, their goals and that's it.

Unfortunately a lot of the writing that's coming out doesn't really lend itself to that, because there is also a diversity deficit in what gets commissioned for stage and screen and we all know that. Once again, we have to keep talking about it, shouting about it, and actively working to change it. While there's been a lot of talk about racism and sexism, that's just two aspects — there's socio-economic background, age, religion, disability, sexuality . . . the challenge is huge. Just focusing on one part doesn't make sense is we want to see true balance in the industry.

So maybe there's always been an element of the agent being a force for change if only because it makes sense to get more people on your books into work.

We're all individuals in our own different area of expertise working on whatever, but if we pool our efforts, even if it's just ten per cent that collectiveness will make a difference and it will make a change. But when people say change comes from the collective, what does that actually mean? If we all change individually, that's when it becomes a collective change. You can't just have a collective change out of nowhere and then expect things to happen. It doesn't work that way. So it's a mindset linked to each of us and how we work on a daily basis, and then we act on that.

For example, as agents most of us are signed up to membership organisations such as PMA, the Entertainment Agents Association or similar, and casting directors also have their industry bodies and networks. *[A talent agent represents the actor etc, while a casting director represents the producer.]* If those bodies were to say "Okay, agents and casting directors we want you to be more aware of taking on actors of all diversities", and then everyone respects that and acts on it individually, then logically it becomes a collective action. But it still starts with those one or two people who actively champion it and start to make the difference.

To be a little more positive, I would say that there are areas where things are more open than it before. For one thing, actors aren't getting boxed into a particular genre anymore. This generation of actors, they're more confident about what they want to do. You'll find an actor who's doing theatre suddenly say, "Actually I want to do film or now I want to do TV." In the past a casting director or producer would have looked at their CV and said, "Oh, you've only done theatre . . ." — but these days they don't really mind. The reason being that firstly you usually have to audition in front of the camera anyway. They get to see what you look like onscreen and because they have that opportunity, they're not really too fussed if you've been doing theatre for the last ten years. Of course, there are other factors that you need to take into account, such as the confidence an actor needs to want to cross over to other sectors, and also how much they are prepared to invest in fresh training to learn the required skills.

Sometimes casting briefs are highly specific in terms of height, age and so on. It all boils down to what the brief is. For example, we get lots of briefs for people who 'look American', whatever that means, as well as really odd briefs coming through, which we're now seeing more and more of, like they want someone who is a real doctor who's now an actor — they want that background of authenticity. Or they may say in a brief that they want an actor who has been a nurse or is a nurse in their day job. So then you have the other actors saying, "That's not fair because we trained at drama school so that we could *play* the nurse or the doctor!"

Things are opening up in one way and in a way they're not, so it's a really interesting balance. What we also have coming through is producers or casting directors now saying, "We don't mind if they're not actors." An actor may be asked to bring their family to do a scene with them, so that way the rest of the family become actors. Everything's about authenticity, they want something that's 'real'. For example, I had an actor who was a barrister in real life — I say 'real life', in other words it was his day job. They quickly took him because they felt he would bring the realism that they wanted to a lawyer character because he actually was a lawyer.

But what does that mean for the actor who has only ever done acting? Who doesn't have the other day job beyond the usual waitering or call centre? I am always saying to actors that your acting probably won't be your 'main' career, but it should be your 'lead' career. Look for anything that will give you a different range that makes you stand out from what everybody else brings to the table. Again, awareness of diversity is important. A producer will say, "The reason why we're doing this is because we want to open it out." But how does that actually work? I think if anything this tight reliance on 'real experience' closes it, because now you're saying you only want people who have actually done this.

It's interesting how theatre, TV & film are one of the areas that has pushed and tested legislation in the UK. You can specify requirements for roles that aren't legally possible in other sectors — which works both ways.

It's a big industry and that's why diversity and inclusion can have a wide range of meanings and interpretations for any number of people that create all sorts of barriers. Like you said, there's legislation to make it clearer, but it's also very easy to work under the radar. Some producers and casting directors at the end of the day will always want to work with the people who they are comfortable with. No matter how many people they see, if they decide that a particular person fits the bill, that's who gets the job, and talent is often just one factor in that decision.

It's obvious, but anything that hinders you from doing your job also affects the people you represent because you are indelibly part of part of the chain.

I am part of a chain. And there are things that frustrate me. What I will say is I often find it hard getting through to the casting directors and other industry folk in the UK. It's actually easier for me to get through to industry based in the US and abroad and I'll tell you why. It's very often not race, or at least not race alone, that counts against you as such, but with TV and film in particular it's more to do with an industry that's very closed and very incestuous. Everybody knows each other. I was recently at an event for casting directors and as soon as I stepped into the room I saw that I was the only person of colour in a room packed with white people who all knew each other.

So the UK industry is very closed in the sense that you always have the same people getting the same roles on all the TV dramas, for example. It's the same people because the agents and producers are all known to each other, and often represent casting directors too, and they keep themselves that way.

What I've found in America is that if you have an actor who can do the role, they don't care whether that person has been in a highly rated TV show previously. If that actor is having an audition at that moment and the producers like what they see, they will take the actor. I find it easier to get people to pick up the phone in the USA, to speak to casting directors there or set up meetings when I visit because I find they are always open. They don't need to know whether you've been in *EastEnders* or *Downton Abbey*, whereas here if you haven't been at the top, they're very wary which means they always call the same person every time.

I do find it frustrating because we've done well as an agency to get to the level we are at, but when you're faced with that combination of closed shop *and* racism, then at times I just have to say to John *[Byrne, Lola's husband & agency co-director]*, "You contact them because you're a white middle-aged man. If they see you, they'll most likely want to talk." I know that if I call them or send my details, they won't want to know. It shouldn't be that way, I shouldn't have to use John in that way but there are times when I'll have to say that to him.

That's my job occasionally too — at the same time I have a surname that often gets taken to be Nigerian, which leads to some interesting situations. But in an uneven world, I appreciate that's my role.

And that's John's role and he understands his privilege in that, but there are times when he opens the door for me and then I will follow up from there. But, like I said, it shouldn't be that way. I know he has had to do that for many colleagues of colour over the years, and he will still do it but he gets very frustrated too, because it should have changed long before now. But apart from that type of situation, I tend to knock down the doors I'm knocking on until I get a result — I'm bold in that sense.

It all affects people like theatre and filmmakers of colour in getting their stuff out there because of the amount of times it'll be rejected here in the UK. The people doing the rejecting will have all sorts of reasons but in reality what they have is a disinterest in wanting to look at stories that are related to people of colour because it's *perceived* as being not interesting to the wider scheme of people. Whereas in America, despite the fact that they do have deep racism, there's more opportunity in the TV and film world. People want to see those stories and they accept that. And though we may be opening up a little in the UK, it's not enough at all.

Well, you do wonder how relevant Downton Abbey is to anyone.

Exactly. You will definitely get something like *Downton Abbey* commissioned. But if it was a programme where it was a bit more multi-racial, they'd say, "Well there's only ten per cent that would really watch it, so it just won't sell." In the industry, race is now playing a larger role because it has become more visible. We get noticeably more custom briefs where clients say we need a black male, a black female for a particular role. But again there's the difference: in the UK historically it would be tied to a specific character type, like the gangster, however in the USA you watch television drama and you'll see a person of colour in high profile roles like the lawyer. In a lot of British shows that are produced it's very rare for you to see a person of colour playing the role of a lawyer, unless it's an assistant to whoever the lead is. In their heads they simply can't see it, even though in reality you have many senior lawyers of colour here, but their perception is that people won't accept it despite the society that we in.

In America, of course they will cast *judges* of colour — and they have many in real life. In the UK you can usually count senior figures of colour in any area of the establishment on your fingers. That sort of attitude in turn translates into the drama scripts, so in the UK you will get those gangster, thug roles, and you'll get a type of casting for certain ethnicities where some of the castings that come in will say we want someone who 'looks Middle Eastern' who will play a terrorist. Some actors who are from that background will play the roles, either because they don't take it seriously, or because they do, but can't see any other way of advancing their careers. But even if they don't, somebody who 'looks' like them — even if it is just because they tan well — will always be found to do it, even if they are from some other culture.

Yes I understand that some scripts reflect society and what's happening around us. We are in an era of where international terrorism is in the news, so yes that will translate into movies and films. I get that, but there's the other side: the normal life, the dramas that should just let anybody have a role in them.

So how did you get into all this?

It's an interesting journey. I wanted to be an actress when I was younger and went to drama school. I was born in Manchester, growing up in Longsight, and then my parents decided to go back to Nigeria and took us with them to Lagos — I was about 12 and had just started secondary school here. In Nigeria, I did drama at the University of Benin, got a degree in theatre arts, and then came back to England where I started working as an actress. I took my own advice to find a sustainable income source and ended up taking an MBA, which is how I got into the business and corporate side of things. I did very well in the corporate world, becoming a consultant to different organisations, charging them good money, and fitting in my acting around that.

But my heart was still with the arts and theatre. Then, you know, you have children and all that stuff and you're busy parenting. But once our boys were grown, I suddenly thought, I want to go back to what I first loved. Because I had been a consultant in the transformation business, managing people and managing businesses and all that for a number of years, I thought I could take that skill and add it to what I know of the industry and become an agent. There was also my husband John and his background in the industry to draw on, so that's why I decided to set up the agency.

We've done well as an agency now, with a lot of actors especially in mainstream TV like Netflix and Amazon, but it hasn't been easy. It's a lot of knocking down doors, but my skill from the corporate world has helped me a lot as an agent, particularly as the industry is changing all around us. Social media has definitely been part of that change. Traditionally it was very much, "You, the actor don't call me. I the agent will call you when I have a role." So you'd just be sitting there by the phone waiting.

Now it's a different, inclusive concept where you need to collaborate with the actor, it has to be a 50-50 relationship. You still have your role as an agent of course, but you have to work together. Part of the reason why it's changed is because it's harder to get work, and it works better if you come together. So we will sit down, say for a six-month review, and say look this is what we need to do, this is what you're going to do, you're going to be more proactive, you're going to go to workshops or do training or add this or that to your reel, while on our side, we're going to do this. I had to do that in a corporate environment where it was all very much "you've got to achieve this by that date". I've just transferred those skills to what I do at the agency and it has grown as the industry changes.

The increase in awareness of the economic and artistic value of diversity and collaboration within the industry is noticeable. It has to be linked to the increase of UK actors in American film and TV, black actors in particular which has caused some pushback from American black actors. But the way the Americans are complaining is interesting because they know the UK actors can hold their own. And, pertinently, the UK actors on those US screens are all theatre people.

I can see both sides of that story, American actors are very good and I can understand the frustration of an African American actor when a role goes to somebody from over here. I definitely wouldn't claim there is a difference in talent, but what I would say is that the black British actors who have done well in America have one thing in common: flawless American accents. Which is interesting because even though you get a much wider range of roles being offered to actors of colour in America, you very rarely see an actual black British character, or indeed a black character from any European country, unless that is a big plot point in the show.

How does live theatre fit into the agent's world? Is it like a second string to help prioritise people's skills. To give them that extra edge for that Netflix role?

I use Netflix as an example, but theatre is pretty much up there with the new television platforms. Theatre is big. And theatre is making great strides in committing to diversity. One thing I will say is that the Royal Shakespeare Company in terms of diversity have been spot on. They're one of the only organisations so far that when it comes to castings they're not just prescriptive. You have a chance is basically is what I'm saying.

From an agent's point of view, we're not just looking at actors for film and TV. It's not about what we want — a good agent will call up the actor and say, "What do you want?" Because at the end of the day it's their career and not yours. You facilitate and you profit off that facilitation, but ultimately you should really be saying to the actor, "What is your vision? What are your goals?" If they say, "Actually theatre is my passion", you're not going to turn and say, "Well no, I want you to go and do Netflix." Absolutely not — it's their vision, it's their career. If they want to do theatre then it's my job to facilitate how I can get them into theatre. Once again, if we're talking about diversity, especially inclusion, it's in that change, from the old hard-nosed agents, where it's all about what they want for you — to the reality now that some actors are doing perfectly well without agents. That said, if an actor has a far too narrow list of what they will do, that makes it hard for us to get them work and maybe an agent isn't what they need to be looking for right now.

The role of the agent over in the next 20 years or so will change, and I think numbers will probably diminish. The reason is because actors can just as easily go to a website, join a network listing lots of casting briefs and they can just go it alone, do themselves without the agent. And people are getting roles. Casting directors are now approaching actors direct so there won't be agents as we know them, to be honest. That doesn't mean agents won't exist, just that how they work and who they work with will be more focused.

Most smart agents are already diversifying their activities. So for example, at some point some of us are going to move into production. There's so much information out there for people to make their own careers, just having an agent isn't the be-all-and-end- all it used to be, and as agents we need to be

542

Equal Stages

confident in what we can offer and work with actors who appreciate that. Seeing it as a collaboration is in the long-term interest of both parties.

In the meantime we need to solve that problem of access, to help the actors who just don't understand 'why am I not getting seen?' The agent knows there are only a few agents who the old school big players like BBC or ITV or West End theatres, for example, will prioritise — because they've known them forever. But as an agent, you can't afford to spend all your time trying to get into that little clique. You need to be diverse and look for opportunities. Go where the work is and take your actors with you. It's the reality of life.

*

39
Kate Wood

'The arts create an emotional connection to the landscape'

Kate Wood, artistic & executive director of Activate & co-artistic director with Bill Gee of Inside Out Dorset festival. Based in West Dorset, she was born in North London & raised between there, Essex & West Sussex. • insideoutdorset.co.uk

Putting the global into the rural must be an interesting proposition post-Brexit?

The context for Inside Out Dorset, as an international festival, has changed post-Brexit and we think the festival is even more relevant now than ever. There's a set of challenges facing us that is different from before and we now find ourselves in new territory. It will be interesting to see how many obstacles we have to tackle because we are determined to retain the international aspect of our programme, bringing in and working with artists and partners who are mainly within the European area.

It's important personally too because I still see myself as European. Just because we are out of the European Union doesn't mean we're not European. A lot of us across the UK are now working in places where Brexit is divisive culturally in communities and families. There's therefore a lot of talk about how important it is to bring people together from all walks of life in spaces linked to cultural activities and festivals.

The festival takes place across the whole county of Dorset, where there was a higher percentage who voted Leave. It is important that Inside Out Dorset is open to absolutely everybody, bringing them together in the community.

We have been working with Oerol *[meaning 'Overall' or 'Everywhere', an arts festival on the island of Terschelling in the Netherlands]* for some years now and we are just finishing a Creative Europe-funded project with them called LAND *[Land Stewards AND Artists]*. It brings together land stewards, organisations like Dorset Area of Outstanding Natural Beauty (AONB) and the Staatsbosbeheer *[the Dutch equivalent to Forestry England]*.

LAND brings artists, producers, directors and land stewards together to explore what our relationship is to the landscape through performance and installation. It is a pilot project with lead partner Oerol, us, a creation space called Le Citron Jaune in the Camargue in the south of France and Artopolis and the PLACCC International Arts Festival which it runs in Budapest, Hungary. The pilot project has been really successful and now we've created a charter about how we want to move forward. We were able to work with UK artists, Dutch artists, universities in both the Netherlands and Hungary, really building the confidence of the land stewards we're working with. We had two conferences where we talked about our purpose, our shared interest, and what's really significant is that an organisation like Dorset AONB now has a crossover with a publicly funded organisation like Activate. They want to broaden their reach and encourage a more diverse range of people into the landscape.

Julian Glover *[journalist & former government aide]* was recently talking about his Landscapes Review: National Parks and AONBs *[2019 government report on the next steps for national parks & areas of outstanding natural beauty (AONBs) in England]* in terms of how the landscape doesn't feel welcoming to the population as a whole. It feels very similar to the conversations we are having in the publicly funded arts sector around ensuring that our work is accessible to the full community.

We have started working with the National Association of AONBs and we took the chief executive across to Oerol in the Netherlands last year to one of the LAND conferences. The trip was also very much about going to see the art works in the landscape, experiencing the work, meeting the artists, then sitting in the room and talking with other land stewards, with scientists, with academics and with artists and producers. We also took one of our board members who works with the National Trust *[National Trust for Places of Historic Interest or Natural Beauty charity for environmental and heritage conservation in England, Wales & Northern Ireland]* and who previously worked with the RSPB *[Royal Society for the Protection of Birds charity]* here in Dorset, as well as a member of the Dorset AONB team.

This was pretty new for some of the group and they were a bit unsure at first, not knowing quite what to expect. In fact, it proved to be an inspirational visit — they had experienced and supported our work before but on the island of Terschelling they were fully immersed in conversations about how we could work together while at the same time experiencing the theatre and installation art for which Oerol is incredibly respected. This has led to the National Association of AONBs securing some investment from Arts Council England to create their own arts strategy. AONBs are not arts organisations, but set up to preserve and enhance natural beauty in their various designated areas, of which there are 46 across England, Wales and Northern Ireland.

That sort of collaboration with organisations that are outside the arts sector — and lots of us in the arts have been doing this of course — is really really important because we have a shared interest in reaching new audiences. We both want to encourage and welcome people into the landscape. The National Association of AONBs recognises that the arts can create an emotional connection to landscape and this in turn can help us understand why we need to look after it. Our work with the National Association is to help them create an arts strategy. Of course Inside Out Dorset and Activate has its roots in the performing arts, but because of our crossover into installation and of my co-artistic director Bill Gee's background working with various visual artists, we are ensuring that the approach they take to creating an arts strategy is cross-art form.

As part of our research we have been looking at other organisations such as National Trust, Forestry England and the Canals & Rivers Trust, that have worked closely with the Arts Council and have created a memorandum of understanding with them. All three have a long history within public and visual arts and are more recently expanding further into commissioning and programming across other art forms. We are also talking to a number of AONBs who are already working with producers, directors, curators and artists, some who work in the visual arts and some who also encompass performance.

For those that are more familiar with the idea of public art and visual arts the incorporation of performance will be new. Last year I was invited to an internal conference of the National Trust to talk about our work. One question that was posed was, "Do you ever get asked about the fact that the work that you do in the landscape and in the public realm isn't permanent, it's temporary, and is that harder to secure investment for?" My response was that I think the permanent work created by artists in the public realm is often brilliant and our work is centred around creating permanent *memories* — experiencing something transformational in the public realm, be it urban or rural.

That idea of permanent memories is important for us because the permanence is within the people and that experience can be transformational. The majority of those people in the room that I was talking to at the conference were visitor experience managers and property managers. They are used to being approached because they may perhaps have a visual art collection in the houses that they run, so they will be far more familiar with the idea of curators working with them and being approached by Trust New Art to explore a contemporary art project.

There is a real overlap in interest between Inside Out Dorset and organisations like the National Trust that have a large property portfolio and thus a series of venues. We are not a venue-based organisation. The landscape whether it is a town or city is our venue, so we always need to work with partners such as a local authority, the National Trust or a private landowner — with our aim of inviting everyone into the space, many of whom may not regularly attend the theatre or go to a gallery space. This is very important to us.

One experience linked to that which has really stayed with me is a piece we presented as part of the 2012 Cultural Olympiad, called *Harmonic Fields* by *[French composer & street theatremaker]* Pierre Sauvageot. We had chosen these incredible aeolian instruments to be on the front cover of our festival programme and some of the residents in Portland didn't quite know what it was. Some of them made a point of coming to see us at our front of house, at the beginning and at the end of the experience, saying things like, "Do you know what, I looked at it and I had no idea what it was, I really didn't understand this, but I spoke to my neighbour and my neighbour said 'you have to go', and I've come down and this is absolutely fantastic. Can it stay here permanently?"

So there's a way of connecting with people who wouldn't ordinarily go to a contemporary art event like *Harmonic Fields*. It's important to note that the event was outside and free, open to all. Tickets can sometimes be barriers and for us it is vital that we try and break down those barriers. There are times when we do need to ticket: *The Rock Charmer* by *[Finnish musician]* Kimmo Pohjonen and The Paper Cinema is a good example. We commissioned them to work together down in Winspit *[abandoned quarry in the sea cliffs of Purbeck]*, over three nights. We took the audience from a small village called Worth Matravers where there's a fantastic Walker's pub that puts on all sorts of really great events called the Square & Compass. It's quite a well-trodden path for people interested in music, theatre and walking in Dorset, and there is a path that goes down through the landscape on to the cliff edge.

Since we were taking hundreds of people down in the dark to the edge of a cliff, of course for health & safety and to manage the audience, we had to ticket it! We made sure that the ticket price was affordable. But if we ticket anything, even when it's free, we do see a change in the audience, so we know that it can be a barrier. The audience was full each night for *The Rock Charmer* and we had ensured that we went out into the local community and set aside one additional free night for local residents.

If you remove tickets and people stumble across the work in the countryside or if we present it in the centre of a town or within a community, you see those people staying to watch or experience it. This is the most amazing thing: you can programme a piece of surreal or experimental contemporary dance in the public realm and people will stay and be absorbed in it. I remember us presenting ExNihilo's *Trajets de Ville, Trajets de Vie* from France in the middle of Bournemouth Square and it was an hour-long performance. The joy was seeing people engaging for the whole duration. It's very easy for them to walk away because, unlike a theatre where it is much more embarrassing if you get up if you are not enjoying it and you walk out, if people come to see work in the public realm and they aren't enjoying it they can simply walk away. We had a thousand people sit and watch the show.

It shows the quality of the work. We know within our industry that ExNihilo are a leader in creating site-responsive outdoor dance work, but an audience here won't necessarily know them, it's not a familiar name. So trying to attract a thousand people into a venue to see a company that they don't know and who don't have a public profile would be a challenge because of demands on the audience's time. It is also an indication that the work is really strong and the interest is really there.

What's important about our relationships with our international partners, particularly within Europe, is that our budgets aren't huge but we do an enormous amount of work to secure funding to ensure that they visit Dorset and that the performances are free. If you live in London it can be much easier to get access to international work, but people cannot always afford to travel to London — and it isn't as regularly programmed here.

So from the outset, Inside Out Dorset has always had that mix of local, national and international?

It took time to build up to that. The festival was first conceived by the Dorset Theatre Promoters' Consortium, a group of small-scale promoters and arts centres that wanted to reach a different audience and a larger audience. The focus was on rural Dorset — when we came onboard we brought in the conurbation of Bournemouth and Poole. The group included the Rural Touring consortium, a college with a theatre space, small market town arts centres. They had access to venues that seated between 60 and 200 and they recognised that if they tried to place work in public spaces they might reach a different audience.

They did exactly that and piloted the festival in 2001 with theatre and dance across different locations in rural Dorset. But it stretched them as a consortium and so when we ourselves changed from being Dorset Dance to

Activate in order to broaden our remit from dance to dance and theatre, one of the first things that we did back in 2005 was to review the festival, which was then called Inside Out — and which we then renamed Inside Out Dorset. We did some research and development on whether we could restage it, and that's when we brought in *[outdoor and site-specific arts producers]* Bill Gee and Simon Chatterton.

We also expanded the Dorset Theatre Promoters' Consortium to bring in Lighthouse Poole, which is the largest arts centre outside of London, and the local authorities of Dorset County Council and what was back then the Borough of Poole and Bournemouth Borough Council. It was the first time those three local authorities had worked together on a project like this. So we commissioned Bill and Simon to look at what the opportunities were — they had an established background as directors and programmers in the outdoor arts for some years. Bill had set up the Independent Street Arts Network (now Outdoor Arts UK). They proposed two programmes: an ambitious programme with an ambitious budget which could animate a number of different sites across rural and urban Dorset, and if we got a smaller amount of funding, they proposed an alternative programme. The consortium then asked Activate to manage the festival on their behalf because our remit was pan-Dorset.

So that's really where the partnerships started. We put a large bid into the Arts Council and we secured the money, and with local authority and some Heritage Lottery funding and other partner funding we had the first festival in 2007. It absolutely surpassed expectations and each of the performances and art works that we presented were responding to the sites — and we have continued to do that.

Our first festival set in train the idea of creating 'Extraordinary Events in Extraordinary Places'. We presented Compagnie Carabosse and their musicians, a French company who created *Fire Gardens* in Bournemouth in the Lower Gardens, reflecting their history of Empress Eugenie *[wife of France's exiled emperor Napoleon III]* in Victorian times of her route down to the sea being lit by the gardeners. It was the first time that people brought their mobile phones down — you can't imagine it now but they were relatively new then *[note that the first smartphone, the iPhone, was launched the same year]* — and were taking photos and calling their friends saying, "You must come down here *now!*" It was a bit of a phenomenon for us all in fact.

We wanted to test whether, if you put a compelling and international programme together that is accessible and free, people will travel from urban to rural Dorset. From Lighthouse's box office, the statistics showed that people were travelling from rural Dorset into Poole, but we couldn't see if they were doing the same in the opposite direction. We could see that

Lighthouse Poole brochures were displayed across rural Dorset, places like Bridport and Dorchester, but we weren't seeing the brochures of our rural venues in Bournemouth and Poole. We commissioned external evaluators from Bournemouth University (MRG: Market Research Group) to test this programming model and whether audiences would travel from Bournemouth and Poole into Weymouth for example where we had presented Polish company Teatr Biuro Podrozy — and they absolutely did.

Key to all this has always been the fact that this festival is distinctive to Dorset. Most of our colleagues producing outdoor festivals across the country are predominately in urban areas with a growing number based rurally like the Wye Valley River Festival. But — and I say this cautiously because you can never be 100 per cent sure — I think we are the only festival in the UK that is always both rural and urban. You need both in order to create these extraordinary events in extraordinary places because that combination really is the make-up of Dorset and what makes it distinctively set here. And we are one of the very few arts organisations in Dorset that have these European partnerships.

Currently we are in two. There's LAND, which is just coming to an end and we're talking about our next steps now. We are also in another unfunded partnership called Green Carpet, which is focused on commissioning small-scale performance work for green spaces internationally. The partners are from France, Belgium and the UK — we are the only ones from the UK. The first company we commissioned was Les Souffleurs Commandos Poetique, introduced to us by our French colleagues at Le Citron Jaune. The company created site-responsive work across all the partners during the course of the year.

We wanted to open the opportunity and raise the profile of the partnership, so our next commission was selected through an open call. As a result, we have commissioned a UK company Red Herring to create a new site-responsive performance called Whistlers. We are really pleased to be commissioning a UK company and support them touring our European partner festivals. They were competing with a lot of companies in France, Belgium and the Netherlands where there is a lot more investment in the creation of street arts and the public realm.

Although we here at Inside Out Dorset knew the company, Red Herring were unknown to our Green Carpet partners. We're just at the beginning stages of the new commission and they'll present their work this year at our festival in September [rescheduled due to the Coronavirus crisis]. As a result, the company will also tour France and Belgium and we feel it's really important to keep these partnerships strong post-Brexit. Technically we've looked into all of the changing legalities around visas because we weren't sure what the impact of leaving the European Union was going to be, but it is business as usual until the end of the year *[2020]* as far as we know. As early as 2016 we had a Dutch circus company approach us around the time of the Referendum, asking "Does that mean you are not going to be able to programme us in the future?" We told them that we were committed to programming international work and of course we will continue to be. I was just talking to a UK circus company who said that their bookings reduced just after the Referendum but they have picked up again — although they are not really sure how it's going to be next year.

So there are challenges but we are absolutely committed to working together as a sector to try and overcome them, because touring overseas into Europe, as many of our companies have been doing, and bringing companies here from mainland Europe is really important to us. We've had lots of companies from France, Belgium, Spain and the Netherlands. We have also been part of a project in Sri Lanka called Sura Medura, a residency programme supporting UK mid-career artists, who for six weeks interrogate their practice by working solo and in collaboration with each other and with the local community. It created a point where they can reflect on what they are doing and invest in future new ideas. The setting is taking them out of their comfort zone from making work in the UK to a completely different culture — and climate — working with artists in non-traditional settings and very cross-art form. All three artists we have supported in Sura Medura have gone on to develop new work as a result of being in Sri Lanka — in different ways and with new partners. The project is also linked with In Situ, a major European network *[for artistic creation in public space]* of which Oerol is another partner.

Those dualities of arts-landscape, rural-urban, national-international along with the concept of free performance seem obvious but, as you say, it's not a combination you'll find elsewhere even though there must be so many other counties in the UK that offer a similar setting. And you've built this up through a collaborative structure, which must be working well because you haven't complained about funding so far!

[laughs] That's true I haven't, have I? Clearly it's a concern, it's a worry, it's something that we always have to consider and work hard to secure. Your first challenge is money. The backbone of making this type of work happen is public investment, and we all know that public investment is getting tighter and tighter.

I remember one of the members of our team being surprised when she first joined because we have so many different investors. But we just have to, because we aren't in a city, we don't have the potential to have large sponsors and philanthropy. It's so much harder out in the regions to ever have those kinds of investments in your funding portfolio. This type of work means that we have to have lots of different stakeholders. We do secure varying amounts from the traditional areas that our sector applies to — Arts Council England, local authorities, trusts and foundations — and we have started to get investment from business improvement districts *[BIDs]*, in the larger towns that we work in. We also have investment with the AONBs and continually working hard to see where there are opportunities to find support for the work.

The National Lottery Project Grants (formerly Heritage Lottery Fund) had what was called a Landscape Partnership Scheme and Dorset AONB secured this funding for their South Dorset Ridgeway Partnership Scheme. It enabled them to partner with a number of arts organisations. Our partnership with them in this project came under the strand of 'Celebrating the Ridgeway' because they wanted to raise the profile of this major archaeological site in the South Dorset landscape. It has the same significance as Stonehenge and Avebury archaeologically and the way that they described it as a ceremonial landscape was beautiful. The wonderful thing about working with Dorset AONB is their knowledge and ability to convey their knowledge almost through storytelling.

We are lucky to be working in partnership with passionate people, so when you bring in a group of passionate artists with passionate archaeologists and geographers, that room is a really rich place to be. I wasn't surprised when I found out that the project manager from the South Dorset Ridgeway Partnership had gone to art school originally. Right at the beginning of the partnership, when he brought arts organisations together with environmental organisations, the first thing this facilitator did was to go around the table and connect us emotionally to the landscape — what was it that interested us in the Ridgeway? We all talked about how it made us feel and suddenly there were all these academics, artists and scientists sitting in a room talking about how we feel about it. The rest of the day went brilliantly because we had found a place of connection through how we emotionally connected to the place, and that's exactly why the AONBs want to work with the arts because they see there is an emotional connection there.

The interesting challenge for people in either sector before they start working together is that there's a worry about not really understanding geography and or not really understanding the arts, thinking these are completely different languages. But if you come in as people first and not organisations, and then talk about it as a shared interest without using industry-specific language, then it's about understanding each other.

We want to work in sites of special scientific interest or World Heritage

552   Equal Stages

Organisation sites with ancient scheduled monuments. So we need to understand what we can and can't do, like where we can take an audience or site a temporary installation or production equipment. We've learnt this through the process of talking to people through partners at organisations like the AONB. It is important for them to know that we want to have a greater understanding of the place — we've got some really protected landscapes that we work in as well as nearby towns. As soon as people realise that you are going to respect where they're from, the opportunities appear despite the challenges.

Where you're from, however, is all over Dorset — and you don't have a venue!

We don't have a venue no, and the festival is every two years. Because of that we felt we needed to do some additional audience development. We decided to create what we internally call 'signature events' to keep audiences aware of what we are doing. Last year we produced two signature events. We toured Luke Jerram's *Museum of the Moon* with the Dorset Festivals Consortium and commissioned some performance and artworks underneath it, touring to three places, Bournemouth, Sherborne and Weymouth. We worked with two other festivals on that, Bside and Bournemouth Arts by the Sea Festival. We also co-presented Michael Pinsky's *Pollution Pods* with Cape Farewell, which was installed on Brownsea Island with National Trust and focused on experiencing air pollution. The two projects very much lifted our profile with audiences because even though Inside Out Dorset only happens every two years, apparently according to Audience Agency research most people engage with the arts like this once every two years. Well that's what I heard two years ago! However, most people engage with culture on a daily basis through the internet, radio, music, but engaging in publicly funded arts of this kind is apparently biennial.

Do you think you have a model that's exportable to other places outside of Dorset, or is it simply that every area is different and has to evolve its own model?

That's a really interesting one. I think in principle we do have a model that can work in other places — potentially. My co-artistic director Bill is based in London and I'm based here in Dorset so already there's an interesting combination of perspective of city and county brought to the festival. We work with a lot of other arts organisations and partners locally — it might be a youth music organisation or a community organisation, and sometimes it depends on the locations or themes of the work in relation to the outreach programmes we run. Local relationships are very important.

We've recently finished a big project with the National Association of AONBs that lasted three years called Life Cycles and Landscapes, and commissioned a company, And Now, to make a large-scale installation performance piece called *Wayfaring*. We worked across an ancient superhighway called the Icknield Way, running between Dorset and north Norfolk — and actually across the old Doggerland into the Netherlands, so it connected to Oerol. There were various strands that we produced in the project, but from the performance aspect there were performances on the north Norfolk Coast AONB, in the North Wessex Downs AONB which is in between Reading and Newbury, and Dorset AONB.

We were the lead producer on the project, but it was really important in the making and the presentation that we worked in partnership with the local arts organisations that co-commissioned *Wayfaring*. We were working with AONBs that had less experience of working with artists than Dorset AONB, so we really focused on the outreach to ensure that there was a local organisation involved. We worked with Norfolk & Norwich Festival in Norfolk, with the Corn Exchange's 101 creation space in Newbury in the North Wessex Downs, and in Dorset it was part of Inside Out Dorset.

So in each location it was about connecting to what's happening locally. In the North Wessex Downs, the Corn Exchange supported the AONB there to deliver educational and outreach work with schools that the AONB had never done before. This is a more regular practice in our sector, but for them it was very new — one of the reasons is because they are a very small team, like many AONBs. In fact, the manager of North Wessex Downs AONB openly said that he needed to be 'converted' to take on an arts project, and at the end of the project he was completely converted! It was a really positive experience and deeply connected many new audiences to the landscapes that the work was presented across.

So in answer to the question is there a model? I would say yes there is, and it depends on the extent of what you want to produce. If it's a series of events like Inside Out Dorset, then you definitely want to discover the roots of where you are and want to be.

*

40

Kat Woods

'It takes a team to make theatre – and it takes representation'

Kat Woods is a writer & director. After living in London, she is based in Enniskillen in County Fermanagh, Northern Ireland, where she was born & raised.
• *kat-woods.com*

Coming as you do from a council estate in Fermanagh, you really are from the far extremes of the UK, and you've become a champion for the benefit class.

There's a middle path of experience and a massive division that we don't talk about enough, between being working class and being benefit class. It's a completely different level of shame, a completely different level of poverty. You grow up with 'bog fighter' syndrome where you're always fighting for your place. When you grow up in an area where poverty and the Troubles are interlinked, you so often see families like mine left at the wayside, and it seems remarkable that I have forged a career in the arts because it's unheard of in my housing estate.

So often we are the demonised class in the media and the performing arts, be it *Shameless* on Channel 4 or the plays in theatre where the narrative of demonisation is solely concerned with people that have grown up as the underclass. This term 'the underclass' is so often bandied about as an insult but I want to reclaim it, because it's something that the government tagged us with, and when you have that kind of a title you're constantly fighting against it.

It's especially in the arts that you really see how that this community was divided from the rest of society. When I started to forge a career within the arts, I'd see people getting monetary help from family or having the ability to live at home rent-free. That's not something I have access to — I don't even have access to a community at home that I can *talk* with about art or the theatre. In Fermanagh we don't really have an arts 'scene', so you have to travel two and half hours up the road to Belfast to get to see anything that would be close to what would be going on in London. So not only are you compounded by poverty on a daily level with not having access to economic advantages that can help you in life, you just don't have the access of it being on your doorstep.

That's something that gets overlooked so often. I look at my peers and they would say things like, "When I was six I went to see my first play" or "I got taken to the National when I was ten and that's when I knew that I wanted to get into theatre." But for someone like me I got into the theatre late in life. I only started doing drama at 25, and my trajectory was shaped by the family tragedy of my father's brutal murder when I was 20. That really made me strive for a place in society that would make me feel a little bit worth something — and also to help people like me that come from my background to highlight our voice on stage because we are the only oppressed community that doesn't have a voice onstage, we're so often silenced, so often grouped in with the working classes which is really irritating, because we're not working class.

My mum did her best with what she had, but she had five children and she was just vulnerable to circumstance. My father had been in a bad accident when he was younger so he couldn't work, and we grew up in an environment without any monetary advantage. I don't think people understand what that means. It means things like not going to a private school, it means not having access to extra-curricular activities that can enhance your educational performance. So anything from music lessons, drama lessons, extra help from a maths tutor, all of that plays in to how you succeed in school. And school is inherently set up for the middle classes to succeed.

I put an example of that in *Killymuck*, an autobiographical play. My father was an alcoholic and he had issues with violence. There'd be days when he'd've been taken away by the police and so my homework wouldn't have been done. And so when we'd be going into school late the next day, we'd be double-punished because we also wouldn't have had our homework done. But no one took into account the situation that we were coming from, and we'd would be put outside the class or would get detention or even the ruler across the hands *[laughs]* because we was taught in a different time I guess. It wasn't that long ago but it feels like now it's a totally different situation.

Having that sort of monetary advantage in the arts is like taking a performance-enhancing drug in athletics. You know you are not equal by any means when it comes to class structure. Even if you're from an upper working class background, you have no idea how oppressive it is not to have access to things that money can buy. Things like sanitary products, where you have no money to buy sanitary products and you're not able to leave the house, which means you miss a day off school or work. *You miss out.* You can't go to work in a restaurant with a scrunched-up bit of toilet roll in your pants. It's unhygienic and you're there for a ten-hour shift.

It's things like that that people don't realise go on in the background. And with the work I produce I want to redefine the narrative whenever we talk about poverty and people from poverty, because so often people define us as being lazy, as layabouts, who benefit from benefits — whereas I don't think I know anyone who grew up in the situation that I grew up in that would want to remain in that situation. To dispel that myth, we need to start by looking at the education structure.

And also — *[laughs]* I sound like I'm just complaining! — we also need to look at theatre and the arts. I hate seeing especially in theatre the villainisation of the impoverished, and it's revealing to see how writers from the privileged classes document people from impoverished areas. It's not a surprise really if you look at how the arts itself is set up in a way in terms of access. Take for example playwrighting competitions like Theatre 503 and the Bruntwood Prize, they're all entered with your name withheld. But I have a massive issue with the blind read on that, because you're going to cut away a lot of people from that pile who are from lower class categories that have social-economic factors that oppress their writing capabilities. I'll use myself as an example. I entered one of those competitions and I got on the longlist. But at the time I had nowhere to live and I was sofa-hopping so I was technically homeless and I was trying to write the play during my break in my full-time job which was managing a restaurant and I wrote it over the space of three days. I also didn't have any confidence, I didn't think that there was a point in me entering it, I didn't think that I would be able to get anything from it. When you enter competitions like that and they are blind, none of those factors are taken into consideration. You're going up against people that don't have full-time jobs, that perhaps have parents in the industry, that have big networks.

So often you see a playwright winning that sort of award, yet is already in the industry, has parents in the industry, has already had success to date. When you're going up against somebody like that who has all that access it feels like you've already lost. I will go out on a limb and say there are very few people from the benefit class structure that have got anywhere in those competitions, let alone got into the top three. So it would be interesting to see the class breakdown in those competitions — in fact I'm not sure how helpful they are for someone from my class background.

Which is why you've felt you needed to become more than just a writer . . .

Of course. You see I've just moved back home to Fermanagh because I can't afford to live in London after ten years there. It's been an incredibly tough decision but I was in that rut, that cycle of doing a job, paying rent, paying debts. In 2014 we took *Belfast Boy* to the Edinburgh Festival Fringe based on me taking a bank loan of £5,000 plus interest — which means it has taken me five years to pay back £6,500 or so. *And* I was still playing that back when I took up other plays but I used credit cards to help me pay for them.

So I got myself into loads of debt over the years but I had no other way of getting recognised in the industry other than putting on my own work because no one would take a chance on me. I couldn't get into any of the writers' groups. I applied year on year to get into the Soho Theatre or the Royal Court Theatre writers' groups. When I wrote *Belfast Boy* I entered it into the Royal Court and I was told that I had already found my voice and the group wouldn't help me. *[laughs]* If there are rungs being offered on the ladder, you need to forge relationships, it's not only about mining your craft, it's about being given access to a space like that.

Mind you, there's quite a queue for spaces like that, so the statistics are working against you in any case for gaining entry. Now you're back in Northern Ireland, have you found that the spaces there have changed?

We do have a space in Fermanagh, the Ardhowen in Enniskillen, but if you have five kids and you live on benefits and a theatre ticket is 15 quid and your benefits are a hundred pounds a week to pay to get food for seven people you are not going to go to the theatre. Even if a theatre ticket is £3, if you have five kids you need to get there, you need to have a packed lunch, because they sell refreshments and there is nothing worse than going to a building and getting access to get into the building and having money to get there in the first place, but then getting there and not being able to afford to *be* there. Like going to the bar and requesting a glass of water much to the dismay of the bartender. "Can I have a glass of water, I can't afford your £3 glass of Coke."

It's just so expensive and, like I said, we don't really have an arts scene in Fermanagh. I didn't have any drama outlet. I was sort of the class clown but I think that I acted out in class very much because of my circumstances at home and I was never told that maybe I should do something in drama. It was never an option for me. Even doing A-levels I think was a surprise to my teachers because though I always had the ability — I was never expelled from school because I was bright and they knew I was bright so they kept me in — I was naughty and I was never given another option of what I could possibly do. An English teacher once told me that I reminded her of *[English comedian &*

writer] Jennifer Saunders, but she never said to me. "Maybe you should do drama." The next sentence didn't come out of her mouth.

Looking back on that, I think she knew I was poor and that it wasn't for me. It was never given to me as an option. And how would you know that it's an option if you're never told about it, if your world is so insular and you have no exposure to the arts?

So that plays into the notion that when you come from a lower class you often get into these things later in life. But then you go up against ageism, so you end up left out of a lot of things that are for new or emerging people coming into the arts. So much is capped by age, where it's 'under-25' or 'under-30' for so many things — and I am not 'under-either' *[laughs]* because I started this when I was 25. So even though I'm 'emerging' I can't apply to things like that because I'm automatically excluded. That's yet another exclusionary factor where it's almost like you're punished for not starting off when you're young. You don't have to be young to be new or emerging, that is definitely not the case.

And so exclusion can lead to isolation, which is why you've ended up directing and producing your own plays.

When we did *Belfast Boy* I didn't have access to anyone that had done the fringe before, because I started to write to employ myself because I was never part of a writing community — which is what competitions like the Royal Court and the Soho give you, a community that you can bite things off and get advice from. So I was very isolated but I wanted my career to progress and I didn't know how else to do get my plays on except by doing them myself. When I raised all that money and took all the financial costs on myself I was working at one stage 50-60 hour weeks as well as writing, directing, producing and marketing my own work — and of course getting myself into a cycle of debt every year.

So eventually I've had to leave London and move back to Northern Ireland, but I'm home in Fermanagh now still trying to get myself out of the debt that I put myself in. But I have no access to art to help me progress. I don't drive — I probably couldn't afford a car anyway — and I am a good half-hour walk from the local bus station, which is fine, I need the exercise. But there's really nowhere to go. Beyond our local theatre, there is nothing here in my county, and that's to do with being a regional county in the North of Ireland, we are all forgotten in terms of art. And when there is something you can go to, everything is 15 or 20 quid anyway and there are no concessionary rates that match your income. If the ticket price is £15 and the concession's £13, what concession is two pound off for somebody that is on benefits, you know? It doesn't match and it doesn't give you any provision for travel to the theatre space — and if you're a family, like I've said, forget it.

So in a situation like that, it's no surprise that our local theatre is not in a position to be open for the entire community, to include people from the housing estates. Theatres in Northern Ireland don't seem to be representative of our society. Now *Killymuck* is a play that is representative, it deals with suicide in that society, it touches on the Troubles — in fact it's impossible to write a play about the landscape of Northern Ireland and not write about the Troubles because they shape who we are and how we've grown up. They're still here, they never went away and everyone from Northern Ireland has always known that, that it has always shaped our culture and our society, and it deals with poverty and it deals with murder.

When we wanted to tour the play, we got rejected for funding from my local council to bring it to my local county. Even though it is about the county and the place that I grew up in, we were unable to have the chance to show a slice of reality that reflects society on a stage in Fermanagh because they don't have the infrastructure to add a follow-on to help anyone that has been triggered by things that have been in the play, which is insane because these things are happening today in our society. I think Northern Ireland has the highest suicide rate in the UK, its PTSD rate is shockingly high. We don't have any resources for that because when we didn't have a sitting government *[the Northern Ireland government was suspended because of political infighting over economic policies from January 2017 to January 2020]*, but the prime minister or anyone from head office in Westminster wouldn't get involved because it was seen as a 'devolved issue', which meant that things like resources for schools and mental health have all gone completely under, along with massive Arts Council funding cuts. The government has just reformed but I'm not sure there'll be any changes soon, there's such a backlog of stuff to deal and it's going to take years for them to sort out the financial and social mess that the Six Counties are in at the moment.

Of course this has a massive impact on people from the lower echelons, the benefit class in particular, because of that trickle-down economy effect. Who gets hit the most in times of austerity? The poor. Who suffers the most? The poor. Who have least access to everything? The poor. I love my home county, it's absolutely stunning, it's a beautiful place to have grown up and there was beauty even in my housing estate where I formed friendships that I will have for life, but coming back here now I realise that we are still excluded — especially for the arts.

Enniskillen has only the one theatre, and your next nearest town is not mentally your next nearest town, as many parts of the UK might otherwise see it, because distance doesn't work that way in the Counties. You don't just 'pop over' to Omagh, Newry or Derry~Londonderry. And there's also the buses in non-urban areas, which can be a significant contributing factor to exclusion — like in Morecambe where the buses are more expensive than the train. If you want to keep a population in its place, give them a bus route in the name of access, privately run of course, and only give them two a day — and only one that comes back. And certainly not at the beginning and end of the working day. At prices that no benefits can sustain. It's an alternative UK reality that people who are not trapped in this way may well not understand. So how have you dealt with those combined barriers to arts and mobility on your return to County Fermanagh?

I've been working in Malformation *[25 miles away in the Republic of Ireland]* on a crossbearer initiative that's run by County Leitrim. It's a school project with funding for workshops for young people aged nine to 16 and then they create a piece of theatre. It's the odd Saturday because they have to organist the schools so it's just a couple of hours a week, and of course it is a schools project and there are specific things that we have to do within that remit. So it's not as free as creating your own piece of theatre. But I can only go to there if somebody else from the town is going. In Enniskillen, there's people like Sally Rees, the local drama teacher who is one of the people who drives the arts in Fermanagh at the moment, and Dylan Quinn as well who has his own dance company *[Dylan also walked 90 miles from Enniskillen to Stormont in 2019 in protest at the lack of devolved government]* — but he has had his funding cut, which when you're from a rural community is catastrophic to try and to make a living or do your job. We've got other arty people here but I think I'm the only benefit class person. Well, to be honest, I'm probably not the only benefit class person, I just like to think I am.

In the time you've been away, Arts Over Borders has grown into a major event, a lo-tech highbrow crossborder festival between Northern Ireland and the Republic with a particular focus on Enniskillen and Derry~Londonderry up the road. They do the Happy Days: Enniskillen Beckett International Festival, A Wilde Weekend: Wildetown, Home of the Happy Prince, and the Lughnasa FrielFest in the summer months and get in top Irish actors who for next to nothing do things like read Godot on the moors.

Yeah, 'on the moors'. I find this really exclusionary. The Beckett festival and the Oscar Wilde festival that they've also done would be the Fermanagh elite that organise it. It's by the middle classes and it's for the middle classes and they get people like Adrian Dunbar *[actor & director from Enniskillen]* and Ciarán McMenamin *[actor also from Enniskillen]* to come over, yet I don't see them approaching local people.

But they're not in a position to do that, are they? They need the big names to put the borders on the map.

It is great because it's a boost for our economy, and Adrian is brilliant and why not have him over? But why not have him just direct one play and give another to someone local, or at least have an assistant. Open it up. So it's not criticising Arts Over Borders, but the reality of something that is that, is that it's exclusionary, it's not inclusive. And it's not it's fault, I know, but things like Beckett and Wilde, as much as I love them, coming from the background that I come from, they're not my first go-to point if I want to read a play. I want to read something that speaks more to me, that speaks to my community. Beckett and Wilde are written in a format that isn't accessible for certainly myself, it's something that I would need to read about ten times to understand it, the staged versions are often boring. It's disengaging because Beckett and Wilde are tied up with class and that's just how it is. And I don't know how you break that, because they are two of the greatest and they were educated in Fermanagh and that's a great thing, but in terms of access it's not something that I feel comfortable with.

We can and should celebrate both their legacy in the area and the creativity that's there today in the community that actually lives there. It would be pointless to look for a magic wand and, as you've said, the festival is a welcome initiative because without it there would be nothing, but the issue of representation that it throws up to the general area is pretty glaring. However, I suspect that Arts Over Borders is not significant in some ways because it's seasonal and fleeting. In fact it's down to the local, regional and national bodies responsible for culture who are there all year round to organise representation for you and all the others — there are many borders after all in Northern Ireland. That way they could, should create a context where a more accessible festival in the spirit of Arts Over Borders and the community can meet in the middle to work within as much of the limited spectrum that you could find in an area with that economy, non-urban population and a long way away from the West End. But there's also what you said about Wilde and Beckett not being not your first port of call — plays like Belfast Boy might be the first to-go texts if you've grown up in Fermanagh but definitely not the only ones. If people want to see The Lion King in the language of Fermanagh set on an Enniskillen housing estate, you could also contemplate The Importance of Being Earnest and reclaim it the same way, or even a Shakespeare. So how do you bridge the gap by opening your own work and voice for the community that you're a conduit for?

It's about breaking down the myth that theatre is for the middle classes. What we need to do, especially in Fermanagh, is we need to provide a space. We don't have a black box space here to experiment. We are told that the Ardhowen is the theatre and there is nothing else. Unless of course you fit into the category that they're wanting at the minute — their programme is predominately based around country & western music, which is fine, there is a market for that apparently . . .

Well we are talking about Northern Ireland, obviously.

It is Northern Ireland! And it falls into the over-50, maybe over-60 bracket white middle class that buy those tickets. My issue with this is that theatres are sitting back on the model that works for them at the minute, but they have never tried anything else. So if you were to give them *Romeo and Juliet* set in a housing estate, we don't know if that will be successful because nobody has ever trialled it and you can't just trial something for one night. You need to build up a community for that, you need to do outreach work, you need to do something within the communities to make them want to come to a theatre space that is inherently not built for them.

I've done projects where we've set the bar in terms of what local theatre can do, where we've said this is what theatre is, this is what we do. Because where you *do* theatre *is* a theatre. But when you come from a housing estate and you have no access to the theatre in town anyway, and their programme comes through your letterbox, what they are telling you is this is what theatre is, this is what theatre does, and if you're not there, you feel that is not for me.

So what theatres need to do is to break down that preconception that still exists that theatre is for a certain segment of society, and instead to make it for all. We then need to get people in from those other segments to create their own art, because there is absolutely no point putting on art for people and then not having those people in the audience. So the work needs to reflect the audience, the theatre needs to make that work accessible in terms of the ticket pricing, there needs to be a plan that would encourage people to come, there needs to be a sponsored bus to go out to the housing estates to pick people up to come in.

It's not giving them equality in that terminology, it's about *equity*, it's about meeting your needs, it's about providing the resources in order to match what other people have in society so then you too can have access to it. So when we talk in terms of creating artwork that is reflective of the community we still need those communities in to see that artwork otherwise you are playing to the echo chamber of the middle classes that can buy those tickets.

Now of course you can do it yourself, but it's really difficult for somebody like me to offer open access and ticket prices because they're generally set by the venue, and you have to pay the venue. But when we did *Killymuck* with the Bunker Theatre *[in South Central London]* I asked for three pound tickets and for specific days that we could provide free tickets for a number of people. Instead of shouting that from the rooftops, I was putting out tweets if people wanted to come and see the play and if they had not enough money for the ticket price, they could DM me and we would stand them the ticket, because I would rather have people in seeing the work than not having access to it if it is speaking to them.

That's the economics of access, isn't it? It's the major underlying problem and one of the reasons why I find it difficult to take my seat in so many venues — all that amazing representation is there on the stage and then you look around the audience. And that diversity onstage is a bit like the circus in town — when it's over, it's gone until it's back next year. The community you're building up may wait till then, but they probably have better things to do.

That's why it's so important to have spaces like the Bunker, even if it's in London. I think what Chris Sonnex did as the artistic director was revolutionary. For example, he partnered with the Black Ticket Project where he provided a number of seats for free to ensure diversity not only amongst the cast and creatives but amongst our audience, and I think that's vital for highlighting to people that are from oppressed communities and underrepresented communities that these spaces are for you, it is about opening up your space and saying to somebody, "Come in, because we're reflecting society, and that is what theatre does and we want you to see the work because it's for you, it's about you."

It's also about telling people that these jobs are for them. I didn't have that growing up, I didn't have anyone within my near community that had worked in the theatre or had access to anything like that. It's such a shame that the Bunker theatre is closing — the irony is that it's being bought out to make room for some beautiful flats in London Bridge for prime real estate.

But that's not the shame of it. That's the reason for it, since the Bunker was an upcycled underground carpark after all. The economics of access again. If you went off and found yourself a regular space to do that in Central London, you couldn't do it the same way. This was the way to create a space that wasn't beholden to economics, and a limited lifespan came with the concept (which actually be a useful frame). It just needs a canny individual or two to spot the gaps in the shifting economy and grab it, even if it's just for a year or two. At the Bunker they created a space unique for its time — and, importantly, I'd say the audiences were too. And that's been part of a particularly interesting period in London where empty office blocks and municipal buildings have offered a home to theatre, as the traditional warehouses and older buildings have priced artists out — and 2020 probably marks the end of that wave as the developers run out of this latest generation of real estate to knock down. So you might say you've left London just as a lot of it's closing down. The revolution comes from what you're all going to do next. But going back to the beginning of it all, what was it that gave you that first spark, what made you think fuck this, I'm going into theatre?

I actually studied a sociology degree first, in Jordanstown *[Ulster University]*, just outside Belfast and I was living in Belfast at the time, like 1999-2000. I still worked in Enniskillen at the weekends so I used to come home and work at the restaurant. I also worked in the student union during the week. *[laughs]* I was never at college, I was just always working for money. I'd always been I suppose 'performative' in things that I did, even in things at the restaurant where I worked in for eight years. You almost had to perform at every table because they had a really small kitchen and some people used to wait and hour to an hour and a half for their food and I used to do a little routine at each table to keep them happy so that they wouldn't leave until their food had come down. I became duty manager when I was 17 — I started working there when I was 14-15 and got £1.55 an hour, totally exploited, it really shaped me!

While I was studying, the guy that I was dating was the chef and his mum worked in the social work environment and also would have spoken at events in America for *[republican political party]* Sinn Féin, so she was quite a prolific person the community. One day she was driving myself and her son up to Belfast, and she just stopped the car and turned to me, and she was like, "I just don't understand why you're pursuing this sociology. You should be doing drama." It just came out of nowhere, no one had ever said it to me before. No one. And I was like, *what?* And she kept on and gave me a monologue of why I should be doing some type of drama, some type of theatre course, some type of performance or something within that realm.

I went on to work in a couple of call centres, I worked for an insurance company and BT, and I suddenly realised, "Oh my God, what am I doing with my life?" And then I remembered what she had said to me in the car, I looked up drama courses and went and did a drama degree at Magee *[Ulster University]* in Derry. Just to see, because I wanted to do something that included everything with a performance element, directing element, and stage management, because at that point I didn't know that I wanted to write but I didn't actually know what I wanted to do. And because I had never had any access to it before, I thought if I'm going to do a degree I might as well get a taste of everything just to see what element I wanted to go into. I didn't even know that stage management was a thing, I'd never heard of it. I didn't know what a director did. I didn't know how the elements of performance and theatre worked, I didn't realise because you see the actor and you assume it's all them, which sounds really stupid but they're the ones you see and they get all the praise. And then you slowly begin to study it, to research it, and you realise that actually the acting is like a small cog in this amazing machine.

So I studied a drama degree and I specialised in theatre directing and my lecturers encouraged me and I discovered that I loved reading plays. I was never a great reader but I discovered Irish playwright Enda Walsh and *Disco Pigs*, which is my all-time favourite play. I'd never seen or heard anything like it, and I had never read anything like it. And it was done in a language was just so beautiful, and the community that they speak of was one I related to. It was the first time that I had related to a piece of theatre. I find Shakespeare very alien because of the language and its world, and I couldn't believe that here was something that I was, like, oh my God, this is like my community when they talk about the fictitious City of Pork!

My lecturers took me aside and told me that I needed to move to London and I was like, "No are you mad? I do *not* want to go to England." *[laughs]* But they insisted and they helped me with applying, I came over to London for an audition at the Drama Studio in Ealing *[West London]* and I got into their directing course — but I had to delay it by a year, because I couldn't afford to go. I spent the year working in a restaurant and fundraising and saving a couple of thousand pounds but it still wasn't enough to pay the tuition fees.

But at the end of the year I had saved enough to go, and I gave up my job, I had booked my flights, I was going to sofa-surf between a couple of cousins in London just to get me through, I had all this planned out. And then I got a letter from the college saying that the course was cancelled. And I was like *what?*

I sent them back an email, and I was like, "No you don't understand I *have* to go now, I've given notice on my accommodation in Derry, I've given up my job, I've done all this, and I can't stay here now because I'd told everyone I've done fundraising things, I'll have to give back the money, like you don't understand, this is so shameful. It feels like I've failed before I've got started."

So they set up a year of me shadowing directors which was *eye-opening*! So I sofa-surfed at my cousins' and I would go to places like the Gate and White Bear theatres and sit in on rehearsals and watch theatre directors do their thing. But all of the directors that I seemed to work with were either Oxford or Cambridge-educated with loads of money, with access to putting on their own work where money was never an issue. And I worked with one director and it was an awful experience. I became the sandwich girl, even though I probably had more experience than him as a director putting on work in Ireland — but I couldn't direct anything when I came to London because I had no English experience and no one took me seriously. I always felt like the stupid person in the room.

It was little things. They had hit a block in rehearsals and I raised my hand to offer a suggestion, but I was taken aside and told that there was only one director in the room and that if I had to suggest anything that I should take the director aside to suggest it. And then they used my suggestion in any case. I would have to go to Sainsbury's on the lunch break and get the director his baguette and brie. That's what he would have, fresh French baguette with brie cheese — in fact, an interesting combination of the white stuff. *[laughs]*

So it was eye-opening in the sense that I felt it made me feel like I didn't belong. I was working full-time in a restaurant as well because I had to get money. I had signed on *[register as unemployed]* when I first came to London but then it became a problem whenever I had to earn something to pay the bills. The officer where I signed on was absolutely lovely. I had to explain that I was trying to do work in theatre but I had to do work for free so I couldn't actively look for jobs, and she was like, "Right, well don't be saying that you will be looking for jobs." And that was okay, but then it became that I could no longer sign on because I couldn't go to the interviews because I was working full-time in these free positions, so I had to just get a full-time job in a restaurant which meant then I could no longer commit to go to those rehearsals.

It was in those time periods that I began to think, well should I write for myself and then direct it myself, and then I'll show them that I can direct? It was that kind of mentality. And then what happened was thanks to Michael Kingsbury, artistic director of the White Bear Theatre in Kennington *[South London]*. I had read some scripts for him and he said that if I found anything in the pile that he gave me, he would let me direct it on a Sunday and Monday night for a box office split. And I was like amazing, yes! So I quickly went home and read all these scripts and . . . they were all awful. And I said to Michael, "Listen, what if I write my own work? I think I could write something that works." I was really blunt and said, "I think my crap will be just as crap as this. So I might as well put on my own shit than someone else's shit. And then at least it's mine." Importantly, none of the plays that I had read spoke to my community, none of them spoke to me or where I came from. They were all English too, so that was a barrier anyway.

So I wrote a play called *Skin Town*, and Michael let me put it on over a few nights and it did really well. But I didn't have a dramaturg or anyone to provide me with information of where to go next. I sent the play to theatres and I got no response, six months passed and I'd get a rejection email. I was like, is this how this industry works? This is actually insane. I realised that in the time it had taken to get that rejection I could have had the play on again at another venue. If somebody could have just helped me to rewrite it, tell me where I need to improve it — because I didn't train as a playwright and I'd always had bad imposter syndrome.

So I wrote something else, *Dirty Flirty Thirty*. I wanted to write a comedy for my friends, a group that I worked in restaurants — I didn't have any theatre community people because of the way the drama school thing turned out, because I was on my own. I didn't know anyone in the theatre, and the people I had met doing that year it was very much apparent that they were not my friends because I was not the same as them.

Also most of them had never made me feel part of what was happening because the college had approached them and asked them for me to sit in, so I was very much not accepted into their productions. Maybe that was something I could have worked on myself more, but I felt excluded even from the way they were talking, like their vocal tone and, I suppose, that middle class English accent. Every time I opened my mouth I didn't feel smart, I didn't feel like that was an area that I would be able to fit in. Now, as I've said, at lot of that could be very much my own imposter syndrome and the narratives that I created in that moment in my own head as opposed to just the same way everyone else in the hierarchy gets treated, but there was something *assumed* in that act of sending me out for sandwiches, making me feel like the server in the situation as opposed to an equal and intelligent equal. The assistant director wasn't asked to go out to get sandwiches, it was me, who wasn't actually part of the company. The assistant director went to the same school as the director. He probably would have told him to fuck off, get your own sandwich. The director is a successful one now and hats off to him because . . . that's how it works!

So I wrote *Dirty Flirty Thirty* for my friends, and it did really well and somebody said I should take it to Edinburgh. At the time I didn't know how to access Edinburgh — I'd never been, I didn't know what it involved — so I didn't pursue it. But we did bring it to Enniskillen and to Derry. We had the play on in a few places which I was able to do with box office splits and guarantees. I came up with a financial model based on me working full-time in restaurants, so I forfeited any payment for myself and made sure that the actor and stage manager would get something, and obviously I would pay their flights and get accommodation sorted for them.

So I was able to do little mini-tours and get my work seen in my own home community where we were part of a festival called Fermanagh Live. We did it at the top of a night club in Enniskillen seven floors up with no lift. But we sold out, we got over a hundred people to see it. It didn't get picked up and off the back of that I returned to London, worked in restaurants and started work on *Belfast Boy*.

Now I've worked in nearly every restaurant in London, mainly because I can only last a year and then my brain nearly explodes because it's too much responsibility to manage a restaurant while trying to do your other full-time job in theatre. But I can't be a waitress because I have all this managerial experience, *[laughs]* but sometimes I do. So I was working in a restaurant in King's Cross and I had a fare for a table of Americans and I had four plates on my hands of food and I was thinking the whole time how will I tell *Belfast Boy*? One of the ladies said to another lady at the table, "Oh my God, girlfriend you need to see my *therapist!*" And that was my lightbulb moment of, oh my God, it's set in a psychology office. And to this day I don't remember what I did with the food! I must have put it down on a random person's table and run away to type into my phone like mad. When I came back, my boss is like, "Where the hell have you been?" I was like, *[innocent voice]* "I've just had a breakthrough with my play so I decided to run off the floor and neglect my section for half an hour, is that okay?"

Belfast Boy was definitely my breakthrough play in the industry, where I was able to get reviews — I had never been reviewed before — and we brought it to Edinburgh. A guy that came to see it in London at the Etcetera Theatre in Camden for three nights — again this would be not paying anyone but on a box office split. It was just for exposure but in a situation like that you have to have everyone feel that they are involved, so you pay the stage manager a fee and then you split the box office with the actors, which is usually not very much. Probably about 20 or 30 quid which is awful, but that's just the model that worked for me at the time because I didn't know how to access funding forms. That's another big thing. The language that they use in funding applications I find really exclusionary. The forms are designed to fail and they're super time-consuming. My brain just automatically thinks, "Why would I invest days applying for a funding opportunity when I know that I'm not going to get accepted?"

So off the back of *Belfast Boy*, I was asked to write *Wasted* by Serena Jennings and Will Merrick from No Prophet Theatre. It went to Edinburgh and as a result it transferred to New York as part of the Encore Festival in 2015. We were invited back out on tour by Center Stage in Baltimore and went to Washington DC and Connecticut. So it's out of just pure stubbornness that I've forged my way — I've always had this thing that I don't want to be seen as a failure having moved from Fermanagh. And I think that's why I stayed in London for so long. I was ready to leave London five years before I did because I physically I couldn't afford to live there. But I stayed and just kept repeating the same model that has worked for me but again feeling isolated from the theatre community.

Then I found a community with the Bunker. I've found people that were like me. Chris Sonnex programmed *Killymuck* as a double-bill with Monsay Whitney's *Box Clever [in 2019]* and that was the first time I've ever spoken to a playwright that has come from a similar background to my own. I felt so safe in that environment. Even the little things, like I remember I turned up to the first meeting with the Bunker and again I was in one of those compromising situations: I had lost a job and I was in a bit of a tizzy and I was called in for this meeting and I had barely the money for the Tube and I didn't want to fight them because I didn't want to be a big sweaty mess turning up and I was in a hooded top. And I was like oh my God what am I doing, going to a theatre meeting in this, shit should I change? I had a credit card with me and shit should I go into Topshop and get a shirt or something and I was like, no don't get yourself into more debt getting something to wear.

It's little things like that, like questioning your clothing or the words that come out of your mouth or how you speak in those spaces. But Chris is from a working class background and he grew up in a single parent family and he's from Pimlico *[in London]*, and I just felt like he just got it. It didn't feel like he was judging me, I felt so safe in those surroundings. It has taken ten years for me to get to there, but I had already made the decision to move back by then. But yeah, it felt like I'd found my community but now that's being dissolved, *[laughs]* because the Bunker has closed down.

But those people are still going to be there. They are not being dissolved obviously, so I can bounce things off them I can send them scripts to read. There's also *[scriptreader & dramaturg]* Louise Stephens who has been absolutely incredible. She worked at the Royal Court and she has seen everything I've written since she came to *Belfast Boy* in Edinburgh. Even though she didn't teach me on a playwrighting course she's always kept in contact. So I used to send her scripts to read and she would give me a few paragraphs of feedback because obviously I wasn't paying her to be a dramaturg. I'd say I met her in 2016, so it took five years to find her, but she's been incredible

For me it has been about finding a community because, as they say, no person is an island. If you are in theatre you do need that support, it takes a team to make a piece of theatre. And I guess that's what I've been striving to find the whole time, that support network, but a support network that is of the that same ilk as me. I obviously have middle class friends but it's not the same as finding somebody you see like yourself in your close circle of support for a piece of theatre you're doing. So it's about representation I suppose there.

Representation of your culture — and your language.

And the little references. When we took *Killymuck* to Edinburgh, I made a bit of a mistake financially. Again I didn't have anybody to give me indepth financial advice and, as we all know, the main thing when you're poor is that you make stupid mistakes with money and finances. I spent on extra things like PR and an expensive venue, and though we were okay ticket-wise we made a £3,500 loss or something like that. It was all on my credit card, and I had to take that financial hit myself.

Looking at other theatre companies that have done well and had the pay-off at the same profile of venue, I thought well why can't I have that? Maybe that's what I need to take my work to the next level. But I guess when you put a play on about class at a middle class festival, who the hell's going to come and see the play to take it on to the next level? You're also putting on pieces of theatre from a world that the critics don't see themselves in, so they often question that world. What happened with *Killymuck*, we got a couple of three star reviews from middle class white men that just didn't get it, they thought that it was Other. I don't know whether they realised that it was an autobiographical piece of theatre, but they spoke about the character as though this was totally alien — because they didn't have those life experiences so how could that be true? There is no real poverty in the West, if you talk in terms of poverty it's the droughts in Ethiopia and the malnourishment there. But poverty is relative and I think people sometimes miss that. And I think that happened a bit with *Killymuck*.

One of the several reasons I don't review any more is that critics also have a voice and my voice means nothing if my fellow critics aren't looking out for what they should be looking out for. I'm not contributing to a context, the shows I should be seeing won't have a context, and the audiences become more blinkered as a result.

Especially with Edinburgh, reviewers come in and expect your play to be like one at the Traverse *[permanent theatre in Edinburgh, considered the festival's most prestigious venue]*. So it's unfortunate to be pitted off like that, where your work in the 30-seater kitchen space is valued in the same regard as the work that is going on in the Traverse which has loads of money — well, not loads of money but more money, properly funded and access to things like rehearsal space. Whereas I rehearse plays by taking all the furniture out of my bedroom, everything from *Belfast Boy* to *Killymuck*. I always wondered what the neighbours thought we were doing, especially with *Belfast Boy*, they probably thought Jesus . . .

But *Killymuck* is the first thing that I've had published. I've struggled for publishers to take my work seriously and there's also the fact that I write in my mother tongue, I write the way that I would talk to my friends and family, to my community, so it's seen as 'colloquial', as 'dense' language. With *Belfast*

Boy we were super well reviewed at Edinburgh, we won the Stage Award for Acting Excellence and the Fringe Review Award for Outstanding Theatre and I thought I'm going to get published, I'm going to feel like a proper playwright, this is going to be the play, this is it. And I couldn't get a publishing house to take that on board. Couldn't get it!

It took *Killymuck* to get me published but the reason it was published because we started to have the 'trend of class' because, before, class was something that wasn't really looked upon, whereas when we did *Killymuck* there had been a couple of other plays that were specially on about class — one from Ireland called *Class* by Iseult Golden and David Horan in 2017 and then you had Scottee, in 2019 he did a piece also called *Class*. So it became the trend.

It's a class issue as well, I don't know how to sell myself and I find it really hard going into those situations telling someone how amazing you are just to get them on side to publish your work. But I was published in 2019 by Samuel French so it's taken me eight years from the time that I started writing to get published. Which is mad.

But you're going back to Fermanagh with a massive ticklist of career stuff under your belt, so it sounds like it's neither a right nor wrong decision to have decided to go back. And since London has degenerated in some ways into a massive echo chamber for theatre, maybe Northern Ireland's ready for you now.

[laughs] Hopefully that! I think being accepted to the BBC Writers Room now has really helped after applying a number of times. When I did the interviews, I told them that I wanted to move back home and I was like, I'll not move back if I have to be here for this opportunity. Because the BBC Writers Room isn't paid. It's two or three days a month and if this was a paid thing I would stay, but it's not paid and I need to get my synapses and finances in order. So I really wanted to move to Fermanagh. But they told me that if I did move home they'd pay my travel over, so that was the sealing point for me. Even though it's not paid I get my travel paid and a hotel,

I had that opportunity open to me, that access was offered, and that's why I took the plunge then and moved back because I felt less of a failure, because I had the option to come back to London once a month. It has made the transition for me easier mentally — because I have this hope of trying to break into something that will provide more money.

*   *

*

Good uses for a theatre, No. 97

Nick Awde
23 December 2017 · 🌐 ▾

Shoes – and none of them lonely or lost...
There have been so many donations of clothes, toys and food this week that
our wonderful volunteer team have moved everything into the Alhambra
Theatre's main space.
Tell everyone we're back open Wednesday Jan 3rd.
Merry Xmas all!!

👍❤️ 44   10 comments 11 shares

"Almost one in three children in the North West is estimated to be living in poverty. Two-thirds of children in poverty are growing up in households where at least one parent has a job, and that number is rising."

In the second week of December 2017, Morecambe was the focus of ITV's *Granada Report*, which ran a series of special reports by political correspondent Daniel Hewitt and producer Mat Heywood into in-work poverty and child poverty in the North West of England: 'The children from working families falling into poverty', 'Schools are frontline in fight against child poverty' and 'Teaching staff say they're seeing children arrive hungry at school'.

After the reports aired, there was an overwhelming response from people in the area who came to the two primary schools featured in the report to donate thousands of Christmas presents, clothing, food and money.

The response of Morecambe's Tory MP David Morris was to accuse the schools and the GP's surgery headed by Dr Andy Knox (featured in the reports and who is director of population health and engagement for Bay Health & Care Partners in Morecambe Bay) of being "politically motivated" (ITV report: 'Morecambe MP questions poverty claims by local schools as our report sparks huge community response').

When the schools closed for the Christmas holidays, the donations didn't stop, and the Alhambra Theatre stepped in with its team of volunteers headed by our wonderful manager at the time Tracy Brown, who was also a Morecambe Town & Lancaster City councillor and the council's Champion for Children & Young People. Within the space of a few days the theatre filled up and we think at one point it was the country's biggest clothes bank. We opened the theatre early and closed it late until after the schools opened again in January, for all people to drop off donations and for others to take whatever they needed. There were a lot of people in need that Christmas and in January we redistributed everything back into the community to continue meeting that need.

A bit of background: 1. The schools and the theatre are in the West End of Morecambe, which at the time was one of the top ten per cent most deprived places in the UK. 2. There was an unprecedented cold snap that December/January and things were glacial. 3. The theatre had no resources to put on shows (there wasn't even the mood for carol singing) that Christmas or New Year, nor to switch on the heating.

Shortly afterwards, the Alhambra helped to flip the narrative further by opening the theatre's doors to a people's meeting of more than 500 from the West End and wider Morecambe — led by Andy Knox, and the biggest gathering of the community in decades — to discuss how to tackle the area's poverty, to defend the community, and to restore its identity and pride. And that's a process which started that night and continues successfully to this day.

• *morecambe.me, othernationaltheatre.org.uk*

On leadership

A February 2020 piece by Nick Awde on the plight of migrant practitioners in the UK, reflecting the deeper issue of theatre lacking any credible industry leaders. Although rejected for publication, it's probably not going to go out of date any time soon.

The threat of ending freedom of movement between the UK and EU, looming in January 2021, reveals the devastating implications of restricting international borders for the performing arts. It also reveals the fact that no one is fighting theatre's corner — unsurprising for an industry that has long lacked meaningful leadership.

Where indeed are theatre's champions? Despite the Tory government's trumpeting of arts and culture as a £10.8 billion jewel in the UK's international trade crown, the performing arts are looking like yet one more industry swept under the carpet in the Brexit trade-offs.

But for all the headlines and opinions, what do we actually know? Only what has been publicly listed, i.e. that freedom of movement is 'planned' to cease from January 1, 2021, to be replaced with a new UK points-based immigration system restricting movement. And that's honestly all we know in the current information vacuum.

Obviously what's likely is that EU-national artists from the EU will be subject to restrictions, and UK-based EU nationals will be restricted too.

And, since movement of labour is pivotal to the negotiations, it is likely that UK demands for control will provoke an escalation on both sides of the red line. The EU, which wants to keep freedom of movement and a level playing field (sound familiar?), will respond by imposing a tit-for-tat Schengen visa/work permit that includes the carnet system, unpopular yet less draconian than the UK's Tier 5 regime currently aimed at non-EU creatives wanting to come here.

Meanwhile entry requirements for the rest of the world's artists wanting to come to the UK remain the same — as do visas required by other nations for UK artists to go to the rest of the world. But, whatever the EU outcome, UK visa/permit thresholds may rise across the board, making it harder for non-EU artists to access the UK — and for UK artists in return if retaliatory measures are imposed.

It's a two-tiered, invisible wall outcome that may turn out to be pay-to-play on a scale never seen before in this country.

But we don't actually know any of this. When they sit down to negotiate, the EU and the UK will use the crossborder exchange of our respective performing arts sectors as a bargaining chip. It could go either way.

To complicate things further, there's growing doubt about the future status of Irish artists under the continuation of the mutual Common Travel Agreement with the UK.

But again we just don't know.

Now, if things do go the way of punitive visas and work permits, what we do know is that without representation, it'll be business as usual for the big fish, who will pass on the cost and inconvenience to their funders and audiences (and many have already taken large chunks of their business out of the UK), while the small artists lose out on the right to travel for work or study. For them 'caps', 'thresholds', 'sponsorship' and the rest of the terms that drive the existing UK system are Cummingspeak dogwhistles that will translate into crushing delays, costs and exclusion.

Unbelievably in all of this there is no one actually making a convincing case for the performing arts at that negotiation table. Correction: film, music and dance seem to be making their case, very vocally, very informed. The rest of the performing arts far less so. It's understandable if sectors like circus and street arts are struggling to be heard, but a well-connected behemoth like theatre?

Predictably, there has been a degree of complaining and blaming, consultations and reports from theatre's logical points of reference — the Arts Councils (where is ACE's director of international?), Equity (what's happening with their Seat at the Table campaign?), the self-serving Creative Industries Federation, the ephemeral fringe and venue networks. But judging from their actions so far, they're not hearing the same alarm bells as the rest of the industry.

These key bodies need to prove they are lobbying MPs, ministers, the Creative Industries Council, the DCMS and the people in government they hang out with or went to university with, they need to prove that they are talking on official levels with their European counterparts, to prove they are actively defending the channels that provide our international balance of culture, explaining clearly why keeping them open matters.

But ask around the industry and you'll encounter few at the top who will go on record and list what they want to see happen in the various scenarios. What appears timidity might simply be that they don't care . . . or don't know.

There's a hermeticisation that has always lurked in theatre, and one only has to look at the way its leaders allowed the USA's harsh and imbalanced visa system for creatives be imposed without a real fight. The suspicion therefore is that our leaders don't actually know what to do.

The UK is hailed as a net exporter of culture, a world leader, but none of these bodies can convincingly quantify the reality of what we stand to lose.

£10.8 billion is a meaningless figure if no one can actually identify and value the people who make it happen.

Europe is indelibly built into our arts, it's a part of our DNA now, it creates jobs, it creates opportunities — the open interchange between Europe and the UK means our practitioners are in demand worldwide. But we're already seeing a negative effect as theatremakers from Europe are increasingly made to feel unwelcome — as are European theatremakers based in the UK.

And it's shameful that for some years now top European theatremakers have already got the message to avoid the trouble of including the UK in their world circuits. Will any new or emerging talent be bothered to come over?

It's not all doom and gloom. Looking outwards, the UK will continue to export solo and fringe shows, workshops and knowhow, it will carry on helping create festivals and venues overseas. There's a world circuit being set up with UK creatives linking to Australia and New Zealand via non-EU countries such as the Emirates, Singapore, Hong Kong, China and Taiwan. British-driven organisations like dance's Spring Forward are creating amazing networks in Europe. Our migrant artists here in the UK are mobilising — and gathering statistics to fill the void.

And it may actually transpire that the UK and EU find a win-win compromise after the bargaining process ends — and then theatre can start to adapt in response.

But it can't adapt without a plan. There is no voice without a plan. And even if there is a plan, it means nothing if there are no leaders to champion it.

This matters. Isolation comes in many guises, and guaranteed free cultural interchange is a two-way process that no one on earth should allow to disappear and replace instead with, well, isolation.

Unless maybe you're an employee of the National Theatre, protesting or striking will change little here. Theatre's strength must come from identifying its leaders whose positions give them real voice and influence. It's not too late to press those leaders every minute to account for they are doing to convince their peers in government, in the media, in Europe that there is an economic price to be paid that far outweighs the political.

Those leaders need to fight for a guaranteed seat for theatre and the performing arts at that table, to detail the impact that the removal of freedom of movement will have on programming and budgets, touring and festivals, national and international, on the individual practitioner and the company, the student and the professional, on UK nationals and UK-based European nationals, on their counterparts in the EU.

In times of crisis, what else are leaders for?

*

Glossary

Readers may be unfamiliar with technical terms used within the performing arts & the various genres, or perhaps with some cultural terms specific to the British Isles — obvious to a Brit or Irishperson but a mystery to the rest of the world. Here then is a list of simple definitions used in this book (not exhaustive) relating to theatre & society, which hopefully will answer your questions.

A note on the UK & Ireland: The two countries are spread across the British Isles. The United Kingdom is made up of the nations of England, Northern Ireland, Scotland & Wales, which have their own local governments & different (but sometimes shared) educational, health & cultural funding systems. Additionally, the Isle of Man & the Channel Islands are sort of part of the same country but not quite, since they're not legally part of the United Kingdom & have their own governments. There's a good argument for the City of London also being sort of but not quite (historically it's the financial 'Square Mile' of London & whose bounds more or less sit on the original Roman fortified town).

academy — an independent institution, or undergraduate &/or graduate department at a college or university, that teaches the performing arts. Also known as drama school, stage school, theatre school, with different shades of meaning.

access — *see* **open access**.

ACE — Arts Council England.

actor *vs* actress — **actor** is the preferred gender-neutral term. **Actress** is still used by many female performers to describe themselves, & it is also found in acting awards categories.

agent — someone who finds jobs for people working in the performing arts, the majority of them being actors. Also variously known as talent agent, acting agent, booking agent. *See also* **casting director** (a talent agent represents the actor etc, while a casting director represents the producer).

agitprop — promoting political ideas or arguments through theatre, art & literature.

A-levels — exams done in the final year of school at 18 years old.

alt-cabaret — irreverent provocative cabaret, comedy & circus, spread & established by Australian artists through the major Angloworld fringe festivals.

applied theatre — taking theatre beyond traditional theatre spaces & audiences, including schools, the community, prisons & streets. Also used in areas like therapy & hospitals.

ASM — *see* **stage manager**.

artist — performer.

artistic director — the person with overall responsibility for the selection & interpretation of work performed by a theatre, ballet or opera company. Often simply called director, & can also have duties as the CEO, manager etc of an organisation.

arts — 1. The performing arts, visual arts & literature. 2. creative culture. 3. *See also* **performing arts**.

Arts Council — the national funding body for the arts, currently split across the UK as follows: Arts Council England, Arts Council of Northern Ireland, Creative Scotland, Arts Council of Wales.

Asian — people of Bangladeshi, Indian, Pakistani or Sri Lankan descent.

austerity — after the financial crisis of 2007–2008, austerity was launched in 2010 by the Conservative & Liberal Democrat coalition government under David Cameron & Nick Clegg. The austerity programme included cuts to health, education & welfare spending, reductions in local government funding & an increase in VAT. Spending on the police, courts & prisons was also reduced. The effects of austerity continue to divide the country.

audition — a short performance or interview for a role or job in the **performing arts**.

backstage — the areas behind a venue's stage such as the wings, dressing rooms, storage & workshops.

BAME — abbreviation for Black, Asian, & minority ethnic, used to refer to people in the UK who are not white. It's an official term that has not been well received by the communities it seeks to describe.

benefit, benefits — the government system of money given to people who need financial help, e.g. if they are unemployed, sick or disabled.

Big Four — the four (or five, depending how you look at it) main paid-for venues at the Edinburgh Festival Fringe: Assembly, Gilded Balloon, Pleasance, Underbelly, who all print a common programme. Some people add C Venues as the fifth.

black box — a small theatre space, usually a studio added to a larger theatre or converted from a large room, e.g. above a pub, where the walls, floor & stage (often just the floor) are painted black & have fixed or removable seating.

borough — administrative unit that is either an area of a city, a town or a district.

box office — **1.** the place where you buy tickets at a theatre or venue; **2.** the revenue earned by ticket sales for a show.

BSL — British Sign Language is used mainly by people who are deaf in the UK. It's one of the seven indigenous languages of the British Isles but was only recognised by the government in 2003.

British Council — the United Kingdom's international organisation for cultural relations & educational opportunities. They don't have much in the way of funding but do help with UK shows wanting to go to various countries & vice-versa.

BTEC — pronounced 'BEE-tech', an educational qualification mainly for vocational subjects, taken at GCSE, A-level & degree levels. It stands for 'Business & Technology Education Council'.

casting director — a person or organisation that organises the casting of actors for film or TV. *See also* **agent** (a casting director represents the producer, & a talent agent represents the actor etc).

community centre, community hall — a public building available to a community for group activities, performances, exhibitions, fairs, social support, public information, etc.

community theatre — theatre made by & for members of a community. It can be existing works created by the community, performed by the community, or original work that reflects the community.

company — a group that makes theatre.

Conservatives — the Conservative Party, one of the UK's two main political parties, traditionally right-wing with capitalist values. Also called the Tory Party.

co-production, co-produce — a joint venture between two or more companies to make & stage work.

Coronation Street — long-running ITV TV soap opera set in Manchester (North West of England) since 1960 that has become a key reference point for culture & society in the UK.

council — **1.** a body of people elected to manage the affairs of a city, county, or other municipal district. **2.** the organisation they control. Seen in such forms as borough council, town council, city council, district council, county council. Often called 'local council'.

council estate — area of houses or blocks of flats built & rented out at a low rent to tenants by a local council. Traditionally associated with working class communities, & the main part of the UK's low-rent 'social housing' system.

council flat, council house — a dwelling that is owned by a local council (possibly built by it) & rented to tenants at a low rent.

county — administrative area of the UK. It has the same meaning as **shire**.

a creative — member of the creative team that makes new productions from existing or new works, including directors, musical directors & choreographers, as well as designers of sets, props, costume, lighting & audiovisual media.

Creative Europe — the European Union's programme to support the cultural, creative & audiovisual sectors, launched in January 2014. Based across the UK in London, Manchester, Edinburgh, Glasgow, Cardiff & Belfast, pre-Brexit, Creative Europe Desk UK promoted awareness & understanding of Creative Europe, & free advice & support for applicants from the UK & organised workshops, seminars & industry events.

criminal justice system — the legal & social institutions that enforce criminal law: the police, law courts, prisons & probation agencies.

cross-arts — mixing different art forms together, e.g. painting & theatre, video & opera.

culture — a universal word that takes different shades of meaning across the world. In the UK it has more the sense of what you find in museums & art galleries, & is therefore often associated with the elites & treated with suspicion in a class way. In the UK, the **arts** tends to be the preferred term, although 'culture & the arts' is also commonly used.

cultural centre — an organisation, building or complex that promotes culture & arts, e.g. somewhere you can see theatre, catch a concert, view an art show, buy a croissant & coffee.

curated — fringe festivals are either curated (the shows are chosen by the organisers), or open to anyone depending on venue availability. The opposite of **open access**.

DCMS — the government's Department (i.e. ministry) for Digital, Culture, Media & Sport.

designer — someone who creates the set, costumes &/or lighting for a show.

devised theatre — collectively writing & staging a show, where the script or movement is built on ideas & improvisation by some/everyone involved.

director — **1.** the person in charge of creating a show & staging it. **2.** the person who runs an organisation. **3.** both. **4.** *see* **artistic director**

drama — **1.** the practice or subject of theatre, as opposed to dance, circus, opera, etc. **2.** a play that isn't a comedy.

dramaturg — a literary adviser or editor who works on other people's scripts, duties vary from company to company. A bit like a **literary manager**.

EastEnders — long-running BBC TV soap opera set in East London (South East of England) since 1985 that has become a key reference point for culture & society in the UK.

Edinburgh — the Edinburgh Festival Fringe, the world's first & largest fringe festival, which is **open access** (not **curated**) & takes place every August at the same time as other festivals such as the Royal Tattoo & the Edinburgh International Festival.

education *see* **theatre in education**

11-Plus — exam some students take at the age of 11-12 in their last year of **primary school** for admission to **grammar schools** & other **secondary schools** (system currently existing in England & Northern Ireland).

the Establishment — a broad term that today is best summed as the closed-shop dominant sociopolitical group of the UK, formed of an entrenched core elite with more porous outer circles.

estate *see* **council estate**

free — **1.** shows that don't require you to buy a ticket to see them. **2.** fringe shows that aren't **paid-for**.

free fringe, free festival — fringe venues that do not charge audiences for tickets or charge acts or companies to hire or use the venue. Under Peter Buckley Hill at the Edinburgh Festival Fringe it became a movement under the banner of PBH's Free Fringe.

fringe — theatre that is produced outside of the main theatre institutions, often small-scale, low-budget & non-traditional in style, technique or subject. The term comes from the Edinburgh Festival Fringe, the original fringe. In London, the fringe means small-scale theatres, often in pubs. Usage: a fringe festival, a fringe venue, a fringe show. 'The fringe' means either the whole genre, or sector, or specifically the **Edinburgh Festival Fringe**.

Fringe Society — the Edinburgh Festival Fringe Society is a charity that supports participants & audiences, printing the main festival programme & running the main box office. Its role is often confused as that of running the fringe, when in reality no one does.

front of house — **1.** the parts of a venue open to the audience. **2.** the people who sell tickets, programmes, drinks etc & who show you to your seat.

GCSEs — the exams you do at school aged 16.

get-in — moving set, props etc into a venue before starting production on a show.

get-out — moving set, props etc out of a venue after ending a show there.

gig theatre — a fusion of plays with contemporary live music, where the musicians are part of the ensemble, often with a strong storytelling social message.

gig economy — labour market made of short-term contracts or freelance work as opposed to permanent jobs, of which the performing arts are a classic model. *See also* **zero hours**.

GP — general practitioner, a doctor who provides general medical treatment for people who live in an area.

grammar school — an academically-focused secondary school that selects its pupils by means of the **11-plus** exam taken by children at age 11. There are only about 163 grammar schools in England, out of 3,000 or so state secondaries, & a further 69 grammar schools in Northern Ireland. There are no state grammars in Wales or Scotland

Grenfell — a fire broke out on June 14, 2017 in Grenfell Tower, a council housing 24-storey block of flats in West London, causing 72 deaths, the worst UK residential fire since the Second World War & caused by the building's inflammable cladding.

guarantee: box office guarantee — where a theatre guarantees that revenue from ticket sales will be a certain amount, that this amount will be paid over to the company, & the theatre will make up the difference if this amount is not earned at the box office.

hall — performance space on the large size, usually the main halls intended for gathering people such as community halls & school halls, & often used as part of festivals. *See also* **room**, **space**.

health & safety — regulations & procedures intended to prevent accident or injury in workplaces or public environments.

Home Counties — the commuter counties that surround and feed the UK's capital London.

housing estate — a **council estate**.

HS2— multi-billion-pound high-speed train line being built from London to parts of the North, controversial because it's running late, massively over-budget & doesn't actually connect up the rest of the country with each other.

immersive theatre — theatre that removes the idea of the stage & immerses audiences within the performance, often by using a specific location (**site-specific**) indoors or outdoors.

improv, improvised theatre — theatre & comedy where most or all of the performance is unplanned or unscripted, created spontaneously by the performers, ideally collaboratively, often taking plot, situation or character suggestions from the audience. Improv is used in drama courses, workshops & rehearsals. As 'applied improvisation', it is used in schools & businesses to develop communication skills, creative problem solving & supportive teamwork.

industry — the theatre sector, the performing arts sector, which after all 'manufactures' entertainment & much more. Also called 'show business'.

Labour — the Labour Party, one of the UK's two main political parties, traditionally left-wing with socialist values.

level playing-field — a desired situation in which everyone has a fair & equal chance of succeeding. The Edinburgh Festival Fringe uses the term to address inequalities caused by the year-on rising cost of putting on a show there, while the Arts Council periodically adopts it as a funding or consultation banner.

literary manager — a literary adviser or editor who works on other people's scripts, duties vary from company to company. A bit like a **dramaturg** but usually it's a more formal position at a mid-size or large theatre.

local government — usually means **councils**.

mainstage — refers to the largest or most prestigious space of a theatre & to the productions performed in that space. Sometimes also used as a term for a country's top theatres/opera houses.

mid-scale — venues or work that fall in scale between the small-size fringe venues & the large theatres.

the Midlands — the inland counties of Central England.

multiculturalism — a word that describes a society where many different cultures live together, i.e. cultural diversity. In the UK this formed the basis of government initiatives from the 1990s onwards to integrate communities with varying success.

National Theatre — the UK's main publicly funded theatre is the **National Theatre of Great Britain** (officially the Royal National Theatre), centrally based in London on the South Bank of the River Thames by the Southbank Centre. Scotland has the **National Theatre of Scotland** ('theatre without walls') with no venue but offices in Glasgow. Wales has **Theatr Genedlaethol Cymru** (the Welsh language national theatre of Wales) in Carmarthen, & its English language counterpart the **National Theatre Wales** in Cardiff. Northern Ireland has the **Lyric Theatre** in Belfast, which is the only full-time producing theatre in Northern Ireland. England has no national theatre as such. Ireland's national theatre is the **Abbey Theatre** in Dublin.

new writing — original plays that are relevant to society & the issues facing it. Also called **new work** in order to include **devised theatre**.

NHS — the National Health Service

non-verbal theatre — expressing the narrative with movement, sound, props & projections instead of words.

the North — the north part of England, definitions vary.

NPO, national portfolio organisation — a organisation given major funding by Arts Council England over a guaranteed period of years to support their significant contribution to culture & the arts.

O-levels — now called **GCSEs**, an older form of the exams you do at school aged 16.

one-man show — a show, usually theatre, performed by a single performer. Since it's not gender-neutral, it is variously called one-woman show, one-person show, **solo show** &, outside of the Angloworld countries, monodrama.

onstage — the same as 'on stage' in this book.

open access — the Edinburgh Festival Fringe is an open access arts festival, meaning that anyone who can find a venue or space to perform in can put on a show. The opposite of juried, programmed or **curated**.

open call — an audition, especially for actors or dancers, open to anyone wishing to try out.

Other — **1.** disturbingly or threateningly different (capped up in this book to distinguish it from the regular meaning of the word). **2. to other** means to view or treat a person or group as different from & alien to oneself, via the process of 'othering'.

Oxbridge — the universities of Oxford & Cambridge, the top two in the UK. Associated with perpetuating class-based elitism & privilege on social, economic & cultural grounds in UK society.

paid — a fringe venue that offers paid tickets to see shows. Opposite of **free**.

paid-for — a fringe venue that charges you to put on a show there. *See* **pay-to-play**.

panto, pantomime — a Christmas family show, often based on popular fairy tales with stock characters who sing, dance & tell jokes.

Patois, Patwa — the language spoken in Jamaica, which was evolved & adapted in the 17th century from English. Mostly spoken, it has been gaining ground as a written language.

pay-to-play — a fringe venue that charges you to put on your show with them, usually venue hire but also things like marketing, programme, fliers. *See* **paid-for**.

pay-what-you-want (PWYW), pay-what-you-can, — a show where you pay at the end (e.g. popping your cash into a bucket as you leave), giving what you think the show deserves or what you can afford.

performing arts — theatre, music, dance, opera, circus, comedy, spoken word & performance art, i.e. performance with a live audience present. (The visual arts are things like painting, sculpture, ceramics, video art.)

piece — a show.

physical theatre — performance that tells a story through techniques such as movement, mime, gesture & dance, it crosses between music, dance & visual art as well as theatre, & doesn't require a formal script or plot.

playwright — someone who specifically writes plays for the stage, the term **writer** being used for people who write for other genres. It is also used instead of playwright of course.

post-show discussion/Q&A — session held onstage after a show has finished, where the audience stays on to hear the creatives or performers talk about the show & to take questions from the audience.

PR — **1.** publicity for a show. **2.** the individuals or agencies who provide this service.

practitioner — someone who creates a performance in the performing arts or creates a theoretical discourse that informs their work. Their collective work is called 'theatre practice'.

press release — the description of a show & details about its cast, venue, dates etc that is sent out to the press & listings sites.

primary school — state-funded school from age 5 to 11.

producing theatre/house — a venue which produces & programmes its own shows. *See* also **receiving theatre/house.**

a production — a show.

programme — **1.** the brochure or leaflet given to the audience with details of the show: cast, creatives, technical team, synopsis, etc. **2.** for fringes & festivals, the booklet/brochure (printed &/or online) that lists all the shows, dates, locations & ticketing details.

promoter — a person or organisation who organises &/or finances a show for venues or tours.

pub theatre — a theatre, usually **fringe** & **black box**, in a separate room isolated from the rest of the pub, usually on the first floor or in the basement.

R&D — research & development, the experimental stage of a project where different ideas are tried out to see what works.

receiving theatre/house — a venue which receives touring shows. *See also* **producing theatre/house.**

repertory, rep — **1.** a **repertory company** is a permanent ensemble of performers & creatives who tour with shows from a specified repertoire. **2.** a **repertory theatre** is a theatre that has a resident company that stages shows from a specified repertoire, usually in alternation or rotation.

regions, regional — **1.** roughly anywhere in the UK that's not London & its surrounding counties. **2.** one of nine official sub-divisions of England (not the UK): North East, North West, Yorkshire & the Humber, West Midlands, East Midlands, East of England, South West, South East & London.

regional theatre — although regional theatre has a broad definition, it's generally used to refer to the main theatres outside of the London heartland.

ROH — the Royal Opera House, in Covent Garden, Central London, which puts on opera & ballet.

room — a performance space, usually small converted spaces in pubs, community buildings etc, especially when part of fringe festivals. *See also* **hall**, **space**.

RP — Received Pronunciation, a 'standard' (Southern) English that in practice is still used as a class distinction that protects unmerited privilege. Other terms used are Queen's English, Oxford English, Public School English, BBC English, all or some of which may or may not be the same thing.

RSC — the Royal Shakespeare Company, which focuses on producing the plays of William Shakespeare in his hometown of Stratford-upon-Avon, West Midlands.

rural touring — taking theatre beyond the cities & towns where there are rarely dedicated venues to be found. The performance spaces usually take the form of a village hall or community centre, but can be schools, pubs, libraries, barns, outdoors, etc.

Scouse — from Liverpool. The person is a **Scouser.**

seater — a 100-seater, for example, is a space with 100 seats for the audience.

set — the scenery & furniture onstage.

school — performing arts college or **academy**.

secondary school — state-funded school from aged 12 to 18.

shire — administrative area of the UK, has the

same meaning as **county**.

showreel — a short video showcasing the skills & work of a practitioner, usually a performer.

to sign on — to register as unemployed.

site-responsive — shows created stylistically & thematically to reflect the 'architecture' or spirit of the space where you perform it. Usually not in a standard theatre.

site-specific — shows designed to be performed at a unique & specially adapted location other than a standard theatre.

solo theatre — a show, usually theatre, performed by a single performer. Also variously called **one-man**, one-woman show, one-person show, solo show &, outside of the Angloworld countries, monodrama.

Southbank Centre — a complex of artistic venues, centrally based in London on the South Bank of the River Thames by the National Theatre. It comprises three main performance venues: the Royal Festival Hall including the Poetry Library, the Queen Elizabeth Hall & the Purcell Room. Together with the Hayward Gallery next door, it is reputedly Europe's largest arts centre.

South East — London & the commuter counties that surround the capital. Often called the **Home Counties**.

space — anywhere defined as a place where you can perform.

split: box office split — the agreed percentage to divide box office revenue between the performing artist or company & the venue.

spoken word — poetry intended for performance.

stage-manager — the person who deals with the majority of the administrative duties involved in a production, assisting the director during rehearsals, & being responsible for all backstage activity once the show opens. In smaller productions there is usually one stage manager, while larger productions have a stage management team with a head stage manager/production stage manager, & one or more ASMs (assistant stage managers).

stand-up — comedy performed by comedians who stand in front of audiences & deliver jokes, usually with a microphone.

studio — a small theatre within which the stage & seating can usually be rearranged, often where experimental & innovative productions are staged.

surtitles — translated or transcribed lyrics/dialogue projected above a stage or displayed on a screen, especially used in opera, & now increasingly for theatre, particularly in Europe.

tech — 1. a **theatre technician** is responsible for setting up & running lighting, sound & other technical aspects of a show. **2. technical theatre** covers scenery, lighting, sound, props & costume. Sometimes also called stagecraft. **3.** a **tech rehearsal** is the main rehearsal before opening a show where you check all the technical aspects, such as lighting, props & set changes.

Margaret Thatcher — the Conservative prime minister from 1979 to 1990, whose political & government policies are known as Thatcherism, an ideology that emulates the anti-welfare state system of the United States, involving free markets, privatisation of national assets, reduced government spending, nationalism & the destruction of social structures.

theatregoer — someone who goes to see theatre.

theatre in education, TIE — taking a theatre company to perform, give workshops & create work in schools.

theatremaker — a theatre director, writer or producer, often a combination.

Theatre Workshop — theatre company mixing politics & popular entertainment that started in 1945 under director Joan Littlewood in East London.

tickbox — relating to a procedure or process carried out to satisfy convention, rules, or regulations.

Tory, Tories — another name for the **Conservative Party**.

transfer — when a show proves popular & moves its run from one venue to start a run at another venue, e.g. a West End transfer means a show moving from a smaller London or regional theatre to run for several weeks or months, possibly years at a West End theatre.

The Troubles — the 1968-1998 ethnopolitical conflict in Northern Ireland between nationalists (mainly self-identifying as Irish or Roman Catholic) & unionists (mainly self-identifying as British or Protestant), which ended with the Peace Process of the Good Friday Agreement in 1998.

UKIP — the UK Independence Party, a Eurosceptic right-wing populist political party that promotes & is synonymous with racism & nationalism.

uni — university.

union: student union — as a university or college building, it's the main meeting & recreational building for students where you'll find a cafe, bar, supplies shop, gym & often a hall where shows & gigs are put on.

venue — a building or part of a building where performances take place.

Welsh — the Celtic language spoken in Wales & one of the seven indigenous languages of the British Isles. It gained official status in Wales in 2011, making it the only *legally* official language in the UK (English isn't legally defined as an official language).

West End — **1.** the main area for theatres in Central London, also known as Theatreland. **2.** a benchmark term for top quality popular theatre, e.g. a 'West End musical'.

Westminster — used to refer to the UK government, since the Houses of Parliament & government ministries are located in the London borough of the City of Westminster.

Windrush — the Windrush generation are the half a million people who came to the UK from the Caribbean between 1948 & 1971 (the Caribbean nations were part of the British Empire & Commonwealth), & named after the Empire Windrush, the first ship to arrive

carrying the migrants in 1948. In 2012, under the Conservative-Liberal Democrat coalition government of David Cameron & Nick Clegg, the Hostile Environment policy came into effect & was used to treat people of the Windrush generation as 'illegal immigrants'. As a result they started to lose their jobs, homes, benefits & access to the health service. Some were placed in immigration detention, deported or were refused the right to return from abroad.

work — a show. In the industry, if you 'make work', it means you create a show or performance.

working men's club — a type of private social club first started in the 19th century in industrialised areas of the United Kingdom, particularly the North of England, the Midlands, Scotland & many parts of the South Wales Valleys, to provide recreation & education for working class men & their families. Clubs also began at this time in Australia, with a small number in Ireland, primarily Dublin.

workshop — **1.** a technique class involving practical exercises. **2.** a **workshop production** is a performance where a show is staged in stripped down way, e.g. without costumes or sets. **3.** **to workshop a show** means to try out ideas before finalising its final shape & structure.

writer — someone who writes a script or structure of a show, includes the more specific term **playwright** which is usually used for the writer of spoken plays for the stage.

zero hours — a job involving a type of contract between employer & worker, where the employer is not obliged to provide any minimum working hours, while the worker is not obliged to accept any work offered. *See* also **gig economy**.

A demographic note

Age-wise, the interviewees represent a generational range from their 20s to their 80s, spanning seven amazing interconnected decades of ages and experience.

In terms of cohorts, there's a consistently even spread across the whole year, with the older generations born in September-April, and the younger generations born April-August. However no one was born in July nor, like the interviewees in my Mellotron book, in November. In terms of birth year, there are two major clusters: the mid/late 1960s and the late 1970s/early 1980s.

There's an even spread too across the country for place of birth and place where raised (the latter being the best indication of culture and worldview, I think), with London, the North West, the Midlands and Overseas representing larger clusters of similar size, with mobility from region to region not particularly evident.

However, in terms of where people are based currently because of their professional work, the shift is to London, even if that work is carried out elsewhere, with the numbers taken mainly from the North West, the Midlands and Overseas rather than the other regions. Note that London, a world hub where almost 15 per cent of the UK's population live and which is easily accessible from the densely populated/prosperous surrounding Home Counties of the South East, is an irresistible destination for any sector in the UK and even Ireland. Less than a third of the interviewees were born or raised there, but almost half are now based there. Significant or not, no one in this book was born, raised or is based in West London.

Rather than look at the origins of the migrants and non-UK nationals based in the country, I think it's more revealing to look at the influence of time spent out of the country by everyone. Regardless of nationality or origin, around 35 per cent have had the experience of being raised or part-raised Overseas or have lived as an adult Overseas for a long period. Additionally, of course, one interviewee was raised as a nomad within the UK.

Another good indicator of identity and values is religious upbringing (i.e. culturally as opposed to belief), which can be especially influential in developing awareness of social issues — Quakers are a good example (though there are none in this book). Among the major religions represented here, there is a large over-representation of Catholics, in a British/Irish sense, of 30 per cent (while comprising only 6 per cent of the population).

A lot of these patterns, of course, more than likely reflect my own British Catholic/Overseas upbringing & culture, but then I suppose that's another handy identity filter we could apply!   **— Nick Awde**

Index